CHRONIC POVERTY IN ASIA

Causes, Consequences and Policies

John Malcolm Dowling
University of Hawaii, USA

Yap Chin-Fang

World Scientific

NEW JERSEY • LONDON • SINGAPORE • BEIJING • SHANGHAI • HONG KONG • TAIPEI • CHENNAI

Published by

World Scientific Publishing Co. Pte. Ltd.
5 Toh Tuck Link, Singapore 596224
USA office: 27 Warren Street, Suite 401-402, Hackensack, NJ 07601
UK office: 57 Shelton Street, Covent Garden, London WC2H 9HE

British Library Cataloguing-in-Publication Data
A catalogue record for this book is available from the British Library.

CHRONIC POVERTY IN ASIA
Causes, Consequences and Policies

ISBN-13 978-981-283-886-5
ISBN-10 981-283-886-4

Typeset by Stallion Press
Email: enquiries@stallionpress.com

Printed in Singapore by B & Jo Enterprise Pte Ltd

Dedication

There are a few dedicated scholars who have devoted their lives to studying chronic poverty and developing programs and policies to address this challenging problem. This book is dedicated to them and their tireless efforts to uplift those who have suffered for so long.

Preface

The subject of chronic poverty has challenged researchers and policymakers for many years. The chronically poor are everywhere, in industrial and developing countries alike. Their numbers are larger and more apparent in Asia and Africa, yet there are pockets of households that have been poor for several generations on all continents and in many different countries. Asia is the focus in this volume for two reasons. We are most familiar with Asia, having lived and worked in the region for many years and Asia contains the most chronically poor of any of the developing regions.

We approach the subject by first outlining the dimensions of chronic poverty in Asia in Chapter 1. It is important to begin by finding out who the poor are, how they became poor and where they live. In this chapter, the characteristics of poor households are discussed and the geographic, economic and social dimensions of poverty analyzed. Many of the observations are self evident. The bulk of the poor live in rural areas and these rural poor are the primary focus of this book. The poor have low skills, are poorly educated, live in regions where soil fertility is low and connectivity with urban centers is limited. The poor are often minorities that suffer from discrimination, neglect and social isolation. The poor have limited stocks of physical assets, low levels of savings and are vulnerable to the vicissitudes of nature and to illness, both of which can be devastating to those who have little to begin with. The chapter also considers the major factors responsible for chronic poverty in rural areas — limited education and skill, low income, limited capital and availability of social services, lack of capital and low savings. Differences between the chronically poor and the transient poor are also discussed and ways that the non-poor can sink into chronic poverty.

The determinants of chronic poverty in Asia are addressed in more detail in Chapter 2. Lack of human capital including lower life expectancy and higher morbidity and infant mortality are characteristics of the chronically poor. They also have limited earning power, tend to live in geographic and political isolation and lack financial capital and physical assets. They often suffer from gender, religious, race, class and caste discrimination. Because they have few physical assets, low levels of education and literacy, they are hindered in their ability to move or to otherwise uplift their living standards. The chronically poor are also adversely affected more than their richer counterparts by economic shocks, wars and natural disasters. Children are trapped in the swirl of chronic poverty, unable to extricate themselves by their own efforts. They are too often bound to the wheel of poverty for their generation and generations to come by debts incurred by their parents and grandparents that they and their children are forced to repay.

The dynamics of chronic poverty are discussed in Chapter 3. The yoke of poverty is transferred from generation to generation in different ways. Uneducated parents are sometimes too poor to send their children to school and so illiteracy is passed on, food shortages can result in children's cognitive impairment and when income is limited, girls receive less food than boys. The poor have few physical assets and further fragmented as these are split up among the children. Those poor that have sufficient resources send their children to school either for selfish or altruistic reasons. Often, parents care for children to ensure that they will have someone to care for them in old age. When life is hard and risks of survival to adulthood are high, parents, where possible, seek to ensure this support by bearing as many children as possible, taking care of their health and sanitation needs and sending them to school so that they can earn a living that will support themselves and their parents when they grow up. Too often, debts rather than assets are transferred through a bondage system, particularly in South Asia and sometimes children are sold into debt bondage by parents who are strapped for resources or in debt to other creditors. There has been little systematic analysis of risks to children or policies suggested to provide better coping mechanisms in chronically poor environments. Similarly, the topic of resilience to trauma has received little effective analysis.

Chapters 4, 5 and 6 consider policies to address chronic poverty. Chapter 4 considers microeconomic policies, Chapter 5 looks at sector policies and finally Chapter 6 reviews macroeconomic policies.

Chapter 4 considers a wide variety of government policies that are designed to aid individual households and villages. These include social safety nets and entitlements; cash transfers and food subsidies, public works programs that are geared toward poor villages and localities; social funds; conditional cash transfers and educational and health subsidies. Each of these programs usually has a specific objective and sometimes narrowly focusing on the poor and chronically poor. In other cases, the focus is broader and the transient poor and non-poor may also benefit from these programs. The effectiveness of each of these programs is considered with reference to individual country experience and lessons learned. The chapter reviews five modalities that are being used to assist the poor: cash transfers, universal food subsidies, rationed food subsidies, public works and social funds. Each of these programs is designed to help individuals and families that are poor to escape from poverty and their effectiveness is increased as the focus on the poor and chronically poor is maintained and improved. The costs and benefits of food subsidies, which have been used as a policy to relieve poverty for many years, are discussed and suggestions offered for improving their focus. Cash transfers to the poor either through direct cash transfers, food stamps or other government vouchers are also reviewed. Public works programs, sometimes called work fare, can have two objectives. The first is to provide income for the poor in exchange for work contributions to a government project. The second is that workers can benefit from the project itself through skill enhancement and experience. Social funds mobilize local community involvement in projects that develop infrastructure in poorer communities. Educational and health subsidies are often used in conjunction with public works programs to induce families to send their children to school. Alternatively, cash or sometimes food is offered to chronically poor families in exchange for the family commitment to send their children to elementary school. There are also subsidies to children from poor families which generally takes the form of government subsidized education. Such subsidies are generally available to all children and there are only a few examples where the chronically poor might be targeted. The chapter concludes with a discussion of labor mobility as a way for poor families to break the cycle of poverty, either by internal migration, usually from rural to urban movement or, less likely, through international migration.

Sector policies to reduce chronic poverty are the focus of Chapter 5. The role of transportation and communications in improving the connectivity of high poverty by-passed regions is considered. Improved communication with others is an important way to spread the availability of new information and technology to poor communities. For example, telecommunications access can be improved by the use of cellular phones, where usage is increasing by leaps and bounds. New applications for cell phone use will develop as new technology evolves like recharging from solar batteries, lower prices and more sophisticated instruments. Rural electrification also plays a critical role in facilitating the flow of information and commerce to these regions and there were a variety of other benefits that have accrued from electrification. Security and mobility at night was enhanced by the availability of electricity which also afforded more time for work and leisure. Access to the news media also increased awareness of the importance of education, personal hygiene, inoculations and consultations with qualified medical personnel. This resulted in a reduction in the number of infant and child mortality, improved hygiene and better school attendance. Electricity played a catalyst in the educational process by extending the time period for study and creating a comfortable learning environment. The role of regional infrastructure including irrigation, agricultural extension and the transfer of new technologies to the rural poor is also reviewed and policies suggested. Irrigation benefits the poor through providing more food at lower prices and stimulating the shift from subsistence farming to higher value crops for sale to the market. Micro irrigation systems also have strong potential for reducing poverty. Even greater poverty reduction can be achieved by targeting irrigation to poorer communities by reducing the unequal distribution of water rights as well as reducing the inequality in land holdings. Regarding the relationship between rural poverty and spending on roads, studies show that investment in roads had a significant impact on non-agricultural economic activities which in turn helped to reduce poverty. Pumping for irrigation and potable water along with lighting and TV for homes and health centers are also ways in which electricity has improved living conditions for the chronically poor throughout the Asian region. Discussion of land reform and technological innovation conclude the chapter. The chronically poor, many of whom are illiterate or have limited education, will probably not be involved with the leading edge advances in agricultural science. Nevertheless, some of the newer aspects of agricultural extension and cropping systems may be relevant to some chronically poor who either own a little land or who can benefit from these developments as members of the agricultural sector work force. One of these developments is *no-till* farming. No-till farming is a system where fields are not tilled after the harvesting of the previous crop but rather seeded immediately with plant residues and some mulching material. No-till farming has the advantage of water conservation, time saving, reduced sowing and soil preparation costs, reduced reliance on tractors and burning of fossil fuels. Regarding land reform, there have been few reforms that have been subject to rigorous analysis. However, the evidence that does exist suggests that land reform that change tenancy laws and regulations that make tenure legally binding have a powerful positive impact on poverty reduction. While the poor are not directly involved in technology and technological transfer, they benefit from new research and adoption of new varieties indirectly through higher yields and greater income. In recent years, there has been a slowdown in rice yield growth and this is partly the result of a slowdown in the rate of public investment in agricultural research and development, primarily by international agencies. This trend needs to be reversed by greater efforts to develop and disseminate new technologies.

Macroeconomic policies to reduce chronic poverty are the focus of Chapter 6. Clearly, overall economic growth is the most important macroeconomic variable that could impact poverty. There is ample evidence that rapid economic growth results in a decline in poverty. There has been strong growth in income in Asia since 1990 along with a significant reduction in the overall level of poverty. Despite the strong relationship between poverty reduction and income growth in Asia in this 15 year period, income growth alone does not fully account for the reduction in poverty. Other factors and policies, both at the sector and macroeconomic level have also worked to reduce chronic poverty. The pace of infrastructure spending is considered in Chapter 6, following the discussion of individual components of infrastructure spending in Chapter 5, the point being that lags in infrastructure can introduce bottlenecks that retard the overall expansion of economic activity. Fiscal deficits can reduce the pace of poverty reduction if they have a negative impact on the pace of development spending. India is a case in point. The fiscal deficit remains substantial (7 percent to 8 percent of GDP) which could pose a problem in addressing poverty reduction issues. How can India finance greater capital investment as well as development spending while keeping the deficit in check? Excessive regulation of labor markets can also prove to be an impediment to poverty alleviation. Restrictive labor laws are particularly burdensome to small and medium scale industries. For example, Indian textile plants have lower capacity than Chinese plants and hence operate at lower efficiency and higher costs. Compared to other countries, there are smaller firms in India than in other countries and labor laws protect only a few well paid salary workers. Such a dualistic system also perpetuates discrimination against women and minorities and helps to perpetuate existing poverty traps and low living standards for the chronically poor. Despite the conventional belief that minimum wage legislation reduces the supply of labor and tends to increase poverty, there is limited evidence for the impact of minimum wage legislation on the chronically poor. To the contrary, there are some results that suggest that in particular circumstances, minimum wage legislation can result in a win-win outcome where wages for the poor increase without a commensurate reduction in employment. Government development spending can have a salutary impact on poverty, particularly in specific areas where expenditures can be increased or targeted to reach the chronically poor, particularly education and health and rural road investments. While the pace of international migration by the chronically poor is likely to be slow, policies regarding internal migration can help the chronically poor by focusing on providing information on job opportunities to villages in rural locations and the development of information networks including the internet, particularly in poor villages. While some government departments can be involved, the private sector is already doing a good job of providing information for prospective job seekers. Which social programs are most relevant for the chronically poor? First are policies which can help families to break out of the poverty trap by educating the next generation. These include subsidies for education at the primary level, either through workfare or the introduction of small subsidies to families for shoes, uniforms and free lunches to reduce out of pocket costs for parents. Second are social programs and expenditures that protect assets and income by smoothing consumption and income for the vulnerable poor who can't get out of poverty given their current occupation, education and geographic location. Work fare programs can provide employment for the poor during these gaps with work on public schemes to build and rehabilitate infrastructure in their villages or surrounding areas. Selective food subsidies can be used to bring health outcomes up to standard for those families with nutritional deficits. Another initiative is needed to help poor household get out of debt that are indebted to landlords or money lenders and may even have some family members in virtual bondage to these landlords or money lenders. Imaginative schemes which serve to break this debt bondage are critical if this cycle of chronic poverty for literally millions of farmers and other rural families is to be broken. Third are social programs that both protect against shocks and provide assistance after shocks occur. Since the shocks are unanticipated, much of what has to be done here is preventative or reactive in nature. For the chronically poor, it only takes a major shock to have devastating impacts on the chronically poor. Crop failure, either from pests or adverse weather (drought or flood) or escalating prices for food and other essentials poses the most significant risk.

Chapter 7 provides an extensive review of 11 individual country experiences with a focus on the incidence of poverty, determinants of poverty and micro, sector and macroeconomic policies which have been adopted to deal with these chronic poverty challenges. The countries reviewed include the three most populous economies, China, India, Indonesia; four countries in South Asia, Bangladesh, Nepal, Pakistan and Sri Lanka, one economy in Southeast Asia that have significant numbers of chronically poor, namely the Philippines; and lastly the three Mekong countries, Cambodia, Laos and Vietnam. The Chronic Poverty Research Center has tagged China, Indonesia Vietnam as a "consistent improver" with their fight against chronic poverty. Some of the poverty reduction policies that proved successful at targeting the so-called "invisible" chronic poor are particularly highlighted. Lastly, each country review concludes with a section on future policy agenda and challenges.

Final thoughts on policy are presented in Chapter 8. An overview of the policies and challenges covered in Chapters 1 through 7 is provided. Where chronic poverty fits into the overall poverty reduction picture and an analysis of the cost of eliminating chronic poverty in Asia is presented. The cost, estimated to be $64 billion, is not that high considering the scope of suffering that the chronically poor endure every day. A summary of issues for social protection and social assistance, assisting isolated poor communities, migration as a strategy for the chronically poor, creation of assets for the chronically poor and discrimination and gender empowerment are also provided. The chapter concludes with two sections that are forward looking; an analysis of chronic poverty and the global financial crisis as well as medium term prospects for reducing chronic poverty. Governments need to prepare further for this contingency by setting aside some funds to protect the poor, should the global recession deepen further. They also need to adopt appropriate countercyclical macroeconomic policies to compensate for the slowdown in exports by way of compensatory monetary and fiscal stimulus. Governments also need to be ready to provide resources to protect the chronically poor from further deterioration in their living standards. In our view, a deeper recession scenario becomes more probable every day the global crisis persists and the possibility of further contagion spreading to stock markets and banking systems in Asia increases. In light of these developments, it is unlikely that much progress will be made in poverty reduction in the immediate future. Nevertheless, projection made by the Asian Development Bank present an optimistic medium term scenario whereby pro-poor policies stress more equitable distribution of income and policies that address the problems of the poor. Under this scenario, South Asia can reduce poverty from 42.5 percent in 2005 to around 16 percent by 2015. Estimates for Southeast Asia which includes the Mekong countries goes from 18.8 percent to 7.3 percent and China (and Mongolia) from 15.9 percent to 2.6 percent within the same time period. For the Asia and Pacific region, poverty will fall from around 900 million in 2005 to 342 million if pro-poor policies are adopted. On the other hand, 160 million fewer people will be raised out of poverty if pro-rich policies are adopted.

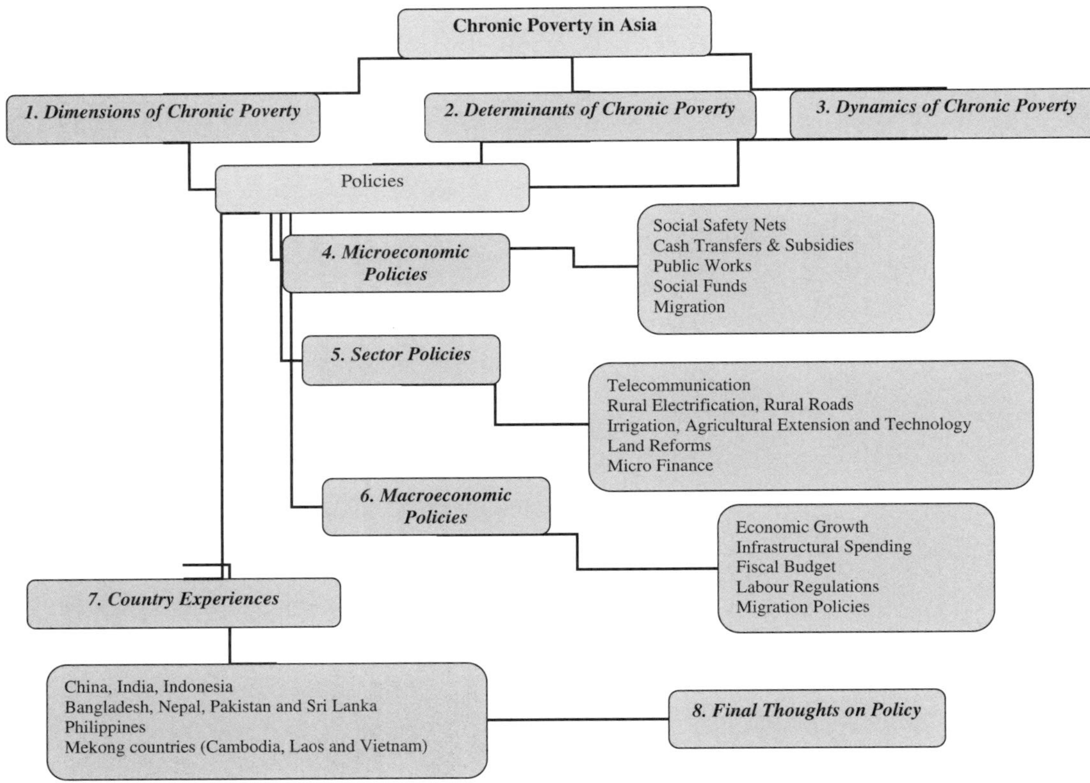
Chronic Poverty in Asia
1. Dimensions of Chronic Poverty
2. Determinants of Chronic Poverty
3. Dynamics of Chronic Poverty
Policies
4. Microeconomic Policies
Social Safety Nets
Cash Transfers & Subsidies
Public Works
Social Funds
Migration
5. Sector Policies
Telecommunication
Rural Electrification, Rural Roads
Irrigation, Agricultural Extension and Technology
Land Reforms
Micro Finance
6. Macroeconomic Policies
Economic Growth
Infrastructural Spending
Fiscal Budget
Labour Regulations
Migration Policies
7. Country Experiences
China, India, Indonesia
Bangladesh, Nepal, Pakistan and Sri Lanka
Philippines
Mekong countries (Cambodia, Laos and Vietnam)
8. Final Thoughts on Policy

Acknowledgments

We would like to thank Armin Bauer, Wei Ge, Ernesto Pernia, Pradumna Rana, M.G. Quibria, Peter Warr, Rebecca Valenzuela and the editors of World Scientific for their continued encouragement, and helpful comments. We are also grateful to the Chronic Poverty Research Center at the University of Manchester for their ongoing efforts to investigate chronic poverty around the globe and suggest policy solutions. We thank Ms Helen Choo, Mr Balamurugan, Mr Inderjit Singh and friends at Tampines Junior College for their kind support. We also want to thank our families for their unwavering support throughout the duration of this project. We want to particularly thank Maribeth Boritzer who was unstinting in her editorial comments which were instrumental in making the book concise, readable and to the point.

Contents

Acronyms

AAY	*Antyodaya Anna Yojana* (*India*)
ACC	Administrative Committee on Coordination (*United Nations*)
ADB	Asian Development Bank
ADBL	Agricultural Development Bank Limited
AFD	*Agence Française de Développement*
AFP	Agence France-Presse
AFTA	ASEAN Free Trade Area
AIDS	Acquired Immune Deficiency Syndrome
AKRSP	Aga Khan Rural Support Program (*Pakistan*)
AP	Andhra Pradesh
APIS	Annual Poverty Indicators Survey (*Philippines*)
APP	Agriculture Perspective Plan (*Nepal*)
ARMM	Autonomous Region in Muslim Mindanao
ATM	Automated Teller Machine
BAAC	Bank for Agricultural Cooperatives (*Thailand*)
BIDS	Bangladesh Institute of Development Studies
BMZ	*Bundesministerium für Wirtschaftliche Zusammenarbeit und Entwicklung*
BPS	Indonesian Central Body of Statistics
BRAC	Bangladesh Rural Advancement Committee
BRI	Bank Rakyat Indonesia
CARP	Comprehensive Agrarian Reform Program (*Philippines*)
CCT	Conditional Cash Transfers
CDRI	Cambodia Development Resource Institute
CEIC	Center for International Studies and Cooperation
CGIAR	Consultative Group on International Agricultural Research
CIA	Central Intelligence Agency

CIDDS	*Comprehensive and Integrated Delivery of Social Services (Philippines)*
CPRC	Chronic Poverty Research Center
CPRGS	Comprehensive Poverty Reduction and Growth Strategy (*Vietnam*)
CSES	Cambodia Socio-Economic Survey
CSIS	Center for Strategic and International Studies
DALE	Disability Adjusted Life Expectancy
DFID	U.K. Department for International Development
DSWD	Department of Social Work and Development (*Philippines*)
ECD	Early Childhood Development
EGS	Education Guarantee Scheme (*India*)
FAO	Food and Agriculture Organization (*United Nations*)
FATA	Federally-Administered Tribal Areas
FBS	Federal Bureau of Statistics (*Pakistan*)
FDI	Foreign Direct Investment
FFA	Food for Asset (*Bangladesh*)
FFE	Food for Education Program (*Bangladesh*)
FIES	Family Income and Expenditure Survey (*Philippines*)
FSP	Food Support Program (*Pakistan*)
FSSSP	Female Secondary School Stipend Program (*Bangladesh*)
FUG	Forest User Groups (*Nepal*)
GDP	Gross Domestic Product
GMS	Greater Mekong Sub-Region
GNP	Gross National Product
GTZ	German Technical Cooperation Agency
HCP	Health Coverage Plan (*Cambodia*)
HDI	Human Development Index
HDR	Human Development Report
HEF	Health Equity Fund
HEPR	Hunger Eradication and Poverty Reduction (*Vietnam*)
HIES	Household Integrated Economic Survey (*Pakistan*)
HIV	Human Immunodeficiency Virus
HRS	Household Responsibility System (*China*)

HRSA	Health Sector Reform Agenda (*Philippines*)
ICT	Information and Communication Technologies
IDE	International Development Enterprise
IDT	*Inpres Desa Tertinggal* (IDT) or "Presidential Instruction for Village Left Behind" (*Indonesia*)
IFAD	International Fund for Agricultural Development
IFPRI	International Food Policy Research Institute
IGR	Income Gap Ratio
ILO	International Labor Organization
IMF	International Monetary Fund
IMR	Infant Mortality Rate
IRRI	International Rice Research Institute
JFPR	Japan Fund for Poverty Reduction
JPS	*Jaringan Pengaman Sosial* (*Indonesia*)
KALAHI	*Kapit-Bisig Laban sa Kahirapan* (Linking Arms against Poverty)(*Philippines*)
KDP	Kecamatan Development Program (*Indonesia*)
Lao PDR	Lao People's Democratic Republic
LGPR	Leading Group for Poverty Reduction (*China*)
LSMS	Living Standards Measurement Survey
MDG	Millennium Development Goals (*United Nations*)
MOLISA	Ministry of Labor and Social Assistance
MP	Madhya Pradesh
MRD	Ministry of Rural Development
MSSRF	MS Swaminathan Research Foundation
MTPDP	Medium Term Philippines Development Plan
NAPC	National Anti-Poverty Commission (*Philippines*)
NCAER	National Council of Applied Economic Research (*India*)
NCR	National Capital Region
NEDA	National Economic and Development Authority
NEDO	New Energy and Industrial Technology Development Organization
NFA	National Food Authority (*Philippines*)
NFBS	National Family Benefit Scheme (*India*)
NGO	Non Government Organization

NGPES	National Growth and Poverty Eradication Strategy
NMBS	National Maternity Benefit Scheme (*India*)
NOAPS	National Old Age Pension Scheme (*India*)
NPCC	Nepal National Planning Commission
NREGS	National Rural Employment Scheme (*India*)
NSAP	National Social Assistance Programme (*India*)
NSO	National Statistics Office (*Philippines*)
NSSO	National Sample Survey Organization (*India*)
NTP	National Targeted Programme (*Vietnam*)
NWFP	North West Frontier Province
OBA	Output Based Approach
OBC	Other Backward Castes
ODA	Official Development Assistance
OPEC	Organization of the Petroleum Exporting Countries
OPK	*Operasi Pasar Khusus* (*Indonesia*)
P4K	*Pembinaan Peningkatan Pendapatan Petani-Nelayan Kecil* (Income-Generating Project for Marginal Farmers and the Landless) (*Indonesia*)
PAF	Poverty Alleviation Fund (*Nepal*)
PAP	Poverty Alleviation Programs
PDS	Public Distribution System (*India*)
PES	Parents' Effective Services (*Philippines*)
PGR	Poverty Gap Ratio
PIDS	Philippine Institute for Development Studies
PODES	Village Potential (*Indonesia*)
PPAF	Pakistan Poverty Alleviation Fund
PPP	Purchasing Power Parity
PPP	Pantawid Pamilyang Pilipino (*Philippines*)
PRF	Poverty Reduction Fund
PRSP	Poverty Reduction Strategy Paper
PV	Photovoltaic
REF	Rural Electrification Fund (*Cambodia*)
RMP	Rural Maintenance Program (*Bangladesh*)
ROSCA	Rotating Saving and Credit Association
SC	Scheduled Castes
SCN	Standing Committee on Nutrition (*United Nations*)

SDS	Society for Development Studies (*India*)
SEAK	Self-Employment Assistance Kaunlaran (*Philippines*)
SEDIP	Secondary Education Development and Improvement Project
SEDP	Socio-Economic Development Plan
SESC	Socio-Economic Survey of Cambodia
SEZ	Special Economic Zones
SLF	Short-Term Liquidity Facility
SOE	State-Owned Enterprises
SPFS	Special Programme on Food Security (*Cambodia*)
ST	Scheduled Tribes
SUSENAS	National Socio- Economic Survey (*Statistics Indonesia*)
TANGO	Technical Assistance to Non-Governmental Organization
TFP	Total Factor Productivity
TRIP	Tertiary Rural Roads Improvement Programme (*Cambodia*)
TUP	Targeted Ultra-Poor (*Bangladesh*)
TVE	Town and Village Enterprise (*China*)
UN	United Nations
UNDP	United Nations Development Programme
UNESCAP	United Nations Economic and Social Commission for Asia and the Pacific
UNICEF	United Nations Children's Fund
URDI	Urban Research Development Institute of Indonesia
UXO	Unexploded Ordinance
VASS	Vietnam Academy of Social Sciences
VDF	Village Development Funds (*Laos*)
VND	Vietnamese *Dong*
WHO	World Health Organization
WTO	World Trade Organization

Chapter 1

The Dimensions of Chronic Poverty in Asia

1.1 Introduction

Poverty has several different dimensions. At any given time poverty can be measured as a shortfall in a minimum level of income needed to provide a sustainable level of consumption of food, clothing and affordable housing. There is also illiteracy due to lack of access to education; poor health due to inadequate services and access to potable water and little or no representation in the community. Often these dimensions of poverty become apparent when family income falls below some minimum income standard.

The World Bank in its comparative work around the world has used the standard of one US dollar a day per person as a benchmark for measuring poverty. Those whose income is below US$1 a day fall into the poverty category. While it leave out many factors, this simple income standard for measuring poverty is useful in making comparisons between different locations in a country as well as among different countries. The dollar a day standard made its debut in 1990 (World Bank, 1990) and has remained the standard for poverty line estimation until recently.

In mid-2008, the World Bank unveiled a new estimate of the poverty line, in light of inflation since 1980 and new estimates of purchasing power parity (see Ravallion *et al.*, 2008; Ravallion *et al.*, 2008a; and *The Economist*, 2008). One simple way to account for inflation would be to factor in US inflation which would bring the poverty line to about $1.45 in 2005. However Ravallion *et al.* (2008a) thought this estimate was a bit too high. Rather than abandon the poverty line concept Ravallion *et al.* (2008a) re-estimated the poverty line using similar methodology and better data. They gathered national poverty line data from 75 national estimates and picked the 15 lowest (13 sub-Sahara African countries and Nepal and Tajikistan). Averaging out they came to an estimate of the poverty line to about $1.25 per day using 2005 purchasing power parity terms.

How much difference does this make in poverty for Asian countries? It is hard to say right now, although the level of poverty will probably be a bit higher for most countries. Ravallion *et al.* (2008) made a first cut for China and found that poverty increased substantially using the new estimation procedure, from 74 million to around 200 million in 2005. However using the new standard developed by Ravallion *et al.* (2008) to measure poverty changes over time, the level of poverty fell by over 400 million between 1990 and 2004 compared with a previous estimated decline of around 250 million.

The most recent estimates of povety in Asia are displayed in Table 1.1. There are about 740 million people in poverty in this panel of countries and about 900 million in all of the Asia and Pacific region. The bulk of the poor are in three countries — India, China and Bangladesh.

Table 1.1 Head Count Ratio and Numbers in Poverty in Asia

Country	Head Count Ratio — Proportion of Population in Poverty	People in Poverty (millions)
Bangladesh	0.51	75
Cambodia	0.40	5.6
China (rural)	0.25	200
China	0.16	210
India (rural)	0.44	342
Indonesia (rural)	0.25	27
Lao PDR	0.35	2
Nepal	0.55	14.8
Pakistan	0.22	35
Philippines	0.22	19
Vietnam	0.23	19

Source: Asian Development Bank (2008) and Bauer *et al.* (2008).

To augment this approach adopted by the World Bank, the Asian Development Bank, other multilateral agencies and individual countries also have developed their own indices of poverty based on local standards and data sources.

An interesting approach has been suggested by the International Food Policy Research Institute (IFPRI, 2007) which has broken down poverty incidence into three separate income categories that shows the depth of poverty as well as the absolute level. Measuring income in purchasing power parity terms they are the subjacent poor whose income is between \$0.81 and \$1.08 per day per person; the medial poor whose income is between \$0.81 and \$0.54 per day; and the ultra poor whole income is less than \$0.54 per day. Estimates for selected countries are displayed in Table 1.2.

The estimates are somewhat different from the figures reported in Table 1.1, particularly for Pakistan and less so for India and Bangladesh. Nevertheless, they are interesting because they show the level of severe deprivation (ultra poor category) is less than 5 percent in all the countries sampled.

Who are the poor in Asia? Economic growth in East Asia has resulted in the reduction of poor households, especially for rural households over the past two decades. However the number of poor rose in South Asia over the same period. Furthermore the total number of households in rural poverty in South Asia was almost double that of sub-Saharan Africa. (World Bank, 2008 and Ravallion, Chen and Sangraula, 2008).

Table 1.2 Incidence of Rural Poverty by Depth of Poverty — Head Count Ratio (%)

Country	Subjacent Poor	Medial Poor	Ultra Poor	All Rural Poor
Bangladesh	27.5	22.9	4.8	55.2
India	22.1	13.2	1.8	37.1
Pakistan	9.5	3.0	0.3	12.8
Sri Lanka	3.8	1.2	0.2	6.8
Vietnam	19.8	12.0	3.3	35.1

Source: IFPRI (2007).

That brings us to the next question, which is the focus of our work in the remaining chapters of this monograph — what causes chronic poverty and what can be done about it? Causes of chronic poverty depend on (i) maintainers that keep households in poverty and (ii) drivers that cause households to fall into poverty traps. We will explore into greater depth the various causes of chronic poverty as we look into the respective country experiences over time in Chapter 7 and more generally in Chapters 2 and 3.

If a family is diagnosed as suffering from the shackles of chronic poverty, how can they break free? Exit routes are generally fastest when the chronic poor have the opportunity to participate in "new patterns of transformative growth" and when the government has sufficient revenue from taxation to spend on pro-poor expenditure (Chronic Poverty Research Center, 2008). Access to infrastructure, education and information are of vital importance especially for the poor residing in landlocked areas. Table 1.3 ranks the various efforts of Asian countries in reducing chronic poverty over the past 30 years. China, Indonesia and Vietnam have consistently improved their chronic poverty situations. Pakistan, Bangladesh, India are considered as partially chronically deprived. Lastly, Cambodia has the greatest degree of chronic deprivation. Chronically deprived countries are characterized by relatively low initial levels of welfare (relatively low GDP and relatively high child and infant mortality) and by their relatively slow rate of progress over time. They account for over 30 percent child and infant mortality and 17 percent of population earning less than US$1 day per day than their share of total population. Partially chronically

Table 1.3 Country Classifications of Poverty for Selected Asian Countries, 1970–2003

Chronically Deprived Countries	Cambodia
Partially Chronically Deprived Countries	Pakistan, Bangladesh, Laos, Nepal, Philippines, India, Thailand, Mongolia, Myanmar
Partial Consistent Improvers	Malaysia
Across-the-board Consistent Improvers	China, Indonesia, Vietnam

Source: Chronic Poverty Research Center (2008, p. 15), Table 2.

deprived countries show relatively low levels of welfare but have shown at least relative slow rates of improvement. Consistent improvers would show faster rates of progress over time.

The further income is below the poverty line, the greater the depth of poverty experienced. By adding up the shortfalls in income relative to the poverty line we can develop a measure of the depth of deprivation. This total represents the income required to raise the income of everyone who is below the poverty line up to the poverty line. This poverty gap ratio (PGR) tells us the income required to raise everyone's income to the poverty line divided by the total income of the entire population:

$$\text{PGR} = \sum \frac{(y_i - p)}{total\ income}$$

where y_i is the income of the ith individual and p is the poverty line. All of the shortfalls in income of the poor are added and then divided by the total income of the community (GDP) in a year to arrive at the PGR. Alternatively, we can use the total income of the poor if all of them were to have income at the poverty line as the divisor. For example if the poverty line is US$1 per day and there were 1,000 poor people the divisor would be US$365,000. This ratio of the shortfalls in income for the year divided by the total income of the poor (US$365,000 in our example) is called the income gap ratio (IGR):

$$\text{IGR} = \sum \frac{(y_i - p)}{total\ income\ of\ the\ poor\ (if\ they\ were\ all\ to\ have\ incomes\ at\ the\ poverty\ line)}$$

While the depth of poverty is a useful concept, it is not widely used since data on the relative poverty gap are not easy to generate.

We can also look at poverty over time. If a family is below the poverty line for a sustained period of time, five years or longer, we can say that the family is chronically poor. If a family comes in and out of poverty depending on circumstances that are temporal in nature such as temporary illness or unemployment, then the family is characterized as being temporarily poor. Families can have several bouts of poverty and still not be chronically poor.

Chronic poverty can be mild or severe, depending on how far the family is below the poverty line. Generally however, all chronically poor are below the poverty line for an extended period of time. The Chronic Poverty Research Center (2008) has recently estimated the extent of chronic poverty for countries around the world where there are large numbers of chronically poor. These are reported in Table 1.4.

Who are the chronic poor in Asia? To be diagnosed as chronically poor, the household will have to be persistently poor and experience multidimensional deprivation for an extended period of time. However the length of time is arbitrary. According to Adams and He (1995), chronic poverty is indicated if the family is in the poorest quintile of the income distribution for three successive years. Other studies, such as McCulloch and Baulch (1999) put chronic poverty to being poor in all five years. It is also not easy to identify chronic poverty at a point in time as poverty trends can mask poverty dynamics. Some

Table 1.4 Poor and Chronically Poor in East Asia and South Asia

Country	Proportion of Poor Who are Chronically Poor Over Five Years — Low Estimate	Proportion of Poor Who are Chronically Poor Over Five Years — High Estimate	Proportion Poor — US$1.25 Per Day	Number of Poor — US$1 Per Day (rounded to millions)
China	0.15	0.25	0.25	200
Indonesia	0.15	0.25	0.25	27
Philippines	0.30	0.40	0.22	19
Vietnam	0.35	0.45	0.20	19
Bangladesh	0.20	0.30	0.50	75
India	0.25	0.35	0.44	342
Nepal	0.50	0.60	0.55	15
Pakistan	0.25	0.35	0.22	35

Source: Chronic Poverty Center (2008), Annex E; Asian Development Bank (2008).

households could have moved out of poverty while other households moved into poverty and are still struggling to escape from poverty. Once they have fallen into poverty, intergenerational transmission of poverty is likely to occur unless they have access to educational and social capital.

According to the estimates from Chronic Poverty Research Center (2008, p. 9), the likelihood of households in South Asia suffering from chronic poverty is quite substantial. Estimates range between 126 million and 176 million. South Asia alone accounts for close to 40 percent of chronic poor in the world. For estimates of chronic poverty in selected Asian countries, see Tables 1.4 and Table 1.5.

Notice that there are some differences between the chronic poverty estimates in Tables 1.4 and 1.5. Aside from methodology, these differences highlight the difficulties in determining who are actually chrononically poor.

While the number of chronically poor is substantially less than the total number of those in poverty at any one time, the numbers of chronically poor are still high. The total number of chronically poor in the four countries in East Asia (China, Indonesia, Philippines and Vietnam) is estimated at between 50 and 80 million while in South Asia (Bangladesh, India, Nepal and Pakistan) the number of chronically poor is substantially higher at between 126 million and 176 million.

Since we are focusing on chronic poverty it is important to begin by asking the question — who is chronically poor in Asia? To answer this question we need to examine whatever information and research

Table 1.5 Chronic and Transitory Poverty in Recent Panel Studies (%)

Country	Dates	Observations	Chronic Poverty	Transitory Poverty	Never Poor
China	1985–90	2	6.2	47.8	46.0
India	1968–1971	3	33.3	36.7	30.0
India	1975–1984	9	21.8	65.8	12.4
Pakistan	1986–91	5	3.0	55.3	41.7

Source: Baulch and Hoddinott (2000) and Shaffer (2001, p. 33) Table 1.2.

is available on the poor. It is also difficult to differentiate between the chronically and the temporarily poor. Nevertheless it is useful to concentrate on those who are chronically poor. Most importantly, persistent or chronic poverty has intertemporal effects on those who are trapped in a poverty cycle. There are physical and psychological impacts that are not necessarily felt by those who fall into poverty for a short period of time. These aspects of chronic poverty include: (i) a lack of incentive and feelings of hopelessness brought on by persistent poverty, (ii) shortage of food and other material goods, illness and diseases that are passed on from generation to generation beginning at conception (iii) and a continual struggle for survival.

Chronic poverty has many different and interwoven aspects, which will vary from country to country and location to location, within a country. These specific features of chronic poverty need to be spelled out in some details if those in poverty traps are to free themselves. While avoiding overgeneralization, it is useful to introduce a few features which are common in many different situations.

1.2 Poverty and Hunger

While there is a definite relationship between hunger and poverty, not all the poor are hungry and not all the hungry are poor. Nevertheless we would expect the two variables to be highly correlated over time both within countries and between different countries. However comparing proportions of poor and hungry compiled by IFPRI (2007), there are some glaring discrepancies between the two variables for the Asian economies. In particular the hunger proportions are much higher than the poverty proportions for Pakistan and Sri Lanka. The discrepancies are particularly striking in Sri Lanka, where the proportion of the population that is ultra poor is less than one percent while the proportion that is ultra hungry is 24.2 percent (see Table 1.6).

Since all of the South Asian countries had food surpluses at the time of the surveys, IFPRI (2007) argues that food deficiencies in South Asia are the result of an inability to access available food rather than food shortages The disconnection between hunger and poverty

Table 1.6 Incidence of Rural Hunger by Food Energy Deficiency — Head Count Ratio (%)

Country	Subjacent Hungry	Medial Hungry	Ultra Hungry	All Rural Hungry
Bangladesh	30.9 (27.5)	12.8 (22.9)	4.8 (15.9)	59.6 (55.2)
India	28.9 (22.1)	12.1 (13.2)	1.8 (17.1)	37.1 (58.1)
Pakistan	21.8 (9.5)	9.9 (3.0)	16.5 (0.3)	12.8 (48.2)
Sri Lanka	23.4 (3.8)	10.9 (1.2)	24.3 (0.2)	6.8 (58.6)

Source: IFPRI (2007) percentages in brackets from Table 1.2.

statistics for Pakistan and Sri Lanka is reinforced by additional data collected by IFPRI (2007) which shows the incidence of poverty among the hungry to be very low in Pakistan and Sri Lanka (19 percent and 10 percent respectively). This is further evidence that in these two countries there must either be some food distribution shortages or consumption habits that stress other basic needs — health, education, transportation or housing — that kept food consumption low and the food energy deficit high.

But this would be seemingly inconsistent with budget surveys reported by IFPRI (2007) for the two other Asian economies in the survey. These show the share of food in the budgets of the poor in Bangladesh and India — but not Pakistan and Sri Lanka — to be between 60 and 70 percent of income. Without further data and analysis it is difficult to reconcile these results of large hunger deficits and low rates of poverty. One possible aspect of the hunger data is that meals eaten out of the home, either at restaurants or elsewhere, cannot be reliably estimated. But, there is no reason to believe that the rural poor in Sri Lanka and Pakistan ate many meals out of their own homes than the rural poor in the other two countries.

Due to these discrepancies between hunger and poverty data for South Asia and also because hunger statistics are not collected as systematically as information on poverty, for many countries, our analysis in the rest of this book will be confined to the analysis of poverty rather than hunger.

1.3 Poverty and Discrimination

Groups caught in the trap[1] of chronic poverty are often the object of discrimination. The amount of discrimination is difficult to determine because there is a feedback loop operating that makes identifying the degree of discrimination difficult. Are they poor because of discrimination or are they discriminated against because they are poor?

Discrimination takes many different forms, some obvious and others more subtle. Discrimination results in disadvantages to the poor that result from the lack of a level playing field at many different levels. We can generically group all of these various kinds of discrimination with one word — status. By status we mean any disadvantage that can be ascribed to race, ethnicity, gender, religion, social class or age. Generally such discrimination can occur in the work place, in markets for goods and services, in civil society or in legal matters. A few separate groups are analyzed below.

1.3.1 *Minorities including indigenous people*

Some minorities and indigenous people include marginalized groups that have been denied access to education, health and other social services and who have been relegated to the ranks of the unskilled in labor markets. For example in China there are more than 50 ethnic groups. These ethnic groups comprise less than 9 percent of the total population but around 40 percent of these minorities are in poverty (see World Bank, 2001). In Vietnam ethnic minorities make up only about 14 percent of the total population and 30 percent of these

[1] The term "poverty trap" has been widely used to describe a situation where a self-reinforcing set of circumstances result in persistent poverty. Poverty traps have been used to describe low growth scenarios for countries as a whole and also for segments within societies. Recent developments in growth theory feature models with increasing returns to scale as alternatives to the standard neoclassical model. These models include blocks to adoption of new technology, risk and liquidity constraints among others to explain low level equilibrium growth paths for many poor countries in Africa and South Asia (See Azariadis and Stachurski, 2006 and Barrientos, 2007).

Table 1.7 Rural Poverty Head Count Ratios by Social Group in Orissa and India, 1999–2000

Province	Scheduled Tribes	Scheduled Caste	All
Orissa	73	52	48
All — India	44	35	27

Source: de Haan and Dubey (2003).

minorities are poor (see Baulch and Masset, 2003). In India poverty rates for Scheduled Tribes and Scheduled Classes were up to 40 percent greater than for other ethnic groups (see Mehta and Shah, 2003 and 2006 and Table 1.7).

In Thailand about 1 million hill tribe members earn an average of around $100 per year per capita, less than a third of the poverty line of $1 per day (see FAO report available at http://www.fao.org/DOCREP/0040AC385E). In Bangladesh, Hindus comprise around 12 percent of the population while ethnic minorities (called Adavasi) comprise around 2 percent. Both groups are discriminated against, although there are few hard figures since the government has not recognized the Adavasi as a separate group and there are no data on income by religious affiliation.

In Pakistan, there is also a Hindu minority (although not as large as in Bangladesh) and a Catholic minority. Both groups are subject to discrimination. In the Philippines there are several hill tribes, indigenous people that were forced into the mountains and marginal agricultural lands by the Spanish over 400 years ago. While in Burma there are hill tribes that were similarly forced into marginal areas by the British.

In the Mekong countries of Vietnam, Laos and Cambodia there are also a sprinkling of indigenous tribes that share some of the same characteristics as the tribes in Thailand. In Vietnam approximately eight million or about 10 percent of the population comprising 51 ethnic groups live in the remote areas of the North, Northeast and the Central Highlands (see http://www.offroadvietham.com/eng/13-46.php and Minot, Baulch and Epprecht, 2006).

Poverty rates are significantly higher for these people than those living in more fertile lowland regions.

Laos and Cambodia (see Dasgupta *et al.*, 2003 and World Bank, 2006) have fewer ethnic minorities than the rest of Southeast Asian countries and there appears to be less ethnic discrimination. In Cambodia, the Cham account for around 2 percent of the population. They are somewhat different in dress and occupation from the Khmer majority yet their living circumstances are not noticeably different from the Khmer. Their incomes are also not at the lower end of the per capita consumption distribution. Other ethnic minorities including Chinese and Vietnamese are typically wealthier than the Khmer majority. The poorest are the highland tribal groups living in forested upland areas. There are 17 main tribal groups numbering only around 100,000.

In Lao PDR (see World Bank and IMF, 2001) the Lao Loum, or lowland Lao, constitute the majority of the population — 66 percent and speak the Lao language. The Lao Theung, or midland Lao migrated northward in prehistoric times and account for about 24 percent of the national population. The Lao Sung makes up about 10 percent of the population and live on upper slopes of the northern mountains. The Hmong are the most numerous Lao Sung group, with villages spread across the uplands of all the northern provinces. There are no statistics on the relative incomes of these three groups (Lao Loum, Lao Theung and Lao Sung). However it does not appear that the minority Lao Sung are discriminated against although their land is the least fertile of the three groups.

There are other ethnic minorities in Asia that also suffer from systematic discrimination. These and the minorities mentioned briefly above will be discussed more fully in the country reports in Chapter 7.

1.3.2 *Unfair labor practices*

Unfair labor practices help keep the chronically poor below the poverty line. The most widespread form of unfair labor practice is bonded labor. The practice comes about when a worker goes into debt to his employer and agrees to work for the employer in order to repay the debt. Bonded workers are usually poorly educated and work for a landowner as a share cropper but more often as a laborer. Bonded laborers are not guaranteed full time work or wages. A poor harvest can mean lower wages or intermittent employment. Any shock such as illness or bad weather can result in further borrowing and increased indebtedness to the landlord. Sometimes new migrants looking for work become bonded when they borrow money for subsistence or emergencies. Often the worker is duped by the employer and is charged high rates of interest on the loan from the employer. Over time the worker can no longer hope to repay this loan and his entire family becomes bonded to help repay the loan.

Bonded labor is widespread in South Asia. The system is perpetuated because the landowners may also be elected officials and are protected by or have influence with law enforcement officials. Conservative estimates of the numbers of bonded laborers indicate there are at least 2 million in India, approximately 1.7 million in Pakistan (mostly in southern Sindh and southern Punjab) and over 100,000 in Nepal. In India and Nepal, scheduled castes and scheduled classes and other poor groups form the bulk of the bonded. The Hindu minority in Pakistan are often bonded. An example of the extent of poverty endured by bonded labor is the Tharu community in western Nepal which typically gets 2 meals a day and a sack of grain at harvest time as the only form of payment. (See www.The southasian.com/Nov 2002/bonded_labor.htm).

Genicot (2002) has shown that abolition of bondage would be beneficial to the laborer in a rural village economy where bonded laborers work exclusively for the landlord. Being free from bondage would enable laborers to avail of a variety of borrowing and saving opportunities rather than exclusive reliance upon the landlord. Because it provides work security, laborers that are bonded voluntarily accept the exclusive relationship with the landlord. But this leads to a vicious cycle of poverty. Substituting access to credit from local credit institutions for an exclusive relationship with the landlord, the chain of bondage can be broken and more opportunities developed for increasing welfare of the chronically poor.

1.3.3 *Child labor*

The children in chronically poor households are often forced to work to help families survive. The bulk of child labor in Asia is in the agricultural sector. In Bangladesh it is estimated that over 80 percent of economically active children are working in agriculture and the figures are comparably large for India and other South Asian countries (see ILO, 1997). As a result of poverty in the family, child labor is widespread. Children are subject to bonding in South Asia to help their families pay off debts to the landlord. They are also forced to work long hours and face risks of snake and insect bites. They also suffer from a high incidence of respiratory infection from working outside in damp fields without proper shoes and clothing. Child labor statistics displayed in Table 1.8 show the estimated relationship between the total number of children and the number of child workers. These reported figures are also likely to be underreported and percentages are likely to be substantially higher among the chronically poor.

Children are forced into the labor market to help out with the family. Work can exist in a variety of occupations including as domestics, in export oriented industries, particularly textiles, apparel and hazardous industries such as brick kilns, glassware and stone quarrying. Child labor is also widely observed in parts of Southeast Asia. Children are kidnapped, smuggled and forced into prostitution or slavery. (See Nickolas Kristof's blog at http://www.facebook.com/Kristof and Nickolas Kristof, 2009).

Table 1.8 Child Labour Statistics

Country	Working Children	Total Children	Percent Who Work
Bangladesh	5.05 million	35.06 million	14
India	11.2 million	210 million	5
Nepal	1.660 million	6.225 million	25
Pakistan	3.3 million	40 million	8
Sri Lanka	0.475 million	3.18 million	15

Source: http://www.ilo.org/public/english/region/asro/newdelhi/ipec/index.htm.
Note: Children ages 5–14.

Child labor is prevalent in the Philippines, particularly in industries producing and exporting garments and wood products. (See http://www.dol.gov/ilab/media/reports/iclp/sweat/philippines.htm). In Indonesia over 2 million children under the age of 15 are employed, primarily in rattan and other furniture manufacturing and in the garment industry (see http://www.dol.gov/ilab/media/reports/iclp/sweat/indonesia.htm).

Childhood deprivation appears to be rather serious especially in the Mekong countries of Cambodia, Laos and Vietnam. According to Moore (2005) above 35 percent of children are severely deprived of two or more basic needs (i.e. access to shelter, sanitation and safe drinking water). Using a two wave panel data from the Vietnam Living Standard Survey conducted in 1992 and 1997, Gunther and Klasen (2007) reported that 38 percent of children in Vietnam were suffering from chronic poverty (Figure 1.1).

The well-being of children appeared to be less stable than that of adults. Despite the decline in absolute poverty in Vietnam due to

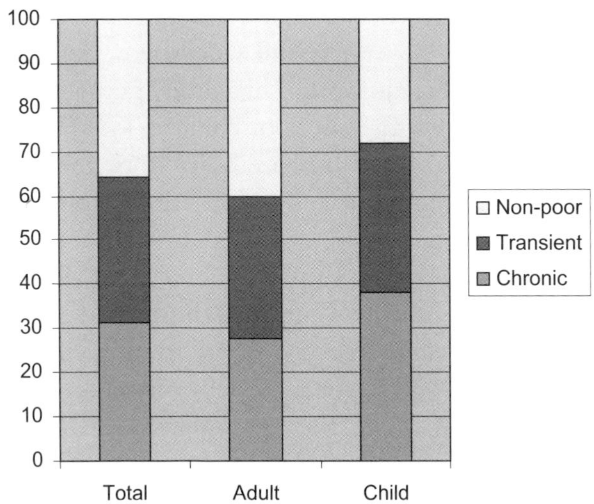

Figure 1.1 Poverty Rates in Vietnam, 1992 to 1997

Source: Data from Gunther and Klasen (2007, Table 1).

Note: Survey of 4,305 households tracking 17,829 individuals over a 5 year period.

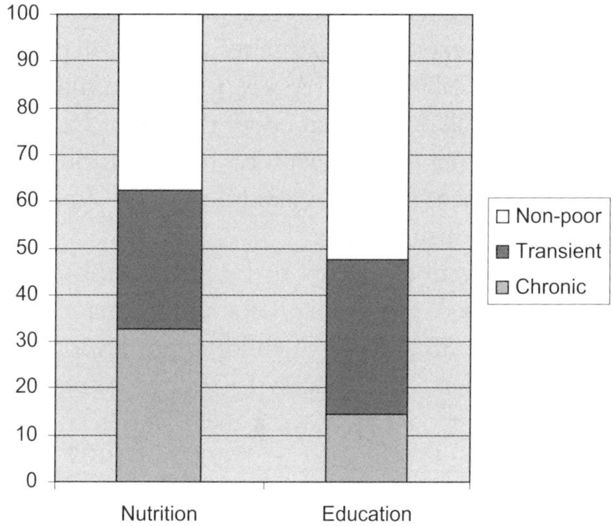

Figure 1.2 Non-Income Poverty Rates for Children in Vietnam in 1992 to 1997

Source: Data from Gunther and Klasen (2007, Table 1).

Note: Survey of 4,305 households tracking 17,829 individuals over a 5 year period.

significant economic growth between 1992 and 1997, the high ratio of children in chronic poverty is still worrisome. Educational well-being was a mere 15 percent for the chronically poor children as compared to over 50 percent for non-poor children (see Figure 1.2).

Efforts to ban child labor are based on the premise that parents are selfish. The evidence presented above suggests that decisions to send children to work are based on family survival. If parents act out on the need to ensure this survival, Basu and Van (1998) show that banning child labor is not the solution. Where child labor and adult labor are substitutes there are two equilibria — one where child labor persists and another when adult labor is paid enough so that children do not have to work. Rather, higher wages for parents will result in children going to school rather than working or even working after school, as suggested elsewhere. Basu and Van (1998) extend the multiple equilibria framework to show that women can be prompted to work outside the household if incentives are sufficiently attractive.

Basu (1999) goes a bit further and suggests that children should be prevented from working in dangerous occupations and that collaborative interventions can be used. These interventions involve restricting the number of hours children can work and making school attendance compulsory. At the same time, schools can be improved and free lunches provided. To prevent capital flight to countries which have not adopted child labor legislation, Basu (1999) also suggests the adoption of international labor standards for child labor that embody suggestion for safety and compulsory education while at the same time allowing children to work after school if needed to support their families. The evidence and theoretical models of Basu (1999) and Basu and Van (1998) suggest that the key to eliminating or reducing child labor lies in raising incomes for poor families so that they will have to rely less on their children to supplement family income.

1.3.4 *Gender*

There are several types of gender discrimination that result in the perpetuation of chronic poverty. Women and girls are often discriminated against within the household. Boys receive more human capital investment than girls and boys are given more education, food and health care. Birth weight, general health, literacy/education and life expectancy are also much lower for girls and infant mortality, stunting, anemia are higher. The cycle is perpetuated from generation to generation. Girls who grow up in such deprived environments are much more likely to be illiterate, sickly and die at an early age. They are also likely to pass these characteristics onto their own children.

> It is clear that girls who grow up stunted or anaemic are more likely to be underdeveloped for childbirth and face higher risks of maternal and child mortality and of low birthweight and stunting among their own children. (ACC/SNN, 2000).

It is also more likely that children born into such environments will have a greater probability of being mentally challenged as they receive less than adequate levels of nutrition and choleric intake. Global gender discrimination, including abortion, female infanticide poor health care, overwork and neglect have resulted in a stark imbalance in gender. Klasen and Wink (2003) estimate that as many as 80 million women in India and China are "missing" in the sense that the observed number of women is 80 million lesser than expected if there was no gender discrimination. This is 6.7 percent of the expected female population in China and 7.9 percent of the expected female population of India (see Klasen and Wink 2003, p. 264 and also Chronic Poverty Research Center, 2004 Chapter 2).

The one-child policy in China has resulted in further discrimination against girls. Orphaned and abandoned children are predominantly girls and the incidence of abortion has increased even though the one-child policy permits rural households to have a second child if the first is a boy. Families who violate the one-child guidelines are subject to severe penalties including higher taxes, ostracism and loss of jobs. As a result, there are strong social reasons for aborting the first born if it is a girl. Infanticide has also increased but it is difficult to obtain good estimates of the incidence of infanticide although the number of missing women suggests that it is high.

In a study of mother's education and survival of female children in Bangladesh, Bhuiya and Streatsfield (1991) found that girls infant mortality was about the same as boys in a section of rural Bangladesh until the age of 6 months, when girls mortality began to increase. The authors surmise that 6 months is the age at which babies begin to eat solid food and when differential gender treatment begins. They were able to document that baby girls received less food and health care which resulted in higher infant mortality for girl babies. Logit analysis for nearly eight thousand births showed that mother's education reduced the risk of infant mortality for both genders but still remained higher for girls. The age of the mother was not an important explanatory variable in explaining infant mortality differences.

The gender gap in adult literacy is also high, particularly in South Asia. Table 1.9 shows the extent of this discrimination. Female literacy rates are over 20 percent lower than male literacy rates in all countries.

Table 1.9 Adult Literacy Rates by Gender

Country	Adult Illiteracy Rate for Females — As Percent of Cohort	Adult Illiteracy Rate for Males — As Percent of Cohort	Gender Gap — Difference Between Female and Male Literacy Rates
Bangladesh	70.1	47.7	22.4
India	54.6	31.6	23.0
Nepal	76.0	40.4	35.6
Pakistan	72.1	42.5	29.6
Sri Lanka	11.0	5.6	5.4

Source: Chronic Poverty Research Center (2000).
Note: Data is from most recent year available.

Women are illiterate at a rate of over 70 percent in three out of the five South Asian countries.

Women and girls are also discriminated against in the workplace. Since they receive less education they are automatically excluded from many jobs. They are forced to work as manual labor or in farming related chores such as animal husbandry, cooking and collecting firewood and gardening. They are exposed to carcinogens from inhaling smoke from wood burning fires and injuries from carrying heavy loads. In many parts of India women serve as beasts of burden, pulling plows and carrying heavy loads on their heads at construction sites. They also receive lower pay for equal work. Trade unions in four Indian states reported wage rates for women that are 50 percent to 60 percent of male workers for the same job (see ILO, 2008).

Teenage pregnancy also tends to be higher among females with little formal education. Poor adolescent girls who get pregnant are likely to have many children, contributing towards high dependency rates and increased poverty. Moore (2005) points out that the birth rate among teenage girls from the lowest income quintile in Philippines is comparable to that in poorer developing countries like Bangladesh. The low level of maternal human capital for the young mothers could result in chronic poverty for their children thus feeding a vicious cycle of poverty.

1.4 Income and the Ability to Work

Those with limited earning capacity — the young, the disabled, the victims of conflict and displacement, the sick, the aged, the uneducated and illiterate are most likely to be chronically poor. All of these groups suffer higher than average rates of chronic poverty because they lack the earning power to lift themselves to a higher standard of living. This kind of income poverty is quite pervasive and hits all demographics including those subject to discrimination. While those without education can still work, they often do not make enough to escape poverty.

One large group, agricultural laborers having low levels of education and literacy, are subject to high rates of chronic poverty. 90 percent of the lowest caste in India, the dalits (formerly known as untouchables), work as laborers and many are in chronic poverty. Similar rates of chronic poverty are found among the uneducated and illiterate in other countries in South Asia. Without any formal social security, the poor elderly who are unable to work are dependent on relatives for support. The young who are living in poor households without any access to public health or education are more likely to be sick, suffer from diseases such as malaria and dysentery and to remain illiterate as they grow up. Many children are forced to the streets as orphans or beggars, working for low pay in the garment industry or in other occupations. Among those that can work, income poverty is primarily caused by a dramatic shortfall in the human and physical capital required to earn enough money to feed, clothe and house themselves and their families. Those who are too young, too old, disabled or sick also suffer from income poverty although they are essentially unable to take any actions on their own to change their situation.

1.5 Vulnerability

Households are vulnerable to poverty for a number of different reasons. Markets can collapse; workers may become sick or disabled. Weather factors can reduce crop yields. Price fluctuations can result in loss of income or higher prices for products purchased in the market. There are a number of research papers dealing with vulnerability (see Calvo and Dercon, 2005, and Sarewitz *et al.*, 2003, for references and discussion). Simply, vulnerability can be viewed as the exposure to downward risks. Risk is the probability of loss resulting from a specific outcome. Vulnerability pertains to the possible losses that could arise from changes in an existing condition or state of nature while risk is a more focused chance of loss from a particular event.

Vulnerability can be expressed, but not necessarily confined to, in terms of probabilities. Vulnerability can also be a more general term designed to describe an environment of susceptibility to undesirable changes. For example, New Orleans was vulnerable to flooding before it was hit by Hurricane Katrina, and the World Trade Towers were vulnerable to attack before September 11, 2001. However the vulnerability to such a flood or attack was difficult to assess. It is also difficult to insure against losses resulting from these incidents.

If one group is subject to higher downside risks that result in poverty, they are more vulnerable. Furthermore, the greater the risk that they will experience severe poverty, the greater is their vulnerability. Vulnerability is an ex ante concept and will supplement the ex post measures of poverty such as being below the poverty line. If the probability of entering into poverty increases then the vulnerability to poverty also increases. Other things being equal, a family will try to avoid as much risk as possible by opting for a living situation where it is less vulnerable to poverty in the sense that its chances of experiencing poverty in the future will be lower.

However households will balance vulnerability and risk with the possibilities of earning higher incomes. Vulnerability is related to risk. However vulnerability cannot be easily translated into expected outcomes as the New Orleans flood and the twin towers attack demonstrate. At the same time people will try to avoid vulnerable situations and they do this by pursuing less risky alternatives. Farmers working the slopes of volcanoes in Indonesia can expect higher yields since the soil is more fertile than in river valleys where farming has been going on for centuries and the soil may have become less fertile.

However, these farmers are more vulnerable since they will lose everything is there is a volcanic eruption. In general rural villages often choose planting options that minimize vulnerability that can arise if prices of inputs required to cultivate new varieties varies or if there is a crop failure and they fail to repay loans used to buy these inputs. Similarly, moving from subsistence to cash crops may introduce vulnerability to market fluctuations, exchange rates and other variable factors (see Sen, 1981, p. 126; Calvo and Dercon, 2005). There have been numerous studies of how households react to changes in these vulnerability factors and the perceived risks that accompany them (see Ramousset, 1976). Because of volatility in income and (to a lesser extent) the availability of social services, the vulnerability to poverty is significantly higher than the level of poverty at any time.

In a study of Indonesian poverty (Chaudhuri *et al.*, 2002) used a regression model to predict the level and volatility of poverty at the regional level. They found that the proportion of the population facing a non-negligible level of poverty was considerably greater than the observed fraction of the population that is poor. The main source of vulnerability for rural households and for the less-educated was the persistently low level of consumption. The most vulnerable groups reside in the outer islands of Indonesia, east of the major islands of Sumatra, Java, Sulawesi and Kalimantan in the Maluku and Papua provinces. Poverty levels are also high (over 30 percent) in Aceh and East Nusu Tenggara. The 1997 financial crisis had a significant impact on the most vulnerable groups in the outer islands.

The incidence of poverty and chronic poverty for the provinces of Indonesia are displayed in Table 1.10 for the years 1996, 1999 and 2004. Chronic poverty rose in every province between 1996 and 1999, more dramatically in the provinces with the highest incidence of chronic poverty and more rapidly than transient poverty (not shown). By 2003, overall rural poverty had declined pretty much across the board with the exception of Aceh, Riau and Northern Sumatra where the 2004 Tsunami did so much damage. The crisis also had a much larger than proportional impact on the poorly

Table 1.10 Poverty Incidences in Indonesia 2004

Province	Rural Poverty 2004	Rural Poverty 1999	Chronic Poverty 1999	Chronic Poverty 1996	Difference in Chronic Poverty 1999–1996
Aceh	33	13.6	1.2	0.5	0.7
North Sumatra	17	15.1	2.2	0.3	1.9
West Sumatra	10	9.4	1.4	0.0	1.4
Riau	18	9.4	3.3	0.8	2.5
Jambi	10	17.1	4.4	0.9	3.5
South Sumatra	21	23.5	6.0	1.1	4.9
Benkulu	21	20.6	7.2	1.9	5.3
Lampung	23	38.1	17.2	2.1	15.1
West Java	13	26.8	7.2	1.0	6.2
Central Java	24	32.9	9.9	2.4	7.5
East Java	24	33.6	10.3	2.4	7.9
West Nusu Tenggara	21	41.6	20.1	13.5	6.6
East Nusu Tenggara	30	62.0	51.4	39.9	11.5
West Kalimantan	14	29.4	14.7	5.1	9.6
Central Kalimantan	12	12.2	5.0	0.1	4.9
South Kalimantan	8	20.0	7.3	0.4	6.9
East Kalimantan	19	21.8	10.2	0.8	9.4
North Sulawesi	12	24.9	14.1	5.2	8.9
Central Sulawesi	23	28.0	16.1	3.5	12.6
South Sulawesi	19	36.6	19.9	10.9	9.0
Maluku	40	48.2	36.8	22.6	14.2
Papua	49	58.0	54.5	40.2	14.3

Source: Sussenas reported in Asian Development Bank (2006) and Suryahadi and Sumarto (2003).

educated and those making a living in agriculture. Chronic poverty among those without a primary education rose from 6.4 percent to 19 percent nationwide and from 7.2 to 18.7 percent among agricultural workers. Analysis of poverty vulnerability by gender showed virtually no difference between men and women, a result that is consistent with findings in other countries (see Dreze and Srinavasan, 1997). Overall the crisis raised the chronic poverty rate from 3.2 percent to 9.5 percent.

The average vulnerability to poverty, that is the probability that a person will be poor in the future rose to 27.2 percent in 1999 from 16.6 percent in 1996. Furthermore, the proportion of the highly vulnerable — those who have at least a 50 percent chance of falling into poverty rose from 7 percent before the crisis to 18.4 percent after the crisis.

In a study of poor villages in two of the poorest provinces of India (Uttar Pradesh and Bihar) Parker and Kozel (2007) found that lack of social capital and savings, together with susceptibility to illness and disease were the main factors responsible for high volatility in income and consumption, mainly in a downward direction. They also found that the persistence of long term poverty and its volatility were closely related to social classes and status. Scheduled castes and scheduled tribes lived in segregated areas within their villages which restricted their access to a wide variety of infrastructure and social services that were available to others in the village.

> ... resources such as drinking and irrigation water, schools, health posts, infrastructure projects, Public Distribution System (PDS) shops etc become concentrated in the wealthy or dominant-caste communities. When the school is at the far end of the village, the poor are less likely to enroll their children (especially girls) and low caste people have expressed unwillingness to brace the insults and humiliations they receive when attempting to utilize PDS fair price shops and other resources located in high-caste neighborhoods. (Chaudhuri *et al.*, 2002, p. 20).

Lack of access to government services and the isolation of particular classes contribute to the inability to obtain outside help when someone in the family becomes ill, injured or incapacitated with a long term disease such as tuberculosis or diabetes. Lacking support from family or friends, poor families either have to sell assets or resort to borrowing which drives them further into poverty and often to bondage relationships for themselves and their families. Many of the resources intended for the poor such as basic public health services and education are co-opted by the wealthy and powerful, leaving the poor without any hope for using these resources to better their lives. Scheduled tribes and scheduled casts are particularly vulnerable to shocks that can come from illness, poor weather, a poor harvest, accidents, violence and volatility in prices for cash crops. The vulnerability of the poor is reinforced by their lack of job stability. Few members of the lower caste households in rural Uttar Pradesh had permanent or secure job. Over 50 percent were employed as agricultural labor or non-farm labor while another 20 percent were self employed in the farming sector. Few of the lower castes have a significant amount of land (Chaudhuri *et al.*, 2002, p. 14).

Chronically poor farmers are usually unable to get access to irrigated land and the rain fed land they cultivate is often marginal and vulnerable to droughts or floods. As a result, crop yields and farmers earnings are quite volatile. When the harvest is bad chronically poor farmers often are forced to resort to borrowing from the landlord or from friends or family. The chronically poor have limited access to formal credit markets where interest rates would be substantially lower than rates charged by money lenders or their landlords. As a result, the chronically poor fall into the trap of bondage, where they sell their labor to the landlord at below market rates and become more like indentured servants than free workers (see Suryahadi and Sumarto, 2003).

Unexpected events often affect those who are already poor. IFPRI (2007) reports that consumption of households in the lowest income deciles fluctuated much more than consumption of families in the richer deciles in Pakistan (see Alderman, 1996) and China (see Jalan and Ravallion, 1999)., This suggests that those families in the lowest deciles were less able to protect themselves against shocks and would have probably had borrow to smooth consumption. These shocks are usually unavoidable. In Pakistan, for example, a large proportion of variation in household expenditure was the result of weather shocks (World Bank, 2002).

The lesson that can be drawn from the above analysis of vulnerable groups in Indonesia, India, Pakistan and China is that social protection for the vulnerable should be a high government priority. In the poorer deciles of the income distribution, many households are only a few steps from a disastrous downward spiral into poverty that can only be avoided by some form of social protection.

1.6 The Confluence of Forces and Poverty Dynamics

Surely income poverty takes center stage when looking at headcount ratios and summary statistics about poverty. Income is a key variable in assessing what progress is being made in reducing poverty. The substantial progress in reducing poverty in the 1980s and 1990s was primarily the result of raising incomes for the rural poor. As a result of the green revolution, total factor productivity increased along with the marginal product of labor (see Lipton, 2005). This helped to lower the rate of unemployment as well as prices of staple goods for the poor. Without raising income chronic poverty cannot be effectively reduced in the long run.

Nonmonetary factor are also important in and of themselves and also as they interact with monetary factors. Chronic health, nutritional and educational poverty often result in reduced ability to do productive work which results in lower earning capacity. Stagnant income and poor health and nutrition combine to put a stranglehold on the poor that is so tight that successive generations are trapped in its noose.

In other settings, low income and poor health and nutrituion may not always be closely associated. In a study of chronic poverty in Vietnam, Baulch and Masset (2003) found that chronic food poverty in reflecting income poverty, are not always correlated with stunted growth and lack of any primary school education. While low income, poor health and low nutrition are all found in the ethnic minorities living in the mountainous North and Central Highlands, there are also many chronically malnourished adults in the richer Red River and Mekong deltas.

While it is true that generally over time both monetary and nonmonetary indices of chronic poverty do tend to move together, it is important to recognize the multiple dimensions of poverty and the interrelationships between monetary and nonmonetary factors.

It is also important to understand the dynamics of chronic poverty. The answer to the question "Who are the chronically poor?" will change over time. Some families will escape the poverty trap while others will be driven into poverty. In a study of Bangladesh, Sen (2003) found a number of factors helped to lift families out of poverty over time. These factors include a decrease in the dependency ratio (fewer children and more working adults per family), crop diversification, rapid acquisition of human resources (more education), adaptation of high yielding rice varieties, increased access to land and diversification of employment out of agriculture (into transport, construction, agro processing, petty trading and business) and better access to credit. As these indicators of the status of the poor have changed, so has their status. Those falling into poverty experienced changes in the opposite direction — reduced access to land and credit, greater concentration on traditional planting methods, higher dependency rates and smaller additions to the stock of human capital. Natural disasters and other crises also played a role in driving families further into poverty.

1.7 Where do the Chronically Poor Live?

The bulk of the poor in Asia are caught it a cycle of poverty that has a number of special location features. The term poverty trap has been widely used to describe location factors relating to poverty and chronic poverty. The chronically poor in rural Asia live in widely disperse locations in different countries. In China many of the chronically poor are found in the mountainous provinces of Guangdong, Guangxi, Guizou and Yunnan in Southwest China. In India, the provinces of Andhra Pradesh, Assam, Bihar, Kerala, Orissa, Madhya Pradesh, Rajastan, West Bengal and Uttar Pradesh have the highest concentration of the poor. In India more than 70 percent of the poor live in these states and the concentration of poverty in these states is increasing (see Table 1.11). In Thailand, Burma, Vietnam and the Philippines hill tribes have high concentrations of the chronically poor while the outer island have high concentrations of the poor in Indonesia. Nevertheless irrespective of country these locations have a number of features in common.

Table 1.11 Concentration of Poverty in India in Percent of Poor Below Poverty Line

State	1983	1993/94	1999/2000
Poor states	70	71	76
Richer states	27	26	22

Source: World Bank 2003.
Note: Poor states are Andhra Pradesh, Assam, Bihar, Kerala, Orissa, Madhya Pradesh, Rajasthan, West Bengal and Uttar Pradesh. Rich states are Gujarat, Karnataka, Haryana, Maharastra, Punjab and Tamil Nadu.

1.7.1 *In remote areas*

The chronically poor often live in remote locations that are far from the centers of commercial activity as well as political influence and power. This distance is measured not only in miles or kilometers but in the time that it takes to reach them. Roads in and out of these areas can be dangerous and sometimes even impassable during the rainy season, or located in treacherous mountainous areas filled with switchbacks and subject to landslides. This leads to high transportation costs and reduced ability to sell surplus agricultural products in market towns. In countries where there are many different islands, the chronically poor often reside on islands that are far away from the main centers of commerce and trade. These include the outer islands of Indonesia and some of the smaller islands in the Visayas in the Philippines and parts of Mindanao. These remote islands have few ports, limited sea traffic and few air links.

1.7.2 *Where agricultural productivity is low*

Agricultural land occupied by the chronically poor rice farmers is in low yielding rain-fed locations, in mountainous terrain with limited opportunities for irrigation or in relatively dry soil where the chances of drought are high. Soil quality is poor and land can be on slopes requiring extensive civil works such as rice terraces to create level fields. Low yielding rice varieties are common, since high yielding varieties require more reliable rainfall and irrigation. The poor farmers living in these regions often cultivate other low yielding crops such as sorghum and pulses. Natural hazards including flooding and drought are common. In Bangladesh the *char* communities along the river and coastline are periodically flooded. In Pakistan's Baluchistan, Northwest Frontier Province and parts of Sindh the mountain environment results in variable growing conditions and low yields. In the poorer provinces of India, drought and variability in monsoon rains results in periodic crop failures. Poverty is high, and labor bonding is extensive despite being prohibited by law. Rice yields are a fraction of those obtained on more fertile irrigated land and in river valleys. Wage rates are correspondingly low and variability in productivity as a result of weather factors often result in workers in agriculture not being fully employed.

Jalan and Ravallion (2000) found that low food-grain yields were positively associated with chronic poverty in China. In addition, Sah (2007) found that the possibility of a household in Southwestern Madhya Pradesh being chronic poor is 2.5 times more likely if agricultural production is low. Furthermore, households without irrigation are 5 times more likely to be chronic poor. Falling agricultural incomes also can result in households being caught in a poverty trap and forced to consider migration out of rural areas. However, migration does not necessarily imply rising income for the households that do migrate.

1.7.3 *In political and social isolation*

The concentration of minorities in these remote rural locations is high and they have a limited voice in the political life and in the decision-making process of the community. As a result public resources directed to these areas both by local, provincial and the national government is limited. Their access to markets is restricted by the lack of efficient, rapid and convenient transportation which is costly and often unreliable. Buses and trucks often break down and goods have to be offloaded increasing delivery time and spoilage. Furthermore integration with urban markets can be weak. All of these factors result in high transportation and transactions costs. Social isolation is reinforced by language and social customs that differ from surrounding communities. In many cases hill tribes speak many different languages and may have difficulty communicating with each other. Social isolation also keeps members of local communities from seeking employment outside of their villages and/or migrating to small nearby urban centers or to larger cities. This social isolation compounds the physical isolation that results from geographic remoteness.

1.8 Why are They Poor?

"Why are they poor?" may sound like a rhetorical question. Obviously they are poor because they fall below the poverty line. Those that are chronically poor are below the poverty line for significantly long periods of time to qualify to be in this chronic category. The main reason for chronic poverty is lack of earning power and the inability to avail of social services such as education, health and sanitation and satisfactory housing. Without the wherewithal to achieve a sustainable standard of living, families in chronic poverty are mired in a long lasting poverty trap. The perpetuation of this poverty trap is the result of a combination of factors, many of which are common to those immersed in this trap in countries throughout the region.

1.8.1 *Income poverty*

We can start with income poverty of primary income earners. The chronically poor are subject to multiple poverty traps relating to their lack of a sustainable income. The first trap is illiteracy. The bulk of the chronically poor are unable to earn enough income to bring themselves and their families out of poverty. The illiterate and poorly educated are forced to work in menial jobs as laborers earning very little. They have few possessions and no physical capital to speak of, not even farm implements or means of transportation. Since they have no saving to fall back on or a network of social services the can rely on, they are vulnerable to shocks that can drive them even deeper into poverty. Poor soil fertility is a characteristic of chronically poor rural areas where agriculture is rain fed and soil fertility is low. Rice grown in upland conditions subject to variable rainfall without appropriate inputs will have yields that are as low as 20 percent of yields on irrigation land where there is appropriate irrigation and application of fertilizers.

They lack access to credit since they are judged poor credit risks by both formal and informal lenders. As a result they turn to their landlord employers in times of poor harvests, drought and floods or when they are subject to spells of unemployment for other reasons. This cycle of fluctuations in income often results in rural agricultural workers becoming bonded to their employer. Their children are in turn, forced to work and subsequently become bonded as well.

Discrimination also plays a role in keeping the chronically poor from escaping poverty. Lower social classes and castes suffer disproportionately. 90 percent of the dalits, the lowest social class in India are either illiterate or have low levels of numeracy and literacy. They work as laborers for the lowest possible wages. For example, in Bihar, the poorest Indian state, 16.5 percent of the population is Moslem and subject to discrimination and 87 percent of the population lives in rural areas. Generally low levels of education and training lead to a skills trap whereby employers in the region are not interested in developing products and services requiring higher levels of skill. As a result, the region stagnates technologically and workers have few incentives to uplift themselves or their families. This is also the case in Orissa and other poor states as well.

The practice of subsistence farming in chronically poor areas results in isolation from outside markets and a low level of trade with surrounding communities. Subsistence farmers have very little disposable income and bring a limited amount of their production to market. Specialization is not rewarded since there are few opportunities for trade and few middlemen to facilitate sales with other markets. Subsistence farming can also result in farming practices that focus on short term gains rather than longer term soil viability thereby reducing soil fertility by over cultivation.

1.8.2 *Lack of capital and social services*

Isolation and neglect by various levels of government results in a dramatic shortfall in the level of social services provided to regions which are experiencing chronic poverty. Many chronically poor are undernourished and suffering from poor health. Tuberculosis, malaria, dysentery, stunting, infant mortality and malnutrition levels are significantly higher in poor areas compared with the non-poor. The chronically poor suffer from intergenerational transmission of poor health and sanitation. Mothers unable to get enough nutrition to feed themselves while they are pregnant have smaller babies who are more susceptible to disease and can be mentally challenged from birth. Families have large families in order to provide a social safety net of support for the parents in old age. Instead this often results in a lower standard of living for the family as a whole and increased infant mortality and increased susceptibility to diseases. Lacking working capital small businesses operate inefficiently on a hand to mouth basis, selling little and purchasing and stocking small quantities for inventory. As a result they are unable to take advantage of economies of scale in purchasing or to buy new product lines for fear that they will not sell. As a result there is little innovation and business dynamism in poor regions. Farmers are unwilling to try new methods of cultivation or experiment with new high yielding varieties. High levels of risk aversion constrain the agricultural community to traditional methods and varieties that have a better chance of surviving floods and droughts.

1.8.3 *Environmental degradation*

Common property resources are often mismanaged in chronically poor regions. Many of these regions are already fragile ecosystems. Although logging is a far bigger source of deforestation hill tribes in mountainous areas that depend on firewood for warmth and meal preparation can also contribute to deforestation. Shifting cultivation requires land to be left fallow for a certain time to regenerate the soil and provide protection against soil erosion, landslides and flooding. Shifting cultivation may also result in further incursion into virgin forests and this is a long record of these incursions in the Philippines, Thailand and Burma.

Population pressures and the need for more food can destroy the natural balance between nature and agricultural practices and can also lead to further deforestation of virgin forests. As environmental damage escalates it also causes further deterioration in living standards on the chronically poor through reduced crop yields, increased risk of landslides, flooding and other natural disasters.

1.8.4 *Lack of diversity, low saving, growth and limited technical transfer*

Isolated agricultural communities that live in chronic poverty are generally risk averse. Living from hand to mouth they do not plan for the future, thus they are unable to amass saving to upgrade farm equipment or livestock or diversify to crops other than rice. Often they are tied to landlords through loans which are not available from other sources. They are income constrained to the extent that they find it difficult to send their children to school. Poor roads and inadequate health and educational facilities also make education and preventive health care expensive. This limits the formation of human infrastructure at an early age. Rather, children often start working instead of going to school. Investment opportunities in business finance and commerce in such communities is limited by the lack of nearby and accessible markets. Because of the lack of resource, physical infrastructure may crumble over time exacerbating the other challenges that face those trying to rise out of poverty.

1.9 Chronically Poor, Transient Poor and Non-Poor

The fundamental difference between the chronically poor and the transient poor is the depth of poverty which persists for an extended period of time (see Table 1.12). The transient poor can come in and out of poverty while the chronically poor remain for years. For the working poor the level of chronic deprivation is pervasive and extends to every corner of their daily lives. It is widespread both in terms of levels of income, physical assets necessary to earn more money and social services such as education, housing, sanitation and health care. Without physical assets, income, education and suffering from potential bouts of illness and disease the chronically poor have no way to

Table 1.12 Chronic Poverty, Transient Poverty and Non-Poor

	Chronically Poor	Transient Poor	Non-Poor
Definition	• Chronic inability to generate sufficient income to leave poverty trap • Poverty persistence as defined by the length of years being poor (more than 5 years)	• Vulnerability to income shocks and risks • Temporal slip into poverty for a given time period	• Living above the country's poverty line
Over time	• Intergenerational transmission of poverty	• Ability to lift themselves or children out of poverty	• Bequest of income or wealth to future generations
Causes	• Permanent multidimensional deprivation such as lack of assets (physical and capital); trapped in low productive activities; high dependency rates and/or location in remote areas	• Exposure to uninsured income risk such as random shocks like natural disasters and accidents to bread earner of the family	• Accumulation of physical and human assets that generate income for the individual or household
Proposed solutions	• Policies to increase long term investment in physical and human capital	• Policies to allow smoothing of income/ consumption such as access to credit schemes and insurance options	• Not applicable

Source: McKay and Lawson (2002).

lift themselves out of poverty by themselves given the current regulatory and policy environment and the lack opportunities to earn more income and obtain better education and health services. These families desperately need a way to earn more income and raise their levels of human capital.

There is a culture of poverty among the chronically poor that focuses on everyday survival. There can be no thought of educating your children or uplifting your own skills, health and literacy if it is a daily struggle to survive. There can be no thought of planting higher yielding varieties when you are already deeply in debt to your landlord. Laborers have little hope of finding a better job when they cannot read and write and belong to a tribal minority or lower caste. There may be an option to send children to school to learn to read and write but the cost of doing so is usually beyond the reach of the chronically poor. As a result children of the chronically poor remain in poverty and the intergenerational transmission of poverty persists.

1.10 Rural and Urban Poverty

The major focus of this book is rural poverty. This is because the vast majority of the chronically poor in Asia are living in rural settlements. In the year 2000, the Planning Commission of India estimated that around 70 percent of the poor including both transient and chronically poor lived in rural areas. Nearly 200 million people in rural areas were poor while around 67 million people in urban areas were poor. Furthermore, the level of chronic poverty in rural areas is probably even higher. This is because the rural poor often reside in poverty trapped regions while many of the urban poor live in more fluid circumstance where the children of the chronically poor have a better chance of getting out of the poverty trap. The situation in other countries in South Asia is similar as urban poverty is dwarfed by rural poverty.

This is not to minimize the plight of the urban poor, many of whom live in poverty stricken circumstances in large and growing urban slums, near garbage dumps and along railroad tracks in overly crowded circumstances without proper sewage, clean water, adequate housing or primary health care. Nevertheless, the problems of the urban poor have more to do with the rapid growth of cities and the rapid immigration from the countryside where conditions are even worse and chances of being chronically poor are even higher. Therefore, while recognizing the challenges of urban poverty we focus more on rural poverty.

1.11 Dimensions of Chronic Poverty in Asia

Estimates of chronic poverty differ from traditional estimates of poverty. Chronic poverty will be somewhat lower since only families that have endured poverty from some time are counted as the chronically poor. McKay and Baulch (2003) estimate the number of chronically poor using the World Bank estimates of US1 dollar per day poverty (World Bank, 2003b) and combined these estimates with the likelihood that those in poverty will stay poor for five years or more. Panel data for many countries were used to estimate the transition matrix which shows the likelihood that a person will stay poor for five years or more.

The transition probabilities are displayed in Figure 1.3 and the estimates of Chronic Poverty and Extreme Poverty (US$1 per day) are displayed in Table 1.13 for Asia and the rest of the globe. Table 1.14 contains chronic poverty and extreme poverty estimates for selected countries in Asia. These estimates are somewhat different from the

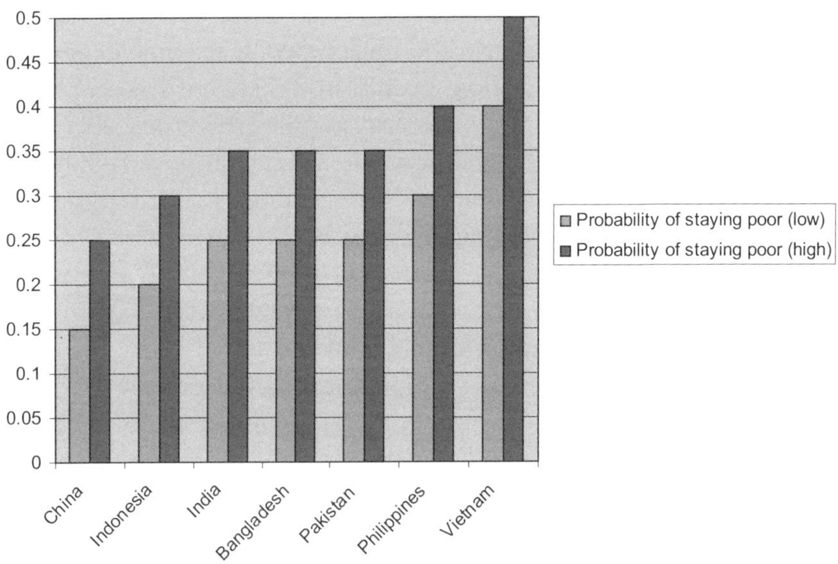

Figure 1.3 Probabilities of Staying Poor for 5 Years Using Panel Data Estimates

Source: Data from McKay and Baulch (2003, p. 6).

Table 1.13 Estimates of Chronic Poverty and Extreme Poverty by Region in Millions

Region	Poverty Measured by US$ 1 Per Day Poverty Line	Chronic Poverty (low)	Chronic Poverty (high)	Proportion of Poor Who are Chronically Poor (low)	Proportion of Poor Who are Chronically Poor (high)
Sub-Sahara Africa	303.3	100.0	121.3	30%	40%
East Asia and Pacific	312.8	53.7	84.9	17.2%	27.2%
South Asia	535.6	133.9	187.5	25.0%	35.0%
Rest of World	88.0	19.8	28.0	22.5%	31.8%
Global	1,239.7	298.3	412.7		

Source: McKay and Baulch (2003, p. 8).

Table 1.14 Chronic Poverty and Extreme Poverty for Selected Asian Countries in 2000

Country	Extreme Poor (in millions)	Chronically Poor (in millions)
India	450	155
China	230	60
Bangladesh	45	20
Vietnam	18	10
Pakistan	20	9
Indonesia	18	7
Philippines	14	7

Source: McKay and Baulch (2003, p. 12), interpolated from Figure 2.

figures reported in Table 1.2 and Table 1.3, which were compiled using a slightly different methodology.

From Table 1.15 the chronic poverty estimates are for the number of poor who have been chronically poor for at least five years, living on US$1 per day or less for this entire period. The figures in Table 1.15 are point estimates of the proportion of the poor who are

Table 1.15 Estimates of Very Poor and Poor in Rural Areas of India, 1993–94 (%)

State	Very Poor	Poor
Bihar	27.7	58.2
Madhya Pradesh	17.1	40.7
Maharastra	16.2	37.9
Orissa	21.8	49.8
Uttar Pradesh	19.6	42.3
All India	15.3	37.1

Source: Datta and Sharma (2000), cited in Mehta and Shah (2006).

very poor. Families in chronic poverty are highly likely to have transition probabilities that are substantially higher than those in the larger extreme poverty group. It is highly likely that they will not be able to break out of the poverty trap and that their children will all be doomed to live a life of chronic poverty with almost no hope of breaking out. Furthermore the concentration of poor in the poorest states has increased over time and that the number of people in poverty has increased as well. Fan *et al.* (1999) report that in two of the poorest states, Bihar and Uttar Pradesh the proportion of total poor in India increased from 11.4 percent in 1960 to 18.5 percent in 1993 (Fan *et al.*, 1999, Table 20) and in Uttar Pradesh from 15 percent to 18 percent. These two states alone accounted for nearly 40 percent of all the poor in India by the early years of this century.

Several estimates of the level of chronic poverty are reported for Pakistan in Chronic Poverty Research Center, 2003, Chapter 7. There is some variation in these estimates. They are, however, lower than the estimates for India — ranging from 6 to 10 percent of the population being chronically poor for 3 to 5 years in a row as measured by falling below the poverty line.

East Asia has approximately 54 to 84 million of the chronic poor and most of them live in China. Chronic poverty in China tends to be concentrated in remote areas of low agricultural productivity and away from the dynamic coastal cities (Chronic Poverty Research

Table 1.16 Estimates of Chronic Poverty in Four Selected Provinces of Southern China, 1985–1990 (%)

Province	Chronic Poverty (%)
Guangdong	15.8
Guangxi	43.4
Guizhou	57.2
Yunnan	51.0

Source: Data from Jalan and Ravallion (1998, Table 1).

Center, 2004, Chapter 10). There are four main groups of chronic poor. They are mainly the ethnic minorities living generally in remote areas, households with older, sick or disabled members, orphaned and abandoned children and the newly poor due to dismantling of state-owned enterprises or resettlers for major infrastructural project or rural to urban migrants. Chronic poverty accounts for approximately 45 percent to 60 percent of poverty in Guangxi, Guizhou, Yunnan but only 16 percent in the more prosperous province, Guangdong (Table 1.16).

Chapter 2

What Determines Chronic Poverty in Asia?

As we learned in Chapter 1, there are a number of factors that contribute to chronic poverty in Asia. In this chapter we explore the determinants of chronic poverty in greater depth. Each of the individual factors by themselves is an important marker for chronic poverty. However the condition of persistent poverty cannot exist without the presence of several factors working together to further reduce the chances of families rising out of poverty and achieving a more fulfilling, happier and healthier life. In this chapter we discuss each of the important factors contributing to chronic poverty separately. In the next chapter we will look more carefully at the dynamics of chronic poverty and how these individual factors work, interact and reinforce each other to keep families in chronic poverty.

2.1 Lack of Human Capital

We define human capital as the acquisition of literacy, numeracy and other forms of education, job market skills, on the job training, good health and nutrition, proper sanitation and satisfactory clothing and housing. The chronically poor are lacking in such stocks of human capital and are unable to acquire additional human capital. They are poorly housed, clothed, fed and they have low levels of education and are generally in poorer health that the non poor and the transitory poor. As a result their productivity as workers and wage earners suffers; they are often ill and unable to work efficiently. They do not qualify for jobs that require anything more than minimal skill and have few prospects for finding more productive work.

The United Nations prepares an annual document that assesses human capital developments in many countries around the world. This Human Development Report's Human Development Index is comprised of three variables of equal weight comparing nations' human capital performance stressing literacy, education and level of income. The first variable is an indicator of whether the residents of a country can look forward to a long and healthy life. This expectation is proxied by a measure of life expectancy at birth. The second variables is a measure of knowledge and education proxied by a weighted average of the adult literacy rate (with two-third weight) and the combined primary, secondary and tertiary gross enrollment rate (with one-third weight). The third variable is the standard of living in the country which is proxied by the gross domestic per capita measured at purchasing power parity.

Is it possible to develop a similar index of well being for the chronically poor? So far, no efforts have been made to do this for a wide range of countries. What we can do is to list some of the social indicators for chronically poor areas in Asia that are currently available from local and international sources. We will then focus on life expectancy, infant mortality (which we have added as an additional indication of health) and literacy/education. We can start with life expectancy at birth from country data and then try to see how these figures can be adjusted for the chronically poor.

2.1.1 *Life expectancy*

Countrywide figures for life expectancy and infant mortality are displayed in Table 2.1 for the countries in Asia where there are likely to be large numbers of chronically poor. How can these figures be adjusted to reflect these human development indicators for the chronically poor? One approach would be to look at poor regions where life expectancy and infant mortality statistics have been collected. In India these figures are reported in Table 2.2.

Comparison of life expectancy and infant mortality in the poorer states of India in Table 2.2 with the India average in Table 2.1 indicates a significantly lower state of health in the poorer states. Life

Table 2.1 Life Expectancy and Infant Mortality

Country	Life Expectancy at Birth in Years 2001	Infant Mortality Per 1000 Live Births 2004
Bangladesh	62	56
India	63	62
Pakistan	63	80
Sri Lanka	73	12
Cambodia	54	97
Indonesia	66	30
Lao PDR	54	65
Philippines	70	26
Thailand	69	18
Vietnam	69	17
China	70	26

Source: UNESCAP (2004) and Save the Children (2006), available at http://www.savethechildren.org/

Table 2.2 Demographic Indicators by State

State	Female Life Expectancy (1992–94)	Infant Mortality Per 1000 Births (1992–94)
Poorer states		
Assam	54.4	78
Bihar	56.4	69
Madhya Pradesh	53.2	102
Orissa	55.1	109
Rajasthan	56.7	85
Uttar Pradesh	54.5	93
Richer states		
Andhra Pradesh	61.5	66
Gujarat	60.5	63
Haryana	63.2	69
Karnataka	63.6	68
Kerala	73.4	15
Punjab	67.2	55
Tamil Nadu	62.5	58
West Bengal	62.3	61

Source: Government of India, Population Census and Registrar General of India.

expectancy is about 10 years longer for India as a whole than it is in the poorer states. Infant mortality rates are higher by as much as 40 percent in Madya Pradesh and Orissa (62 versus 102 and 109). For the chronically poor, these figures would have to be adjusted even further. In the poorest districts in the poorest states the infant mortality rates are even higher than the rates for the provinces with the highest infant mortality. Mehta and Shah (2006) report that one district in Assam, seven districts in Uttar Pradesh, seven in Orissa and 23 in Madhya Pradesh had infant mortality rates higher than 109; two districts the IMR had rates over 150.

This suggests that the IMR and perhaps life expectancy need to be adjusted for the chronically poor. The World Health Organization has developed a concept they call Disability Adjusted Life Expectancy (DALE). DALE summarizes the expected number of years to be lived in what might be termed the equivalent of "full health." To calculate DALE, the years of ill-health are weighted according to severity and subtracted from the expected overall life expectancy to give the equivalent years of healthy life. WHO rankings show that years lost to disability are substantially higher in poorer countries because some limitations — injury, blindness, paralysis and the debilitating effects of several tropical diseases such as malaria — strike children and young adults. People in the healthiest regions lose some 9 percent of their lives to disability, versus 14 percent in the worst-off countries.

How many more years are lost by the chronically poor? Unfortunately there are no reliable estimates. As an approximation lets suppose that the chronically poor lose an additional five percent of their life expectancy as a result of the risks that come with being chronically poor. In Table 2.2 the average life expectancy for women in the poorer states is 55. For the chronically poor life expectancy would be reduced by about 2.5 years. This brings the life expectancy for women in the poorer Indian provinces down to around 52. If the loss is 10 percent, the life expectancy for women in the poorer Indian states would be around 50.

2.1.2 *Infant mortality*

Since the poor often live far from hospitals, many births take place at home with the sole help of a midwife and often in unsafe and unsanitary conditions. These conditions often lead to sickness among the very young. Rates of infant mortality (measured as deaths before age 2) for the chronically poor is likely to be 5 to 10 percent higher than the average rates in the poorest provinces of India. This is borne out by figures compiled by the World Health Organization (World Health Organization, 2000, p. 12) where infant mortality is broken down by population quintile as displayed in Table 2.3. The figures for the lowest two quintiles are similar to the IMR for the poorest state in India and the chronically poor are more likely to be in the lowest decile with even higher IMRs. Notice that the IMR for the bottom quintile is the same as the IMR for Orissa in Table 2.2.

The Family Planning Foundation in India conducted a survey (Family Planning Foundation in India, 1988) to investigate the factors responsible for high infant mortality among the more vulnerable sections of the population in 800 villages of 33 districts in five states in India. Pregnancy rates for women younger than 18 were quite high — 50–58 percent in Madhya Pradesh, 26–38 percent in Uttar Pradesh, around 46 percent in rural Karnataka and the slums of Bombay, and 29–33 percent in tribal Orissa. The infant mortality rate was significantly higher for children whose mothers were younger than 18 years as compared to those older than 18. The infant mortality rate was

Table 2.3 Infant Mortality Rates for India

Population Quintile	Infant Mortality Rate (IMR)
Top quintile	44
Second quintile	65.6
Third quintile	89.7
Fourth quintile	106.3
Bottom Quintile	109.2

Source: WHO (2000).

2–3 times higher when there was a premature delivery. For those families earning less than Rs 500/month (just over US$1 per day per person) the infant mortality rate was 2 times higher than those earning more. This high rate can be attributed to the elevated level of poverty in the villages where early deliveries were recorded.

Many researchers have observed that poor women marry early and have children before they turn 18. There are many possible reasons to support these observations including lack of availability and education about contraceptives and widespread illiteracy among the poor. Children in this setting are likely to be undernourished and mothers are unable to afford pre- and postnatal care. As a result their babies run a higher risk of mortality. The cycle does not stop there since the young girls get pregnant again and the poverty trap of high fertility and infant mortality continues.

The inadequate level of primary medical care in the poorer states compounds high infant mortality and lower life expectancy. Using absentee rates for health care workers as a proxy for primary medical care Table 2.4 displays the relationship between primary medical care and income in the states of India. Absentee rates are high in all states and particularly so in Assam and Bihar, two of the poorest states.

Do other countries in South Asia, Indonesia, Philippines and the Mekong countries have similar experience to those just described for

Table 2.4 Absentee Rates in States of India for Healthcare Workers (2003) and Per Capita Income (2001)

State	Absentee Rate for Primary Care Health Workers	Rank of Income Out of 15 States
Assam	58	4
Bihar	58	1
Rajasthan	39	6
Karnataka	43	10
West Bengal	43	7
Gujarat	52	12
Haryana	35	13
Orissa	35	2

Source: World Bank (2003a) and Government of India, Indian Population Census (2001).

India? In Vietnam (see Wagstaff and Nguyen, 2007) infant mortality (age 0 to 5 yrs) was around 50 per thousand births throughout the early 1990s for all quintiles of the income distribution but it has fallen dramatically for the upper quintiles of the income distribution by 1997 and 1998 to around 25 per thousand. From these figures it is apparant that progress in reducing infant mortality has been concentrated among the rich.

It is also quite likely that infant mortality among the chronically poor is substantially higher than 50 per thousand births, although there is no hard evidence to support this conclusion. More detailed analysis is reported by Wagstaff and Nguyen (2007) who undertook a statistical analysis to examine which factors are important in determining infant mortality. They concluded that mother's education significantly improves survival prospects, having access to satisfactory drinking water also significantly improves a child's survival prospects although sanitation does not have a significant effect. Deliveries attended by someone with medical training had a positive and significant effect on survival prospects of poor children while vaccination was not significant.

In Bangladesh, recent work by Koenig *et al.* (2003) suggests that the poor do derive significant benefit from vaccination. These results are consistent with a prior reasoning and supports the conclusion that lack of minimal health care has a further negative impact on infant mortality.

In Indonesia, a study relating family welfare and infant mortality was conducted by Poerwanto *et al.* (2003) for a sample of women of reproductive age between 1983 and 1997 using 1997 Indonesian demographic and health survey data. They found that infant mortality was associated with a family welfare index and maternal education. The risk of infant death was almost twice as high among families which had low family welfare scores compared with high family welfare scores. Also, the risk of infant death was threefold higher among mothers who had fewer than seven years of formal education compared with mothers with more than seven years of education. Furthermore, younger mothers, lack of contraception, short birth intervals, and absence of or poor prenatal care are correlated with an increased probability of infant death.

Each of these studies pinpoints similar factors responsible for high infant mortality including lack of family planning, low literacy and education rate for mothers, low birth weight, poor nutrition and pregnancy at a young age. Infant mortality rates for the young women in the poorest provinces of India and the poorest sections of Pakistan and Bangladesh could easily be over 150 and perhaps as high as 200. Breaking the cycle requires a stronger family planning program to lower fertility combined with greater emphasis on women's education and better nutrition (see Chapter 5 for further discussion).

2.1.3 *Literacy and education*

As we explore literacy and educational levels for the chronic poor in Asia, we begin with a survey of national literacy and educational attainment for the poorest countries in the Asian region including some richer countries in the region for comparison. Literacy rates for most countries outside of South Asia are quite high; particularly literacy rates for the young (see Table 2.5). Only Bangladesh and Pakistan have male youth literacy rates less than 80 percent. China and Vietnam have a strong history of promoting literacy and this is reflected in much higher levels of literacy than for other countries with similar levels of per capita income. Outside of Sri Lanka literacy rates in South Asia are much lower. Youth literacy is highest in India, although 16 percent of males are still illiterate.

Literacy rates for Dalit children are still much lower than even the average literacy rates for the poorest provinces in India. Mehrota (2006) notes that in Bihar dalits are subject to systematic practice of "untouchability" by other casts and that the literacy rates for girls belonging to the Dalit class are as low as 10 percent. Corrie (1995) compiles a human development index which shows dalits have a significantly lower level of human development than Indian citizens as a group. Are other scheduled castes and classes in India subject to the same level of discrimination? It is difficult to evaluate without more information.

There is more complete information on school attendance for children belonging to scheduled tribes and scheduled casts as well as

Table 2.5 Literacy Rates for Adults, Females and the Classes (SC) 2001/2003

Country	Adult Literacy Males (Those Older Than 15)	Adult Female Literacy (Those Older Than 15)	Youth Literacy Male (Percentage of People 15–24)	Youth Literacy Female (Percentage of People 15–24)
Bangladesh*	41	31	51	33
India	73	48	84	68
Nepal	63	35	81	60
Pakistan	63	36	76	55
Sri Lanka	92	89	95	96
Cambodia	85	64	88	79
Indonesia	94	87	99	99
Lao PDR	77	61	83	75
Philippines	93	93	94	96
Thailand	95	91	98	98
Vietnam	94	87	94	94
China	95	87	99	99
Korea*	98	na	100	na

Source: World Bank (2007).
*UN ESCAP (2004) and Save the Children (2006).

more general school attendance in Asian countries where persistent poverty is high. Table 2.6 displays these school attendance rates for scheduled casts in seven of the poorest provinces of India.

Scheduled class enrolment is lower than total enrolment for both boys and girls. While there is widespread discrimination against girls, the gender differences between scheduled casts and the total enrolment figures are not that large except in Bihar where differences are about 15 percent.

In Bihar poverty among scheduled classes is also substantially higher than total poverty rates. For the other provinces differences in the incidence of poverty between scheduled classes and the aggregate poverty proportions are much larger than the disparity in education. This suggests that efforts to improve the delivery of education to the poor are meeting with some success.

Table 2.6 School Attendance of Scheduled Classes (SC) and Others

Province	Percentage of children attending school age 6–13						
	% SC Population	Male Total	Female Total	Male SC	Female SC	Below Poverty Total	SC Below Poverty
Assam	6.9	65.6	62.4	72.4	68.4	45.0	45.4
Bihar	15.7	52.6	40.4	39.0	25.0	58.2	70.7
Madhya Pradesh	15.2	76.0	66.8	76.7	67.1	40.6	45.8
Orissa	16.5	74.3	65.9	72.7	62.3	49.7	49.0
Uttar Pradesh	21.1	68.0	58.3	67.6	57.1	42.3	59.0
Maharashtra	10.2	87.7	85.5	88.0	85.5	37.9	51.6
Tamil Nadu	19.0	89.4	88.1	89.0	87.4	32.5	44.1

Source: Jenkins and Barr (2006).

Primary school completion rates tell a somewhat different story. These rates are quite low for the lowest quintile of the income distribution in the poorer countries in South Asia where chronic poverty rates are relatively high. Average years of schooling are even low in Indonesia and the Philippines where general education outcomes are good (see Table 2.7). In these two countries teenagers and young adults in the poorest quintile who are already in the workforce have, on average, completed primary school. Educational attainment is much lower in South Asia where the average person has completed only two or three years. Whether it is two or three years or completion of the primary grades, this level of schooling is hardly enough to achieve basic literacy and certainly not sufficient to help these individuals get out of poverty and obtain skilled positions in the work force. For the chronically poor, education performances are probably even lower. As noted elsewhere in this book the illiteracy rate for Dalits is as high as 90 percent.

In addition to low completion rates the quality of education provided at the primary level can be substandard. Overall estimates of educational quality are notoriously difficult to measure even for industrial countries. However teacher absenteeism is one measure that has been used as a marker for general efficiency of primary school systems. The absentee rate in India is quite high by any standard.

Table 2.7 Primary School Completion Rate and Average Years of Schooling

Country	Primary School Completion Rate by Lowest Quintile of Income Distribution — Percent of Relevant Age Group	Average Years of School Completed for Ages 15–24 by Poorest Quintile of the Income Distribution — Percent of Relevant Age Group
Bangladesh	26	3
Cambodia	4	2
India	31	3
Indonesia	75	7
Nepal	18	3
Pakistan	11	2
Philippines	46	6
Vietnam	58	5

Source: World Bank (2006a) Table 2.13.

The absentee rates for primary school teachers in India are displayed in Table 2.8. They are high — over 20 percent in all but on state — and there is some correlation between the absenteeism rate and the level of poverty in the state. Absenteeism rates are likely to be even higher in villages where the chronically poor reside.

Low levels of social capita are highly correlated with high rates of poverty in an extensive study of rural villages in Bangladesh. Kam *et al.* (2005) found that the level of education and access to health services were important determinants of the severity of rural poverty even after controlling for access to physical capital such as land ownership, better quality land and irrigation in a model on a nationally representative sample survey data set of 1 million households. Poverty indices were mapped for 415 rural subdistricts. There were distinct areas where the incidence of poverty was high which corresponded to ecologically depressed areas — arid land, poor soil or subject to flooding (see the section below on access to physical capital.)

Bhide and Mehta (2004) looked at poverty over time for a panel of households in India. They found that households with literate heads in the initial period had a greater probability of moving out of

Table 2.8 Absentee Rate of Primary School Teachers (2003) and Rank of Per Capita Income (2001)

State	Absentee Rate for Primary School Teachers	Rank of Per Capita Income — Low to High out of 15 States
Andhra Pradesh	26	8
Assam	34	4
Uttar Pradesh	26	3
Bihar	39	1
Rajasthan	24	6
Karnataka	20	10
West Bengal	23	7
Gujarat	15	12
Haryana	24	13
Kerala	23	9
Punjab	37	15
Tamil Nadu	21	11
Orissa	23	2

Source: World Bank (2003a) and Indian Population Census (2001).

poverty, more particularly in the case of households that were severely poor initially. In addition acquiring literacy over time does help moderately poor households escape from poverty completely. However these latter results were ambiguous for the severely poor. Some managed to escape poverty completely. Others did not. On the other hand, continued illiteracy is almost a sure guarantee of continued poverty for generations to come.

In summary, various studies of education and income in India, Indonesia, Malaysia and Vietnam show that children from poor families are less likely to complete as many years of school as children from households where income levels are higher. Furthermore, when household incomes fall unexpectedly children from these households are either withdrawn from school or spend less time in school (see King and Lillard, 1987; Deolalikar, 1993; Behrman and Knowles, 1999).

One lesson to be learned from a review of these data is that we know little about the chronically poor by looking at averages for countries as a whole. Using the lowest quintile as a proxy for the chronically poor gives added insight into their plight and the shortfall in the delivery of social services to them. However even more precise methods of targeting the chronically poor are required to effectively deliver the appropriate level of social services to raise the level of human development in South Asia, Indonesia and the Philippines and the Mekong countries.

2.2 Limited Income and Earning Power

There are few estimates of the wage or earning income of the chronically poor in Asian countries. Agricultural farm workers comprise the bulk of the poor in South Asia. In Pakistan, for example over 60 percent of the poor are made up of landless agricultural workers and the nonfarm rural poor (see Dorosh *et al.*, 2003); in India the proportion of the poor in agricultural is similar. Therefore it is important to determine the earnings of field crop farm workers in order to get a better handle on the relationship of income to chronic poverty. The ILO reports earnings of field crop farm workers which could serve as a benchmark for earnings of the chronically poor. These data are compiled in Table 2.9. For India earnings are less the US$1 per day and have been stagnant for many years. In real terms and converted into US dollars, these earnings have actually been falling. Furthermore a study of migration in two states in India found that poor landless laborers who migrated earn roughly Rs 30 per day transplanting paddy fields. At these low rates of pay it is likely that

Table 2.9 Earnings of Field Crop Farm Workers

Country	Year	Earning Per Day in Local Currency	Earning Per Day in US Dollar Equivalent
India	2001	20	$0.50
Bangladesh	1998	40	$0.98
Pakistan	2004	88.3	$1.51
Indonesia	1992	2500	$1.23
Philippines	1987	32	$1.56

Source: ILO (2007).

such temporary migration does not insure that poor families escape the poverty trap (see Deshingkar and Start, 2003). In Pakistan field crop workers earn slightly more than US$1 per day and in Bangladesh slightly less. This is barely enough to keep the worker or his family out of poverty. There were no data reported for field crop workers in Nepal or Sri Lanka.

In Southeast Asia the situation is somewhat brighter. In Indonesia the minimum earnings were equivalent to $1.23 per day in 1992 and in the Philippines $1.56 per day. Of course these earnings could still be far below the poverty line if there is only one breadwinner in the family and there is no supplementary income from other sources. At the very least these figures would have to be divided by two if there is another family member that is not earning income.

In a study of the poor in India Parker and Kozel (2007) suggests the presence of a male child who contributes to family income is one of the major factors raising income Even if this is the case that additional worker would also be earning very little. Any illness or loss of work for any other reason including lay off during the slack season would depress earnings even further and could result in poor families being forced to borrow for consumption. Data gathered by the World Bank (Narayan, 1999) suggests that around half of all landless and marginal farmers in India borrowed from informal lending sources — usually the landlord or a money lender — in the last year, possibly as a continuation of the *jajmani* system that establishes a close relationship between client and patron.[2] This system also leads to a potential for bonded labor as the worker becomes indebted to the landlord and is unable to ever extricate himself from this obligation.

---

[2] In a jajmani system villagers exchanged their respective produces between themselves under a customary system of trading and swapping. The food producing peasants played the pivotal role in the game. The artisans, weavers, boatmen, barbers, cleaners, doctors, etc supplied their products and services to peasant families in return for some share in their harvest which cleared everybody's dues accumulated during the crop season. The peasants, like the religious husbandman, who fed the Brahman under a different type of exchange system, became the jajmans of all non-farm elements catering to their needs. The jajmani system survives in villages in India through the patron client relationship between peasant cultivators and the patron or land owner.

It is even possible, as Dasgupta and Ray (1986) have argued, the poorest of the poor are not able to get work even if they underbid healthier workers because their marginal productivity is so low as a result of poor health. These workers are in such poor health that they cannot earn a living wage. Dasgupta and Ray (1986) suggests that one way out of this trap is to redistribute enough land so that even the destitute can survive by growing enough food to feed their families.

In a study of Bangladesh which is primarily concerned with gender discrimination in the workplace, Rahman (2005) shows that a healthy male working in agriculture can sustain 2.1 people above the poverty level on the average day wage of an agricultural laborer in 1989. By 2000 this had improved somewhat to 2.5 persons. Nevertheless since family size in Bangladesh is over four and probably closer to five or six (two to four children) then there would have to be more than one breadwinner to sustain a level of consumption that is above the poverty level. For women the story is even grimmer. Agriculture earnings for women fell from 1.5 persons that could be sustained on a day's wages in 1989 to 1.4 persons by 2000.

Additional income for the family suffering from chronic poverty could come from other family members. Wives in families suffering from chronic poverty are able to earn additional income to supplement the earnings of the major breadwinner by gardening, raising chickens, joining a handicraft group, being a housemaid for one of the larger landowners or a variety of other informal work to supplement family income. Once children are old enough to work they are often hired out as day laborers or as housemaids for the rich. School is often an unaffordable option for the poorest of the poor. It is difficult to quantify these contributions to the income of the poor on a systematic basis since records for the informal economy are sparse and often not comparable across cultures. The chronically poor are also at risk of losing any assets or be faced with debts as a result of lack of work due to poor harvests, bad weather, illness, disease and other hardships to the family In Bangladesh, for example agricultural wages declined sharply in regions suffering severe flooding and remained depressed in these regions even in the post-flood months during a period from 1979–2000 (Banerjee, 2007).

Another factor is the growing importance of non-agricultural income to poor families. Data accumulated by ILO (2008) indicates that for families in Bangladesh, India, Philippines and Thailand non-farm income contributed less than 50 percent of household income in 7 out of 8 instances in the 1980s. By 2003/04 non-farm income surpassed that derived from agriculture in 5 out of 8 instances and often by significant amounts. In Bangladesh, for example, the annual rate of growth in agriculture income was only 0.3 percent per annum between 1987 and 2000 while non-agricultural income, mostly from trade and business and remittances, grew by 4.3 percent per annum. There was also a shift away from rice farming to other crops and non-crop agriculture even as agricultural wages were falling at an annual rate of 5.5 percent. These trends are also reflected in the percent of households reporting farming as their primary occupation, the rise in trade and business and other services and the shift in the proportion of households reporting income from sources other than agriculture (see Table 2.10).

Table 2.10 Distribution of Workers by Primary Occupation Bangladesh in 1987 and 2000

	% Households Reporting as Primary Occupation 1987	% Households Reporting as Primary Occupation 2000	% Households Reporting Some Income from Occupation 1987	% Households Reporting Some Income Fro Occupation 2000
Farming	44.6	36.7	64.0	69.9
Agricultural labor	22.4	11.8	51.6	28.2
Other agriculture	1.2	0.9	78	86.2
Trade and business	8.3	12.2	31.9	32.3
Services	14.7	21.7	21.9	28.0
Non-agricultural labor	8.7	16.8	29.2	23.7

Source: ILO (2008).

2.3 Geographical Isolation

Geographical isolation is one of the characteristics of many locations where chronic poverty levels are high. This isolation results in reduced access to markets for goods and services as well as job opportunities outside of agriculture. Educational and health facilities are often rudimentary and physical infrastructure such as irrigation, sanitation and transportation limited. There is also limited contact with urban centers and limited access to advanced agricultural technology, new seed varieties and cropping techniques, uses of fertilizer and other developments in agricultural technology and innovation. Alternative employment opportunities outside of agriculture are also limited by geography.

Many chronically poor areas are located in mountainous terrain where road access is difficult and may be closed for some periods of the year due to rainy conditions, flooding and landslides. Power, telephone and internet service may also be weak and subject to interruptions in service in poor weather in their homes and surrounding areas. The ethnic minority tribal people in central Luzon, in northern Thailand and Burma, parts of Eastern Indonesia, particularly Papua where the level of rural poverty level is close to 50 percent and in the southwestern provinces of China are examples of such geographic locations that are isolated from the rest of the country.

Landless and often illiterate laborers in these isolated upland villages are often locked into a continuing cycle of low income and limited employment prospects. Employment opportunities in other villages or in larger urban areas are difficult to access without reliable transportation. Handicraft work in the home, while possible among ethnic minorities with a tradition of weaving, embroidery, basketry and other indigenous crafts, is limited by access to markets and high intermediation costs.

Much of the available literature relating to spatial inequality and geographic isolation has focused on differences between different regions (see Bird *et al.*, 2007 and references contained therein). There are a few exceptions such as Bird *et al.* (2007) that draw on information at the district level such as physical remoteness, access to infrastructure, availability of services, facilities and means of communication to develop a model of poverty intensitivity for Uganda. Their results suggest that about 25 percent of the variation in income can be explained by these regional factors while the rest is due to variations in the characteristics of individuals within the region — literacy, skill, age etc. Results are likely to be similar for the poor in Asia.

In a study of poverty determinants in the Philippines Monsod *et al.* (2004) found that poverty is higher in the cordilleras region of Luzon and muslin Mindanao, two ethnic minority regions where topography and proximity to markets along with weather conditions were also contributing factors to the extent of rural poverty. Interestingly two provinces where there are provincial political dynasties also had higher rates of poverty, other things equal. Thus we should add local and regional commitment to reducing chronic poverty as an additional factor contributing to geographic isolation.

In China, a more aggregated study Benjamin *et al.* (2005) suggests that the poorer regions of interior China have grown faster than the coastal provinces in recent years. The tentative conclusion that can be drawn from their analysis is that China generally seems to be dealing aggressively with income inequality. However more detailed work suggests this may not be wholly accurate.

In a more detailed study of a few poor provinces in China, Ravallion and Jalan (2002) reviewed consumption patterns in Guangdong, Guangxi, Guizhou, and Yunnan. The latter three provinces are in southwest China, widely regarded as one of the poorest regions in the country. By comparing assets and consumptions between the poor regions with the relatively richer coastal regions of Guangdong, adjacent to Hong Kong and using a sophistical econometric model Ravallion and Jalan (2002) were able to test whether geography has a significant impact on consumption with aid of an econometric model. They concluded that:

> living in a poor area lowers the productivity of a farm-household's own investments, which reduces the growth rate of consumption..., Ravallion and Jalan (2002, p. 343).

Infrastructure access is a contributing factor to lower productivity of farm households and it is interrelated with geographical isolation. The two combine to increase the burden for the chronically poor. For example, Warr (2006) notes that family access to social and physical infrastructure such as health to education facilities, to communications through improved roads and telecommunications as well as access to cheaper consumer goods by reducing transportation costs are other ways to aid the poor. Lack of these services is apparent in Bangladesh where 7 of the 64 districts in the country are home to half of the country's serverely stunted children (Khandker, Bakht and Koolwal, 2006). In Laos, for example, barter trade accounted for as much as 80 percent of trade in the most remote areas and fell when villages had access to all weather roads and were closer to major towns (see Hill *et al.*, 2006). Electricity access also allows consumers to use a range of consumer goods at a lower cost. Without these infrastructure upgrades the chronically poor will continue to be constrained.

Bhide and Mehta (2004) provide further evidence regarding economies of scale and geographic isolation. Larger villages provide relatively more diverse opportunities for employment than the smaller villages. Therefore residence in a bigger village can be expected to reduce the incidence of poverty for this reason alone. This result was confirmed by regressions determining the incidence of poverty. While the initial size of the village does not have a significant impact on the mobility of the poor out of poverty, living in a larger village does reduce the probability of the persistence of poverty and the ability of families to break out of the poverty trap. This result is particularly relevant for those who are in severe poverty.

Taken together, these studies suggest that poverty traps were created as a result of a shortage in infrastructure such as rural roads and social capital including health and education expenditures as well as limitations in size and access to markets. By detailing the impact of the isolation created by the lack of social and physical capital on poverty, they prove that the impact of geographical isolation is significant and needs to be addressed from a number of different perspectives. We will examine these alternatives further in Chapters 5 and 6.

2.4 Lack of Physical Assets

The chronically poor are handicapped by having to rely almost exclusively on labor to earn income as they generally have few other assets. Most of the chronically poor own little or no land, livestock or farming implements. As a result they have no resources to help them smooth consumption should there be crop failures, loss of wage employment, sickness or death in the family. Furthermore any wealth that is accumulated is often held in unproductive assets. (see Rosenzweig and Wolpin, 1993). As a result, these chronically poor households are unable to insure against risks and are usually unable to pursue the coping strategies available to more well to do families such as storing grain, diversification of farming activities or looking for off farm employment opportunities.

These conclusions are reinforced by regression equations used by Bhide and Mehta (2004) designed to measure the determinants of chronic poverty in India using national cross section data from the 1970s and 1980s. They found that chronic poverty was negatively related to household holdings of land, livestock and dwellings. An improvement in households housing and livestock assets and an increase in the crop area cultivated by the poor household were significant determinants of the probability of a reduction in persistence of poverty. This was determined by comparisons of poverty incidence in 1970 and a decade later.

Furthermore, information collected for land poor and land rich households in two provinces in southwestern China, Hunan and Yunnan, suggest that:

> even a minor increase in land holding can help to considerably improve household's ability to smooth total consumption (Rozenzweigh and Wolpin, 1993, p. 1347).

In Bangladesh, several factors were important in determining the extent of rural poverty in a large panel of villages. They included a variety of physical capital assets as reflected in land holdings, agricultural area under tenancy, holdings of livestock and net cropped area under irrigation. In addition access to main roads and land characteristics were also included as regressors. The results suggest that the extremely poor households are particularly adversely affected by land-related factors such as landlessness and the prevalence of low-lying land and high land which is either difficult to irrigate or subject to flooding (Kam *et al.*, 2005).

Taken together these various studies using microeconomic data from different countries highlights the importance of having or obtaining some physical assets to break out of the poverty cycle. These physical assets include land and farm implements, as well as farm animals.

2.5 Lack of Financial Capital

The chronically poor are unskilled and they rely on their own labor as farm laborers for the bulk of their income. The majority of the poor do not have any capital or land. If they do own any land it is a very small plot. In Pakistan 75 percent of the poor do not have any land of their own and statistical analysis shows that land is the most important factor in reducing poverty (World Bank, 2002). In Bangladesh, data compiled by IFPRI (2007) Table 4.9 shows that land ownership declines dramatically as the depth of poverty increases. 75 percent of the ultra poor own no cultivable land and another 20 percent own less than 0.5 hectares. Landlessness decrease somewhat to 50 percent among the subjacent poor and the average size of land holding among the 30 percent of the subjacent poor who own some land also increases. Furthermore the inability of poor households to acquire land are because of lack of credit and saving as well as the reluctance of larger farmers to sell any of their land. These farmers are reluctant to see any of their land both because of the status value of land in developing countries and the option to pass the land on to family members.

As a result of lack of land and other financial assets the poor live day to day and often have no savings. As a result when they suffer setbacks as a result of poor harvests, illness or other shocks they are often forced to borrow from their landlord, moneylenders or friends. Often this results in the chronically poor being constantly in debt.

This is a barrier that prevents them from ever escaping the chronic poverty trap (see Rosenzweig and Wolpin, 1993). In some cases, particularly in India the chronically poor are forced into bondage with their employer that perpetuates the poverty trap for generations. While these bondage arrangements are illegal they persist where there are powerful landlords and a large supply of landless chronically poor. Srivastava (2005) defines bonding as:

> Bonded labor is characterized by a creditor-debtor relationship between the employer and the employee which can then spill over to other members of the family, be of an indefinite duration, and involve adverse contractual stipulations not justified by law or even by the prevailing state of the market. Bonded labor relationships are also usually reinforced by custom or force. Thus bonded labor relationships are not purely economic contracts, even though employees may enter into them voluntarily because of economic necessity. Once employees enter into these relationships, they are characterized by multiple asymmetries and high exit costs, which were not a part of the contract, as understood by the employee, at the outset. We would argue that bonded labor refers to a long-term relationship between employee and employer which is cemented through a loan, by custom or by force, which denies the employee various freedoms including to choose his or her employer, to enter into a fresh contract with the same employer or to negotiate the terms and condition of her/his contract. (Srivastava, 2005, p. 2).

This form of bondage is the severest type of relationship between a debtor and a creditor. Milder forms of bondage exist when the poor borrow from the landlord or the informal credit market at high rates of interest with little prospect of ever paying off the principal. Even when there is no apparent bondage tenants may be paid less than the market wage in return for some debt forgiveness or simply by the fact that the tenant is dominated by the landlord.

Srivastava (2005) supplies some estimates of the number of bonded laborers in different provinces. As expected, the highest levels of debt bondage are found in the poorer provinces of Andhra Pradesh, Bihar, Madhya Pradesh, Maharashtra, Orissa, and Tamil Nadu but also in Haryana, Punjab and Karnataka. Migrants and women have been identified as most often victims of bonded labor relationships as well as scheduled tribes.

Genicot (2002) argues that bonded labor provides more security for the borrowing peasants who might not be able to access credit from a local credit institution particularly if they had defaulted in the past. In entering into bondage, the peasant forgoes access to the local credit institution in favor of the guarantee of credit afforded by the landlord even though this arrangement binds him. Genicot argues that a ban on bonded labor would be desirable because it would result in the development of greater credit opportunities for the peasant.

Nevertheless, the chronically poor have historically had little recourse other than to money lenders and landlords for borrowed funds to smooth consumption in the face of crop losses or other shocks much less to build up assets and break out of the poverty trap. In recent years however, a number of financial institutions began to specialize in lending to the poor. The most famous of these is the Grameen Bank in Bangladesh. News of its success spread within the region and beyond, and there are now a number of Grameen Bank look alikes. Financial cooperatives among the poor have also started in India and elsewhere. We will discuss these new entities later in Chapter 5. For now, suffice to say, the bulk of the chronically poor in Asia are not yet able to avail low-cost loans from financial institutions, even from lenders like the Grameen Bank, and are still relying on money lenders, pawnshops and landlords when they have to borrow.

2.6 Political and Social Isolation

It seems that discrimination wears many faces. It manifests in lower provision of public services, lower quality of land and other resources and also in the limited access that the disadvantaged have to the existing facilities. Disadvantaged chronically poor minorities are isolated in many different dimensions including politically, socially, ethnically and racially. In the political realm the chronically poor suffer from lack of access to the political process. As a result they do not benefit from government programs, some of which are directed to them but which are diverted by other more powerful interest groups. In a detailed study of Palanpur, a village in Uttar Pradesh the World Bank (2006b) found that:

> The dominance of privileged groups over collective institutions has had far reaching consequences. Between the late 1950s and early 1990s no fewer that 18 types of government provided programs were introduced to the village: a public works road building program, free schooling, free basic health, old age pensions, a fair price shop, a farmers' cooperative and so on. Most of them remained non-functional, particularly where there was a redistributive component. Only programs that enjoyed strong backing from the politically advantaged in the village were allowed to succeed. (World Bank, 2006b, pp. 26–27).

As a result the village did not grow as rapidly as it could have and the poor remained outside the loop of available social services and subsidized activities. The lesson here is that unless these deep seated discriminatory practices are stopped, well meaning government programs directed to help the poor can easily be undermined by powerful local interests. In some villages and towns groups subject to discrimination have organized and been able to wrest some of the financial controls of government sponsored programs away from the traditional power centers. But these have been few and far between.

Discrimination against minorities often interferes with the provision of social services and political clout. In an attempt to differentiate between regional variations resulting from poor access to the market economy and poor infrastructure with overt discrimination, Kijima (2006) found that scheduled tribes and scheduled casts had lower earnings and consumption even after accounting for the fact that they lived in areas where road connectivity, electricity access, education and public health were poor. He concluded that differences in consumption expenditures between tribal/ethnic minorities and others is not just a matter of geographical differences although geography does also play a role. He tentatively identified the quality and level of educational facilities provided for the minorities as a key reason why earnings and consumption were lower for them. A much larger proportion of the minorities worked as laborers than the rest of the men in the villages studied and their levels of education were lower than that of other men in the village. Kijima's study does not quantify the extent of the disparity in earnings in rupee terms although it makes a strong case that discrimination has continued for the entire sample period. The differences in income between SC/ST and other workers is partially because of their more limited stocks of human and physical assets in terms of education, skill, land and other capita. It is also a result of geography. SC/STs live in marginal areas with lower rainfall and poorer soil condition and more limited infrastructure. SC/STs are usually the poorst in their villages. On reason for this is because of labor market discrimination and lower returns to labor for SC/ST workers, even for the same skill set as other groups. Kijima (2006) argues that improving nondiscriminatory access to labor markets would be a good way to raise living standards for the SC/ST families. Discrimination within the village also works to reduce the earnings of the poor and their levels of human and physical capital. Discrimination is manifest in access to good educational opportunities as well as to health facilities, potable water and other social services.

Other studies (see Probe Team India, 1999 and Jenkins and Barr, 2006) have noted that minorities often live on the outskirts of villages on the most undesirable pieces of land. They are far from the center of the village and also some distance from schools and the rural health clinic. Minority children are taunted by other children and adults as they go to school. While in school they also suffer discrimination from their teachers and school administrators. Most teachers in India are from upper castes and bring their own views into the classroom (see Kabeer, 2006).

While much of the evidence presented by Kabeer (2006) is based on anecdotes it does appear that social distance from the school is much greater than geographical distance. However this anecdotal evidence is supported by data from the National Family Health Survey of 1998/99 which has been analyzed by Jenkins and Barr (2006). Using regression analysis they concluded that children who are from Scheduled Castes or other lower casts are at a distinct disadvantage

Table 2.11 Odds Ratio Among Castes

Caste	Ever Been to School (7–17) Years of Age	Completed Grade 5 for Age Groups 11–17
Scheduled caste	1.0	1.0
Other backward classes	1.07	1.1
Other Hindu castes	1.35	1.33

Source: Jenkins and Barr (2006), Table 9 based on regression results from International Institute for Population Sciences (1999).

over the entire spectrum of education. Children aged 7–17 from other castes (not Scheduled Castes) are 1.35 times more likely to have been to school as SC children and these higher caste children are 1.33 times more likely to have completed grade 5 even after controlling for working status, number of children in the family, adult male and female education levels, urban or rural residence and a standard of living index. See Table 2.11 for further details.

The chronically poor also have a narrow and less affluent social circle and as such their stock of social capital is limited. These "ties of cooperation and mutual assistance" (Parker and Kozel, 2007) were found to be strongly related to poverty. Access to short term financial assistance was lower among the poorer castes and they had a less extensive extended family network that could be supportive in time of need. On the other hand, Parker and Kozel (2007) report that many of the upper caste families in the same village could not only draw assistance from close family members but also other relatives or other members of the same caste in case of an emergency.

In Indonesia, minorities were discriminated against during the Suharto era which lasted over 30 years, ending in 1999. There are about 500 ethnic groups speaking more than 600 languages and the regime saw them as a threat to national unity. There may be as many as 70 million people belonging to enthnic *adat* groups according to AMAN (Aliansi Masyarakat Adat Nusantara.). Literally *adat* means tradition. However the word has come to mean autonomous communities that follow traditional rules and customs. Many of these traditional communities have been integrated into the mainstream of Indonesia cultural life while others have not.

Of these, the government has identified nearly 300 isolated communities with approximately 800 thousand residents that are not yet integrated. These *adat* communities are poor and with no systematic recognition of *adat* rights over their land and natural resources, they have been, and continue to be, marginalized. Furthermore, there is no government bureau that takes responsibility for their well being. Poverty reduction strategies may include *adat* communities but they are not separated out for special treatment. For example *batak* is a term used to describe a loosely related number of ethnic groups with distinct, albeit related, languages and customs located in North Sumatra around Lake Toba. While there is a high concentration of *bataks* in this region of Sumatra, there is no government program that is designed to directly assist these indigenous people.

2.7 Ethnic, Gender and Other Forms of Discrimination

There are a number of other ways that ethnic, gender and other forms of discrimination have negatively impacted the chronically poor, aside from political and social isolation or indirect or direct discrimination in access to social services such as education.

We begin with a discussion of gender discrimination. There are two general theories that have been proposed to explain changes in gender choices over time. The modernization theory suggests that economic growth and higher family incomes lead to greater gender equality as the incentives to make gender choices are reduced. Evidence for a number of industrial and developing countries suggests that gender differences narrow as economic development progress and those countries that have grown most rapidly have also narrowed the gender gap more quickly (see Schultz, 1995). When incomes are low in the early stage of development and most people are employed in agriculture, scarce resources make the choices between educating boys or girls critical. Decisions are usually made to educate boys, since their labor productivity in agriculture is expected to be higher. These constraints are less onerous as income increase and opportunities for women in the workplace expand. There is evidence that girls' education responds more rapidly to changes in wealth (Schultz, 1995).

An alternative approach argues that incentives to have boys increase with growth as more employment opportunities open up for them (see Boserup, 1989; Hannum, 2005). There is evidence that such a process has taken place in Vietnam and China in recent years. In China, women's work in agriculture and in the home has intensified as more men have become employed in the industrial sector. A third alternative explanation is that discrimination has local and regional dimensions that can involve historical, ethnic or cultural precursors. For example, gender disparities have not narrowed much in India over time, although there is more discrimination in the poorer provinces.

Each of these different perspectives on gender discrimination can manifest within the household, at school and in the workplace.

Beginning within the household women and girls can be discriminated against by getting smaller portions of food, being denied education and receiving less health care than their male counterparts. Within the rural village they are subject to prejudice and humiliation, are forced to live on the poorest land and denied social services including water, electricity and medical care. As a result they have fewer economic, educational and social abilities than their male counterparts. With regard to discrimination in the classroom, girls' education has a number of economic and non-economic benefits or externalities. It can reduce gender inequalities in the labor market. As the education gap is closed in the future, greater emphasis on girls' education can reap benefits in reducing infant mortality and the incidence of childhood illness, slowing the rate of population growth and increasing labor productivity.

Discrimination against girls can provide some *prima facia* justification for the fact that they are paid less than men. In the work place women can be denied jobs because of their gender (between job discrimination) or they can be denied the same pay for the same work (within job discrimination). The different kinds of discrimination can interact. Women may be less productive than men not only because of their different physical characteristics but also because they have been the subject of discrimination at home and within the community.

Turning to country experiences within Asia, in Bangladesh there is evidence that there are movements of labor out of agriculture and that wage rates for woment in non-agricultural employment have been increasing. There is also strong evidence that females are discriminated in the work place (see Table 2.12 and Rahman, 2005).

Non-agricultural employment wages for women have increased dramatically between 1989 and 2000, from sustaining only one person in 1989 to 2.2 persons in 2000. Much of this increase has to do with the increased employment in the textile industry in recent years (see Table 2.12). Wage differentials between men and women are still substantial and have widened in agriculture although they have narrowed in non-agriculture.

In India the ILO has also made some comparisons between earnings for men and women (ILO, 2003) for the agricultural sector. These are displayed in Table 2.13. The rates of pay are slightly lower than in Bangladesh. 40 rupees is about US$1 per day so the average man can support between 1 and 1.5 persons on a days wages. The level of discrimination against women is about the same. These rates of discrimination are similar to the general figures quoted by the Department of Labor in India which puts the pay differential at 60 percent.

Table 2.12 Bangladesh — Male and Female Wage Rates Relative to Poverty Line in Terms of Number of People Who Could be Sustained Above the Poverty Level by a Day's Wages

Year	Sector	Male	Female	(Female/Male) Times 100
1989	Agriculture	2.1	1.5	71
	Non-agriculture	2.1	1.0	48
1995–96	Rural	2.2	1.3	59
	Urban	2.5	1.5	60
1999–2001	Agriculture	2.5	1.4	56
	Non-agriculture	3.2	2.2	69

Source: Rahman (2005).

Table 2.13 Male/Female Wages Rates in Indian Agriculture in Rupees

State	Wage Rate for Men in Rupees Per Day	Wage Rate for Women	(Women/Men) Time 100 Using Midpoint of Wage Range
Haryana	50–60	25–30	50
Uttar Pradesh	60	35–40	62.5
West Bengal	40 (6 hours of work)	25 (6 hours of work)	62.5
Andhra Pradesh	40–50	25–30	61

Source: ILO (2003).

Since the levels of many socio-economic indicators, particularly education and health, are strongly associated with per-capita income, gender comparisons of these indicators is an indirect way to gauge the level of discrimination against girls. It provides strong evidence of poor social performance by chronically poor girls.[3]

Alderman *et al.* (1996) found that the shortage of local schools for girls in Pakistan (boys and girls are schooled in gender specific schools) accounts for about a third of the total cognitive achievement gender gap and over two-fifths of the gap in numeracy.

Liu (2004) reports results from a probit model estimation of the probability of girls and boys being in school. He used the two rounds of the Vietnam Living Standards Surveys on children whose highest attained degree is primary education. Discrimination against girls accounts for most of the gap predicted by the model over and above other demographic and socioeconomic factors that were included in the model. Liu's results suggest that education of girls is a luxury good and the cost of schooling has an adverse impact on girls' education rates. Liu suggests that cultural values, including Confucianism, are largely responsible for the disparity between gender differences in education rates. Boys are expected to provide old age security for parents while girls are a liability since they marry and move away. The external

[3] There have been a number of studies of discrimination in access to social service including education and health, in the work place and also within the household. See King and Hill (1993) and Filmer (2000) for general discussion and examples.

benefits to girls' education noted above are being ignored at the household level although recent evidence suggests the gender gap is closing somewhat in Vietnam and in South Korea.

On a more positive note Phan and Reilly (2007) find that *Doi moi* reforms in Vietnam were associated with a sharp reduction in gender pay gap disparities for those earning wage incomes. The average gender pay gap for these workers halved between 1993 and 2002 with most of the contraction evident by 1998.

More generally, aggregated data for South Asia and Southeast Asian countries also demonstrates the gender disparity between literacy/educational attainment and per capita income. Female to male enrolment ratios are highly correlated with per capita income — discrimination against females is highest in the poorest provinces in South Asia (see Table 2.14). This suggests that girls are more heavily discriminated against in the poorer regions and that this would probably be true for chronically poor girls as well. Bangladesh has a better disparity ratio than Pakistan and India, probably because it has had a subsidy program for girl's education in place since the early 1990s.

Table 2.14 Ratio of Female to Male Enrolment Ages 11–14

State/Province or Country	Female/Male Enrolment Ratio	Poverty Rank in Country (Poorest is Lowest)
India		
Rajasthan	0.49	6
Bihar	0.55	1
Kerala	1.0	9
India total	0.86	
Pakistan		
Baluchastan	0.34	1
NWFP	0.37	2
Punjab	0.69	3
Pakistan total	0.64	
Bangladesh	0.93	

Source: Dowling (2007) and Filmer *et al.* (1998).
Note: Poverty rank is out of 15 provinces in India and four in Pakistan.

Table 2.15 Literacy and Per Capita Income in Poor States of India

States of India	Percent of Illiterate Females (6 Years and Over) — Rank out of 15 States in Parenthesis (1992–93)	Rank of Per Capita Income (2001) Lowest to Highest out of 15 States
Assam	61.5 (5)	4
Bihar	71.4 (2)	1
Madhya Pradesh	65.7 (4)	5
Orissa	58.6 (6)	2
Rajasthan	74.6 (1)	6
Uttar Pradesh	68.5 (3)	5

Source: Dowling (2007).

This inference that gender discrimination is greatest among the poorest villages and regions holds up in a wider sample that Filmer *et al.* (1998) analyzed and it also holds for rankings of literacy by province and income per capita in India as displayed in Table 2.15. The six states that are ranked highest in terms of percentages of illiterate females in the 15 states of India also have the lowest per capital income.

Gender discrimination manifests in many ways including lower pay for the same work, lower levels of education and health, lower caloric intake and nutritional deficiencies. Furthermore gender discrimination tends to be greater among the poor although there are some exceptions. Progress in gender equality has been slow although Vietnam and Korea have made strides in reducing the pay gap between men and women.

2.7.1 *Infant mortality and gender discrimination*

Infant mortality rates (IMR) are generally substantially higher in poorer countries and regions than in their richer counterparts. The relationship between the IMR and per capita income continues in Asia and among the chronically poor with a few interesting exceptions. While overall infant mortality is not a direct marker for gender

Table 2.16 Gender Infant Mortality Rates in India and Pakistan

Country or Region	Female/Male IMR
India	1.44
Pakistan	1.52/1.66
Nepal	1.24
Sri Lanka	0.99
Punjab	2.06 (Pakistan)
Baluchistan	1.79
Sindh	1.24
NWFP	0.86
Harayana	2.35
Punjab	1.81 (India)
UP	1.70
Goa	1.11
Kerala	0.94
Tamil Nadu	0.80

Source: Filmer *et al.* (1998).

discrimination we also note that infant mortality for girls is higher than for boys (see Pritchett and Summers, 1996; Filmer and Pritchett, 1997; and Filmer *et al.*, 1998). This is true for South Asia as well: the level of income has a strong relationship with the level of child mortality in most instances. Table 2.16 displays the infant mortality rate for children less than 5 years of age for several regions in Pakistan and India as well as Sri Lanka and Nepal as measured by the ratio of female to male infant mortality. Table 2.17 shows per capita income and sex ratios for the Indian state for an earlier period. The northern states have higher rates than the southern states. For example two of the poorest ranking states Uttar Pradesh (15) and Punjab (16) had sex ratios of women to men of 0.88 and 0.87 respectively.

These observations about the Indian experience have been further analyzed by several economists in terms of a variety of social and economic factors including lower female literacy in the north as well as lower labor force participation rates. Furthermore men in the southern states generally take their wives from within the village (endogamy) while in the north wives generally are from other villages

Table 2.17 Per Capita Income and Sex Ratios of Indian States

State	Ranking of Per Capita Income 1983–84 — Highest to Lowest	Ranking of Sex Ratio — Females Per 1000 Males 1981 — Highest to Lowest
Punjab	1	16
Haryana	2	17
Maharashtra	3	11
Gujarat	4	9
West Bengal	5	13
Himachal Pradesh	6	5
Karnataka	7	7
Andhra Pradesh	8	4
Rajasthan	9	12
Tamil Nadu	10	3
Jammu and Kashmir	11	14
Kerala	12	1
Manipur	13	6
Madhya Pradesh	14	10
Uttar Pradesh	15	15
Orissa	16	2
Tripura	17	8
Bihar	18	8

Source: Das Gupta (1987).

(exogamy). All of these factors help to explain why women are less valued in the North than the South (see Dyson and Moore, 1983).

Take the case of the Punjab. The Punjab, both in Pakistan and India as well as Harayana province in India (which used to be a part of the Punjab in India and has many geographical and ethnic features in common) have much higher levels of IMRs for girls than one would expect from their socioeconomic status. For example Punjabi women have comparatively high status using measures of literacy and age at marriage. Das Gupta (1987) argues that the primary reason for such high levels of gender difference in IMR is that the patrilineal kinship and the dowry system combined with exogamy to render females a liability to the parents in the northern states of India. As soon as the daughter marries she moves away and her husband takes the dowry. (See Miller, 1981; Bardan, 1974; Bardan, 1982; and Bardan, 1984 for further discussion of gender mortality differences between northern and southern regions of India.)

Extending this line of reasoning, Sen (1990) makes a penetrating argument that puts gender IMR in a broader perspective. He argues that gender discrimination is not a function of poverty alone but about the perceived value of women in society and this is primarily a function of the value that society outside the home puts on her work. In societies where women are able to find work outside the home gender discrimination is lower and this is reinforced by the educational status of women. If labor force participation and women's education is high, there is noticeably less gender discrimination, even in poor countries or regions. Sen (1990) notes the example of Kerala in India. It is a poor to middle income state of India yet it has a gender IMR of 1. In Punjab state in India gender ratios are very low, about 87 women for every 100 males, yet it is the richest state in India (see Table 2.17).

Furthermore, gender ratios in Southeast Asia where women's education is prized, are close to 1 or even higher than 1 while in Pakistan, where women's literacy and educational levels are low, IMR rates are among the highest in the world. We will touch on these issues later on in Chapters 4, 6 and 7 when we discuss the interrelated nature of chronic poverty and the need to attack it on a number of different fronts at the same time.

An interesting footnote to the results of gender discrimination and infant mortality is provided by a recent study of Korea (Chung and Das Gupta, 2007). The author's analyzed the socioeconomic status of families in 1991 and 2003 in response to the women's sex preference for their children: "I must have a son". Chung and Das Gupta found that gender preference for sons has moderated between 1991 and 2003 as a result of several socioeconomic factors including education of the mother, residence in urban areas, age of the woman (younger women show lower gender preference for sons), parental pressure and a strong secular trend not explained by any of the independent variables which may be due to changing social norms. The authors infer from this analysis that the gradual liberation of women in Korean society is largely responsible for the shift in preference for sons. They found that 25 percent of the decline in preference for sons is due to high rates of education for men and women as well as a trend toward higher levels of urbanization. With respect to India and China the authors argue that changes in social organization and production including circular migration to the cities, the growing availability of employment outside agriculture along with public policies that guarantee women's rights are crucial and can augment increased emphasis on women's education as a vehicle for social change, including a reduction in son preference bias.

A further comment on the missing women phenomena is provided by Das Gupta (2005), who examines whether changes in IMR could be the result of childhood diseases that affect boys and girls differently. Focusing on India and China, Das Gupta (2005) concludes that cultural attitudes are responsible for variations in IMRs. She examines birth order for a number of countries and finds a close association between IMRs and birth order. In China, for example IMRs are significantly higher for girls born to a mother who already has a girl while first born IMRs are much lower. These results extend to other countries in Asia including Bangladesh and South Korea. Furthermore, ethnic factors are responsible for differences in IMRs. Minority groups in China have much more equal IMRs than Han Chinese, who have a particular preference for boys. This is similar to the findings by Das Gupta (1987) that IMRs are similar for boys and girls in northwestern provinces of China. Finally, variations in IMR were found to depend upon economic and social conditions. During the Japanese invasion of China during World War II boys were much preferred. However at the beginning and during the early years of the communist regime, there was a shift toward more gender equality as IMRs began to equalize. After the one-child policy was introduced the male selection bias increased again.

In another micro study of women in 1995 covering five districts in Karnataka in south India and five districts in Uttar Pradesh in north India, Rahman and Rao (2004) looked at responses of 800 married women and found that historical differences in marriage practices became blurred between northern and southern India. More marriages in Uttar Pradesh were within the local community and the differences in distances between the marriage and natal family were similar in both regions.

This new evidence also suggests that social mobility in the North and South, as reflected in these comparisons is more uniform than it was a few decades ago. The authors suggest that social mobility has generally improved in both regions as village infrastructure has improved, particularly the introduction of physical infrastructure such as street lights, more schools, better roads and improved public transportation which increased the mobility and independence of women in the countryside. There may also be indirect impacts on poverty as a result, through increased involvement with the market economy and higher labor force participation rates for women in both north and south.

It has also been suggested that discrimination against female children is higher among the wealthier classes and less among tribal groups. This view is supported by a careful, though somewhat dated study of 296 districts of the 1981 Census by Murti *et al.* (1995) as part of a larger study of fertility, mortality and gender. The analysis of the relationship between female discrimination and class builds on the ideas of Dreze and Sen (1995), while the lack of discrimination within scheduled tribes is based on the observation that male children have no special cachet in tribal societies.

In a related study, Das Gupta (1987) investigates sex bias in rural villages in the Indian punjab. Her analysis suggests that sex bias focuses on higher birth order girls and these biases are stronger among the higher classes. She also finds that recent downward trends in fertility intensify these biases against girls among the upper classes but not among the poor.

Clearly the determinants of gender discrimination and the impact of gender discrimination on chronic poverty are complex. Changes in society that give women more freedom to work, move about freely and without fear, become educated and learn more about how to care for and raise their children to be healthy and literate are all beneficial for society in general. They also have salutary impacts on chronic poverty. It is, however, difficult to single out the extent of these impacts directly without a more thorough understanding of the dynamic interactions among the various forces that determine gender discrimination. Further analysis should help in determining the mix of policies required to reduce discrimination in particular circumstances

2.7.2 *Gender discrimination at work*

Turning to the work place discrimination against chronically poor women, a study of rural poverty in Bangladesh by Akter (2005) confirms the work of several other economists. The bulk of job discrimination (estimated to be 75 percent) is manifest through the occupational distribution which constrains women to work in a limited range of low paying jobs rather than within a particular job classification. These results are obtained from the analysis of an eight village census in Bangladesh conducted by the Institute of Development Studies in the United Kingdom using multinomial logit analysis.

Hare (1999) came to a different conclusion. Uing data collected in 1989 for China she analyzed sample response from 249 farm households from Qingyuan County in central Guangdong province, a county that is a typical middle level rural village. She found that young women's wages were 40 percent below that of men in comparable occupations, typically agriculture. The fact that Hare's study focused on agriculture provides some control on difference in job classification since both men and women in these villages were working in the agricultural sector. Hare's analysis demonstrates that discrimination against women occurs within individual occupations as well as between occupations in different industries.

In a study of Malaysia, Milanovic (2006) examined Household Income Survey data for 1984–1997 and found that the shortfall of women's earnings relative to men's decreased from 36 percent in 1984 to 28 percent in 1997. Controlling for the structure of earnings in different occupations the shortfall fell to 21 percent in 1997. The Milanovic study does not tell us much about chronic poverty though it is likely that gender discrimination is also substantial among chronically poor women. Whether gender discrimination declined among chronically poor women between 1984 and 1997 as well as among women generally is not known. We do know that the chronically poor in Malaysia, though relatively few in numbers, are more likely to be Malay than Chinese. Milanovic also looks at discrimination against Malays generally and against women of Malay and Chinese extraction. Adjusting for individual characteristics including education, occupation and location, discrimination against Malays generally was about 25 percent. For women without any adjustments for individual characteristics there was more discrimination against Chinese than Malay women. Earnings for Chinese women were 41 percent lower than for ethnic Chinese men whereas the gender difference was only 34 percent between Malay women and men.

In another study for Malaysia using data from the Second Family Life Survey of 1998–99, Schafgans (1998) found discrimination against Malaysian women of between 21 and 23 percent, a figure that is similar to the results from the Milanovic study. However, when a different (and preferable) econometric technique is used, the ethnic bias disappears. These results for Malaysia provide a cautionary note on the interpretation of econometric estimates when evaluating ethnic and gender bias.

These studies for China, Malaysia and Bangladesh suggest that discrimination against women at work is widespread and pervasive.It is unclear whether we can draw any general conclusions as to the size of this discrimination as between the occupational distributions or between men and women in the same occupation. Similarly it is difficult to determine whether there is more discrimination among the poor than the rich or between different ethnic groups.

2.7.3 *Class and caste based discrimination*

Turning to caste and class based discrimination there are a number of studies that provide details of the magnitude and extent of this kind of discrimination. In India, Borooah (2005) has analyzed a 1994 survey of nearly 29,000 households. The survey was conducted by the National Council of Applied Economic Research of India. In order to isolate the impact of discrimination against scheduled castes and scheduled tribes Borooah controlled for other socioeconomic variables in a log-linear model of income determination. In the model household income depends on whether the household owned land (a dichotomous variable), the amount of land owned in acres, number of adults in the household, an index of the amount of productive assets outside of land owned by the household, educational level of the household head — low (illiterate), moderate (primary school), high (above primary school), and social groups (Scheduled Caste, Scheduled Tribe or other Hindu classes, region of residence (central, south, west, east, north).

Most of the socio economic variables were significant and served as useful control variables. SC and ST were more heavily discriminated in the northern region states of Maharastra and Gugarat, two of the poorest states. The poorest states of Bihar and Orissa, where SC and ST represent a significant share of the population were lumped with other states in the Central and Eastern regions and so it was difficult to gauge the level of ST and SC discrimination in these states. Several interaction terms were introduced in the model to allow for unequal treatment discrimination (for the same job) as opposed to occupational discrimination (between different jobs). Borooah (2005) was able to differentiate between unequal treatment two ways, based on what SC and ST households would have received if they were to be treated as "Hindus" and what Hindus would have received if they were treated as SC or ST households.

The extent of discrimination differs, but not significantly. The results are displayed in Table 2.18. The extent of the discrimination is between 30 and 40 percent of the total income differential between the scheduled tribes and scheduled casts and the Hindu majority.

Table 2.18 Decomposition of Inter-Group Differences in Mean Household Income

SC Treated as Hindus	ST Treated as Hindus	Hindus Treated as SC	Hindus Treats as ST
36	46	32	39

Source: Borooah (2005).

Note: Table values represent the "unequal treatment" proportion of the differences in income between SC/ST and Hindus in India.

Table 2.19 Decomposition of Inter-Group Differences in the Proportion of Households in the Bottom Income Quintile Using Multinomial Probit Model

SC Treated as Hindus	ST Treated as Hindus	Hindus Treated as SC	Hindus Treats as ST
36	53	22	47

Source: Borooah (2005).
Note: Table values are probabilities of being in the lower quintile of the income distribution of different ethnic groups in India.

The remainder of the differential in income is due to socioeconomic attribute differences such as education, land ownership, which are also indirectly related to discrimination. Borooah (2005) goes on to analyze the difference between Hindu and SC households in terms of probabilities of being in different income quintiles using a multinomial probit model where the dependent variable is the income quintile. The results are similar to the decomposition of household income and are reported in Table 2.19. The probabilities of being in the lower 20 percent of the income distribution is much greater for the SC/ST. Overall discrimination against scheduled tribes is somewhat greater than scheduled castes in both sets of results.

Finally, Borooah reports results relating to the proportion of poor households in the total number of SC/ST and Hindu households. These results are reported in Table 2.20. Assuming medium income is the top of the second quartile of the overall income distribution (the 50th percentile) then the breakdown of the four categories would be (i) above 37.5 percent (ii) between 25 percent and 37.5 percent (iii) 12.5 percent and 25 percent and (iv) below 12.5 percent. The poorest of the poor are mostly in the lowest decile of the income distribution, which is about 5 percent of all households in the Indian sub sample examined by Borooah (2005). This is about half the proportion of chronically poor estimated by McKay and Baulch (2006), who argue that between one quarter and one third of the number of people in US$1 a day poverty are chronically poor.

Based on data from Table 2.20, 36 percent of all households are poor (the sum of mildly poor, moderately poor and very poor in

Table 2.20 Proportion of Poor Households in India by Ethnic Breakdown (%)

	All Households	Hindu Households	SC Households	ST Households
Not poor	64	71	54	53
Mildly poor	17	14	21	22
Moderately Poor	14	11	19	19
Very Poor	5	4	6	6

Source: Borooah (2005).
Note: Not poor are households with incomes above 75 percent of median income for sample of 28,922 households; Mildly poor includes households with between 50 and 75 percent of median income for the sample; Moderately poor are households with between 50 and 25 percent of median income and Very Poor are households with income below 25 percent of median income. In any event a significant proportion of ST/SC households are chronically poor.

column 1 of the table). If we take this to be those living on US$1 dollar per day then a quarter to a third would be 9 percent to 13 percent of all households in India. In terms of discrimination, Borooah (2005) estimates that for SC households 36 percent of the probability of being in the bottom income quintile came from discrimination while for ST households the probability of being in the bottom income quintile coming from discriminationit was an even higher 53 percent.

Turning to Vietnam, the per capita expenditure of ethnic minorities are 14 percent lower than the expenditures of the ethnic majority Kinh or the Chinese, even holding other factors such as family size, asset ownership and education constant. (see World Bank, 2004). In another study of Vietnam, van de Walle and Gunewardena (2001) uses a similar methodology to that employed by Borooah to examine discrimination against ethnic minorities in northern Vietnam using the 1992–93 Vietnam Living Standards Measurement Survey for 2720 rural households. The sample was comprised of provinces in the Northern Uplands, North Coast, Red River, the Central Coast and the Central Highlands. The analysis focused on differences in consumption between the tribal minorities and the ethnic majority. They found that the tribal groups had lower living standards and consumption because they lived in mountainous terrain, had less access to education and geographic isolation as the result of poor road access and other infrastructure which also meant they had less access to off farm employment. Aside from these geographic factors the biggest determinant of differences in the consumption pattern of the ethnic minorities is the poor quality of the land they tilled and the equally poor quality of the education they received. Measuring the precise size of these differentials was not possible yet they seemed to be responsible for the lion's share of the difference in consumption between the two groups. Still there are differences in consumption that can not be traced to social or economic characteristics which may be due to discrimination. These were not quantified precisely. Van de Walle and Gunewardena argue that the minorities have learned to specialize in activities where they can not be discriminated against, such as subsistence farming and gathering forest products and perhaps cultivation of non-traditional crops. But this means that they have to be content with living on the margin of the market economy where standards are low. Where discrimination exists, in terms of sales of traditional crops and off-farm employment, the tribal minorities are less likely to be successful in making a living because of overt discrimination.

> A rational response to the social or economic exclusion of an ethnic subgroup is to retreat into specific activities, or strive to obtain higher returns to certain characteristics that cannot be easily discriminated against. (Van de Walle and Gunewardena, 2001, p. 19).

Van de Walle and Gunewardena stress that the preferred approach to raising living standards and breaking the bonds of discrimination that have resulted in social exclusion among the hill tribes is by providing more opportunities for off-farm employment and by reducing labor market discrimination. These suggestions would apply equally to hill tribes in the Philippines and Thailand. We will discuss possible policies further in Chapters 5 and 7.

In Thailand, Neef *et al.* (2003) draw on various case studies as evidence of the failure of the state paradigm in the management of natural resources, such as forests and agricultural land in protected areas. They discuss the ambiguous achievements of the land reform process in the most poverty-stricken areas of North and Northeast regions of the country. Their analysis suggest that local communities and ethnic minorities have reacted to top-down planning, corruptive land allocation and repressive forest policies by initiating their own reforestation activities — often supported by NGOs — with local management and control structures. They have initiated resource protection measures, such as planting fruit trees, and reviving religious traditions of sacred forests. Thus, rural communities in Thailand have demonstrated that the conventional paradigm of the Royal Forest Department of "forest without people" is alien to their local concepts of natural resource management. Recently, in North Thailand's desperate attempts to reclaim rural people's lands from speculators who either grabbed the land illegally or supposedly bought the land from the government have resulted in massive public pressure forcing the government to reconsider its resource policies. While some promising attempts of decentralization of natural resource management have been initiated, the nature of these policies remains highly controversial and ambiguous. Neff *et al.* (2003) conclude that the reluctance of government agencies to devolve control over natural resources to local communities seriously jeopardize their drive for food security and sustainable livelihoods. A number of alternative policy approaches are discussed, such as the redistribution of private land bought for speculative reasons, establishment of community land trusts and co-management arrangements for common-pool resources, such as forestland in protected areas.

In Lao, there is discrimination against ethnic minorities. They have less land and fewer assets. Even controlling for these endowments the Mon-Khmer minority remain poorer than the Lao majority (see World Bank, 2006c) and they are also discriminated against even when these factors are taken into account.

All of these policies and issues have particular relevance for the chronically poor who derive their livelihood from agricultural activities in mountainous and forested regions in Cambodia, Lao, Thailand, Burma, Philippines and Vietnam. They are discussed further in country studies reviewed in Chapter 7.

In terms of hard numbers the evidence from India is most compelling. Around 30 to 40 percent of income differentials were as a result of overt discrimination against ST/SC for the same job while the remaining differentials were the result of discrimination that kept ST/SC from jobs in higher paying occupations. The latter form of discrimination is also documented in the other studies reviewed in this section.

As a final note on how discrimination and prejudice can have a pervasive toxic impact on the social fabric of society consider the case study of Uttar Pradesh, where a history of such discrimination can have a persistent impact on test score performance in school When caste was hidden low-caste and high-caste students performed equally on tests but when caste was announced beforehand the low-caste students had scores that were 23 percent lower on average. The conclusion was not that lower caste students were less confident but rather that when their caste was know they would be treated prejudicially so it really didn't matter how well they performed on the test. (see Hoff and Pandey, 2004).

2.8 Limited Mobility and Migration

Out migration provides a significant outlet for poor families to increase their earnings by augment farm labor with employment outside of agriculture. Restrictions on mobility will have a detrimental impact on their poverty status and the probability of a continuation of chronic poverty. In most of the poorest regions in South and Southeast Asia the chronically poor are cut off from access to markets and the flow of commerce. Geographic isolation is compounded by neglect of infrastructure development such as roads and telecommunications. Since transportation and communications are limited, these chronically poor areas have not developed strong linkages outside their village communities. As a result they have no voice in the political process or in the allocation of development assistance to their villages. Policies pertaining to their welfare are too often made by government officials living the cities who seldom, if ever, visit the remote areas were the chronically poor reside. The situation is compounded by the interaction between increasing land scarcity, reduced soil fertility, environmental damage and growing poverty.

The entire family feels the impact of severe and protracted chronic poverty although the differential impact will be borne by women and young girls particularly in South Asia, where gender discrimination is greater than in Southeast Asia. Isolation and lack of job opportunities outside of agriculture all have detrimental impacts for all of these isolated areas populated primarily by ethnic minorities in Thailand, Vietnam, China and India.

Farm to market roads, sometimes called feeder roads, are a good way to improve access to remote areas. Studies of the effectiveness of rural road improvements show that physical isolation, poor and insufficient access to social services and markets are important impediments to raising incomes and are closely related to poverty (see Warr, 2007). Improved road access is correlated with a reduction of poverty in rural areas. Travel time decreased and purchases of bicycles, motorcycles and small pick up trucks increased in regions where the rural transport network has improved.

Warr (2007) argues that there are too many farmers in Asian agriculture and that the young in rural areas have to be encouraged to migrate. This can only be accomplished by raising the quality of education so that migrants can qualify for jobs in the cities. For example, Warr (2007) notes that the vast majority of Thailand's poor are uneducated, nearly 95 percent of the poor have only a primary school education or less. Additional education is not valued because the quality of education in rural areas is deficient. Yet it is just that educational upliftment that is one of the important key to unlocking to door out of poverty for the rural poor in Asia.

The results of a recent study of child health in Pakistan highlights how transportation constraints can have wide reaching impacts on chronic poverty and the relief that outmigration can provide in depressed in depressed areas. It also shows how gender discrimination can react with other variables to moderate the impact of improvements in diet as the result of migration. Ghazala (2006) found that the girls of migrants from rural areas had significant gains in weight and height compared with their counterparts that did not migrate. The results were validated by looking at weights of children in families before and after migration. The results for boys did not show any significant differences which suggests that stunting of girls is a result of gender discrimination.

In another study, Jacoby (2000) analyzed the value of rural roads in Nepal, The value of land is used as a means of measuring the value of upgrading and extending the rural road network. The argument states that farmland will be more valuable the closer it is to markets for agricultural products. The results of Jacoby's work suggest that road access to markets increases benefits to rural communities and many of these benefits might accrue to the poor. There was, however, no evidence that these benefits would serve a redistribution function. The results give partial support to the contention of the World Bank (World Bank, 1994) that rural roads are not necessarily designed to benefit the poor alone but rather to open up more isolated rural communities in general. To the extent that these rural communities are primarily composed of the disadvantaged, rural roads could provide a useful way for the poor to obtain better access to education and health facilities, a wider variety of consumer goods and greater employment opportunities. However, none of these options was part of the study and their exclusion exerts a possible downward bias on the impact of rural roads on the chronically poor.

Taken together, these studies of rural road impacts on the chronically poor suggests gains from providing better communications access to isolated rural communities have a number of benefits, some of which need to be investigated further in order to fully assess the advantages that accrue to the chronically poor who live in these isolated communities.

2.9 Unfavorable Household Characteristics

There are a variety of socioeconomic characteristics of households that are associated with poverty and which contribute to the perpetuation of poverty. We list them first and then discuss them in turn. They include large households, households headed by women or children, poor health of the main wage earner and of others in the household, poor nutrition, low education and literacy of adults and children, unfair allocation of resources within the family.

There is wide agreement that larger households in developing countries tend to be poorer (see Lipton and Ravallion, 1994; Lanjouw and Ravallion, 1995, for additional discussion and sources). The correlation has been observed in a number of developing countries in Asia and elsewhere. The pattern of causation has been subject to even more discussion. Clearly household size at any point in time is determined by a number of factors including the age and education of the mother, education of the father, infant mortality, and perhaps some other socioeconomic factors, ethnic and geographic factors. Larger families are a result of planning that reflects high infant mortality, the need for support of parents in old age and requirements to augment family income when children mature. Family size will fall as education, earnings, potential employment outside of agriculture and use of contraception increase and infant mortality decreases. However those in chronic poverty who have not made the transition to a higher income and education level are still likely to have large families. Lanjouw and Ravallion (1994) also argue that there are some economies of scale for large families which offsets the additional costs of more children. Welfare measures for the family are complicated by the presence of adults and children of different ages.

To investigate the relationship between family size and income further Lanjouw and Ravallion (1995) use regression analysis of the log of total household expenditures on the log of household size for a large sample of families in Pakistan. While the possibility that some families could benefit from economies of scale of consumption the general conclusion is, other things being equal, larger families will be poorer. The relationship between nutrition and family size was examined by including two nutritional variables in the analysis, namely stunting (as indicated by child height-for-age, relative to international standards), and wasting (as indicated by weight-for-height). While wasting was not significant Lanjouw and Ravallion found that stunting tends to be higher in large households, even after the inclusion of other socioeconomic variables.

In a study of rural Bangladeshi households, Mahmud and McIntosh (1980) examined consumption per capita and family size in a sample of villages using information collected by the Bangladesh Institute of Development Studies. Despite some economies of scale they found that consumption per family member and family size are negatively related.[4] One explanation for this inverse relationship suggested by the research is that the distribution of consumption within the family becomes more unequal as family size increases. Females are the subject of this internal family discrimination, receiving less food in larger families. This is also reflected by a decline in the sex ratio for women, who are less likely to survive to adulthood as a result of food deprivation as well as less health care. This is despite the fact that infant mortality for girls is nearly the same as for boys. The situation perpetuates because large families provide additional benefits, particularly security in old age.

> The importance of this to peasants cannot be overestimated. Thus, the fact that present consumption per head might be lower is probably seen by many farmers with large families as a very small price to pay for this security. Moreover, it has been suggested that greater numbers of children minimize the risk of economic decline of the household, especially during periods of crisis. (Mahmoud and MacIntosh, 1980, p. 506).

In addition, the negative relationship between consumption per head and family size appears to increase with the level of poverty. This further reinforces the potential poverty trap wherein short term well being is sacrificed for the longer term security of the head of poor households.

Looking into female headed households and chronic poverty some studies suggest that the ratio of female headed to male headed households in poverty could be as high as 2 to 1. UNDP (1995) suggests that only 30 percent of households in poverty are headed by men However Marcoux (1998) examines this claim carefully and suggest the ratio is more like 55 percent of households are headed by men.

There are only a few detailed studies at the country level in Asia and the evidence of higher poverty rates for female headed households is mixed. After controlling for cultivated area and education for

[4] See also JC Caldwell (1976, 1977 and 1978).

the period 1987–88, Gangopadhyay and Wadhwa (2003) found there were significantly higher levels of poverty for female headed households in rural areas. There were significantly higher levels of poverty for female headed households However when the sample for 1993–94 was examined there was no significant effect on poverty for female headed households relative to men. This evidence suggests that female headed households in India have become less vulnerable as incomes have risen and development has accelerated in the intervening decade between the two surveys.

In a broader study of 10 developing countries Quisumbin *et al.* (2007) found weak evidence that female headed households experienced higher incidence of poverty than male headed households. They caution against drawing quick inferences about the relationship between female headed households and poverty. There are other factors that are equally important in determining poverty aside from the gender of the household head which they don't explore in the paper.

IFAD (1999) notes that female-headed households constitute a significant proportion of households in Cambodia (35 percent) and in parts of Nepal. Out-migration of men to work in urban areas or outside of agriculture is a major cause for the shift to female-headed household. IFAD (1999) argues that women remain as household heads and the main farmers. IFAD (1999) goes on to say that in many countries, such households are poorer than households with male heads. Female headed households constitute 16 percent of the landless and marginal households in Bangladesh. Furthermore, 96 percent of female headed households are poor, and 33 percent are hard-core poor. IFAD doesn't define what hard core poor is but we can assume this would comprise families some distance below the poverty line and perhaps also chronically poor.

Female-headed households in rural areas have also migrated to urban areas to improve their standards of living, particularly in the garment industry in Bangladesh, India and the Philippines. In a study of garment workers in Bangladesh Kabeer *et al.* (2004) found that more than half of the young women working in domestic garment factors in Dhaka were single, separated or divorced. While some were temporary migrants and were sending part of their earnings home to their families, these female headed households were an important component of the overall female headed workforce and were contributing to both their own well being and that of their families that were living in rural communities.

The relationship between family size and chronic poverty is compelling. In addition there is also evidence that children in large families have a greater chance of having dietary deficiencies.

On the other hand, summarizing the literature on the specifics of chronic poverty as it relates to differences in the gender of household heads is not easy. First there are few studies designed to specifically investigate the poverty map for female versus male headed households. There are many studies that observe some aspects of gender and poverty but virtually none that deal with chronic poverty and female headed households. The detailed studies that are available find some evidence that female headed households are poorer than their male counterparts. There is evidence for India that these differences have been falling over time. It is important to recognize that only carefully crafted studies with extensive cross section information would be able to isolate gender after controlling for age, education, family size and family characteristics, asset holdings and other household characteristics. It makes intuitive sense that women who have become the only bread winners after some family tragedy where the father has died or is injured will suffer a major setback and could sink further into poverty. It is another matter to conclude that female headed households are systematically subject to chronic poverty. So far the evidence is extensive, though not compelling, that females are more likely to be chronically poor than men once other factors have been accounted for.

2.10 Children and Chronic Poverty

Most information on the status of children and chronic poverty is anecdotal. Conventional wisdom says that the number and proportions of economically active children between the ages of 7 and 14 (10–14) will be larger in poorer countries and the adolescent fertility rate will also be higher in poorer countries. The consensus is that young children in poorer countries are more likely to be drawn into the work force to help support their families. This holds for both boys and girls. Whether girls or boys are more likely to join the work force is debatable. Some observers would contend that boys are more likely to drop out of school to work because they are stronger and more productive in the agricultural sector. Others maintain that girls are more likely to drop out because they are subject to educational discrimination and have lower rates of return to further schooling. It is also claimed that adolescent fertility is higher among the poor since literacy rates are low and knowledge of birth control less widespread. Furthermore the opportunity cost of postponing child bearing is lower for the poorer women since they have few prospects for more education or work.

Broad country evidence is consistent with these conjectures. The evidence in Tables 2.21 and 2.22 and Charts 2.1 and 2.2 suggests that the relationships are highly nonlinear. Rich countries have much lower levels of adolescent fertility and labor force participation rates for the young than the poor countries. If we confine our attention to China, the Mekong countries and South Asia the relationship is more linear

Table 2.21 Adolescent Fertility and Income Per Capita

Country	Adolescent Fertility 15–19 Per Thousand Women (2007)	Income Per Capita in US Dollars (2003)
Bangladesh	123	470
Cambodia	48	430
China	5	1740
India	73	730
Indonesia	54	1260
Korea	3	15880
Lao PDR	89	450
Malaysia	18	4970
Nepal	53	270
Pakistan	69	690
Philippines	36	1290
Singapore	5	26620
Sri Lanka	19	1170
Thailand	48	2720
Vietnam	20	620

Source: World Bank (2007).

Table 2.22 Economically Active Children Ages 7–14 and Income Per Capita — Countries in East Asia, Southeast Asia, Mekong and South Asia.

Country	Economically Active Children as Percent of Age Cohort (10–14) 2005	Yearly Income Per Capita in US Dollars (2003)
Bangladesh	26.5	470
Cambodia	23.2	430
China	4.0	1740
India	10.7	730
Indonesia	6.8	1260
Korea	0.0	15880
Lao PDR	24.3	450
Malaysia	1.2	4970
Nepal	40.2	270
Pakistan	14.0	690
Philippines	2.7	1290
Singapore	0.0	26620
Sri Lanka	1.0	1170
Thailand	10.0	2720
Vietnam	2.6	620

Source: ILO (2007) and World Bank (2007).

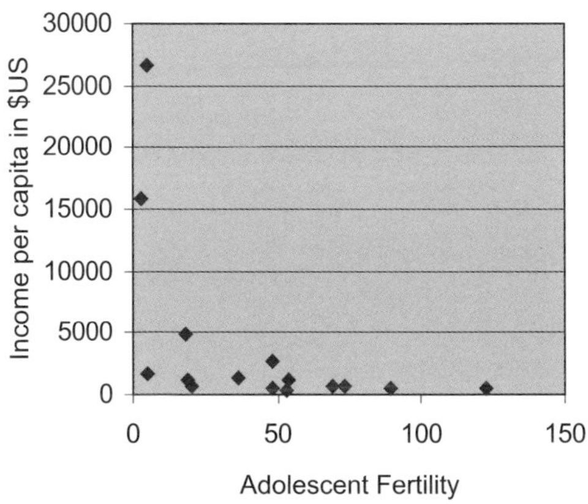

Chart 2.1 Adolescent Fertility and Income per capita — countries in East Asia, Southeast Asia, Mekong and South Asia.

Source: Table 2.21.

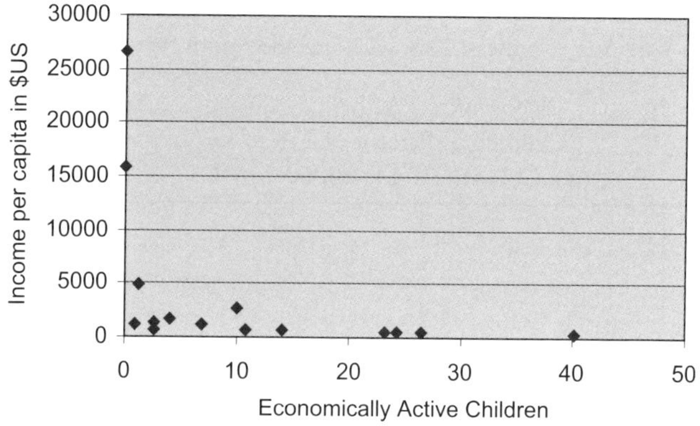

Chart 2.2 Economically active children and Income per capita — countries in East Asia, Southeast Asia, Mekong and South Asia.

Source: Table 2.21.

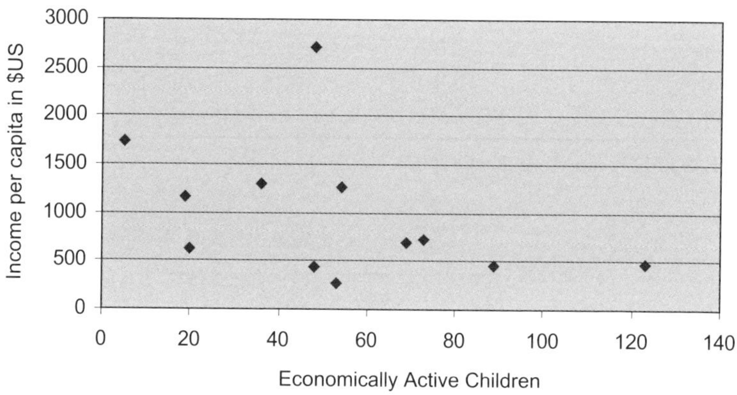

Chart 2.3 Economically active children and income per capita — Countries in Southeast Asia (excluding Malaysia), Mekong and South Asia.

Source: Table 2.22.

and while the fit is not particularly tight there is still a negative realationship (see Charts 2.3 and 2.4).

There are some in-depth studies of the relationship between poverty and labor force participation by children. Theoretically we would expect the incidence of child labor to be directly related to poverty. Poor families have to decide between short term gains in

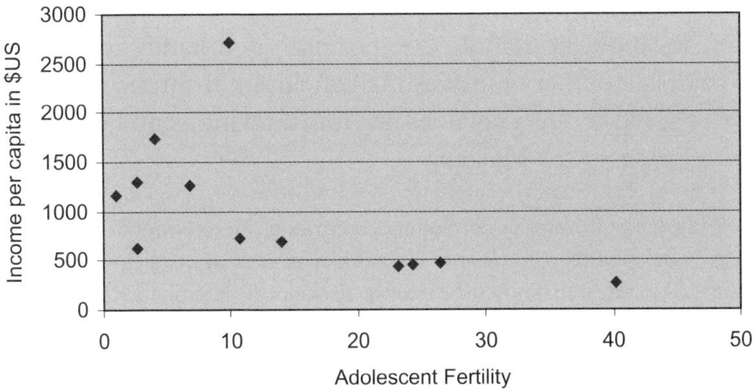

Chart 2.4 Adolescent fertility rate and income per capita — countries in Southeast Asia (excluding Malaysia), Mekong and South Asia.

Source: Table 2.23.

income from sending their children to work or the longer term returns to providing them with education. Continued expectations that the family would still be in poverty in the future and the presence of imperfect capital markets that prevent them from borrowing to finance their children's education, poor families are likely to choose the work option. There is considerable evidence that this is indeed what is happening although there can be other reasons for child labor including lack of good schooling opportunities, parental indifference related to their own lack of education along with the ready availability of job opportunities for children (see for example, Edmonds, 2001). Ray (2000) finds a strong negative correlation between household income and child labor as well as a positive relationship between household income and school enrolment in Pakistan (see also Udry, 2006). However he does not find such a relationship in Peru, a higher income country.

The inference that household income and child labor are related for poor but not richer countries is confirmed by a study drawing on data compiled from a family life survey for 1976 in Malaysia, Dennis De Tray (1983) examined the time use profile of children in 1262 households. Multivariate analysis was used to determine the impact of a series of independent variables on the use of time. These included socioeconomic variables relating to the child (gender, age), parents (education, age), and household characteristics (ethnicity, income sources, location, household composition, and family income). The study draws a number of interesting conclusion from the probit analysis of this data set. De Tray does not find a relationship between child labor and poverty for Malaysia.

> The burden of poverty in developing countries is often thought to fall most heavily on children who must begin work at an early age to help make ends meet. This research finds no evidence to support that picture. Malaysian children from poor families neither participate more in productive activities nor work longer hours when they do participate than children from more well-to-do families. (De Tray, 1983, p. 452).

While the direct evidence for Malaysia strongly suggests that there is no relationship between poverty and child labor, the evidence from Pakistan and casual observation of poverty and income in India (see below) suggests that child labor bears more heavily on the poor than the non poor, primarily because of its impact on the level of children's literacy.

Doanne (2007) compiled evidence on literacy rates and the incidence of child labor for a variety of occupations in South Asia displayed in Table 2.23. The incidence of child labor is quite high for all occupations in the four poorest South Asian economies. Aside from garments, where reading and writing may be required, literacy rates are also quite low for most home based occupations. It is hard to believe that these households are not poor. Doanne provides further earnings information of these households based on occupation, lean and peak employment periods (Table 2.24). In most cases the lean period is the norm and peak periods are short and focused on festivals or other yearly events that only last a few days. Earnings are low, although providing some supplemental income to poor families where the main bread winner only earns enough to feed between two and three people at the $1 per day poverty minimum (see Table 2.12). Child or female earnings could supplement primary earnings by as much as 50 percent, the difference between near starvation and a reasonably full belly. This added income can also prevent growth stunting and ensure normal childhood development of younger siblings or younger workers.

Table 2.23 Child labor and Illiteracy Rates in South Asia of Households Surveyed

Home Based Occupations	Child Labor Rate (5–14) as Percent of Respondents Who Started Doing Home-Based Work Before Age 15	Illiteracy Rate (Percent of Respondents Self Reporting)
Bangladesh		
Garments	22	16
Weaving	58	70
Pottery	72	24
Pearl/shell	72	92
India		
Garments	54	26
Weaving	42	55
Incense stick rolling	42	47
Nepal		
Garments		40
Weaving	2	32
Handmade Paper		26
Pakistan		
Garments	63	26
Weaving	68	80
Pottery Survey 1	82	38
Pottery Survey 2	61	78
Sri Lanka		
Yarn	22	5
Batik	5	19

Source: Doanne (2007, p. 19).

There are also some additional studies on the relationship between age at marriage and per capita income that throws further light on the relationship between poverty and female child labor. In a cross-section study of age at marriage for Asian countries, Singh and Samara (1996) found a close correlation between per capita income and age at first marriage. (see Table 2.25 and Chart 2.5). The authors also found age at marriage closely related to woman's education, urbanization and women's labor force participation rate. Where education levels were low and the women had a low rate of participation in the work force

Table 2.24 Average Earnings Per Month of Home-Based Workers Surveyed

Country and Occupation	Lean Period Earnings in US Dollar Equivalent Per Month After Deducting Costs	Peak Period Earnings in US Dollars Per Month After Ddeducting Costs
Bangladesh		
Garments	11	25
Weaving	4	7
Pottery	20	35
Pearl/shells	4	8
India		
Garments	16	26
Weaving	19	28
Incense stick rolling	7	11
Nepal		
Garments	30	49
Weaving	21	38
Handmade paper	21	38
Pakistan		
Garments	24	40
Weaving	22	30
Pottery	22	56
Sri Lanka		
Yarn	13	23
Mat making	14	27
Rattan weaving	12	24
Batik	39	58

Source: Doanne (2007, p. 7).
Note: Earnings rounded to nearest US dollar.

and lived in rural areas they were more likely to marry and bear children at an early age.

This suggests that poor families have two choices when it comes to their daughters; marry them off at an early age to shift responsibility of the daughters support to the husband; or continue to work and contribute income to the family. The downside of the second option is that the daughter might never marry creating a social stigma for the parents.

How do these choices impact on the poverty status of the family and of child labor? Poverty puts stress on the family to either marry

Table 2.25 Percent of Women Aged 20–24 Married by 15, 18 and 20 Along with Median Age at First Marriage for All Women

Country	Married at 15 (%)	Married at 18 (%)	Married at 20 (%)	Median Age of All Women at First Marriage	Yearly Per Income Capita 2003 in US Dollars
Bangladesh	47	73	82	14.1	470
India	18	51	70	16.1	730
Indonesia	10	34	51	17.7	1260
Pakistan	11	32	49	18.6	690
Philippines	2	14	29	21.4	1290
Sri Lanka	1	14	28	22.4	1170
Thailand	2	20	37	20.5	2720

Source: Singh and Samara (1996).

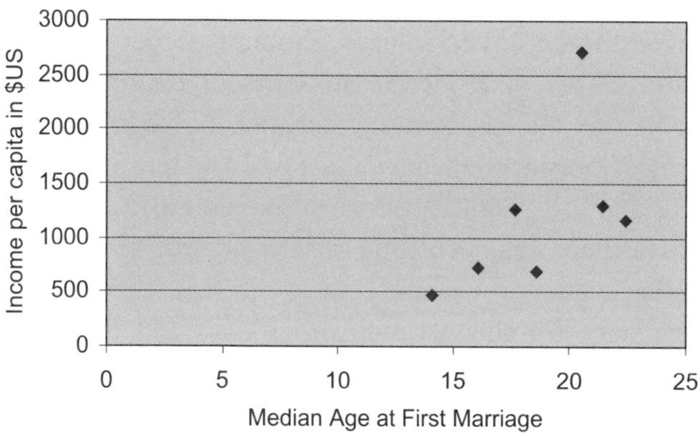

Chart 2.5 Median age at first marriage and annual per capita income in US dollars.

Source: Table 2.25.

off daughters or encourage them to work to support the family. When women marry early their chance of escaping poverty are reduced, since they will probably forgo further education and bear more children over their lifetime than if they were able to continue schooling and/or enter the labor force. Many girls are employed in home based occupations at low wage rates. They usually do not continue their education beyond a few years of elementary school. Both of these options tend to perpetuate the cycle of poverty and keep these young women and their families locked in the poverty trap.

We return to the issue of child labor in Chapter 4, where we consider policies to subsidize poor families to send their children to school (see section on Human Capital Subsidies through Conditional Cash Transfers).

2.11 Shocks, Wars and Other Disruptions

In recent years there have been a number of unexpected disruptions that have had an adverse impact on chronic poverty within the Asia region. These include the Asian financial crisis of 1997–1998; the Tsunami that hit Indonesia, Thailand, Sri Lanka and India at the end of 2005; the eruptions of Mount Pitatubu in the Philippines in 1995 and Mount Merapi in Indonesia in 2005; ongoing classes between India and Pakistan over dispute territories in Kashmir, a border skirmish between Vietnam and China in 1979 the atrocities of the Pol Pot regime in Cambodia in the 1970s; domestic turmoil in Pakistan following the assassination of president Bhutto and his daughter; and the draconian social, economic and political policies of the regime in Myanmar. Due to a lack of data there has been little systematic analysis of the impact of many of these events on chronic poverty. In this section we review the available evidence for the Asian financial crisis and the impact of the Tsunami, each of which impacted several countries in the Asian region.

2.11.1 *Asian financial crisis*

The Asian financial crisis of 1997–98 had a severe impact on several countries in Southeast Asia (Thailand, where the crisis started, Indonesia, Malaysia and Philippines) and also on Korea. The overall extent of the crisis can be understood by analyzing macroeconomic and poverty data for these countries. Looking first at GDP growth in GDP, the five countries most affected experienced a sharp downturn in GDP as shown in Table 2.26. Along with the sharp decline in GDP growth there was acceleration in the rate of growth in poverty.

Table 2.26 Growth in Real GDP 1994–2007

Country	94	95	96	97	98	99	00	01	02	03	04	05	06	07
Thailand	8.6	8.8	5.5	**–0.4**	**–10.5**	4.4	4.8	2.1	5.3	7.1	6.3	4.5	5.0	4.0
Korea	8.6	8.9	7.1	5.5	**–6.9**	9.5	8.5	3.8	7.0	3.1	4.7	4.0	5.0	4.5
Malaysia	9.3	9.4	8.6	7.7	**–7.4**	6.1	8.5	0.3	4.4	5.5	7.2	5.2	5.9	5.4
Indonesia	7.5	8.2	8.0	4.6	**–13.1**	0.8	4.9	3.5	4.5	4.8	5.0	5.7	5.5	6.0
Philippine	4.4	4.7	5.8	5.2	**–0.6**	3.4	4.4	3.0	4.4	4.9	6.2	5.0	5.4	5.4

Source: World Bank (2007) and Asian Development Bank (2008a) Statistical Annex. Years of negative growth in bold.

Hong Kong Singapore and Taiwan were also affected but the impact on poverty was less pronounced. Thailand had two years of negative growth while the rest of the region had negative growth in 1998. By 1999, all countries were back to positive growth.

Knowles *et al.* (2000) documented a variety of social impacts on the countries affected by the Asian financial crisis including an increase in unemployment, reduced incomes and a reduction in the supply of social services. They note that the level of poverty also increased during the crisis. The poverty level in Korea more than doubled from a low 3 to 7.5 percent. In Indonesia they report that the poverty incidence increased from 11 to 14 percent or perhaps even higher. Poverty levels in the other affected countries also increased. There is, however, limited information on the extent of the impact of the crisis on chronic poverty.

Suryahadi and Sumarto (2003) conducted a more detailed study of Indonesia based on two large surveys, the SUSENAS survey of 200,000 households and PODES village data sets for nearly 69,000 villages in 1996 and 1999. The data sets were merged to give consumption, household characteristics and village level characteristics for over 57,000 households in over 3400 villages. In addition to estimates of chronic poverty the authors also developed a vulnerability to poverty measure which calculated the probability that a family will have income below the poverty line. Using a probability of 0.5 that a family will fall into poverty, they report a number of different statistics for various group combinations — low vulnerability, high vulnerability, poor and non–poor and various combinations. They also looked at gender specific poverty rates as well as occupational, geographic and educational differences using the socioeconomic characteristics of their sample households.

By comparing the 1996 and 1999 results, they drew a series of inferences regarding the impact of the financial crisis which can be summarized as follows: The poverty impact was most severe in the agricultural sector, among the chronically poor and the poorly educated (Tables 2.27 and 2.28). The chronically poor in agriculture had a total vulnerability probability of being poor of 51 percent and those with less than primary had a higher vulnerability probability of

Table 2.27 Poverty Categories in Indonesia by Sectors of Occupation of Household Heads 1996 and 1999 in Percent

	Transient Poor	Chronically Poor	Total Vulnerability
1996			
Agriculture	19.1	7.1	31.6
Industry	10.1	1.3	13.1
1999			
Agriculture	21.7	18.7	51.0
Industry	17.2	6.8	28.4

Source: Suryahadi and Sumarto (2003).

Table 2.28 Poverty Categories in Indonesia by Education Level of Household Head 1996 and 1999 in Percent

	Transient Poor	Chronically Poor	Total Vulnerability
1996			
Not completed primary plus primary	31.5	8.2	46.7
Lower secondary plus upper secondary	9.0	1.3	10.9
1999			
Not completed primary plus primary	44.2	26.6	88.0
Lower secondary plus upper secondary	22.0	3.4	28.3

Source: Suryahadi and Sumarto (2003).

88 percent. Those with higher levels of education were much less vulnerable. The fact that the chronically poor were also more likely to be poorly educated increased their vulnerability in a highly nonlinear way. Their vulnerability to poverty nearly doubled between 1996 and 1999. Suryahadi and Sumarto also found that the more remote eastern provinces were the more adversely affected than Sumatra, Java and Kalimantan. This is consistent with the results on the impact of isolation on chronic poverty discussed in section 2.8 above. There was no differential impact of the financial crisis between

female and male headed households. This particular result is consistent with the general findings of Dreze and Srinivasan (1997) for India, where they conclude that there is no gender bias in India in the sense that on average female headed households are not poorer than male headed households.

2.11.2 *2004 Tsunami*

Turning to the impact of the tsunami that hit many countries on the Pacific Rim on 26 December 2004, we begin with a summary of the devastation which is reported in Table 2.29 for the three countries most affected Other countries, including Thailand, Malaysia, Maldives and Somalia were also hit by the tsunami; however they sustained less damage. The affected residents lived near the water and were primarily rice farmers, artisanal fishermen and their families, tourists and tourist industry employees as well as those engaged in activities related to the farming, fishing and tourism industries.

Artisanal fishermen are among the poorest groups in the region while rice farmers and employees in the tourist industry were probably earning more. In Aceh province of Indonesia where the tsunami first hit there was significant damage to infrastructure including houses, roads, schools, hospitals and heath centers, rice fields, forests and industry. Poverty increased dramatically following the disaster. Before the tsunami it was estimated that 30 percent of the households in Aceh were in poverty. This swelled to over 50 percent after the tsunami (see Athukorala, 2005). Food prices also increased after the

Table 2.29 Damage from the 2004 tsunami in India, Indonesia and Sri Lanka

Country	Damaged	Dead and Missing	Displaced
India	$1.56 billion in assets, 897 villages	16,423	647,556
Indonesia	1550 villages	294,509	811,409
Sri Lanka	119626 houses damaged	36,603	502,268

Source: Athukorala (2005) adapted from Table 1.

tsunami increasing the stress on the poor and those who were displaced as a result of the devastation caused by the disaster. Disaster relief began immediately after the extent of the devastation became widely known. Aceh began to recover in the 2006 and the region returned to near normal by 2007.

In Sri Lanka, the tsunami reached the eastern part of the island between 2 hours and 15 minutes and 2 1/2 hours after the earthquake that caused the tsunami. There was little warning and residents had no time to flee despite the time delay. Women, children and the elderly accounted for approximately 2/3 of the fatalities which confirms the pattern of natural disasters in other parts of the world and also reports from Indonesia regarding the composition of fatalities in Aceh. The fishing and tourism industries were the hardest hit. 80 percent of the fishing fleet was destroyed as was 30 percent of tourist room capacity. As a proportion of the size of these sectors in the economy of Sri Lanka; the damage was more extensive than in Indonesia. The poverty rate rose as the tsunami pushed a quarter of a million people into poverty, implying a significant increase in the overall poverty rate for the country. Reconstruction and disaster management in Sri Lanka were complicated by the ongoing political conflicts between the government and the Tamil Tigers that controlled portions of the northern part of the country. Pledges from foreign donors to aid the rebuilding efforts caused some currency appreciation and inflation, resulting in further stress for the chronically poor.

In Indonesia, Sri Lanka, Thailand and other countries hit by the tsunami, the poor as well as the young, aged and women suffered the most from the devastation. Loss of life and property could have been avoided to a significant extent if environmental regulations that are designed to preserve coral reefs and mangrove forests were enforced. These coral reefs and mangroves could have acted as effective barriers to the tsunami. Since the poor are most affected by natural disasters it is important to be able to provide immediate assistance through some sort of disaster management fund. Greater understanding of the macroeconomic impacts of natural disasters is needed including currency appreciation and inflation as well as the impacts on the local economy. These topics are considered in greater depth in Chapter 6.

Chapter 3

The Dynamics of Chronic Poverty

The focus of this chapter is the intergenerational transmission of chronic poverty. Poverty, like power, wealth and social position, is transferred to the next generation in a number of different ways. Kings bestow their throne to one of their children, usually the eldest male, through well-established rituals that transfer the powers of the king to his successor. These powers are vested in the sovereign and cannot be usurped by another. The head of a wealthy family similarly transfer his family's power, property and social position to his children through legal instruments and tradition. Middle-class families project their values and life style on their children through their work and social contacts, educational orientation, entertainment and leisure activities as well as through inheritance of assets.

Poverty is also subject to intergenerational transfers. Poor health and improper diet are transferred beginning at conception and continuing within the womb and into infancy. Lack of proper health care and sanitation threaten infants born into poverty and the risks of nutritional deprivation are transferred from mother to child. Infant mortality is higher for the chronically poor than for any other social group. Low levels of literacy and education are also transferred from parents to children along with lack of proper sanitation and potable water, low levels of basic services, shelter and education. The probability of illiterate parents having illiterate children is much higher than if the parents are educated. Social skills and contacts are also passed on from one generation to the next. Those born in a village are likely to stay, bear children, raise a family and die in the village. The rhythm of life in rural Asia has followed an unchanging pattern from generation to generation and for the chronically poor it is soaked in the cloth of continued deprivation.

Intergenerational transfers of physical and social capital assets are typically characterized by the passage of those assets from parents to children or other relatives which are part of the extended family such as cousins, aunts and uncles. These kinds of intergenerational transfers are more likely to occur within extended family groups in poor countries. In richer countries where the nuclear family is more typical, intergenerational transfers are more often between parent and child or grandparent and grandchildren.

Breaking out of the poverty trap requires changes in the pattern of intergenerational transfer of assets. If families are able to transfer more assets than they initially had when they were growing up there is some hope of breaking out of the poverty trap. For poor families, education is probably the most important asset that parents can pass on to their children. If parents do not understand, appreciate or value their children's education then there will be limited intergenerational transfer of assets and poverty will be perpetuated. Lloyd (1994) and Desai (1993) argue that the demand for schooling is likely to be low where poverty rates are high and where the value of reading and writing skills is minimal. This is because there are few jobs for the poor that require even these minimal educational skills (see also Kabeer, 2000). We will now explore further the evidence regarding transfer of assets by the poor and its impact on the perpetuation of chronic poverty.

We begin with an analysis of general nutrition and food allocations within the family including care of young infants and mothers during pregnancy. We will also discuss transfers of social capital such as health and education; social status including involvement in local groups; information about careers; mobility; and political action.

3.1 Intra Household Food Allocations

Food allocation within a family is not determined by a simple matter of income and and is not necessarily correlated with family income. In some cases allocations to some family members may be negatively related to income. There is evidence, for example, that females are more food deficient in some higher income families in parts of India than in poorer families. This also holds for medical and nutritional discrimination (see Miller, 1997). On the other hand, the very poor do not discriminate as much between boys and girls in terms of food allocation. The evidence assembled by Miller suggests that the amount of gender discrimination in allocation of food in India is complicated and inconclusive. When speaking of discrimination between genders among the young, Miller argues that it is difficult to generalize about food allocations within the household. What pervades is the consistent difference in infant mortality for girls. Part of the explanation has to do with being clear about differences in rates of mortality between social classes and the disparity between gender mortality rates across income classes. Furthermore, overall statistics on gender mortality are generally couched in aggregate terms and not broken down by income. Therefore it is possible to have higher gender mortality rates for girls while at the same time having greater gender equality in terms of mortality and nutrition among the poor. This is the same argument made by Miller (1981, 1997).

There is evidence that nutritional intervention programs may help redress differences in gender nutrition. In West Bengal, for example, where girls from Scheduled Tribes and Scheduled Casts in one village were targeted for food subsidies, the malnourishment ratio was lower and girls were less discriminated against than in other villages where minorities were not singled out for subsidies (see Miller, 1997). However, there have been no comprehensive studies of the success of nutritional intervention programs for India as a whole and there is little systematic evidence for other poor countries in Asia. There is, however, general agreement that boys are generally fed more than girls and that male household heads eat more than their wives and children.

3.2 Transfers of Human Capital

If the chronically poor have few assets to transfer to their children, is there anything that they can pass on? The answer to this question is health and education. If health and education are the building blocks for improving the human capital foundation for the next generation and a possible exit from the circle of poverty, then we can ask the question: What are the motivating forces behind providing better health and education for the young in poor communities?

Collard (2000) argued that there are two possible motives, altruism and strategic self interest. In the altruistic model parents defer their own consumption to provide resources for educating and providing health care for their children because of an altruistic imperative to care for their close relatives; biological reasoning loosely termed as *genetic fitness*. Parents want their children to survive and prosper to ensure that their genes are passed on to future generations. These altruistic motives have been codified in what has become known as sociobiology or evolutionary psychology. See for example Edward O Wilson's pioneering work (Wilson, 1975).

Strategic self interest, on the other hand, provides a more practical and selfish motive. Parents care for children to ensure that they will have a close relative to care for them in old age. When life is hard and risks of survival to adulthood are high parents seek to ensure this support by bearing as many children as possible, taking care of their health and sanitation needs and sending them to school so that they can earn a living that will support themselves and their parents when they grow up. Of course the cost benefit equation can be biased toward sending them off to work instead of school, particularly for girls who will be married off into another family. Then girls' responsibilities to their own parents will be suppressed in favor of their husband's parents. It could also be that their lifetime discounted earnings are projected to be higher if they work rather than attend school.

For the chronic poor the implicit cost benefit calculations by parents make school the choice a small fraction of the time. In India the literacy rate for tribal women is 8 percent and for lower cast women (dalits) it is 10.9 percent (see Sainath, 1996). There are few teachers from these two groups to serve as role models or mentors for young girls from the lower castes and classes. Further, girls from lower caste and scheduled tribes suffer discrimination from other castes and classes.The grinding reality of poverty is also reflected by health indicators (See Table 2.2). Is it no wonder, then, that chronic poverty levels remain high in the poorest sectors of society in South Asia and in parts of China, Indonesia, Philippines and the Mekong countries?

The choice for work versus school is also highly influenced by and weighed by considerations of the time horizon. Out of necessity the chronically poor have a short time horizon. They cannot think of the long run possibilities when they are continually faced with the prospect of immediate deprivation. Decisions about the benefits of children's education in the future are discounted heavily and children are forced to work instead of attend school. As a result the lack of parental investment in children causes poverty to be passed on from generation to generation as adults without education are more likely to be poor.

3.3 Transfer of Other Assets

If the chronically poor have any physical assets, they are likely be transferred to their children. Tradition would dictate how these assets are divided. In some cultures all the assets would go to the oldest male heir and in others it would be divided among the male heirs. In the latter case there is a risk of further fractionalization of land holdings and other assets which could result in further impoverishment. Other asset transfers by the chronically poor could include work animals and farm equipment. Bondage and assumption of family debts is another negative aspect of asset transfers. In the model suggested by Genicot (2002) laborers choose to enter into a long term relationship with the landlord rather than risk the possibility that they would not be able to borrow from other sources in times of need. This obligation to the landlord — characterized as bonded labor by some — can also be passed on to future generations. Whether the next generation honors the commitment will depend upon local customs, the perceived power of the landlord to enforce the contract (either thru legal or illegal means) and the existing legal system that can either side with the landlord or the tenant. In many cases the bonding has continued for several generations although there is limited systematic evidence of the extent of these practices.

> The bonded laborer is technically free wage laborer whose state of servitude may be terminated by payment of the debt. So, although once bonded, a worker is unfree, the act of choosing to be bonded is usually one freely made to avert acute poverty or starvation. (Genicot, 2002, p. 102).

This bonding agreement is often interpreted to pertain to the family of the indebted farmer as well as to the farmer himself. This is often done using strong arm tactics and without the agreement of the farmer or his family (see Box 3.1). Children are also sold into debt bondage in exchange for money (or perhaps release from their bondage if there is some payment) by parents in need of income or to pay off other debts (see Box 3.2).

Box 3.1 Debt Bondage in Pakistan

Millions of workers in Pakistan are held in contemporary forms of slavery. Throughout the country employers forcibly extract labor from adults and children, restrict their freedom of movement, and deny them the right to negotiate the terms of their employment. Employers coerce such workers into servitude through physical abuse, forced confinement, and debt-bondage. The state offers these workers no effective protection from this exploitation. Although slavery is unconstitutional in Pakistan and violates various national and international laws, state practices support its existence. The state rarely prosecutes or punishes employers who hold workers in servitude. Moreover, workers who contest their exploitation are invariably confronted with police harassment, often leading to imprisonment under false charges.

While some NGOs estimate that the numbers range into the millions; there is little doubt that at least thousands of persons in Pakistan are held in debt-bondage, many of them children. Bondage is particularly common in the areas of agriculture, brick-making, carpet-weaving, mining, and handicraft production.

Bonded laborers in Pakistan suffer a range of violations of internationally recognized human rights. These include the right not to be

(*Continued*)

Box 3.1 (*Continued*)

held in slavery or servitude, the right not to be imprisoned merely on the ground of inability to fulfill a contractual obligation, the right not to be arbitrarily arrested, the right to liberty of movement, and the right to freedom of association, including the right to form and join trade unions. The government of Pakistan is complicit in these violations, both by the direct involvement of the police, who consistently arrest bonded laborers under false charges, and through the state's failure to enforce its obligation to protect the rights of bonded laborers guaranteed under national and international law. Furthermore, the ability of workers to collectively address their exploitation is constrained by legislation which restricts trade union activity.

This report is the product of a long-term investigation that started with a mission we undertook in late 1993. During this investigation, more than 150 adult and child bonded laborers were interviewed at or near their work sites. In particular, thirty-nine bonded laborers were interviewed individually at brick-kilns on the outskirts of Lahore, Kasur, Peshawar, Faisalabad, and Hyderabad; twenty-two at carpet-weaving centers and private homes with carpet looms in and around Lahore, Faisalabad, Peshawar, Karachi, Hyderabad, and Mithi; and twenty-four at agricultural sites in the interior of Sindh, rural Punjab between Lahore and Faisalabad, and rural sections of the Northwest Frontier Province between Peshawar and Swabi. Throughout this report, examples are drawn from these interviews with pseudonyms substituted for the real names of the laborers. Human rights activists, development workers, lawyers, labor organizers, government officials, Muslim and Christian religious leaders, police officers and academics were also interviewed.

While this report seeks to document debt-bondage specifically in Pakistan, it is clear that debt-bondage is a worldwide phenomenon, and that the specific forms of bonded labor which exist in Pakistan are also found in India and Nepal. The latter two countries have carpet industries that employ bonded child laborers as well as agricultural sectors which depend on bonded agricultural workers

(*Continued*)

Box 3.1 (*Continued*)

The most common types of tenancy contract in Pakistan are sharecropping and fixed-rent tenancy. Under sharecropping, the rent is a contracted percentage (usually half) of the output of the rented land. A fixed-rent contract involves a specified rental either in cash or in kind. Under another type of tenancy contract, the "rent" is fully or partly paid in labor services. Other things being equal, these forms of tenancy have different implications for the contracting parties' incomes and incentives. In particular, the landowner's share under a sharecropping arrangement depends directly on the level of output, so that the consequences of a change in output, whatever its cause, are shared between the landlord and tenant. In fixed-rent tenancies, however, any reduction or increase in output affects only the tenant cultivator.

Where markets for capital and credit are imperfect or undeveloped, the only way that a person without assets may gain access to such resources is to enter into a tenancy contract. However, as all tenants must provide landlords either rent or a partial payment for inputs, they enter a vicious cycle of debt. They must borrow money from landlords to cultivate their land, and during poor harvests they must borrow more money to repay landlords. Landlords take advantage of this situation and in particularly difficult financial times convince peasants to enter into debt-bondage arrangements with them.

"Suleiman," a Muslim Sindhi man in his thirties, worked with his entire family in sugarcane fields near Hala. He was told that he would receive Rs. 300 [$9] per month for his work. After three years of work he was told he owed the zamindar Rs. 3,000 [$90]. He attempted to leave the employ of the landlord but was tracked down and forced to continue to work.

"Lal," a Hindu Sindhi man in his forties, and his entire family of ten have worked for a landlord for their entire lives in a sugarcane field in Sindh. His parents had worked for the same landlord. He was told that he could not work anywhere else until he paid off the family debt of over Rs. 100,000 [$3,000] that he inherited. As he earns subsistence wages, it is impossible for him to repay the debt.

(*Continued*)

Box 3.1 (*Continued*)

"Meeran," a Muslim Sindhi man in his thirties, was given a small percentage of the harvest in exchange for his and his family's work at a sugarcane farm. As this was not enough to survive, he would take advances from the landlord. The longer he worked, the greater his debt became. Eventually his debt became so high that he had to sell himself into debt-bondage to the landlord. His initial landlord no longer needed his services. Thus, without "Meeran's" acquiescence, he and his entire family were sold to another landlord.

Source: Edited from Human Rights Watch (1995).

Box 3.2 Debt Bondage of Children in India

Most or all of these children are working under some form of compulsion, whether from their parents, from the expectations attached to their caste, or from simple economic necessity. At least fifteen million of them, however, are working as virtual slaves. "Bonded child labor" refers to the phenomenon of children working in conditions of servitude in order to pay off a debt. The debt that binds them to their employer is incurred not by the children themselves, but by their relatives or guardians-usually by a parent. In India, these debts tend to be relatively modest, ranging on average from 500 rupees to 7,500 rupees, depending on the industry and the age and skill of the child. The creditors-cum-employers offer these "loans" to destitute parents in an effort to secure the labor of a child, which is always cheap, but even cheaper under a situation of bondage. The parents, for their part, accept the loans. Bondage is a traditional worker-employer relationship in India, and the parents need the money-perhaps to pay for the costs of an illness, perhaps to provide a dowry to a marrying child, or perhaps — as is often the case — to help put food on the table.

(*Continued*)

Box 3.2 (*Continued*)

The children who are sold to these bond masters work long hours over many years in an attempt to pay off these debts. Due to the astronomically high rates of interest charged and the abysmally low wages paid, they are usually unsuccessful. As they reach maturity, some of them may be released by the employer in favor of a newly-indebted and younger child. Many others will pass the debt on, intact or even higher, to a younger sibling, back to a parent, or on to their own children.

Source: Human Rights Watch (1997).

Many of those forced into bonded relationships in Pakistan, India and Nepal are from the scheduled tribes and scheduled castes, mainly dalits. The UN (2001) estimates that over 20 million workers are in debt bondage in India, 6 million or more in Pakistan and many more thousands in Nepal. In all three countries the vast majority of the bonded workers are dalits or other outcast Hindus. There is no legal recourse for those enslaved by the bondage system since they are legally bound to repay their debts. Usury laws are not enforced and as a result debts accumulate at a much faster rate than their earnings or the ability of the bonded laborer to repay. Rather than accumulating assets to allow succeeding generations of the chronically poor to exit poverty this system of bonded labor creates an indentured underclass than can never hope to be free of debt under the existing social and legal system. The bonded labor system is prevalent in agriculture but also in the brick kiln industry, textiles, silk and carpet weaving. (See http://www.hrw.org/reports/2003/india/for a discussion of the silk industry and bonded labor of children in India.) If the young want to leave and go to school the employer will either force them to stay or will tell the parents to send another child to work in the factory. So the family is forever bounded one way or another. (See Human Rights Watch, 2003, and Human Rights Watch, 1996.) Even when NGOs become involved in trying to get children out of silk factories they are met with stiff resistance on the part of the owners.

> The failure to enforce the law makes the work of NGOs and other internationally funded organizations that are trying to withdraw children from work and keep them in school difficult and, in some cases, impossible. It also handicaps the government's own education programs, which, in any event, cover only a tiny fraction of working children. ... NGOs can lobby employers to release non-bonded children, but for bonded labor, a multi-pronged approach that includes political and legal mechanisms is needed. "Without [enforcement of the] bonded labor law, we cannot create fear in the employer's mind, and if employers don't fear, then we can't stop exploitation. It has to be dealt with as a crime." (see http://www.hrw.org/reports/2003/india/India0103-05.htm#P1330_294375)

What proportion of the chronically poor are not subject to some form of debt obligation either in the form of bonded labor or debts to landlords, money lenders or family members that will have to be repaid by someone in the family? There are no reliable estimates except records of bonded labor in India, Pakistan and Nepal. However it is likely to be a substantial proportion of the chronically poor interpolating for under reporting and estimating other debts other than those resulting from direct bonding. As a result, rather than accumulating physical assets and human capital to pass onto the next generation, the chronically poor are more likely to make intergenerational transfers of red ink and contractual obligation that condemn future generations to some form of bondage and a continuation of chronic poverty.

3.4 Transfer of Social Capital

The wealthy and well positioned in society develop a circle of friends, relatives and colleagues who are often influential and helpful in establishing contacts that can enhance business and social prospects for others with wealth. Those with extensive contacts have an extensive list that they can call on to access appropriate contacts in any situation. These contacts are the components of individuals' social capital network. Economists, sociologists and psychologists have explored various aspects of this "social capital". Putnam (1995, p. 67) defines social capital as "norms values attitudes and beliefs that predispose people to cooperate", and Dowling and Yap (2007) as:

> a network of cooperating individuals sensitive to the needs of reciprocity operating within a social framework where such cooperation is energized, enforced and encouraged (Dowling and Yap, p. 254).

Therefore social capita has two components. One involves individuals who are able to take advantage of social networks to increase opportunities. The second is the existence of such networks which are characterized by

> trust, concerns for one's associates, a willingness to live by the norms of one's community and to punish those who don't (Bowles and Gintes, 2002, p. 419).

Are there social capital networks available to the chronically poor? If so, what are their characteristics and how do they help the chronically poor to exit poverty and help their children and families get access to a better life? In societies where there are close family and cultural ties it is sometimes possible to build consensus for group action that serve to uplift and reinforce the status of the group that contribute to more rapid growth and lift the group out of poverty. Informal financial institutions or informal credit markets including chit funds[5] and informal savings associations can provide access to credit at reasonable rates as an alternative to borrowing from landlords, pawn shops and other informal lenders (see Ghate, 1992). Eventually such schemes can also link poor borrowers to the formal financial system.

Microfinance instructions such as the Grameen Bank and other microfinance institutions help fund small projects that produce handicrafts in poor villages. Scheduled tribes and castes have also been the

---

[5] A chit fund is a savings scheme where individuals come together to pool money at periodic intervals. At the end of each period the money is auctioned to the highest bidder. See Ghate (1992) for further details.

beneficiaries of affirmative action programs that protect the rights of indigenous people to control their land and natural resources and to protect their traditional way of life. Some placement in institutions of higher education and in business establishments are also reserved for minorities.

The success of these programs is mixed and there are many cases where the laws protecting and encouraging minorities have not been enforced. NGOs have played a key role in championing the rights of these and other minorities but sometime meet with stiff opposition from entrenched interests. Modern technology is being used to mobilize and connect the poor to each other and to markets. For example Grameen Telecom, a spin off from the Grameen Bank, has provided poor landless women in Bangladesh with cellular telephones. Such telephone linkages help link poor buyers and sellers to markets in urban areas. The founder of the Grameen Bank, Muhammad Yunus, winner of the Nobel Peace Prize, has developed a number of other projects that create opportunities for the poor (Yunus and Weber, 2007). These projects not only provide likelihood projects for the poor but also educational opportunities for the children of the poor. These efforts have lifted many families out of poverty in the past two decades.

Efforts to address caste and class discrimination in India have been made by many different organizations. A recent report by Human Rights Watch (2007) lists a long series of abuses of human rights against dalits and urges government action. These abuses range from discrimination in employment and education; denial of access to social services and infrastructure; denial of access to places and services freely available to others; discrimination against women and children; intimidation of political candidates; bribery and corruption to prevent dalits from due process and civil rights. The report compares the treatment of dalits to the apartheid regime in South Africa before the end of segregation. The conclusions begin with the following statement:

> Under-educated, severely impoverished, and brutally exploited, Dalits struggle to provide for even their most basic daily needs. Dalits must also

> endure daily threats to their physical security from both state and private actors. The violence by upper-caste groups against Dalits have two major causes: the "untouchability" and discrimination upper-caste community members practice on a daily basis and the desire of upper-caste community members to protect their own entrenched status by preventing Dalit development and the fulfillment of Dalits' rights. (Human Rights Watch, 2007).

By mobilizing public sentiment such efforts can contribute to removing the barriers to participation in government and to help integrate these groups into the mainstream of social and political discourse. Civil action efforts by those who are the subject of discrimination can also help promote the establishment of a system of government that is not based on prejudice and discrimination.

The efforts of the Grameen Bank and other similar financial sector initiatives by NGOs have helped to overcome market imperfections and improve efficiency and profitability of small agro businesses run by the poor. Civil action groups have also been successful in making government accountable for the success or failure of its programs. For example, citizen groups in India have filed an independent report on the status of primary education that has been disseminated widely and forced remedial action. In Rajasthan, civil pressure for public disclosure has led village governments to disclose government funds received and spent on public bulletin boards (see Narayan, 1999). Civil action can also work to get candidates elected to champion the rights and access of the poor. Revamping of government including decentralization seeks to bring government decision making to the local level. Poverty interest groups can work to support their own agenda as these processes unfold and decision-making is done closer to home. Community projects have been undertaken for public works in cooperation with government such as water works, sewers and roads.

In socialist or communist societies such as China and Vietnam, the mechanisms for developing a civil society are different from those in countries where there are more democratic institutions in place. In a study of Vietnam (Dalton *et al.*, 2002, and Dalton and Ong, 2005) found that group participation stimulated political engagement in Vietnam. They found that the relationship between social trust and political engagement is weak and even negative — that is those who are less trusting of their neighbors are more interested in political activity. Furthermore the relationship between involvement in groups that serve to build up social capital does not necessarily result in support for democratic institution. They mechanisms for seeking redress of grievances of the poor does not necessarily take place through the political process directly as it might in a more democratic system. This is not to say that civil society has no impact on decision making of government. *Doi moi* reforms and social modernization seem to be increasing the development of an independent civil society in Vietnam (see also the work by Dalton *et al.*, 2002, and Kerkvliet, 2001).

In Chapter 7, we will discuss how the chronically poor can effectively mobilize themselves to achieve a greater degree of social inclusion and political power with reference to the experience of individual countries.

3.5 Reversibility, Resilience and Coping Strategies

Children raised in chronically poor environments are vulnerable to a number of risks including poor nutrition, inequities in the allocation of resources and emotional support within the family and discrimination and possible abuse within the family or in the society. This section focuses on how children survive and negotiate through these risks and what coping mechanisms and support are available.

Nutritional deficiencies are well documented. In South Asia it is estimated that 60 percent of children are undernourished (see Engle *et al.*, 1996). The poorly nourished are also subject to iron and iodine deficiencies as well as Vitamin A, an important building block for good vision. The child who is poorly nourished may receive less attention from his parents or other caregivers, particularly if the child is irritable or lethargic. Research in India showed that smaller babies received less affection and loving care than larger babies although they may have to be fed more often (see Engle *et al.*, 1996; Arya, 1989). Even in a relatively homogenous but poor environment where there is limited nutrition, some babies will show adequate growth rates while others will be stunted and underweight.

Research suggests that in these environments more intensive care giving can compensate for poor nutrition to some extent. Malnourished children who were exposed to relative high levels of care and interaction with parents scored as well as better nourished children in tests of cognition in a study sponsored by USAID in Egypt and in a study in Jamaica where young mothers were taught to play and interact with their young children Supplementary feeding programs also achieved similar results (see Engle *et al.*, 1996). Based on this evidence we are tempted to draw the conclusion that increased emphasis on women's education would be helpful in compensating for diet deficiencies insofar as the mothers realize that such compensations do exist. Furthermore, more educated mothers may be more able to address the nourishment deficiencies. However, neither of these ideas has been tested through field trials. Of course the preferred alternative is better nutrition for all children.

Within the family children's risks will depend to a considerable extent on the status of their mother in the household as well as the child's relationship to his or her mother. Engle *et al.* (1996) argue that young mothers are less likely to have as many resources available for the care of their children as older mothers who have higher status and who are in the later stages of their child bearing years. Similarly mothers in societies where women are less educated and are more subservient to their husbands have less control over resources within the family. Thus, where there is discrimination against younger mothers and perhaps those coming from a distant village would have fewer resources for their children even in wealthier hierarchial households. Children in these settings are subject to the whims of fortune, having little control over their own destiny. In some cases these children and their mothers are able to seek protection from domineering family circumstances with social support from other care givers, external networks sponsored by churches, NGOs or even informal financial institutions and their members. Women with some education may be aware of these options and also more likely to take advantage of them.

Whether children in female headed households are at greater risk than children in traditional families where both parents are present has been debated by researchers. There is no clear evidence that children in families headed by women are subject to more deprivations or ill treatment than children born into more traditional families. Much will depend on local circumstances as well as whether the father is deceased, has abandoned the family or is working elsewhere. In households where the woman is the operational household head there is some evidence from Africa that children received better care (Engle *et al.*, 1996).

How resilient are children to the risks and threats that face them? There is very little evidence aside from anecdotes and reports from the abused children when they grow up. Certainly those children raised in violent circumstances are prone to develop psychiatric abnormalities. Episodes of trauma in early childhood are more likely lead to such abnormalities than when the child has reached adolescence. For details, see Davidson and Smith (1990) and also the account of a boy soldier survivor of violence in Sierra Leone (Beah, 2007).

Engle (1996) notes that systematic analysis of institutions such as schools and health care and village life with regard to the risks that these children face have not been systematically analyzed; nor policies been suggested to reduce these risks and provide better coping mechanisms for the children in chronically poor environments. Similarly, the topic of resilience to trauma has received little systematic analysis although it has become a fashionable topic among child psychologists. The adaptation of behavior that increases resilience may also have unrecognized costs (see Luthar, 1991).

In some instances villagers have formed groups that are able to address problems of natural disasters such as floods, droughts and drinking water security like the initiatives in Sri Lanka and India noted by Ariyabandu, 2000. In the aftermath of disasters there can be discrimination against women and children as survivors confiscate the land formerly tilled by those that have died in the disaster (see Ariyabandu, 2000). In urban areas street children are the group often studied and the most often at risk to suffer from abuse, violence and become involved in crime, sexual abuse, prostitution and drugs. Their resilience and coping mechanisms are their main hope of survival (Panter-Brick, 2002).

Chapter 4

Microeconomic Policies to Reduce Poverty

From this chapter onwards, we will focus on policies to reduce chronic poverty. In this chapter we will discuss programs directed to the alleviation of chronic poverty of individuals, households and to higher aggregation levels of the village and local governments. The emphasis of this chapter is on specific microeconomic policies that focus on particular households or groups of households and their behavior. Attitudes towards these families or individuals by other members of the community as well as the behavior and policies of government are also considered.

It should be noted at the outset that policies that address the poverty of individual households and groups of households, commonly known as social safety nets, have not historically been seen as a critical element in the fight against poverty. This is because perceived benefitis to the poor are often co-opted by the non poor or misdirected by well meaning government agencies. Furthermore some argue that there is a trade off between growth and income distribution; reducing poverty by improving the distribution of income reduces the rate of growth of income.

These negative views about the safety nets have been repudiated by recent research. New evidence from these studies suggests that effective targeted poverty reduction programs have been successful in many countries and that there are considerable benefits to economic growth by improving the distribution of income (see Dasgupta and Ray, 1986; Ravallion, 2006). The introduction of some sort of safety net is also important in reducing risk and the real possibility of being trapped in poverty. For example if a worker with no saving or other source of income than his own labor falls ill and loses his job or fails to earn enough to maintain his ability to work and sustain his strength his or her health and stamina may further deteriorate unless he receives a boost to his income from an income transfer, thereby placing him in a poverty trap. Also when incomes are low workers do not earn enough to have adequate housing and clothes to participate in the work force, effectively excluding them socially as well.

In what follows we present the case for appropriately structured targeted transfers that have a salutary effect on chronic poverty without adverse impacts on economic growth. These transfers help to prevent poverty traps from arising and help those already trapped in poverty to escape. Furthermore redistribution of income and assets which result from policies that provide assistance for the poor has both short and long term benefits through a dynamic which lifts the burden of poverty over time (see Holzman, 1990).

4.1 Social Safety Nets and Entitlements

Safety nets and entitlements are often the first line of defense for individuals and families that are experiencing chronic poverty. In this section we look at how governments in Asia provide social safety nets and entitlement programs. Such programs are generally designed to address the problems faced by households in chronic poverty as opposed to transient or temporary poverty. Safety nets serve to protect the poor from continuing to suffer from persistent poverty or from sinking deeper into poverty. This role differs from providing programs whereby households exit poverty by either improving their endowments of physical capital and land or by raising their human capital stock through higher education, better health and sanitation or population programs that reduces fertility.

A number of social safety nets and entitlement programs have been implemented in South and Southeast Asia to achieve the objective of protecting the chronically poor. Sen (1981) and Sen (1990a) has suggested an entitlement approach which would provide every family an income or entitlement to ensure that the household would not suffer from famine or severe deprivation. Sen (1990a) highlights

Table 4.1 Relative Advantages of Different Subsidy Programs

Program	Targeting Performance Median Rating	Targeting Performance Range	Cost Benefit Ratio Median Rating	Cost Benefit Ratio Range
Cash Transfers	1.4		2.2	1.2–3.4
Universal Food Subsidies	0.93	0.6–1.0	3.3	3.0–5.0
Rationed Food Subsidies	1.3	1.0–1.6	2.4	1.9–2.9
Public Works	1.85	1.5–4.0	1.6	1.25–2.0
Public Works with foregone earnings included	2.18		3.2	
Social Funds	1.2		2.75	2.4–2.8

Source: Coady (2004, statistical appendix). The figures in the table refer to the general cost benefit ratio of the program. The higher the ratio the higher is the payoff of the program in reducing poverty.

the Bangladesh famine of 1974 where landless rural laborers could not find jobs planting rice as a result of flooding.

More generally we look at the role of government in providing support for chronically poor households and review five modalities that are being used to assist the poor; cash transfers, universal food subsidies, rationed food subsidies, public works and social funds. Each of these programs is designed to help individuals and families that are poor to escape from poverty and their effectiveness is increased as the focus on the poor and chronically poor is maintained and improved (for example, see Elbers *et al.*, 2004, for the importance of geographic targeting). The relative advantages of different forms of subsidies can be referenced in Table 4.1 and are discussed in the following sections.

4.2 Cash Transfers and Food Subsidies

Food subsidies have been used by governments in South Asia and Southeast Asia for many years. In this section we explore the impact of these subsidy programs on the chronically poor. There are a number of issues that have been raised regarding the impact of these subsidies on efficiency and equity, on agricultural production, the distribution of income and on various aspects of macroeconomic and microeconomic performance (see Ahmad and Mellor, 1988). Our primary emphasis is on the impact of subsidies on the chronically poor and the kinds of policies that have been adopted in different countries in the Asian region.

Social safety nets, of which food subsidies are a component, have generally been criticized for several reasons. First it is argued that they are not targeted effectively and often fail to reach the poor. Second, most countries have a number of related but uncoordinated programs that either duplicate each other or collectively omit some components of the poor community. The programs are costly, inefficient and often do not involve enough resource transfer to make a dent in the overall level of chronic poverty. Furthermore government programs have multiple and sometimes contradictory objectives that reduce their effectiveness.

Nevertheless it is possible to design effective, efficient and well targeted systems. A good knowledge of the target population and a focus on programs that address these groups is needed. There are a number of reasons for choosing subsidies to achieve social protection in general and protection of the chronically poor in particular. Alderman (2002) makes a case for using pricing policies and subsidies rather than income transfers to aid the poor. Lower prices for staple foods that are key components in the expenditures of the poor will raise their real incomes. Such subsidies also do not require budget allocations to fund poverty program and provide a minimum level of consumption of these basic goods for everyone in the society. These basic goods would qualify along with education as merit goods which are beneficial for the society as a whole. It may also be easier to administer subsidies for commodities than to deliver an income transfer to the poor. Income transfers to the poor would require a means test or other method for identification of the target group. Normally when the historical role of the state has been strong, there may be a feeling that allocation of resources by commodity markets may not work well because of monopoly elements, trade restrictions or poor infrastructure. In such cases a government agency is created to distribute key staple commodities.

There are several kinds of price subsidies. Generalized or universal consumer price subsidies have been the most widely used in the Asian region including all the countries in South Asia. Since these subsidies are applied to all consumers of the targeted products they did not have poverty alleviation as their fundamental objective. There is, however, tacit recognition in these general subsidy programs that staple items should be subsidized. The products selected would be self targeting in the sense that it is a substantial component of the budgets of the poor. The products often mentioned are coarse grains, wheat and rice. However, even when this selection criterion is used universal food subsidies are rarely progressive and can even be regressive (see Coady *et al.*, 2002) One reason for this is that the poor often produce the products such as rice that are subsidized. There will be significant leakage to higher income groups that will be consuming these staple products too.

Different distribution and targeting methods have be suggested to reduce this leakage. A simple method would be to impose limits and allow the targeted commodities to be sold on a first come first served basis. Since the opportunity cost of time is supposedly, lower for the poor, they would queue up first. There are several objections to this rationing scheme. First the rich may be willing to wait longer if they are going to purchase more. The poor may be income constrained and would not be willing to queue for a small purchase or where the poor can not afford their full ration entitlement (see Alderman and von Braun, 1984, and references in Coady *et al.*, 2002, p. 19). The chronically poor may also have more logistical problems than the rich although the outlets can be located where there is better access for the poor.

Cash transfers are made to the poor either through direct cash transfers, food stamps or other government vouchers that can be exchanged for (specific) goods and services. Eligibility criteria vary. Transfers could be to families that pass a means test, by categorical targeting such as number of children, household headed by a woman, the elderly, and residents in targeted villages among others. The design of the targeting system should avoid disincentive effects that arise from means tests that offer incentives to reduce work in order to qualify. The direct benefit of cash transfers is an increase in consumption and improvements in nutrition of poor families. Such transfers also provide a stable source of income and offer a cushion in case of emergency or fluctuations in other earning sources that would otherwise require sale of assets or withdrawing children from school. A more dependable source of income also relieves anxiety and allows families to pursue alternative strategies that might involve taking more risk or exploring alterative farming opportunities that could provide higher yields and more income. A cash transfer also addresses the needs of those who cannot work and who have no other means of support like the sick and elderly.

Countries in South Asia have adopted various cash transfer schemes. In India the National Social Assistance Programme (NSAP) provides cash transfers through three different schemes. The first is a pension scheme for those men and women over 65 living in households below the poverty line. Those who qualify receive 75 rupees per month, about $2. Secondly there is a National Family Benefit Scheme (NFBS) that gives a lump sum benefit of 10,000 Rupees (about $250) to those in households living below the poverty line following the death of the primary breadwinner. Finally, the National Maternity Benefit Scheme (NMBS) gives 500 rupees to poor women to support her in raising her first two children. State governments also provide additional benefits for the poor depending on the extent of budget support. Poorer states provide less than richer states. For example in Maharashtra, one of the poorer states, the elderly receive 175 rupees per month and some poor widows also receive benefits.

The level of benefits from these programs is so low as to be laughable if the situation of the poor was not so desperate. As a result none of these cash transfers alone can hope to raise families above the poverty level. Furthermore many eligible families are either not aware of the programs or are subject of extortion by government officials administering the programs, particularly those who cannot read or write. For example the illiterate hire scribes who to help them fill up the appropriate paperwork for a fee which varies from 50 rupees to 250 rupees (see Pellissery, 2008, for further details).

A national public distribution scheme (PDS) to provide food security has been in place in India for many years by subsidizing prices for six commodities — wheat, rice, sugar, edible oils, kerosene and soft cake. These commodities are distributed through a network of 424,000 fair price shops distributed throughout the country. Over 75 percent of these shops are located in rural areas (see Roy and Chai, 1999).

The program was not originally intended as an anti-poverty program and has been criticized for its lack of focus, bureaucratic inefficiency and variable impacts in different states. The program has been redesigned to have a greater poverty impact. Recently the program was revamped to address those below the poverty line by increasing the allocation to those in poverty at a more highly subsidized rate. However the means test for qualification has been criticized and studies of the impact of the subsidy program showed negligible welfare gains to the poor with the exception of a few states — Kerala, Tamil Nadu and Andhra Pradesh (see Dev, 2006, for further details). Furthermore the costs of the program are high. It costs two rupees to deliver a rupee worth of food to the intended recipient. (See Farrington *et al.*, 2003; Dev, 2006; and Table 4.1).

The subsidy system in India has also been criticized for other reasons. B Ramaswami and P Balakrishnan (2002) argue that inefficiencies in the food distribution system in India inadvertently hurt the poor by diverting valuable resources that could be used for poverty reduction to other programs. They suggest that reforms are needed in the agencies that administer the state procurement and distribution of food grains and other commodities. Using the results from an economy-wide multisector model. Praveen (1994) finds that targeted production subsidies are more beneficial to the poor than food subsidies. Krishna and Chibber (1983) argued that by nationalizing inventory and trade policies the government could reduce the cost of the food distribution by two thirds compared with the result if current policies were continued. Furthermore in the current price subsidy system about 85 percent of food grains are going to urban consumers rather than to poor rural families. George (1988) analyzes food subsidies in three Indian states and finds that much depends on the administration of the subsidy system in the different states. For example there is wide variation in the distribution of food grains among different income groups. In Kerala, nearly 87 percent of food grains were distributed to families with annual family income below Rs 3600 while in Tamil Nadu, only 50 percent of the food grains were distributed to this income group.

As a response to these and other criticisms an alternative to the PDS program called the Antyodaya Anna Yojana (AAY) was introduced in 2001. The AAY program gives special ration cards to very poor families. These ration cards give households an entitlement to 35 kg of wheat and rice at highly subsidized prices (Rs 2 per kg for wheat and Rs 3 per kg for rice). This program may have been inspired by a program introduced in Maharastra after a drought in 1972–1973 which guaranteed employment at minimum wage to anyone who wanted work. This program is discussed in more detail in the next section.

The AAY program has been expanded recently and now reaches 25 million families across India and is focused on the poorest states (see Table 4.2). 25 million is far short of the estimated 370 million poor and 150 million chronically poor from a population of 1 billion people (see Table 1.7). The program as it exists now covers only a fraction of the chronically poor. Column 6 of Table 4.2 shows the estimated proportion of the very poor covered by the AAY program. The rate of coverage averages 16 percent for three of the poorest states and somewhat lower for the other two, except for Assam where the coverage is over 100 percent.

There are however, plans to further expand the program. Those eligible now include landless agricultural laborers, marginal farmers and those working in the informal sector as well as households headed by a widow, the disabled and aged with no visible means of support and primitive tribal households. The AAY program seems to be working more effectively at targeting the poor than the PDS scheme (see Dreze, 2002). It may be useful to consider further expanding this program to cover a larger proportion of workers in the 5 states with the highest rates of chronic poverty.

Table 4.2. Number of households covered by the AAY program in selected states of India, state population and estimated poverty count

(1) State	(2) Number of Households in Millions — Covered by AAY 2000	(3) Population in Million 2007	(4) Estimated Poverty in Rural Areas — Very Poor 1993–94 in Percent (Rounded)	(5) Million People Who are Very Poor (column 4 Multiplied by Column 3)	(6) Percentage of Very Poor Covered by AAY Program $[(1)/(5)] \times 100$
Andhra Pradesh	1.6	76	4	5.0	32
Assam	0.70	27	13	0.5	140
Bihar	**2.5**	**83**	**28**	**23.2**	**11**
Gujarat	0.8	51	7	3.6	22
Haryana	0.3	21	9	1.9	16
Karnataka	1.2	53	11	5.8	21
Kerala	0.6	32	9	2.9	21
Madhya Pradesh	**1.6**	**60**	**17**	**10.1**	**16**
Maharashtra	**2.5**	**97**	**16**	**15.5**	**16**
Orissa	**1.3**	**37**	**22**	**8.1**	**16**
Punjab	0.2	24	3	0.7	29
Rajasthan	0.9	56	9	5.0	18
Tamil Nadu	1.9	62	13	8.1	23
Uttar Pradesh	**4.1**	**166**	**20**	**33.2**	**12**
West Bengal	2.0	80	14	11.2	18

Source: Datta and Sharma (2000) for percentage of the very poor, Wikipedia for population. Percentage of very poor calculated as income that was equivalent to 75 percent of the poverty line. Highlighted data reflect the poorest provinces.

In China responsibility for the social safety net now belongs with rural government at the county and township level. Subsidies from the central government have decreased along with fiscal equalization transfers to poorer regions in the past. As a result, these local administrative entities have resorted to off-budget resources. Local governments have been forced to levy taxes or impose ad hoc fees on households in the agricultural sector in poorer areas with few sources of revenue from industries (see West and Wong, 1995; Roy and Chai, 1999). The quality of social services has deteriorated in these poorer regions and the level of poverty has not decreased as rapidly as in the coastal regions. Nevertheless, analysis of a household panel data set concluded that the subsidy program raised long term consumption growth (see Jalan and Ravallion, 1998).

In Bangladesh the food subsidy program is primarily directed to urban residents, the army, police and government officials in particular. Its impact on rural poverty is quite small.

A small pilot program introduced in three provinces in the Philippines that has shown promise focuses on low income families with preschool children or pregnant and lactating women from poor villages. About half of typical consumption of rice and vegetable oils were subsidized and ration cards were issued. To provide incentives for the private sector shops involved in the subsidy program, commercial banks reimbursed retailers who offered the subsidized goods and gave them a 3 percent share of the traded volume. There was little government involvement aside from selecting the villages and issuing the ratio cards. The program was relatively cheap to administer since the private sector handled the marketing and distribution, and rice and vegetable oil are cheap and readily available using existing infrastructure. Still households on the fringes of the villages sometimes had problems getting food. To further improve the delivery system of such a subsidy program it could be tied to children's education and health seminars for the mothers. (See Kennedy, 1988, for further discussion of food-as-medicine programs and Garcia, 1988, for discussion of the Philippines study.)

Effective targeting of the chronically poor is a challenge that has to be overcome by all cash transfer and public subsidy programs. It is therefore essential to develop accurate data bases that highlight the characteristics of the chronically poor. Targeting poor areas and/or minority groups is a powerful way to uplift living standards and may well have a wider impact on the community. Furthermore assistance to one set of beneficiaries can have beneficial external impacts on others. For example assistance to the elderly can have beneficial impacts on children's health within recipient families (see Duflo, 2000; Ravallion, 2006).

4.3 Public Works Programs

Instead of making direct grants to the poor through food subsidies, cash transfers or food stamps, a program that involves work for pay has been suggested as an alternative. This would help avoid the dependency culture that characterizes direct grants. While such a program may breed a dependence on the state to provide work for the poor, it can also confer a degree of skill enhancement, achievement and self worth that simple cash transfers can not supply. In cases where the recipient of subsidies is unable to work either because they are too young, too old, sick, injured or otherwise unable to enter the labor force subsidies could continue to be offered. For others that can work a number of public works schemes have been suggested and implemented throughout Asia. There are several issues involved. What kinds of projects should be involved? How much workers should be paid? What will be the impact on work effort and incomes if those who qualify are already working? What are the best ways to ensure success and what should be the indicators of success?

Public works programs, sometimes called work fare, can have two objectives. The first is to provide income for the poor in exchange for work contributions to a government project. The second is that workers can benefit from the project itself through skill enhancement and experience. In the past the first component was given greater emphasis. The work programs themselves were generally designed to benefit the wider community. Roads, irrigation systems, sewers and other civil works infrastructure were the focus of these social projects. Recently such projects have included components of the village infrastructure such as schools and primary health care facilities that can directly benefit the poor and the local communities where they live.

Direct assistance to the chronically poor comes from wages received by those who work on the project.

If the poor have to give up other jobs to participate in the project, it will subtract from the overall benefit. Therefore projects should be designed to be implemented during the slack season when agricultural workers, who make up the bulk of the chronically poor involved, are not employed elsewhere as day laborers. Secondly, the wage rate should be enough to attract poor laborers yet not too high to attract the non poor. (See McCord, 2008, for further general discussion of these programs in Africa and Asia.)

In India, for example, looking at the poorest households defined as those where the family head is an unskilled casual worker supplying unskilled labor in the market, primarily in agriculture, we note that the average wage for these workers was around 40 to 50 rupees per day in India about 10 years ago or about $1 or a little more (see Table 2.12). In Maharashtra, a government scheme was implemented in the 1980s that employed laborers at these kinds of wage rates to work on small scale projects constructing and maintaining roads, irrigation facilities and undertaking reforestation.

The project was successful and recently India has implemented a Maharastran type scheme for the entire country which has been phased in over a three year period beginning in 2006. It is called the National Rural Employment Guarantee Act (NREGA) and guarantees one person in every poor household in the country employment 100 days out of every year. In 2007, it provided 30 million families with an average of 43 days work (see the Economist, 2007). The program is eventually designed to provide 100 days of work per year for up to 60 million families per year. The wage per day is about $1.50, low enough to attract only the poorest but high enough to make a difference in their living standards (see Green, 2008, and the Oxfam web site www.fp2p.org for further details).

In the past, unscrupulous contractors have often subverted funds from similar poverty programs. To avoid such misuse and potential corruption, NREGA has instituted a series of safeguards including roll calls being read aloud each morning to discourage ghost workers and a requirement that at least 60 percent of the funds devoted to NREGA projects be spent on wages for manual labor.

Rajasthan has been at the forefront in implementing the NREGA system, offering two million households an average of 85 days work. This is a three fold increase in the public works employment offered by the state. Furthermore, most of the beneficiaries of the program have been Dalits and poor women. Even though they earn only 73 rupees a day it is more than wages for agricultural workers, which averaged out to 48 rupees a day (*The Economist*, 2007). Some other states including Bihar, the poorest state, have been slow to adopt the scheme although Madhya Pradesh is hoping to implement the program in 2008. Despite success in Rajasthan there are complaints in other states, such as Jharkhand, of corruption. It is claimed that many poor have not been able to avail of their 100 days, entitlement and there has been a shortage of engineers to implement projects. Officials say that these problems will be sorted out as the program matures.

Progress has also been made in Andhra Pradesh with the help of new computer software. Computers now generate pay slips and automatically deposit earnings into bank accounts of the workers. This avoids the possibility of bribery and corruption and has reportedly prevented misappropriation of funds. This process eliminates the involvement of local village level government (Panchayats) or district officials. Adult members of rural households register for assistance by submitting an application with their name, age and address with photo to the Gram Panchayat. The Gram Panchayat makes some inquiries, registers households and issues a job card. The job card contains the details of adult member enrolled and his/her photo. The registered person can submit an application for work in writing (for at least fourteen days of continuous work) either to the Panchayat or to the Programme Officer. Computers issue job cards to families and generate each worker's pay slip based on work accomplished. All information is put online and payments are being made into postal accounts created for villagers. The choice of works that these projects address is related to the infrastructure needs of the chronically poor, including drought relief, deforestation and soil erosion.

The computer software was developed by Tata Consultancy Service in partnership with the Andhra Pradesh government. It is designed to reduce drudgery of paper work, make work available on demand by maintaining an inventory of projects and monitor the works through measurement books and muster rolls. It also does funds management by tracking wage payments, material payments and administrative costs, facilitates social audit and right to information. (See www.stockholdchallenge.se/data/468 for more details of the software program.)

The cost of programs such as NREGA will depend on the scale of the direct benefits to poor households and communities from projects as well as the foregone earnings. In the employment guarantee scheme in Maharastra these foregone earniings were estimated at 25 percent of the total wage bill. When non-wage costs of administration are added to wage costs including leakage from foregone earnings the program was not very efficient in transferring resources to the poor. This is reflected in the public works with foregone earnings included in Table 4.1, which shows an even larger average cost benefit ratio of 3.2 when foregone income is included.

This is not to say that well targeted programs of this sort can not be efficient. If the poor are well targeted and good infrastructure projects that can employ surplus labor during the slack season are selected these projects can be very beneficial. The new India program would do well to take note of some of the successes that have been recorded in other countries (see examples in Rawlings *et al.*, 2002) and to focus their attention on the poorest states rather than spread their net too wide by including states where there are fewer poor families.

One key to achieving greater success involves community involvement in both the planning and implementation of social programs. This is particularly pertinent when communities involved take ownership of the projects and the workers families are shown to benefit from the completed projects. Dreze and Sen (1989) have argued that cash transfers of the sort that we have been talking about in this section are particularly beneficial to vulnerable populations when food supplies may be costly and *a fortiori* should be also beneficial in more normal circumstances. Geographical targeting of poor communities with physical and social infrastructure needs will also raise the overall effectiveness of these kinds of projects. Project preparation and implementation should be organized in consultation with and also with the support of the local communities that will benefit from the completion of the project. Local financial support, even token amounts, is also helpful in establishing ownership of the project and ensuring its completion and utilization by the community. Providing employment when other jobs may be scarce provides an income smoothing function for the chronically poor and reduces the risks of income shocks which would force them to take drastic actions that could harm their chances of raising incomes and escaping poverty such as selling assets, taking children out of school to work and borrowing from landlords or money lenders to meet current expenses.

The labor intensive projects that such social programs undertake are likely to be under supplied by the market and yet beneficial to the poor communities where the projects are taking place. The sense of community is stressed by Adato and Haddad (2002) who also argue that there might be a trade off between higher wages and added employment and also between the cost of the project and the benefit to the community which will see the physical evidence of their work on the project. Rawlings *et al.* (2002) evaluated a number of social programs and concluded that human capital improvements were observed in some of the projects where education and health were involved. While there is no evidence to suggest that the chronically poor received the bulk of the benefits from these projects, they did benefit at least in proportion and sometimes more to their contribution to the project. This was, to some extent, due to the lack of capacity of the poor to compete with other interest groups for such programs within their local communities (see Rawlings *et al.*, 2002).

A virtuous cycle of self help, human development, ownership and increased productivity can be generated by developing infrastructure projects that have community roots such as schools, health facilities, sewage and water projects. Work by Pradhan and Rawlings (2002) and Paxson and Schady (2002) in Latin America reinforces these ideas.

4.4 Social Funds

In addition to public works programs, international donors such as the World Bank, the Asian Development Bank and the European Union have developed projects classified as social funds. Originally these projects were developed in Latin America and more recently implemented in Asia and Africa. These projects are funded primarily by development banks and international donors and operate outside of the usual bureaucratic apparatus. In Asia about 10 percent of the total project cost is financed domestically (see Asian Development Bank, 2001).

Many of the objectives of social funds are similar to the public works projects described in Section 4.3. They mobilize local community involvement in projects that develop infrastructure in poorer communities. There have been projects in several Asian economies including Pakistan (Pakistan Poverty Alleviation Fund), Mongolia (National Poverty Alleviation Program) and Vietnam (Rural Infrastructure Development Fund). The primary objective of these funds is poverty reduction. This objective is achieved thru various programs including short term employment in public projects, private sector promotion, and decentralization and strengthening of civil society. Local interest groups play a role in project preparation and focus while target groups are involved in planning and implementation. For example, to address poverty concerns in ethnic minority communities in Vietnam, the World Bank and the European Union have developed small infrastructure projects including feeder roads, irrigation and village water supply taking care to involve the poorest groups in the villages even though they may not be the most vocal interest group. Women's participation has been encouraged in the Sri Lankan Poverty Alleviation Project and their empowerment encouraged. In Mongolia a credit funds was set up to help vulnerable women by supplying health and schooling facilities (see World Bank web site for further details of Social Funds activities

(at http://web.worldbank.org/WBSITE/EXTERNAL/TOPICS/EXTSOCIALPROTECTION/EXTSF/)

The ability to target needy geographic groups is an advantage of these social funds as well as their ability to operate outside the mainstream administrative structure of the development banking community. However the size of the projects is also limited and it is difficult to scale up to the national or provincial level. Although they are financing rather than implementation agencies social funds are still able to develop a sense of local ownership and are also able to pinpoint target groups. In several cases social funds have been instrumental in building social organizations and civil societies although these benefits are hard to quantify. Externalities such as best practices in terms of transparency and simplicity can be copied by governmental line agencies. Social funds also provide additionality to local resources in fighting chronic poverty. Communities handle their own procurement and financing of projects which builds confidence, ownership, efficiency and capacity building. However there are disadvantages to this approach where funding is provided by outside agencies. Staff remuneration is often higher than in the public sector and the establishment of a more permanent system of service delivery has to be worked out which involves domestic funding.

There are also some criticisms. Social funds have also been accused of undermining local agencies that also deliver social services to these target communities. Furthermore project evaluation for these projects are still weak. For examples see Subbarao *et al.* (1999).

4.5 Conditional Cash Transfers

There are other ways to extend social programs mentioned in Section 4.4. These programs combine the traditional preventive role of social safety nets with a new role of promoting social development in targeted communities, primarily through educational subsidies.

Most programs of aid designed to address chronic poverty come with certain conditions. Cash (or sometimes food) is offered to chronically poor families in exchange for the family's commitment to send their children to elementary school. Such programs, commonly called conditional cash transfers (CCT) have become quite popular in Latin America, particularly Mexico.[6] Brazil, Chile, Colombia, Honduras and Nicaragua also have similar programs. These programs have recently been extended to Asia. For example in Bangladesh a food for education program began in 1993 and continued for 10 years until 2002, when it was replaced by a similar program using cash transfers. Indonesia had a school scholarship and grant program implemented in 1998/99 as a social safety net in response to the Asian financial crisis which lasted two years and has recently begun a pilot CCT program (See Coady, 2004; Asian Development Bank, 2006a; de Janvry *et al.*, 2006 and Reimers *et al.*, 2006 for further discussion of these programs).

Simply put, CCT programs give cash transfers to targeted poor households. They offer cash transfers to households as a carrot to induce households to send their children to school and adopt more progressive health care treatment regimes. Families also attend nutrition and hygiene classes. The objective is to focus on the children's health, nutrition and education. The programs target families and villages which have been identified as locations where chronic poverty is most prevalent. The grants are conditional upon the participation of the households in education and or health programs for their children. These programs are designed to build up human capital of the younger generation of these families as a way to break the unending cycle of chronic poverty and prevent the transmission of poverty to the next generation.

CCT programs have a number of advantages besides the human capital components. They work both to build up the supply of human capital and satisfy a demand side need for funds to meet household expenses as well as expenses of children going to school. They instill a feeling of mutual responsibility and doer ship among the recipients. Households feel that they are investing in their own future and that of their children. The programs can also build support within the local community by building pride in the students

---

[6] See Rosenberg (2008) for an interesting account of the very successful Mexican program Opportunidades.

and in the school system. Such programs are designed to balance current poverty reduction objectives against future reductions in poverty for the next generation.

CCT programs are beginning to be recognized within the international community and have drawn support from donors. However Bangladesh and Indonesia are the only countries in Asia that are currently developing such a program. Many other programs have already begun or are in the planning stages in Latin America and the Caribbean with the help of the Inter-American Development Bank. The program in Mexico has proved to be very effective (see Skoufias, 2001). These programs as well as the Bangladesh Food for Education Program (FFE) have resulted in improvements in educational outcomes, increased family income, reduction in child labor, better nutrition and health (for the programs in Latin America, see Skoufias and McClafferty, 2001; IFPRI, 2002; and Coady, 2003; for Bangladesh, see Ravallion and Wodon, 2000; and Ahmad and Ninno, 2002).

The programs in Latin America are usually implemented by the central government with the expressed purpose of streamlining bureaucracy as well as avoiding possible corruption. Cash transfers are sent directly to participating household from the central government. These households are targeted by a combination of different screening techniques, including geography, socioeconomic characteristics including ethnicity, gender, age, occupation and proxies for income. The transfers are conditional on households participating in the various components of the program. Those who do not participate are dropped. Supporters of the programs use the catch phrase a *hand up* rather than a *hand out* to describe it. The poor have as much right to a better life and a responsibility to achieving that life through their own self effort.

The Bangladesh study found that the subsidy program had strong and significant positive effects on school attendance.

> A stipend with value considerably less than the mean child wage was enough to assure nearly full school attendance among participants. The impact was strongest among families where the parents were poorly educated. (Ravallion and Wodon, 2000, p. 173).

The enrolment subsidy also reduced the amount of child labor. However the impact was small compared with that of the enrolment effect, somewhere between one eight for girls and one fourth for boys. It seems that many children can find part time work while attending school. Primary schools in Bangladesh are in session on the average of around 17 hours per week while government statistics suggest the average workforce participation of children including work on the family farm or related farming activities was 26 hours for boys and 20 for girls.

The subsidy program did result in some shift from work to school. It did not support the stereotypical suggestion that poor children do not go to school because they have to work and that this results in a poverty trap for the poor. Primary school enrolment in Bangladesh is over 70 percent for boys and girls irrespective of participation in the subsidy program and many of these children also work. The Ravallion and Wodon study also concluded that families where the parents were more highly educated would have sent their children to school without the subsidy.

Subsequent programs might consider finer targeting of poor families with little education. In selecting the poor villages a number of socioeconomic characteristics were identified. However parental income was not one of them. Nevertheless the selection process seems to be on target. Higher rates of primary education also raise expected future income for participants. After controlling for socioeconomic characteristics, Wodon (1999) found that completing primary school in Bangladesh increases expected per capita consumption by 9 percent and the program increased school attendance with modest forgone income from displaced child labor (see Ravallion and Wodon, 2000, and Ravallion, 2006).

The results of food for school programs in countries where the enrolment rate in primary school is lower can be even more powerful, including the poorer states of India where enrolment rates, particularly for girls are lower and also perhaps also in Nepal and Pakistan.

Effective targeting of poor households is a challenge that faces all countries that are implements CCT schemes. Targeting reduces costs, increases efficiency and provides showcase value that attracts further financial support. Targeting strategies include isolating the chronically poor by socioeconomic characteristic and geographic location. These could include the identification of poor villages, education level or literacy of the household head, income proxies such as employment as well as ethnic factors that could identify minorities or other groups that are suffering from discrimination. CCT programs also have evaluation components so that feedback can help improve the impact of the programs. By raising the attendance rate in primary school CCT also reduce the incidence of child labor and raise health and nutrition outcomes. CCT programs have the advantage over supply side programs alone that build more schools. Infrastructure programs are common in many countries in South Asia and Southeast Asia. While increasing the accessibility of primary education without tuition fees, these supply side initiatives alone are costly in terms of household expenses for uniforms, shoes and other materials as well as the opportunity cost of child labor.

For example in Mexico, CCT programs were 10 times more effective than school building programs that took place simultaneously (see Coady, 2003). CCT programs can be more useful compared to public works programs that provide work employment and income but do not require raising human capital with education and health components. Evaluation of CCT programs have demonstrated the positive impacts made in reducing the level of poverty and chronic poverty. However poor households are often not able to take advantage of increased school access simply because it is too expensive for them to send their children to school. Subsidies for these families should also be considered for CCT programs to reach all of the chronically poor more effectively and ensure their participation in CCT programs

Many of the elements of these intervention programs such as CCT have been employed before. These new programs are successful because they incorporate components from previous programs into a single coherent and focused endeavor. The programs employ local point people who are also beneficiaries and will provide information to others in the program about theirs responsibilities as participants as well as benefits they will receive. The programs also have evaluation components that provide useful feedback for improving the system of delivery, outcomes and suggestions for improvement. This feedback is useful for gathering further political and financial support from domestic and foreign donors. The recent feedback suggests that these programs have had a substantial impact on human development indicators.

Because the cost of access to education and health services is so high, poor families choose the alternative of poor health and illiteracy for their children, further perpetuating the cycle of chronic poverty. This is why these CCT programs in Latin America and Bangladesh appear to be more effective than interventions to increase the availability of social services on the supply side alone. Schooling expenses including uniforms, tuition travel time, and foregone earnings is often too much of a financial burden for poor families. Better health care also requires travel time, small initial fees and waiting time to see a health professional. Even if poor families make the effort, the quality of the health and educational services provided are often substandard or low quality.

To be effective, supply side improvements need to be made in many countries so that the health and education subsidies are not wasted on inferior delivery of health services and poor teaching by unqualified instructors.

4.6 Education and Health Subsidies

Education and health are the most important components of human resource development for the chronically poor. Improvements in the delivery of quality educational and health services to the chronically poor are the primary tool for lifting them out of the poverty trap and starting them on the road to a better life. The successful Bangladesh subsidy program for children who attend school was reviewed above in 4.5. In other countries in Asia subsidies to children from poor families generally takes to form of government subsidized education. Such subsidies are generally available to all children and there are only a few examples where the chronically poor might be targeted. We focus primarily on these programs in this section while also commenting on the general delivery of education services and how it impacts on the chronically poor. We begin with a discussion of the poorest states of India.

Four of the six poorest states of India (Bihar, Madhya Pradesh, Rajasthan and Uttar Pradesh) along with two other relatively poor states (Tamil Nadu and West Bengal) were the subject of a large project by UNICEF conducted in 1999 and 2000 the results of which were summarized in Mehrotra (2006). The experience of Madhya Pradesh is also discussed in Narayan and Glinskaya (2007).

The experience of Madhya Pradesh has received the most attention for the success of an innovative program that has increased the enrolment rate in primary education quite dramatically over the past decade or so. The Education Guarantee Scheme (EGS) was launched in 1997. The program guarantees that the state government of Madhya Pradesh will provide a school within 90 days if a panchayat (village) forwards a list of 40 children or 25 to 30 children in a tribal area who have no school facilities within one kilometer walking distance. The state government also guarantees a teacher-pupil ratio of 1 to 40 and a curriculum that is on par with government schools. An important feature of the EGS approach is that it forges a partnership between the local community, the state government and the parents of the students that are involved in the program as well as the teachers. An interesting result is that many of the new schools are in locations where there are heavy concentrations of scheduled tribes and scheduled casts. Before the program was put in place the enrolment rates of scheduled castes, scheduled tribes and other backward castes were quite low — 31 percent, 25 percent and 24 percent respectively who had not previously been enrolled in primary school. These new school facilities resulted in enrolment rates in primary school of 62 percent, 60 percent and 65 percent respectively in 2000 (Mehrotra, 2006, p. 194). Over 90 percent of the over 1.2 million children enrolled in the EGS are from these three groups. The community also has the responsibility of identifying a teacher candidate to be trained by the education department. Many of these teachers are from one of the lower castes or scheduled tribes, breaking barriers that exist in the formal school system against teachers from these groups. There are also more female teachers. These teachers are known as *gurujis* (teacher) and are paid much less than regular teachers, a bone of contention that is now being addressed. The EGS system runs in parallel to the government system of primary schools and turned out to be cheaper to operate. The number of schools increased rapidly — more than 7500 new schools between 1994 and 1998 — with lower operating costs than government schools. As of 2000 there were over 26,000 EGS schools, nearly one–third the number of government schools. Attendance rates are higher than in government schools and performance is as good or better (Mehrota, 2006, p. 210). Still, much remains to be done. Facilities are Spartan. There are generally no bathrooms or potable water in the schools and teacher training needs to be continually upgraded. Household costs are still high even though lower than in government schools, where families have to buy uniforms and shoes. The most significant achievement of the EGS has been a sharp drop in the number of children out of school. Between 1996 and 2003 the number of children out of school between ages 6 and 14 in Madhya Pradesh fell from over 29 million to just over 4 million (Mehrota, 2006, p. 285). There have also been concomitant increases in literacy. Female literacy increased nearly 21 percent according to the national census between 1991 and 2000 and probably even more in the last few years as the impact of the EGS increases. EGS has also been responsible for a sharp increase in the enrolment rate of scheduled tribes and scheduled castes where it is now nearly equal to that of the general population.

Can the experience of EGS in Madhya Pradesh be replicated in other states? Observers suggest that it would require administrators, teachers and community leaders to develop a similar system. In Rajasthan, a similar scheme was introduced. Ramachandran (2007) argues that the Rajasthan program, called Rajiv Gandhi Pathashala, was not as successful because it did not channel local community support through the local village hierarchy. Nevertheless, Sunil

Ray (2006) argues that this program was largely responsible for the surge in literacy in Rajasthan in the 1990s.

Nevertheless there remain a number of challenges to improving the educational access for the chronically poor in all states of India and elsewhere. The educational response in Rajasthan was not as strong as in Madhya Pradesh despite adequate funding. Enrolment of girls is still substantially below that of boys, particularly at the upper primary and secondary levels (only 29 percent of all students at the upper primary level in 1997–98 (Ray, 2006, p. 164, Table 4.2). Household costs of elementary education in government schools is about the same as in Madhya Pradesh, around Rp 1000 per child per year, somewhat lower in the early years and higher in upper primary. For a worker earning at the poverty line level for a family of four that is the equivalent of two weeks' salary. To have two children in school costs a month's earnings. The survey by UNICEF suggests that the poor and illiterate would still be willing to send their children to school, despite the expense, if they had confidence that their children were being educated.

Even in the Rajiv Gandhi Pathashala alternative school set up where the minimum qualification of teachers is class 8, there is interest on the part of parents because they believe it provides a better alternative to the government schools which, although having generally well maintained physical infrastructure, have been widely criticized on several grounds. The school system lacks proper administration and security, lacks teachers who are committed, fosters an environment where teacher absenteeism is rampant and where teachers that do show up are ill prepared. Furthermore many schools have no toilets or safe drinking water and children often go home during the day to drink liquids. Also there are reported cases of minority children being abused by their classmates and/or by teachers who are usually of higher caste; and of teachers smoking and drinking in class.

Serious efforts must be made to lift the quality of teaching and the general educational environment in Rajasthan. In addition to building schools in villages where there are high concentrations of scheduled classes and scheduled tribes, particularly in the desert regions of the state. Efforts can also be made to refine the delivery system of Rajiv Gandhi Pathashala along the lines of the very successful EGS in Madhya Pradesh.

The educational challenges facing Bihar are of a different nature from Madhya Pradesh and Rajasthan. Bihar is the poorest of all the states in India and has the largest proportion of families in poverty and chronic poverty. Education receives a little over 20 percent of the state government's budget and close to 70 percent of this goes to elementary education. These funds are almost exclusively used for recurrent expenses, mostly wages and salaries, and there are few funds left for capital improvements. There are some allocations for capita spending in the plan budget but they are meager compared with needs. Furthermore the share of education in total spending has been trending slowly downward for the past two decades. In per capita terms the declines are even sharper although there have been some reversals in the last decade or so. Though Bihar is poorer than its neighboring states the household costs of primary education are similar (see Table 4.3), and even higher than four other states with higher per capita income. As a result, households in Bihar bear a larger average financial burden of primary education than households in other states. Therefore it is not surprising that Bihar has the lowest elementary attendance rates of any Indian

Table 4.3 Average monthly household expenditures on elementary education (Rs per month by Indian State)

State	Expenditure for Primary Education
Andhra Pradesh	42
Assam	47
Bihar	63
Madhya Pradesh	46
Rajasthan	79
Tamil Nadu	76
Uttar Pradesh	72
West Bengal	52

Source: Unicef Survey 1999–2000 reported in Mehtrotra (2006, p. 145).

state (54 percent versus over 72 percent for Madhya Pradesh which is the next lowest and ranging to over 90 percent in Kerala, Himachal Pradesh and Tamil Nadu) and its literacy rates are the lowest in the country. Female literacy rates among the Dalits are estimated to be around 12 percent in rural areas. Nearly two–thirds of all Dalit children are not in school.

The delivery of primary education to the chronically poor in Bihar also lags behind other states. The percentage of children in the relevant cohort age group from 6 to 14 that never enrolled in any educational institution by social groups is shown in Table 4.4. SC, ST and Other Backward Castes and Muslims is much higher than other Hindus. Furthermore these groups have lower rates of attendance at private sector institutions although the unaided proportion is comparable to the attendance proportions for other castes. It is surprising that the ratio of private aided enrolment for more prosperous classes is much higher than for poorer minorities, a clear case of discrimination (see Table 4.5). Nevertheless it seems that a significant percent of minorities attending school are able to afford private school in Bihar (column 4 in Table 4.5). Still, for a majority of the poorest classes, improvements in the government school system are their main hope for raising their levels of human capital and prospects for a better life. As it stands the elementary school system continues to deteriorate as class sizes increase and the number of schools is not keeping up with the growing number of school age

Table 4.4 Percentage of children by social group who were never enrolled — Bihar

Social Group	Percentage Never Enrolled — Children 6–14
Scheduled Tribe and Schedule Caste	58.8
Other Backward Castes	43.0
Muslims	53.3
Other Hindu	14.9

Source: Karan and Pushpendra (2006).

Table 4.5 Percentage distribution of enrolled children by caste and type of institution — Bihar

(1) Caste	(2) Government	(3) Private Aided	(4) Private Unaided	(5) Total Private
SC	80.3	7.0	12.7	19.7
ST	74.2	5.0	20.8	25.8
OBC	76.6	6.4	17.0	23.4
Other	49.9	23.4	26.7	50.1

Source: Karan and Pushpendra (2006).

children. The pupil–teacher ratio increased from 60 to 90 between 1980 and 1999 and the quality of instruction is low. Teachers often miss classes or leave the village during school hours and the school curriculum is not standardized. Many schools lack bathrooms and potable water. Furthermore, discrimination against Dalits continues to hold back progress in addressing their educational needs. The misallocation of resources and the sizeable administrative bureaucracy also creates additional problems. The World Bank has done a careful analysis of these problems and made a number of useful suggestions for improving the delivery of education and health service. One of the glaring administration problems is that allocations from the federal government are not released due to institutional constraints imposed by both the federal and state governments. For example only 65 percent of the allocation to Bihar in the Ninth Five Year Plan was released (see World Bank, 2005).

Some observers have suggested that Bihar introduce an Education Guarantee Scheme (EGS) similar to the successful experiment in Madhya Pradesh to address some of the shortcomings of its existing primary education system. If successful it would address many of the difficulties that the current government system is encountering including an increase in the supply of schools and teachers and better attendance of minorities.

After Bihar, Assam is the poorest state in India. It is a state that is dependent upon agriculture and aside from two oil refineries has no significant large scale industry. Enrollment rates are much higher than in Bihar, falling in the middle range of attendance by state. Gross attendance rates are 81 percent compared with Kerala at 98 percent and Bihar at 54 percent (see Karan and Pushpendra, 2006, Figure 3.1, p. 113). As in other states the net enrolment rate is much lower — 47 percent, 41 and 42 percent for SC, ST and OBC respectively for children ages 6–10. Girls from scheduled classes and other backward classes have generally lower enrolment rates than boys — about 5 percent and 2 percent respectively. Gender enrolment rates for ST are somewhat higher for girls. Dropout rates for those who started school and rates for those who never attended school are high among the three disadvantaged groups (ST, SC, OBC) siting financial constraints as the main reason for never attending or dropping out. The UNICEF study estimated that 67 percent or SC boys, 50 percent of ST boys and 40 percent of ST girls belong to families with income below Rs 6000 per annum, a figure substantially below the poverty line of a dollar per day equivalent earnings (around Rps 10,000 per year working 22 days per month and earning 40 rupees per day). At a 37 to 1 student–teacher ratio in primary school, it is lower than in Bihar, where it increased to 90 to 1 in recent years or in Uttar Pradesh where it is 67 to 1. Schools are far apart and difficult to access for many minorities, particularly for ST in the hills. Primary education costs to households average 544 Rps per annum for primary education in Assam, about 10 percent of household income for a family earning Rps 6000 per year. About half of this spending is for uniforms and shoes, a similar range of average household expenditure for these items in Rajasthan and Madhya Pradesh (see Table 4.6). For the poor this is a substantial economic burden, particularly if there are several children in school.

There are also widespread complaints of teacher absenteeism and lack of teacher supervision. 5 percent of total education spending by the states is supposed to be allocated for free textbooks, midday meals and scholarships. In Assam and other states there is little coverage of the midday meal (4 percent of students in Assam) and there are no scholarships at the primary level. Suggestions for addressing the deficiencies in the delivery of primary education in Assam include redirecting some

Table 4.6 Average household spending on uniforms and shoes as a percent of total household spending for primary education per student

State	Average Household Spending on Uniforms and Shoes as a Percent of Total Spending per Student
Assam	50
Bihar	25
Madhya Pradesh	50
Rajasthan	54
Tamil Nadu	33
Uttar Pradesh	20 (not including shoes)
West Bengal	18

Source: Various country reports in Mehrotra (2006).

funds from other levels of education in urban areas to primary education in rural areas. Upgrading and extension of the primary school network is needed so that children do not have to walk long distances to school. Furthermore, poor teacher attendance and lack of supervision keep parents from sending their children to school particularly when it imposes a significant financial hardship for the poor. Free midday meals would also help to attract students. Rebates for uniforms and shoes would also reduce the financial burden on poor families.

West Bengal has benefited from increased spending on education and a general appreciation of the value of education and literacy. As a result literacy increased substantially between 1991 and 2001 — from 67.8 percent to 81.3 percent for men and from 46.6 percent to 63.9 percent for women. Dropout and never enrolled rates are much lower than in Bihar, Madhya Pradesh and Assam. Furthermore attendance rates SC, ST and OBC are not appreciably different from other groups. (see Mehrotra, 2006, p. 262). Household expenses on uniforms and shoes are also a much smaller percentage in West Bengal than in other states (see Table 4.6).

In West Bengal the increased commitment to reducing poverty of the government since 1977 is one the reasons why the poor are faring better recently (see Sengupta and Gazdar, 1996). It has helped

West Bengal to achieve greater poverty reduction and better educational outcomes than other states in eastern India including Orissa and Bihar. However, as Majumdar (2006) argues.

> West Bengal's political will has not extended to wider public action in the social sphere. State politics have not generated the Kerala-type public action that could have wrested and extracted from the schools and hospitals elementary education for all children and primary health for all persons... Nor was there clear and positive policy discrimination in favor of the girl child. (Majumdar, p. 274).

As a result West Bengal's record in providing elementary education for the chronically poor falls short of the exemplary performance of Kerala, which stands out relative to all other Indian states. However, there is much more to do. Shortages is schools and teachers is being addressed by a cost effective community–based alternative to government schools called Shishu Shiksha Karmashuci or SSK, which is similar in nature to the Shiksha karmi program in Rajasthan and the Education Guarantee Scheme (EGS) in Madhya Pradesh. The SSK is now being primarily funded through the central government program Sarva Shiksha Abhiyan (SSA) program which is designed to universalize elementary education by community ownership of the school system. In West Bengal more than 1.2 million children are now enrolled in about 18,000 schools. Schools are set up in any village where there are 20 or more children aged 5–9 who do not have access to the formal school system. The instructional regimen is shorter than in the government schools (3 hours a day for 200 days a year) and there are 2 female teachers older than 35 years of age hired on an annual contractual basis with a salary of Rs 1000 per month, which is less than 20 percent of what government teachers earn.

For many, including Amartya Sen and Tapas Majumdar (see Majumdar, 2006, p. 276) this is a temporary solution and should not make us lose sight of the need for reforming and expanding the government school program. One indication of increased interest in elementary education in West Bengal in recent years is the increase in expenditures per student, which more than tripled between 1998–99 and 2000–2001. Still West Bengal ranks lower in terms of allocations to elementary education as a percent of state income or as a percent of the budget (see Table 4.8).

Tamil Nadu has a historically higher rate of elementary school attendance and concern for the poor than many other states. Education for girls was promoted very early and Madras State, as Tamil Nadu was formerly called, gave local authorities the responsibility for elementary education. ST and SC benefited from early social movements. Enrolment in primary education increased. In 1998–99 enrolment was higher than the population share in the state (see Mehrotra, 2007, p. 23). Tamil Nadu also introduced midday meals, free textbooks and uniforms. Better and more comprehensive elementary education for girls also helped to bring down the infant mortality rate and total fertility rates and reduced the burden of building more schools at a rapid pace to absorb the rapid growth of new entrants. However much remains to be done to reduce drop out rates and high household expenditures per child (mainly on uniforms and shoes) which is as high as some other states (see Table 4.6).

In summarizing the experience of elementary educational subsidies in India and how these subsidies have impacted on the poor we will focus on scheduled tribes, scheduled classes and other backward classes as representing the bulk of the chronically poor in the rural economies of the Indian states. There are a number of successful programs where these chronically poor groups have benefited from government sponsored programs and from self help efforts of local communities in some states. Although not mentioned specifically in the review above, the states of Kerala and Maharastra as well as Punjab, Haryana and Karnataka have achieved strong literacy and nearly universal primary education. As a result, chronic poverty is probably lower in these states.

Nevertheless, the inequalities that drive persistent chronic poverty have generally been perpetuated by the school system in India and the rest of South Asia that provides well for a few and nearly nothing for most. A power balance that favors the rich and well connected classes has not shifted in more than a handful of Indian states. While the growth of community based schools in Madya Pradesh, Tamil Nadu and Rajastan and their raising of teaching and learning standards is to be applauded, the fundamental weaknesses of the government school system remain. State governments are unable and/or unwilling to tighten teacher oversight and reduce teacher absenteeism and lack of commitment. While salaries are low it does not excuse moonlighting, absenteeism and ill treatment of students. The bureaucracy has to become more responsive to the parents and the community and discipline teachers where weaknesses and rules violations are reported. State government budgets are stretched and funds to significantly increase the flow of resources to primary education are unlikely to increase. There needs to be additional funding either from the federal government or external donors or both. The central government is committed to increasing its allocations to elementary education but it needs foreign assistance or additional funding if the goal of universal elementary education is to be reached.

The poorest families are generally willing and anxious to send their children to school but only if they have the resources and are convinced that the schools are also putting in the effort. When they see classrooms without toilets, high rates of absenteeism and schools that are many kilometers from their homes they are often discouraged and either take their children out of school or decide not to send them in the first place.

In Southeast Asia similar attitudes regarding the importance of community involvement are reflected in reviews of the educational system. In Thailand, the local community was viewed as an important element in the delivery of better education and in the work of school administrators gleaned from analysis conducted following the Asian financial crisis. (Gamage and Sooksomchitra, 2004.)

In Vietnam primary school is compulsory and the rate of attendance is high. However, there is room for improvement. A survey of girls who are serving as domestic servants in Hanoi reflects the low value put on education and the perception that more education would not be beneficial in getting a better job (Rubenson *et al.*, 2004). Most of the girls interviewed came from poor families and the girls moved from rural villages to Hanoi to work in order to support their families. Of the 13 girls interviewed, 3 had completed third grade, 1 fourth,

1 fifth, 3 sixth, 2 seventh, 1 eighth and 2 ninth grade. Also household work in Hanoi was viewed as being less demanding than work in the farming communities they had come from although many were psychologically affected by being away from home and the work day was long. Some said that life at home was also dull and not challenging and so they were anxious to try something new in an urban setting. There was, however, little emphasis on the importance of more education or of accumulating more human capital to get a higher paying and more interesting job.

Nevertheless household work in Hanoi did provide a stable income and food, board and clothing. Therefore it would seem that even their limited level of education had enabled them to forge a somewhat better life than if they had not gone to primary school. This anecdotal evidence lends partial support for the view that more education results in higher income. The girls in this study and in other settings reviewed by Rubenson *et al.* (2004) suggests that where the relationship between the employer and the girls was based on a family connection the experience was positive and contributed to their independence and building up of positive habits including saving and planning for future employment. However where the girls or their families did not know their employers previously there was more anxiety and tension. None of these girls reported any abuse.

Regarding the delivery of education and health services to the chronically poor in rural areas, the experience of Malaysia is instructive. Malaysia had numerous advantages as it embarked on a path of economic development following independence. It had a large and productive agricultural sector and low population density. A series of strong government initiatives stressed universal primary literacy and this process resulted in steady improvement in the extension of primary education. The Razak Report (Government of Malaysia, 1956) set the agenda to bring the children of all races under a national education system where the national language was the main medium of instruction but where the common curriculum could be taught in other languages. Budget allocations were between 7 and 8 percent of government spending and some of the funding came from taxes on agricultural exports.

Primary education in peninsular Malaysia (excluding Sabah and Sarawak where progress was slower) was extended to over 90 percent of school aged children by the late 1960s (see Leong and Tan, 2006, Table 10.4). Care was taken to ensure the program was multi-ethnic and funding was generous. Teacher training colleges and centre were also expanded to provide enough teachers. Private schools (Chinese, Tamil and Christian mission) were also provided assistance. School fees were eliminated in 1962. The success of the Malaysian experience was the result of the commitment to several basic principles — access to quality education for all ethnic groups without prejudice, the commitment to gender equality and sufficient funding of school buildings and qualified teachers. As a result human capital built up quickly. This ensured the growth of a skilled and healthy labor force along with expansion of the health delivery system which followed with a short lag. Fertility declined along with infant mortality while life expectancy increased. Poverty rates in the rural sector fell from 58.7 percent in 1970 to less than 20 percent by 1990 and to close to zero using $1 per day poverty by 2008 (see Asian Development Bank, 2008). Rapid economic growth combined with the development of a healthy and educated labor force provided rapid growth in employment and incomes.

A similar result for poverty reduction was achieved by Thailand, where $1 per day poverty fell to negligible levels by 2005 as a result of strong economic growth over the previous several decades combined with a strong commitment to education and public health (see Asian Development Bank, 2008).

4.7 Success Stories

The experience of Kerala in India and Sri Lanka demonstrate the importance of public spending on education and health for the eradication of poverty in general and chronic poverty in particular. By focusing on these kinds of social investment, poverty has been reduced, human indicators improved and economic growth sustained. In Kerala, social involvement and public action to raise the quality of education have played a critical role in the success of the primary education delivery system (see Krishnan, 1997). Public spending for social security and welfare programs is nearly 3 percent of the budget whereas for India as a whole it is slightly over one percent. Primary health care is available for everyone through government health care centers and there is a public distribution system for food and supplemental nutrition schemes for the poor. There are old age pension schemes for widows, the disabled and informal sector workers including rural laborers and social insurance through welfare funds for those working in the informal sector. Education is free up to 10 years of school and there are housing schemes for the poor.

Despite income per capita that is only about average for the states of India, Kerala has been able to forge an exemplary record of achievement in education and health services and the highest human development index (0.775) in the country. Infant mortality is 17 per thousand, a level achieved only by developed countries with much higher per capita income. Fertility has fallen as the effect of higher women's literacy has had a salutary impact on family size. There has also been significant progress in reducing the level of poverty. Private sector resources have also been forthcoming as the awareness of the importance of education and health care have spread throughout the community.

The Kerala model shows that a high degree of social development and a strong human capital index can be achieved if sufficient resources are devoted to improving education and health care. In Kerala, these resources came first from the public sector and later with the cooperation of the private sector by way of the growth of private health clinics and the integration of private education into the overall educational system. Private school teachers are now paid by the government and tuition fees have been eliminated. This merging of private and public educational streams is one reason why there is a higher proportion of current expenditures on education in Kerala than in other Indian states. Further acceleration in economic growth has also contributed to an increase in quality of both the educational and health delivery systems. Flows of remittances from international migrants to the Middle East have also raised the consumption levels in Kerala. These remittances came from migrants who were prized because of their high level of education relative to other potential migrants from other Indian states.

The success of these various socioeconomic programs is reflected in social indicators for Kerala. Infant mortality is the lowest of all Indian states and on a par with industrial countries at 17 per 1000. Life expectance is much higher than the India average (67.6 versus 52.1 for women and 63.5 versus 52.5 for men) and the adult literacy rate is also significantly higher than the Indian average (86 and 71 percent for men and women respectively in Kerala and 55 and 26 for India). Gender bias which is high for India is nonexistent in Kerala. The ratio of females to males is just over 1 (see Dreze and Sen, 1989).

There is a good deal of evidence that health services and public food distribution as well as education have played an instrumental role in raising living standards and reducing poverty in Sri Lanka. Social indicators are much more favorable than in the rest of South Asia (see Tables 1.3, 2.1, 2.5 and 2.24) and are similar or even more favorable than those found in Kerala. Overall literacy is high (89 percent for women and 94 percent for men, infant mortality is 12 per 1000 births, population growth is low as is the incidence of early marriages and child labor (see Dreze and Sen, 1989). Free rice distribution began as early as 1942 and the provision of health and education began earlier than in other countries in South Asia and has continued despite budgetary difficulties and civil disturbances (see for example S Samasinghe, 1988).

> Sri Lanka's strategic experience as a pioneer in overcoming the major penalties of low income remains one of great significance for understanding the prospects for support-led security in poor countries. (Dreze and Sen, 1989, p. 229).

4.8 Labor Mobility — Migration and Remittances

One way the chronically poor can break out of the poverty trap is by migrating to another part of their homeland or by immigrating to another country. This path out of poverty will be successful only if they can make a better life for themselves and their families in another place. What are the chances that the chronically poor will break the poverty trap in this way? While there is a good deal of evidence regarding migration in general there is very little evidence regarding specific migration movements of the chronically poor either locally or regionally. However many of the arguments regarding general migration can also apply to the chronically poor.

Our earlier discussion of migration focused on the development of rural roads and telecommunications as a way of opening up potential pathways to urban centers and some anecdotal accounts of gains made by girls who moved to Karachi to work in textile factories. Infrastructure is but one of many factors that impacts on the general pattern of migration from rural areas and of migration of the chronically poor in particular.

A general discussion of migration needs to look at specific economic and social factors including education and geography. Only then can a general assessment of the impact of migration on chronic poverty be made.

4.8.1 *International migration*

The World Bank has provided evidence of a strong relationship between international migration and poverty. Evidence on the pattern of international migration assembled by the World Bank and analyzed by Adams and Page (2005) report regression results for 71 low and middle income countries using survey research data. Their results suggest that a ten percent increase in the share of international migrants in a country's population results in a 1.4 percent decline in the number of people living on less than $1 per day. How do these results help with establishing the impact of international migration on the chronically poor in our target countries in South Asia, the Mekong and Southeast Asia? The answer is probably not very much. It is unlikely that many of the chronically poor have been able to amass enough saving to afford the cost of traveling overseas. In the Philippines, remittances are lowest in the poorest provinces and only 15 percent of those who migrated have less than a high school education (see Holmvall, 2007, and Capistrano and Sta Maria, 2007). There may be some indirect benefit to the chronically poor in rural areas as the more well to do are able to migrate and subsequently send remittances to their relatives, some of whom may be chronically poor or live in villages inhabited by the chronically poor where living standards are rising. This alone may be enough to raise the living standards of the chronically poor a little. In the long run there may be some substitution of unskilled or semiskilled rural labor for skilled urban or rural labor that migrated and this also could have an indirect effect on rural poverty.

Another possible strategy for the poor is to offset the costs of international migration in other ways either by pooling of assets among family members or giving loans to migrants by members of their extended families to facilitate paying these costs. Ilahi and Jafarey (1999) explore this behavior using data from a survey conducted in 1987 by ILO and ARTEP. While their results are interesting we are more concerned with the financial position of the migrants as well as average annual earnings. Pre-migration income of those who borrowed to migrate is compared with those who didn't borrow along with their holdings of financial assets. These results are displayed in Table 4.7. Using a dollar a day poverty figures as a benchmark and a five day work week these yearly earnings convert to around $2 per day. This is about double what the chronically poor would have been making at the time in most of the Indian subcontinent. It is also unlikely that those who were chronically poor would have had the nearly two thousand rupees required to finance the migration.

Nevertheless it is possible that families would have been able to pool resources to send one family member to, say, the Middle East to work as a day laborer for an extended time period. The education

Table 4.7 Pre-migration income of international immigrants from Pakistan in 1986 in thousand rupees

Income and Assets	Borrowers	Non-Borrowers
Pre-migration income	11.6	15.9
Pre-migration assets	1.9	9.6

Source: Ilahi and Jafarey (1999).
Note: Exchange rate was 16 Rps/$ in 1986.

level of those surveyed for the Pakistan study was not high. A third had no education, a quarter had a primary education and 20 percent had some secondary education. It's unclear as to the educational attainment of the remaining 22 percent. Although we don't know their level of education, nearly half were skilled. It could be that a similar pattern is observed in the rest of South Asia. This suggests that the chronically poor could increase their chances of migration if they obtained some training in a skilled occupation.

It is also possible that improved infrastructure will connect isolated rural communities with high concentrations of chronically poor to small or medium sized urban areas which serve as migration destinations for the young and better educated chronically poor and also serve as jumping off points for international migration.

The international flow of Indian migrants is the highest in the world. Over 5 million people immigrate annually. What proportion of these immigrants are likely to be chronically poor? The four poorest states of India (Orissa, Bihar, Madhya Pradesh and Uttar Pradesh) contributed about 9 percent of total out migration from India in 2001. Further analysis of international migration flows from India suggests a bimodal distribution. Skilled and professional migrants move to industrialized countries, primarily the English speaking countries of Australia, Canada, UK and the US. Very few of these migrants would be chronically poor. Most of the remaining international migrants went to work in the Middle East.

The Government of India's Ministry of External Affairs, estimated that 3 million of the total of 5 million immigrants from India in 2000 went to the Middle East (reported in Srivastava and Sasikumar, 2003). Assuming that 10 percent of these came from the poorest Indian states, about 300,000 migrants from these 4 states would have migrated to the Middle East. This is less than 1 percent of the total population of over 340 million. It is hard to tell how many of these immigrants were chronically poor or how much they remit to their families at home.

We can get some estimate of the size of remittances by looking at nonresident Indian remittances. Total remittances from nonresident Indians totaled $24.5 billion about three percent of India's GDP.

Even if a fraction of this went to the poorest states it could make a big difference to living standards. However it is likely that the chronically poor in the least developed states of India have very low rates of international migration simply because of their poverty status. There is also little evidence that chronically poor families have been able to form groups and pool money to send one of their members overseas to work. It is possible that in some Indian states chronically poor laborers with an elementary education might have migrated to the Middle East to work on construction sites; yet information is sketchy. Nevertheless, if international migration rates of the chronically poor could be raised even a little it would mean so much to their families at home.

Erfe (2007) used Uttar Pradesh and Bihar Survey of Living Condition in 1997/98 to develop a model of remittances. However the analysis was confined to internal migration, suggesting that few survey households reported any international remittances from the poorer states. Another study of Bihar by Deshingkar, Kumar, Chobey and Kumar (2006) reported very little international remittance income. What international remittance there were came mostly from Moslems who probably had migrated to the Middle East based on family ties.

The Philippines is another country where international migration rates and recipients of remittances are among the highest in the world. The Philippines ranks fourth after India, China and Mexico in total remittances (see World Bank, 2006b) and second after Mexico in remittance income per capita. Analysis by Pernia (2007) suggests that the poor derive substantial benefits from remittances. Pernia analyzed data from Family Income and Expenditure Surveys for 2000 and 2003 for around 40,000 families. He concluded that the lowest quintile of the income distribution benefits from remittances to the tune of a one percent increase in income in both years as a result of spillovers from the recipients of remittances in their villages. For those families in the lowest quintile of the income distribution that were direct beneficiaries of international remittance income (about 4 percent of the sample), incomes were raised by 35.1 percent in 2000 and 21.5 percent in 2003. When these figures were adjusted downward by removing estimated foregone domestic earnings these returns were moderated somewhat, but incomes were still raised by close to 10 percent in 2000. Estimated poverty incidence was reduced slightly in the lowest quintile of the distribution and more significantly in the next highest quintile by between 45 and 50 percent in 2000 and 2003 respectively for those with remittance income and 7 and 13 percent respectively for all households.

This evidence suggests that remittances were a powerful force in raising incomes for those close to the poverty line. This additional income enabled these families to break out of the poverty trap. However remittances alone were not sufficient to lift those in the lowest quintile out of poverty and the impact on chronically poor is unclear. The chronic poor are probably still in the lowest quintile where the incidence of poverty was over 99 percent.

Pernia (2007) also analyzed the impact of domestic remittances on households by quintile (sample size of around 13,000 households in 2000 and 17,600 households in 2003). A fraction of households in the lowest quintile in the sample (about 4 percent) received domestic remittances. The impact of domestic remittances on income was not as strong as in the case of international remittances and the impact dropped off in the three highest quintiles. Household incomes were raised by 21.6 percent in 2000 and 16.2 percent in 2003. This is probably due to the fact that much internal migration is from rural to unskilled urban jobs such as housemaids and laborers. It is likely that a larger proportion from these internal migrants would be remitted to poorer families than income remittances from international migrants.

The differential impact on the overall income distribution between international and domestic migrations is also interesting (See also the next section on internal migration). Remittances to the top three quintiles is substantially higher for international migrants while domestic remittances by quintile falls as a proportion of income (See Table 4.8). Migrants from higher income rural households are better educated and earn high incomes overseas and these household do not need to send family members to the city to work, except as a favor to relatives now living in urban areas.

Pernia also developed an econometric model to assess the impact of remittances on human capital formation. He found that remittances

Table 4.8 Impact of international and domestic remittance flows on household income of those receiving remittances by quintile 2003 — Philippines

Quintile	Income Increase from International Remittances in Percent	Income Increase from Domestic Remittances in Percent
1	21.5	16.2
2	23.4	12.1
3	29.7	9.6
4	37.7	8.1
5	46.3	5.5

Source: Pernia (2007, Tables 2 and 6).

strongly influenced education and health care spending on per school-age members of the household. Other things equal households receiving remittance were also able to raise their savings rates by about 2 percent.

There also seem to be some positive impacts on local economies as a result of spill over effects on aggregate regional income as a result of remittance flows. These developments suggest that a 1 percent increase in remittances per capita to the lowest quintile of the income distribution led to a 1.8 percent increase in overall per capita spending, a multiplier of a little less than 2. Finally, Pernia draws a general conclusion that the elasticity of poverty reduction to a change in remittances is about 0.26. A 10 percent increase in remittances results in a 2.6 percent increase in the proportion lifted out of poverty.

These results for the Philippines are powerful evidence and support the general conclusion that international migration by the chronically poor is an excellent way to raise their living standards.

There is some information on migration and the impact of remittances on chronic poverty in other countries. Generally it suggests that the chronically poor have so few resources that they are left behind even as those in their villages with a few more resources will be able to migrate. This conjecture is partially supported by the results of Pernia's study of the Philippines for international migration.

8.6 percent of households in the second quintile received remittances suggesting (but not conclusively) that the remitters were also from this wealthier cohort group. This compared with 3.8 percent of households receiving remttances in the first quintile. And there were even more households receiving remittances in the highest three quintiles — 15.7, 24.2 and 35.8 respectively. Of course there is the possibility that higher remittances resulted in higher incomes the next year.

While it is hard to draw conclusion about the incidence of chronic poverty from income breakdowns by quintile it is likely that most households in the lowest quintile are chronically poor. This is particularly true in Bangladesh, India and Nepal where poverty rates are over 40 percent and chronic poverty over 15 percent (see Table 1.2, Tables 1.4 and 1.5). However, most families in the 2nd quintile would be poor but not chronically poor.

Turning to India, Lipton (1988) argues that high emigration rates — destination unspecified — are observed in villages where there is a high degree of inequality. He argues that better off migrants are pulled out toward fairly firm prospects of a job or education while the poor are pushed out by rural poverty. Stark (1991) makes similar argues regarding the push factor on the poor in Mexico.

4.8.2 *Rural to urban migration*

Turning to migration from rural to urban areas within the home country, many of the reasons for migration are similar to those for international migration. For example Croll and Huang (1997) compiled domestic migration for China based on information from several different villages. They cite the importance of land scarcity and rising costs as reasons for out migration from rural to urban locations. Croll and Ping do not consider the incomes and living standards of migrants as factors impacting on patterns of migration.

In India there is considerable information on internal migration into cities from the countryside. For the poorest state of Bihar the remittances from migrants, while meager in total value, often constitutes the difference between severe deprivation or starvation and survival. A variety of information on migration and remittances were obtained and reported in *The Bihar Times* by Anup Karan based on surveys from 18 villages and census data for 38,000 individuals from 6400 households. Available at http://www.bihartimes.com/poverty/anup.html.

Nearly half of the households reported at least one migrating member. The percentage distribution of migrating and non migrating households by caste is reported in Table 4.9. There is little difference in the pattern of migration by caste *vis-à-vis* the general population. Upper castes make up only 19 percent of the population with the same percentage of migrating households. A slightly larger proportion of Muslims migrated.

The number of migrants was slightly biased toward men — around 53 percent to 47 with the age groups from 15 to 39 dominated. 57 percent of the migrants from rural areas were laborers (agricultural and non-agricultural) and 23 percent were non-workers. There were few migrating businessmen or government officials.

The vast majority of migrants moved to find a job or get a better job (87 percent). Many migrants in Bihar migrated to Delhi or to other urban locations in Bihar. Average reported monthly income was between US$1 and $2 per day equivalent in Rupees for laborers and for those with primary education or less. Despite these meager earnings, remittances accounted for a substantial proportion of household income for most classes and for the landless. These results are summarized in Table 4.10.

Table 4.9 Percentage distribution of migrating and non-migrating households by caste — Bihar

Caste	Non-Migrating Households	Migrating Households
Upper caste	19	19
Other Backward Castes	41	40
Scheduled Caste	16	14
Muslims	23	27

Source: *The Bihar Times* (2007).

Table 4.10 Income from migration as a percentage of total household income — Bihar

Caste and Land Ownership	Percent Contribution of Remittances to Household Income
Upper caste	23
OBC	24
ST and SC	30
Muslim	30
Landless	33
Less than one acre	34
Between 1 and 2.5 acres	27

Source: *The Bihar Times*, numbers rounded.
Note: All migration is assumed to be rural to urban.

Connell *et al.* (1976) provide a thorough analysis of migration patterns of rural households from a global perspective with many examples from South Asia. From their analysis of the migration patterns of residents from 40 villages in India they conclude that there are three main variables responsible for migration from rural to urban areas — the man to land ratio, yield per acre and the distribution of land in the village. When land is poorly distributed those without land have more pressing motives to migrate. Greater yields and richer soil reduce the propensity to migrate and the smaller the average size of land holdings the greater is the motivation to migrate. Connell *et al.* (1976) also note that unemployment and underemployment within the village is a push factor that encourages migration and poor young laborers are the most likely to migrate (between 15 and 35). Aside from these common factors they note significant variations in migration behavior from village to village depending on local factors and socioeconomic differences. Therefore they stress the importance of framing migration policies to reflect these factors rather than adopting blanket programs that do not allow for flexibility to match the needs of different kinds of villages.

Evidence regarding the migration pattern of the poorest village groups is mixed. Some authors argue that the poorest are income constrained and can not afford the initial expenditures required to migrate. Larger families tend to have more migrants because there is more likely to be an extra young male that can be a designated migrant and family income can be pooled to send him off to the city. If there is more than one the oldest will stay home to help with farming chores while the younger sibling will migrate with the goal of sending remittances that will allow the family to build up some financial assets and smooth out consumption patterns for those left behind.

The pattern of migration by education varies. In northern Indian villages the more educated tended to migrate — only 42 percent of migrants were illiterate as compared with 80 percent of all village residents. Having said this there is no hard and fast rule that says the more educated will migrate. There are local variations in the returns to formal education. Sometimes, skill can substitute for formal education as in the case of "diggers" discussed in a subsequent section of this chapter. There is clear evidence that the more educated earn more but it is not a guarantee that their remittances contributed more to their families left in the village.

For the chronically poor with little education migration of someone in the family can be the most significant force to lift the family above the poverty line. In many cases the migration pattern is bimodal. The poorest and the richest in the village migrate, although for different reasons. Distance factors are important. Remote and inaccessible villages will have fewer migrants, other things equal. Costs of migration are higher and knowledge of alternative could be limited by distance. Better transportation and telecommunications are keys to improving access and knowledge of employment opportunities. Step migration is also a pattern followed by some migrants, first moving from a rural village to a small accessible town and then eventually to a larger urban area.

A quantitative analysis of the data from these villages suggests that low migration villages were poorer than other villages. They had less land per adult male, lower yields per hectare, less irrigated land, higher debt per household, fewer cattle, a higher proportion of village agricultural production sold in the market as opposed to home consumption and less crop diversification. Proportion of product sold as a proxy for commercialization of agriculture was the most significant of the urban factors related to migration. It is unclear whether villages with good access to towns were more likely to have higher migration rates or commercialization resulted in fewer job opportunities for the landless. It is probably the former. There were also more agricultural laborers as a percent of total workers and with a greater population density and of landlessness among migrants. In interpreting these results it is important to note that there was a lot of variation within each of these variables as well. Not all variables were important in every village and multicollinearity often resulted in the authors being unable to separate the influence of particular variables.

Analysis of the migration results by sex and education strongly suggests that the vast majority of migrants were young, male and married. Few of the women migrated to work; rather they went to study or to follow their husbands. As for education, the rate of literacy is somewhat higher among migrants, although still not high. 42 percent of migrants were illiterate as opposed to nearly 80 percent of the adult population in the villages. 15 percent had a primary education as opposed to 6 percent of all adults in the villages.

While data on caste and class were not comprehensive the marginal social groups (SC, ST, Muslims and Christians) were more likely to migrate.

Connell *et al.* (1976) argue that because they concentrated on individual migrants, the results may be biased toward richer families since poor families tend to move together more often than the more well-to-do who can afford to send one or two family members to the city. As a result the migration pattern shows that fewer laborers migrated than self-employed agricultural workers.

As far as policy goes, the Connell *et al.* (1976) study has several recommendations designed to lift living standards in rural areas including land redistribution, greater irrigation, double cropping and infrastructure development, which include roads. The study does not seem to encourage rural to urban migration but rather stresses the development of stronger rural technology and human resource development. In recent years, the emphasis has shifted towards a more balanced policy of encouraging migration of those with the appropriate skill set which would provide higher incomes and possibly remittances from the migrants as well as lifting productivity in the rural village by reducing population density and increasing resources devoted to better farming techniques, land redistribution, irrigation and new varieties.

In a more recent study, Oberai, Prasad and Sardana (1989) explore the migration pattern in three provinces of India. They conclude that those residents from the lower income deciles are more likely to migrate than the general population in all three provinces. Their results are shown in Table 4.11.

This evidence is consistent with the educational attainment of the migrant pool and the results of the Connell *et al.* study. The education evidence also demonstrates the different mix of educational attainment by state.

In Table 4.12 we note that most migrants in all three states had a minimal level of education, although their average level of education was still higher than the average education level in the sample populations in Bihar and Uttar Pradesh. However for the less than secondary category (probably completed primary and some secondary) there were more migrants in the category than in the general population. Religion and caste play a small role in the pattern of migration. Rates reflected the general population aside from a slightly lower rate of out migration from Kerala of ST/SC members.

In the Bihar state of India there is some evidence that there were disproportionately many more out-migrants from the lowest income class. Oberai *et al.* (1989) note that 15 percent of out migrants belonged to the lowest income class while only 7 percent of the sample population belonged to this class. Given that poverty rates in Bihar are quite high — 28 percent from Table 4.2 — it is quite likely that these migrants were from the chronically poor. The remittances from this group of migrants were also very high and contributed 93 percent of the income of the migrant households in the lowest income group. Nevertheless this income class remained poor, although perhaps not as poor as they would have been otherwise. Perhaps it is desperation that led them to migrate even though their prospects for getting out of the poverty trap did not improve

Table 4.11 Percentage distribution of out-migrants and sample populations 10 years and older by household income excluding remittances

Income Class (Decile)	Bihar Out-Migration	Bihar Sample Population	Kerala Out-Migration	Kerala Sample Population	Uttar Pradesh Sample Population	Uttar Pradesh Sample Population
1	15.8	6.5	17.2	7.9	13.2	7.7
2	12.9	7.5	14.0	6.5	10.7	8.0
3	11.8	8.7	9.0	8.8	7.6	7.4
4	8.2	9.2	6.8	9.0	10.8	10.1
5	8.5	9.0	6.8	9.2	9.2	9.5
6	8.0	10.0	8.2	10.7	9.6	10.9
7	7.9	11.3	8.7	10.8	8.1	10.1
8	8.1	11.7	8.6	10.8	10.7	11.3
9	10.0	12.6	8.8	11.9	8.7	11.8
10	8.9	13.5	11.9	14.4	11.4	13.1

Source: Oberai *et al.* (1989, p. 35, Table 3.6).

Table 4.12 Percentage distributions of out-migrants and sample population by educational attainment and religion/caste

Education	Bihar Out-Migration	Bihar Sample Population	Kerala Out-Migration	Kerala Sample Population	Uttar Pradesh Sample Population	Uttar Pradesh Sample Population
None	43.4	64.3	0.8	9.0	8.5	39.2
Less than secondary	38.7	28.5	61.7	71.2	56.5	39.1
Secondary	14.8	6.1	27.8	15.1	21.6	16.6
Graduate	3.3	1.2	9.7	4.7	13.5	5.1
Religion/caste						
SC/ST	39.4	38.7	4.6	8.1	17.5	18.1
Hindu	52.4	54	51.0	49.9	81	80.1
Muslin	7.3	7.1	12.8	12.4	1.2	1.7

Source: Oberai *et al.* (1989, p. 28, Table 3.2).

Note: There is a large Christian community in Kerala; 31.2 percent migrated out of a sample population with 29.5 percent.

that much. In the other two states studied by Oberai *et al.* (1989) the pattern of migration was different. In Kerala the middle peasantry migrated more while in Uttar Pradesh the landed groups tended to migrate.

In two other studies by Mallee (1995/96) and Connell *et al.* (1976), the poorest do not have high rates of migration. There is still little evidence as to whether the migration led to a reduction in poverty for either the migrants or those left behind. Without further evidence it is impossible to evaluate whether migration, either international or domestic, has resulted in a significant reduction in poverty. In the poorest states of India including Bihar and Assam, it is plausible that migration to urban areas resulted in some diminution in rates of chronic poverty, although the level of poverty has remained high. This is probably because the out-migration did not result in a significant increase in remittances or reduce labor pressure enough to make a perceptible difference in poverty incidence.

Remittance and migration flows from Kerala demonstrate the potential gains that can be made in India if human resource development is highly valued. A study by Kanan and Hari (2002) concluded that remittances to Kerala average 21 percent of state income in the 1990s. Although per capita consumption was below the national average in the late 1970s it substantially exceeded the national average by 2000. Most of these remittance flows from international migrants sent back to Kerala residents were used for consumption and education (see also Sasikumar and Hussain, 2007).

The pattern of rural to urban migration depends on geographical and weather factors as well as the state of the local economy. Deshingkar and Start (2003) report migration patterns for Andhra Pradesh (AP) and Madhya Pradesh (MP) based on census data from 4647 households in AP and 1297 households in MP. 25 percent of all households in AP had at least one migrating member and 52 percent in MP. Migration is defined as any movement to earn income outside the village from short term visits to other rural or urban locations to longer term migration.

There was significant variation in the rate of migration by village. There were six villages sampled in each state, with varying numbers of households sampled in each village. The villages were spread out in different locations so as to reflect different geographical and socio-economic characteristics and their impact on migration patterns. The village in AP with the highest migration rate of 78 percent is in a very dry and backward part of the state. Migration to Hyderabad is common as well as to sugarcane fields in close proximity. Casual labor is virtually the only occupation in the state for the chronically poor and available work is limited. During the *Kharif* or autumn harvest (also known as the summer or monsoon crop grown between April and September) the average number of days of work reported was 35 out of a possible 100 or so work days.

The village in MP with the highest migration rate was also in a region with poor agricultural potential and a high incidence of marginal holdings. The migration rate there was 75 percent. Other villages with high migration rates were either located close to urban centers and/or limited agricultural potential. In some cases land productivity was high but ownership was polarized leading the landless to migrate. The more well endowed villages also experienced some migration but at a much lower rate — between 10 and 20 percent. These villages had strong labor demand throughout the year for high value, labor intensive crops particularly horticulture.

Although there were wide variations in experience from village to village, total earnings from outside the six villages in MP from both farm and non-farm work slightly exceeded income from within the villages. In AP, where several villages benefited from green revolution technology and a high level of irrigation there was little migration and overall earnings from migration were only 15 percent of total earnings of the combined six village income. There were also large variations in migration between the Kharif and Rabi seasons (November to April).

The evidence assembled by Deshingkar and Start (2003) suggests that migrant and local agricultural work is combined by many households to yield a smoother annual income stream than would be possible from season work within the villages. An econometric model was constructed to look at the determinants of migration in both states. Those with less land were more likely to migrate in MP but land was not significant as an explanatory variable in AP. The significance of agricultural assets differed. In MP more farm assets meant less migration while in AP more assets were associated with more migration. Having an extra working member in the household increased the probability of migrating — by 17 percent and 19 percent respectively in AP and MP and the ratio of working to non-working members in the household also increased the likelihood of migrating.

In both AP and MP the chronically poor, as proxied by Scheduled Tribes and Scheduled Castes, are five to six times more likely to migrate as "higher" castes (not counting OBC). However, there are those ST and SC who are not poor and they also migrate while the extremely poor many not have the resources to migrate. Also to the extent that SC/STs are excluded from higher paying jobs at home, they could migrate with lower expected returns.

Land ownership could be considered another proxy for chronic poverty. As noted above regression results for AP suggest that those without land do tend to migrate more. While we don't know how many chronically poor migrated from these two Indian states, we do know that many from the chronically poor groups including minorities and the landless, do migrate with greater frequency than the landed. We also know that while the chronically poor migrate often and for low wages, those that do migrate probably send remittances that are extremely helpful to their families.

In both MP and AP some poor families have been able to lift themselves out of poverty by learning rudimentary construction skill including stone cutting and well and trench digging while others have been able to either hire or purchase bullocks and carts to become sugarcane cutters (see Deshingkar and Stark, 2003, pp. 22–28). Social cohesion has helped these migrant groups survive and flourish and overcome harsh physical conditions while forging bonds with local contractors in locations to which they migrate.

Women from lower casts (SC/ST/OBC) are more likely to migrate and this willingness to move with their families has been a support for households in the districts studied by Deshingkar and Start (2003). However children's education has often suffered. Recent efforts have been made to start schools for migrants by an NGO and the UNICEF office in Hyderabad. However, these efforts have not been extended to other groups that have established a consistent internal migration pattern and could be assisted by similar support.

Finally, we summarize results on migration for India from an ILO rural survey of 2000 households in 24 villages in the Indian Punjab (Oberai, 1979). The findings are broadly consistent with other surveys reviewed above. Males have a higher propensity to migrate and migrants are younger than average. Migration rates for single workers are higher than for those that are married. The very poor cannot generally afford to migrate although there is no conclusive evidence relating migration to the depth of poverty. Migrants who return home to their village because they were unable to find a job are from the poorest and least educated households. Other things equal members of lower castes (ST/SC/OBC) have higher migration rates than other castes.

Turning to China the variables determining the rate of rural to urban migration are similar to those in other Asian countries (see Zhao, 2005). Young, educated males are the most likely to migrate with higher incomes as the biggest attraction for potential migrants. Migrants have to work in the informal sector because the *hokou* system keeps them from establishing permanent residency required for employment in the formal sector. Only 1 percent of migrants hold managerial and technical positions compared with 19 percent of local residents (Knight, Song and Jia, 1999). Still per capita incomes are 2.5 to 3 times higher in the cities than in rural villages and this provides a strong incentive to migrate for young adults in general.

Typical migration patterns are from the poorer western regions to central and eastern regions. Those rural families with limited land are the most likely to migrate. Those in rural villages with higher income are also attracted to non farm work in the rural economy rather than to run the risks of migrating to an unfamiliar urban setting. In this connection having an established network in the city also increases the changes of a successful migration. Many young male migrants work in the construction industry where residence papers are not required.

In China housing costs are an important barrier to migration particularly for families with children. According to Zhao (1999) the monthly rent for a one-bedroom apartment in Beijing is around 1000 yuan whereas the average monthly wage is only 553 yuan. There is also discrimination against rural migrants once they have reached the city. They are geographically segregated, politically ignored and financially discriminated against. The Zhejiang village on the outskirts of Beijing which is occupied primarily by migrants is a good example of this social exclusion (see Yao, 2001; Zhao, 2005). There is evidence that wage discrimination against migrants is rampant. Meng and Zhang (2001) find that over 80 percent of the hourly wage differential between urban and rural workers is due to unequal pay within occupation. The remainder is due to inter occupational differences.

Since the *hukou* system shields the formal labor market, there is a premium for working in the formal sector even though it is inefficient compared with the informal market which is more competitive. SOEs which are large formal sector employers are notoriously inefficient. Nevertheless, these labor market differences are changing rapidly as market forces are bringing competition and flexibility to all labor markets.

Pulling together the results from studies of India and China it is evident that rural to urban migration provides an important outlet for the young to earn more money and develop skills that will enhance their job opportunities. Although lack of education and low incomes impede the pace of migration the chronically poor often find ways to send a young male member to the city to find work. The remittances sent home by these migrants may be small and intermittent but it is an important source of income for the chronically poor in rural villages. Policies should be further developed to encourage continued rural to urban migration. These possibilities are further discussed in Chapter 8.

Chapter 5

Sector Policies to Reduce Chronic Poverty

In this chapter we turn to an analysis of sector policies that can be applied to address the continued persistence of chronic poverty in Asia. This approach shifts focus from programs and policies designed to help individual families or small communities which have been poor for a long time. Instead, sector policies are designed to address chronic poverty from a broader perspective by looking at poverty in the context of the physical and social environment. The focus is on public spending to address the physical and social infrastructure needs of poor villages and communities. These include programs to reduce social, cultural and physical isolation and to give the chronically poor more voice in the political arena. This involves increased connectivity to others both geographically, economically, culturally and politically. It focuses on physical infrastructure such as roads and telecommunications as well as ways to increase productivity in rural areas, including irrigation, agricultural extension and adoption of progressive farming technologies. It also addresses the need to improve the delivery of human capital resources such as education, health and sanitation to the poorest of the poor.

5.1 Increase Connectivity of By-Passed Regions

There are many ways that isolated regions can be better integrated with the rest of the economy. Integration enhances the ability of the regions left behind to forge commercial links with nearby urban areas as well as other rural communities. Better linkage leads to greater exchange of information and technology and provide pathways to further integrate these communities into the economic fabric of the region and the rest of the country.

5.1.1 *Communications*

Improved communication with others is an important way to spread the availability of new information and technology to poor communities. For example telecommunications access can be improved is by the use of cellular phones, where usage is increasing by leaps and bounds. Furthermore new uses are being found all the time (Corbett, 2008). In villages in rural China cell phones are being used by children to keep in touch with their parents working in urban areas as far away as Beijing. Aside from keeping families in touch it also provides added incentives for parents to send money and to keep fathers and husbands that are away for long periods of time from forming new attachments away from home. More generally cell phones can also be used by migrants from rural villages to keep in touch with friends and family at home. In India, where teacher absenteeism is rampant cell phone networks can help supervisors track teachers' movements. A support network of observers can be developed to notify appropriate supervisors when teachers are missing. Students can also contact this network to see if the teacher is present.

Commercial use of cell phones have also been reported by fishermen who use them to connect with different markets to check out where demand is strongest and where prices are high when they are ready to deliver their catch. This has improved the efficiency of delivery to market, increased earnings of fishermen and reduced spoilage (see Corbett, 2008 for more details). Cell phones could also be used to assist farmers in remote locations improve the efficiency of marketing produce by connecting them with operators of vehicles that could transport their goods. The vehicle operators could organize several pick ups in the village or different villages to reduce travel time and ensure a full load for the trip to market. Families of children going to school where teacher absenteeism is high could monitor teacher movements by contacting point persons in or near the school. This could also serve as a substitute for site visits by supervisory personnel in charge of monitoring teacher attendance. Other uses will undoubtedly arise as prices come down, technical relay networks and grids grow and more people gain access. Sharing of phones will increase and Nokia and other manufacturers are already devising memory access where several different people can keep contact lists on the same phone.

Use of texting, which is cheaper but not as flexible in transmitting information, is also becoming more popular. In the Philippines, many young people are so good at texting that they can text a verbal message as fast as a person can speak. Also in the Philippines a text network was responsible for mobilizing large protests and eventually forced the ouster of President Estrada. Health information can also be made available through cell phone networks and the internet. This would improve the ability of households in remote locations to make contact with health professionals, receive advice and become aware of needed vaccinations, outbreaks of disease and other pertinent information relating to health and sanitation.

New applications for cell phone use will develop as new technology evolves like recharging from solar batteries, lower prices and more sophisticated instruments. A recent study by World Resources Institute and the International Finance Corporation suggests that expenditures on information and communication equipment will increase more rapidly than any other consumer spending component, not only among the rich but more particularly among the poor. The principal author of the study says that the poor are buying cellphones and prepaid cards at a faster rate than any other category, including heath, education and housing (see Corbett, 2008, and Hammond *et al.*, 2007). To quote from the conclusion of Jensen's paper on fishing in Kerala

> We find that the addition of mobile phones reduced price dispersion and waste and increased fishermen's profits and consumer welfare. These results demonstrate the importance of information for the functioning of markets and the value of well-functioning markets; information makes markets work, and markets improve welfare. And it is again worth emphasizing that the results represent persistent rather then one-time gains since market functioning should be permanently enhanced by the availability of mobile phones. (Jensen, 2007, p. 892)

Jensen goes on to argue that cell phones

> increase earnings, (and) those increased earnings (or increased purchasing power, due to reduced consumer prices), in turn, can be expected to lead to improvements in health and education. In addition, because mobile phones in Kerala are a private sector initiative rather than a development project ... they do not crowd out investments in other projects..., the service is self-sustaining; mobile phone companies provide service because it is profitable to do so, and fishermen are willing to pay for mobile phones because of the increased profits they receive ... (and) the private sector may be better suited to identifying such opportunities.

Jensen argues that the perishable nature of fish makescell phone use so profitable. He argues that this profitability can be extended to other markets.

> While there is evidence that even markets in nonperishable commodities, such as grains, are often not well integrated spatially, the biggest gains will likely be for other perishable commodities, such as milk, eggs, fruits, and vegetables, and possibly even day labor, where spot labor markets often only clear locally (within villages).

He further argues that transportation and related infrastructure can improve market performance, lower costs, improve efficiency and raise income. There may be shifts in the profitability of cell phone use as these developments move forward.

> In Kerala, improvements in communication have lowered the cost of land transport, leading to more arbitrage by wholesalers on land (and less by fishermen) since transport is now in many cases cheaper by road than by sea. In other cases, poor quality roads may limit the ability of improvements in information to enhance market performance because arbitrage remains prohibitively expensive. However, the widespread, voluntary adoption of ICTs for marketing by producers and traders observed in many developing countries suggests similar gains are likely to be found elsewhere.

Finally, Jensen argues that there are spillovers from the innovators of ICT technology in developing countries and the poor.

> While it was primarily the largest fishermen who adopted mobile phones in the present case, there were significant spillover gains for the smaller fishermen who did not use phones, due to the improved functioning of markets.

Thus, rather than simply excluding the poor or less educated, the "digital provide" appears to be shared more widely throughout society.

Aside from commercial use to connect the chronically poor to markets and provide information that is useful for them and their children, Waverman *et al.* (2005) argue that the spread of telecommunications capital in the form of cell phones is similar to the rates of return to human capita suggested by Romer (1986) and Barro (1991). Waverman *et al.* (2005) estimate that in low income countries an average of ten more mobile phones per hundred people resulted in an annual increase in GDP of 0.59 percent. More work will have to be done to verify this relationship since the sample was small and the difficulties of simultaneity were not dealt with in a well specified econometric model. Nevertheless these results are suggestive of a long run relationship between economic growth and ICT technology in developing countries that needs to be both studied and exploited. The beauty of this relationship is that it depends primarily on the private sector and needs no government support aside from the infrastructure required to implement the transmission of signals.

There is evidence that farmers and others in the agricultural sector including the chronically poor are beginning to use cell phones to gain access to valuable market information as well as research findings to enhance economic efficiency and increase yields. Farmers in Madhya Pradesh state in India are gaining access to soil testing services and market price trends to help them decide appropriate crop selection and where and when to sell crops. Small scale village entrepreneurs now use cell phone networks to build networks of shops and other vendors. In the Philippines, McDonalds's franchises serve as points of delivery for remittances sent by phone from overseas while Smart Communications, an operator in the Philippines sells text messages for as little as $1.80 per 100 messages and allows subscribers to pass airtime to others at a cost of less than $0.03 per minute. In Bangladesh hand sets are rented out a call at a time. Costs have also been cut for phones, led by Motorola, and also for infrastructure as small low-cost equipment-makers have developed base-stations used in developing countries. In China, the telecoms industry is being restructured to introduce more competition with China Mobile merging with a smaller company, and six companies regrouped into three, each spanning all three telecommunications modalities — fixed, broadband and mobile networks. Hopefully this will result in further competition and cost reductions for service. (see *The Economist*, May 29, 2008).

Knowledge of low-cost filtering systems that prevent the spread of dysentery, cholera and other water borne diseases are being spread with the help of cell phones. (More clean-water technology for poor villages is discussed further in the next chapter.) Knowledge of other technology such as low cost solar powered lights and multi-fuel cook stoves that can burn a variety of fuels including biomass and plants are also being made available to rural villages. In Bangladesh, Grameen Telecom generates revenue by providing service to entire villages thru village phone entrepreneurs that serve over 80,000 villages (See Hammond *et al.*, 2007, for additional discussion of these ideas).

Cellphones can also be used to warn against hazards like flash floods, tsunamis and other safety warnings as well as notification of food shortages and possible epidemics.

Taxation of mobile phones has remained modest in Asia and this should continue rather than follow the example of countries in Africa where taxes have been raised and the spread of the telecommunications network penalized.

5.1.2 *Rural roads*

Market access in South Asia is better than in other developing regions, with more than 50 percent of the rural population within 1 hour to market compared with only around 30 percent in East Asia and the Pacific and even less in other regions (see Sebastian, 2007). Nevertheless extension of the transportation network by expanding access to isolated rural villages is an efficient way to increase the mobility of residents in these villages as well as a way to increase their connectivity to nearby rural towns and larger urban areas. Traditionally road projects have been appraised based on the road networks ability to increase economic efficiency by reducing travel time, facilitating and reducing handling time and increase load limits by building road surfaces to handle large trucks. (See, for example, Gannon and Liu, 1997). More recently equity considerations have been incorporated in project evaluations of road projects. This shift in emphasis reflects a growing realization that traditional project evaluation techniques tended to favor the rich and road projects bypassed poorer areas whereas these by-passed regions might not have had the volume of traffic flow necessary to justify extension or improvement of the transport network based on efficiency grounds alone. As a remedy the World Bank and other international agencies have adopted alternative evaluation criteria that incorporate potential health, nutrition and educational benefits, enhance transfer of agricultural extension and new technology as well as greater opportunities to migrate and commute to rural towns or urban areas (see Van de Walle, 2002). Proponents of such an approach suggest gathering information from subject villages in order to pinpoint rural road projects that will address poverty reduction in the most effective manner. Analysis of data from villages in Vietnam demonstrated the importance of assessing poverty, accessibility and economic potential to obtain the best candidates for rural road extension and upgrading. In many regions this could involve insuring that roads are passable year around and in others it could involve access during part of the year. Many rural roads are impassible during the rainy season and would require significant upgrading to increase access for the entire year.

Aside from the topic of project selection and evaluation there have been a number of studies of the rate of return on rural road projects in Asia. However, only a few have focused on the explicit relationship between roads and rural poverty. IFPRI economist Fan and his associates have carried out three studies of the impact of government spending on poverty in Asia. Rural road investment was one of the key variables analyzed (see Fan, Zhang and Zhang, 2002; Fan, Hazell and Thorat, 1999; Thorat and Fan, 2007). These studies developed a system of simultaneous equations to determine the interaction of government expenditures on poverty, growth and productivity change. Regarding the relationship between rural poverty and spending on roads, all of these studies show that investment in roads had more impact on non-agricultural economic activities which in turn helped to reduce poverty. In India (Fan *et al.*, 2002) investment in roads has the largest impact on rural poverty. Spending on roads had nearly twice as large an impact as R&D investment in agriculture, the next most important expenditure variable. Investment in roads also was an important factor in raising productivity. In China road investment was also a significant variable in a simultaneous model of economic activity including poverty determination. Similar results were also obtained for Thailand. Altogether these three studies provide strong evidence for the general impact of road investment on poverty, they do not have much to say about the impact of road spending on chronic poverty nor do they explore what kind of roads have the most impact on poverty.

In an analysis of road projects several studies have concluded that secondary and feeder roads results in greater poverty reductions than primary highways, particularly chronically poor villages that are cut off from road access during the monsoon season. For example the study of China conducted by Fan *et al.* (1999) found a much greater impact on poverty by spending on "low" quality as opposed to "high" quality roads even though the estimates suggest that the expenditures on roads in general is not particularly effective.

In Lao PDR two studies by Warr (2006a and 2005) suggest strongly that road investment has a significant impact on rural poverty. Between 1997/98 and 2002/2003 rural incidence of poverty in Lao PDR declined by 9.5 percent of the rural population. The analysis of the impact of road development during that period suggests that 13 percent of this decline in poverty was the result of improved road access. Other investments, particularly in irrigation also contributed to the decline. Road improvements took two forms. First there were improvements to give wet season access to roads that already had dry season access, making them passable all year. Secondly, investments were made to grant at least dry season access to villages that previously had no road access. The studies both suggest that both investments yield a significant reduction in poverty. Most of the investments during this period took the form of providing year round access was previously limited during the wet season. However there are also substantial benefits to be gained by providing road access to more than 30 percent of rural households who still do not have any road access. According to Warr's estimates providing these families with dry season could reduce poverty incidence by more than 3 percent and another 3 percent by providing all weather access. Warr's work also suggests that providing roads for households without road access is more pro-poor than upgrading of other roads to all weather usage. Even though road construction for villages without any previous access is more expensive than upgrading of existing roads to year around use, the benefits in poverty reduction are worth the added cost as suggested by Warr's simulation results.

Road construction is expensive particularly in countries where the road network is already well developed and further road construction could yield different results. Nevertheless in countries like Lao PDR where almost a third of the population has no road access at all, it makes good sense to invest heavily in rural roads. In Lao PDR, only 4 percent of the road network is paved and the local road network is impassable for parts of the wet season, In Bihar, the state of India with the highest rate of poverty and the least progress in reducing poverty (the state's share India's poverty increased from 11.4 percent in 1960 to 18.5 percent in 1993) the road network is in a deplorable state of repair. In the 1990s, Bihar was the only state that had no increase in the extension of the road network. Mohanan (2003) and *The Bihar Times* (2007) estimated that 15 percent of harvested crops were lost between the farm gate and the consumer because of poor roads and inadequate storage. A report by the special Bihar task force (Government of India, 2007) says that villages with more than 500 residents will have all weather roads connecting them to the wider road network by 2009. However 10 percent of the villages in the state of Bihar are still without roads. On the surface this is a much better record than the work of Warr suggests for Lao PDR. However, 57 percent of the village connector roads in Bihar are in poor shape.

In a study of Bangladesh, Khandker *et al.* (2006) found that rural road investment reduced poverty through increases in efficiency resulting in higher wages, low input and transportation costs and higher output prices. Rural road investments also facilitated transportation of children to school and resulted in more schooling for both boys and girls. Gains in income were proportionally greater for the poor than the non-poor. Khandker *et al.* estimate that poverty in subject villages fell by about 1 percent per year solely as a result of road improvements.

The International Labor Organization (ILO) has undertaken a wide ranging study of the rural road network in Asia concerned with analyzing the extent of the network and expenditures needed to maintain rural access in the future (Donnges, Edmonds and Johannessen, 2007). In Asia the rural road network represents between 70 percent and 80 percent of the public road network yet it only accounts for between 15 and 20 percent of the traffic volume. Nevertheless road access is critical for rural villages that depend on them for marketing, communications and information. There are still many villages in Asia that have no road access. Figures assembled by ILO are presented in Table 5.1. Between 1980 and 2004 the road network in South Asia and East Asia has increased dramatically, 88 percent and 83 percent respectively. China accounted for the bulk of road network expansion in East Asia.

While the network has increased in size the same can not be said for road conditions. Rural road maintenance has failed to keep up with need and there has been a serious deterioration in road surface conditions in recent years. Table 5.1 suggests that substantially more than half of rural roads are in poor condition. In countries experiencing monsoon or typhoon conditions during the wet season this implies that these roads would be impassible for some of the year, a view that is consistent with the Warr studies of Lao PDR. Impassable roads mean loss of income and communication for those villages and significantly impact chronic poverty.

How did this situation come about and what can be done? Maintenance funding is a major challenge for all countries in the Asian region and particularly so for the poorer countries. Part of the problem lies with who is responsible for maintenance of the rural road network. In some countries maintenance responsibility is split

Table 5.1 Condition of Rural Roads in Asia

Country and Region	Percentage of Villages/ Population With No Road Access	Percentage of Rural Roads in Poor Condition
India	50	60
Madhya Pradesh	62	80
Uttar Pradesh	50	80
Jharkhand		81
Himachal Pradesh	52	55
Philippines		65
Lao PDR	38	73
Bhutan	40	86
Pakistan	34	>50
Indonesia	10	50
Sri Lanka		>70
Vietnam		35

Source: Donnges *et al.* (2007).
Note: For Bhutan, Pakistan and Indonesia percentages in second column are for population. For other countries figures are for villages. Blanks in second column reflect lack of data.

between various government agencies or local authorities. These are described in some detail in Table 5.2.

In nearly every country implementation for rural roads is devolved to local governments and the bulk of funds are allocated to main roads which have the most traffic. Unless road funds are established specifically for rural roads, funding will be unreliable. In some cases this means individual villages that are charged with building and maintaining roads in the vicinity of the village. This can lead to uneven road development where some sections are well maintained and others are not. Compliance is hard to enforce because of limited funding from provincial authorities and villages have to fund road maintenance or upgrading in their area of responsibility.

Separate budgets for main road and rural road maintenance are not available. However, overall budgets for maintenance are generally less than 2 tenths of a percent of GDP (0.2 percent), whereas annual capital investment is in the neighborhood of 2 percent of GDP.

Table 5.2 Responsibility for Road Construction and Maintenance

Country	Main Roads	Rural Roads
Philippines	Dept. of Public Works and Highways	Provincial governments for provincial roads and villages for rural roads
Indonesia	Ministry of Public Works	Ministry of Home Affairs — Implementation devolved to local government
Cambodia	Ministry of Public Works	Ministry of Rural Development
Lao PDR	Ministry of Communications, Transport, Posts and Construction	Ministry of Communications, Transport, Posts and Construction
Thailand	Dept of Highways	Ministry of Interior — Implementation devolved to local governments
Vietnam	Roads Authority and Ministry of Transport	Provincial and District Departments of Transport responsible to provincial authorities
Bangladesh	Roads and Highways Dept.	Local Government Engineering Department, Ministry of Local Government
Indian states	State Ministry of Public Works	State Ministry of Rural Development and local government (village roads)
Pakistan	National Highway Authority	Provincial authorities — implementation devolved to districts
Nepal	Ministry of Physical Planning and Works, Dept of Roads	Ministry of Local Governments — implementation devolved to districts
Sri Lanka	Ministry of Highways	Ministry of Home Affairs, Provincial Councils and Local Governments — implementation devolved to local government

Source: Donnges *et al.* (2007, p. 27).

Industrial countries spend more than twice as much on maintenance relative to new road construction than the average developing country in Asia (Donnges *et al.*, 2007, p. 33).

How much money is needed to maintain the rural road network? Donnges *et al.* (2007) suggest the ratio of the length of the rural road network to GDP as a measure of need. The larger this ratio the larger the budget required for rural road maintenance. These ratios are presented in Table 5.3 arranged from low to high. The size of the budget required is roughly inversely related to the country's income, although there are exceptions like China and Sri Lanka. Nevertheless these ratios are a reasonable indication of the cost of maintaining the rural road network and a countries ability to finance these costs. It seems reasonable to assume that poorer countries are the biggest beneficiaries of improvements in the rural road network. There are more

Table 5.3 Ratio of Rural Road Length to GNP

Country	Ratio of Rural Road Length in Km to GNP in US$ Millions.
China	1.0
Thailand	1.3
Indonesia	1.7
Philippines	1.9
Pakistan	2.1
Bhutan	3.1
Vietnam	3.4
India	3.5
Bangladesh	3.7
Nepal	3.8
Afghanistan	3.9
Sri Lanka	4.1
PNG	5.4
Cambodia	6.8
Lao PDR	11.2
Mongolia	31.9

Source: Donnges *et al.* (2007, p. 34).

poor people in rural locations in these countries but at the same time the cost of maintaining the road network strains their budgets more than richer countries. For example the cost of maintaining rural roads in Lao PDR represents 2 percent of GNP while in the Philippines it is only 0.3 percent of GNP.

Another factor to remember is that, other things being equal, countries with more widely dispersed populations such as PNG and Mongolia will spend more than countries where population density is high. As we saw in Warr's analysis of Lao PDR (Warr, 2005, 2006) the rate of return to road development and maintenance is high. Therefore Lao PDR and perhaps Cambodia seem like good candidates for external financial of rural road development and maintenance.

The benefits of all weather rural roads are many. In an evaluation of such projects in Pakistan (www.pakistan.gov.pk/divisions/lgrd-division/media/project/farm2road/farm2road.html) the following changes in the local village environment were noted. Many new businesses developed including: rice mills and flour mills, shopping centers and other commercial activities. Marketing of agricultural products improved as total costs, as well as transportation costs, fell while product quality increased. Worker mobility increased which could have resulted in more migration to urban areas. Education, health and other social services improved, land value increases, vehicular traffic increased and the construction industry benefited. There were also new employment opportunities created as the economic well being of the community improved.

In analyzing the impact of road developments on poverty reduction it is important to look into the general relationship between infrastructure spending and other sector and even macroeconomic variables and overall economic growth. We will have more to say about this in the next chapter. Here it is useful to recognize that such interactions do exist and that there are synergies that analyzing spending on individual infrastructure projects would not capture. For example using household panel for Bangladesh, Khandker and Koolwal (2006) point out that growth in rural incomes supported by pro-growth policies led to a significant reduction in poverty particularly those in the poorest categories. This reduction in poverty came from the implementation of policies that had been traditionally associated with pro-growth such as infrastructure investment including proximity to rural roads, commercial bank expansion and higher agricultural output prices. Another interesting result is that poverty reduction was particularly responsive to non-farm income growth.

These results suggest a complicated and sometimes reinforcing interaction among several variables which includes road investment and also possible small scale lending to agricultural households and expansion of employment opportunities either in rural industry or perhaps in circular migration to urban areas. In a study for India, Binswanger and Khandker (1993) suggest that infrastructure (including for education) spending and expansion of the banking system results in greater investment in agriculture and higher output prices. This improved economic environment subsequently results in a decrease in poverty.

Another paper by Chaudhury and Hammer (2004) spells out the interaction between health services, rural roads and rural electrification. We know that absenteeism is a problem in rural South Asia (see Table 2.4 and Chapter 2). Chaudhury and Hammer find that there is less absenteeism among health professionals in rural Bangladesh where villages are electrified and rural roads are in close proximity to the village. The authors suggest that the proportion of households with electricity serves as a proxy for wealth as well as a measure of the comforts of having conveniences that go with electricity — TV, radio, appliances. Road access is important as an indirect indicator of willingness of health practitioners to live in the village. Those that live in the village have much lower rates of absenteeism. Their study shows that if road access is more than a kilometer away from the village there is less likelihood that the health professional would be willing to live in the village.

5.1.3 *Rural electrification*

Universal access to electricity is a policy goal for most developing countries. India has a plan to electrify all villages by 2008 and all households by 2012. Currently this plan is behind schedule although efforts continue to extend the network. The poorer states lag behind as reflected in household access shown in Table 5.4. Only a fraction of households in Bihar, Assam and Orissa had access to electricity in 1999 (Das, 1999). Good progress in rural electrification has been made in both Bangladesh and Pakistan Both countries say that all villages will be electrified by 2008 although the proportion of households connected will be considerably smaller (see WAPDA web site www.wapda.gov.pk/htmls/power-development.html for Pakistan and Kahn *et al.*, 2002, for Bangladesh). In Sri Lanka and Indonesia, plans are also in place to offer complete access to the grid for all villages (see Dasuki, Djamin and Lubis, 2001). In Indonesia PLN the state electricity company plans to electrify most villages in the next few years with the help of solar technology. In other countries such as Nepal and the Mekong countries, rural electrification is not as advanced. In Nepal, less that 15 percent of rural

Table 5.4 Household Access to Electricity by Indian State (%)

State	Percentage of Households with Electricity 2004
Andhra Pradesh	67
Assam	19
Bihar	10
Gujarat	80
Haryana	83
Himachal Pradesh	95
Karnataka	78
Kerala	70
Madhya Pradesh	70
Maharashtra	78
Orissa	27
Punjab	92
Rajasthan	55
Tamil Nadu	78
Uttar Pradesh	32
West Bengal	37

Source: Das (1999).

households are electrified despite abundant hydroelectric resources and the poor consume only a fraction of the electricity used by the rich. In the Philippines and Lao PDR, the bottom forty percent of the income distribution consumed around 15 percent of the electricity generated (see Independent Evaluation Group, 2008). Connection fees along with bias against poor communities are two reasons why the poor, particularly the chronically poor have limited access. Cost effectiveness criteria used to rank potential grid extension include population size, average community income and potential use. The poor rank high on only the first of these criteria.

The impact of rural electrification on chronic poverty is complicated. It is acknowledged that the poor and particularly the chronically poor are less likely to have access to electricity (see Independent Evaluation Group, 2008). However Independent Evaluation Group (2008) argues that the distribution to the poor improves as coverage expands. Whether this is a cost effective way to address chronic poverty in rural areas is another matter. Certainly having electricity increases the quality of life and has secondary impacts on infant mortality and overall health outcomes. Based on statistics compiled from interview with nearly 4,000 people, Khan *et al.* (2002) suggest several reasons why rural electrification has had a positive impact on reducing chronic poverty in Bangladesh. They note that households that have had electricity for a longer period of time (four to six years) have a significantly lower rate of poverty incidence, from 42 percent for those who had electricity for three years or less down to 34 percent for those who had access for six years or longer. They also note that electrified households had poverty rates of 40 percent on average while the corresponding figure for non-electrified households was 51 percent. While these figures seem suggestive, they prove nothing since other factors could have also contributed to lower incidences of poverty among households with electricity. Hook up fees are substantial and serve as a deterrent to the poorest households and this would serve as an initial screen that could account for poverty differentials. Other aspects of the analysis of Khan *et al.* shed light on a variety of other benefits that have accrued from electrification. Security and mobility at night was enhanced by the availability of electricity which also afforded more time for work and leisure. The access to the news media also increased awareness of the importance education, personal hygiene, inoculations and consultations with qualified medical personnel and, knowledge of availability of contraceptive devices. This resulted in a reduction in infant mortality and child mortality, improved hygiene including use of hygienic latrines and better school attendance. Electricity played a catalyst in the educational process by extending the time period for study and creating a comfortable learning environment. The study also argues that interplay of factors that arise when a household has electricity, including more time, less drudgery and information from the media created opportunities for overcoming the hardships of poverty. These include working at night to earn money either by the household head or women in the household, learning of possible employment opportunities and better agricultural practices. There was also evidence that households in villages where others had electricity also benefited from the changes in patterns of behavior and information obtained by those with electricity. There was also evidence that the presence of electricity in a village made it more attractive to outsiders. As a result there was significant in-migration to villages with electricity creating more employment opportunities and raising property values. Human development indices also increased as a result of rural electrification. Finally, bias against female children was much smaller in electrified villages as evidenced by a smaller disproportion in the male to female birth rate. This could be the result of a significant decrease in infant mortality to age 5 for electrified villages. Assured of surviving children families are less prone to make choices that endanger survival of female infants.

The perceived benefits of rural electrification in Bangladesh have also been touted in other countries with longer experience with rural electrification including China Indonesia, Philippines and India (see Munasinghe, 1990). While the direct impact on chronic poverty may be hard to measure (see Table 5.10 and Table 5.11), the indirect benefit on health, education and the quality of life provide convincing evidence for the benefits of rural electrification.

> Viable and reliable electricity services result in increased productivity in agriculture and labor, improvement in the delivery of health and education, access to communication ... improved lighting after sunset, facilitating the use of time and energy saving mills, pumps and motor and increasing public safety through outdoor lighting ... and can increasingly meet the aspirations of the rural populations ... (Modi, 2005, p. 13).

In India the question of the impact on chronic poverty is moot. While government and other researchers emphasize the importance of rural electrification most of the chronically have no or very limited access to electricity. This shortfall is most apparent in the poorest states and among the ST/SC. Table 5.4 shows the extremely low level of rural electrification in the poorest states of Assam, Bihar and Orissa. Furthermore, Vijay Modi (2005) points out that these same states have the lowest level of government funds made available for rural electrification. Furthermore the poorest states also have the lowest usage of electric pumps for groundwater extraction for agricultural usage — typically less that 15 percent or between 15 and 30 percent. In addition to lack of connectivity power supplies are available only for a few hours during the day and not often at night. SC/ST classes were the least likely to have electricity access.

> ... in the village of Gurariya, where the harizan basti (dalits) living conditions were pathetic compared to other parts of the village. The harizan basti had no water source or electricity connection illustrating that, in this instance, the schemes targeting the most vulnerable segments in society are, in fact, not benefiting them. (Modi, 2005, p. 39).

Connection fees are another barrier for the chronically poor. Should these fees be subsidized in full? Should there be subsidies for low volume users — a lifeline fee — and how much should the subsidy be?

There are a number of other difficulties with the delivery of and utilization of power in rural India, including lack of metering of ground water drawdown — the so-called Energy-Water Nexus (see Shaw *et al.*, 2003), shortages of engineers to implement further extension of the rural electrification network, issues of pricing service to the poor and the benefits of decentralization of the power network.

However, the pressing need is to facilitate greater electricity access for the chronically poor.

By waiving connection fees the cost of electricity in India can be made very attractive to the chronically poor and by charging a small fee for minimum usage to run a few lights and appliances. The chronically poor are unlikely to be irrigating their land, since land ownership is low. However if they do have the option of using electricity to run irrigation pumps, additional subsidies can be developed so that variable costs for irrigation would not be prohibitive. By providing subsidies, supplying electricity to the chronically poor will be costly, particularly in mountainous and remote regions (or islands) where population density is low and extension of the power grid is expensive.

Several challenges have to be overcome if electricity is to be provided for significant numbers of rural residents that do not have access, including wide dispersion of population, low levels of demand, limited purchasing power and billing, and maintenance difficulties as well as demand concentrated in the early evening hours and high levels of power loss. Therefore, conventional rural electrification by extending the power grid may not be cost effective.

Solar power is an alternative that has been developed in pilot projects in Indonesia and some other Asian economies where extension of the power network is expensive and would involve a significant and costly subsidy (see Dasuki, Djamin and Lubis, 2001). The Indonesia project has focused on villages in the eastern part of Indonesia. Pilot programs and capacity development for photovoltaic deployment in rural areas are also being carried out in Bangladesh, Cambodia, Lao PDR, Nepal and Vietnam (see Kumar *et al.*, 2003). The Food and Agricultural Organization of the United Nations (FAO) has reviewed the use of photovoltaic systems (PV) stressing not only possible household use for lighting but also for agricultural use in pumping irrigation, potable water, cottage industries, health care and education (van Campen, Guidi and Best, 2000). PV can be used as stand alone systems or in hybrid systems with diesel fuel.

The various possible uses for PV were assembled as responses to an FAO survey in a number of countries around the world and are displayed in Table 5.5.

Table 5.5 Uses of PV Systems as Percent of Survey Respondents

Pumping for irrigation	30
Livestock watering	9
Pumping potable water	35
Water purification	12
Electric fences	16
Lighting for poultry/livestock	14
Office equipment e.g. computers	16
Radio or cellular phones	42
Health centers — refrigeration, lighting	44
Veterinary services — refrigeration, lighting	9
Refrigeration — households, stores, agricultural products, fish	16
Lighting, TV, radio — for commercial establishments	47
Lighting, small power tools for micro enterprise	19
Lighting, TV, radio for household use	81
Tourist facilities — lighting, TV, refrigeration	21
Lighting and audiovisual for schools	37
Street lighting	28

Source: FAO survey in connection with van Campen *et al.* (2000).

Pumping for irrigation and potable water along with lighting and TV for homes and health centers were the most often mentioned uses of electricity by respondents and this is consistent with the current usage in pilot projects in Asia. If PV systems could be widely distributed at low cost to chronically poor villages there is likely to be a substantial improvement in the quality of life, particularly for home lighting and TV as well as cell phone access. Those chronically poor families with land could benefit from solar pumps and all families would benefit from health centers with refrigeration and lighting as well as possibilities of making potable water. Furthermore a significant proportion of respondents believe that PV systems could make a significant impact on agricultural productivity (35 percent of survey respondents), off–farm productive use in rural industries and commercial and business services (40 percent), social and community services (60 percent) and households (81 percent). Van Campen *et al.* (2000) detail the various uses in countries around the world. In Asia

Table 5.6 Some PV Systems Currently in Use in Asia

Type of Application	Examples of Systems	Countries Where Used
Lighting and cooling for poultry factory	Battery, lights, fan	India, Indonesia, Vietnam
Irrigation	Small pumps	India
Cooling for fruit preservation	PV/wind system	Indonesia
Egg Incubation	Heating element for hatching	India, Philippines
Crop spraying	sprayer	India
Handicraft workshop	Lighting small tools	Nepal, Vietnam
Health clinics	Refrigerators, freezers	Many countries
Potable water pumping	Electronic solar pump	Many countries
Water purification	Power to ozone water purifiers	China and other countries
School and training centers	Lights, TV, PCs, VCR	China, Philippines other countries
Street lights	Electronic battery	India, Indonesia, Philippines

Source: FAO survey in connection with van Campen *et al.* (2000) and literature review by van Campen *et al.* (2000).

a few systems are worth mentioning as they pertain to chronic poverty reduction are listed in Table 5.6.

PV systems have similar positive social impacts on households as conventional rural electrification mentioned at the beginning of this section including impact on work and education and recreation (TV, reading) as well as on health and time for leisure, particularly for women. In addition PV electrification had a positive impact on attitudes, pride and self esteem.

Cooperatives have played a role in augmenting rural electrification capacity in certain parts of Bangladesh and the Philippines using conventional technology and have been suggested in Nepal (see Adhikari, http://www.smecc.org/rural_electrification_in_nepal.htm) Subsidies, usually provided by an international donor, are based on the efficiency of performance by the cooperative in reducing system losses from transmission, generation or distribution of electricity. Pilferage is often a problem that can be better addressed by a local cooperative than a national power company. The performance of the cooperative and the subsidy is also based on increasing sales, meeting connection targets and improving collection rates. In Bangladesh, achievement of targets is also the basis for annual bonuses to cooperative employees (see Tomkins, 1997). There are distinct advantages of involving local cooperatives in rural electrification. They are in touch with local conditions and are more easily able to respond to local needs and deal with pilferage and other problems. To achieve wider distribution of service in poor and thinly populated areas these programs and subsidies should focus more on increasing access to electricity rather than consumption. Introducing competition for grants to operate in a particular region will give added incentives for bidders to provide efficient and affordable service.

Biofuels and Minihydro are also possible alternatives to conventional power generation and have been suggested for different countries in Asia. Hydro and Minihydro plants are now in use to generate electricity in Nepal. Biomass has been suggested for Cambodia, where systems losses and low capacity systems make for high costs (see e-Newsletter Biofuel for Rural Electrification in Cambodia (2007), available at www.bio2power.org/dmdocuments/Biofuel%20for%20 Rural%20Electrificaiton%20Newsletter_Feb_eng.pdf).

5.2 Irrigation

Water availability is a key determinant of productivity in the agricultural sector and a major driver in chronic poverty reduction. Generally South Asia has been able to take advantage of irrigation potential compared to other developing regions. 60 percent of the rural population in South Asia has access to irrigation. This compares with 50 percent in East Asia and the Pacific, around 30 percent in Middle East and North Africa, and less than 20 percent in the rest of the developing world. Market access is also better in South Asia, with more than 50 percent of the rural population being within 1 hour of a market compared with only 30 percent in East Asia and the Pacific (see Sebastian, 2007).

Nevertheless, there remains additional irrigation potential that can be tapped. This section focuses on the impact of tube well and canal irrigation on chronic poverty. Larger irrigation schemes involve complicated movements of residents in building large dams. As a result it is difficult to measure the impact on the chronically poor. Furthermore there are many smaller schemes that are pertinent in areas where the chronically poor reside. Research reviewed by Lipton and other on an FAO team (Lipton and Litchfield, 2003) investigated returns to farmers and workers in villages where tube wells and canal irrigation schemes were introduced. For India they found that irrigation enabled farmers to plant two or more crops rather than just one. There were also positive impacts on employment and earnings for both resource poor farmers with marginal lands as well as landless laborers. For those farmers with marginal lands the effect of irrigation generally manifested in increased production, whether for home consumption or for sale in the market. This appreciably raised incomes and living standards. Because of the second (and occasionally third) crop there is employment more days during the year. For landless laborers there was also a positive net benefit as a result of higher and more consistent rates of employment. There is also possible additional income for some who were put in charge of some aspects of maintaining the irrigation system including care of canals or management of communally owned tube wells. These findings are based on 25 micro studies in India and 20 in other countries. (see Chambers *et al.*, 1989) . The impact of irrigation on employment was even stronger than the adoption of higher yielding varieties. There was a tendency for higher yields to suppress food prices and reduce earnings for farmers. However this effect was smaller than the gains from irrigation and was also offset to some extent by lower food costs for landless laborers.

The impact of irrigation is highlighted by comparisons between irrigated and non-irrigated villages in West Bengal. In the non-irrigated villages there were two periods when there was little or no work which created severe problems. Laborers either had to find low paying subsistence work locally or migrate to find employment and some families suffered serious deprivation as a result. In the irrigated villages employment was more or less continuous and no cases of severe deprivation were reported. Reports by Hussain and Hanjra (2003) and Hussain and Hanjra (2004) based on research conducted by the International Water Management Institute in Sri Lanka as well as a review of the literature suggests that irrigation increases agricultural productivity and generates higher incomes and higher yields while reducing the risk of crop failure and increasing the level of year around employment. Irrigation benefits the poor through providing more food at lower prices and stimulating the shift from subsistence farming to higher value crops for sale to the market. Micro irrigation systems also have strong potential for reducing poverty. Even greater poverty reduction can be achieved by targeting irrigation to poorer communities by reducing the unequal distribution of water rights as well as reducing the inequality in land holdings.

Irrigation also had a salutary impact on women in irrigated villages. In Bangladesh women benefited more from the increase in employment opportunities than men (Jordans and Zwarteveen, 1997) as a result of higher incomes and more employment opportunities in agriculture. Irrigation made it easier to care for livestock as well as providing convenient access to water for home use. Furthermore many women who might have previously worked as poorly paid servants in rich household are now able to find employment in villages that have access to irrigation and several crops per year. Women have also been empowered to assist in managing tube well equipment and in constructing earthen irrigation channels in the tube well command area.

Hussain *et al.* (2004) looked at large scale irrigation projects in the Walawe Ganga basin about 200 kilometers southwest of Colombo, Sri Lanka and the upper part of the Indus basin in Pakistan. In Sri Lanka, household incomes and expenditures were higher in the irrigated areas because of double cropping as well as higher worker productivity, increased employment and greater stability in income as well as higher wages. Irrigation also contributed to food security more balanced diets and reduced vulnerability to poverty. There were spillover effects on incomes and poverty reduction in nearby villages where there was no irrigation. There were also measurable increases in the effective use of water resources which helped improve equity in water distribution as well as incomes throughout the irrigated region.

In Pakistan poor governance and inequality in the distribution of land holdings and widespread landlessness exerted a drag on the impact of irrigation on poor households. Irrigation infrastructure was not improved uniformly and was not targeted at the poor. As a result, the irrigation project benefited richer households and villages and the impact on chronic poverty was minimal. The study concluded that unless significant redistribution of physical assets and particularly land was to occur, it would be difficult for irrigation projects to have any appreciable impact on chronic poverty in the study area. In both of these studies of large scale irrigation, the issue of downstream water use has arisen. Without proper analysis of the water use pattern for the entire irrigation network it is likely that users at the end of the line will run out of water or to be forced to conserve water at the cost of higher yields and productivity. Therefore it is important to introduce pricing and other control measures to ensure that upstream users conserve water.

Even if those at the end of the line do receive less water several imaginative schemes have been devised to reallocate or conserve water. In central Java, Indonesia a village is located near the end of a local irrigation system constructed infrastructure to divert and use drainage water that previously flowed into the sea. As a result the village farmers now get three crops a year (Hussain *et al.*, 2004, p. 68).

In another example, villagers in Sri Lanka arranged for farmers to exchange land to achieve a more equitable distribution of water year around (see Box 5.1). This illustrates how win win solutions can be achieved thru cooperation.

While research is still ongoing further work in Bangladesh, PRC, India, Indonesia, Pakistan and Vietnam, by Hussain and Hanjral (2004) and Hussain and Hanjra (2004) had reached some preliminary conclusions. Of the rural irrigation systems reviewed the incidence of poverty is highest in Bangladesh and Pakistan and lowest in the PRC. The distribution of land and water resources is least equitable in South Asia, particularly Pakistan and more

Box 5.1 Adaptation of the Bethma system of irrigation in Sri Lanka

Villages located in dry areas in Sri Lanka are often located near man-made water tanks. Water is distributed outward from the tank to different fields. Those closest to the tank receive water first and the furthest last. In periods where there is sufficient water all fields will be irrigated. In drought periods only fields closest to the tanks receive water. This arrangement is known as the Bethma system in Sri Lanka. To rectify these imbalances in water availability that can arise in dry periods land is now reallocated by the Sri Lankan water authority so that some land closest to the tank is temporarily given to farmers furthest away from the tank during periods of drought or other water shortage and vice versa. This result in all farmers sharing in the water shortage not just those furthest removed from the water tank. (Hussain *et al.*, 2004, p. 70).

equitable in PRC and Vietnam. Productivity levels are fairly high with cropping intensities ranging from two to three crops per year. Crop diversification could bring added productivity gains as well as better management of water resources in these countries. It provides indirect benefits to the landless poor in terms of more employment opportunities and higher earnings and would also be of considerable benefit to poor small land holders. Productivity in India and South Asia generally is still quite low and substantial gains could be made from further extension of the irrigation network, by more efficient use of water resources and better integration of water resources with cropping patterns and new agricultural technology including new varieties and different crops. These will be further discussed in the next section of this chapter which deals with agriculture extension and new technology.

Aside from large irrigation projects, small scale irrigation schemes have been implemented in a variety of ways including diesel and solar pumps, treadle pumps, bucket, drip and micro sprinklers. The private sector plays a key role in distributing these technologies to poor farmers with initial help of some subsidies. High value horticulture crops including papaya, gourds, pumpkins and other vegetables can be grown with the help of kits that include seed, fertilizer, pest control and other information. Water requirements can be as little as 2 to 10 buckets of water per day was with as little as 10 square meters of land. The chronically poor would need subsidies to buy the kits and the requires active involvement of the private sector in marketing these products. Drip irrigation technology and expertise would also be needed in some cases (see Winrock International and International Development Enterprise, 2001). One of the most efficient and cheapest methods of obtaining water for the rural poor is through the use of treadle pumps. Treadle pumps are foot operated and use bamboo or other flexible pipes for suction to pump water from shallow acquifer or bodies of water. The pump is useful for lifting water from ponds, tanks, canals, tube wells up to 7 meters deep although they work best at shallower depths of around 3 meters or slightly more. Treadle pumps are easily installed for less that $30, can be shared by several users and are particularly affordable for the poor. A survey of 2,400 households in parts of Bangladesh, eastern India and the Nepalese Terai was conducted by Shah *et al.* (2000). This region is characterized by tiny land holdings and has one of the world's best groundwater resources available at a reasonable shallow depth of 1.5 meters to 3.5 meters, which is perfect for treadle pumps. More than 1.5 million treadle pumps have been sold in this region and International Development Enterprise estimates that as many as 10 million treadle pumps can be sold in eastern India and Nepal alone. Shah *et al.*, 2000 estimate this would raise net annual incomes of the poorest households by a billion dollars. Currently treadle pumps result in an increased of average net income of $100 per year per pump with gross incomes of $300–400 not uncommon (see Hussain and Hanraj, 2004). Using the 10 million treadle pump forecast, the $100 per head increase would amount to a billion dollars additional income per year. $100 per year may not sound like much but for those at the $1 per day poverty threshold it is equivalent to more than 3 months income.

This analysis ignores the possible draw down in the aquifer as the result of increased treadle pump usage and we do not know of any research yet undertaken to ascertain this possible environmental impact.

To further enhance the poverty reduction impact of irrigation projects, poverty reduction objectives must be given more weight than in the past. Various technologies have to be considered to achieve poverty reduction objectives as well as the more traditional objectives of raising yields and farm output. This could include choosing labor intensive methods as opposed to capital and fertilizer intensive approaches. Efficiency has to be weighed against equity perhaps by estimating the poverty reduction impact per dollar of irrigation investment. More research is necessary in order to reflect the appropriate modalities of irrigation given the distribution of the rural poor, particularly the chronically poor, the different agricultural cropping patterns that exist in each poor area and other benefits that groups can derive from irrigation and new technology.

The indirect benefits of irrigation on the livelihood of the chronically poor in rural areas is difficult to measure, particularly for groups that have been by passed or have been isolated from the rest of the rural community. The standard argument that the rising tides lifts all boats needs to be carefully assessed. While it has been observed that the introduction of new technologies in crop cultivation including genetically modified crops along with irrigation have resulted in substantial increases in rural incomes and living standards, it is not always clear how the chronically poor have benefited from these new cropping technologies and practices. These impacts need to be further documented in order to obtain a clearer picture of both the direct and indirect impacts of irrigation on chronic poverty.

5.3 Agricultural Extension and New Technologies

Agricultural extension and the adoption of new technologies and cropping systems are directed to farmers who own land and who are open to new ideas. The chronically poor, many of whom are illiterate or have limited education, will probably not be involved with the leading edge advances in agricultural science. Nevertheless some of the newer aspects of agricultural extension and cropping systems may be relevant to some chronically poor who either own a little land or who can benefit from these developments as members of the agricultural sector work force.

Globally a new development has been introduced in cropping systems called *no till* farming. One of the major challenges in Asia is to sustain and even enhance long term productivity gains in the face of continued population growth, reduction in soil fertility and growing resistance to herbicides. No till farming is a system where fields are not tilled after the harvesting of the previous crop but rather seeded immediately with plant residues and some mulching material. No till farming has the advantage of water conservation, time saving, reduced sowing and soil preparation costs, reduced reliance on tractors and burning of fossil fuels. In experiments in Haryana province in India no till farming showed no reduction in yield and a few farmers have adopted this system in India and Pakistan. One region where no-till technology has possible potential is the Indo-Ganges Plain, a region that extends from Pakistan across northern India including Afghanastan and down into Bangladesh. It includes the Nepalese Terai, areas in Pakistan and parts of the Punjab, Harayana as well as Uttar Pradesh, Bihar and West Bengal provinces and also Bangladesh. There is evidence that more farmers in India, Bangladesh and Pakistan are beginning to adopt no till farming techniques. How no till farming will impact chronic poverty is still unclear. Bihar is one of the states mentioned for possible adoption of no till farming. Since it requires double cropping of already irrigated land it is unlikely to have a substantial impact on the chronically poor right away but could have a long term impact if it raises incomes and agricultural productivity. One issue that has not yet been fully resolved is how to generate enough dung and crop residue to fuel a no till farming crop cycle as well as provide cooking fuels for rural households. Solar technology, as suggested in the section on information technology above is one possibility to address this problem (see Lal *et al.*, 2002; Soil Research, 2007; Malik *et al.*, 2004 and also www.cropscienc.org.au).

Government agricultural extension services are another way for farmers to lift productivity. Extension programs have a long history in developing countries with mixed results. There are a number of issues and problems that can reduce the effectiveness of extension services. These include difficulties in tracing the effectiveness of extension, particularly when new technology is being disseminated to farmers as well as reaching enough farmers to ensure proper dissemination of information. One of the complications is that extension services can have both public and private goods characteristics. Marketing information, cropping patterns, new varieties and recommended fertilizer, pesticide or field preparation information (for example, no till) are public goods, whereas specific information for a particular field or farm would be private information. The former information is probably best provided by extension services while the latter could also be provided by the private sector on a fee paying basis.

With widely available mass media including the internet, radio and television many farmers do not need extension services with face to face interaction as much as poorer farmers with lower levels of literacy and education. At the same time these farmers are most in need of knowledge of ways to increase yields and productivity even for small plots that they are most likely to be tilling. The scale and complexity of extension where there are many farmers with small plots (which characterized agriculture in South Asia, the Mekong and parts of Southeast Asia) is difficult to deal with. And where there are large numbers of agricultural extension field agents, centralized and hierarchical bureaucracies arise which are not particularly flexible in responding to farmers' needs. There is also typically a lack of knowledge about current research findings and best practice technology. It is often difficult to find a direct link between extension service, productivity and yield improvements. This inability to measure the impact of extension reduces incentives to "make a difference". Instead time is spent collecting data that is easier to collect but not particularly relevant to the outcome of the extension process. Furthermore extension is often under funded and workers are given additional duties that detract from their commitment to increasing yields and productivity (see Anderson and Feder, 2004, and Feder *et al.*, 1999, for additional discussion on this point).

To overcome these difficulties a number of different modalities have been tried. Some of these modalities include training and visit extension (TVE) which provides in depth training for a few farmers in a set schedule of training sessions; decentralization of the extension process by moving delivery to local governments; introduction of fees for special extension services; field schools that teach a number of aspects of agricultural ecosystems including water management, weeding, disease and pest management. These skills are then supposed to be transferred to other farmers. Such systems were implemented in Philippines and Indonesia (see Rola *et al.*, 2002, and Feder *et al.*, 2004, for details). Some of these programs were successful and others failed for a variety of reasons as discussed by Anderson and Feder (2004).

The impact of extension on the rural poor of South Asia, the Mekong countries and the Philippines and Indonesia is difficult to assess. Several studies using econometric methods have been conducted to measure the benefits of extension. Most of them focus on productivity gains as a result of the introduction of new technology and its related cost benefit analysis. High rates of return have been reported by some and disputed by others. Alston *et al.* (2000) report estimated returns to R&D of around 50 percent in Asia and 43 percent in all regions (see Anderson and Feder, 2004, and World Bank, 2008, Chapter 7, for discussion and further references). In any event none of the studies address the impact of extension on the chronically poor.

In the case of India, farmers seem to get their information about farming from other sources. Birner and Anderson (2007) report on the results of farmer surveys taken by the National Statistical Office. The percentage of farming households accessing information on modern agricultural technology are reported in Table 5.7. Extension workers are far down the list, below other progressive farmers, input dealers and the media.

Some NGOs have developed programs that distribute materials on horticulture which can easily be adapted by the chronically poor with small plots of land around their houses. Pulses, vegetables and fruit trees are possible ways to supplement income of poor families particularly when water is plentiful.

In Pakistan successive governments have adopted different approaches to agricultural extension starting with decentralization of

Table 5.7 Where Farmers Accessed Information on Modern Agricultural Technology in India

Information Source	Percent of Households Reporting
Other progressive farmers	16.7
Input dealers	13.1
Radio	13.0
Television	9.3
Newspaper	7.0
Extension service	5.7
Cooperatives	3.6
Output buyers and food processors	2.3
Government demonstration	2.0

Source: Birner and Anderson (2007, p. 7) based on date reported in National Sample Survey Organization (NSSO) (2005). Situation assessment survey of farmers: access to modern technology for farming, National sample survey 59th round Report 499 (59/33/2, New Delhi Government of India, Ministry of Statistics and Programme Implementation).

authority in the 1960s followed by integrated rural development in the 1970s and training and visit system (TVE) which stressed a systematic approach to extension by selecting certain contact farmers who were trained and revisited by government extension workers. The system focused more on richer farmers and surveys indicated that as many as 85 percent of farmers had little faith in extension (see Davidson *et al.*, 2001, p. 5). Recently the private sector has become more involved in the provision of agricultural extension services, particularly with respect to cotton. Ciba, a Swiss firm provides the bulk of agricultural extension in Pakistan, working primarily in Punjab. The Punjab is the main producer of agricultural commodities in Pakistan (83 percent of cotton, 72 percent of wheat and 95 percent of rice). According to Davidson *et al.* (2001) Ciba's extension work is biased toward large farmers since it is these farmers that buy the most inputs that Ciba sells. Extension in Baluchistan and NWFP, where the bulk of the chronically poor live, has been limited. These conclusions are supported by the work of others including Alkire

Sofranko and Khan (1992) for Northwest Frontier Province. While government extension workers have less of a large farmer bias than Ciba's extension workers there is still very little extension to the rural poor in Pakistan.

In Bangladesh agricultural extension has both government and NGO components. In a country where over 70 percent of arable land is devoted to rice farming, most of the chronically poor are rice farmers or landless farmers working for rice farmers. Forty percent of agricultural households are either categorized as landless (20 percent with less than 0.02 ha or less than 2,150 square feet) or marginal farmers (19 percent between 0.02 ha and 0.2 ha).They operate only 4 percent of the total arable area (see Bangladesh Agricultural Extension Manual, 1999). With the help of NGOs and external lenders the focus of agricultural extension for these poorest groups is on crop diversification away from grains with emphasis on horticulture and cottage industry. Generally extension is directed to larger farms and richer farmers (see Hamid and Frank, 1993.) The Grameen Bank and its affiliates have been instrumental in extending financial assistance to these small farmers. The role of the Grameen Bank and other micro-financial institutions is discussed below.

5.4 Land Reform

It is widely thought that land redistribution and/or changes in share tenancy arrangements is a powerful way to increase the share of agricultural income of poor farmers (see World Bank, 1993, and Binswanger *et al.*, 1995). However Banerjee *et al.* (2002) argue that there have been few comprehensive land reforms not involving revolutions or widespread social disruption. They analyze one such reform which was undertaken in West Bengal in the late 1970s. Other reforms in Taiwan, Korea and the Philippines have been analyzed by Putzel (2000). Besley and Burgess (1998) investigate the impact of tenancy on poverty and growth in India for 16 major states from 1958 to 1992.

Banerjee *et al.* (2002) found a highly significant impact of land reform brought about by a new government in the state of West Bengal elected in 1977 which enforced tenancy laws that regulated rents and security of tenure. Tenants were assured of permanent and inheritable rights on land they sharecropped as long as they paid their landlords at least 25 percent of output as rent. There was no transfer of land. Banerjee *et al.* (2002) found that other things equal these changes resulted in a nearly 30 percent increase in rice productivity (p. 276). These productivity gains compare favorably with the work of Sharma (1987) who analyzed changes in ownership status from tenant to owner cultivator in 8 Indian villages. He found that such changes would increase productivity by 16 percent. Putzel (2000) also reported the positive impact of land reform in both Korea and Taiwan. Results for the Philippines were not conclusive.

The analysis by Besley and Burgess (1998) considers changes in land ownership as well as modifications in tenancy relationships. They consider three alternatives

(i) regulating tenancy contracts to provide legally binding share tenancy rights as well as transfer of ownership to tenant.
(ii) abolish intermediaries who formerly worked for feudal landlords (Zamadari) and who still take a share of the crop despite legislation in most states that have abolished these intermediaries.
(iii) Implement land ceilings that require land ownership to fall within certain boundaries combined with redistribution of land above these ceilings to the landless.

Besley and Burgess (1998) found that attempts to implement land ceilings either had no or even negative impact on poverty. This was because landlords were able to spread ownership among family members by cutting large land holdings into smaller parcels. This sometimes gave them even greater leverage on the poor laborers. On the other hand changes in tenancy had a significant impact on poverty reduction as did reducing the power and output share of intermediaries. These changes in tenancy also had a positive impact on wages of agricultural workers many of whom are poor or chronically poor. There was also evidence from another related study by Banerjee and Ghatak (1996) (see also Banerjee, Gertler and Ghatak, 2002) that more secure tenancy also had a positive impact on farm investment with possible further benefits for poverty reduction. Besley and Burgess (1998) estimate that about 10 percent of the reduction in the poverty gap in India can be attributed to these land reforms over and above poverty reductions from other sources like economic growth and other policy interventions,. Besley and Burgess (1988) have compiled a comprehensive list of land reform legislation for the 16 major states and there is no evidence that land reform legislation was less ambitious or more biased toward landlords in the poorer states of India.

While there have been few land reforms that have been subject to rigorous analysis the evidence that does exist suggests that land reform that change tenancy laws and regulations that make tenure legally binding have a powerful positve impact on poverty reduction. Transfer of ownership to tenants has a similar impact to reduce poverty as does any reduction in the role of intermediaries that put a wedge between the farmer and the market.

5.5 Technological Innovation

The green revolution has brought dramatic increases in yields to farmers in Asia and other developing regions over the last four decades. These developments were spearheaded by international research centers of the Consultative Group on International Agricultural Research (CGIAR), particularly the centers in the Philippines and Mexico where semi dwarf varieties of rice and wheat respectively were developed. More than 8,000 improved crop varieties have been released since the early 1960s (see Evenson and Gollin, 2003). What is less well known is that developments since 1980 have been even more significant than in the previous 20 years. Area planted in improved varieties of rice, wheat, maize, sorghum and potatoes has increased quite dramatically, reaching the bulk of area planted as displayed in Table 5.8.

Higher yields have also kept prices from rising. Evenson and Rosegrant (2003) estimate that world cereal prices would have been 18–21 percent higher in 2000 without these improvements in yields, that over 10 million children would have been malnourished and that more forest and other fragile ecosystems would have been brought under cultivation.

Table 5.8 Area Planted with Improved Varieties as a Percent of Cropped Area

Crop	Percent of Cropped Area Planted With Improved Varieties
Rice	76
Wheat	88
Maize	60
Sorghum	68
Potatoes	75

Source: Estimated from World Bank (2008, Figure 7.1).

While originally developed for irrigated areas, new high yielding varieties have also been recently adopted to rain fed conditions. About 80 percent of the cereal area in India is now planted with high yielding varieties (mostly wheat and rice) although only 50 percent is irrigated (see http://www.indiastat.com). These advances were made possible by understanding the relationship between new varieties and the crop environment along with better crop management by farmers.

Current governmental interest and environment for research and technology in agriculture has shifted toward other priorities. The budgets for CGIAR and other research initiatives have been cut and there is widespread concern that agricultural productivity gains will be threatened. To exacerbate the problem, in the first half of 2008 prices for food grains, particularly rice began to rise with adverse effects on the chronically poor in Asia as well as other consumers. Even a small increase in rice prices can mean a substantial drop in real income, since rice purchases constitute a significant share of consumption expenditures for the poor, as much as 40 to 50 percent for poor households.

As concern mounted, the media and government officials have expressed an interest in exploring alternative solutions (see for example Bradsher and Martin, 2008). There are a number of interrelated factors that were responsible for this spike in prices including a long term imbalance between supply and demand over the past 7 or 8 years which has been partially masked by a reduction in rice stockpiles that in the middle of 2008 were at low levels (See IRRI, 2008).

Since area cultivated has not changed much, the slowdown in the growth of yields is probably the major reason why this imbalance has grown. In South Asia average yield growth decreased from just over 2 percent per year from 1970 to 1990 to 1.4 percent per year from 1990 to 2005. Similar declines were experienced in Southeast Asia. At the same time population growth has continued to rise as has the demand for rice, which is projected to increase by around 5 million tons per year in Asia. (IRRI, 2008).

The slowdown in rice yield growth is partly the result of a slowdown in the rate of public investment in agricultural research and development, primarily by international agencies such as the CGIAR institutions. Declining rice prices and comfortable buffer stocks in the 1990s led to some complacency on the part of governments responsible for funding agricultural research and development. This was reflected by slower growth in investment. Irrigation investment is not increasing much and additional irrigation infrastructure maintenance is needed. Although rice has not been directly impacted yet, the supply of grains is also threatened by the recent interest in biofuels.

In the short term natural disasters including droughts in India and China in 2002, typhoons in the Philippines in 2006 and major flooding in Bangladesh in 2007 have resulted in recent supply disruptions. There have also been outbreaks of plant hopper pests that are threatening rice crops in China, Indonesia, Japan and Korea.

To accelerate the rate of growth in rice productions cropping intensity and yields have to increase. This can be achieved by increasing the rate of irrigation and multiple cropping. However, IRRI estimates that the bulk of the increase will have to come from higher yields. A nine point program is suggested which will aid the chronically poor by keeping rice prices down and also increase incomes of the chronically poor that depend upon rice for their livelihood, either on their own small plots or as agricultural laborers working on rice paddy farms. The essential components of the IRRI program are as follows:

- Reduce yield gap between potential yield and actual yield which can be as much as 1 to 2 tons per hectare. This can be achieved by improving farmers skill in land preparation, water and nutrient management and pest and disease control.

- Improve post harvest technologies to reduce losses including storing, drying and processing of rice.
- Accelerate introduction and adoption of higher yielding rice varieties including those under development that are flood and drought resistant.
- Strengthen rice breeding and rice research activities including resistance to disease, flood, salinity and drought resistant strains (see Box 5.2).
- Increase investment in agricultural infrastructure, particularly irrigation and farm to market roads.
- Strengthen food safety nets for the poor.

Box 5.2 Rice Research to Increase Productivity

Several flood resistant rice varieties called Swarna Sub-1, IR64 Sub-1 and BR11 Sub-1 have recently been introduced by IRRI that survive despite being submerged for several days. These varieties are able to "hold their breaths" for such a long time because of a gene implanted in a high yielding Indian rice variety through conventional breeding. These new varieties will be critical in reducing flood damage to crops amounting to about 10 million hectares each year. In addition to the direct benefit to flooded crops these new varieties will reduce risk and create a secure environment for farmers that should create incentives for them to undertake additional investments that will further enhance productivity. IRRI is also developing drought resistant rice varieties that can be introduced in densely populated countries such as China, Indonesia and India. The timely use of these varieties should not be delayed and might even be accelerated by secure funding which is now being threatened. Plant hopper problems could also be addressed if IRRI funding is maintained. IRRI director Robert S Ziegler emphasized that "cutting back on agricultural research today is pure folly".

Source: Brasher and Martin (2008) and IRRI (2008).

In addition to a shift in emphasis away from agricultural research into other areas there are other, more fundamental reasons why agricultural research and development has been under funded despite the demonstrated high rates of return to such research. The World Bank (World Bank, 2008) offers three main reasons. First, public expenditure decisions are often based on short run visible payoff spending. Agricultural research is longer term and can be risky. Furthermore farmers, and particularly the chronically poor, have limited political muscle. Second, trade distortions and national policies that reduce incentives for farmers are a disincentive to both private and public investment (see Chapter 7 below for more details.) Third, because there are spillover effects of research and development spending, small countries would rather free ride on the spending of large countries. While CGIAR research centers were created to provide such spillovers the current funding crunch means that research and development programs are being under funded. It is important that the larger countries in Asia step up their efforts. China and India have been building up their public research systems and more needs to be done.

Alternatives to the traditional dissemination of innovations in agronomy and food science can also be introduced to increase the efficiency and speed of transmission of new developments. The internet is one way to spread information. Indian expertise in information technology is being used to extend agricultural information farmers. A good example is ITC Limited, traditionally a tobacco and cigarette producer that has grown into a conglomerate dealing in hotels, packaging, agribusiness, information technology, and consumer goods. ITC is developing its internationally competitive agricultural business by working with independent small farmer. It has deployed a network of internet-connected kiosks, known as e-Choupals, in many agricultural locations in India. (An e-Choupal is a high-tech version of the traditional "choupal", or "village gathering place" in Hindi). Through these e-Choupals farmers are provided with the latest weather reports, local and international produce prices, and farming best practices. These e-Choupals are not cheap, costing between $3,000 and $6,000 each to set up. In addition to providing information they also allow farmers to sell their products to ITC and allow households to buy agricultural inputs and consumer goods. ITC purchases as many as 13 agricultural commodities through these e-Choupals and bought wheat, soybeans, coffee, shrimp and pulses valued at $400 million through the network in 2006/2006 according to the World Bank 2008. More information on e-Choupals is contained in Box 5.3.

Box 5.3 ITC Limited and IT Developments in Product Marketing and Distribution

Each e-Choupal is managed by an ITC-appointed "Sanchalak", a respected farmer of the community who takes a public oath of office upon accepting the position. While ITC covers equipment costs, the day-to-day operating costs, which consist primarily of electricity and internet connection charges, are paid for by the e-Choupal Sanchalak. These costs vary depending on usage, but average about US$ 60 and US$ 160 per year respectively according to information provided by ITC on its web site Miscellaneous travel and equipment maintenance costs add another US$ 20 in yearly fixed costs. ITC, for its part, spends an average of US$ 100 annually on each kiosk, which goes toward training and infrastructure management. Such activities include maintaining a helpdesk, addressing equipment and software complaints, and repairing or replacing broken equipment.

The premise of ITC's expanded business model is backward integration, a form of virtual vertical integration that involves the direct purchase of produce from farmers, thereby reducing ITC's dependence on middlemen. In many sectors of India's unorganized economy, middlemen involved in procurement typically make large profits by blocking market and price information.

(*Continued*)

Box 5.3 (*Continued*)

Up until now they have been indispensable even so, because they compensate for infrastructure gaps along the supply chain. The e-Choupal network, by deploying IT innovatively, reorganizes the roles of these intermediaries by leveraging their strengths in physical transmission of goods, yet disintermediating them in the flow of information along the chain. In the process several non-value-adding activities in the traditional farm to factory leg of the value chain, such as redundant transportation, bagging, handling and labor, are eliminated.

This reorganization of the role of middlemen results in lower procurement costs for ITC, despite having to pay higher prices to the farmers. Transaction costs are also minimized for the farmer by buying output at the farmers' doorstep, and through transparent pricing and weighing practices. 120,000 MT of various commodities has already been procured through this channel, resulting in overall savings over a million dollars. The savings are shared between ITC and the farmer. According to company officials, the average soya farmer saves US$5 per ton of beans when he sells through the e-Choupal network. ITC, for its part, saves US$4 per ton, even after paying transportation costs.

On the marketing front, ITC is able to maintain and grow the trust of its farmers by enhancing their productivity and wealth. ITC leverages this position of trust among farmers, as well as its distribution capabilities, to market its own consumer good brands and those of partner companies offering products and services that ITC does not. Sales of consumer goods through the e-Choupals have been particularly successful because the cost-savings associated with dealing directly with the manufacturer allow Sanchalaks to offer goods at lower prices than other village-level traders or retailers can afford to do.

Through his close relationship with other farmers, the e-Choupal Sanchalak is also able to gain market information not otherwise available to a big company, such as preferences or specific needs, thus

(*Continued*)

Box 5.3 (*Continued*)

giving ITC the ability to customize products to provide increased convenience at a lower cost. Brand marketing by a trusted name (e-Choupal) in a market without brand leaders leads to improved market penetration and reduced cost of advertising new products. By cutting costs and increasing revenues both to ITC and to farmers, the e-Choupal network demonstrates the possibility of convergence between shareholder value creation and social good. This "win-win" business model helps ensure its sustainability, while also making it highly scalable.

Source: Adapted from www.digitaldividend.org/pubs/pubs_01_echoupal.htm

It should be noted that the e-Choupals are active in markets for secondary food crops and shrimp not staple grains such as wheat and rice. Nevertheless, these intermediaries seem to be playing an important role in using IT to smooth out the inefficiencies in the sale, marketing and distribution of these crops. Some chronically poor would benefit directly and even indirectly as the farmers around India benefit from the increased efficiency of this new system based on internet technology.

In another venture the MS Swaminathan Research Foundation in Pondicherry in cooperation with the Indian Space Research Organization connects villages throughout India via a satellite hub. The centers are managed by women's self help groups who receive micro credit loans to start small businesses. The self help groups also use the center to manage their business accounts and coordinate their activities using video links with other villages. Farmers can use the data base to access technical information in their local language with the help of technical experts from local agricultural institutions. An alliance of more than 80 partner institutions extends the concept through India (see MS Swaminathan Resesarch Foundation, 2005).

As noted above it is not clear how relevant these NGO/private sector initiatives are for the chronically poor. This is an important task for the future. There is a risk that without upgrading of skills, education and connectivity, the chronically poor will be left further behind as the information technology revolution requires skills that they do not have and have difficulty obtaining.

5.6 Small Scale Industry and Micro Finance

The poor, particularly the chronically poor in rural areas, have problems in smoothing consumption patterns and in being able to invest. They are unable to obtain credit from commercial banks and other formal lending institutions such as savings and loan cooperatives or rural development banks. As a result, in cases of emergency or illness or to start up a small business, they are forced to borrow from the informal sector. Money lenders, pawnshops, landlords and friends and relatives may charge higher rates of interest but they do not require collateral. As we learned in previous chapters the use of informal credit markets at high interest rates can result in financial ruin and further descent into debt and poverty traps. The poverty trap results in a chain of debt that can be sustained for generations to come and result in continued illiteracy as children are kept out of school to work.

To fill the financing gap a number of microfinance schemes have been operating in South and Southeast Asia for the past few decades. Microfinance is often directed to poor women who make small loans to start and maintain handicraft production, poultry farms and other agricultural based businesses that supplement incomes of poor families in South Asia. The Grameen Bank is the most famous of these. Its founder Mohammad Yunus was awarded the Nobel Peace Prize in 2005. There are literally hundreds of articles dealing with microfinance. Morduch (1999) has written a useful review of many of these studies from a global microfinance perspectives. He touches on a number of issues including a review of the Grameen Bank and other successful microfinance institutions, mechanisms for lending to low income households, profitability and financial sustainability, credit subsidies and the social and economic impacts of microfinance. The World Bank also reviews microfinance in connection with their thorough study of issues in the agricultural sectors of developing countries (World Bank, 2008). Aside from microfinance for ancillary agricultural activities such as handicrafts by the Grameen Bank and other microfinance institutions there is little evidence on how much microfinance addresses the needs of chronically poor families in the agricultural sector. Both Morduch (1999) and the World Bank (2008) find that microfinance (MFIs) has not yet been able to address these financial needs.

The World Bank (2008) states that

> The inadequacies of rural financial markets reflect real risks and real transaction costs that can not simply be wished or legislated away ... Many MFIs lend to local groups whose members select one another and share their liability for repaying loans ... This shared liability creates powerful incentives for peer selection and borrower monitoring ... However it works less well where all producers are subject to a common set of weather risks (when one cannot pay, often no one can pay) ... Weather risk ... undermines the financial stability of local MFIs and more explicitly limit their share of lending to agriculture to reduce exposure to risk. Moreover, many microfinance organizations have targeting criteria ... that restrict lending to agricultural activities (p. 146).

Morduch (1999) finds

> ... microfinance has yet to make real inroads in areas focused sharply on highly seasonal occupations like agricultural cultivation. Seasonality thus poses one of the largest challenges to the spread of microfinance in areas centered on rainfed agriculture, areas that include some of the poorest regions of South Asia ... (p. 1585).

and

> ... microfinance programs targeted to poor households may offer only limited benefits ... and that poorer households should be served by other interventions than credit (p. 1599–1600).

Even where agriculture yields are more predictable and less prone to yield fluctuations such as irrigated areas with double or triple cropping MFIs have not been doing much business. Of course the incidence of chronic poverty is much lower as well for farmers with irrigated land and the ability to double crop.

There are two rural development banks that have a good record in reaching out to the agricultural community. In Thailand, the Bank for Agricultural Cooperatives (BAAC) has an extensive rural network with over 500 branches and 850 field offices. BAAC makes loans to individual farmers through agricultural cooperatives and farmers associations at low interest rates. Loans for cottage industries and some non-agricultural related projects are also permitted. It's unclear how many of these loans go to the chronically poor or even the poor. BAAC says it concentrates on small and medium scale producers but there is no information available on the size of the average loan or the income status of the borrowers. There are some provisions for risk. In the case of natural calamities loans can be restructured over a longer repayment period without penalties. Repayment rates by individual farmers are lower than the defaults and arrears rates of agricultural cooperatives and farmers associations. However arrears are still unacceptably high at 12 percent (see Fitchett, 1999).

In Indonesia the Bank Rakyat Indonesia (BRI) extends micro loans to rural borrowers. BRI has 3855 outlets, mostly in rural areas servicing over 30 million small savers and 3.1 million small borrowers. Only 5 percent of the BRI portfolio is at risk from arrears or possible default. BRI lending portfolio caters to rural households who are relatively poor but above the poverty line. The average loan size is around \$500 although 60 percent of its loans are less than \$300. There was a small-scale lending product introduced in 2000 to extend lending to the poorer segments of the population but there is little information available (see Maurer, 2004.)

Is this the end of the story? What other means to evenout income streams should the chronically poor focus on? We have discussed temporary migration, extension of irrigation to previously rain fed areas or exploring alternative crops or cropping patterns such as no till or genetically modified crops that require less water as possible alternatives or solutions.

Alternatively, some rural areas have developed self-help groups at the village and district levels. There are an estimated 2.2 million groups in India that collect savings from their members and either deposit them in rural banks or lend them to members (see World Bank, 2008, p. 146). Once these groups have demonstrated a capacity to collect on loans over a six month period, the rural banks can leverage a groups' savings by a factor of four, providing additional capital that is mostly used for agricultural purposes. The self-help group is responsible for screening, processing and collection of payments which reduces banks' costs while providing additionality to the rural borrowers. The Indian self help story is an example of a recent development in the financial area — financial cooperatives.

Another saving and investment scheme that has been around for a long time is the rotating saving and credit association, typically called a ROSCA. A ROSCA is a group of individuals who group together with the mutual interest of saving and investing. The group can be ethnically, geographically or language based and has to have mutual trust in order to work well. The members make regular contributions to a common fund which is given to one member at the end of a cycle. For example each person in a group of 10 members regularly contributes $10 to a fund. At the end of 10 periods the $100 lump sum is given to a selected individual. The cycle then repeats and a second individual is given the $100 at the end of the cycle. There are three variations on how the winner of the lump sum is determined. The recepient can be decided by consensus of the members or the winner can be decided by bidding and the highest bidder receives the lump sum. Or the winner can be decided by drawing lots. With ROSCA there is no additionality. There may also be default risk when one or more members do not contribute their shares on time. Nevertheless ROSCAs are widespread in developing Asia and measures could be taken to provide insurance against fraud as well as facilitate the formation of ROSCAs in poor communities where other banking type facilities are not available.

Sri Lanka has a relatively thick network of savings and lending institutions. A survey in 2005 found that 78 percent of households had access to formal credit. A rural cooperative called SANASA has the most extensive network with over 8,000 offices and over 850,000 members, about one out of five households in the country. Transactions are not generally computerized and it is unclear how many of these borrowers are chronically poor aside from statements that a large number of loan products serving social needs are provided and that

> members are drawn from all ethnic communities and are middle to low income entrepeneurs, farmers, workers and civil servants (Nair and Kloeppinger-Todd, 2007, p. 17).

This leads one to believe that not many chronically poor are clients. Even with a richer clientele SANASA still has collection problems. 23.5 percent of loans were past due in 2004.

Insurance is one alternative that has been suggested but which has so far gotten little traction in reducing chronic poverty. If poor farmers could insure themselves against crop failures and other emergencies there would be no need to borrow and risk falling into a cycle of chronic poverty and debt. Lack of capital is a constraint to insurance because the chronically poor don't have the resources to pay premiums. Dercon, Bold and Calvo (2008) discuss the various problems and challenges facing programs that seek to insure the poor. Costs of administration are high, potential losses are hard to quantify because of data problems and the poor have limited ability to pay the required premiums to attract private insurance companies. Covariant risks, i.e. the chance that many insured will file claims at the same time, are also high in the case of drought or floods. Mutual insurance is a way to pool risks although systemic risks when crops fail may reduce the payout or bankrupt the insurer. Microfinance institutions can help by collecting small amounts which can serve either as saving or as payment of insurance premiums against crop failure or even health and disability insurance. The development of even these rather unsophisticated insurance modalities is limited although there are successful cases where NGOs played a critical role in the process (see World Bank, 2008, p. 148).

In India a micro finance company BASIX serves as an intermediary between insurance companies and its clients purchasing unsubsidized weather insurance. While individual poor farmers are unable to afford the insurance premium a large group of farmers together can offset some crop loss risks. See Brown and Churchill (2000) and Dercon *et al.* (2005) for further suggestions regarding how governments could support insurance schemes for the poor.

A variety of imaginative and innovative ideas have been suggested for mobilizing savings of the poor although it is again unclear how the chronically poor would ever be able to save much. These schemes could be packaged with micro credit for the more well to do poor or as a separate financial service. The latter is currently being tried by BRI and Grameen Bank. This saving serves as a cheap source of funds for relending as well as a way for the poor to build collateral. However these programs and ideas are still in the experimental stages and currently there are no plans to scale them up to meet the needs of the chronically poor on a larger scale.

5.7 Returns to Alternative Infrastructure Investment — A Summary

Using the results of their previous work Thorat and Fan (2007) have analyzed the relative returns to rural government spending on infrastructure in India, China Thailand and Vietnam. Their results are summarized in Tables 5.9, 5.10 and 5.11.

While there is some variation in the rates of returns to different infrastructure investment schemes, there are five major conclusions that can be drawn from this comparative analysis of public invesments in India, China, Thailand and Vietnam by Fan and his colleagues. First, investment in the less developed regions of China and India offer the largest poverty reduction impact per unit of spending as well as the highest rate of economic return per unit of investment. This result suggests that a much more focused and clearer regional perspective of investment priorities is called for. Particular emphasis should be put on the rainfed areas of India and the areas of China that are less fertile and not well irrigated.

Second, the direct impact of anti poverty programs are weak and their indirect impact in the agricultural sector are also ineffective

Table 5.9 Returns to Rural Government Spending in India — State Level Analysis

Program	Return in Rupees Per Rupee Spent	Number of Poor Reduced Per Million Rupees Spent
Research & Development	13.45	84.5
Irrigation		9.7
Roads		123.8
Education		4.1
Power		3.8
Soil & water conservation		22.6
Health		25.5
Anti-poverty programs		17.8

Source: Fan, Hazell and Thorat (1999).

Table 5.10 Marginal Returns to Public Investment in Rural India — District Level Analysis of Number of Poor Lifted out of Poverty Per Unit of Investment

Type of Investment	Irrigated Areas	High Potential Rainfed Areas	Low Potential Rainfed Areas
High yielding varieties per Ha	0	0.02	0.05
Roads in km	1.57	3.50	9.51
Canal irrigation per Ha	0.01	0.23	0.09
Private irrigation per Ha	0.01	–0.15	0.30
Electrificaiton per Ha	0.01	0.07	0.10
Education per worker	0.01	0.23	0.01

Source: Fan, Hazell and Thorat (1999).

Table 5.11 Returns to Agricultural Investment in China — Provincial Level Analysis of Number of Poor Reduced Per 10,000 Yuan Expenditure

Type of Investment	Coastal	Central	Western	Average
R&D	1.99	4.4	33.12	6.79
Irrigation	0.55	0.77	4.04	1.33
Roads	0.83	3.61	10.73	3.22
Education	2.73	5.38	28.66	8.8
Electricity	0.76	1.65	6.17	2.27
Telephone	0.6	0.75	1.94	2.21
Poverty loan	0.88	0.75	1.49	1.13

Source: Fan, Zhang and Zhang (2002).

Table 5.12 Returns to Public Investment in Agricultural Production — Relative Ranking in China, India, Thailand and Vietnam

Type of Investment	China	India	Thailand	Vieitnam
Agricultural R&D	1	1	1	1
Irrigation	5	4	5	4
Education	2	3	3	3
Roads	3	2	4	2
Telecomms	4			
Electricity	6	8	2	
Health		7		
Soil and water conservation		6		
Anti-poverty programs		5		

Source: Fan, Zhang and Zhang (2002), Fan, Hazell and Thorat (1999), Fan, Jitsuchon and Methakunnavut (2002) and Hao and Fan (2001).

Table 5.13 Returns to Public Investment in Reducing Poverty — Relative Ranking in China, India, Thailand and Vietnam

Type of Investment	China	India	Thailand	Vietnam
Agricultural R&D	2	2	2	3
Irrigation	6	7	5	4
Education	1	3	3	1
Roads	3	1	3	2
Telecomms	5			
Electricity	4	8	1	
Health		6		
Soil and water conservation		5		
Anti-poverty programs		4		

Source: Fan, Zhang and Zhang (2002), Fan, Hazell and Thorat (1999), Fan, Jitsuchon and Methakunnavut (2002a) and Hao and Fan (2001).

because of poor project selection. Better targeting of these programs is required if they are to make a substantial impact on poverty reduction. In particular, better focus on education of the chronically poor is required along with better targeting of rural infrastructure. Expansion of water resources for the poor is also critical.

Third, research and development yielded the highest rate of return for agricultural production in all four countries and was second highest in three countries when it comes to poverty reduction. This suggests that further R&D with focus on the chronically poor in by-passed areas would yield high returns in raising output in the agricultural sector and in reducing poverty.

Fourth, roads yielded the next highest rates of poverty reduction and were also effective in raising agricultural production. As we have seen above road investments are also instrumental in increasing connectivity between isolated rural locations and in stimulating rural to urban migration.

Fifth, education yielded the highest rate of poverty reduction in China and Vietnam and was ranked third in India and Thailand. This result is consistent with our findings in Chapter 4, where particular emphasis on elementary education for the poorest groups was stressed.

Other investment projects in irrigation placed far down the list, although it scored well in the poorer western section of China and in low potential rainfed areas of India. Electricity and health investments along with soil conservation also ranked low both in rates of return to investment and in poverty reduction impact. Better focus on the chronically poor is required for these investments to be profitable either by raising output in the agicultural sector or in reducing poverty, or both.

Chapter 6

Macroeconomic Policies to Reduce Chronic Poverty

6.1 Introduction

There is ample evidence that rapid economic growth results in a decline in poverty. See for example, Dollar and Kray (2001 and 2001a), Roemer and Gugerty (1997) and World Bank (1993). The World Bank (2000) and Ravallion and Chen (1997) conclude that on average one percent of growth will bring about a 2 to 3 percent reduction in the number of people living below the poverty line (see also IFPRI, 2007, Chapter 4). The Dollar and Kray paper and the Roemer and Gugerty paper conclude that once the impact of economic growth on poverty has been taken into account there are no other measurable impacts on poverty from other macroeconomic variables.

In a broader context, analysis of economic growth through either neoclassical production functions or extensions of the Solow model by Mankiw, Romer and Weil (1992) and Lucas (1990) among others conclude that growth is determined by a combination of factors including labor, capital and total factor productivity. Mankiw *et al.* (1992) and Lucas (1990) both highlight the importance of human capital in augmenting the ability of labor to raise productivity and economic growth. Barro and Sala-i-Martin (1995) provide a useful summary of the empirical evidence that throws light on the process of economic growth.

Several studies of the effects of economicl growth on poverty in developing countries have been conducted for large cross section panels of developing economies, including East Asia and South Asia. Studies by Ghura *et al.* (2002), Collier and Dollar (2001) and Easterly and Fisher (2001) argue that other macro variables aside from economic growth have an impact on poverty reduction. Easterly and Fisher (2001) find inflation has a negative impact on poverty by reducing the value of real consumption of the poor. Higher prices for food stuffs are particularly burdensome on the poor since such a large proportion of their consumption is for food. The same conclusion has also been reached by Ravallion and Datt (2002), Cardoso (1992); and more recently by Martin and Ivanic (2008), who analyzed household surveys and found that the poor are adversely affected in seven out of the nine countries studied.

After examining a broad cross-section of developing countries Ghura *et al.* (2002) found that in addition to inflation, the level of financial development and level of schooling and educational attainment are important determinants of poverty reduction. They also concluded that human capital on its own plays a critical role in poverty reduction in addition to its separate impact on poverty through more rapid economic growth. Mallick (2008) found extension of bank credit to agriculture and higher levels of government spending on economic development are also important factors in poverty reduction.

A recent study by Gill and Kharas (2006) focuses more on East Asia. They argue that while the rapid development of this region (including the NIEs and Southeast Asian economies to include the Mekong countries but excluding South Asia) has resulted in a sharp reduction in poverty over the past decade and a half, a divide has arisen that runs the risk of creating a further spread between the rich and the poor. This development divide, while articulated by Gill and Kharas for the East Asian region, also applies to South Asia as well. The arguments are familiar and echo many of the issues that we have been discussing in previous chapters of this book. As an example consider China in the decade of the 1990s where the income of the richest 1 percent of the population grew nearly 4 times faster than the income of the poorest 1–11 percent per annum versus 3 percent per annum (see Chen and Wang, 2001).

To address this developmental divide Gill and Kharas stress the importance of enhancing education and health opportunities for the poor. This is crucial for the poor so they are able to compete for jobs that require greater skill and education as the information technology revolution spreads through the region. Gill and Kharas also mention the further development of credit market for the poorer segments of society to address the challenges of small businesses and consumer financing to facilitate consumption smoothing and avoid burdensome consumer debt. They also investigate problems with the growing gap between the rich and poor by lagging and possibly geographically isolated regions in western China, the eastern provinces of the Philippines, mountainous areas of Vietnam and poor regions within countries in East Asia. Infrastructure projects are needed to provide greater connectivity for these regions. Furthermore Gill and Kharas stress the importance of building up social protection as well as providing mechanisms for poor farmers and others in rural areas to be able to migrate to small urban areas or larger cities.

Following this line of thought, Ravallion (2007) has argued that growth has less of an impact on reducing poverty in economies where income inequality is high. This means that in countries where the development gap is greater, the poorest have the least share of resources and are less likely to benefit from economic growth. It also means that growth will have a more powerful impact on poverty when macroeconomic policies are in place that redistribute income and when the poor are given access to better jobs or more education.

In another recent publication the World Bank refocused its attention on agricultural development from a global perspective (World Bank, 2008) and reviews the relationship between agricultural development and poverty. The report stresses the importance of shifting some spending from industry and urban areas to the rural and agriculture sector. The report concludes that agriculture was a key factor in reducing rural poverty in both India and China Sustained growth in agricultural production and yields were the main ingredient for poverty reduction in both countries. The World Bank also found that industrial growth was not a key ingredient in sustaining poverty reduction in either country. The World Bank (2008) does point out that recent reforms in India were not directed towards agriculture and as a result the reduction in rural poverty has slowed. There are also regional issues that have to be addressed when speaking of poverty reduction in both China and India. These are addressed in Chapter 7.

Aside from inflation, trade openness might be the only "pure" macroeconomic policy that has a direct impact on poverty. The prevailing belief of international donors including the World Bank and the IMF is that the opening up of the trade regime through lower tariff barriers and stimulation of the flow of foreign direct investment is beneficial for economic growth and for poverty reduction. Evidence to support the importance of trade openness on economic growth is persuasively argued by Dollar and Kraay (2001). From a broad cross section analysis of developing countries they estimated that increases in the trade share of GDP from 20 percent to 40 percent over a decade would raise real GDP per capita by 10 percent. For example if a country with a trade share of 20 percent and 1 percent growth were to raise its trade share to 40 percent, it would also raise growth to 2 percent.

Of course these are only notional examples. Most countries have not raised their share of trade by so much in such a short period of time. Nevertheless the impact of trade on economic growth is strong and compelling (see Berg and Krueger, 2002). Berg and Krueger also argue that there is no evidence that the poor would be either better off or worse off than the average citizen as a result of trade openness although there might be specific cases where the poor are either helped or hindered. Berg and Krueger did find that poor countries with small home markets may benefit the most from trade liberalization. There may also be some spillovers from openness to the extent it can encourage institutional reform and reduce corruption by raising the level of competition and probity.

With regard to the Asian economies, Topalova (2007) found that rural areas in India with high concentrations of industries disproportionately affected by tariff reductions experienced slower progress in poverty reduction. This is because in the short run labor is immobile across geographic districts in India. Internal migration in India is also inhibited by rigid labor laws in the formal manufacturing sector. Although there is selective migration of the chronically poor and poor, the overall rate of migration is not that high (around 20 percent of rural residents have changed residence at least once in their lifetime) and the data revealed that most migrants were women who relocate at marriage. When migration movements in the past ten years were sampled only 3 to 4 percent of rural residents reported migrating and less that 1 percent moved for economic reasons. This is despite the growing disparity in incomes across states in the past two decades.

Clearly there has been strong growth in income in Asia since 1990 along with a significant reduction in the overall level of poverty as displayed in Table 6.1. Despite the strong relationship between poverty reduction and income growth in Asia in this 15 year period income growth alone does not fully account for the reduction in poverty. There are still some aspects of poverty reduction that remain unexplained. For example how did Indonesia achieve such a dramatic reduction in poverty in the face of modest GDP growth? In percentage terms the reduction in poverty was higher than any other country in Asia including China. Yet its GDP growth rate ranked 7th out of 12 countries sampled. Sri Lanka is another puzzle. It ranked third

Table 6.1 GDP Growth and Poverty Reduction in Asia 1990–2005

Country	Poverty Head Count Ratio 1990 Dollar a Day	Poverty Head Count Ratio 2005 Dollar a Day	GDP Growth 1990–2000	GDP Growth 2000–2005
Bangladesh	53	36	4.8	5.2
India	36	26	6.0	6.2
Nepal	41	24	4.9	2.5
Pakistan	26	17	3.8	4.1
Sri Lanka	26	6	5.3	3.7
China	31	9	10.6	9.4
Cambodia	32	17	7.1	6.3
Indonesia	21	4	4.2	4.6
Laos	53	20	6.5	6.0
Philippines	19	11	3.4	3.9
Thailand	13	2	4.2	5.4
Vietnam	51	8	7.9	7.2

Source: Gill and Kharas (2006, Table 6.1), World Bank (2008a).

behind China and Indonesia in terms of poverty reduction yet it was racked with civil strife and managed a growth rate just above Indonesia for the period from 1990 to 2005. The third puzzle is India, with the lowest percentage reduction in poverty of only 28 percent over the 15 year period reported while at the same time achieving rather robust growth of just over 6 percent per annum. This rate of growth ranked fourth in the Asian region behind the four socialist states of China, Vietnam, Cambodia and Laos.

These puzzles of growth and poverty reduction will be addressed in more detail in Chapter 7. For now we will consider several policy issues from either the macroeconomic or sector point of view that promote growth and at the same time address poverty alleviation/reduction. They augment growth as factors impacting on poverty and chronic poverty. We focus our attention on India primarily as a case in point for South Asia. Other countries in the region are experiencing similar challenges.

6.2 Infrastructure[7]

We discussed the components of infrastructure investment in Chapter 5. In this section we look at the oveall pace of investment with particular reference to India and China. Infrastructure spending in India has lagged behind that of China over the past 15 years although India had higher stocks of infrastructure in terms of power, roads and telecommunications in the 1980s. By 2003, China's infrastructure had outstripped India by a large margin. From 1990 to 2000, China's installed power capacity increased by 136 percent compared with 51 percent in India. Road investment and telecommunications in China also exceeded investment in India. Power outages in India are estimated to cause over 8 percent loss in sales volumes for manufacturers compared with an estimated 2 percent in China. Over 60 percent of Indian manufacturing firms own generators compared with 27 percent in China. Power costs are nearly 40 percent higher in India compared with China. The infrastructure constraint is borne most heavily by

[7] This and the next two subsections are based on World Bank (2006d).

exporters of manufactured goods. India's share of global trade in goods in services is around 2.5 percent. China's share is over four times larger at 10.5 percent. Despite these difficulties, India's mix of exports is very high quality, similar to countries with per capita income nearly five times higher (Hausmann *et al.*, 2005).

While it has a talented and rich labor pool, India will have to improve its transport and production capabilities in order to compete in the growing dominance of firms operating in a complex network of supply chains. These networks are characterized by firms which source production inputs to final products from many different countries. Margins are low and competition is stiff and high transport costs can serve to offset the advantages of a skilled work force and low wages. There is substantial potential for Indian manufacturers becoming players in these markets if transport bottlenecks and labor markets constraints (see below) can be overcome. These markets require semi-skilled labor that could be drawn from the lower income groups, although perhaps not the chronically poor.

In telecommunications India is still far behind China in the number of fixed lines. However it has developed a rapidly growing cell phone and internet capability that has synergies with its growing global power in telecommunications. Here the role of private public partnerships can be useful for further infrastructure expansion and bringing these communications to the chronically poor as well as to the business community.

The lag in infrastructure spending, paticularly in remote and by-passed areas where chronic poverty is high, may also account for some of the shortfall in progress in reducing chronic poverty in India. Financing infrastructure spending particularly for roads and power in India will be a challenge and will require imaginative solutions requiring users to pay for services and greater participation of the private sector in financing infrastructure projects.

6.3 Fiscal Deficits and Fiscal Adjustment

While it has come down in recent years the fiscal deficit in India remains large at 7 to 8 percent of GDP due to an increase in government debt.

To some extent the acceleration in growth reduces the danger of a financial crisis that a large deficit may pose to a less vibrant economy; it still poses a problem for a government that has so many spending priorities that need to be addressed. India's ratio of public debt to GDP is around 80 percent, substantially higher than China's. The big question is how India is going to finance greater capital investment as well as development spending while keeping the deficit in check. One approach is to increase the efficiency of delivery of public service, by reducing corruption, simplifying the tax code and at the same time broadening the tax base (on corruption see Dowling, 2008, Chapter 5). This is a tall order that needs to be addressed if growth in India is to continue at high rates. Salary savings have been suggested by Howes and Murgai (2004) particularly for lower level civil servants. Subsidies are both inefficient and regressive and need to be redirected or eliminated. The food subsidies on rice and wheat are largely spent on storage and the subsidies themselves go primarily to Haryana, Punjab and Andhra Pradesh. Farmers in these states receive subsidies and guaranteed sales that are much higher than in other states where the governments purchasing agent, the Food Corporation of India, is not active. Generally little progress has been made in making the general thrust of the subsidy program redirected towards the poor. This is not unexpected since once in place subsidies are hard to remove.

6.4 Labor Laws

Flexible labor markets are important to ensure the ability of firms to adjust quickly to changing patterns of production and demand as well as adopt new technology. This is particularly important in manufacturing for export where there is intense international competition and dynamic innovation. Investment surveys and labor market research suggest that the Indian labor laws are complex and restrictive. A World Bank research (World Bank, 2004) of large firms employing more than 100 workers, consider labor regulations equal to power shortages as key constraints to their operations and the investment climate in India. An ILO (2004) suggests that labor laws have been

> criticized as being ad hoc, complicated, mutually inconsistent, if not contradictory, lacking in uniformity of definitions and riddled with clauses that become outdated and anachronistic (ILO, 2004).

Court decisions create uncertainty about how labor laws are interpreted and many observers contend that regulations prevent new jobs from being created and serve only to protect the jobs of existing workers. The labor law environment should protect the interests of all workers rather than the small number of workers, about 7 percent of the work force, already employed in the formal sector. Restrictive labor laws are particularly burdensome to small and medium scale industries and create diseconomies of scale and raise costs. For example, in the textile industry, manufacturers often set up multiple small plants instead of a single large operation in order take advantage of more lax labor laws governing small operations. As a result Indian textile plants have lower capacity than Chinese plants and hence operate at lower efficiency and higher costs. Compared to other countries there are smaller firms in India than in other countries whch could be more efficient if they were operating at the economically optimal plant size (see Mazumdar, 2005). These laws protect only a few well paid salary workers that earn around 30 percent more than a similarly qualified casual worker of the same age and experience. Such a dualistic system also perpetuates discrimination against women and SC and ST workers. The labor market distortion shows up as a shrinking premium between wages for casual urban labor and casual rural labor. The convergence in these two markets is resulting in fewer incentives for rural workers to migrate to urban areas for better jobs. This in turn keeps pressure on the rural economy and tends to perpetuate existing poverty traps and low living standards for the rural poor and chronically poor. Without the urban migration safety valve future prospects will be even dimmer.

What is needed is a labor law code that protects the rights of all workers and provides for a salary scale that rewards workers based on the value of their marginal product as determined by their skill, education and experience. Such a system will allow firms to operate at their most efficient plant capacity, lower costs, increase competitiveness and scale of production. It will also reduce discrimination against those who are qualified and eliminate the premium currently being paid to those already employed. It will raise average wages in urban areas as it stimulates the industrial sector, particularly if combined with reforms that reduce the cost of power and relax other infrastructure constraints. As this process unfolds the chronically poor, particularly those with enough skill and education to qualify for jobs, will be drawn into higher paying occupations in the newly energized industrial sector.

While national labor regulations have been the focus of attention the bulk of regulations are at the state level (47 national versus 157) and there is scope for reform there as well. A few states including Gujarat and Andhra Pradesh have begun the reform process while others let companies evade the laws by using contract labor. The number of strikes and lock outs has also decreased. While labor laws do not need to be completely overhauled. there are strong incentives to undertake reforms at both the state and national level (see Economist, 2008c).

6.4.1 *Minimum wage laws*

Minimum wage laws exist for formal sector employees in developed economies and in some developing countries. In Asia there are few minimum wage standards in the informal sector where many are self employed or employed by landlords who are not covered by minimum wage legislation While minimum wage legislation in developing countries does not target the chronically poor, it is useful to review some of the evidence regarding the impact of minimum wage legislation on poverty to see if there are any indirect impacts of such legislation on the chronically poor.

Analysis of the impact of minimum wage legislation on poverty has been conducted by several authors. Lustig and McLeod (1997) investigate the relationship between minimum wages and poverty for a cross section of developing countries including India, Indonesia, Philippines, Sri Lanka and Thailand in Asia and 18 other countries mostly in Latin America. Contrary to the World Bank view (World Bank, 1995) that minimum wages do not protect the poor in developing countries, Lustig and McLeod (1997) find that an increase in minimum wage is accompanied by a fall in the rate of poverty. Additional support for this view is provided by Saget (2001) who found a strong positive effect of minimum wage legislation on poverty in Thailand and the Philippines. In his model raising the minimum wage by 1 percent implied a reduction in poverty of 0.46 percent. In Latin America, Maloney and Nunez (2001) found a "demonstration effect" where mininum wage legislation in the formal sector seems to provide a "fair" benchmark for remuneration in both sectors.

Theoretical evidence for this positive relationship between minimum wage legislation and poverty reduction is provided by general equilibrium analysis which argues that in small open economies a rise in formal sector wages causes a reduction in profits and the rate of return to investment in the formal sector. Capital investment shifts to the informal sector driving up wages and employment. While there are many caveats to this sort of analysis (see Lustig and McLeod, 1997, and Leamer, 1995) the empirical analysis of Lustig and McLeod (1997) supports these theoretical results and it is also consistent with the argument put forward by Card and Krueger (1995) that if formal sector labor demand is inelastic in a Harris-Todaro type model then formal sector wage increases can drive up wages in the informal sector. In a related paper, Dessing (2004) argues that when the labor — supply response is negative at low wages, raising minimum wages may work to reabsorb this excess supply of labor and stabilize the labor market. In these circumstances minimum wage policies could work to increase wages in both formal and informal sectors. Dessing cites evidence from Costa Rica to support this argument.

Another possibility is that employers are monopsonistic and pay workers less than the value of their marginal product and so they hire up to the point where the marginal cost of labor equals their demand for labor. This type of labor market is typical of poor countries where the supply of unskilled labor exceeds labor demand. In these circumstances minimum wage laws can increase aggregate employment (see Alatas and Cameron, 2003). Devereux (2005) also argues that since low paying sectors are characterized by poor working conditions and negligible benefits, minimum wage legislation should be complemented by policies to improve working conditions.

Within the formal sector Harrison and Scorse (2005) find that pressure to raise wages for unskilled workers in the textile, footwear and apparel industries in Indonesia during the early and mid-1990s (before the Asian financial crisis) resulted in an increase in real wages of 20 percent. The effects of minimum wage legislation and anti-sweatshop lobbying was most effective in multinational plants while there was no reduction in employment, perhaps because of the high mark up on these products, particularly brand names like Nike. Negative employment impacts might be greater in more competitive markets where markups are not as high, brand loyalty is not as strong and labor costs are a larger proportion of the final product price.

Taken together these results suggest that in particular circumstances minimum wage legislation can result in a win-win outcome where wages for the poor increase without a commensurate reduction in employment. How these results impact the chronically poor is difficult to ascertain. There may be spillovers into labor markets in the informal sector as suggested by Lustig and McLeod (1997) and Leamer (1995). There may also be demonstration effects as knowledge of the salutary relationship between minimum wage legislation and poverty spreads to policy makers and other decision makers translating into greater lobbying for higher wages by the poor and greater receptivity on the part of employers. To ensure that minimum wage legislation is appropriate in particular circumstances Devereux (2005) suggests a checklist for ensuring that minimum wages have the intended poverty impact while minimizing side effects. They include:

1. Adopting minimum wage legislation in markets where there is chronic poverty and an excess supply of unskilled labor.
2. Employees earn less than the value of their marginal product.
3. Labor demand is relatively inelastic so that raising wages does not result in loss of employment.
4. Uncovered sectors are not adversely affected as might happen if

workers displaced from covered sectors drive down wages in uncovered sectors.

5. Compliance with minimum wage legislation is monitored and enforced by the government.

6.5 Financial Sector

We have already discussed the role of informal and micro finance as it pertains to the chronically poor. From the point of view of the formal banking system it is important to improve the delivery of financial services to small and medium sized businesses. The ratio of private credit to GDP is much lower in India than in other Asian economies (40 percent compared with over 100 percent in China, Korea and Malaysia). Only a little over half of small businesses have active credit lines. Credit appraisal mechanisms are weak, the legal framework for loan recovery, bankruptcy and contract enforcement are also weak and credit checks are minimal. As a result it is difficult to assess the risks of lending to small businesses. Because of these weaknesses and the continued strength of informal lenders in rural towns, banks have a limited presence in rural India. Fewer than 40 percent of rural households have a bank account and the figures are probably much smaller for the rural poor and chronically poor Reform of the Indian financial sector will go a long way towards helping the chronically poor to enter mainstream financial life, particularly if these reforms include contract enforcement for the poor, better credit information and laws regulating financial transactions of the poor as well as the non poor. Similar reforms should also be adopted in other Asian economies in order to give the chronically poor better access to the formal banking and credit system and not have to rely on money lenders and the informal credit system.

6.6 Government Development Spending

Some details of government spending and poverty were discussed previously in Chapter 2. Here we investigate the impact of different components of development spending on poverty as well as the distribution of the federal government's spending across different provinces or states in individual countries.

The International Food Policy Research Institute (IFPRI) has assembled a data set for Bangladesh, China, India, Malaysia, Myanmar, Nepal, Philippines, Sri Lanka, South Korea and Thailand that shows total government spending increased at an average rate of 5.7 percent between 1980 and 1990 and 9.1 percent between 1990 and 2000. This represents a significant rise in public spending growth compared with earlier years. Education spending had the highest share of total government spending, at 12 percent followed closely by defense (8 percent) and agriculture (7 percent) (see Fan *et al.*, 2008). Because agriculture spending is important in the rural sector it is noteworthy that agriculture expenditures rose at a rate of 4.2 percent in the past two decades (between 1988 and 2008), a healthy rate of increase that helped fund programs to raise agricultural output and productivity. China and Thailand both spent the equivalent of 11 percent of agricultural GDP on the sector.

However spending allocations to agriculture in other countries in Asia such as Bangladesh, Sri Lanka, Nepal and Indonesia and Myanmar have fallen both as a percent of the total national budget or in terms of agriculture GDP. This is a worrisome trend which we will come back to later in this chapter and also in Chapter 8. Another important aspect of government spending for agriculture is the allocation of resources devoted to research and development. Agricultural economists suggest a benchmark of spending such that one percent of agricultural gross domestic product (or value added by agriculture) should be devoted to research and development in order to sustain growth in productivity over time. This is the case in many industrial countries even though agriculture is a now a small fraction of the overall economy in these nations. Table 6.2 shows that in Asia only Malaysia has reached that benchmark and most countries fall far short. Most countries in Asia are devoting between 0.2 and 0.5 percent of agricultural sector GDP to research and development.

Table 6.2 Agricultural Research and Development Expenditure 2002

Country	Percent of Agricultural GDP Devoted to R&D
Bangladesh	0.4
China	0.5
India	0.4
Indonesia	0.25
Laos	0.3
Malaysia	2.0
Nepal	0.3
Pakistan	0.275
Philippines	0.45
Sri Lanka	0.5
Vietnam	0.2

Source: Nienke and Steds (2002).

We begin our discussion of government development spending with India. Table 6.3 displays the ranking by state for GDP per capita, poverty and several human development indicators. The table also displays the ranking by per capita development expenditures in 1970 and 1993. The poorest states have the lowest Human Development Index rankings as well as the lowest levels of per capita development spending. The latter has changed relatively little in over twenty years. Rich states grow faster and are able to increase the tax base more rapidly and to raise the level of government spending on a per capita basis.

This pattern of spending pays little attention to poverty and is similar to the thinking of agricultural economists such as Binswanger Kandker and Rosenzweig (1989) who believe that governments allocate more resources to areas with high potential than low potential. By placing efficiency over equity what this has done is to ensure that the poorest states received fewer funds than richer states resulting in a continuing growth in the gap between richest and poorest states. Despite this bias there are a couple of anomalies. Maharastra is the

Table 6.3 Indian State Rankings by Per Capita Income, Human Development Index, Per Capita Development Expenditures and Under Weight Children

State	Rank by Gross State Domestic Product Per Capita 1999	Human Development Index Rank 2001	Per Capita Development Spending Rank 1970	Per Capita Development Spending Rank 1993	Underweight Children Rank 1998/99-Percent Under 3 Years Old
Bihar	13	13	13	14	11
Orissa	12	10	11	10	12
Uttar Pradesh	11	12	12	13	10
Madhya Pradesh	10	11	11	9	13
Rajasthan	9	8	8	8	9
West Bengal	8	7	10	12	7
Andhra Pradesh	7	9	9	4	4
Kerala	7	1	6	9	1
Karnataka	6	6	6	4	5
Tamil Nadu	5	2	5	3	3
Haryana	4	4	4	7	2
Gujarat	3	5	1	2	6
Punjab	2	1	2	6	1
Maharastra	1	3	2	1	8

Sources: World Bank (2006e) and Fan, Hazell and Thorat (1999).

richest state yet has a high incidence of underweight children because of the disparity between Mumbai and the much poorer eastern villages in the state. Also the success of Kerala in attaining high human development achievements should be noted despite only average income and government spending per capita.

Fan *et al.* (1999) estimated a simultaneous equation system to explore the interaction between government spending, technology, infrastructure, productivity, rural employment and wages and poverty for India. Their model used annual data from 1970 to 1997 and employed a number of lagged relationships to capture the response of poverty to changes in rural investment and other infrastructure variables. They found that research and development spending for agriculture along with rural road investment provide the most effective way of reducing poverty in the Indian states. They were also able to measure the impact of development spending on total factor productivity. Road investment had a number of secondary effects on rural development in addition to its direct impact on poverty.

These results of Fan *et al.* (1999) echo the discussion on road infrastructure spending and its impact on poverty in Chapter 4. Roads improve agricultural efficiency and productivity and raise rural wages as a result. Agricultural prices are lowered as a result of increased productive efficiency and lower costs. There are also salutary impacts of wages and employment. The total productivity impact on poverty arises from the direct impact of roads on raising income (about 75 percent of the total) while the remaining 25 percent from lower agricultural prices (15 percent) and increased wages (10 percent). Research and development spending has a somewhat smaller impact on poverty probably because it has not been targeted toward the poor. Still it has an impact through improved productivity. It is estimated that an additional 1 million rupees spent on R&D would result in an increase in TFP by almost 7 percent and reduce rural poverty by 0.5 percent.

The Fan *et al.* (1999) study does not address the issue of chronic poverty directly but it provides additional and compelling evidence of the importance of infrastructure spending in reducing chronic poverty. We should also mention that Fan *et al.* found that education also had a significant impact on reducing poverty, primarily through increased employment and higher wages. Rural development and irrigation spending had smaller impacts on poverty. Public irrigation spending did raise productivity and provided some stimulus for additional private investment in irrigation. Spending on power had a minimal impact on poverty reduction, perhaps because poor villages continue to fall outside the power grid as noted above in our discussion of the power sector. The clear message from the careful work of Zhang *et al.* (2002) and Fan *et al.* (1999) and Fan *et al.* (2008) is that reorientation of infrastructure spending toward the poorer states of India is a high priority in the fight to reduce chronic poverty.

In other work by IFPRI staff, similar results on the impact of government spending on poverty are observed although the order of importance may vary (see Zhang and Zhang, 2002; Fan and Chan-Kang, 2005; Fan, Brzeska and Shields, 2008). For China government expenditure on education has the largest impact on reducing rural poverty as well as regional inequality. Education spending also had a significant impact on growth in agricultural production. Agriculture spending on research and development had the most significant impact on agricultural production growth and a secondary impact by reducing rural poverty. Government spending on rural infrastructure, particularly roads (see below) and also telecommunications and electricity, impacted poverty primarily by boosting rural wages and opening up opportunities for non-farm employment. Investment in the western region of China, where chronic poverty rates are higher than in the rest of the country, tended to reduce regional inequality while similar investments in the coastal provinces exacerbated inequality. In a related study rural road investment was found to have much higher cost benefit ratios — four times — than high grade urban roads. Investment in rural roads also had extremely high returns. Every yuan invested in these rural roads yielded more than a 5 yuan increase in non-farm GDP.

In Vietnam investment in education had the highest return followed by roads. These investments both raised non farm employment opportunities which had a significant salutary impact on poverty reduction (see Zhang and Zhang, 2002, for details). The results for

Thailand are somewhat different from the impact studies in India, China and Vietnam. While agricultural research and development expenditure and road investments were important drivers of poverty reduction in Thailand (second and third in order of importance), investment in rural electrification had the highest impact on rural poverty and the second largest impact on growth. Power and electrification had minimal impacts on poverty in China, India and Vietnam studied by IFPRI. Rural electrification and secondary road construction in the northeast of Thailand were instrumental in reducing the level of poverty and chronic poverty in this region. The lesson from the Thai experience is that well positioned infrastructure investments of all kinds can be beneficial in reducing chronic poverty if they are appropriately designed and targeted.

In Pakistan, economic returns to education are high and further investment should yield consistent payoff since educational attainment is significantly below India and Sri Lanka. (see World Bank, 2007a, and discussion in Chapter 2). Irrigation investment also plays a key role in the development strategy of Pakistan, including water pricing issues related to water logging and salinity. Returns to investment in irrigation and to agricultural research in this area should also have a high payoff.

In order to achieve infrastructure upgrading to address needs discussed in this section further funding will have to be made available in government budgets, by increased spending or by reorientating and increasing efficiency of existing programs. The World Bank and the IMF together have suggested a few measures that can be considered in order to accomplish this objective (see, for example, Heller, 2005). These suggestions are by no means the last word but rather a starting point for addressing the budgetary needs of poverty programs in conjunction with other government spending and revenue measures.

Heller (2005) notes that government revenue as a percent of GDP tends to rise with income. Low income countries in Asia have average revenue share of GDP of around 18 percent whereas the share rises to around 27 percent in upper middle income countries. Therefore, in Heller's estimation some of the lower income countries, particularly Laos and Bangladesh have room for further resource mobilization by the government. Similarly, for Pakistan, Indonesia, Philippines and Vietnam where revenues were higher in the past, there is now room for additional revenue generation (Pakistan is down from 12 percent at its peak to 11 percent currently, Philippines from 17 to 13 percent Indonesia from 15 to 11 percent). Poorly targeted fuel subsidies can be reduced in India, Vietnam, Laos and Pakistan, although this would depend upon the price of oil, which has been volatile in 2008 and early 2009. Food and fertilizer subsidies should be reoriented in India. State enterprise losses need to be cut and management of these enterprises should be redirected as follows: energy and manufacturing in Bangladesh, Laos Airlines in Laos, transfers and subsidies in Pakistan, power and utilities in Philippines and rail road subsidies in India.

We have noted specific areas where expenditures can be increased or targeted to reach the chronically poor, particularly education and health and rural road investments. In addition, wage increases for public sector officials in Bangladesh and increases in health and education expenditure focused on the poor in Laos are required. According to the Heller study, these programs in Laos and Bangladesh need to have concessional assistance to help them get started and quickly address urgent needs.

Continued fiscal discipline is needed to reduce government debt and interest payments. For India, Indonesia and Philippines fiscal prudence is needed to maintain credibility in international capital markets. Despite these caveats debt to GDP ratios both domestically and internationally are within manageable levels and have come down in several countries (see Table 6.4 for details).

6.7 Migration Policy

International migration is not likely to attract the chronically poor in Asia because of the income required to pay agents and transportation costs. Nevertheless the numbers of chronically poor who do migrate is predicted to increase as the demand for overseas workers in the Middle East and other higher income Asian countries rises.

Table 6.4 Debt to GDP Ratios in Asia 2003

Country	Debt to GDP Ratio (Domestic) as a Percent	Debt to GDP Ratio (External) as a Percent
Bangladesh	40	32
Pakistan	15	32
India	58	2
Philippines	32	30
Indonesia	Less than 1 percent	35
Vietnam	na	30 (mostly concessional)
Laos	na	90 (mostly concessional)

Source: Heller (2005).

Some chronically poor are now migrating from Indonesia to Malaysia and also from northern Malaysia to southern Thailand and from the Mekong countries and Myanmar to Thailand. To provide protection for international migrants, governments need to have a set of policy objectives for migration and also for remittances (see Dowling, 2008, and Chapter 2 for further discussion.) These objectives should include

- Providing information on living conditions, logistics and other important information to potential migrants before they leave their country;
- Keeping a registry of migrants in the sending country including age, gender, medical records, residence and contact in case of emergency.
- Establishing a government agency in sending countries that licenses and regulates recruiters.
- Reducing the cost of migration by curbing monopoly practices of recruiters.
- Establishing a policy of reducing domestic unemployment through migration from sending countries.
- Establishing a policy to generate foreign exchange through migration.
- Improving wages and working conditions of employed nationals overseas through diplomatic channels based on feedback from recent immigrants.

- Establishing a policy to recruit the chronically poor for possible foreign employment opportunities.
- Considering subsidies for the chronically poor to facilitate their migration.
- Focusing on issues concerning female migrants, particularly in entertainment and household services where the unskilled are employed and risk abuse.
- Helping migrants save and invest wisely.

Policies regarding internal migration should focus on providing information on job opportunities to villages in rural locations. Development of information networks using both government agencies and informal channels including the internet are proving to be valuable sources of information not only for labor force opportunities but also commercial activities including costs and availability of goods in local markets and weather conditions for farmers. While some government departments can be involved, the private sector is already doing a good job of providing information for prospective job seekers. The government can help by continuing to expand internet access to more villages particularly in poor villages. For migrant families or groups that are relocating to villages where housing, health and sanitation and education facilities may be strained by the influx of new migrants local governments and NGOs can be ready to assist by providing local support and help these migrants integrate into the local community. Experiences of migrants in India and elsewhere suggests that migrants are often discriminated against and denied access to proper housing, health care and education. This can destroy the incentive to migrate and force the chronically poor to return home which discourages additional internal migration. The *hokou* system in China acts as such a deterrent to internal migration by denying access to health, education and housing subsidies to migrants from rural to urban areas.

6.8 Social Protection

Social funds, food subsidies and public works programs were discussed in Chapter 4 and country programs in India and China were mentioned as examples of how these social protection ideas have been implemented in Asia. In this section we take a broader view of such programs within the context of Asia and social protection priorities. If we think of the ways that chronic poverty arises then we can devise social protection initiatives to address these issues. There are three groups to consider:

First there are those without ability to protect themselves from deprivation and chronic poverty — infants, young children, the elderly, the physically and mentally disabled.

Second, there are those who work but don't earn enough to rise out of poverty. They stay chronically poor because they are subject to discrimination, are landless and work as poorly paid agricultural laborers, live in a village where soil conditions and fertility are low, are illiterate, can't get full time work, are the only working member in the household, there are many mouths to feed in their household, they till land which is rain fed with one crop a year and no work in the dry seasons, their livelihood is subject to the vagaries of the weather, are in to debt and bonded to their landlord.

Third, there are households that are normally not poor but have been subject to risks and external shocks. Prices for food have shot up faster than their earnings and they can no longer make ends meet. They had a bad harvest or even two or three and they have no saving and are in debt. The household head has been ill and unable to work and their savings are gone. Because of bad harvests there is no work for the household head or any of the family. A flood or drought or pests have wiped out their harvest.

There are a variety of social protection measures that are available to aid households in each of these groups. There are two basic types of measures — livelihood protection and livelihood promotion. Programs that provide work to smooth out the pattern of income over time and keep households from going into debt or that supply resources to the young, the elderly or disabled would fall into the livelihood protection category. Programs that subsidize children's education and health through school lunch programs, and educational subsidies and programs that help build village social infrastructure such as irrigation and school would fit into the livelihood promotion category. Information about possible opportunities for migration and microfinance or programs that offer training and adult education would also fall into the livelihood promotion category.

These various programs and type of beneficiaries can be further broken down into different categories and existing governmental programs can be analyzed for strengths, weaknesses and gaps in coverage. The Asian Development Bank (2006a, Chapter 17) has developed these three groupings of risk categories into four categories:

Lifecycle — which includes illness and disease as well as children's health and nutrition;

Economic factors — includes unemployment, inflation, loss of job or livelihood because of crop failure due to pests etc, low and unreliable income;

Environmental factors — which includes droughts, floods, earthquakes, landslides;

Social and governmental factors — which include discrimination, corruption, political instability, loss of status, loss of capital or land through expropriation.

The Governmental programs in Asian countries which have large numbers of the chronically poor were compiled by the Asian Development Bank and are displayed in Tables 6.5 and 6.6.

While these tables give some indication of the breadth of the various social protection coverage schemes in Asia, it does not tell anything about the intensity of the commitment or the details of coverage for each program. Baulch *et al.* (2006) developed an indicator for six countries that compiles measures for

Expenditure — which calculates the percent of GDP spent on social protection activities

Program coverage — includes unemployment and underemployment insurance, health care, social assistance to the poor, micro credit to the poor, disability assistance and protection for poor children, aged 5–15.

Table 6.5 Social Protection Programs in Asia — Labor Market Programs

Country	Employment Generation	Unemployment Insurance	Labor Standards
Cambodia	X		X
China	X	X	X
Indonesia	X		X
Lao PDR			X
Philippines	X	X	X
Thailand	X		X
Vietnam	X		X
Bangladesh	X	X	X
India	X		X
Nepal	X		X
Pakistan	X		X
Sri Lanka	X		X

Source: Ortiz (2001, Chapter 17, Table 2).

Poverty targeting — shows the percentage of the poor in each country that receive social protection benefits or transfers.

Impact of the social expenditures — measures the proportion of the poor who benefit from social protection without measuring the impact of the programs on household welfare.

These four measures are then scaled to produce the overall social protection index. The results for this exercise in Bangladesh, Indonesia, Mongolia, Nepal, Pakistan and Vietnam are displayed in Table 6.7.

Coverage is varied with Mongolia standing out with the most comprehensive coverage dating from its membership in the Soviet Union. It has health insurance, pensions and disability schemes that are near universal. For Pakistan and Nepal membership in the main social protection schemes is confined to government and formal sector employees and there are major programs to provide subsidized food or to reduce costs of education and health coverage for the poor. Bangladesh, Indonesia and Vietnam fall in between with extensive social assistance, subsidy and micro-credit programs but with social security schemes that are largely restricted to the formal sector and

Table 6.6 Social Insurance and Assistance, Agriculture Insurance, Child Protection

Country	Old Age, Disability and Death	Sickness and Maternity	Medical Care	Work Injury	Social Assistance	Agricultural Insurance	Social Funds	Family Allowances
Cambodia						X	X	
China	X	X	X	X	X			X
Indonesia	X							
Lao PDR								
Philippines	X	X		X	X		X	
Thailand	X	X		X	X	X	X	X
Vietnam	X	X			X	X		
Bangladesh	X	X		X	X	X	X	X
India	X	X		X		X		
Nepal	X				X			
Pakistan	X	X		X	X			
Sri Lanka	X				X	X	X	X

Source: Ortiz (2001, Chapter 17, Table 2).

Table 6.7 Social Protection Indicators by Country in Percent

Country	Expenditure on All Social Protection as Percent of GDP	Coverage as Percent of Reference Population of Total Poor	Poverty Target as Percent of Poor Receiving Some Social Protection Benefits	Impact[8] is the Proportion of the Poor Who Benefit for Social Protection Measured as Percent of National Poverty Live
Bangladesh	3.8	10.2	34	15
Indonesia	1.9	34.6	73	11
Mongolia	10.5	53.6	60	21
Nepal	2.2	10.5	26	7
Pakistan	2.0	6.5	5.3	2
Vietnam	3.5	21.7	51.9	11.6

Source: Baulch *et al.* (2006, Table 3).

government employees, excluding the poor. Column 4 shows that in Indonesia, Mongolia and Vietnam more than half the poor receive some social protection while column shows that the impact of poverty programs is highest in Mongolia followed closely by Bangladesh, Indonesia and Vietnam. Poverty impact in Nepal and Pakistan is much lower. The ranking of these six countries vis a vis their ranking in the Human Development Indicator Index prepared by UNDP shows some similarities but also some differences as summarized in Table 6.8.

There are distinct differences between the social protection index rank and the human development. Human Development Index is not focused primarily on the poor and the social protection index adds valuable information to policy makers in developing countries. As a companion to the human development index the UN and World

[8] Impact = $(\Sigma e_{i \cap P})/z$ where z is the poverty line, e_i is the expenditure per beneficiary for program s. There are S programs to be summed over and p is the number of poor people. $\cap$ is the intersection of total expenditure and the poor. For details see Baulch *et al.* (2006).

Table 6.8 Ranking of Social Protection and Human Development Indices

Country	Social Protection Index Rank	Human Development Index Rank	Human Development Index GDP Rank
Bangladesh	4	4	5
Indonesia	2	2	1
Mongolia	1	3	4
Nepal	5	5	6
Pakistan	6	6	3
Vietnam	3	1	2

Source: Baulch *et al.* (2006, Table 4).

Bank could consider developing a social protection index for all developing countries.

Which social programs are most relevant for the chronically poor? Based on our discussion from this and earlier chapters there are three classes of policies that are of interest. First are policies which can help families to break out of the poverty trap by educating the next generation. These include subsidies for education at the primary level, either through workfare or the introduction of small subsidies to families for shoes and uniforms to reduce out of pocket costs for parents. They also include free lunches for school children, better monitoring of teachers attendance and provision of more teachers to cut classroom size. Capital spending for more schools as appropriate to cut down distance traveled for young children in isolated and remote areas is also critical. Furthermore general education of the adult population particularly women can have salutary impacts on family health, fertility and nutrition.

Second are social programs and expenditures that protect assets and income by smoothing consumption and income which also supplement income for those who can't get out of poverty given their current occupation, education and geographic location. These programs would apply primarily to agricultural labor who are uneducated or illiterate and live in remote areas and may be members of a minority religion, class or caste. These households are likely to have a primary earner who either works on marginal rain fed farm land or has a small plot of rain fed land of his own. These farmers and agricultural laborers are vulnerable to the vagaries of the weather and do not have much income during the dry season. These households need income and employment when there is no work available in agriculture. Work fare programs can provide employment for the poor during these gaps with work on public schemes to build and rehabilitate infrastructure in their villages or surrounding areas. As we saw in Chapter 4 these programs have had a strong and focused impact on households and their village communities and at the same time help to build up social and physical infrastructure. Selective food subsidies can be used to bring health outcomes up to standard when nutritional deficits are observed either because of childhood stunting, underweight or lack of important nutritional components such Vitamin A which can cause blindness.

Another initiative is needed to help poor household get out of debt that are indebted to landlords or money lenders and may even have some family members in virtual bondage to these landlords or money lenders. None of the existing programs in any of the developing countries of Asia that we have studied directly address these households. Imaginative schemes which serve to break this debt bondage are critical if this cycle of chronic poverty for literally millions of farmers and other rural families is to be broken. In many cases the debts are relatively small, given overall national income and the growing tax base of the middle class. It may require efforts by donors to galvanize action to address this critical problem.

Third are social programs that both protect against shocks and provide assistance after shocks occur. Since the shocks are unanticipated much of what has to be done here is preventative or reactive in nature. For the chronically poor it only takes a major shock to have devastating impacts. Crop failure, either from pests or adverse weather (drought or flood) or escalating prices for food and other essentials pose the most significant risk, There are programs to reduce risk that relate to farming practices, new crops and agricultural extension that are reviewed elsewhere in this chapter and in previous chapters. In this section we are primarily concerned with programs needed in place now which can be implemented as needed. In terms of crop failure the biggest impact seems to be on prices for agricultural products. Much of their spending is on food so when prices rise their purchasing power plummets and the poor can starve even in the face of plentiful food. Dreze and Sen (1989) discuss many aspects of famines and hunger. In the Bangladesh famine of 1974, for example, flooding caused a loss of employment and also created expectations that food prices would rise in the future. This led to hoarding and further price increases in food prices. Higher unemployment rates and lower incomes combined with higher food prices caused a catastrophic decline in real purchasing power for the poor and starvation for many.

In their analysis of the Bangladesh famine and other similar episodes Dreze and Sen (1989) stressed the importance of policies that give food entitlements to the poor rather than the overall availability of food. To ensure that the poor get their fair entitlement of food and other necessities when a shock occurs there must be plentiful stocks on hand or else mechanisms are in place to insure that food stocks are available for distribution to the poor. Alternatively monetary subsidies can be introduced to allow the poor to buy food. These measures have to be developed ahead of time when supplies are plentiful and buffer stocks can be created and emergency action plans are place. This will reduce reaction time and ensure a smooth response to the shock. Early warning systems that report potential crop failures, poor weather and other possible shocks can also be introduced so that policy makers can be ready to act as the crisis unfolds.

Chapter 7
Country Experiences

This chapter focuses on the experiences of various Asian countries with chronic poverty over time. In addition, we also highlight some of their poverty reduction policies that proved successful at targeting the so called "invisible" chronic poor. The countries reviewed include the three most populous economies China, India, Indonesia; four countries in South Asia, Bangladesh, Nepal, Pakistan and Sri Lanka, one economy in Southeast Asia that has significant numbers of chronically poor, namely the Philippines; and lastly the three Mekong countries Cambodia, Laos and Vietnam.

7.1 China

With impressive economic growth in China over the past 20 years, there has been an increase in the standard of living and corresponding reduction in poverty. How the extent of poverty is calculated depends on whether the national official poverty line or the international level of households living below US$1 per day is used. International estimates of US$1 per day for the poverty line show the number of households living in poverty declined by 63 percent to 97 million between 1978 and 1999. Using the official government estimate of the poverty line of approximately US$0.67 per day, the number of poor households fell even further to only 34 million by 2004, an 86 percent decline (CPRC, 2004). By this yardstick China accounted for the bulk of global reduction in poverty between 1990 and 2004. The Gini coefficients of rural China have fallen from almost 0.5 in 1980 to 0.35 in 1999 (Bramall, 2001) although CPRC (2008) shows it to be 0.447 (see Box 7.1).

Box 7.1. A Snapshot of China's Chronic Poor

- China has over 200 million people living on less than US$1.25 per day. The poor make up close to 16 percent of its population and 25 percent of the population in rural areas.
- The chronic poor accounts for approximately 15 percent to 25 percent of the poor. Due to its huge population, China has the largest number of chronic poor in East Asia.
- China's chronic poor are concentrated in rural areas and generally in the northwest, west and southwest areas and away from the coastal region. In 2002, rural per capita income in the Shanghai province was 6244 yuan, but less than 1500 yuan in Guizhou province.
- The chronic poor include ethnic minorities such as the non-Han population; households burdened with older, sick, disabled people or high dependency ratios; orphans and "new poor" such as those who recently lost their jobs due to state-owned enterprise restructuring and rural migrants to the cities.
- China has consistently stepped up efforts to reduce poverty and has improved its well-being over the years. CPRC (2008) has categorized China as a consistent improver.

Table Box 7.1 Selected Indicators

Proportion of poor who are chronically poor over 5 years (low estimate)[1]	0.15
Proportion of poor who are chronically poor over 5 years (high estimate)[1]	0.25
Population	1.3 bn
Percentage of poor living on less than US$1.25 per day (2005PPP)*	15.9
Average depth of poverty (number of % points by which the poor fall below the poverty line[2] in 2001)	23.5
Income share held by lowest 20 percent	4.7
Gini index of inequality	44.7
Healthcare indicators	
Under-5 mortality rate (per 1000 live births) in 2004	31
Infant mortality rate (per 1000 live births) in 2004	26

(*Continued*)

Box 7.1 (*Continued*)

Proportion of children under five who are stunted (2002)[2]	14
Life expectancy at birth, 2004	71.9
Educational indicators	
Adult illiteracy rate for women aged 15 years and above (2000–2004)	13
Adult illiteracy rate for men aged 15 years and above (2000–2004)	5
Child labor	
Percentage of children aged between 7–14 in the labor force (1999–2004)	7.9

Sources: CPRC (2008) Annex E and F and *Bauer *et al.* (2008).
Notes: [1]Based on McCulloch and Calandrino (2003): [2]Most recent year.

Recently the World Bank embarked on a major comparison of purchasing power in many countries in 2005 and its findings show that prices in China appear to be higher than previous estimates. The Chinese income in 2005 could buy less than previously thought (*The Economist*, 22 May 2008) and this has resulted in a revision of poverty figures. Chen and Ravallion (2008) find that around 200 million Chinese people were poor in 2005, about 170 million more than the previous estimate. The CPRC figures quoted for 2008 in Box 7.1 estimate poverty at 217 million. Whatever the actual poverty figure, the achievement in poverty reduction in China is still quite remarkable.

Chronic poverty in China tends to be concentrated in the rural areas and generally increases as we move to the inner provinces of China and away from the coastal cities. One vulnerable group is the ethnic minorities. They make up 9 percent of its population and tend to dwell in remote mountainous areas. Educational attainment among minorities tends to be extremely low. Other high-risk groups include households burdened with older, sick, disabled people or high dependency ratios, orphans and "new poor" such as those who lost their jobs due to state-owned enterprise restructuring and rural migrants to the cities.

7.1.1 *Incidence of poverty*

Due to the vastness of China, there are tremendous differences in geographical factors and economic conditions. As a result estimation of poverty incidence is difficult at both the provincial and national level. Previous studies mainly concentrated their efforts to specific provinces. McCulloch and Calandrino (2003) investigated chronic poverty in rural Sichuan. Around 6 percent of households were persistently poor and deprived of food in rural Sichuan. Transient poverty was high at 44 percent. However poverty trends often mask movements in and out of poverty, so we cannot be sure if the 6 percent of households that were diagnosed as persistently poor were the same households interviewed over the survey period. Despite measurement difficulties, most observers have concluded that households mired in chronic poverty face often insurmountable difficulties in escaping poverty.

Jalan and Ravallion (1998) focused their attention on 4 southern provinces, namely Guangdong, Guangxi, Guizhou and Yunnan using a consumption-based poverty line. They found that almost two-thirds of poor households were chronically poor. Only the Guangzhou province which were relatively well-off had less than 20 percent of chronically poor households (see Table 7.1). In another study, Jalan and Ravallion (2002) highlighted the problems of geographic poverty traps. They also studied how the chronically poor may be impeded by their lack of mobility and low levels of human and physical capital. They found that household's asset holdings, family size, education level and health status were important determinants of chronic poverty.

Jalan and Ravallion (1998) also found widespread differences in the determinants of transitory and chronic poverty in China. Variables which are often associated with chronic poverty, such as household size, health and education have no apparent bearing on transitory poverty. However their study does not differentiate the chronically poor from the transient poor, but simply observes chronic and transient

Table 7.1 Incidence of Chronic Poverty in Southern China, 1985–1990

Province	Chronic Poverty (%) as a Percent of Total Poverty
Guizhou	57
Yunnan	51
Guangxi	43
Guangdong	16

Source: Reprint of Table 1.16.
Note: Sample size of 5845 households over the six year period 1985–1990.

components of the poverty gap for each household. The poverty gap for each household is decomposed into a time-mean (chronic), and a time variant (transient) component. As a result the degree of chronic poverty could have been under estimated.

More recent studies have been able to expand the scope of analysis by incorporating new data that covers more provinces from the middle 1980s to early 2000s. Gustafsson and Li (2002) found great divergence of mean income among the three regions of eastern, central and western China. Their findings support the hypothesis that most income inequality is spatial in nature. Industrialization in the eastern provinces contributed to increasing job opportunities and income levels for their citizens, while the central and western regions experienced slower growth in income. Since 2000, the government has tried to emphasize development in the western region as a way to reduce income inequality.

Duclos *et al.* (2006) attempted to unravel the extent of chronic poverty and transient poverty in several provinces in different parts of the country using a 17 year panel data set from the Research Center on Rural Economy in Beijing and National Bureau of Statistics. Household level surveys were gathered from provinces in eastern, central and western regions from 1986 to 2002. Income and daily expenses were collected from around 4000 households per year and deflated to 1990 prices. Estimates of chronic poverty were sensitive to model specification, making it difficult to draw strong conclusions regarding the extent of chronic poverty by province and region. Chronic poverty was estimated to average 20 percent over all provinces.

Using the same data source as Duclos *et al.* (2006), Benjamin *et al.* (2005) challenged the popular notion that inequality is mainly due to geographical factors. Benjamin *et al.* (2005) decomposed rural inequality by geography (village, province and region) and source of income (e.g. farm and non-farm). They concluded that most rural inequality is found within villages rather than between villages. They hypothesize that rising income inequality is due to a wider trend of falling farm incomes and rising non-farm income as a result of industrialization. Rising inequality results from the inability of poor households within villages to access higher paying opportunities from non-agricultural jobs that were becoming available to those with more skills and education. While they did not look explicitly at chronic poverty it seems plausible that their results would also hold for the chronically poor.

While income and living standards within villages are factors in explaining chronic poverty, Gustafsson and Li (2002) and Duclos *et al.* (2006) look into village income differences and the relationship between geography and poverty. Borooah *et al.* (2006) also found geographic factors are important, recognizing that China deliberately implemented significant restrictions on labor mobility and favored development of coastal regions. The personal registration (*hukou*) system imposed by the local authorities restricts rural to urban migration. Rural inhabitants of remote areas are hampered by the local geographical conditions (e.g. land quality and limited access to markets) and by government intervention on migration issues.

Owing to decentralization and differences in the cost of living in different provinces, the local provincial authorities would determine their own poverty line. Better off cities tend to have a higher poverty line than remote western provinces such as Inner Mongolia. Table 7.2 shows the food poverty line by province.

Table 7.2 Food Poverty Line by Province, 1998

Food Poverty Line (% with Regards to the National Line)	Province
121%–170% above national line	• Beijing, Tianjin, Shanghai, Zhejiang, Guangdong and Hainan. • Ranges from 1693 to 2361 yuan per head per year.
101% to 120% above national line	• Jiangsu, Fujian, Guangxi, Yunan and Tibet • Ranges from 1448 to 1572 yuan per head per year
100% national line	• 1392 yuan per head per year
81% to 100% national line	• Heibei, Liaoning, Anhui, Jiangxi, Shandong, Hubei, Hunan, Sichuan, Guizhou and Chongqing • Ranges from 1127 to 1355 yuan per head per year
60% to 80% national line	• Shanxi, Inner Mongolia, Jilin, Heilongjiang, Henan, Shaanxi, Qinghai and Ningxia. • Ranges from 941 to 1085 yuan per head per year

Source: Data from Hussain (2003, p. 14, Table 3) based on 1998 urban household data for 31 provinces.

Rural and urban poverty. Though the emphasis of our study is on chronic poverty in rural areas, it is interesting to explore urban poverty in China. The peculiar difficulties of China with its rural-urban divide lie in its definition. There are two divisions, both at the spatial and demographic level (Hussain, 2003). Chinese cities are divided spatially, into urban districts and rural counties. Chinese residents are classified at the demographic level into "agricultural" and "non-agricultural". "Non-agricultural" refers to urban status. Both spatial and demographic divisions partially overlap, creating anomalies in what is termed as rural and urban (see Table 7.3). For instance, an individual may be officially registered as having urban status; however he could be residing in a rural area (urban status, rural

Table 7.3 Definitions of Rural and Urban Locations

	Spatial Division (by Citizen's Residence)	
Demographic Division (by citizen's personal registration status)	[1]Non-agricultural, Urban Districts	[3]Non-agricultural, Rural Counties *Estimates of 160 million in 1999.*
	[3]Agricultural, Urban Districts *Estimates of 101 million in 1999.*	[2]Agricultural, Rural Counties

Source: Data from Hussain (2003, pp. 2–3).
Notes: [1]Citizen holding an urban registration account and residing in urban districts (distinctly urban) and [2]citizen holding an rural registration account and residing in rural areas (distinctly rural) and [3]overlaps.

resident). Or a long term urban citizen may be officially registered as an agricultural resident despite having left the farming community long ago (rural status, urban resident).

Such rural-urban registration anomalies are due to the personal registration (*hukou*) system. Local authorities tightly monitor and control labor mobility although constraints on labor mobility have eased with the economic reforms since 1978. Nevertheless urban registration especially for larger cities such as Beijing and Shanghai is not easy to obtain, unless inherited from the mother. This creates a further possible distortion to the quality of the official rural poverty estimates (see Chapter 4, Section 4.8.2). Chan and Buckingham (2008) argue that devolution of responsibility for the *hukou* policies to local governments in 2005 have often made permanent migration of peasants to cities even harder than before.

Urban poverty. Recently an emerging class of "newly poor" has arisen in China. A large proportion of these newly poor are willing and able to work but unable to find jobs. Approximately 5 percent of urban population survives on less than US$1 per day (CRPC, 2004). The chronic poor are likely to earn much less than that figure.

According to a survey conducted by the local government in late 2000, a total of 14 million urban residents earn income less than the local poverty line. These include the urban population characterized by the "three nos", namely no ability to work, no savings or incomes, and no relatives to depend on.

Rural to urban migration. One in five workers in China is a migrant worker (Metraux and Yoxall, 2007). The Chinese government uses six months as the cut-off period to distinguish between short term and long term migrants. Long term migrants could be granted temporary registration that allows them the right to stay but with limited or no access to housing and educational services that full-time urban resident enjoy. Official statistics put the number of floating population (migrants) at 40 million in 1999, but it is likely to be underestimated. The Centers for Strategic and International Studies (CSIS) reports migrant numbers to have increased to over 140 million in 2004 and continues to grow at an astounding rate (CSIS, in Metraux and Yoxall, 2007, p. 46).

Many of the floating population are illiterate, speak only non-Mandarin dialects and are often relegated to low-paying jobs or illicit employment. These unskilled rural laborers get menial jobs as construction workers, cleaners and restaurant waiters. Many of them go from job to job or set up illegal business on the streets to sell items from food and cheap watches to clothing. They are unregulated, their work is often demeaning and their living conditions are poor. As the floating population increased, homelessness and petty crime have risen.

Also, since most migrants are young to middle aged men and women in their most sexually active stages of life, they are also vulnerable to exposure to HIV infections. It is estimated that more than 650,000 people in China are living with HIV/Aids. The largest concentrations are in Henan, Yunnan, Guangxi, Xinjiang and Guangdong, also provinces with the highest concentration of chronically poor identified in Table 7.1 (see the United Nations report on the Aids epidemic update for 2006 in Asia located at http://data.unaids.org/pub/EpiReport/2006/05-Asia_2006_EpiUpdate_eng.pdf).

In addition since it is often the father who migrates to the city for a job, the wife is left with the added burden of caring for the family and running the farm. Children left behind lack proper care and discipline since their mother is busy trying to make ends meet. While there are social safety nets for urban poor such as the Minimum Living Standards, it is limited to those with disabilities, no incomes/savings and no relatives. Support given to the emerging urban poor who are likely to be recent immigrants from rural areas is extremely limited (See Ge, 2009, for further details of the urban employment challenge).

Information on rural to urban migration of the chronically poor is not available. However Duclos *et al.* (2005) found that the members of poor households do not consider the *hukou* system to be a significant barrier to migration. They estimate migration has increased per capita household income in rural areas by between 8.5 and 13.1 percent as remittances have helped to improve living standards of the poor. They also conclude that the poorest rural households have few laborers and limited human capital so that migration is less of an option than it is for richer families.

Poverty dynamics. How does one measure the dynamics of poverty reduction? One good indicator would be the level of asset holdings a household has accumulated *over time.* If asset holdings of the household have increased over time, it would imply that the level of income of the household has increased and that their living circumstances have improved. If household assets declined or remained stagnant it is highly unlikely that households would have escaped from poverty. However inter-temporal measures of assets per household are relatively limited. Children's height over time would be another possible measure of poverty dynamics. This could aid in assessing individual nutritional history and provide information about past living conditions. A child whose growth has been stunted is indicative of previous dietary deficiencies and positively associated with malnutrition due to chronic poverty. Anthropometric evidence indicates that the average height of children has increased with family incomes in China over time.

According to this key measure of nutritional status, there has been declining level of chronic deprivation in China.

7.1.2 *Determinants of poverty*

As discussed earlier, Jalan and Ravallion (1998) found that the household's average wealth holding is an important determinant for chronic poverty. Other important determinants include household size, levels of education, and the health status of household members. Chronic poverty is reduced when families have more physical assets and able bodied workers in the family. Other studies also confirmed the importance of geographical poverty traps and the status of household wealth (see Jalan and Ravallion, 2002; Gustafsson and Li, 2002). As we noted in Table 7.1 poverty is quite a severe problem in the western provinces of Guizhou, Yunnan and Guangxi and also Qinghai.

7.1.3 *Government commitment to reduce poverty*

Overall, the Chinese government has actively stepped up efforts to alleviate poverty in China. The Chinese government established the Leading Group for Poverty Reduction (LGPR) in 1986 to support poverty reduction initiatives and in particular, to expedite economic development in lagging areas. LGPR is the key agency responsible for coordinating more than US$2 billion in annual funding for poverty reduction programs under China's 1994 "8–7 Poverty Reduction Plan" to overcome absolute poverty in 592 poor counties.

The 8–7 plan aims to lift the remaining 80 million poor people in rural areas out of poverty in 7 years (i.e. by the year 2000). The LGPR coordinates and oversees initiatives from various sectoral initiatives such as subsidies from the Agricultural Bank of China, a food-for-work infrastructure program run by the Planning Commission and from grants by the Ministry of Finance. China was the only country to have realized ahead of schedule, the United Nations Millennium Goal of slashing poverty levels in half by 2015. The Deputy Director of the LGPR announced recently that China had lifted 228 million rural residents out of extreme poverty since 1978 and had cut their numbers to 21.48 million in 2006. The rate of extreme poverty in these areas fell dramatically from 30 percent 1987 to 2.3 percent in 2006 (*People's Daily*, May 29, 2007).

It is unclear how these figures relate to the overall thrust of poverty reduction reviewed above and whether the reduction of extreme poverty from 30 percent to 2.3 percent is believable. One criticism of LGPR is that it oversees the initiatives but not the direct implementation of poverty programs and there have been concern that resources have been allocated to inefficient and unprofitable enterprises in poor counties rather than to poor households. It is alleged that needed resources are drained away from poverty reduction.

One of the major measures instituted in the 8–7 program is the partnership method, where the central government mobilizes financial resources from developed provinces to support targeted poor provinces and regions. Beijing helps Inner Mongolia, Tianjin helps Gansu, Shanghai helps Yunnan, Guangdong helps Guangxi, Jiangsu helps Shaanxi, Zhejiang helps Sichuan, Shandong helps Xinjiang, Liaoning helps Qinghai, Fujian helps Ningxia, Shenzhen, Qingdao, Dalian and Ningbo help Guizhou. For example, the mayor of Shenzhen allocated $26 million to support developmental projects in Guizhou (Zhang, 1993).

In all, the government takes the lead in mobilizing all social forces, and encouraging poor people to be self-reliant. Since most of the poor are farmers who are vulnerable to changes in climate, market access and economic conditions, the anti-poverty strategies outlined in the 8–7 program focus on strategies to increase agricultural growth and incomes of the farmers. Strategies include: the initiation of new commercial ventures in livestock, forestry, fruit trees and plantation crops; development of rural infrastructure (roads, power and water supply), increasing access to markets as well as provision of basic services like health, education and family planning. There has not been any clear analysis of the successes of these initiatives.

7.1.4 *Microeconomic policies*

Historically there have been no systematic cash transfer efforts or food subsidy programs (including food stamps) in place in China to assist the chronically poor who have very low paying jobs or who are unable to help themselves including children, the elderly and the disabled. Recently a program to provide food subsidies to poor families and basic public services under China's Eleventh Five-Year Plan (2006–2010) was introduced. There is a food for work program in place designed to mobilize the under employed in poor areas to improve infrastructure including water and irrigation projects, roads and provide power and other communications to poor rural areas. Funds for these programs totaled 43 billion yuan between 1984 and 2001 (see Riskin and Bouche, 2004, for details).

To improve educational facilities basic skills are being upgraded. It was estimated that approximately 85 million primary students were not receiving compulsory education by end of 2000 (see Park *et al.*, 2003) and this figure is an underestimate since the study did not include children of migrant workers. Educational reforms include increases in teachers' salaries, reconstruction of run-down schools and funding for programs targeting China's rural illiteracy problem. Tuition and incidental fees for rural students during the compulsory education period of K to 9 are to be eliminated. The effectiveness of the reforms depends on minimizing rent-seeking activities and corruption by officers in charge. In the wake of devastation from an earthquake in Sichuan where many schools collapsed, 2500 people including school headmasters were convicted on charges of corruption.

Complete rural healthcare and medical aid are also emphasized in the Government's plans. New rural cooperative medical care's coverage is expected to cover 80 percent of the target population. China will also need to provide for vulnerable groups such as orphans and handicapped (Metraux and Yoxall, 2007, p. 164). Only 1600 schools out of nearly 30,000 elementary schools in China are devoted to special education.

NGOs. A number of projects have been set up by charity organizations to enable children in China's rural poverty-stricken areas to attend school. They include the Project Hope launched by the Youth League and the Chunlei (Spring Bud) Program by the All-China Federation of Women and the Children's Foundation of China. Such projects rely on overseas donors. By 2005, Project Hope had raised over 3 billion renminbi and allowed almost 3000 children to go to school. They also built nearly 13,000 Hope schools (Metraux and Yoxall, 2007). The Chunlei program encourages female enrolment in schools. Between 1992 and1993, classes have rapidly grown from 14 in four provinces and regions to over 1000 in 23 provinces and regions (Zhang, 1993).

7.1.5 *Sector policies*

China has designated 592 poor counties for development and has had a modicum of success in pursuing strategies to raise farmers incomes in these counties; the average income of farmers has risen from less than 52 percent of the national average in 1985 to nearly 60 percent of the national average by 2000 (see Riskin and Bouche, 2004). However there are some problems with the designation of these counties (see Box 7.2). There have also been systematic efforts to improve physical and social infrastructure, particularly access to potable water and primary education as well as medical services despite some leakage to the non poor in these counties. Funds have also been made available for agricultural extension programs to raise productivity and undertake research and development. Most of the poorest counties are in the western region and China has set in place various initiatives to develop the western regions such as Gansu, Qinghai and Guizhou, where chronic poverty levels are high in mountainous terrain and remote areas. The government has spent on development of infrastructure including transport, hydropower plants, energy and telecommunications and access to services such as education. One example is the Qingzang railway which allows easier access to Tibet and could promote the tourism industry in future. Efforts to attract FDI have been stepped up.

Box 7.2 Defining Poor Counties in China

The definition of poor counties is problematic for several reasons. First, the poverty lines chosen in 1986 for defining poor counties were arbitrary and inconsistently applied, mixing political concerns with poverty alleviation goals. In addition to preferential treatment for minority counties and old revolutionary base areas, political appeals by individual counties sometimes affected designations. Political factors also prevented counties from losing their poor county designation even when they were no longer poor. Second, efforts to maintain balance among provinces in the number of designated poor counties may have hurt provinces in which the vast majority of counties were poor, especially in the initial designations. Third, regional targeting based on the definition of poor counties necessarily gives rise to incomplete coverage and leakage. Even with accurate targeting at the county level, the poor in non-poor counties are not helped. On the other hand, most of the populations in poor counties are not poor. Jalan and Ravallion (1998) reported that about half of the poor in four southern provinces did not live in poor counties in the late 1980s. Riskin (1994) reported, based on a 1988 national survey of over 10,000 rural households in 28 provinces, that only 37 percent of poor households were located in an officially designated poor county.

Source: Riskin and Bouche (2004, pp. 22–26).

To analyze the role of public investment on rural poverty Fan *et al.* (2002) developed a simultaneous equation model which related provincial infrastructure spending in China to poverty for the period 1970–1997. The study came to several conclusions. For the country expenditure on education had the largest impact on poverty alleviation. Every additional 10,000 yuan spent on education raised an average of 6.3 people above the poverty line (p. 40). Education also raised growth in production in the rural sector, providing a win-win strategy for the agricultural sector. R&D had the largest impact on agricultural production and the third largest impact on rural poverty. Investment in rural telecommunications had the third largest impact on production growth and the second largest impact on poverty reduction. Road and rural electrification investment was also an important factor lifting both production and reducing poverty ranking fourth and fifth in overall importance. Telecommunications, roads and rural electrification contributed to poverty reduction by increasing non-farm employment as well as through growth in agricultural production. Surprisingly, investment in irrigation had the smallest impact on both production and poverty alleviation.

Regionally, the highest returns to poverty reduction from additional infrastructure spending were realized in the western region. The major growth potential for agricultural production was in the central region where land is relatively abundant and agricultural production is still the major source of income. All types of infrastructure investment had their largest impact on the western region and the study concludes that the western region should be the major focus for poverty reduction. There is a measurable trade off between growth and poverty reduction. However in the western region the gains from poverty reduction more than offset a small reduction in economic growth. See Table 7.4 for details of the poverty and production impact on different regions.

While the western region is indeed the focal point for poverty reduction China also needs to consider the Chinese heartland areas too. It also persists in places like Henan, where population densities are among the highest in China. Henan and other heavily populated parts of the Chinese heartland are often excluded from the financial support and any antipoverty measures in place have little effect. Residents of those areas say, money intended for them is appropriated by corrupt local officials, who pocket it or divert it to business investments. Paradoxically they are overlooked precisely because of their proximity to the major economic centers of the east. It is assumed that residents in Henan and other central provinces can make do with income sent home by migrant laborers and other forms of trickle-down wealth. In Henan's rural Gushi County 73,000 of 1.4 million farmers fall below the official poverty level of

Table 7.4 Impact of Infrastructure Spending on Poverty and Productivity

	Coastal Region	Central Region	Western Region
Returns to agricultural production — yuan return per yuan invested			
R&D	7.33	8.53	9.23
Irrigation	1.40	0.98	0.93
Roads	3.69	6.90	6.71
Education	6.06	8.45	6.20
Electrification	3.67	4.89	3.33
Rural Telephone	4.14	8.05	6.57
Returns to poverty reduction — number of poor reduced per 19,00 yuan invested			
R&D	0.97	2.42	14.03
Irrigation	0.15	0.23	1.14
Roads	0.70	2.80	14.60
Education	1.79	5.35	21.09
Electrification	0.92	2.64	9.62
Rural Telephone	0.98	4.11	17.99

Source: Fan *et al.* (2002, Table 6).

$94 a year, which is supposed to be enough to cover basic needs, including maintaining a daily diet of 2,000 calories. (*New York Times*, 13 January 2008).

Certainly, China needs to strike the right balance between regional development and poverty alleviation measures at the household level. Some projects do not have high rates of return and McCulloch and Calandrino (2003) argue that participation in such agricultural projects has prevented households from undertaking more lucrative alternative schemes that could have sped up their exit from poverty. In addition, China should also explore alternative indicators which proxy for chronic poverty instead of solely focusing on income and consumption levels in individual years (McCulloch and Calandrino, 2003). It should also include educational levels, asset and geographical characteristics for database gathering and the implementation of effective targeting. Infrastructure spending in the Western region seems to be headed in the right direction to foster economic growth and reduce poverty.

7.1.6 *Macroeconomic policies*

Macroeconomic policies have favored economic development zones such as coastal cities and government support for development of those areas has left remote areas with insufficient funding. Government officials in richer areas are also inclined to extend their jurisdiction to increase access to government funds and resources while ignoring poorer areas.

Nevertheless the Chinese government has effective systems in place to foster the domestic economy and create local employment opportunities, namely through the household responsibility system (HRS), Town and Village Enterprise (TVEs) and Special Economic Zones (SEZs).

The household responsibility system (HRS) was introduced in the early 1980s and marked the transition from communal farms to family farms. Under the HRS, farmlands were sub-contracted to rural families. They were responsible for meeting the production quotas set by the officials. They were free to trade any excess surplus on the free market where prices fluctuate according to the forces of demand and supply, and keep their personal profits. As a result, this greatly increased farmers' incentives to increase productivity and technological progress. The agricultural sector flourished rapidly under the HRS. Average growth rate between 1979 and 1984 was 7.1 percent, and almost three times that from 1970 to 1978 and growth was generally sustained in the next decade as well (see Table 7.5). The increase in rural families' income which allowed them to purchase industrial goods provided the impetus for the growth of the industrial sector.

In 1998, to further strengthen the rights of rural families tending arable land, China embarked on the second stage of land tenure reform by passing a revised Land Management Law. Under HRS rights to arable land were not clearly defined and the terms of use

Table 7.5 Growth in Production in Agriculture, Industry and Non-farm Rural Enterprises

Growth	1970–1978	1979–1984	1985–1995	1996–2000	2001–2005
GDP Growth	4.9	8.5	9.7	8.2	9.5
Agriculture	2.7	7.1	4.0	3.4	3.9
Industry	6.8	8.2	12.8	9.6	10.7
Non-farm rural enterprises (TVEs)	n.a	12.3	24.1	14.0	

Source: Dowling (2007, Table 7.1).

were typically short term. This often created uncertainty and insecurity for farmers in the past. The new law states that collectively owned arable land be contracted to collective members for a term of 30 years and that a written contract be executed detailing the rights and obligations of both parties. It also restricts land readjustment. Land readjustment used to occur in about 80 percent of rural villages where village land was redistributing periodically (some times annually) to reflect changes in household population size since the previous land allocation. For instance, in a major land readjustment exercise, all land is given back to the village and redistributed so that families receive new parcels of land. This type of frequent land redistribution reduces incentives to improve productivity and raise output. In another kind of redistribution land could be taken from households who have lost members and given to households who have new members. As a result farmers whose incomes have increased could easily return to poverty as a result of such land readjustment exercises. The new law aims to provide nearly 200 million Chinese farm households with long term, assured land use rights. It also aims to facilitate long-term, productivity-enhancing investments and the development of markets for rural land use rights (World Bank, 2001a). Efforts to improve land quality are of essential importance. Even with access to land under the HRS, it may not be possible for the poor to subsist on farms with inferior quality land where yields are low or where the possibility of drought or flood is high.

Non-farm rural enterprises also known as town and village enterprises (TVEs) have successfully promoted economic growth and employment in rural areas. Employment has grown from 28 million in 1978 (7 percent of workforce) to 140 million (25 percent of workforce) in 2005. TVEs are a cooperative enterprise between town and village authorities and local rural businessmen, and are likened to small and medium enterprises with less than 50 employees. Incomes of farmers under the HRS started to rise. Rural businessmen started by producing simple consumer goods to satisfy demand from rural families. Later they moved on to produce manufactured products such as air conditioners, fans, refrigerators and television sets etc. Domestically, they served to increase the availability of cheap consumer goods and help reduce inflationary pressure. Today, they contribute more than 55 percent of industrial output, more than 30 percent of GDP and more than 50 percent of exports (Dowling, 2007). The growth in TVEs has also drawn labor from agriculture and contributed to further reductions in poverty in rural areas.

Although TVEs enjoyed little government support, unlike state-owned enterprises (SOEs), they had ready access to credit (via bank or rural credit co-operative loans and investments of other collective TVEs), productive inputs, and information, and possessed an advantage when applying for legal permits and arranging market linkages. The growth in TVEs also helped to absorb surplus rural labor as a result of rising productivity in the agricultural sector and contributed to further reductions in poverty. TVEs also allowed the smoothing of the seasonal work cycle in rural areas by providing off-season work. With the on-going industrial reforms of large scale SOEs, TVEs also help absorb displaced workers to some extent and provide alternative employment opportunities. This reduced the rural-urban income gap.

Special Economic Zones (SEZs) are designated geographical regions that emphasize free market trade and use tax and business incentives to attract foreign investment and technology. They are intended to function as zones of rapid economic growth. Most of the SEZs in China are located at the coastal regions such as Shen zhen,

Zhuhai and Shantou in Guangdong Province and Xiamen in Fujian Province. The entire province of Hainan is a special economic zone. Since the opening up of the economy there has been a dramatic increase in Foreign Direct Investment (FDI) and export-oriented labor-intensive industry. This has successfully transferred the surplus agricultural labor to the industrial sector. For instance, the province of Guangdong which have several SEZs, accounts for a large share of the industrial labor force for the entire country (Hu *et al.*, 2003). The SEZs have been extremely successful and have generated new wealth and prosperity. As a result poverty has fallen dramatically in the coastal region.

7.1.7 *Future policy agenda and challenges*

Despite rapid progress in poverty reduction following the opening up of the Chinese economy in the 1980s, regional disparities in living standards have increased. The Gini coefficient for the country rose from 22.4 in 1958 to close to 40 by the early years of the 21st century (see Dowling, 2007 and Morgan Stanley, 2006). Comparisons between India and China also show wide disparity in income per capita between the richest and poorest regions in the two countries (see Table 7.8). The western region in China has about the same level of per capita income as the poorest region in India ($555 per capita in the western region of China and $536 in the Eastern region of India). However the richest region in China has a per capita income nearly 40 percent higher than the richest region in India. Furthermore poverty rates are in the neighborhood of 50 percent in Guanxi, Guizhou and Yunnan (see Table 7.1).

Raiser (1998) also suggests that income per capita has been diverging across the provinces of China. Restrictions in internal migration through the regulations imposed by the *hukou* system combined with the allocation of government resources to urban residents have created a dual labor market that needs to be addressed. More resources have to be allocated to the poorer provinces located in the western part of the country. Some movements in the direction have already begun. However further relaxation of the *hukou* system is required to increase labor mobility and give migrant workers greater access to urban services.

Resources are being allocated to extend development westward along the upper reaches of the Yangtze River. Further infrastructure development in the western region designed to support poverty reduction efforts as well as industrial development to further attract rural workers to higher paying jobs are under way. Under China's Eleventh Five-Year Plan outline 2006–2010, additional resources are being allocated to improve the delivery of education and health services in the western region as well as coordinate agricultural development. However, the 8–7 program whereby rich provinces help poor provinces is likely to result in a fragmented and inefficient poverty reduction effort.

Greater efforts have to be made to provide a well coordinated menu of social assistance to the poor that will raise agricultural productivity through agricultural extension and applied research and development. At the same time more off farm employment and better health and education delivery systems need to be created to raise educational outcomes, reduce infant mortality and increase life expectancy. While there are some food subsidy and work fare type programs now being implemented in China, more can be done to aid the chronically poor in the Western region aside from the infrastructure initiatives discussed above. There are many food subsidy and work fare programs now in place in South Asia and it might behoove the Chinese authorities to study such programs to see if they might be appropriate in the Western Provinces and other poorer locations in rural China.

Additional measures have been suggested by Riskin and Bouche (2004). These include greater emphasis on further development of small and medium enterprises and job creation; shifting economic growth policies to focus more on creating employment opportunities for the poor; reforming the fiscal system to make it more progressive; removal of special tax concessions favoring coastal regions and creation of incentives to increase investment in the interior;

ensuring women equality in access to education, land, credit, and socio-economic and political status as well as; timely completion of the new social insurance system.

7.2 India

Box 7.3. A Snapshot of India's Chronic Poor

- India has 455 million people living on less than US$1.25 per day. The poor make up 42 percent of its population.
- The chronic poor accounts for approximately 25 percent to 35 percent of the poor. India has the largest number of chronic poor in South Asia. CPRC (2004) reports that South Asia accounts for about an estimated 135 to 190 million people — including 110–160 million Indians, 9–13 million Bangladeshis, 10–15 million Pakistanis, perhaps 5 million Afghans, and 2–3 million Nepalese. Over one-third of the world's chronic poor live in India.
- Central and eastern India is marked by adverse agrarian relations. Over 70 percent of India's poor reside in six states: Uttar Pradesh, Bihar, Madhya Pradesh, Maharashtra, West Bengal and Orissa.
- The chronic poor include those who eke out a living in extremely low-lying lands and excluded minorities such as the Scheduled Castes (SCs) and Scheduled Tribes (STs) who face extreme discrimination. Another large group of the chronic poor is the casual agricultural laborers who are either landless or near-landless, and highly dependent on wages. Women and girls are also at risk.
- India is categorized as a "partially chronically deprived country". Welfare remains relatively low. Healthcare and educational indicators show deprivation of social services. The extent of child stunting in India is one of the highest in the Asian region.

(*Continued*)

Box 7.3 (*Continued*)

Table Box 7.3 Selected Indicators

Proportion of poor who are chronically poor over 5 years (low estimate)[1]	0.25
Proportion of poor who are chronically poor over 5 years (high estimate)[1]	0.35
Population	1.13 bn
Percentage of poor living on less than US$1.25 per day (2005PPP)*	41.6
Average depth of poverty (number of % points by which the poor fall below the poverty line[2] in 2000)	23.6
Income share held by lowest 20 percent	8.9
Gini index of inequality	32.5
Healthcare indicators	
Under-5 mortality rate (per 1,000 live births) in 2004	85
Infant mortality rate (per 1,000 live births) in 2004	62
Proportion of children under 5 who are stunted (1999)[2]	46
Life expectancy at birth, 2004	63.6
Educational indicators	
Adult illiteracy rate for women aged 15 years and above (2000–2004)	52
Adult illiteracy rate for men aged 15 years and above (2000–2004)	27
Child labor	
Percentage of children aged between 7–14 in the labor force (1999–2004)	7.9

Sources: CPRC (2008) Annex E and F and Bauer *et al.* (2008).
Notes: [1]Based on data from National Council of Applied Economic Research (NCAER). [2]Most recent year.

7.2.1 *Incidence of poverty*

India is the world's second most populous country with approximately 1.1 billion people. CPRC estimates that 41.6 percent of the population is poor, living on less than $1.25 per day (see Box 7.3) and between 25 percent and 35 percent are classified as chronically poor (Sah, 2007 estimates 38 percent). To provide a geographical profile of severe poverty, the number of households unable to consume two square meals per day was highest in Orissa, West Bengal and Assam (Mehta and Shah, 2001). In India the provinces of Andhra Pradesh, Assam, Bihar, Orissa, Madhya Pradesh, Rajasthan, West Bengal and Uttar Pradesh have the highest concentration of the poor. In the year 2000 the Planning Commission of India estimated that around 70 percent of the poor lived in rural areas, 54.6 percent of women and 31.6 percent of men are illiterate. Working conditions of the poor are often hazardous. Those who work in road construction, in factories, and at various cleaning sites are often exposed for long hours to potential toxins and also to heat, noise and air pollution. The poor nutrition that they have offers little resistance against sickness and chronic diseases.

7.2.2 *Determinants of poverty*

Education and health, land ownership and social status are the major determinants of poverty. Geography also plays a role. The poor experience a lower level of human development than their richer neighbors. Life expectancy and earnings are lower and illiteracy and infant mortality rates high. Use of contraceptives is low and total fertility high (see Table 7.6). Women are discriminated against. Their life expectancy is shorter than men's and earnings lower for similar work. Living conditions in the poorest states are grim. In Bihar, the poorest state, 89 percent of households had a mud floor in their house, 1.4 percent had access to tap water while 80 percent had water access from a hand pump. 95 percent used kerosene for lighting and only 5 percent have electricity, 86 percent have no latrine or bathrooms in their homes and 65 percent of those with an outside latrine had no drainage for waste water. Virtually all households used firewood, crop residue or cow dung cakes as cooking fuel. Only 3 percent of households had both a toilet and electricity. More than half of households do not have substantial household assets such as car or other motorized vehicle, no bicycle, no telephone, no television or radio. In Orissa, the next poorest province things were slightly better. 50 percent had a bicycle and 21 percent had

Table 7.6 Demographic Indicators by State of India

	Female Life Expectancy 1992–1994	Infant Mortality per 1000 Births 1993	Total Fertility	Percent of Illiterate Females 1992–1993	Rank of Per Capita Income 2001 Low to High
Poorer states					
Assam	54.2	78	3.3	61.5	4
Bihar	56.4	69	4.6	71.4	1
Madhya Pradesh	53.2	102	4.2	65.7	5
Orissa	55.1	109	3.1	58.6	2
Rajasthan	56.7	85	4.5	74.6	6
Uttar Pradesh	54.5	93	5.2	68.5	3
Richer states					
Andhra Pradesh	61.5	66	2.7	61.5	8
Gujarat	60.5	63	3.2	48.7	12
Haryana	63.2	69	3.7	54.1	13
Karnataka	63.6	68	2.9	53.5	10
Kerala	73.4	15	1.7	17.6	9
Punjab	67.2	55	3.0	48.0	15
Tamil Nadu	62.5	58	2.1	43.9	11
West Bengal	62.3	61	3.0	44.8	7

Source: Dowling (2007, Table 7.13).

a radio. Still 80 percent had mud floors and 44 percent had none of the other amenities just mentioned. (See Dowling, 2007, p. 486).

It only takes one look at the Kerala row to realize that human development indicators need not be so low in India. Even with per capita income ranking in the middle range of all the provinces, Kerala's life expectancy, infant mortality and literacy rates could qualify it as a newly industrialized economy. According to UNICEF infant mortality in East Asia and the Pacific is 26 per 1000 births and life expectancy is 71 years.

Poverty in the remote tribal areas such as southwestern Madhya Pradesh has been especially persistent and remained significantly higher than the rest of rural India. Sah (2007) analyzes causes of poverty in remote areas in the tribal belt of southwestern Madhya Pradesh and found that chronic poverty is negatively related to the level of asset wealth of the household. The lower the level of asset holdings in a household, the higher the probability that the household will suffer from chronic poverty. Family size also matters. The larger the family, the greater the probability of suffering from chronic poverty. Large families are two and a half times as likely to be poor as smaller families. Agricultural production is highly correlated with the incidence of poverty and regions with poor soil and limited irrigation are more likely to be chronically poor.

Past discrimination against scheduled tribes and castes has resulted in low levels of education, poor health and high rates of chronic poverty. Unfair labor practices create damaging patron-client relationships and often leave the worker at the mercy of his employer. For example around 90 percent of Dalits (former untouchable class) work as lowly paid agricultural laborers.[9]

7.2.3 *Microeconomic policy*

To help families at the household and village level India has implemented a Poverty Alleviation Programs (PAP) to assist in poverty reduction in the Indian states. Government spending on poverty reduction is 6–7 percent of India's government budget. However it is still less than 1 percent of GDP (SDS and URDI, 2005). Some policy measures that the Indian government has undertaken to reduce poverty include rapid growth in the agricultural sector, stable prices for the rural consumer and active social sector investment. Rural poverty has been reduced from near 60 percent in the early 1970s to 35 percent by 2001. However progress in poverty alleviation has been uneven. Subsidies are insufficient to lift large numbers out of poverty and there has been a slow build up in human capital among the poorest segments of society.

Despite free access to public schools, there is limited increase in human capital for poor families. School attendance is still low among the poor as families can not afford to send children to school or to pay for the cost of school supplies, lunches and school uniforms. Households

---

[9] Despite these adverse circumstances, Abbott *et al.* (2004) report that income was not a major determinant of emotional well being of chronically poor Indian families. They did not report adverse family interactions or less life satisfaction than richer families.

in remote tribal areas face both spatial and social exclusion and the quality of schools in these areas are also often substandard. (See Chapter 4 and Abbott *et al.*, 2004, p. 21).

Social protection. India has implemented a national public distribution scheme (PDS) to provide food security and subsidize prices for wheat, rice, sugar, edible oils, kerosene and soft cake (see Chapter 4, Section 4.2 for further details). In addition, Antyodaya Anna Yojana (AAY) was introduced in 2001 to distribute special ration cards to very poor families. These schemes provide short-term relief to the general poor against famine risk and chronic malnutrition. To maintain this subsidy system the Indian government incurs an expensive network of food procurement and storage. A pension and rural employment scheme that target the chronic poor might be more effective.

The National Old Age Pension Scheme (NOAPS) provides destitute elderly citizens above the age of 65 years old with a pension of Rs. 200 per month. Approximately 50 percent of intended beneficiaries are now covered by the program (approximately 8.7 million elderly in India). The beneficiaries have difficulties working and often do not receive much assistance from family members. The pension only serves to offset daily living expenses and is not enough for the individual to break out of chronic poverty.

The NOAPS has been successful in reducing rent seeking activities with its direct delivery of payment via the post office to the beneficiaries in certain states. The small size of the individual payment also mitigates corruption. As a result, 96 percent of the beneficiaries reported an increase in their well-being despite the small size of the subsidy. Expansion of the scheme to include greater number of beneficiaries and higher rates of assistance would bring about greater benefits to the chronic poor. Funding caps should be removed and an increase in the centrally sponsored rate would be useful (CPRC, 2007). An increase in the benefit to the equivalent of $1 per day (about Rs. 1200 per beneficiary per month) would go a long way to bridging the chronic poverty gap.

In 2006, India implemented the National Rural Employment Scheme (NREGS) for 200 backward districts. The residents in these districts make up 70 percent of India's poor. They are mainly located in arid and semi-arid regions. The scheme guarantees one person in every poor household in the country employment of 100 days each year. In 2007, it provided 30 million households with an average of 43 of days work. 3 million got the full 100 days between 2007 and 2008 (CPRC, 2008). The scheme aims to reduce severe rural livelihood distress by creating a short-term need for unskilled labor. It also aims to improve agricultural productivity of the arid and semi-arid lands with projects relating to water conservation, drought proofing (including reforestation/tree plantation), land development, flood control and protection works (including drainage in waterlogged areas) and rural connectivity in terms of all-weather roads. Farmers are guaranteed short-term casual employment and with the completion of the NREGS project, the farmers can plant a second crop and earn additional income, thus providing a sustainable livelihood in the long term (see Box 7.4). From April 2008, the NREGS have been extended to all 604 districts of the country.[10] However its effectiveness appears to be varied. The poorer states of Andhra Pradesh (25.37 person days), Uttar Pradesh (22.23 person days), Bihar (18.46 person days), Chhattisgarh (38.65 person days), Orissa (32.27 person days) and Madhya Pradesh (39.9 person days) still fall short of the desired target of 100 days (Center for Science and Environment, 2008). See Chapter 4 for additional discussion of NREGS.

Both the NREGS and the NOAPS are examples of social protection schemes in India. They help to improve both the economic and psychological welfare of the poor. They provide the poor with some degree of financial independence and the poor families enjoy greater respect and dignity instead of relying on assistance from others. Although the current size of the program needs to be upgraded to pull more families out of poverty, the NREGS can aid in reducing or breaking the exploitative relationship between landlords and farmers/bonded workers.

---

[10] See the Center for Science and Environment (2008) for a comprehensive analysis of India's NREGA and suggested reforms needed.

Box 7.4 Double Cropping with Irrigation

The grin on Nepal Singh's face, a 50-year-old farmer in Siddhi district's Barmani village, is unusual. The Siddhi district is facing another drought for the fourth consecutive year. Normally a drought implies anguish for farmers like Nepal Singh as their crops fail and they lose their income earnings.

"This year I have earned more money from agriculture than ever." He has managed for the first time in many decades to harvest a second crop. Wheat cultivation is also possible now with assured irrigation. Under the NREGS, he has been able to renovate a previously abandoned well. Family and village members worked on it for three months and were paid Rs. 2000 each. Although it was less than his earnings as a migrant worker, he was pleased with the results of the renovation. His income has increased from Rs. 4500 to Rs. 20,000 this year.

Within the Siddhi district, up to 8000 wells has been dug in the past two years and 50 percent have been completed. The scheme benefits the large number of scheduled castes and tribes in Siddhi and has reduced severe poverty levels.

Source: Center for Science and Environment (2008, p. 46).

Turning to sectors outside of agriculture, workers in the informal sector, which accounts for a huge proportion of the chronic poor, are especially at risk. They rarely enjoy formal social protection. An exception is the workers in the bidi (hand-rolled cigarette) industry. The Department of Labor implemented a welfare fund based on a levy on bidi exports that provides health care, housing, water supply and recreational facilities. However there is minimal coverage of workers under this program (Mehrotra and Biggeri, 2007). India needs to look at ways to increase its formal sector employment before employment related social protection (social insurance, pension plans, and health insurance) can take off. CPRC (2008) also notes that an increase in formal sector employment would enlarge the tax base for

India, and thus allow greater expenditure on pro-poor policies. Rapid economic growth has been raising fiscal revenue but India's tax system is inefficient and tax exemptions generally benefit the rich at the expense of the poor. The Anti-Corruption Commission of India is addressing these issues but still has some way to go. Government spending at both the national and state level on social development and exclusion issues which directly impact the chronic poor at both the national and state level are often assigned less than 1 percent of the total budget.

On the political front, there are differing levels of state effectiveness in providing human services and infrastructure ranging from Kerala (the best) to Bihar (worse). The effectiveness of social protection schemes also vary from state to state. In certain states, NREGS suffers from ineffectiveness and corruption practices. The main complaints about the NOAPS arises from inept targeting of beneficiaries.

7.2.4 *Sector policies*

Social infrastructure. In 1997, Madhya Pradesh introduced an innovative program designed to increase enrolment in elementary school (see Chapter 4 for additional details). This Education Guarantee Scheme (EGS) guarantees villages that need an elementary school (as demonstrated by submission of a list of children who are out of range of existing schools) that one will be built within 90 days. The EGS forges a partnership between the local community, the state government, parents and teachers. The program has catalyzed the participation of scheduled class and scheduled tribal minority students. Over 90 percent of 1.2 million children enrolled in the EGS are from these three groups.

The EGS system runs in parallel to the government system of primary schools and is cheaper to operate and the introduction of EGS has resulted in a sharp drop in the number of children out of school. Between 1996 and 2003, the number of children out of school has fallen and there has been a measurable increase in literacy. The successful EGS experience in Madhya Pradesh is being experimented with in other states. Rajasthan has also had some success. Future expansion of the program will require keeping costs down and recruiting competent teachers. A survey by UNICEF suggests that the poor and illiterate would still be willing to send their children to school, despite the expense, if they had confidence that their children were being educated.

Health protection also has to be upgraded, with greater attention to prevention of childhood illness as well as malaria, dysentery and tuberculosis. In addition the spread of HIV/AIDS has to be arrested. Two thirds of the reported HIV infections have been in a few states in the industrialized south west, particularly Mumbai and coastal Andhra Pradesh. In the southern provinces of India infection levels are not confined to urban areas as rural and urban populations tend to have similar patterns of HIV infection rates (see World Bank, 2005a and United Nations, 2006).

Physical infrastructure. The spread of new telecommunications technology throughout India has accelerated over the past few years. Cell phone usage has increased rapidly along with the internet and a variety of innovative uses for this technology have arisen in India. For example in the education sector a support network of observers can help supervisors to keep track of teacher's movements. Students can also contact this network to see if the teacher is present. Commercial uses of cell phones have also been reported by fishermen who use them to contact different markets to check out where demand is strongest and where prices are high. This has improved the efficiency of delivery to market, increased earnings of fishermen and reduced spoilage by establishing a network of buyers and sellers. Rural roads have also been a very good investment. As noted in Chapter 4, Fan *et al.* (2002) compared rates of return to various infrastructure programs and found that investment in roads has the largest impact on rural poverty. Spending on roads had nearly twice as large an impact on reducing rural poverty as the next expenditure variable, R&D investment in agriculture. Investment in roads also was an important factor in raising productivity in the agricultural sector.

Migration. Although internal migration is a powerful way for the chronically poor to make a better life for themselves there has been little governmental initiative to promote it. Even though the additional income obtained from seasonal migration may not be large, the evidence suggests that migrant and local agricultural work is combined by many households to yield a smoother annual income stream than would be possible from seasonal work within the villages. Furthermore in some cases migrants can learn new skills that increase their earning capacity.

There is a large amount of temporary labor migration within India as labor needs for harvesting vary from state to state. The migrants are sometimes not welcomed and provision of living quarters for the migrants is often makeshift. Migrants can also be swindled out of their earnings. Legal protection for migrants needs to be increased and migration monitored by local authorities to ensure that their rights are protected. This may be difficult to enforce but is still a critical step in bringing law and order into a sometimes chaotic and unregulated labor market for agricultural laborers who are often among the poorest groups in society.

7.2.5 *Macroeconomic policies*

In Chapter 5 it was noted that trade openness and income distribution are aspects of macroeconomic policy that have an impact on poverty. The federally oriented political structure of India and its impact on federal spending are an additional aspect of the macroeconomic policy environment that has to be considered. Under this federal structure it is difficult for poor states such as Bihar, Orissa and Madhya Pradesh to generate enough revenue to mount effective social programs. India does not have a revenue sharing scheme whereby states are systematically subsidized from federal revenues. Furthermore employment and incomes have grown at a more moderate pace in the poorer states than in richer states providing a slower growth in the tax base and the ability of the states to fund effective poverty reduction strategies (see Dowling, 2007, Table 7.14, reproduced here as Table 7.7) Adopting a revenue sharing system would

Table 7.7 Annual Percentage Change in Public, Private and Total Employment in the Organized Sector of the Indian Economy 1970/71–2001/2002

	Public	Private	Total
Poorer states			
Bihar	1.9	−1.8	0.9
Uttar Pradesh	0.7	−0.5	0.4
Orissa	2.5	0.4	2.2
Madhya Pradesh	0.8	−0.8	0.5
Rajasthan	2.3	2.7	2.4
Rich States			
Tamil Nadu	1.9	1.1	1.6
Gujarat	1.6	1.5	1.5
Haryana	2.8	2.9	2.8
Maharashtra	1.3	0.6	1.0
Punjab	2.1	2.5	2.2

Source: Dowling (2007, Table 7.14).

help address these issues by providing more income for the poorer states. It could also help attract more investment so as to increase the pace of employment generation by the private sector.

One of the reasons why poverty reduction in India has lagged behind that of China is the relative weakness of employment generation in India's manufacturing sector in particular, and industry in general. India's sector share of industry is only 26 percent of total value added compared to 66 percent in China, 46.7 percent in Thailand and nearly 40 percent in Vietnam (see Dowling, 2007). Until the industrial sector in India begins to grow more vigorously and the opportunities for employment generation sufficient to draw labor from agriculture, the likelihood of more rapid reductions in rural poverty in the near future is small.

There are many reasons why industrial sector growth has been so anemic. The regulatory environment is not flexible and it is not easy to enter or leave the market. Starting a business requires many permits and bureaucratic hurdles. Many foreign investors are turned off by this. Less than 20 percent of approved projects were implemented. It is also difficult to hire and fire because of government controls and regulations. It is hard to buy and sell land and there is a history of trade protection. Although trade barriers have been falling, tariffs are still high compared with other Asian competitors. There are also infrastructure bottlenecks and costs of power, telecommunications and water are high and sometimes subject to costly interruption. Finally the web of bureaucracy and controls make bribery and corruption sometimes a necessary evil that some companies are not willing to engage in.

As far as the other macroeconomic factors that have relevance for poverty mentioned in Chapter 5, India has loosened its hold on the financial system. The level of inflation has been moderate and steady at around 5 percent for the past few years. However development spending has tended to favor the richer states (see Table 6.3) and its international trade regime, while continuing to become more liberal, still has some way to go to match East and Southeast Asia.

7.2.6 *Comparison between China and India*

The two largest country contributors to poverty in Asia are China and India. Rural poverty in China tends to be concentrated in the western regions whereas it is more evenly distributed in the states of India. Rural poverty in western China is comparable to that of Indian regions see Table 7.8. However Borooah *et al.* (2006) find that rural poverty in China was mainly due to spatial factors whereas rural poverty in India has been primarily due to discrimination against tribal minorities and lower castes. Ethnic minorities in China make up 9 percent of its population and they are largely concentrated in the remote, mountainous areas in the north-west and south-west regions. India has about 30 percent of its population falling under the minority category. They include Muslims, "untouchable" castes such as Dalit. Access to land is still problematic in India as many rural households in India are landless unlike Chinese households who hold user rights over the lands.

Exposure to uninsured risks such as health costs have resulted in non-poor families falling into chronic poverty. Out-of-pocket health expenditure is said to have increased the poverty rate in China from

Table 7.8 Per Capita Household Income in Rural China, 1995 and in Rural India, 1993–94

	Central	South	West	East	North	National
Rural India						
Mean income (PPP, US$)	606	769	850	536	774	680
Population share	40	20	13	14	12	100
Income share	36	23	16	11	13	100
Gini	0.42	0.48	0.49	0.41	0.41	0.45
Rural China						
Mean income (PPP, US$)	706		555	1352		904
Population share	38		26	36		100
Income share	30		17	53		100
Gini	0.33		0.37	0.44		0.42

Source: Borooah *et al.* (2006, p. 800, Table 1).

13.7 percent to 16.2 percent and in India from 31.1 percent to 34.8 percent (Powell, 2006, and World Bank, 2008a).

There has been less deterioration in income distribution and the share of the lowest quintile in India possibly because of slower growth in the industrial sector. India stands third out of 14 Asian economies (behind Bangladesh and Pakistan) with a Gini coefficient of 32.5 and an income share of the lowest quintile of the population of 8.8 percent. China ranks next to last having a high Gini coefficient (44.7) and a low share of the bottom quintile (4.7 percent) in 2004. Also refer to Table 7.9.

7.2.7 *Future policy agenda and challenges*

India has a number of programs in place to aid the poor, the chronically poor and their families. These include food subsidies, work fare, new schools for villages and conditional cash transfers to encourage students from poor families to attend school. Despite all these programs poverty rates are still going down slowly, particularly in the poorest provinces. It is hard to pinpoint one reason for this. Lack of focus on the poor and

Table 7.9 Income Distribution in Asia — 2004

Country	Share of Lowest 20%	Gini Coefficient
Bangladesh	9.1	31.8
India	8.8	32.5
Nepal		
Pakistan	9.3	30.6
Sri Lanka	8.3	33.2
Cambodia		
Indonesia	8.4	34.3
Lao PDR		
Malaysia	4.4	49.1
Philippines	5.4	46.1
Thailand	8.3	42.0
Vietnam	7.3	37.0
China	4.7	44.7
Korea	7.9	31.6

Source: Dowling (2007, Table 4.17).

subversion of funds to the non poor is one possibility. Discrimination against minorities has also played a big role — in denying educational opportunities, satisfactory health care and sufficient government resources to enable the poorest provinces to generally lift living standards through development of human resources. Slow growth in employment, particularly in manufacturing and related industrial activities is another reason for slow poverty reduction. Reforms governing the investment climate, entry and exit of firms and labor mobility are needed to increase the dynamism of the industrial sector. Some have already been undertaken. More needs to be done to raise economic growth and increase labor absorption. India needs to invest 3–4 percent of GDP on infrastructure to sustain economic growth at around 8 percent per annum (World Bank, 2006e). Remittances have helped reduce poverty for those who can afford to migrate and it would be useful to help the chronically poor to find alternative employment in urban areas or overseas. This can be done through a repayable grant or by developing a program where poor families can pool resources to send some workers to the city or overseas. Those chronically poor with some family members that were able to migrate to urban centers have greatly benefited from remittance income. In cases where there is already circular migration from rural areas government intervention to prevent abuses of the migrants is needed. Agricultural extension policies to raise productivity in drought and flood prone areas as well as increasing connectivity of remote areas will also aid efforts to reduce chronic poverty. Finally, a coordinated social welfare program that provides food and income subsidies for those unable to work and to aid the poor in sending their children to school is needed. Efforts in these directions have begun and need to be strengthened and extended to reach more of the chronically poor.

7.3 Indonesia

Box 7.5. A Snapshot of Indonesia's Chronic Poor

- Indonesia has around 17 million people living on less than US$1 per day. The poor make up 7.5 percent of its population. However according to the latest revised poverty lines from World Bank, magnitude of poverty in Indonesia is much more widespread with approximately 20 percent of the population in Indonesia surviving on less than US1.25 per day.
- The chronic poor accounts for approximately 25 percent to 35 percent of the poor.
- Before the onset of the Asian financial crisis, most provinces reported low levels of chronic poverty. Rates of chronic poverty were generally higher in Eastern than Western Indonesia. Chronic poverty increased by more than 10 percent in Lampung, Papua, Maluku, Central Sulawesi and East Nusa Tenggara between 1996 and 1999.
- The chronic poor were mainly those who had low levels of productive assets, lack education and had limited savings as a buffer against sudden shocks to income.

(*Continued*)

Box 7.5 (*Continued*)

- Indonesia was categorized as a "consistent improver" together with China and Vietnam. Welfare levels have been on the rise especially since 2005. Papua and East Nusa Tenggara have reported large falls in chronic poverty between 1996 and 2005.

Table Box 7.5. Selected Indicators

Proportion of poor who are chronically poor over 5 years (low estimate)[1]	0.25
Proportion of poor who are chronically poor over 5 years (high estimate)[1]	0.35
Population	221 million
Percentage of poor living on less than US$1.25 per day (2005PPP)*	21.4
Average depth of poverty (number of % points by which the poor fall below the poverty line[2] in 2002)	12.0
Income share held by lowest 20%	8.4
Gini index of inequality	34.3
Healthcare indicators	
Under-5 mortality rate (per 1,000 live births) in 2004	38
Infant mortality rate (per 1,000 live births) in 2004	30
Proportion of children under 5 who are stunted	—
Life expectancy at birth, 2004	67.2
Educational indicators	
Adult illiteracy rate for women aged 15 years and above (2000–2004)	17
Adult illiteracy rate for men aged 15 years and above (2000–2004)	8
Child labor	
Percentage of children aged between 7–14 in the labor force (1999–2004)	7.8

Sources: CPRC (2008) Annex E and F, Suryahadi and Sumarto (2003) and Bauer *et al.* (2008).

Notes: [1]Based on various issues of *Indonesia Family Life Survey.* [2]Most recent year.

President Suharto sparked off greater policy attention to pro-poor growth when he announced that 27 million Indonesians (15 percent of the population) were poor in 1990 (Asra, 2000). Before 1993, the method to estimate total poverty line was rather elementary. The food poverty line consisted solely of the amount of expenditure needed to satisfy an energy intake of 2100 calories per capita per day. Some essential non-food items were added to the food poverty line to arrive at the total poverty line.

Over time there has been an improvement to the construction of poverty lines to measure the extent of poverty in Indonesia. The measurement of the poverty line has been expanded to include a comprehensive list of 52 food items and 46 essential non-food needs such as housing, clothing, education, health and transportation etc. Nevertheless, Asra (2000) argues that there remain some limitations to the construction of the poverty line in Indonesia. Firstly, there are disparities between the non-food share in the poverty line and that of the observed consumption expenditure for Indonesian households. The non-food component of the Indonesia poverty line is still much lower than in the Philippines. Secondly, issues of rural-urban comparability arise since the urban-rural differential of the poverty lines appears to be far higher than the cost of living differentials between rural and urban areas. Also, poverty line estimates neglect differences between the consumption baskets of various population groups, and price changes that may have differed. Hence data which suggests that the Gini coefficients have fallen at current prices may be misleading. Asra (2000) argues strongly for collecting disaggregate data such as appropriate price indices for different groups over time and space rather than aggregate data which may mask the dynamics of households moving in and out of poverty. Nevertheless, despite these difficulties, the current poverty measurement methodology in Indonesia is comparable or even superior to other countries in the region.

Between 1975 and 2001, Indonesia was successful in bringing down the level of poverty from nearly 60 percent to around 10 percent (see Quibria, 2002). Indonesia targets to further reduce poverty incidence to 8.2 percent and unemployment rate to 5.1 percent by 2009 (ADB, 2006b and IFAD, 2008). While the Asian financial crisis resulted in some increases in poverty and recent estimates suggest a higher level of poverty, the Indonesian experience continues to offer useful poverty reduction lessons for other countries both in Asia and elsewhere.

7.3.1 *Incidence of poverty*

There is considerable disparity in poverty levels in the provinces of Indonesia. The incidence of poverty is generally higher in Eastern than Western Indonesia (see Table 1.10, a portion is repeated below in Table 7.10). The provinces of Papua and Maluku have the highest incidence of poverty although the greatest numbers of poor people are found in Java. Healthcare, education and infrastructure in Papua and Maluku also lag behind the rest of the provinces (CPRC, 2008). For instance in Java, a poor family has to travel an average of 4 km to

Table 7.10 Rural Poverty in Indonesia, 2004

Province	Rural Poverty 2004 — Percent of population below poverty line
Aceh	33
North Sumatra	17
West Sumatra	10
Riau	18
Jambi	10
South Sumatra	21
Benkulu	21
Lampung	23
West Java	13
Central Java	24
East Java	24
West Nusu Tenggara	21
East Nusu Tenggara	30
West Kalimantan	14
Central Kalimantan	12
South Kalimantan	8
East Kalimantan	19
North Sulawesi	12
Central Sulawesi	23
South Sulawesi	19
Maluku	40
Papua	49

Source: ADB (2006, p. 100, Appendix Table 2).

reach a health clinic whereas they would have to travel over 32 km in Papua. Less than 10 percent of the households in Papua have access to potable drinking water.

To develop a better understanding of the details of poverty and chronic poverty at the provincial level in Indonesia, Alisjahbana and Yusuf (2003) surveyed the consumption expenditure of over 6000 Indonesian households using data from Indonesia Family Life Surveys of 1993 and 1997. They then compared these results with the Indonesian Central Body of Statistics poverty line for urban and rural residents. A household was determined to be chronically poor if its consumption expenditure was below the poverty line for both periods. Using this methodology they concluded that chronic poverty decreased between 1993 and 1997. However approximately half of the poor households in 1993 remained poor in 1997. About 8 percent of the sampled households were diagnosed to be chronically poor in 1997.

Using a different methodology Widyanti *et al.* (2001) classified the population into 4 main categories: the persistently poor, chronically poor, transient poor and never poor.[11] Using the 100 Villages Survey which interviewed a panel of over 10,000 households from 1998 to 1999, households most vulnerable to poverty belong to the persistently poor and chronically poor groups. Using this definition, Widyanti *et al.*, 2001 found that 33 percent of the poor faced problems of continued poverty in 1999 (see Figure 7.1), a much larger proportion than in the Alisjahbana and Yusuf (2003) study.

Impact of Asian financial crisis. Indonesia was hard hit during the Asian financial crisis. Before 1997, Indonesia has been held up as a success story in terms of rapid economic growth and the 50 percent reduction of poverty in less than 20 years. However the sharp contraction of the economy during the Asian financial crisis resulted in rising unemployment and inflation driven primarily by escalating food prices which hit the poor and lower skilled workers hardest. Real wages

[11] Widyanti *et al.* (2001) defined "persistently poor" to be always poor, "chronically poor" as those who were sometimes poor, but whose mean real per capita consumption over the whole period was below the poverty line and "transiently poor" as those who were sometimes poor but their mean real per capita consumption over time was higher than the poverty line.

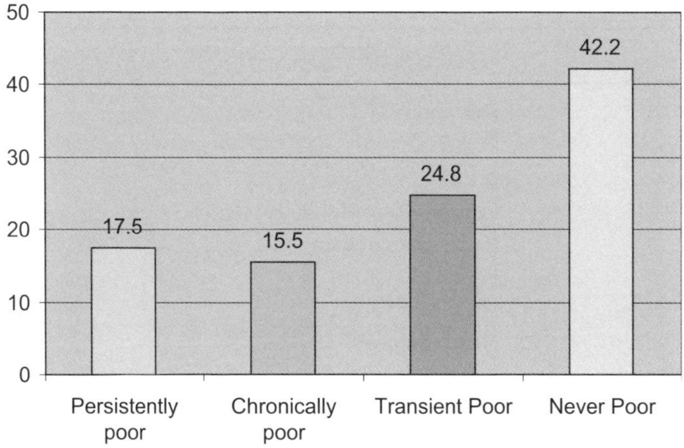

Figure 7.1 Proportions of Poor in Indonesia (%), 1999

Source: Widyanti *et al.* (2001).

Note: Proportion of households who are poor.

fell by 33 percent and both transient and chronic poverty increased. It was estimated that the level of chronic poverty rose from 20 percent before the crisis to 35 percent of the poor after the crisis (Suryahadi and Sumarto, 2003). No single province emerged unscathed from the negative effects of the economic crisis (see Table 7.11).

In comparison to the low incidence of chronic poverty in Jakarta, West Sumatra and Aceh, around 40 percent of the populations in the provinces of Papua and East Nusa Tenggara were chronically poor even in the pre-crisis period. After the crisis, not surprisingly, they were among the provinces that were most adversely impacted by the crisis as chronic poverty increased greatly in Lampung, Maluku and Central Sulawesi. The province of Lampung was the most adversely affected, suffering a 15.1 percent increase in the number of chronic poor.

7.3.2 *Determinants of poverty*

Using a multinomial logit model, Alisjahbana and Yusuf (2003) analyzed the factors determining poverty status of households. Education, size of the household, amount of financial assets and location of residence were key factors affecting households' income and

Table 7.11 Increase in Chronic Poverty Level by Province, 1996–99 (% change)

No	Province	Chronic Poor
1	Lampung	15.1
2	Papua	14.3
3	Maluku	14.2
4	Central Sulawesi	12.6
5	East Nusatenggara	11.6
6	West Kalimantan	9.7
7	Southeast Sulawesi	9.0
8	North Sulawesi	8.9
9	East Kalimantan	8.6
10	Yogyakarta	8.5
11	East Java	7.9
12	Central Java	7.5
13	South Kalimantan	6.9
14	West Nusatenggara	6.6
15	West Java	6.2
16	Bengkulu	5.2
17	South Sumatra	5.0
18	Central Kalimantan	4.9
19	Jambi	3.6
20	Riau	2.5
21	South Sulawesi	2.4
22	North Sumatra	1.9
23	Bali	1.8
24	West Sumatra	1.4
25	Aceh	0.7
26	Jakarta	0.1

Source: Suryahadi and Sumarto (2003, p. 18, Table 4).

their chronic poverty status. Although the incidence of chronic poverty was higher in rural areas than urban areas, the factors determining chronic poverty were the same for both locations.

The increase in chronic poverty was most pronounced for three overlapping groups; those living in rural areas, those working in the agricultural sector and those who did not complete secondary education. Vulnerability was about the same for households headed by males and females. Female-headed households did not seem more vulnerable to poverty than male-headed households (see Table 7.12).

Table 7.12 Chronic Poverty, 1996 and 1999 (%)

	1996	1999
Rural vs urban areas		
Rural	4.7	13.2
Urban	0.6	3.9
Occupational sector		
Agriculture	7.2	18.7
Industry	1.1	6.4
Trade	0.3	2.1
Services	0.4	3.4
Receiving Transfers	0.8	3.7
Educational attainment		
Not completed primary	6.4	19.0
Primary	1.9	7.6
Secondary	1.2	3.4
Tertiary	0.0	0.2
Gender of Heads of Households		
Male	3.3	9.6
Female	3.0	8.2

Source: Suryahadi and Sumarto (2003, Table 5.8).

Approximately 15 percent of the non-poor also slipped into poverty as a result of the financial shock (Alisjahbana and Yusuf, 2003). It remains to be seen if these households continue to be persistently poor in the new millennium or if they adopted coping mechanisms and managed to escape the chronic poverty trap. Their status depends on how well households have dealt with the financial crisis and if those households that slipped into transient poverty have become part of the chronically poor in Indonesia. Preliminary results suggest that most families have recovered and chronic poverty levels have fallen.

7.3.3 *Micro policies*

As a response to the rise in poverty during the Asian financial crisis, Indonesia implemented a range of social safety net packages including

Table 7.13 Major Program of Indonesian Social Safety Nets

Social Safety Net	Program
Food security	• OPK program: sales of subsidized rice to targeted households. This programme has been since renamed Raskin (from Be*ras* untuk Rakyat Mis*kin* — rice for the poor) since 2004
Employment creation	• *Padat karya* (labor intensive) programme that offers employment in selected government departments • PDM–DKE: a community fund that provides block grants directly to villages for either public works or revolving funds for credit
Education	• Scholarships directly to elementary school, junior high and senior high students • Block grants to selected schools
Health	• JPS-BK: a programme providing subsidies for medical services, operational support for health centers, medicine and imported medical equipment, family planning services, nutrition and midwives services

Source: SDS and URDI (2003, pp. 74–75, Table III.3.2).

labor intensive community based projects, subsidies to control the price of nine basic goods and educational and health programs to help the poor maintain a certain level of income security (IFAD, 2008). These projects were supported by financial assistance from international donors like World Bank, ADB and UN. See Table 7.13 for greater details on social safety nets in Indonesia.

Food security. Since 1998, Indonesia has implemented a targeted rice subsidy programme, the *Operasi Pasar Khusus* (OPK), that allows poor households to buy ten kilograms of rice per family per month at a subsidized price. The quantity of rice available for each poor family was later raised to 20 kilograms. The program has since been renamed as Raskin (from Be*ras* untuk Rakyat Mis*kin* — rice for the poor) in 2004. Recipients of the subsidized rice are identified using an eligibility criteria based on asset wealth devised by the National

Coordinating Board for Family Planning. Food is distributed to the community leaders by Bulog, the government food distribution agency, according to number of poor households in their community, which is then distributed to the needy households. Raskin is expected to benefit close to 8.6 million households which supplements about 40 percent to 60 percent of their needs (HDR, 2004). In addition, the World Food Program through NGOs provides subsidized rice to 300,000 poor households each year.

However such food programs often suffer from leakages to the non-poor. Subbarao *et al.* (1997) conducted various cross-country studies and found that for every $1 spent on food distribution programs the administration cost varies from $1.60 to $2.00, and about one-third of the benefits go to the non-poor. The *Indonesia Human Development Report 2004* reveals that about 35 percent of the subsidized Raskin rice leaks to non-poor households. One reason is that the community leaders generally distribute food to all households in their communities on the basis that every household should benefit equally instead of simply targeting needy households. Instead of receiving the full amount of the subsidized rice, the needy households only receive 30 percent to 50 percent of their rice allocation. More needs to be done to reduce such leakages and improve ways to identify the poor.

Cash transfers. Indonesia has also implemented cash transfer programs to help the poor. For instance, the unconditional cash transfer program Bantuan Tunai Langsun provided over 15 million households with over US$2.4 billion in four installments during 2005 (CPRC, 2008). When it was reported that the non-poor also benefited from the program, it was replaced with a conditional cash transfer instead. In view of rapidly rising fuel costs and the pressure to reduce fuel subsidies which disproportionately benefits the well-off, in May 2008 President Susilo Bambang Yudhoyono announced a program to give cash transfers of more than $1.5 billion (14.18 trillion rupiah) to the poor to cope with rising cost of living. With the cut on fuel subsides, the government is expected to spend more on social development projects.

Since 2007, Indonesia has piloted a major conditional cash transfer program, Program Keluarga Harapan, to poor families across 7 provinces to satisfy certain health and educational objectives. Data shows that infant mortality rates are 3 times higher in the poorest quintile than the richest quintile; and only 50 percent of the children in the poorest quintile as opposed to 72 percent in the richest quintile enrol in junior secondary level schools (HDR, 2004). Many school children of poor families drop out even before completion of primary education. Studies also show that the health expenditure of the poorest 10 percent of the population takes up to 2.3 times their monthly income, which is a substantial amount of money for the very poor and likely to affect their livelihoods in the case of a health shock (Thabrany, 2003). Approximately 500,000 very poor families are expected to benefit from the conditional cash transfers (World Bank, 2008b). Results appear encouraging especially in terms of health outcomes for the poor, who are now visiting local health clinics more frequently. The voucher program sponsored by the World Bank has also had some success in increasing school enrolment among the poor and to aid pregnant women pay for midwife services (see Box 7.6).

Box 7.6 Vouchers for Health and Education in Indonesia

World Bank (2006f) assesses the effectiveness of 2 voucher programs in Indonesia — the Safe Motherhood Program and the Jaringan Pengaman Sosial (JPS) scholarship program. It highlighted the importance of benefits being targeted directly at the poor rather than allowing the service providers to select the recipient.

Under the Safe Motherhood Program, vouchers were given directly to poor women in Pemalang district, Central Java, to pay for midwife services during pregnancy. Midwives also benefited from the scheme as they receive money through the vouchers and they were more pro-active in seeking out new clients to supplement their low monthly salary. Usage of midwife services rapidly increased from near zero in the late 1990s to 1,164 in 2000.

The JPS scholarship program did not fare as well as the Safe Motherhood Program in aiding the poor. The JPS program provided

(*Continued*)

Box 7.6 (*Continued*)

scholarships to poor children to enrol in junior secondary school but money was distributed as block grants through the schools. As a result, school principals and treasurers were in charge of the selection of eligible students for scholarships. Most scholarships were given to students who were already enrolled rather than to those who had dropped out. Secondly, there was little incentive on the school administration to encourage drop-outs to come back to school. As a result the effectiveness of the JPS program was limited.

Sources: Ridao-Cano and Filmer (2004), Tan, Kusharto and Budiyati (2005) in World Bank (2006f).

Under the *Kartu Sehat* scheme, health cards are issued to the poor to access health services. The government would then reimburse the service providers. Efforts were also made by the government to provide free referral in-patient care for the poor at district hospitals and free generic drugs and free basic health care at health centers (HDR, 2004). However, service providers were often reluctant to serve the very parties in need and utilization rates by the poorest were quite low as they often have to fork out bribes in order to access the entitled services. In fact for services accessed from state-owned hospitals, the poorest account for the highest proportion of all bribes given — they pay close to 30 percent of all bribes (HDR, 2004).

In an effort to help poor villages to free themselves from poverty, Indonesia has initiated the *Inpres Desa Tertinggal* (IDT) or "Presidential Instruction for Villages Left Behind" program. Community groups in each poor village were provided with 20 to 60 million rupiah as seed funding for development of small local enterprises. The community groups can determine the type of business venture they are interested in. Special training is given to the group members by facilitators. These facilitators are local professionals such as teachers, health workers, social workers and specially assigned young graduates to provide assistance to the group in the development of the business venture. A total of 98,047 IDT community groups has been formed and include around 14 million individuals. Since 1996, over 28,000 villages have received the capital aid. Also, basic infrastructure has been constructed in over 10,500 IDT villages by 2002 and to be extended to cover all IDT villages in the future. It has increased the flow of goods and services between rural and urban areas, and thus improved household incomes of the poor. However the IDT program does face some concerns of ineffective facilitators. The private sector has shown little or minimal interest in the small scale business conducted in remote IDT villages. Hence, the IDT program has limited reach to the geographically disadvantaged villages where the chronic poor are most likely to reside.

In sync with the aims of the IDT program, Indonesia has also recently promoted the Kecamatan Development Program (KDP) to target rural poverty in general. The KDP is a community-development driven project and emphasizes empowerment of the poor. Funds are distributed to directly to the community and the village council empowered with the disbursement of funds to worthwhile proposals from needy groups. Such proposals are assessed openly at the village level. Doing so encourages "healthy competition" between villages within the sub-district level and increases the transparency and efficiency of the funding management. To be eligible for the KDP program, certain criteria has to be fulfilled. First, there must be a high percentage of poor households and a significant number of poor villages in the sub-district. The sub-district must have more than 15,000 people for districts outside Java and 25,000 people for districts on Java. In addition, the village council must be established and in place to assess the group proposals and decide on the disbursement of funds. To date, KDP is one of the largest community-development driven projects in the world and has covered some 34,200 villages, close to 50 percent of the poorest villages in the country (World Bank, 2006f). The poor villages have benefited from the construction of infrastructure including feeder roads and key irrigation channels. Owing to its relative success, KDP is to be expanded to the entire country by 2009. The practice of majority voting within the village has at times neglected the needs of the poorest and this aspect of the KDP program would need to be addressed. McLaughlin *et al.* (2007) recommended the usage of poverty maps to further identify households to make poverty targeting more effective.

Microfinance and banking. The poorest are often excluded from microfinance. The major impediment is the lack of any collateral and banks aren't willing to lend without it. The World Bank (2006) recommends the development of a program for financing household enterprises of rural low-income families. The Income-Generating Project for Marginal Farmers and the Landless (Pembinaan Peningkatan Pendapatan Petani-Nelayan Kecil, or P4K) provides soft loans to poor farmers through self-help groups. The scheme is co-financed by the government and the ADB, and has successfully mobilized savings and improved access to credit that help the rural poor overcome poverty. More than 200,000 marginal farming and fishing households have benefited from the program (World Bank, 2006f).

In addition to microfinance, the government could encourage the development of free online savings products for poor households in underserved areas as a way of supporting capital accumulation and commerce. Online payment services (such as deposit/withdrawal transactions at multiple locations, electronic transfers, overseas and domestic remittances, ATM access, debit/PoS cards, and similar services) have become increasingly important even to relatively low-income households in Indonesia over the past decade. However this kind of project is still in the planning stages. For the chronically poor a minimal level of education and training is necessary so that they are able to access and utilize on line information, assuming that they have access to computers.

Social insurance. Since the beginning of 2005, Indonesia has implemented a national social health insurance scheme (Askeskin) for the poor. The government pays the premiums for 60 million poor. Some studies have shown that this scheme has significantly helped the poor who are more vulnerable to health shocks (World Bank, 2006f). The effectiveness of the scheme in assisting the very poor remains to be seen.

The SDS and URDI (2003) study offers some additional interesting instances of successful cases where progress has been made in reducing poverty and improving income distribution (see Box 7.7).

Box 7.7 Poverty Reduction Schemes in Balikpapan, Bogor and Bandang Lampur

Poverty reduction schemes have been introduced in Balikpapan (East Kalimantan), Bogor (West Java) and Bandar Lampung (Lampung).

Balikpapan in East Kalimantan has enjoyed the lowest poverty rate in Indonesia, only 10 percent of its population is living below the poverty line. The provincial government has also actively developed community-based housing initiatives in Balikpapan, as a result it does not have any marginalized settlements (slums). Some innovative practices for poverty alleviation include the "Nine carry One" program, where every nine better-off individuals donate to support one poor individual in need of assistance. The poor are also identified by a card that gives them access to health education and other forms of subsidies. The scheme offers financial aid and services and also encourages the poor to strive for upward mobility. The program works at the grass root level to provide support and opportunities to escape from poverty. Some other forms of general policies to reduce poverty alleviation include local schemes such as Poverty Alleviation Program (PAP), the social safety network (JPS which includes access to basic services) and targeted schemes to help those hit by the effects of the economic crisis (Pemberdayaan Daerah Mengatasi Dampak — PDMDKE) and school feeding programs for children (under PMT–AS Additional Nutritional for School Children). Block grants are given to poor communities under the PDMKE scheme to fund public works projects and provide subsidized credit to small businesses.

Balikpapan offers a two pronged approach to ensure the poor has access to education. Educational aid is given to the children of poor families attending elementary to high school, with annual aid ranging

(*Continued*)

Box 7.7 (*Continued*)

from 500,000 rupiah for younger students to 1,000,000 rupiahs for high school students (SDS and URDI, 2005) This financial aid helps poor families pay for school uniforms, shoes, stationary, books and etc. Secondly, the operational costs of schools are paid for through an aid fund under the social safety network program and the city government budget. Aid is issued every 6 months through the nearest Payment Point or Post Office, making it convenient for the poor to access the needed funds. A task force was set up for the management of health services and to coordinate with the PAP coordination team. The database of registered poor households are maintained by the task force, and the poor households are assigned to local community health centers (*Puskesmas*) where they can receive treatment from general medical treatment and dental checkups and free medicines. To obtain more advanced health services at the General Hospital, the patient can request a reference letter from his appointed *Puskesmas.*

Capital aid with zero interest is also given to poor households who want to set up a small business. Maximum loan amounts can be up to 2 million rupiah. The borrower can repay in monthly instalments. Skill upgrading programs are also available for the poor. The success of Balikpapan's various poverty alleviation programs over the past five year is reflected in a reduction in the number of poor families.

Bogor is a city of about 745,000 residents located in West Java. Poor families account for approximately 12 percent of total population, located in both urban and rural sub-districts. The urban poor usually live in slums and work as street hawkers or manual laborers in the informal sector. The rural poor depend on farming or small home-based industries to make a living. Since 1999, the local government has launched the Garda Emas program (literally translated as Golden Guard) which involves the cooperation of local government offices, NGOs, micro-finance institutions and local stakeholders. Similar to Balikpapan, government assistance empowers the community at the grass root level rather than being administered by the central government authorities. It involves schemes to increase job and business opportunities by providing

(*Continued*)

Box 7.7 (*Continued*)

access to credit and tackling unemployment with training and productive economic business development. Funds come from the government's budget and additional funding available at a local bank assigned by the Indonesian government. By 2003, the program had assisted over 9000 poor people and provided jobs to 17,769 workers. Between 1999 and 2003 the number of households in poverty fell by almost 50 percent. The initial lending level of 2.84 billion rupiah had doubled by 2003, to 5.6 billion rupiah. The local authorities also implemented other programs such as house and infrastructure upgrading, free health services to poor families that include assistance for mothers during pregnancy and birth, as well as food support for the children suffering from malnutrition. The impact of this program on chronic poverty has not been measured, though it is likely to be strongly positive.

Bandar Lampung, the capital of Lampung province, has about 860 thousand residents in 2002 and a high poverty rate of nearly 50 percent. The local authority made alleviating poverty one of their main agenda items. Data collection to better identify target groups for poverty alleviation programs and in designing ways for community empowerment has been a priority. In 2003, poverty mapping was done in three of the poorest districts of Bandar Lampung detailing (i) infrastructure and physical environmental condition, (ii) local economic potential and (iii) poverty profiles. From the start, Bandar Lampung actively encouraged the involvement of the relevant stakeholders in the community to voice their assessment of their environment and to provide ideas that would aid in poverty alleviation. Discussions and reflections on poverty were conducted at the neighborhood level. Interviews were held with poor households. Agreement among the neighborhood stakeholders was then prioritized at the city level. After ascertaining the target group and their needs, Bandar Lampung set up the P4K (*Perencanaan Program Partisipatif Pengentasan Kemiskinan*) with the support from URDI and Asian Development Bank, to implement poverty reduction programs. The success rate of the P4K has been quite high. Around 50 percent to 60 percent of the community's

(*Continued*)

Box 7.7 (*Continued*)

proposals were accepted. Highly ranked in the priority listing include: (i) upgrading of basic infrastructure such as water supply, roads and waste disposal, housing upgrading and urban management, (ii) socio-cultural programs to improve community welfare (iii) economic development projects to tap into the local economic potential of the district and to provide opportunities for employment.

Sources: SDS and URDI (2005) and McLaughlin *et al.* (2007).

While they do not directly address the problem of chronic poverty in rural areas there are some important lessons to be learned from these three successful microeconomic case studies. First, active engagement of the relevant stakeholders and the local community was of utmost importance. Building awareness of the seriousness of poverty was necessary at all administrative levels from the city, district, sub-district down to the neighborhood level. Second, local governments actively explore local sources of funding. Balikpapan and Bogor were able to garner public support to finance their poverty alleviation schemes. Donor agencies and NGOs also played a part. Third, there was a change in the government paradigm to address local problems and challenges. To illustrate, Balikpapan customized their poverty alleviation plans to suit local needs of poor households. Rather than relying solely on the government's definition of the poor, they also entrusted a local university to conduct a study of their poor, and combined the results to better identify the target groups in their poverty alleviation plans. Also, Bandar Lampung who has a series of failed poverty schemes before P4K also changed their way of formulating plans by incorporating suggestions and feedback from neighborhoods and other relevant stakeholders. Fourth trust was established by engaging the local community and the government. This greatly reduced the risk of corruption and much needed funds from being siphoned off to non-official uses. Lastly, poverty alleviation programs that are comprehensive and identify target groups have a better chance of success.

7.3.4 *Sector polices*

Rural infrastructure. Indonesia has made tremendous progress in improving access to electricity, roads and telecommunications facilities over the past 25 years, but development tends to be uneven especially in rural areas. For example, less than 50 percent of villages in Central Kalimantan were connected by a concrete or asphalt road. (World Bank, 2006f). Road conditions have also deteriorated markedly since the Asian financial crisis. This has resulted in increases in transport costs and lower prices for farm produce for farmers in rural areas.

Hence Indonesia needs to revamp the district level road management system and channel more resources towards repair and routine maintenance of rural roads especially in poorer regions. One possibility is to use performance-based contracts for road maintenance works to ensure quality standards. There are plans to scale up the community driven projects like KDP to improve rural connectivity. Road projects implemented as part of KDP are effective, yielding an internal rate of return of between 33 and 47 percent (Torrens, 2005) and were cheaper by more than 50 percent than equivalent roads built through government contracts (World Bank, 2006). Improvement in road connectivity would allow the rural poor to have better access to urban markets and provide opportunities for non-farm enterprise activities. Evidence from Gibson (2006) showed that rural villages that had their roads upgraded between 1993 and 2000 saw significantly faster growth in non-farm enterprise activities than other villages.

However not all village infrastructure programs were implemented successfully. See Box 7.8 for details.

Social infrastructure. Indonesia has actively increased funding to provide schools and health clinics. However the middle income and rich generally benefited more than the poor. Recent studies by the World Bank have shown that the poor have begun to receive more benefits (see Lanjouw *et al.*, 2001). This is because the poor are now being targeted more effectively (Timmer, 2007).

Box 7.8 Concerns with the PKPS-BBM Village Infrastructure Program

The PKPS-BBM Village Infrastructure Program was developed using savings accruing from the reduction in fuel subsidies in March 2005. The aims of the program were two-fold: (i) to generate labor intensive employment and (ii) improve infrastructure at the village level through a bottom-up decision-making process. More than 12,000 villages received direct grants through the Ministry of Public Works.

However many problems surfaced with the implementation of the program. Firstly, the time frame was extremely tight as all funds had to be expended by end of 2006. Secondly, the implementation schedule did not allow for sufficient discussions among stakeholders. Sixty-seven percent of villagers interviewed knew that their village would receive funding from the fuel-subsidy compensation scheme, and 56 percent knew that the community should be involved in the project. But very few respondents knew what the funds should be used for or what their rights were in terms of participation in the decision-making and implementation processes.

Third, the quality of infrastructure produced by the program was inadequate. Of all the roads built using project funding, 47 percent were ranked of poor quality and unlikely to last more than one year and only 50 percent of all projects were given a good quality evaluation. Only 20 percent of all villages surveyed had established committees to maintain the infrastructure built through the program. Cost-effectiveness was also questionable and one-third of all projects were not cost effective.

Lastly, the choice of using contractors rather than communities to implement projects was a highly risky facet of project design and susceptible to rent seeking activities. The size of the grant at Rp 250 million per village was also considered to be too large for the type of community projects under consideration.

Source: World Bank (2006f, Box 5.4).

Land rights. Land rights have not been effectively established despite forty years of land registration. Only one quarter of Indonesia's estimated 80 million land parcels has been registered according to the World Bank (2006f). The opaque and costly system of land administration has created bottlenecks (AFD *et al.*, 2005). There is a need to accelerate land titling and re-allocate degraded and deforested land to productive use to expand the income and livelihood of the poor farmers.

7.3.5 *Macro policies*

On the macro level, Indonesia has made national poverty reduction a priority in its poverty reduction strategy paper (PRSP). In addition to alleviating poverty for the poor households, it aims to assist those who are vulnerable and at risk of becoming poor (IFAD, 2008). In fact economic growth in Indonesia has been pro-poor for many years (see Timmer, 2007) and Indonesia has been categorized as a "consistent improver" together with China and Vietnam by CPRC (2008). There has been a conscientious attempt to design and implement pro-poor strategies in national plans, even though the term "pro-poor" has not been explicitly stated. Also the growth elasticity of poverty for Indonesia between 1967 and 2002 averaged 1.75, well above East Asia and Pacific average of 1.00 (see Besley and Burgess, 2003). Between 1996 and 2002, growth continued to be pro-poor, despite the negative impact of the Asian financial crisis on the economy. World Bank (2006f) suggested that this was because the crisis squeezed the asset wealth of the rich while having less impact on the poor.

Timmer (2007) argued that Indonesia's post-1967 pro-poor economic growth was strongly due to improvements in agricultural productivity in rural areas. The growth of the rural areas boosted income of the rural poor and created jobs. Furthermore, it facilitated the shift from farm to non-farm rural employment and triggered expansion of the manufacturing industry. Revenues from oil exports were well-managed and re-invested into rural areas to stimulate economic development and raise income. Fluctuations in rice prices which tend to influence consumption expenditure of the poor were well-managed through macroeconomic policy which controlled inflation and the real exchange rate (Timmer, 2007).

The Green Revolution, technology and massive investments in agriculture also catalyzed high rates of pro-poor growth in Indonesia in the 1960s, 1970s and 1980s (AFD *et al.*, 2005). Between 1970 and 2000, agricultural value added per worker increased from about US$450 to over US$700 in 1995 prices (IFAD, 2008). Millions of small-scale rice farmers were able to increase crop output with the introduction of new seed technology from IRRI. This increased incomes of poor farmers and their consumption levels.

The important role of agriculture in poverty reduction has been supported by the research of Suryhadi and Sumarto (2003), who investigated the sectoral disaggregation of the sources of poverty reduction between 1984 and 1996. Their findings confirm the importance of agricultural growth on poverty reduction, which accounted for near two-thirds of the reduction in poverty. The massive investment in rural infrastructure was generally labor intensive and created employment opportunities for the poor (see Timmer, 2007). In addition, growth in the manufacturing sector and the rise in FDI from Japan also contributed to more rapid economic growth and generated substantial labor intensive employment opportunities in sub sectors like shoes, garments, and electronics assembly (Hill, 1996).

Economic growth generally slowed after the onset of the 1997 Asian financial crisis and the poverty headcount rose along with unemployment (AFD *et al.*, 2005). Many formal sector workers lost their jobs and moved back to the rural sector to look for employment. However by the new millennium the Indonesian economy has recovered. Increasing economic efficiency and international competitiveness allowed Indonesia to further accelerate the rate of economic growth and create more jobs.

Indonesia has set forth its targets in its Medium Term Development Plan and aims to attain economic growth of between 6–7 percent per annum and to continue to reduce the poverty headcount to 8.2 percent of the population by 2009 (IFAD, 2008). Plans are in place to target the poorest groups who have not yet participated fully in the country's economic development and mainstream poverty alleviation efforts. It will do this by (i) accelerating rural development through labor intensive agro-industries; (ii) improving rural infrastructure; (iii) increasing participation of the poor in development and improving the quality of life for women; (iv) providing greater opportunities for poor communities especially those living in remote areas and disaster-prone areas; and (v) providing appropriate social safety networks to offer short-term assistance in times of adversity (IFAD, 2008). The importance of equitable development was re-affirmed in Indonesia's Long-Term National Development Plan 2005–2025.

Infrastructure. Public investment in infrastructure has been falling in Indonesia since 1990s, and this trend has to be reversed if economic growth is to accelerate in the future. While capital investment in the 1990s was more or less comparable with Thailand and Malaysia at 30 percent of GDP, it has fallen to 21 percent of GDP in 2004 (World Bank, 2006f). Even Cambodia spends more on infrastructure than Indonesia, not to mention China and India. Plans are in place to build up rural infrastructure by scaling up the community-driven development KDP program as a national priority in 2009.

Budget. Indonesia has set up the Special Allocation Fund to deliver basic services in resource deficit regions and to build up the capacity of the poor. However there are several limitations with the fund (World Bank, 2006f). Firstly, the funds are inadequate as they comprise only 3 percent of central government transfers to the sub-national governments in 2005. Second, with the exception of the health sector the allocation of the fund is often not based on pro-poor considerations. Poverty indicators are not used to determine allocation of funds. The government should reconsider allocation of funding based on attainment of certain desired poverty reduction outcomes to improve the effectiveness of the Fund.

On the government level, regional governments are encouraged to produce their customized Poverty Reduction Strategy Papers before they are eligible to access funds from the central government which accounts for 40 percent of public spending. This has benefited remote regions. For example, Papua and East Nusa Tenggara reported large reductions in chronic poverty between 1996 and 2005 and this has significantly reduced regional disparities within Indonesia (CPRC, 2008). Nevertheless poverty is still much higher in the eastern provinces (see Table 7.10). Furthermore the reduction in the regressive fuel subsidy in 2005 has been encouraging. It has freed up funds for pro-poor spending and US$1.7 billion has been reallocated to pro-poor schemes (World Bank, 2006f).

Labor market and legislations. In the years when Suharto was in power, Indonesia's labor market enjoyed a high degree of market flexibility. This encouraged formal employment and labor intensive growth which provided a pathway out of poverty for many. Rural and urban labor markets were also closely integrated which lowered transaction costs (Timmer, 2007). Since the 1997 Asian crisis, minimum wage increases prompted by union activity have adversely affected growth in the formal sector. Employment growth in the formal sector has been negative since 2000 (Timmer, 2007). Workers have been forced to join the informal sector and work for lower wages (AFD *et al.*, 2005). Indonesia should consider crafting a new social contract with regards to minimum wages, severance pay and methods for settling industrial labor disputes. It also needs to substantially reduce barriers for entry to the formal sector for young and female workers (World Bank, 2006f).

7.3.6 *Future policy agenda and challenges*

Indonesia has done relatively well in fostering pro-poor growth by implementing appropriate macroeconomic policies, successfully lowering transaction cost through investment in rural infrastructure and improving human capabilities of the poor (Timmer, 2007). There are a range of poverty reduction initiatives in place to target the poor and increase provision of basic services. Indonesia has also experimented with various innovative pilot projects like community development driven schemes which encourage self-help groups and conditional cash vouchers that provide incentives for the poor to educate their children.

Despite these successes there are challenges ahead. Spending on infrastructure has been lagging behind since the onset of the Asian financial crisis. Only 1 percent of Indonesians have access to piped sewerage systems, and spending on rural road maintenance has still to recover to its pre-crisis levels. Road congestion has resulted in higher transport costs and reduced earnings for farm produce (World Bank, 2006f). In addition, the MGD target of halving the proportion of people whose income is less than US$1 per day between 1990 and 2015 may have to be reconsidered. Previous estimate of people surviving on less than US$1 was only 7.5 percent of the population. However with the revision to the new poverty lines, the magnitude of the poor has almost tripled to over 20 percent (see Box 7.5).

We summarize some recommendations for further reducing poverty in Indonesia (see World Bank, 2006f):

1. Lowering the price of rice to make it more affordable for the poor. Replacing the import ban on rice with a low specific tariff to prevent excessive increases in rice price that are so damaging to the poor.
2. Revitalize agriculture through investment in infrastructure and rebuilding research and extension services. Help marginal farmers improve productivity or diversify into other higher-margin crops. Develop better marketing and information systems for rural-based businesses.
3. Scale up community development driven projects. Learn from past experiences and further fine tune the system to target the poorest via poverty mapping techniques and improve mechanisms and institutions for monitoring and accountability (McLaughlin *et al.*, 2007).
4. Sustain and fine tune the system of conditional cash transfers for health and educational services. Increase incentives for service providers. Help the poor gain better access to vocational schools and deploy greater numbers of teachers and health care workers to remote areas. Offer formal courses to train teachers and medical workers with monthly pay given during training.
5. Launch a large-scale program to invest in rural and village-level roads particularly in remote areas.
6. Complete development of a comprehensive social protection system that addresses the risks and vulnerabilities faced by the

poor and near-poor. Improve the current household targeting database using a combination of geographic targeting and revised household proxy means-testing. Phasing-out ineffective programs.

7. Accelerate land titling and reallocate degraded and deforested land to productive uses.
8. Make labor regulations more flexible.
9. Extend the reach of financial services to the poor and boost access to commercial credit for micro and small businesses.
10. Improve the poverty focus of national planning and budgeting for service delivery. Ensure greater clarity in functional responsibilities for the provision of specific services. Make general allocation fund and special allocation fund more pro-poor.

7.4 Bangladesh

Box 7.9. A Snapshot of Bangladesh's Chronic Poor

- Bangladesh has 77 million people living on less than US$1.25 per day. The poor make up 51 percent of its population.
- The chronic poor accounts for approximately 20 percent to 30 percent of the poor. After India, Bangladesh has the largest numbers of chronic poverty in South Asia. CPRC (2004) reports that South Asia accounts for about an estimated 135 to 190 million people — including 110–160 million Indians, 9–13 million Bangladeshis, 10–15 million Pakistanis, perhaps 5 million Afghans, and 2–3 million Nepalese.
- Chronic poverty tends to be highest in extremely low-lying lands subjected to frequent flooding (e.g. *chars* — river-islands that seasonally disappear) and in tribal areas with social tensions.
- The chronic poor include those who eke out a living on the *chars* and tribal areas (especially the landless and marginal farmers with less than half an acre of land), ethnic minorities like the Hindus and children who work at a tender age in agricultural lands or on the streets. Households headed by women and households that depend on fisheries and livestock are also at risk.

(*Continued*)

Box 7.9 (*Continued*)

- Bangladesh was categorized as a "partially chronically deprived country" together with India.

Table Box 7.9 Selected Indicators

Proportion of poor who are chronically poor over 5 years (low estimate)[1]	0.20
Proportion of poor who are chronically poor over 5 years (high estimate)[1]	0.30
Population	0.15 bn
Percentage of poor living on less than US$1.25 per day (2005PPP)*	50.5
Average depth of poverty (number of % points by which the poor fall below the poverty line[2] in 2000)	22.5
Income share held by lowest 20 percent	9.0
Gini index of inequality	31.8
Healthcare indicators	
Under-5 mortality rate (per 1,000 live births) in 2004	77
Infant mortality rate (per 1,000 live births) in 2004	56
Proportion of children under 5 who are stunted (2004)[2]	43
Life expectancy at birth, 2004	63.3
Educational indicators	
Adult illiteracy rate for women aged 15 years and above (2000–2004)	69
Adult illiteracy rate for men aged 15 years and above (2000–2004)	50
Child labor	
Percentage of children aged between 7–14 in the labor force (1999–2004)	17.5

Sources: CPRC (2008) Annex E and F and *Bauer *et al.* (2008).
Notes: [1]Based on BIDS 64 Village Panel 1987/88 and 2000 (Sen, 2003) and IFPRI-CPRC-DATA Longitudinal Dataset (Quisumbing, 2007) [2]Most recent year.

In Bangladesh about half of the population is below the poverty line, a poverty rate that is one of the highest in the world (Ahmed, 2006, and World Bank, 2008c). Chronic poverty rates are also high. Rates of child malnutrition, maternal mortality rates and chronic poverty are high.

48 percent of children are stunted and 51 percent are underweight (Sen and Hulme, 2004). Despite these statistics Bangladesh has been placed in the medium human development category according to UNDP.

7.4.1 *Incidence of poverty*

In recent years there has been some acceleration in the rate of economic growth and that has enabled Bangladesh to reduce poverty by about 1 percent point a year for the past five years. However household income of the poor tends to be highly susceptible to external shocks such as floods (Dasgupta, 2007). This is especially true for households residing near low-lying districts prone to river erosion. Low-lying flood prone areas are less costly than drier land that is out of the flood plain.

Depending on the definition and sources utilized, chronic poor households comprise 20 percent to 30 percent of poor households. The corresponding figures for households with less than 50 decimals (10 decimals equals one acre) of land are even higher (Sen and Hulme, 2004). According to spatial maps at the district level the poorest households in Bangladesh are located in the North-West and Western zone: Thakurgaon, Panchagar, Nilphamari, Lalmonirhat, Kurigam, Rangpur, Gaibandha, Sirajganj, Natore, Naogaon, Jaypurhat and Meherpur. Of these 12 districts, up to half are particularly vulnerable to flooding.

7.4.2 *Determinants of poverty*

From a survey of 21 villages in Bangladesh comprising of over 300 households, Sen (2003) was able to draw a pattern of rural poverty, including how households descended into or escaped from poverty over a 12-year period from 1988 till 2000. Only 25 percent of those families interviewed never experienced poverty. Up to 31 percent were always poor. Another 18 percent had recently fallen into poverty. In total up to half of those households interviewed were poor. Using a rural livelihood approach developed by Sen (2003), crisis variables such as ill-health and natural disasters were the most important influences contributing to rural poverty while unfavorable life cycle effects such as the increase in the number of dependents to feed and/or a decrease in the number of breadwinners were the second most important contributing factors. Structural variables such as loss of assets, and adverse market conditions also played a role in the descent of households into poverty.

Using a longitudinal household survey of 1787 core households in 102 rural villages, Quisumbing (2007) confirmed the importance of life cycle and demographic factors in the creation and transmission of poverty. The probability of being chronically poor grows as the proportion of household members below 15 years and over 55 increases. When older household members die it often results in division of property which makes some household members more vulnerable than others (see Box 7.10 for more details). Other shocks such as dowry and wedding expenses also represented forced savings on the part of the bride's family and the transfer of these gifts to the bride groom's family can push the bride's family into poverty. See Table 7.14 for some reasons for deterioration in well-being. As the stories suggest, shocks are a major cause of a decline in income which would be dealt with by better safety nets for health and the introduction on some for of unemployment insurance for the poor.

Box 7.10 Life Histories and Poverty Dynamics in Bangladesh

Using findings from a study in Kushtia District in Western Bangladesh, Davis (2006) investigated life histories of individuals to see clearer the effect of single shocks and its cumulative effects. It also allowed him to see the contribution of informal social protection system and how social protection aids the poor household's survival in times of crisis. He identified eight main life trajectories categories:

The most common was the sawtooth life trajectory experienced by the chronic poor. Sudden shocks to household welfare such as illness and death were common whereas improvements only came gradually over

(*Continued*)

Box 7.10 (*Continued*)

time. Winning the lottery is extremely rare but failing health and losing land, spouse or income is more frequent. The impact of one crisis reduces the individual's ability to cope with the next crisis, leading to a downward trajectory. With reduced resilience minor crisis and ailments then extract a greater toll on family well-being and it may also reflect unsustainable coping strategies. Because of its time series nature the life-history approach can uncover these types of cumulative declines that are hidden from other quantitative research methods.

Level sawtooth: Fujian

Fujian's life story demonstrates features of both "declining sawtooth" (e.g. health crisis and effects of managing dowry expenses) and "improving sawtooth" trajectories (e.g. grown-up sons who started to work and contribute to the family's income).

Fujian was married at the age of twelve in 1981 after her father passed away during the 1974 famine. Both Fujian and her husband came from poor families. In 1984, her mother-in-law was diagnosed with stomach ulcer and her medical expenses came up to 13,000 taka. They had to sell off a handloom. In 1987, Fujian herself fell sick after her baby was stillborn. They spent 20,000 taka for maternal care. In 1991, their position improved after the division of the family property among Fujian's

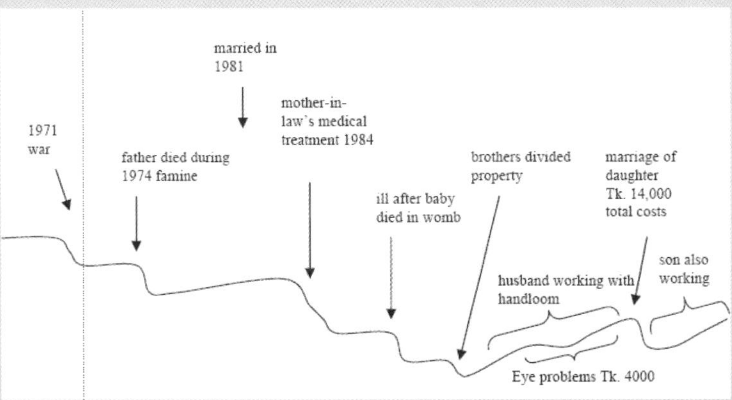

(*Continued*)

Box 7.10 (*Continued*)

husband and his brothers. Fujian's husband works as a loom master. They had 3 boys and 2 girls. In 1998, her eldest daughter's marriage expenses came up to 14,000 taka. They had to sell off a goat, take an advance from an employer, loans from relatives and an NGO loan. With both her husband and eldest son currently contributing to the household income, Fujian is optimistic that her life condition will improve over the years.

Declining single step: Allaudin — Work injury

Allaudin is 44 years old and live with his wife Fatimah. They have a 15-year-old son Ruhul. He works as a day laborer to support the family. In 1993, Allaudin had an accident with a threshing machine and injured his eye. The doctor in the private clinic treated him but had to remove his left eye. He nowadays suffers from bad headaches if he is under the sun. He works as a driver earning 400 taka. The family makes do with the supplementary income from his wife's monthly earnings of 1200 taka from work with the Union Parishad.

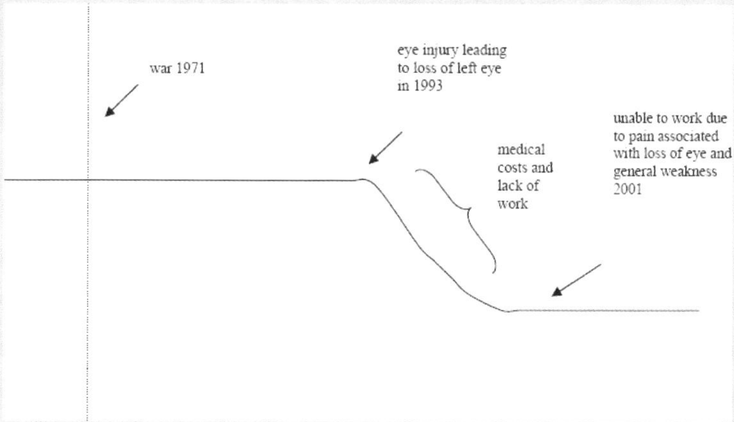

Declining multiple step: Amit — Court case, health and dowries problems

Amit is a 46-year-old Hindu living in the village of Gopalpur. As a Brahmin, he is respected among the Hindu community. However outside

(*Continued*)

Box 7.10 (*Continued*)

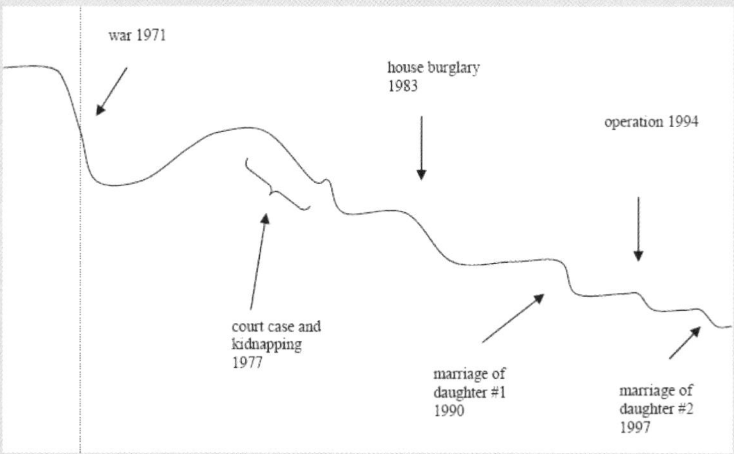

this small and relatively powerless community, he does not have any social capital to depend on within the pre-dominantly Muslim society. He and his father fled from the independence war in 1971, and returned from shelter in India to find their house burnt. After the war, he started a rice trading company and got a wife who gave him 4 children. In 1977, his in laws decided to move to India and gave him 16 bighas (3 bighas = 1 acre) of land as a gift. However, local Muslims illegally grabbed his land and faked papers of ownership. He decided to sue them in court. On his way to attending the court hearing, he was kidnapped by the local Muslims. Another group of Muslims aided him on condition that he give them his land. So he lost his land and had to bear court charges of 17,750 taka.

From then onwards, he suffered a succession of downward steps such as burglary of his house in 1983, a liver stone operation in 1994 and the dowry cost of marrying his two daughters. His first daughter's marriage in 1990 cost 4,000 taka in cash and gold while the dowry expense for his second daughter's marriage was 28,000 taka. To cover these he mortgaged his land, sold his only asset, his cows and also took out two NGO loans (Grameen Bank and Setu). His health suffered and he needed a gall stone removed.

He still has one unmarried daughter living at home. His son is learning the trade as a goldsmith and does not yet earn any income.

(*Continued*)

Box 7.10 (*Continued*)

Amit and his wife survive from agriculture and perform some *puja* for the Hindu community from time to time.

Summarizing these case studies we see that improvement in well being and household income are often associated with work opportunities for the father and/or sons of the family. Loans from relatives and NGOs are taken to start up business. Dowry from the bride's family helps to tide over consumption expenditure and buy productive assets. Inheritance of land and favorable division of property is also a factor contributing to an improvement in standards of living.

On the other hand illness and dowry costs, social conflict and household dissolution as well as land grabbing lead to downward adjustments. To build up the resilience of the poor social programs have to be provided including education and health insurance. At the same time discrimination has to be reduced and steps taken to restore the rights of minorities.

Source: Davis (2006) and Chronic Poverty Research Centers (2008).
Note: interviews conducted between 1999–2001 and total numbers of cases is 90.

Table 7.14 Self-reported Reasons for Deteriorating in Economic Well-being, 1987–2000

Reasons for Deterioration	% of Poverty Groups	Rank of Importance
Crisis	35.2	I
Ill-health	18.4	3
Natural disaster	8.2	4
Personal insecurity	3.7	7
Social ceremony	5.1	6
Life cycle	33.4	II
Negative change in household demography	33.4	1
Structural	31.4	III
Loss of natural assets	19.7	2
Loss of human assets	1.0	9
Loss of financial assets	7.2	5
Loss of social assets	0.7	10
Adverse market conditions	2.7	8

Source: Sen and Hulme (2004, p. 69, Table 4.15).
Note: Estimated from 21-village panel data collected by IRRI-IFPRI project.

The probability that a household could escape or remain mired in poverty was found to be sensitive to the initial asset position, usually the size of land holdings. The vulnerability of households to poverty was the highest for households who had access to 0.2 ha of land and less. Sen (2003) calculated an exit ratio indicating the chance that a household could escape from poverty. The proportion of households that escaped from poverty was much lower for the low-wealth category farmers who had access to 0.2 ha or less than it was for those with more land or other assets. The non-poor have greater access to non-agricultural jobs thus providing opportunities for increase in earned income rather than just being dependent on subsistence wages from farming. Also, the non-poor heavily invested in education. The average years of education of the non-poor was almost triple that of the chronically poor (see Figure 7.2).

Low agricultural productivity is another problem. Arable land per capita is shrinking as population and urbanization are both increasing.

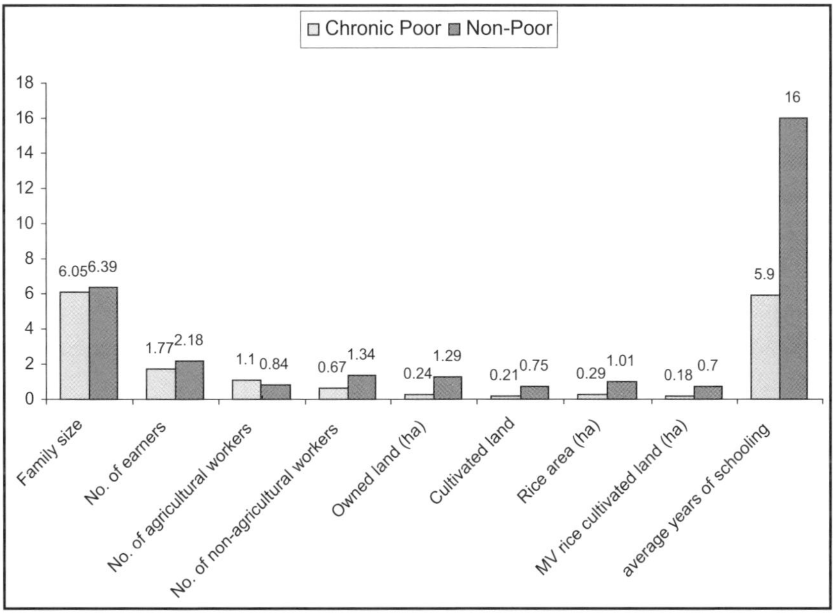

Figure 7.2 Asset Base of Chronic Poor and Non-Poor in Rural Bangladesh, 2000
Source: Data from Sen (2003, p. 42, Table 5).

Cropping intensity is already high. About three quarters of cultivated area now yields two crops per year. To increase rural incomes there will have to be diversification to higher value crops, non-crop activities as well as better storage, processing and marketing.

Vulnerable groups. Generally the poorly educated, those with less land or no land, those with few non-land assets and livestock and with a large proportion of non-working family members (children, elderly, ill, injured) are most likely to be chronically poor. From a geographic standpoint those located in the remote rural areas such as distant *char*[12] lands, *haor*[13] areas and borderlands especially in the North are vulnerable to poverty. As mentioned earlier in Chapter 1, the *char* communities along the river and coastline are periodically flooded. Using data from 1979 to 2000, Banerjee (2007) found that agricultural wages declined sharply where there was severe flooding and remained depressed even in the post-flood months.

The southern coastal region is also vulnerable to cyclones and high tidal waves (TANGO International, 2003). Landlessness and the prevalence of low-lying land and mountainous plots which is difficult to irrigate also played a part in exacerbating chronic poverty in some regions (Kam *et al.*, 2005). These vulnerable areas are mainly located in the coastal, central and north-eastern region and dependent on the vagaries of fluctuating rice production. In the Chittagong Hills villages suffered from political disturbances.

In Bangladesh both Hindus and ethnic minorities suffer from discrimination by the majority Muslin communities. Hindus, comprising around 12 percent of the population and ethnic minorities call Adavasi as they are called in India, are around 2 percent.

Child labor is also widespread. Children are economically active rather than attending school and employed in low skill occupations at low wage rates. Over 80 percent of economically

[12] *Char* land is an area of new land formed through a continual process of erosion and deposition associated with the major rivers which run through the country.

[13] A *haor* is a wetland ecosystem in the north eastern part of Bangladesh which physically is a bowl or saucer shaped shallow depression.

active children are working in agriculture a ratio comparable to child labor in India and other South Asian countries. Also refer to Tables 1.8 and 2.22.

Women tend to marry very young in Bangladesh at an average age of 15 (see Table 2.24). Marriages are generally arranged by their parents which also happens in India and Nepal. Only 35 percent of women interviewed said they had a voice in choosing their husband before marriage (World Bank, 2008d). Generally there tends to be a substantial age gap between women and their spouses, hence raising the possibility that women could live for years as widows. This loss of the income provider often results in a descent into poverty. Dowry is a common Hindu practice in Bangladesh, and dowry rates have been spiraling upward. The dowry price for many women aged 15–25 is now Tk5000[14] or even much more (World Bank, 2006g). This is less than $100, yet a large sum for a poor family. This could be due to shortage of men of marrying age or simply poverty causing young men to push for higher rates of dowry from their prospective bride's family. In poor families, the bridegroom himself takes the dowry and uses it to supplement consumption or purchase productive assets such a rickshaw, van or to start up a business (World Bank, 2008d, p. 119). The payment of the dowry can cause a crisis for the bride's family (see Davis, 2006).

7.4.3 *Micro policies*

After independence in 1971, Bangladesh faced a multitude of problems ranging from high population density, low resource base, high frequency of natural disasters and political unrest. It has successfully slowed fertility rates and curbed population growth through family planning policies, empowerment of women and support from the community (see Chapter 2). Bangladesh's predominantly rural society has a high degree of linguistic, religious and ethnic homogeneity which contributed to the relative success of these human development policies. While there are small ethic minorities such as tribal groups

[14] US$1 equals 69 taka.

and Hindu minority, it does not have the stratification system based on caste as in India and Nepal or biradari (as in Pakistan) that divides villages. The gushtis (kinship based groupings in Bangladesh) do not fragment in the way that caste, clan, biradari or linguistic affiliations do. This made it easier for the government to organize its citizens, bind them with a common goal and design and ensure the success of its programs (World Bank, 2008d).

There has been significant progress in poverty reduction since the 1980s (Sen, 2003). While rural poverty is estimated at just over 50 percent the national headcount measure of those in poverty has fallen from 52.3 percent in the early 1980s to 39.8 percent in 2000. Not surprisingly, urban poverty has fallen more rapidly than rural poverty. However the urban areas have a rising concern of rising urban inequality. Poverty reduction has been unequal across regions with rapid progress in the Dhaka division and minimal progress for the hill people of the Chittagong division. Furthermore reduction in rural poverty appeared to have slowed since the early 1990s.

Within the Asian region, Bangladesh is the only country that explicitly acknowledges and targets chronic poverty under its National Strategy for Accelerated Poverty Reduction. It has set forth its Poverty Reduction Strategy Paper (PRSP) to set up an integrated policy framework for achieving pro-poor growth and meeting the Millennium Development Goals. Its Sixth Five-Year Plan (2003–2008) issued a strongly-worded commitment to improving the lives of the poor, women and other marginalized groups. It identifies key areas of concern such as employment generation, increasing nutrition, quality education, governance, maternal health and criminal justice etc.

Despite this commitment there are only a few government programs directed to the poor at the individual or family level. One such program is a social protection scheme for aged, widowed and destitute women. An unconditional transfer of US$2 is given per month to the intended recipient. It is financed by tax payers and costs about 0.03 percent of GDP. The Ministry of Social Welfare targets a fixed number of the poorest and oldest beneficiaries in each ward and individual selection is then decided by the local communities.

Although it is a small amount of money, and hardly enough to raise these women out of poverty, up to 1.4 million women have so far benefited from this unconditional cash transfer system (CPRC, 2008). Ramping up the program would be needed to make a significant dent in the well being of these groups of needy women. This would be possible without much additional fixed cost because the administrative apparatus is already in place.

Ahmed *et al.* (2007) report that the existing cash and food transfer programs have been effective in reducing extreme poverty, sometimes by as much as 30 percentage points for food security projects. A labor intensive public works program Food for Asset (FFA) offers beneficiaries a combination of food and wages. FFA targets the poorest 10 percent of households and requires at least 70 percent of its beneficiaries to be women. However those far below the poverty line still tend to be trapped in chronic poverty.

To deal with famine, Bangladesh expanded cultivated areas under modern high yielding varieties of rice and has taken steps in achieving food security.[15] However the increased productivity in rice cultivation has not translated into higher incomes. Sen (2003) suggested that this could be due to the slower increase in paddy prices as compared to rising cost of production due to higher wage rate and fertilizer prices. Rice still accounts for 80 percent of the caloric intake of the average family and there is a need to diversify to other food sources not just to increase agriculture production but also to provide a more balanced diet containing needed vitamins, minerals and protein for health and energy.

Hence Bangladesh's rice-centric phase of agricultural development could be approaching its limit. Other development measures should be considered including diversification of agriculture and more high value added crops and livestock sectors (Hossain *et al.*, 2002). It is also important to increase the number of employment

---

[15] However most countries including Bangladesh generally fall far short of targeted spending on agricultural initiatives. Most countries devote only between 0.2 and 0.5 percent of agricultural sector GDP to research and development (refer to Table 6.2).

opportunities such as in small scale industry, animal husbandry and development of cash crops.

NGOs. Various non-government organizations provide micro credit facilities and other social services such as education, health and skill development. Examples include the Grameen Bank, Shakti Foundation and Swanirvar Bangladesh which provides collateral and interest free loans, health treatment and self-employment loans among others (Ahmed, 2006). Their clients are the poorest segment of society, mostly women engaged in food processing, bamboo crafts and household livestock with the assistance of the loan from an NGO (World Bank, 2008d). There is a risk of funds being diverted to husbands who gamble or drink it away (CPRC, 2008).

Bangladesh Rural Advancement Committee (BRAC) is the largest poverty reduction NGO in Bangladesh and works with over 6 million people in villages and slums across the country. Its Targeted Ultra-Poor (TUP) scheme offers a package of assistance to poor women, including asset grants such as poultry, livestock, and horticultural inputs, access to stipends to smooth consumption expenditure, intensive social awareness and enterprise training and health services. Funded by a donor consortium which contributed approximately $US65 million from 2002 to 2006, TUP was in operation in around one quarter of Bangladesh's districts and had reached 100,000 beneficiaries by mid-2006. Preliminary reports suggest the program has been successful. Beneficiaries reported a higher degree of asset accumulations than non-beneficiaries while nutritional status and food security were on the rise. About two-thirds of the beneficiaries had taken and made regular payments for a first loan. To have a greater overall impact the program will have to be expanded to reach more poor families.

Information and communication technology (ICT) can be further harnessed to reach poor families. Currently ICT is being used for distant medical advice especially when clinics are remote. It is also being used to provide some farmers with information regarding prices of agricultural products in different parts of the country as well as agricultural advice. For example Grameen

Telecom, a spin off from the Grameen Bank, has provided poor landless women in Bangladesh with cellular telephones and such telephone linkages help to link poor buyers and sellers with markets in urban areas (see Chapter 3). However the program is still limited in scope.

7.4.4 *Sectoral policies*

Bangladesh's record in human resource development is commensurate with its general level of economic development. It ranks low in the United National Human Development Index ranking as well as income per capita (140th and 138th of 117 countries for HDI and GDP per capita respectively according to the 2007/2008 *Human Development Report*). In the area of human development and social services greater exposure to mass media in Bangladesh has helped to raise demand for maternal health services (World Bank, 2008d). However Bangladesh's record in providing health and education is still poor. For example skilled care for women during delivery has been lacking. Only 14 percent of births in Bangladesh were attended by skilled birth attendants as compared to 43 percent in India and 87 percent in Sri Lanka. Only 6 percent of all facilities offering delivery services were able to provide basic first aid (24 hours services and medicine) for hemorrhage, the principal cause of maternal mortality (World Bank, 2008d). Furthermore, poverty and the cost of services create significant barriers to increasing maternal care. The poor have to resort to loans from relatives, friends or NGOs to fund medical fees. Compared with the rest of Asia Bangladesh has a mediocre record in the human resource areas. It ranks 4th highest in infant mortality and fourth lowest in life expectancy (Table 2.1). Only Nepal and Pakistan have higher rates of child labor (Table 1.8), and nearly 60 percent of children in Bangladesh still suffer from hunger (Table 1.6). Furthermore, Bangladesh has the lowest overall literacy rates, female literacy rates and youth literacy rates of all Asian countries (see Dowling, 2007, Tables 4.13 and 4.14).

The health system has been criticized for widespread corrupt practices. There have been numerous anecdotes about the lack of transparency, bribery and corruption. Checks need to be in place to monitor the quality of the public services (particularly the delivery of health services) and reduce the level of abuse. In many cases health workers seem to be disinterested in the treatment of illnesses and more concerned with collection of bribes. In one case a widow had to resort to begging to provide for herself and child and this led to social ostracism of the family. Box 7.11 outlines an example of how a NGO has been able to improve the health care system in some parts of Bangladesh.

Box 7.11 Gonoshasthaya Kendra

Gonoshasthaya Kendra was established in Savar Upazila in 1972 to ensure that the rural poor had access to affordable health services. It has grown rapidly over the years and is now the second largest service provider in the country after the Ministry of Health and Family Welfare. It provides a wide range of healthcare services to over a million people in 592 villages located in 16 upazilas.

Its features include:

- A range of health care from a specialized teaching hospital to community workers.
- Low unit costs.
- Reliable and accurate database of its patients and backgrounds through 15 years.
- Working closely with the government to allow the model to be replicated across the country.

Source: World Bank (2008d).

In Bangladesh, a food for education program began in 1993 and continued for ten years until 2002, when it was replaced by a similar program using a cash transfer which is still in force. This Cash for Education program covered 2.4 million children in 2000 and has been expanded further in recent years. Targeting is based on geographical location rather than community targeting. Poor locations were identified and children from these areas were selected. Mean transfers of US$2.40 per month are being given to children. The grant is conditional upon the child attending school for at least 85 percent of the school term. Before the program began just over half of the eligible student cohort attended school. The program has resulted in a 9 to 17 percentage increase in school enrolment. The Cash for Education program has also reduced the incidence of child labor. However spending on the program is still a fraction of the level required (less than 0.2 percent of GDP) to raise educational attainment levels to the desired standard and about 40 percent of the funds have leaked to non-poor students (CPRC, 2008). Further improvement can be made by focusing the grants to the chronically poor and raising more money for the program.

Infrastructure spending. Infrastructure spending in Bangladesh tends to focus on areas with higher income. United Nations ESCAP (2008) argues that revitalization of agriculture requires connecting the poor to markets by improving rural infrastructure, improving water management and increasing the dissemination of new technology through agricultural credit and extension. Ahmed and Hossain (1990) find that infrastructure spending increases the incomes and consumption levels of the poor. Under the Rural Maintenance Program poor women work on road maintenance and their families have been able to increase consumption expenditures by 35 kilocalories per individual per day for each taka earned. Khandker *et al.* (2006) found that road improvement projects can reduce the incidence of moderate and extreme poverty by between 5 percent and 7 percent. However the most recent government budget has stressed poverty reduction through building up human resources. A balance needs to be struck so that spending on physical infrastructure, particularly rural roads and irrigation is not neglected.

7.4.5 *Macroeconomic policies*

Gender Discrimination and Governance. Poor women don't usually participate in the economic decision making processes that directly affect their families' well-being. Their decision making is generally confined to aspects of household functioning such as cooking and running of the household's day to day chores. Hence the Government of Bangladesh (2005, p. 135) highlights the importance of the inclusion of women's advancement and rights as a special issue: (i) to uphold fundamental human rights; (ii) to achieve efficiency in poverty reduction; and (iii) to achieve sustainable development. Elimination of gender-based discrimination was also listed as a priority item.

The Female Secondary School Stipend Program (FSSSP), a conditional cash transfer program, has also led to a dramatic improvement in female educational attainment since 1994. Girls completing primary school and wishing to enrol in a junior/high school are automatically eligible for the stipend provided that they: (i) attend up to 75 percent of class in an academic year; (ii) obtain passing grades in the annual examination; and (iii) remain unmarried until passing the Secondary School Certificate examination. This program has had a positive effect on the aspirations of the young females in Bangladesh. The total number of girls enrolled in secondary schools rose from 1.1 million in 1991 to 4 million in 2006. FSSSP success in promoting female enrolment now suggests that boys are being left behind. Given that females have a harder time finding work and generally earn less than males, the FSSSP stipend might result in families sending daughters to school and sons to work. However the percentage of girls enrolling from the poorest two quintiles rose more slowly than other quintiles, perhaps because the stipend is small and poor families may be unable to cover expenses like shoes and uniforms. (World Bank, 2008d).

Spending on physical infrastructure for schools has been increased by the government. In addition, Bangladesh is aided by strong a NGO presence in the country and greater emphasis on the quality of education. Large NGOs like Grameen and BRAC have their own education research units. But there are limitations in improving the coverage for secondary school, such as the quality of teachers and school facilities. Some teachers appear to be unqualified to teach science subjects. For instance, some science subjects are being taught by graduate teachers with a degree in humanities. More than half have not received any training in educational teaching methods. Furthermore close to two-thirds of the class rooms and staff rooms are not equipped with electricity. There are, however, plans to set up an apex institution to be responsible for teacher training (see Chapter 3 for more details).

Some challenges remain such as the women's low access to labor market opportunities. Unlike other neighboring Southeast Asian countries, Bangladesh tends to have low representation of women in the agricultural sector. Furthermore there is low demand for female causal labor. Only 4 percent of women aged between 20–55 years of age work as casual labor in Bangladesh as compared to over 15 percent in India (World Bank, 2008d), perhaps as a result of labor market discrimination in both hiring and remuneration (see Chapter 2 and Table 2.11). Women tend to be employed in a narrow range of occupations including health and community service sectors.

Some projects to facilitate work opportunities for rural women include the Rural Transportation Improvement Project and training workshops for aquaculture. The former allocates five shops in rural markets to women which are equipped with toilet facilities and rooms for their children while they work. In Gabtoli, Upazila of Bogra, 25 out of 100 shops are owned by women. The 6 days training projects on aquaculture which stipulates 25 percent of its trainees to be women, was started in 2002. To date, there are about 1,000 trained fish culturists women in 40 villages. The women prepared the feed and were responsible for feeding the fish. The male members were responsible for harvesting and marketing the fish. On average, female workers feel empowered and claimed they earned as much as 2000 taka per month.

The opening of the export-oriented garment industry in the 1980s increased women's participation in economic activities over the years. However female garment workers continue to have low bargaining power, low wages and poor work conditions. The garment industry is not viewed as a long term occupation and many women leave after marriage.

Property ownership poses another problem. Less than 10 percent of all women have their names on marital property (World Bank, 2008d, p. 73). In Bangladesh, for example, female headed households constitute 16 percent of the landless and marginal households. 96 percent of female headed households are poor, and 33 percent are chronically poor (IFAD, 1999, Chapter 2, p. 62). Chronically poor women are at risk (see Box 7.12). To encourage ownership by women, some NGOs have explicitly granted loans based on the condition that husbands and wives must own the land and house jointly.

Box 7.12 Illegal *Fatwa* (edicts) and Human Rights in Bangladesh

Nurjahan's case was one of the first to be reported. In 1993, Nurjahan was found "guilty" of an illegal second marriage by a self-appointed *fatwa* giver. He passed the sentence to stone Nurjahan and her second husband to death. Her parents who arranged for the marriage were subjected to 50 lashes of flogging each. Although she survived the ordeal, the humiliation drove Nurjahan to commit suicide shortly after.

Under Muslim law, individuals recognized as *muftis* are allowed to issue *fatwa* (an edict). However at times, the manner in which *fatwa* is issued by vested interest groups and self-appointed moralists show how exploitation of vulnerable groups can take place. In most cases, the victims of *fatwa* are poor, illiterate, socially vulnerable, rural persons and almost always females. The perpetuators of illegal *fatwa* are rural elite men. The type of punishment issued under illegal *fatwa* range from disgracing the target in public, physical abuse or even death. Bangladesh government has since stepped up checks against cases of illegal *fatwa* and to prosecute offenders.

Source: World Bank (2008d).
Note: A mufti is institutionally appointed or authorised to pronounce *fatwah* or expound *Shariah* law.

Governance. Currently, the chronic poor tend to be more reliant on NGOs than the state for assistance and relief. At the policy level more needs to be done to involve the Government in the fight against chronic poverty at the policy level. While NGO involvement has been a strong plus in the fight against poverty over reliance on NGOs runs the risk of developing conflicting objectives *vis-à-vis* national policy (CPRC, 2008).

The external debt of Bangladesh is rising especially the non-grant component of official development assistance. Outstanding debt as a percentage of GDP rose from 34.23 percent in 1991 to 43.3 percent in 2004 (Ahmed, 2006). This is going to pose problems to the funding of disaster relief and pro-poor expenditures. Liberalization of trade in services and a more transparent banking and financial system would also allow remittances from Bangladeshi living and working overseas to flow more easily to domestic recipients. This would increase their household income and consumption. Remittances accounted for 8.8 percent of GDP in 2005 (Ahmed, 2006) and are a vital path of the fabric of the social network support upon which the poor depend on.

7.4.6 *Future policy agenda and challenges*

Agricultural development remains crucial for the continued reduction of poverty and chronic poverty in Bangladesh. Since population continues to increase, agricultural land is limited or even declining and further improvement through double and triple cropping are unlikely, increased productivity will have to come from diversification into higher yielding crops, extension of fish farming and aquaculture, horticulture and household farming, expanded production of non staple crops such as pulses, fruits, vegetables, exotic flowers, poultry and dairy products. Essential micronutrients can also be supplied through rice varieties containing an iron supplement and further research into biofortification of other food sources may provide further improvements in nutrition.

The chronically poor in Bangladesh are clustered in the areas in the northern part of the country along rivers that are subject to periodic flooding — the *char* and *haor* areas. To address their special problems development and dissemination of flood resistant varieties being developed at IRRI should be a priority for agricultural extension (refer to Box 5.2). Other technologies might be more appropriate where different conditions exist. The production of such non staple foods has not kept pace with population growth.

It is important to educate poor farmers with small plots and even those with no land at all to these opportunities for agricultural diversification. Major efforts are required to increase yields by intensifying the outreach of agricultural extension and making pertinent information available via media coverage (print, radio, TV, internet) as well as local information networks and word of mouth.

Homestead gardening, called *pusti bagan* in Bangladesh can increase farm income and also provide essential nutrients particularly for children, women and other vulnerable groups. IFPRI suggests targeting women and giving them necessary training for production, processing and cooking. A similar program exists for pulses and oilseeds (see Roos *et al.*, 2004 for details). This would be particularly beneficial to the chronically poor.

In addition to non staple food crops commercial horticulture either in rotation with rice or stand alone as well as orchard farming can serve as additional supplements to a diversified agricultural base. Cultivation of pulses and oilseeds, as well as open water fishing and aquaculture should be encouraged and promoted. Fish supply required protein and Vitamin A; minerals are in great demand for those with affordable income. Poultry and eggs are also a viable alternative even for small land holders where the women can take care of the chickens. Many of these new initiatives can benefit the chronically poor, even those without much land or even no land.

As population densities continue to increase, pollution and environmental degradation is a growing threat in Bangladesh. Agricultural waste puts potable water at risk. Currently there is a growing threat of arsenic poisoning in rural areas which has intensified as ground water tube well irrigation has spread. Arsenic poisoning is now a significant health threat that has to be confronted quickly in order to avoid widespread sickness and mortality from contaminated ground water (see www.sos-arsenic.net for more details).

It is well established that women's education is an important component of a poverty reduction program which has the added benefits of improving nutrition; increasing life expectancy; reducing infant mortality and reducing population growth (see Dowling, 2007, Chapter 4). As a component of its education program the government's Female Secondary School Stipend Program (FSSSP) has been successful in attracting girls to continue their education beyond primary school. Additional resources should be allocated to improving educational opportunities for girls at the primary level and also to educate village women in the rudiments of personal health and hygiene, child care and family planning.

7.5 Sri Lanka

Box 7.13. A Snapshot of Sri Lanka's Chronic Poor

- There is no panel data that reflects on the extent of chronic poverty in Sri Lanka. We can only estimate the extent of chronic poverty based on the 10 percent of the Sri Lanka population who survive on less than $1.25. Uva and Sabaragamuwa had the highest poverty rate (over 33 percent) and greatest depth of poverty (approximately 3 percent) in 2002 (World Bank, 2006h).
- Chronic poverty tends to be located in northern and eastern Sri Lanka where it tends to be mired in violent and escalating conflict. Outside the conflict areas, chronic poverty is concentrated in arid, un-irrigated rural lands.
- Sri Lanka was categorized as a "partially chronically deprived country" together with India. Generally Sri Lanka presents itself as a bit of a

(*Continued*)

Box 7.13 (*Continued*)

puzzle as there has been remarkable improvements in its health and literacy indicators yet progress in poverty reduction appears to be extremely lethargic.

Table Box 7.13 Selected Indicators

Proportion of poor who are chronically poor over 5 years (low estimate)	n.a
Proportion of poor who are chronically poor over 5 years (high estimate)	n.a
Population	19.7 million
Percentage of poor living on less than US$1.25 per day (2005PPP)[1]	10.3*
Average depth of poverty (number of % points by which the poor fall below the poverty line[1] in 2002)	14.3
Income share held by lowest 20 percent	8.3
Gini index of inequality	33.2
Healthcare indicators	
Under-5 mortality rate (per 1,000 live births) in 2000	14
Infant mortality rate (per 1,000 live births) in 2000	12
Proportion of children under 5 who are stunted (2000)[1]	14
Life expectancy at birth, 2004	74.3
Educational indicators	
Adult illiteracy rate for women aged 15 years and above (2000–2004)	11
Adult illiteracy rate for men aged 15 years and above (2000–2004)	8
Child labor	
Percentage of children aged between 7–14 in the labor force (1999–2004)	2.0

Sources: CPRC (2008) Annex E and F, World Bank (2006h), World Bank (2007b) and *Bauer *et al.* (2008)
Note: [1]Most recent year.

Between 1997 and 2003, rapid economic growth of 6.2 percent in the Western Province of Sri Lanka continued to outpace the rest of Sri Lanka which grew at a meager 2.3 percent (World Bank, 2007b). Western Sri Lanka provinces like Colombo, Gampaha and Anuradhapura have become middle class areas. Economic reforms that involved trade liberalization and industrialization led to a boom in manufactured exports such as garments and electronics and successfully halved its poverty rate in Western Sri Lanka. Outside these regions economic growth severely lagged behind and even stagnated. The western province's share of GDP rose from 40 percent in 1990 to near 50 percent in 2002 while those of other regions like Uva and Sabragamuwa fell from 16 to 11 percent (World Bank, 2007b). The situation is further complicated by insurgency issues in the northern and eastern regions where the government is occupied in providing basic security in the north and eastern regions.

The poor and chronically poor are also heavily concentrated in these areas and their economic prospects are further impacted by the failure to implement further agricultural reforms. Farmers continue to grow rice even though they can earn more from planting vegetables and fruits. Fertilizer availability and subsidies to farmers are still biased towards paddy farmers. Furthermore natural disasters like the tsunami in December 2004, which struck the northern and eastern parts of the country also took their toll on the poor.

7.5.1 *Incidence of poverty*

There are no panel data that reflects the extent of chronic poverty in Sri Lanka. Around 10 percent of the population falls below the poverty line (see Table Box 7.13). Chronic poverty tends to be located in northern and eastern Sri Lanka which is mired in conflict. There are around 650,000 internally displaced people in Sri Lanka (CPRC, 2004) although the numbers fluctuate with the level of conflict between the Tamil minority and the Singhalese majority. Refugees from conflict-ridden areas often have no choice but to accept the lowliest paid jobs. They are treated as outcasts and unable to gain entry to formal sector employment. The cease fire agreement between the Government of Sri Lanka and the Liberation Tigers of Tamil Eelam signed in February 2002 has brought some semblance of peace and economic growth in the North and East. However literacy rate and access to amenities like safe drinking water remain below the national average.

Besides the North and the East, other regions like Sabaragamuwa and Uva also have high rates of chronic poverty. Poverty headcount is approximately around 35 percent in these regions and they account for about almost one-third of the poor in the country. Poverty incidence is lowest in the Western provinces like Colombo, Gampaha and Anuradhapura where poverty incidence fell between 1990 and 2002. Some of the poorest districts like Hambantota, Monaragala, Ratnapura and Kegalle actually experienced an increase in poverty, resulting in the widening income gap between districts.

Those who live in the estate sector are also subjected to persistent poverty traps. During the British colonial period, large plantations growing tea, rubber and coconuts developed into self-sufficient enclaves and employed primarily South Indian workers who were not offered Sri Lankan citizenship rights until 1988. Since independence, the importance of the estate sector to the economy has generally declined. However much of the estate sector workforce continues to be isolated from the rest of the economy. The poverty headcount in the estate sector is about 7 percent points higher than the national average. The estates also have a higher percentage of stunted children and lower body mass index of mothers than the national average (World Bank, 2007b).

Sri Lanka enjoys near universal primary enrolment, literacy rates and good health services yet it has made slow progress on poverty reduction. Economic growth in Sri Lanka does not seem to be having the salutary impact on poverty that it has had in other Asian economies. According to the World Bank a one percent increase in the growth of GDP per capita income leads to 0.5 percent decline in the poverty headcount ratio in Sri Lanka whereas a similar increase in the pace of growth in GDP per capita in three other Asian countries led to a 0.9 percent decrease in poverty in Korea, a 1.4 percent decrease in poverty in Vietnam and a 2.6 percent decrease in poverty in Thailand (World Bank, 2007b). From 1991 to

2002, Sri Lanka's per capita GDP grew by 40 percent yet rural poverty declined by less than 5 percentage points. Poverty reduction has been fastest in districts where the incidence of poverty was already low like Colombo and Gampaha in the Western Province, whereas poverty increased in the poorest districts. As a result income inequality has been on the rise. Average per capita consumption grew by 50 percent for the rich income groups whereas it grew by only 2 percent for the poorest group.

7.5.2 *Determinants of poverty*

In general the delivery of education and health services in Sri Lanka tend to be fairly evenly distributed and income distribution was fairly equitably distributed until recently. As with other countries in South Asia rural residents with low levels of education, skills and land access are the most likely to be poor. Geography and political stability also play a role. In areas of conflict in the Northeast where Tamil insurgents have been fighting with the Government on and off for many years the level of poverty is higher than in more settled areas of the country in the South and West. Furthermore estate workers of Indian descent have higher rates of poverty than the Singhalese. The mountainous districts of Badulla and Monaragala in Uva province are among the poorest areas in Sri Lanka. Comparing different districts in Sri Lanka, these two districts reported more than 6 times the poverty headcount ratio of Colombo (World Bank, 2007b).

Factors behind slow decline in poverty reduction. The slow decline in poverty reduction in Sri Lanka has been attributed to the stagnating agricultural growth in Sri Lanka. China and Vietnam has seen remarkable progress in the 1980s and 1990s in reducing poverty due to their agricultural reforms which raised productivity, incomes of the rural poor and allowed employment opportunities. On the other hand, in Sri Lanka agricultural incomes have stagnated for the past ten years. Growth in the agricultural sector has been on a steady decline from 2.8 percent in the 1980s to 1.6 percent in the 1990s and to less than 1 percent between 2002 and 2004. The rural sector accounts for less than one-fifth of the country's economic growth rate yet houses 88 percent of the population and about 3.5 million poor (World Bank, 2007b). About one quarter of all rural households are poor. In the poorest district of Uva, the poverty rate for agricultural households is about 34.3 percent. This is nearly double the rate of poverty for non-agricultural households. Agricultural productivity has also grown slowly and is much lower than its other Asian counterparts (See Table 7.15). India enjoys almost double the rate of agricultural sector productivity growth of Sri Lanka and agricultural sector productivity growth rates are even higher in Pakistan, Vietnam, China and Korea.

Other than the lack of economic growth outside the Western province and the stagnant agricultural sector, the World Bank reported that poverty is due to inadequate infrastructure, restrictive labor practices and civil conflict in the North and East that has hampered the growth of the non-rural sector. Table 7.16 shows a comparison of infrastructure indicators in various Asian countries. Installed infrastructure in Sri Lanka deteriorates the greater the distance from Colombo. Access to electricity generally lags behind all East Asian countries with the exception of Vietnam. Electricity is heavily concentrated in the Western province which has over 80 percent coverage while rural areas like Uva province have less than half the coverage. Frequent power outages increase the cost of doing business and impede economic development in the rural areas. There is

Table 7.15 Agricultural Productivity Growth in Selected Asian Countries, 1990–2000

Country	Agricultural Productivity Growth (%)
Sri Lanka	0.65
India	1.13
Thailand	1.35
Malaysia	1.62
Pakistan	2.56
Vietnam	2.80
China	3.51
Korea	5.89

Source: World Bank (2007b, p. 4, Table 1.1).

Table 7.16 Selected Infrastructure Indicators

Country	Access to Electricity (2000), %	Telephone Mainlines per 1000 People (2003)	Road Density (km/sq. km) (1997–2002)
Sri Lanka	76	49	1.51
Thailand	99	209	0.19
Malaysia	100	538	0.88
Pakistan	97	182	0.20
Vietnam	82	105	0.11
China	36	54	0.29

Source: World Bank (2007b, p. 5, Table 1.2).

low penetration of the telecommunication network with only 49 telephone mainlines per 1,000 people. Road density appears to be high compared to the rest of the Asian countries but there are problems of poor road quality due to lack of proper maintenance. Travel time in poorest districts like Uva and Sabaragamuwa is much higher than the national average. Poor transportation was cited as the top constraint facing rural entrepreneurs. Complaints include poor road quality, lack of access to roads and absence of available transport. Farmers would also be more willing to grow higher-value-added crops such as cinnamon and tea if it were easier to transport the crop to market.

Sri Lanka's labor practices are overly restrictive and prohibit the growth of the non-rural sector. Sri Lanka is one of the most expensive places in the world to dismiss workers. Firing costs amount to 176 weeks worth of wages, nearly double that of any East Asian countries. Excessive job security lowers productivity and strangles private investment. Since the 1990s foreign direct investment in Sri Lanka has been significantly lower than China, Malaysia, Thailand and Vietnam. Net foreign investment to Sri Lanka in the 2000s was only at 1.15 percent of GDP while in China, Malaysia, Thailand and Vietnam it exceeded 2 percent of GDP. The export sector also lags behind other East Asian countries. The overprotection of workers and slow employment growth in the formal sector has pushed workers into the informal sector where earnings and job security are much lower. This has increased the likelihood that some families will fall into poverty.

Civil conflict in the North and East appeared to have ceased since 2002 but there remains significant constraints on economic development and poverty reduction (World Bank, 2007b). Access to certain security zones in the North and East are barred. For example, one third of Jaffna peninsula is a security zone and access to road use is severely limited. Entrepreneurs from Jaffna complain that they spend three days transporting goods to and from Colombo via the A9 highway, where it has to go through four checkpoints. At each check point, they had to undergo the same process of unloading, inspection and reloading. Despite the recent reduction in tension the A9 highway remains closed. Entrepreneurs in the North and East face difficulties in accessing bank credit where the collateral requirements are higher than in other parts of the country. The capital flight from the North and East to the rest of the country reduces the availability of deposits at local banks to be loaned out to local farmers, fishermen and traders, which in turn create a vicious cycle of stringent credit and limited opportunities for the poor to a better life.

7.5.3 *Micro policies*

Sri Lanka has done a commendable job in providing excellent health and educational facilities which are of higher quality than countries with much higher per capita incomes. In 2002 net enrolment ratio in primary education reached 96 percent. The ratio of girls to boys in primary, secondary and tertiary education reached 95 percent, 102 percent and 114 percent respectively and infant and child mortality rates have been falling. Up to 96 percent of births are now attended by a health professional. High enrolment rates have also had a beneficial effect on child labor which is much lower than in other South Asian economies.

Sri Lanka has a fairly extensive social protection system and compares quite favorably with its other South Asian neighbors. Social

Table 7.17 Social Protection Schemes and Expenditure (million Rs.), 2000 and 2004

Social Protection Schemes	2000	2004
Total	20,332	23,086
Ministry of Samurdhi		
Income transfers	9927	8498
Micro credit	1822	3481
Micro insurance	218	201
Small scale infrastructure	548	343
Infant milk subsidy	135	127
Ministry of Women's Empowerment and Social Welfare		
Repayment to disabled soldiers	2282	3860
Rehabilitation & reconstruction — refugees	2658	2532
Flood and drought relief	75	1466
Triposha supplement	320	305
Mother's and child's nutrition	30	100
Rehabilitation drug addicts	15	35
Ministry of Education		
School uniform	980	788
School text books	1000	1100
School season tickets	250	250
Other education welfare	64	...
Provincial Council		
Assistance for indigent elders and disabled	8	...
Memorandum items (% of GDP)		
Social safety net programs — total	1.6	1.1
Samurdhi income transfers	0.8	0.4
Education	2.5	2.1
Health	1.7	1.5
Total government expenditures	27.2	23.7

Source: World Bank (2006h).

safety networks include income transfers to address chronic poverty and individual risks (illness and disability) and shocks (e.g. conflict and tsunamis). One third of its workers, mainly formal workers, benefits from employment protection. About 45 percent of households are covered by social assistance schemes. Table 7.17 shows the range of social protection and their respective expenditures.

7.5.4 *Sector policies*

Social protection. Sri Lanka has implemented a redistributive social protection scheme, called *Samurdhi* transfers, to target poor families. It is the largest social assistance scheme in Sri Lanka and covers close to 45 percent of the population. Over 80 percent of the Samurdhi budget provides income transfers to the poor in the form of food stamps and the remaining on micro credit, small scale infrastructural works and micro insurance to cover emergencies like hospitalization. About 2 million families received Samurdhi transfers in 2005. More than two-thirds of beneficiary families receive Rs. 400 or less per month. Total government expenditure was Rs. 9 billion and approximately 0.4 percent of GDP. The scheme was targeted to move people out of poverty through income transfers.

Eligibility for Samurdhi and the determination of social assistances are based on the household's level of incomes. However it has invited some criticisms as the well-to-do also receives social assistance. The Samurdhi transfer program excludes 40 percent of households in the bottom fifth of the population but spends nearly half of its budget on the richest 60 percent of the population (World Bank, 2006h, and Salih, 2000). Needy estate workers who often do not have a national identity card and families identified with opposing political affiliation often do not get to enjoy Samurdhi benefits. The Samurdhi Development Officers were given too much leeway in targeting recipients and often swayed by the influence of local politicians.

In order to reform the targeting of the Samurdhi transfers, Sri Lanka has enacted a Welfare Benefit Act in 2002 to improve the selection of all beneficiaries for state funded welfare programs. The Act limited the program to the poorest 25–27 percent of the population (approximately 900,000 households) to achieve greater social equity. Given that the current transfer budget is held constant, it is expected that the amount of handouts to the really needy household should double to Rs. 830 per month instead of the current Rs. 320. A Welfare Benefit Board has been set up to develop a formula-based system to identify needy recipients. Rather than to rely on income records of households which are often under-reported, instruments such as demographic data, housing type and ownership of assets are taken into consideration when deciding the amount of cash transfer. Benefits paid to each household also include a variable component such as "vulnerable" household members like children, disabled or elderly so as to ensure progressive payouts. Recent efforts involve the participation of the villagers in the selection of the poor deserving of the Samurdhi transfers, a move that originated from the Samurdhi's predecessor, the Janasaviya Program. The improved targeted system has been set up in two districts in the conflict-affected North.

The Samurdhi banks have become an important source of credit to the ultra poor in Sri Lanka. Small loans of about Rs. 300 are made for emergency purposes. The Samurdhi banks are considered as the principal source of emergency credit for small loans, among friends and relatives and shopkeepers and money lenders. Microfinance coverage in Sri Lanka and also Bangladesh exceed 8 percent of the population, in comparison to most countries where microfinance institutions reach less than 2 percent of the population (World Bank, 2006h, and Salih, 2000).

Other welfare programs. There are other welfare programs in Sri Lanka, though not on the same scale as the Samurdhi transfer program. The Ministry of Social Welfare distributes disability payments of Rs. 100–300 especially for solders injured in the conflict and families of soldiers killed in action. About 41 percent of the disabled are covered under the scheme. The Public Assistance program is targeted towards specific vulnerable individuals like poor elderly, disabled, and families without breadwinners, destitute women and orphans. It covered up to 365,000 families in 2005 with an average monthly assistance of Rs. 135. The Triposha provides nutrition supplement to poor mothers and their young children. About 580,000 recipients benefited from the scheme administered by the Ministry of Health. In addition, there are mid-day meals for children in selected schools including the North and East. Mothers also receive some nutritional assistance in these regions. However, data is lacking regarding the effectiveness of the above welfare schemes.

In view of the vulnerabilities of the poor to natural disasters, the government has set up an emergency cash assistance program of the equivalent of $50 per affected family for a total of four payouts and to be paid up within 3 months of the disaster. The fund is supported by the World Bank's Tsunami Emergency Recovery Project. Feedback and its impact has been positive. Funds have generally reached the affected population and there are signs of longer term recovery in terms of sources of livelihood. Public works were also implemented in tsunami-affected communities to provide work opportunities to affected households. Activities included the cleaning of debris, rehabilitation of rural roads and infrastructure improvement. Drought relief is provided to families with agricultural incomes of less than Rs. 2000 per month. Poor families are eligible if the cultivation of crops have been disrupted for at least 2 consecutive quarters and the family does not have alternative livelihood means to fall back on.

Rural infrastructure. The Colombo district in Western Province and its surrounding areas are well connected to markets. The further the distance from Colombo, the lower is the accessibility index and the higher the probability of poverty. It has been found that each additional minute to a main road increased the probability of unemployment by 3 percent in Sri Lanka. See World Bank (2008e).

In order to increase road connectivity, Sri Lanka has implemented a Roads Sector Assistance Project in 2006 with the support of World Bank. About 160 km of rural roads in nine local government areas will be rehabilitated and maintained based on the recently completed poverty map for Sri Lanka. The government has also collaborated with ADB to improve roads in the poorest district in Sri Lanka, namely, Badulla, Monaragala and Ratnapura. To further develop rural infrastructure in poorest area, Sri Lanka has undertaken rural development projects the Community Development and Livelihood Improvement Project (otherwise known as the "Gemi Diriya" project) with assistance from World Bank. There is active participation by communities in planning and project implementation. About half a million people in the poorest districts of Sri Lanka have benefited from the project. See World Bank (2008f).

Information communication technology. The potential for ICT to reduce rural poverty has yet to be fully harnessed in Sri Lanka. However, pilot ICT schemes to improve the livelihoods of the poor have been implemented in three of the poorest districts in Sri Lanka (ADB, 2007). Beneficiaries include seasonal farmers and fishermen, the unemployed and the disabled living in Gampaha district in the Western Province, Ratnapura district in the province of Sabaragamuwa and Kalutara district. Through community information centers the poor can readily access the Internet and fax machines for information on job opportunities, training, agriculture methods, banking services etc. Between 30 percent and 40 percent of the 60,000 beneficiaries are chronically poor.

7.5.5 *Macro policies*

Macroeconomic policy has been generally conducive to economic growth although recently inflation has accelerated to around 20 percent per annum and is expected to stay above 10 percent although lower oil prices will be a moderating force. Government spending has increased to deal with civil conflict that has reemerged as a challenge to political and social stability and also on post-tsunami construction. Development spending has favored the richer regions of the country, partly as a result of civil conflict which makes it difficult to reach the poor in these regions. Furthermore income growth, the most important macroeconomic variable, does not have a strong poverty reducing impact as noted above, a fraction of the effect in other Asian countries. Educational policies and budgets, mentioned by some as an important component of the macroeconomic environment, have been instrumental in helping Sri Lanka to build a strong record of high school completion rates and gender equality.

To provide alternative livelihoods for the rural poor, Sri Lanka has established "rural industrial villages" to foster the development of small scale industries and creation of non-farm job opportunities in rural areas. Instances include the printing industry in Panaluwa, multipurpose footwear village in Pitipana, and a leather product manufacturing village in Muthiyammagama, and gold, silver, bronze, reed products and domestic equipment manufacturing in Angulmaduwa (Nanayakkara, 2008)

Budget and government spending. Public investment in infrastructure has been low in Sri Lanka. This was primarily due to (i) the need to contain the fiscal deficit and (ii) the long bureaucratic delays in the implementation of infrastructure projects even when foreign funds were available (ADB and World Bank, 2005). Under the 10 year development framework, the government has actively implemented the construction of large scale infrastructure projects like the Colombo Port Expansion Project so as to facilitate trade, stimulate economic development and reduce poverty. There are plans to improve links between poorer provinces and Colombo through road improvements and electrification.

7.5.6 *Future policy agenda and challenges*

Poverty reduction in Sri Lanka has not kept pace with the improvement in healthcare and educational indicators. The poor in Sri Lanka generally fare better in terms of health outcomes compared to the poor in other parts of South Asia. Sri Lanka has a well laid-out network of preventive healthcare services and hospitals as well as universal health care. Levels of infant and child mortality rates are much lower than in the rest of the South Asian region. Stunting is also comparatively lower compared with other South Asian countries. However the stunting among the poor is almost double that of the national average, highlighting the rising income inequality between the poor and the non-poor. Income inequality among provinces will continue to persist if the agricultural sector continues to stagnate and few employment opportunities open up in other sectors.

To address these persistent problems of chronic poverty, Sri Lanka needs to foster growth clusters outside the West Province and reform the labor market. Agricultural reforms[16] are urgently needed if Sri Lanka wishes to improve from its current status of "partially chronically deprived country". Access to agricultural R&D for farmers has been hampered by outdated requirements and costly permits and inspection procedures. The procedures for applying for agricultural grants are complicated and have deterred applicants from applying. Agricultural extension services are inadequate. Many agricultural extension workers are relegated to the role of village facilitator who merely disseminates agricultural information to farmers.

The existing land legislation under the Land Development Ordinance is highly restrictive. Though lands have been transferred to the farmers under various land settlement programs, the farmers are unable to use it as collateral to access credit to buy agricultural inputs, machinery or R&D to improve their crop output and increase farm efficiency. Also, if farmers wish to move into non-farm activities or move to another province, they get no compensation for their land. This has restricted the scope of agricultural activities undertaken by the farmers as well as their ability to move into other sectors.

Sri Lanka needs to work harder on identifying the groups of chronic poor and to tailor appropriate program for them to exit poverty. Although the current social assistance system is fairly extensive, it is subject to leakages to non-poor while some needy groups are excluded.

Budget deficits have been rising and Sri Lanka is reaching a point where these deficits are no longer sustainable. At 93 percent of GDP, Sri Lanka has the highest public debt ratio in South Asian and its debt servicing requirements continue to increase. To complicate matters spending on defense has begun to crowd out pro-poor spending. Security concerns and the conflict in the North and East have also drawn the attention of policy makers away from much needed economic reforms.

---

[16] See World Bank (2007b, pp. 67–75) for more details on the challenges in raising agricultural incomes.

With the rising budget deficit, there is a need for Sri Lanka to reduce wasteful government expenditure on the non-poor and to further revamp the social protection system to target the chronic poor. The World Bank (2006h) has made some suggestions to further improve the scheme to address the vulnerability of the poor. It suggests that Sri Lanka needs to link cash transfers to investment in human development of children and enhance income opportunities for the poor. Cash transfers can be used to provide incentives to improve the schooling enrolment of poor children as well as increasing their participation in nutrition-based programs to reduce malnutrition.

The Sri Lanka government appears to be moving in the right direction as they have started to reduce the cash transfers and increase the micro credit component in recent years (see Table 7.17). More should be done to increase access to skills development and microfinance of the poor. It should also include exit methods for households to leave the program when they have gotten out of poverty. Cash transfers could be distributed via the post office and preferably in the name of the female member especially in certain areas with a high rate of alcoholism. Disability payments could be brought under the umbrella of the Samurdhi scheme instead of the Ministry of Social Welfare to reduce administrative costs. Even though civil conflict in the North and East has fallen in the past 6 years poverty remains high and these regions should continue to be the focus of poverty reduction efforts.

7.6 Pakistan

Box 7.14. A Snapshot of Pakistan's Chronic Poor

- Pakistan has around 35 million people living on less than US$1.25 per day. The poor make up 23 percent of its population.
- The chronic poor accounts for approximately 25 percent to 35 percent of the poor. CPRC (2004) reports that South Asia accounts

(*Continued*)

Box 7.14 (*Continued*)

for about an estimated 135 to 190 million people — including 110–160 million Indians, 9–13 million Bangladeshis, 10–15 million Pakistanis, perhaps 5 million Afghans, and 2–3 million Nepalese.

- Chronic poverty tends to be highest in western and southern Pakistan as well Federally-Administrated Tribal Areas (FATA) territories.
- The chronic poor include (i) those braving the harsh agricultural conditions in the Northern highlands and arid parts of Baluchistan and Sindh in the west and south; (ii) those facing oppression in the Federally-Administered Tribal Areas in the west, Baluchistan, North West Frontier Province and Sindh and (iii) residents of the inner city and urban periphery slums, particularly in areas bordering Afghanistan (CPRC, 2004).
- Pakistan was categorized as a "partially chronically deprived country" together with majority of Southeast countries. Absolute number of stunted children appears to have risen over the years (CPRC, 2004).

Table Box 7.14 Selected Indicators

Proportion of poor who are chronically poor over 5 years (low estimate)[1]	0.25
Proportion of poor who are chronically poor over 5 years (high estimate)[1]	0.35
Population	156 m
Percentage of poor living on less than US$1.25 per day (2005PPP)[2]	22.6
Average depth of poverty (number of % points by which the poor fall below the poverty line[2] in 2002	18.2
Income share held by lowest 20 percent	9.3
Gini index of inequality	22.3
Healthcare indicators	
Under-5 mortality rate (per 1,000 live births) in 2001–2002	101
Infant mortality rate (per 1,000 live births) in 2001–2002	80
Proportion of children under 5 who are stunted (2001–2002)[2]	37
Life expectancy at birth, 2004	63.4
Educational indicators	
Adult illiteracy rate for women aged 15 years and above (2000–2004)	11

(*Continued*)

Box 7.14 (*Continued*)

Adult illiteracy rate for men aged 15 years and above (2000–2004)	8
Child labor	
Percentage of children aged between 7–14 in the labor force (1999–2004)	15.4

Sources: CPRC (2008) Annex E and F and Bauer *et al.* (2008).
Notes: [1]Based on IFPRI Household Food Security Panel annual waves; [2]Most recent year.

7.6.1 *Incidence of poverty*

Despite a relative lack of attention to issues of human development and gender equality, Pakistan succeeded in reducing poverty in the 1970s and 1980s as a result of sustained, if not robust, economic growth. However there was a reversal of trend in the 1990s where there was a disturbing jump in poverty rate (ADB, 2006c) as economic growth rate stuttered, corruption spread and political unrest increased. The poverty situation appeared to have improved in the early years of the new millennium. Real GDP grew at an average of 7 percent from 2002 to 2007 while agricultural output, rural incomes and social welfare indicators showed some improvement. Average per capita expenditure in rural areas rose by 6 percent and per capita expenditure of the poorest two quintiles of the rural population rose by 3.1 percent (World Bank, 2007a). Trade liberalization policies have been implemented and development expenditures have been increased in selected localities. However the trickle down effect to the poor appears to have been minimal. Investigating these trends is complicated by a lack of consistent data on poverty. Furthermore, the literature on pro-poor growth in Pakistan is sparse (ADB, 2006c).

There are two main sources of poverty data, namely the Federal Bureau of Statistics and the Household Integrated Economic Survey (HIES). However these data have to be interpreted carefully. The Federal Bureau of Statistics has frequently changed its data collection methodologies, so the data collected may not always be reliable or comparable. The strength of the HIES has weakened since it was merged with the Pakistan Integrated Household Survey for survey rounds in 1999 and 2001 (ADB, 2006c). Data from HIES tends to be irregular. Estimates of poverty also vary considerably depending on the methodology because of the numerous rural households with per capita expenditure clustering close to the official poverty line (World Bank, 2007a). Studies on provincial poverty have sometimes shown conflicting results.[17]

There are four main provinces in Pakistan, namely Punjab, Baluchistan, North West Frontier Province (NWFP) and Sindh. Punjab is relatively better off than other provinces whereas Baluchistan and NWFP generally suffer from high levels of deprivation. In Sindh, poverty is high in Tharparkar, Jacobabad and Shikarpur while in North West Frontier Province the poor are concentrated in Shangla, Kohistan and Batagram districts. In Baluchistan poverty is highest in Dera Bugti, Jhal Magsi, Musakhel and Kharan districts while districts in the southern Punjab also suffer similar deprivation and low levels of human development (ADB, 2006c).

Security threats arising from conflicts with India and Afghanistan have led to a periodic breakdown of law and order especially at the borders. While necessary to maintain law and order military spending has increased at the expense of pro-poor programs.

Outside the four main provinces, poverty is also an issue in the Federally Administered Tribal Areas (FATA).[18] FATA straddles the border with Afghanistan and is subjected to frequent military skirmishes between the US military, Taliban supporters and the Pakistan guards.

---

[17] See ADB (2006c, Section 2.2) for more details.

[18] Pakistan is sandwiched between India on the east and Iran and Afghanistan on the west and China in the north. FATA is found in between Afghanistan to the west, North West Frontier Province, Punjab in the East and Baluchistan in the South. There are 7 agencies in FATA, namely Khyber, Kurram, Bajaur, Mohmand, Orakzai, North and South Waziristan and six Frontier Regions.

According to Bauer *et al.* (2008), Pakistan has nearly 35 million people living on less than US$1.25 per day. The poor make up 23 percent of its population (CPRC, 2008). Poverty is generally much lower in urban areas than in rural areas where almost 80 percent of the poor reside (World Bank, 2008).

The majority of the poor are non-farm households in rural areas. They are neither tenant farmers nor land owners but rather non-farm households (World Bank, 2007a). These non-farm rural households, which excludes agricultural households, account for more than half (52 percent) of the poor. This rather bizarre situation has been well-documented by past studies such as Arif and Ahmad (2001), Malik (2005) and Qureshi and Ari (2001). See also Table 7.18. These rural poor are either self-employed or engaged as wage workers. The share of non-agricultural households varies from 33 percent of total households in NWFP to as high as 52 percent in Sindh (ADB, 2006c). The poorest 40 percent of rural households derive only about 30 percent of their total income from agriculture.

The chronic poor make up approximately 25 percent to 35 percent of poor households (CPRC, 2008 and World Bank, 2007a). They include: (i) those residing in the Northern highlands and arid parts of Baluchistan and Sindh in the west and south; (ii) those living in the Federally-Administered Tribal Areas in west Baluchistan, North West Frontier Province and Sindh; and (iii) residents of the inner city and urban periphery slums, particularly in areas bordering Afghanistan (CPRC, 2004).

Table 7.18 Rural Poor in Pakistan by Household Group, 2004–2005

Non-farm others	35%
Non-farm self employed	17%
Farmers in Punjab	24%
Farmers in Sindh	11%
Farmers in NWFP	6%
Farmers in Baluchistan	2%
Agricultural Laborers	5%

Source: World Bank (2007a, p. xiii, Figure 3).

7.6.2 *Determinants of chronic poverty*

There are various reasons cited for rising poverty in Pakistan in the 1990s. These include slow growth in the agriculture sector owing to excessive land fragmentation, unequal land distribution among agricultural workers, high unemployment rates in the informal sector, high fertility rates of young mothers resulting in high dependency ratios and existence of local power structures such as caste, religion and biraderi (clan) that have maintained unequal access to resources. Government spending for poverty alleviation has also been stagnant. Additional factors have reinforced the neglect of the poor. These include unequal distribution of land ownership and limited access to water. These difficulties were compounded by the slow rate of agricultural output growth in the 1990s. Although government statistics reported satisfactory agricultural growth of 4 percent during the decade, recent evidence suggest this was over reported since livestock, fishing and forestry value-added were over valued (see ADB, 2006c and World Bank, 2007a).

There is excessive land fragmentation in Pakistan and more than half of rural households do not own any land. Over 40 percent of land belongs to the 2.5 percent richest population (ADB, 2006c). Land inequality is particularly high along the cotton/wheat belts of southern Punjab and Sindh. As a means of survival, the landless poor cultivate others' land as share-tenants and many sharecroppers get easily trapped into poverty and end up as bonded laborers. As many as two-third of the extremely poor have been forced to sell their land in the 1990s to cover urgent consumption needs, marriage expenditure and health shocks (Hussain, 2003a). The continued depletion of assets by the poor impacts adversely on their future stream of income and reduce their chances of escaping poverty. However, it is still unclear why the poverty figures report the predominance of non-farm workers among the rural poor (see Table 7.18). It could be that not all household members work in the agricultural sector even though they are nominally categorized as farmers.

Clearly income from employment as a farm worker is not sufficient to keep most families out of poverty. As a result of the slow growth in jobs and income in farming more households are turning to non-farm employment. This is a trend that has been observed throughout South Asia. In India, for example, employment increased by 16 percent in agriculture compared with 56 percent in rural non-farm activities between 1983 and 2000. In Pakistan declining opportunities for employment in agriculture were the result of mechanization, changes in cropping patterns and conversion of land to non-agricultural use (ILO, 2008) while casual workers accounted for 80 percent of male employment and 92 percent of female employment in agriculture in 2000 (World Bank, 2008).

Access to water usage is highly unequal. Farmers in the dry lands (*barani*), land at the tail end of water courses and areas with saline underground water tends to have lower yields than farmers who work with irrigated fields. Water availability and quality is also a constraint on increasing agricultural output. During drought periods in 2001–2002, wheat output in Sindh shrunk while fluctuation in major cash crops, especially cotton, adversely impacted incomes of farmers in rural Pakistan. This contributed to a rise in rural poverty. Those households adversely impacted with fluctuating incomes and no means of smoothing expenditure faced a rise in transient poverty. If poverty persists for prolonged periods, those same households fall into chronic poverty.

The high unemployment rates in the informal sector have contributed to a high incidence of poverty (World Bank, 2007a). Illiteracy kept many workers from competing for jobs in the expanding service sectors, thus leading to a rise in income inequality and increasing poverty (Naseem, 2005). The promulgation of the Industrial Relation Ordinance 2002 added to the worries of the employed poor as they could be converted from permanent workers to contract workers, a practice common among large scale industrial units in Pakistan. This Ordinance also reduced the bargaining rights of workers. Furthermore bonded labor is commonplace and can be found in many sectors of the economy, including mining, carpet weaving and brick kiln workers, and not just in agriculture. Furthermore employers do not keep accurate records of employment and earnings and these practices are designed to keep workers in debt and in bondage.

In addition to low rates of pay and minimal social protection there are also reported threats of violence against women employees.

The high fertility rates of young mothers in Pakistan have resulted in high dependency ratios among poor families. Average fertility rates have been on the decline since the mid-1980s from 6.8 children per women to 4.1 in 2001 to 3.7 currently (World Bank, 2007a and CIA Factbook, 2008). However Pakistan's current fertility rates are still much higher than they are in neighboring countries of Bangladesh's (3.1) and India's (2.8). Furthermore over 40 percent of Pakistan's population is below 15 years of age and about one quarter comprises females of eligible reproductive age (ADB, 2006c). As a result population growth is likely to be a challenge in the future. As household dependency ratios increase the possibility of being poor increases. The mean number of children in the lowest income quintile is three times more than that in the highest income quintile. This creates undue pressure on the household's consumption expenditure and the bread winner's burden to provide for the family. It might also explain the high percentage of child labor in Pakistan. Approximately 15 percent of children aged between 7–14 years of age are working in the labor force (CPRC, 2008). It may also be partially responsible for poor health and sanitation as well as inadequate diets. In rural Pakistan, children face high risk of stunting. A child in the south-western province Baluchistan has a 75 percent probability of being stunted which is quite high, even compared with other countries in South Asia. (See CPRC, 2004).

The local power structures such as caste, religion and biraderi (clan) form the main pillars of society in Pakistan. Tenants as well as small farmers pay high prices for agricultural inputs as a result of monopoly control by rich middlemen who also keep down farm gate prices. Tenants who borrow from their landlords commonly end up as bonded labor and forced to work in the fields at less than market rates or even without wages in order to repay debts. The landlords also control the use of water on their lands. Agricultural, forestry and irrigation departments are said to assist only the wealthy and ignore the poor. There are also reports of violence, intimidation and abuse of the poor by powerful landlords. The minimum involvement of the police in such cases could be due to the prohibitive fees (bribes) required if the poor want to pursue their complaints with the authorities (World Bank, 2007a).

7.6.3 *Micro policies*

The four pillars of the Poverty Reduction Strategy in Pakistan highlight the importance of economic growth, governance, investment in human capital and integration of the poor, vulnerable and residents of backward regions into mainstream development. Pro-poor expenditure has been picking up in the past few years, rising from 3.8 percent of GDP in 2002 to 4.7 percent in 2004 (ADB, 2006c). It remains to be seen how effective these poverty programs are, particularly in the two poorest provinces and in FATA.

Pakistan transfers resources directly to the poor through schemes like *zakat*.[19] *Zakat* is Pakistan's main social welfare or protection system and depends on charitable donations from Muslims. The system has been in existence since 1980. By 2004, there were over 1.6 million *zakat* beneficiaries. *Zakat* is disbursed for a variety of purposes including subsistence or *Guzara*[20] allowances, educational stipends, health care, social welfare, and marriage assistance and rehabilitation grants. The local *zakat* committee is responsible for identifying vulnerable poor in need of aid. The poor would receive Rs. 500 per month to help them with their monthly expenditures. Since 2002, the *zakat* system has been revamped with emphasis shifting from a subsistence or

[19] *Zakat* are alms and a form of giving to those who are less fortunate. It is obligatory upon all Muslims to give a portion of wealth and assets each year to the poor. The payment of *zakat* is obligatory as it is one of the five pillars of Islam. *Zakat* is a 2.5 percent levy on most valuables and savings held for a full year if their total value is more than a basic minimum known as *nisab*, currently about US $1,000. Cash money in the bank and building society accounts, and the sale value of bonds, securities and shares in any form are *zakatable* if they are purchased as an investment. There is no *zakat* on family home or household furniture, carpets, car, or other personal assets that were not purchased as an investment.

[20] *Guzara* means subsistence in urdu.

Guzara allowance to rehabilitation funds that allows the deserving poor to set up small businesses in one of the 44 approved economic activities. The rehabilitation fund is designed to assist the poor in developing self-reliance unlike the old system of simply relying on handouts from the Guzara allowance. The amount of grant given depends on the type of activity that the poor selects to set up his business. Recipients of the rehabilitation funds are barred from the Guzara allowance scheme. *Zakat* plays a much larger role in the social protection scheme of Pakistan than it does in the other Muslim countries in Asia such as Bangladesh and Indonesia which have a much larger poverty reduction effort funded by the government and NGOs. More needs to be done to supplement *zakat* to help the poor. There are around 7 million households living below the poverty line (ADB, 2006c) and leakage of funds to non-poor parties is a common problem. Furthermore the disbursement of *zakat* has been declining over the years and its sustainability over time is of serious concern (ADB, 2006c).

To supplement *zakat*, the Pakistan Bait-ul-Maal was established in 1992 to provide assistance to minorities — those that do not receive assistance from *zakat*. The Federal government provides the majority of the funding for this program. It has provided financial assistance to the poor for medical care and education stipends. Rs. 327 million was given in 2001 (ADB, 2002). Other safety nets in Pakistan include the Food Support Program (FSP), Child Support Program pilot and Tawana Pakistan school feeding program. The Tawana Pakistan school feeding program aims to improve the health and nutrition of school children. To further encourage long-term human capital investment, Pakistan has also implemented the Child Support Program Pilot to help children of poor households attend schools. The FSP is a cash transfer to the poor to support expenditure on food. It is designed to mitigate the impact of an increase in wheat prices due to withdrawal of government subsidies on wheat flour. It benefits 1.2 million poor households who earn an income of less than Rs. 2,000 per month (ADB, 2002). Cash handouts of Rs. 2,000 are paid to poor households twice a year under the FSP. 3 percent of total funds are reserved especially for minorities, which is a small amount compared with the needs of the poor.

Pakistan Poverty Alleviation Fund (PPAF). Funded by the World Bank, the PPAF is designed to reduce poverty and empower the poor in Pakistan by provision of resources and services to the poor, especially women. It has impacted over 10 million people and has mobilized over 66,000 community boards in 27,000 localities (World Bank, 2008g). Grants has been given for small scale infrastructure projects which include drinking water supply schemes, drainage and sanitation, irrigation, roads, culverts and small bridges. Other schemes include integrated areas up-gradation projects, drought mitigation schemes and technological innovative projects such as micro-hydels, reverse osmoses plant, drip irrigation and solar energy. The projects are labor intensive and generate employment and incomes. It also equips the poor with skills such as management, financial, mechanical and technical skills, water conservation, agriculture, horticulture, livestock and marketing etc. In addition, it has provided disaster relief to the poor who suffered from earthquakes and droughts. Over 100,000 houses are being reconstructed and 300 schemes implemented in the earthquake affected areas.

7.6.4 *Sector policies*

Under the Khushal Pakistan Program, priority has been given to maintenance and rehabilitation of existing roads network in remote areas so as to improve rural access and farm-to-market roads. These projects will create jobs for the rural poor and increase their income levels. In addition, Pakistan's Poverty Reduction Strategy proposes to accelerate distribution of state owned land to small farmers to reduce rural poverty. Priority is to be given to women so that they can benefit from the scheme. About 3 million acre of available land is to be given to poor households. Infrastructure and technical packages are also made available.

Micro finance. Historically, micro finance has been provided by NGOs such as the Aga Khan Rural Support Program. The poor also resort to informal sources of funds by borrowing from friends and relatives to tide over sudden shocks to income. However coverage in Pakistan is generally smaller than in other South Asian countries. Recently, the Pakistan government has intervened and set up microfinance schemes with the support of ADB and the World Bank. Microfinance to the poor is now available from Khushali Bank, through the PPAF and the Zarai Taraqiati Bank.

The Khushali Bank was established in 2000 with the support of ADB. The average loan size ranges from around Rs. 3,000 to 30,000 provided in the form of individual and group loans without the need for collateral. By end of 2001, the Bank has extended loans to 15,000 beneficiaries, of which one-third are female borrowers. The PPAF has also aided in women's microfinance programs and contributed towards reducing female unemployment in Pakistan. Operating through NGOs and the Rural Support Programs, PPAF provides loans to the poor in the range of Rs. 9,500 to Rs. 10,000 with no collateral needed. Its beneficiaries outnumber those of the Khusali banks. Both banks engage in development of physical infrastructure such as water channels and repair of link roads in backward areas.

7.6.5 *Macro policies*

A number of macroeconomic variables including the rate of growth in income, inflation and remittances have been suggested as positive influences on the rate of reduction in the incidence of poverty in Pakistan. Kalim and Shahbaz (2008) developed a regression model to determine the relationship between poverty and several explanatory macroeconomic variables for the period 1973–2006. Their results suggest that the incidence of poverty is reduced as a result of growth in income per capita, the flow of overseas remittance and the pace of urbanization. These results are consistent with evidence accumulated for other countries. The impact of urbanization reflects both the pull factor of higher wages in cities which helps to reduce rural poverty and also the push factor that drives younger Pakistanis to look for employment outside the rural economy. Kalim and Shahbaz (2008) also found that inflation is negatively related to poverty reduction as is the inflow of foreign direct investment (FDI). In the case of FDI the reasoning is that employers in establishments funded by FDI employ higher skilled workers, tending to drive out those with lower skills.

It is certainly plausible that the acceleration in economic growth in Pakistan over the past few years has helped reduce poverty as has the flow of remittances to poor families from overseas workers in the Middle East and elsewhere. However, inflationary tendencies which have resulted in prices rising at around 8 percent per annum in the past two years are likely to squeeze the poor and may have resulted in some increase in the rate of poverty and chronic poverty.

7.6.6 *Future policy agenda and challenges*

Pakistan has the lowest social indicators in South Asia, with the possible exception of Bangladesh and Nepal, and certainly the poorest record of social assistance given its average standard of living (see Dowling, 2007, Tables 4.13 and 4.14). Pakistan has the smallest percentage of the poor covered by social protection schemes and social protection as a share of GDP of all the countries surveyed and reported in Table 6.7 and Table 8.3. This is because membership in the main social protection schemes is confined to government and formal sector employees. There are some programs to provide subsidized food or to reduce costs of education and health coverage for the poor but they are not comprehensive. This governmental neglect is reflected in a variety of human development indicators including limited life expectancy, low overall literacy including female literacy, a high incidence of child labor, a high proportion of stunted children and average depth of poverty. Furthermore there seems to be no evidence of an increase in the motivation of the government to step up its social protection efforts. The preoccupation with military spending to defend against the perceived military threat from India and more recently the growing presence of the Taliban in Afghanistan can explain some of this neglect. Combined with the discrimination against women and the downgrading of women's education, this has created an environment where it has been difficult for the poor and the chronically poor to break out of the poverty trap.

To address these ongoing concerns the Pakistan government would need to rethink its commitment to the poor. In particular it has to realize that it will have to provide a viable supplement to *zakat*. More governmental resources have to be devoted to the development and implementation of social programs to improve health, sanitation, education and promote gender equality, particularly in the poorer regions of the country. It could start by devoting resources to complete the Education for All Plan of Action as part of the education sector reform which plans to increase adult literacy, reduce illiteracy and increase enrolment rates at all levels of education. This program would provide a package of subsidies for poorer students with a view to raising completion rates of primary school to 100 percent (see IMF, 2004)

7.7 Nepal

Box 7.15. A Snapshot of Nepal's Chronic Poor

- Nepal has about 14 million people living on less than US$1.25 per day. The poor make up 55 percent of its population.
- The chronic poor accounts for approximately 50 percent to 60 percent of the poor.
- Chronic poverty tends to be highest in the mountainous regions of the Mid-Western and Far-Western Region. Maoist insurgencies are present in mid-west Nepal.
- The chronic poor include rural farmers, lower social castes like the Janajatis, Dalits, Muslims and bonded laborers.
- Nepal was categorized as a "partially chronically deprived country" together with India.

(*Continued*)

Box 7.15 (*Continued*)

Table Box 7.15. Selected Indicators

Proportion of poor who are chronically poor over 5 years (low estimate)[1]	0.50
Proportion of poor who are chronically poor over 5 years (high estimate)[1]	0.60
Population	27 mil
Percentage of poor living on less than US$1.25 per day (2005PPP)*	54.7
Average depth of poverty (number of % points by which the poor fall below the poverty line[2] in 2000)	22.4
Income share held by lowest 20 percent	6.0
Gini index of inequality	41.1
Healthcare indicators	
Under-5 mortality rate (per 1,000 live births) in 2001	76
Infant mortality rate (per 1,000 live births) in 2001	59
Proportion of children under 5 who are stunted (2001)[2]	51
Life expectancy at birth, 2004	62.1
Educational indicators	
Adult illiteracy rate for women aged 15 years and above (2000–2004)	65
Adult illiteracy rate for men aged 15 years and above (2000–2004)	37
Child labor	
Percentage of children aged between 7–14 in the labor force (1999–2004)	47.2

Sources: CPRC (2008) Annex E and F and *Bauer *et al.* (2008).
Notes: [1]Based on National LSMS Panel 1995/96 and 2003/04; [2]Most recent year.

There has been political unrest and violence in the highlands of Nepal since 1996. It started with the Maoist rebellion in the remote hill areas of the Mid-Western Region which later intensified and spread to other parts of the country. More than 14,000 Nepalese were killed and about 600,000 were displaced or made homeless as a result of this violence (IFAD, 2007). A ceasefire was declared in April 2006 and the domestic situation has remained calm since then. In the past 2 and a half years income and employment opportunities have been on the rise in urban areas such as Kathmandu Valley.

7.7.1 *Incidence of poverty*

Growth has been driven by non-agricultural activities like manufacturing, trade, tourism and services. There has also been a rise in remittances, greater connectivity between rural and urban areas and a decline in the dependency ratio. The poverty rate is extremely low (4 percent) in Kathmandu and the rise in per capita incomes in the Kathmandu Valley is providing markets for products produced in adjacent rural locations. These positive growth spillovers have had a positive income impact on adjacent rural areas like the Central Hills and the Central Terai.

The reduction in poverty has been unevenly distributed not only regionally but across caste and ethnic groups. For the country as a whole the Gini coefficient, a measure of income inequality, rose from 34.2 percent in 1996 to 41.1 percent in 2004. The poorest regions notably the Mid-Western and Far-Western Regions have generally stagnated in terms of economic performance and have lagged behind the rest of the regions. Furthermore, Nepal's Human Development Index (HDI) of 0.534 is the lowest for South Asia and below the average for all developing countries (see *Global Human Development Report* 2007/08).

There are around 14 million people in Nepal living on less than US$1.25 per day and more than half of its population is poor (CPRC, 2008). Furthermore, the chronic poor accounts for approximately 50 percent to 60 percent of the poor, or between 7 million and 8.4 million Nepalese (CPRC, 2004). Many of the poorest families live in the mountains, which are sparsely populated (see Table 7.19) or the hills.

Vulnerable groups include farmers, women and ethnic groups that are subject to discrimination. Poverty is particularly prevalent in

Table 7.19 Population by Ecological Region in Millions — Nepal

Ecological region	Population 1971	Population 2001
Mountains	1.1	1.7
Hills	6.1	10.2
Terao	4.3	11.2

Source: Nepal Central Bureau of Statistics 1996 and 2002 and FAO (2003).

the mountainous regions in the Mid-Western and Far-Western Regions. FAO (2003) estimates poverty rates of 45 percent in the Western Region to 59 percent in the Mid-West to 65 percent in the Far-Western Region. Women generally tend to be poor due to low access to physical and human capital. Only 11 percent of women own land and the female literacy rate (38.2 percent) is much lower than for men (69.3 percent).

Within households, women often have less to eat than men. Insufficient calorie intake often leads to chronic child malnutrition. In addition, traditional Nepali society is extremely hierarchical with the upper caste like Brahmin, Chettris and Newars dominating the hill people (such as the Tamangs, Gurungs, Sherpas and Majhis) and the Dalits (mainly laborers and some semiskilled craftsmen including shoemakers, blacksmiths and tailors). The upper caste own most of the irrigated land (*khet*). The Majhis live along the marginal riverside lands whilst the Tamangs, Gurungs and Sherpas tend to be located at the steep upper slopes where agriculture is solely rain-fed and the soils of lower quality. Most Dalits work for upper-caste farmers as wage laborers. Poverty levels are low among the upper castes such as the Chettris (14 percent) and much higher among the lower castes (over 40 percent). Literacy rates of Dalits is only about two-thirds that of Brahmins and Newars. Primary school enrolment of Dalit and Janajati (ethnic minorities called scheduled tribes in India) are about 17 percent and 37 percent respectively, far below the national average which is now over 80 percent. Life expectancy for Dalits is 51 compared with 62 years for Newars (Nepal National Planning Commission, 2003).

Among the Janajati groups, there are considerable variations in welfare status. Janajati groups like the Gurungs, Limbus and Rais traditionally served in the Indian and or British army and have done well. Thakalis and Sherpas still work in the trading, tourism and business sectors. However other Janajati and scheduled tribes such as the Tharu, Tamang and Kham Magars and 16 other smaller groups are still at the bottom of the income distribution.

Geographically, Nepal is landlocked and mountainous and contains eight of the world's 10 highest peaks, including Mount Everest and Kanchenjunga. Until the East-West Highway was built in the late nineties, there were few road linkages within these two regions. Although there is some limited access with neighboring India through north-south road links, the north-south road linkages between the mountain areas of both regions are lacking. The continued isolation and lack of integration with the mainstream Nepalese economy, coupled with poor access to markets and basic services such as education and health facilities has failed to bring development to the Western and Mountain Regions. In comparison, the Eastern Region is well-served with road links within Nepal and other neighboring countries thereby facilitating trade, commerce and economic development (Nepal National Planning Commission, 2003).

7.7.2 *Determinants of poverty*

High rates of rural poverty in Nepal are the result of continued poor performance in the agricultural sector. There are two reasons for this. First there are virtually no opportunities for expanding cultivated area. Fragmentation of land holdings, coupled with rapid population growth and a fragile ecology does not provide a means for sustainable livelihood. The rate of poverty is particularly severe in the western region. Based on the 1996 NLSS data, the poorer households are consistently handicapped in terms of the quality of the land they cultivate as well as access to irrigation, chemical fertilizer and micro credit. The median landholding of the bottom 25 percent of households is only 0.37 ha, only about three-fourth of the rural average. Only one-third of the land of the poor is suitable for growing rice and irrigation is minimal. Nearly 90 percent of land cultivated by the bottom 25 percent of households is rain fed (Nepal National Planning Commission, 2003).

The second problem is that of agricultural productivity. Agricultural productivity is lowest in the mountains where poverty is most severe and highest in the lowland terai area, a 25 to 30 km wide belt of alluvial and fertile plain in the southern part of the country. There is scope for raising productivity but this requires land improvement, more equipment and purchased inputs including fertilizer and improved seeds. As noted in Chapter 5, no-till farming has potential for increasing yields when wheat is planted after rice. (See also Pathic and Shrestha, 2002, for more on the Nepalese experience). No-till farming is a system where fields are not tilled after the harvesting of the previous crop but rather seeded immediately. It has the advantage of water conservation, time saving and reduced sowing and soil preparation costs, reduced reliance on tractors and burning of fossil fuels. There is potential for no-till farming in the terai in Nepal (and also in the Punjab in India). It is also possible that no-till farming may be appropriate in other parts of Nepal where chronic poverty is more severe than in the terai.

Historical pattern of economic growth in Nepal have not been pro-poor. Most of the growth has been concentrated in urban areas, benefiting only about 15 percent of the Nepalese population. Agriculture grew by about 2 percent a year for the last few decades while industry and services grew three times as fast at around 6 percent (Nepal National Planning Commission, 2003). Small uneconomical farm sizes also prevent farmers from enjoying economies of scale.

Social exclusion and poor governance are other factors that contribute to chronic poverty. Women and ethnic groups are generally left out and denied access to economic opportunities and resources. Labor force participation rates for women are low and they are discriminated against in the work place. Women comprise only a third of the paid labor force and generally earn 20 percent less than their male counterparts. (Nepal National Planning Commission, 2003). There is less discrimination in the mountain regions, perhaps because there is less paid employment and agriculture plays a larger role. About 1 in every 5 households is headed by a female in the mountainous regions, somewhat higher than the national average. There are also sociological factors which impedes female access to household income and resources. Women's legal right to inherit is still limited and their share in even basic food security is far more uncertain than a man's. Adult literacy rate for females in 2000 were just over half that of men.

Poor diets and inadequate nutrition are symptomatic of high rates of poverty. Cereals and root crops supply the bulk of a poor Nepalese diet. There is a deficiency of nutrients, particularly those most available in animal products, including Vitamin A, iron and iodine. FAO (2003) estimates that malnutrition among children is over 50 percent. Half of adult women are anemic as well as three quarters of pregnant women.

Although caste discrimination is officially illegal, it is still widespread especially in rural areas. There has been some progress. Nepal issued a government decree in 2000 freeing indebted laborers from ancestral debt and imposing harsh penalties on employers. It is unclear how effective this legislation has been in making labor markets more open and competitive. Many "freed" Nepal workers still chose to enter into voluntarily contracts with their former employers due to lack of alternative employment opportunities. As a result their livelihoods have not improved.

Frequent changes in government with short time horizons have generally weakened governance, increased corruption and the lack of accountability. The sparsely populated Mid-Western and Far-Western regions lack political representation in the government and have suffered from neglect in the formulation and implementation of government policies. Public expenditure has been concentrated in urban areas. Between 1996 and 2001, the Mid-Western and Far-Western only received 11–12 percent of total government expenditure (Nepal National Planning Commission, 2003) despite the need for more roads, schools, health facilities and other infrastructure.

7.7.3 *Micro policies*

Migration. To augment their income many Nepalese families have sent some family members to work overseas. As we noted in Chapter 4 it is unlikely that a large proportion of chronically poor families would be able to send workers to the Middle East and East Asia because of income constraints. However given the fact that nearly 10 percent of the male work force is employed overseas, and an even larger percentage of the population of Nepal has emigrated in the past, those who are able to afford the fee charged by agents have benefited from the demand for unskilled labor in these markets.[21] Recruiters help to remove the income constraint by paying for passage and then charging high interest rates. There is also a large number of migrants to India each year.

Remittances by Nepalese migrants in India and elsewhere to family households rose by four times to 12 percent of GDP by end of 2004 compared with a decade earlier (World Bank, 2006i). Results of a recent study (Lokshin *et al.*, 2007) indicated that one-fifth of the poverty reduction in Nepal occurring between 1995 and 2004 was because of increased remittances. Internal migration also played an important role in raising incomes although not as much as external migration. While it is less lucrative, migration to urban areas from the countryside is also less costly. In the poorer and inaccessible areas of the Mid-Western and Far-Western Hills there is significant seasonal migration of men from poor households to work as unskilled laborers in India. While earnings are sometimes meager this seasonal migration does reduce the pressure on domestic food supplies while migrants are away. With increasing poverty, migrants stay longer in order to pay debts at home and/or to remit money (see FAO, 2003). Evidence from the national living standard survey suggests that remittance income is highest among the poorest quintile of the income distribution. Other income (read remittance) for this quintile is 25 percent of total income, double the rate for richer quintiles.

Male migration also creates family tensions and puts the burden of sustaining the rural economy on women. Women now constitute more than 60 percent of the agricultural labor force (IFAD, 2007)

---

[21] It was estimated that 4 million Nepalese now reside overseas. This is about 15 percent of the population and close to 30 percent of the male population.

but often face discrimination based on their gender. The findings of Lokshin *et al.* (2007) combined with other data on migration suggest that internal and external labor movements should be considered in the policy mix to reduce poverty and increase economic growth.

Social funds. There is no comprehensive social security system in Nepal although there is a provident fund which is contributed to by both the employer and employee in the formal labor market. The provident fund only covers full time workers and a small fraction of the labor force employed in the modern sector. Workers with three years service or more also get severance pay up to a maximum of one months pay (see Badal, 2005). There are plans to extend and improve the system to cover more employees. There is currently no coverage for workers in the informal sector.

The Japan Fund for Poverty Reduction (JFPR) approved disbursement of $2 million in 2007 and aims to rehabilitate vulnerable families and children in conflict-affected areas of Nepal (ADB, 2008b). In addition, Nepal has set up the Poverty Alleviation Fund (PAF) and aims to institutionalize poverty monitoring. Poverty mapping will be utilized to better provide a database for ministries and targeted programs. As yet Nepal does not have a social security system in place.

7.7.4 *Sector policies*

Rural roads. Nepal's road network is constrained by mountainous terrain and poor access to small population centers in mountainous areas. Less than half of the population has access to all-weather roads and more than 60 percent of the network is concentrated in the terai. To address these deficiencies in the road network Nepal has undertaken a systematic expansion of the road network, which grew at an annual 6.7 percent per year between 1996 and 2004. The Road Network Development Project which began at the end of 2001 is in charge of building new track roads, upgrade existing feeder/district roads and maintaining the highway system.

It has generally improved connectivity in rural areas. While high transport costs and the lack of connectivity are still major impediments to Nepal's development, these new roads have led to increased traffic flow between rural areas and market places and it has also stimulated entrepreneurship. Much of the emphasis has been on rural roads or district roads which grew by 11 percent over the same period. Expansion of secondary and feeder roads also serves as a way to service the poorer regions of the country. As we noted in Chapter 4 these new roads generally increase access to shops, markets, schools and hospitals while opening up to better access to jobs and information in urban areas. Improvements in rural connectivity helped raise non-agricultural employment and incomes.

Despite the continued upgrading and expansion of the road network, lack of all weather surfaces and poor overall conditions hampers the delivery of social services to the remote hill and mountainous districts and retards the reduction in chronic poverty in these areas. Further expansion of the rural road network is critical to the further reduction in chronic poverty.

Micro finance. Since November 1998, the Rural Microfinance Project has been set up to improve women's access of women to financial services and enable them to set up micro enterprises. More than 500,000 families spread across 25 districts have benefited (ADB, 2008b). This includes reform and restructuring of rural finance institutions such as the Agricultural Development Bank Limited (ADBL), the largest rural financial institute in Nepal and the privatization of the Small Farmers Development Bank. The government will also reduce its stake in the five Grameen Bikas Banks in a bid to increase its outreach to rural areas.

How have these developments in microfinance aided the chronically poor? A small pilot project in the western hills of Nepal sponsored by the Center for International Studies and Cooperation suggests that there has been some participation by Dalits and Janajati's (16 percent and 7 percent of the total membership respectively) in the decision making process of saving and credit organizations making loans to village members. Whether these results can be replicated with larger banks and financial institutions will require further monitoring and evaluation (see Sharma and Thapa, 2007).

Forestry reforms. Forestry plays an important role in the livelihood of Nepal's rural population as it is an important source of fuel, fodder, timber and other wood-related products. Forests in Nepal are controlled by Forest User Groups (FUGs) in some piloted districts of Nepal. Community forestry has evolved from tree planting and forest management to issues on governance and poverty reduction. FUGs have developed some programs for the poor who can participate in forest-based enterprises such as small saw-mills, veneer/plywood units and local paper making. The poor and landless mainly use forest resources for fuel and fodder for work animals and as fertilizer (leaf litter). Money earned by FUGs from timber and other forest products can also be used to make loans to the poor (see Springate-Baginshi and Blaike, 2007). Furthermore, the synergy between livestock and forestry resources needs to be addressed, in particular forest resources for livestock feed during movement between summer and winter pastures. As a result of the closing of forests to these movements in livestock has put stress on livestock and on those who depend on livestock for a living (see United Nations FAO, 2003).

Agriculture reforms. Nepal has set up the Agriculture Perspective Plan (APP) in order to increase cereal and cash crop production in the terai and develop livestock, horticulture and specific high value crops in the hills. It intends to further promote commercial agriculture and market-led production of high value crops such as fresh vegetables, vegetable seeds, fruit (e.g. banana, citrus, walnut and mango), spices (e.g. ginger, turmeric, garlic and chilies), fisheries, potatoes, legumes (e.g. chickpea, lentil, pigeon-pea, soybean, groundnut and rajma bean), oil seeds (e.g. mustard, rapeseed and sunflower) and aromatic rice (ADB, 2008b). Package programs include provision of agricultural inputs like fertilizers, access to irrigation facilities and improvement of physical infrastructure like expansion of rural roads and provision of electricity. Other strategies include preparation of land use guidelines and policies, new land ceilings and resettlement of freed "Kamiyas" (bonded labor) on surplus land. The aim is to increase agricultural production growth to 5 percent per annum while lowering food prices and generating jobs in the rural non-farm economy. (see FAO, 2003). Reforms are more likely to meet with success in the terai, perhaps adding no till farming as a possible strategy.

7.7.5 *Macroeconomic policies*

Nepal's Tenth Plan on Poverty Reduction Strategy Paper 2002–2007 is primarily based on four pillars: (i) broad-based high and sustained growth; (ii) social sector development that emphasized human development; (iii) social inclusion programs; and (iv) improved governance. The current plan is to further reduce poverty by 2010. From 2003/2004 onwards, additional "catch up" grants were provided to the Mid-Western and Far-Western Regions. A Highland Livelihood Development Project is to be implemented in 2009. The program aims to enhance ecosystem services and rural livelihoods through applied research and capacity building for community-based integrated watershed management.

Spending on infrastructure with grants from external organizations like ADB and OPEC is in place. An example is the Rural Reconstruction and Rehabilitation Sector Development Program which is financed by ADB and OPEC. The North-South Fast Track Road Connectivity Project is intended for 2009. It will consist of a north-south fast track, to be newly constructed between Kathmandu and the terai, and slope stabilization from Kodari to Kathmandu, part of the north-south corridor.

Social inclusion. With the restoration of democracy in the 1990s, the government has set up structures to increase social inclusion like the establishment of the Dalit Development Commission and Janajati Development Committee. The latter has been recently restructured to a more powerful and independent Adibasi Janajati Utthan Pratisthan (Indigeneous and Ethnic Uplifement Academy) in 2002 (NPPC, 2003). The Gender Equality and Empowerment of Women

Project is meant to help poor rural women through empowerment and livelihood support. However these programs have yet to be effective enough to have a measurable impact on poverty and gender empowerment.

7.7.6 *Future policy agenda and challenges*

The Tenth Five-Year Plan (2003–2008) and the Agricultural Perspective Plan (1997–2017) set out an agenda of agricultural development and poverty reduction for Nepal. Some of these objectives are being achieved and others are not. In order to accelerate the implementation of these two Plans the FAO (2003) suggests a series of policy priorities that are also consistent with Nepal's poverty reduction agenda. These priorities can be summarized in a few points.

First, the agricultural production base has to be strengthened by improving irrigation coverage to match potential capacity, improving fertilizer availability and quality, reorienting agricultural research and raising farm productivity.

Second, affirmative action for women has to be strengthened in all aspects of the rural economy. These include farm extension, female empowerment in the use and exercise of intellectual property rights with regard to medicinal and exotic plants, reduction in bias in schools and health facilities, linking livestock development to women's opportunities and granting women access to land, water, information, technology and skills development.

Third, child development and school feeding programs will have to be promoted, including upgrading of schools and health facilities, improvement in school attendance, free lunch programs and reduction in child labor, monitoring of children's health and reducing hunger and food stress.

Fourth, create social safety nets and welfare support including food supplies to remote regions where chronic poverty levels are high. Public food grain distribution should be supervised to make sure local elites do not control access.

Fifth, develop employment guarantee schemes such as work fare that link infrastructure projects to guaranteed employment by the government for the poorest and more remote regions. These programs could also help to develop infrastructure and to build up the rural non-farm economy.

Sixth, develop better linkages to CGIAR research as a source of agricultural technology particularly for rain fed agriculture and areas where droughts or flood are common or where new multicropping technology like no till can be utilized.

Many of these suggestions are designed to addresses general poverty issues. However the chronically poor should also benefit from these suggestions, even though precise information about the nature and extent of chronic poverty may not be sufficient to develop program that addresses their needs directly. Several suggestions including women's rights, work fare, social safety nets and agricultural research are consistent with general recommendations elsewhere in this volume. One additional suggestion that does not appear in the FAO recommendations or elsewhere in planning documents would be a program to encourage out migration from slow growing or depressed rural locations. Rural to urban migration or rural to international migration has proved an effective way to relieve pressure on the local economy as well as providing extra income for families who remain at home.

7.8 Philippines

Box 7.16 A Snapshot of Philippines' Chronic Poor

- The Philippines has around 19 million people living on less than US$1.25 per day. The poor make up 22.6 percent of its population.
- The chronic poor accounts for approximately 30 percent to 40 percent of the poor.
- Incidence of chronic poverty is concentrated in the Autonomous Region in Muslim Mindanao (ARMM), Bicol, Central Mindanao, Bicao and Northern Mindanao. The poor is also subjected to protracted conflict.

(*Continued*)

Box 7.16 (*Continued*)

- Philippines was categorized as a "partially chronically deprived country" together with India.

Table Box 7.16 Selected Indicators

Proportion of poor who are chronically poor over 5 years (low estimate)[1]	0.30
Proportion of poor who are chronically poor over 5 years (high estimate)[1]	0.40
Population	84 mil
Percentage of poor living on less than US$1.25 per day (2005PPP)*	22.6
Average depth of poverty (number of % points by which the poor fall below the poverty line[2] in 2000)	19.4
Income share held by lowest 20 percent	5.4
Gini index of inequality	46.1
Healthcare indicators	
Under-5 mortality rate (per 1,000 live births) in 2004	34
Infant mortality rate (per 1,000 live births) in 2004	26
Proportion of children under 5 who are stunted (2003)[2]	30
Life expectancy at birth, 2004	70.7
Educational indicators	
Adult illiteracy rate for women aged 15 years and above (2000–2004)	7
Adult illiteracy rate for men aged 15 years and above (2000–2004)	7
Child labor	
Percentage of children aged between 7–14 in the labor force (1999–2004)	13.3

Sources: CPRC (2008) Annex E and F and *Bauer *et al.* (2008).
Notes: [1] Based on FIES-APIS 1997, 1998, 1999. [2]Most recent year.

7.8.1 *Incidence of poverty*

GDP growth in Philippines reached its highest rate in three decades at 7.3 percent in 2007, well above its 5.2 average rate for the previous five years (ADB, 2008). The economy reported strong consumption growth and expansion in net exports and investment. The agriculture sector experienced better weather than in the past 2 years and expanded by a healthy 5.1 percent. Inflation has been reduced, the fiscal position has improved and the peso has strengthened. In addition the current account surplus has increased.

Despite a recent acceleration in growth, per capita income has hardly kept pace with population growth over the past two and a half decades. Between 1980 and 2005, GDP per capita increased at an annual growth rate of 0.63 percent, by far the lowest growth in Southeast Asia and East Asia (see Table 7.20).

The slow rate of growth in per capita income is largely responsible for the failure to satisfactorily address poverty issues. In addition the responsiveness of poverty to economic growth as reflected by the elasticity of poverty reduction in the Philippines has been low. A one percent increase in economic growth resulted in only a 1.3 percent decline in poverty. For other countries the elasticity has been much stronger — 3.5 percent for Thailand and 3.0 percent for Indonesia (Balisacan and Fuwa, 2004).

In addition to slow economic growth the government's direct efforts to reduce poverty have had only modest results. Urban and rural poverty have been on the rise with the agricultural sector accounting for nearly two-thirds of those in poverty. ADB (2008) reports that the incidence of families living in poverty actually

Table 7.20 Growth Rates of GDP Per Capita 1980–2005

Country	Annual Growth in GDP Per Capita 1980–2005
Philippines	0.63
Indonesia	3.70
Malaysia	3.65
Thailand	4.59
Korea	5.53
Vietnam	4.87

Sources: World Bank (2006a) and ADB (2006b).
Note: Vietnam starts in 1985.

increased by 2.5 percent between 2003 and 2006. The Gini coefficient is 0.46 suggesting a high level of income inequality (see Table Box 7.13).

Poverty incidences also vary substantially across regions. Only 4 of 17 regions registered an improvement in the poverty headcount in 2006. Government development spending tends to favor the Metro Manila region and the island of Luzon while discriminating against the islands of the Visayas and especially Mindanao. This has led to substantial regional differences in access to economic opportunities, rates of poverty reduction and incidence of armed conflict as falling real incomes of families and inadequate public spending contributed to the rise in poverty.

Within Asia, the Philippines has lagged behind other countries in eradicating poverty, particularly China, Indonesia, Thailand and Vietnam. Both China and Vietnam started with higher levels of poverty than Philippines in the 1980s, but they swiftly caught up and now their absolute poverty levels are lower than those of Philippines in the early years of the 21st century (ADB 2008). Furthermore, the unemployment rate in the Philippines has remained persistently high at 8–12 percent as compared with 1.5–4.4 percent in Thailand and 2.5–5.0 percent in Malaysia since the 1990s. Even among the employed workforce, there is a substantial degree of underemployment and this is reflected in little improvement in labor productivity.

There is also a lack of rigorous impact evaluation on the various anti-poverty programs in Philippines; hence leading to difficulties in evaluating effectiveness of poverty reducing strategies. In view of this, the Philippines embarked on the Filipino Report Card on Pro-Poor services in 2001 which provides participants' assessment of selected government services such as health care, elementary education, water supply, housing and subsidized rice distribution. It was based on a national client satisfaction study undertaken by the World Bank in collaboration with the Social Weather Station in 2000 to provide a "bottom-up" assessment of pro-poor services. The Report Card is being used by the country's administration to revise the Philippines Medium Term Development Plan and to develop new poverty alleviation strategies and programs.

7.8.2 *Determinants of poverty*

Reyes (2002) is the first study that looks at movements in and out of poverty to distinguish between chronic and transient poverty. Using panel dataset of 17,897 households (1997–1999) from a nationwide survey of the National Statistics Office, she assessed the impact of the Asian financial crisis and abnormal climate changes on income levels of households. Chronic poverty is defined as being poor in the 3 consecutive years 1997, 1998 and 1999. Approximately one in every five surveyed household suffered from chronic poverty.

These figures are compared with the National Statistical Office Family Income and Expenditure Survey of 2003 and are displayed in Table 7.21.

The Reyes (2002) study finds a poverty incidence for the country as a whole of 21.7 percent in 1999 compared with a somewhat higher incidence of 26.1 percent in 2003 from the Family Expenditure Survey. Estimating the number of people who live on less than US$1.25 per day, Bauer *et al.* (2008) reports poverty rate to be at 22.6 percent. Figures from the recently released CPRC (2008) indicate chronic poverty to be around 30 percent and 40 percent. No regional breakdown is provided.

Although there are some differences in estimates of the levels of poverty by region between the Reyes and NSO surveys, the incidence of chronic poverty seems to be concentrated in the Autonomous Region in Muslim Mindanao (ARMM), Bicol, Eastern Viscayas and parts of Mindanao. By comparison, the most prosperous regions with lowest poverty incidence were National Capital Region (Metro Manila) and Central Luzon. Furthermore, compared with 1988 the fall in poverty has been most pronounced in Luzon, followed by the Viscayas. In several parts of Mindanao poverty actually increased — in ARMM by 258 percent reflecting the level of violence and breakdown in law and order.

Albert (2007) estimated the probability that the household will find itself poor in the next time period. His study confirmed the importance of household size, human capital and occupation by sector as crucial determinants of poverty in Philippines. The larger the household size,

Table 7.21 Number and Percentage of Chronic Poor Households, 1999 and 2003

Region	No. of Chronic Poor Households Based on 1999 Sample	% of all Households Based on 1999 Sample	% of all Households Based on 2003 National Statistical Office Income and Expenditure Survey	% of all Households Based on 1988 National Statistical Office Income and Expenditure Survey	% Change in Poverty Between 1988 and 2003 NSO Survey
Philippines	3881	21.7	26.1	34.4	–31.6
Metro Manila	60	3.6	4.8	9.5	–49.5
Mountain Provinces (CAR)	206	27.8	14.8	39.1	–62.1
Ilocos Region I	207	23.3	16.8	25.5	–34.1
Cagayan Valley II	138	18.9	26.9	39.2	–31.4
Central Luzon III	148	8.4	13.7	15.3	–10.5
Southern Tagalog IV	482	17.1	20.9	31.7	–34.1
Bicol Region V	335	34.6	45.6	60.9	–25.1
Western Visaysa VI	343	24.9	26.5	34.4	–23.0
Central Visayas VII	239	22.8	37.5	55.2	–32.1
Eastern Visayas VIII	236	23.5	45.6	53.7	–15.1
West Mindanao IX	176	23.4	48.9	47.6	2.7
North Mindanao X	444	30.5	30.3	44.9	–32.5
South Mindanao XI	251	24.0	27.2	46.9	–42.0
Central Mindanao XII	275	37.1	34.0	35.8	–5.0
Caraga XIII			38.4	30.1	28.9
ARMM	341	38.0	60.5	23.4	258.0

Source: Based on a panel survey of 17,897 households from 1997 to 1999 as reported in Reyes (2002) and on NSO family income and expenditure survey. ARMM stands for autonomous region in Muslim Mindanao region. See also Balisacan (2003) for details.

the more likely a family will be poor. Those with little or no schooling are more vulnerable than those with more education and those working in low skill occupations also have a higher incidence of poverty. According to Reyes (2002), the average educational attainment of the chronic poor is at 7.27 years as compared with the never poor at 13.04 years. In ARRM, nearly two thirds of the poorest 40 percent of the population have little or no schooling (ADB, 2005). Due to lack of education and awareness of family planning, the mean family size of the chronically poor is 6.1 as compared to the never poor at 4.6.

Slow growth in agriculture as a result of limited expansion of cultivated areas combined with low productivity growth is another reason why poverty has remained intractable. In comparison with its neighbors in the region productivity growth in agriculture has been low in the Philippines. While China, Indonesia and Vietnam have experienced good growth in total factor productivity (TFP), TFP in the Philippines has been close to zero between 1980 and 2000 (see Table 7.22).

There is inequality in ownership and control of land as reflected by the high Gini coefficient. Furthermore the Comprehensive Agrarian Reform Program (CARP) has yet to live up to its promise (see below for effectiveness of CARP). In addition, the uncertain incidence of typhoons and dry spells often pose hazards to the crops and farmers' livelihoods. The Philippines has an average of 20 typhoons per year, accompanied by strong winds, intense rainfall and flooding. In recent years, hydrologic events have become more intense and more frequent due to global climate change.

Excessively high population growth. High population growth is another reason why rural poverty has remained high. To study this Balisacan

Table 7.22 Growth of Total Factor Productivity in Agriculture (TFP) in Percent Per Year

Period	China	Thailand	Indonesia	Vietnam	Philippines
1980–2000	4.7	1.0	1.5	2.0	0.1

Source: Balisacan (2007, Table 4).

and Tubianosa (2004) undertook a cross-country analysis of the Philippines and Thailand to investigate the impact of population growth on economic growth, social services and work force participation. Initially in 1975, both Philippines and Thailand enjoyed comparable GDP per capita with similar population sizes. By 2000, the total fertility rate remained at 3.6 in the Philippines while Thailand had cut its fertility rate to 1.9. GDP per capita in Thailand had grown to 8 times its 1975 rate while Philippines' GDP per capita grew only 2.6 fold. While Thailand grew somewhat faster, the bulk of the difference in per capita income growth was due to more rapid population growth in Philippines. There are now 13 million more Filipinos than Thais.

There are several factors contributing to high fertility. The impact of religion is important. Birth control is discouraged by the Catholic Church. Nearly 90 percent of married women aged 15–49 had access to family planning services but less than 40 percent were actually practicing it (ADB, 2005). There is high prevalence of teenage pregnancy and of school-age children dropping out of school to work especially in rural areas. The population pyramid is extremely broad-based. The average Filippino is only 25 years old. Young mothers between 15–24 years of age account for 30 percent of all birth and 74 percent of all illegitimate births (Reyes, 2004).

By reducing population growth Bloom *et al.* (1999) estimate that the demographic dividend earned by lowering population growth in East Asian economies during the 1970s and 1980s contributed to roughly one third of the observed growth in per capita GDP during the so-called East Asian miracle. A higher population growth rate kept the Philippines from enjoying this dividend.

Human capital and natural shocks. As noted above economic growth has not kept up with population growth. GNP per capita has not risen much above $1,000 for the past 20 years (ADB, 2005). Social services have also lagged. The Philippines place in the United Nations Human Development Index ranking has fallen. In 1975, the Philippines ranked 45th· By 1995, her rank was 67th out of 140 countries. Currently in 2008, she ranks at 90 out of

177 countries. Thailand is currently ranked twelve places ahead in the 78th position.

In addition, the economy has been buffeted by natural shocks and man-made shocks that led to variations in the cycle of economic growth (Reyes, 2004). External shocks such as the 1997 Asian Financial Crisis and El Nino[22] conditions have badly impacted the poor. The 1997 Asian financial crisis contributed to a 5 percent reduction in the average living standards and increased in the incidence of poverty by about 9 percent and the depth and severity of poverty by 11 percent and 13 percent respectively (ADB, 2005). El Nino weather conditions are estimated to be responsible for between 47 percent and 57 percent of the total impact on the incidence, depth and severity of poverty.

Poor investment climate and gradual loss of international competitiveness. The World Bank's Doing Business Survey ranks Philippines 133 of 178 economies in terms of the ease of doing business (ADB, 2008). It also fared poorly on control of corruption, political stability and rule of law. Foreign direct investment is low compared with other neighboring countries like Malaysia and Thailand. Macroeconomic instability, corruption, electricity constraints, tax rates, uncertainty of economic policy, crime, theft and disorder and tax administration all contributed to an unfavorable business climate. Transactions at the customs bureau are particularly perceived as riddled with corruption (ADB, 2005). With increased competition from China and Vietnam since the late 1990s, Philippines has been suffering a gradual loss of international competitiveness especially in the electronics and garments markets. The overall weak export performance is due to relatively concentrated export markets and the gradual decline of the competitiveness of the electronics industry.

High unemployment and underemployment. The unemployment rate has declined from over 10 percent of the labor force in 2003 to

---

[22] El Nino conditions are weather patterns than disrupt normal fishing and agricultural yields. These conditions are characterized by unusually dry and warm conditions.

around 7 percent by 2007 (ADB, 2008 and ADB, 2005). Employment generation was generally confined to the construction and services sectors, with few low skill jobs being created in the rural sector or in manufacturing. However, the basic problem of the poor is not so much of a lack of employment as to the low income derived from employment (ADB, 2005). This has to do with both low wage rates and underemployment. About one-fifth of the labor force is underemployed (ADB, 2008). Although the minimum wage rate is still more than the poverty threshold it is not sufficient to keep a family of 4 or more out of poverty. Furthermore wages in rural areas are lower than the minimum wage in urban centers. In ARMM, the minimum wage is not enough to keep the primary wage earner, a spouse and one child out of poverty (ADB, 2005). The minimum wage is only about 40 percent of the family living expenses. Although somewhat out of date Table 2.9 show a minimum wage of just over $1.50 per day for agricultural workers in the Philippines.

Frequent changes in government policies. Under the current Arroyo administration, the 2004–2010 Medium Term Philippines Development Plan (MTPDP) aims to reduce poverty incidence of families from 28.4 percent in 2000 to 17.9 percent in 2010.[23] But to better understand poverty reduction schemes in Philippines, it would be useful to run through an overview of the major poverty programs since 1986.

- MTPDP 1986–1991: Aquino Administration
  Poverty incidence targets are set for the first time. President Aquino launched Tulong sa Tao which was aimed at reducing poverty through creation of employment for "low income municipalities". About 183,500 jobs were created and living conditions of 111,000 beneficiaries improved.
- MTPDP 1992–1997: Ramos Administration
  Under President Ramos, the Social Reform Agenda targeted beneficiaries using sectoral and geographical methods. Focus was primarily

[23] However it does not articulate a clear population policy. Population growth rate will have to be slowed for the Philippines to increase its GDP per capita.

on particularly disadvantaged economic and social groups — farmers, fishermen, indigenous communities, the urban poor, informal sector workers and other disadvantaged groups — women, disabled, youths, the elderly and disaster victims. There was geographical targeting of the country's 20 poorest provinces.

- MTPDP 1999–2004: Estrada Administration
  An attempt was made to develop a Plan that revolves around a common theme of sustaining growth and reducing poverty. Regional poverty targets are also included within the Plan. Under the Estrada Administration, the Lingap Para sa Mahihirap was to identify the 100 poorest families in each local governing unit nationwide for poverty reduction. The emphasis was on the 100 poorest families as the basic targeting unit instead of the village (*barangay*).
- MTPDP 2001–2004 and MTPDP 2004–2010: Arroyo Administration
  The task is to "fight poverty by building prosperity for the greatest number of the Filipino people." Launched in 2001 under the supervision of the National Anti-Poverty Commission (NAPC), it has 5 types of Kapit-Bisig Laban sa Kahirapan (KALAHI) Special Projects that reach out to the poor.

As can be seen, each president had specific poverty reduction projects. This resulted in changes in the poverty framework as well as differing targeting mechanism over the past 20 years. For example, President Ramos preferred a geographical and sector approach while Estrada's Lingap sa Mahirap targeted the 100 poorest families in every province and city while the current KALAHI targets the villages themselves. This shift in priorities has resulted in a waste of energy and resources as even effective programs were discarded just because they were part of the past Presidents' agendas (ADB, 2005).[24] The tenure of the President is also limited to 5 years with the exception of President Arroyo who has held on for two terms, thus providing some stability in the implementation of KALAHI program. Special credit

[24] For more information on the limitations of the various programs, please refer to ADB (2005).

has to be given to certain government agencies that have been inventive in renaming their program to outlast the administration. For instance, the National Food Administration has renamed the Kadiwa rolling store during the Marcos administration to Enhanced Retail Access Program during the Estrada administration. It is now called the Greater Market Access store (Reyes, 2004). However such "long lasting" programs tend to be the exception than the norm.

Furthermore, Balisacan and Fuwa (2004) found a "dynasty" variable (measuring the proportion of Philippine provincial officers related by blood or affinity) that had significantly negative effects on subsequent income growth. There is a lack of a competitive political system in Philippines which leads to suboptimal policy choices and relatively poor economic performance.

7.8.3 *Micro policies*

The Department of Social Work and Development (DSWD) is the governmental body in charge of selecting the targeted beneficiaries based on the selection system developed for a program of social assistance. The Pantawid Pamilyang Pilipino (PPP) provides cash transfers to needy households for health, nutrition and education purposes, especially for children aged between 0 to 14 years old. The PPP targets 300,000 households. Currently 6,000 pilot households from the municipalities of Sibagat and Esperanzo in Agusan del Sur, Lopez Jaena and Bonifacio in Misamis Occidental and Pasay and Caloocan cities in the National Capital Region of Metro Manila have received cash assistance since January 2006. Cash transfers of up to P15,000 per family over a period of 5 years are given if parents keep their children in school and bring them to primary health clinics for full immunization. In addition, pregnant women must get pre and post natal care and be attended during childbirth by a skilled birth attendant. Parents or guardians are to attend family planning sessions, mother's classes and parent effectiveness seminars. Other conditional cash transfers include the food-for-school program where children attending elementary school are given 1 kilogram of rice each day. This program is helpful for the chronically poor. The scope of PPP could be extended to cover more families in Mindanao and parts of the Viscayas where poverty incidence is high.

Subsidized rice. The Philippine government has been supplying rice at subsidized price through the National Food Authority (NFA). The aim is to ensure price and supply stabilization. However it is not targeted specifically at the poor as only 27 percent of the poor buy NFA rice. Mindanao, the poorest region, is excluded from the scheme. NFA's resources would be more effectively utilized by geographically targeting the poor by locating special stores selling NFA rice in poor areas such as Mindanao. The Arroyo administration has developed a number of new food subsidy programs including a Targeted Rice Distribution Program, the Coconut Farmers' Food Access Program, Focus Rice Distribution Program and more retail outlets for the food subsidy program. The effectiveness and focus of these programs has yet to be evaluated.

Employment program. The Self-Employment Assistance — Kaunlaran (SEA-K) Integrated Development Project was started in 1993 and implemented by the DSWD. It is a livelihood assistance program that provided social welfare services to needy families, disadvantaged women, out-of-school youth, and disabled individuals. Annual emergency employment programs are in place for 20,000 out-of-school youth and out-of-work youth in Metro Manila initially and in Regions III and IV (Reyes, 2002). The program has not been extended to the needier regions in the Viscayas and Mindanao.

Social funds. Beginning in 1998, ADB's Secondary Education Development and Improvement Project (SEDIP) has given grants of $53 million to improve quality and access to secondary education in impoverished regions. The project benefits more than 1 million high school students in 26 of Philippines' impoverished districts where school enrolment, completion and student performances generally lag behind the rest of the country. School heads were given training in planning and running the school while teachers were trained in subject content and teaching skills. Textbooks in core subjects such as mathematics, science, English and Filipino were given to students. Alternative secondary education program was provided for students who were unable to attend school regularly. Certain schools also have their own school feeding program to encourage the children to attend school (see Box 7.17).

Box 7.17 Project Effectiveness in Leyte

Southern Leyte is one such province that has benefited from school feeding programs. Recently, under the SEDIP, Southern Leyte ranked first in the recent National Achievement Test, 8 of its high schools made the top 30 for the country (ADB, 2008c). With an average ratio of 40 to 50 students in a class in this province, teachers manage the students well. Rizal National High School ranked first among the region's high schools. This is no small feat considering how difficult it is for the students even to reach school premises. It is located in a remote hill and has approximately 200 students. The students wear rubber flip-flops to walk to school going over mud and over a rugged uphill terrain. Some have to walk an hour or 5 kilometers each day just to get to school. They only change into shoes upon arriving in the classroom. Most of the students are children of poor farmers and are malnourished. The school maximizes students' attendance through a daily feeding program with aid from the parents. The parents take turns bringing simple lunches for the entire school. Hence students do not have to go home for lunch.

In Marayag National High School students also do not wear shoes because they have to cross the sand to reach the school which is just meters from the sea. During Philippines' powerful typhoon season, the waves can get very high. In order to do well in the national examinations, teachers and students alike started intensive study after school hours and on weekends. They were rewarded for their hard work in the success in the national exams.

Source: ADB (2008c).

With support from ADB and World Bank, the Department of the Social Welfare and Development implemented the Early Childhood Development (ECD) project. Since 2000, 3 million children have benefited from the project. ECD provides health, nutrition, psychosocial development and early education for disadvantaged children up to 6 years old. These early years are considered to be the most critical to the child development. Vitamins and medicines, usually for common ailments such as upper respiratory tract infections, gastroenteritis and diarrhea, are also provided by the centers. To motivate mothers to have their children immunized, certain centers also give the mother free groceries and a certificate that shows the child has been immunized. To further educate mothers on family planning, the ECD project also includes a component called Parents' Effective Services. Over 100,000 parents were educated on various issues such as children's rights, responsible parenthood and prevention of child abuse. In addition, the project also constructed or improved facilities such as barangay health stations, day-care centers and mothers' homes. ECD has reached about 1,500 villages where about 50 percent of Philippines' most disadvantaged and vulnerable children are located. At the ground level, ECD field workers were also recognized for their efforts and how well they had utilized their facilities. Both national and regional officials also focused on highlighting the most inspiring efforts among ECD project achievements. It provides a good role model/case studies for the rest to learn from.

In another educational program backed by a $1 million grant from ADB's Japan Fund for Poverty Reduction, poor women vendors were taught new skills to improve their working conditions. It also provided support for them as parents. 1,600 poor women vendors in public markets in eight areas of Mindanao were the targeted beneficiaries. A women's resource center was established in every town and used to conduct training. It also provided a drop in clinic, day care facilities for pre-school children, cold storage lockers and wash room. All these services are available for a minimum fee. Popular courses included training on preparing and handling of food, herbal medicine, hair styling, dressmaking and nail care. The response for training from female vendors in Panabo City was initially dismal because they were reluctant to leave the stall for a full day and forgo potential sales. However once they realized the benefits, attendance dramatically picked up.

ADB has also targeted Mindanao for implementing the Basic Urban Services Sector Project. It involves upgrading and rehabilitating of infrastructure through a $30 million loan. In Panabo City, a new bus and jeepney terminal was completed at the end of 2006. Female market vendors have stalls there as well. In Osamis City, a new two-storey public market is being built to replace the existing dilapidated building where the female vendors sell their wares.

7.8.4 *Sector policies*

Housing. Among the regions, Mindanao and Visayas have the lowest proportion of households owning residential land. The Community Mortgage Program which focuses on security of land tenure and the Arroyo administration's interest in provision of housing assistance to the bottom 40 percent of households through affordable socialized housing is addressing some of the housing needs of the poor (Reyes, 2002).

Energy. The Department of Energy uses ADB funds to rehabilitate old renewable energy systems in remote rural areas. For instance, a pilot project was started to rehabilitate a non-operating solar battery system in Barangay Bunog in Palawan. Since demand for power is low there, it was not economical to connect it to the power grid and the solar-power battery system is sufficient to satisfy current energy requirements. The villagers report their satisfaction with the system. Village children are now able to study and do the homework at night and small businesses like groceries stalls are able to extend their operating hours till 8 pm to augment their incomes and provide more flexible hours of operation for their customers. The solar powered battery is also cheaper than the kerosene lamp which can consume up to a liter of fuel each week and more environmentally friendly than kerosene. It has also created a new line of business for full-time housewives who double up as the *babaeng* (female) energy entrepreneur. They manage the solar battery-charging stations for about 10–15 households. They earn about $5 per month by charging batteries for other households. Some enterprising women earn more by charging mobile phones as a sideline.

The other project which has benefited residents in remote areas is the twin-hydropower system in Balbalan, Kalinga Province. Projects based on renewable energy could be extended to other remote locations where the potential for solar power is high.

Most of the projects described in this section on microeconomic initiatives are funded by external sources. While successful, more needs to be done by the government and local businesses to address the needs of the chronic poor, particularly in Mindanao, parts of the Visayas and Bicol in Luzon.

International migration. Numbering over 1.3 million, the Philippines has the largest percentage of its labor force working overseas of any Asian country. Its remittance income of over $6 billion is now greater than its foreign exchange earnings. Furthermore Capistrano and Sta Maria (2007) show that remittances and the number of overseas workers both have a significant impact on overall poverty. They find that a 1 percent increase in the share of remittances in GDP leads to a 2.55 percent reduction in the incidence of poverty. Similarly, a 10 percent increase in the number of overseas workers as a share of the population results in a 0.73 percent decline in the level of poverty.

The depth and severity of poverty are also reduced in both cases. While this is a powerful result it is unlikely, however, that the poorest families benefit as much as those who are more well to do. Holmvall (2007) notes that remittances per capita from the poorer provinces are much smaller than those from the richer provinces and only a fraction of those who migrate (15 percent) have less than a high school education. Combined with the income constraint and the lack of education, many poor farmers are unable to join the pool of international migrants. The strong positive relationship between poverty reduction and remittance probably is the indirect effect of remittance income on the general standard of living and economic growth.

Agricultural sector. Most of the poor are dependent on agriculture for their livelihoods. To improve social equity, the Department of Agrarian Reform has developed 5 major programs.

- Implementing land tenure improvement programs through land distribution
- Offering support services like credit, infrastructure training, extension and community organizing for rural dwellers
- Implementing a rural-based justice system to resolve rural disputes
- Implementing a program to increase awareness of all the above

Spending on agriculture-related infrastructure has yielded mixed results (ADB, 2005). As of 2002, construction of roads linking farms to markets only managed to achieve 34 percent of the target set in the medium term development plan (MTPDP). Yields were raised by improving the existing irrigation network. However there was less success in raising yields for land that had a newly established irrigation system. The provision of electricity to *barangays* (villages) also fell somewhat short of the MTPDP target for 2003, with only 87 percent of villages being covered.

On the other hand land redistribution through CARP seems to have been an unqualified success (World Bank, 2001b). CARP beneficiaries reported an increase in productivity and incomes, and a higher propensity to invest in both physical and human capital (of the children) as compared to non-beneficiaries. However more needs to be done to accelerate the speed of land distribution and resolve administrative problems of surveying and land valuation. Also effective strategies need to be implemented to lower the resistance of opposing landlords.

7.8.5 *Macroeconomic policies*

The major government initiative originates at the local level. Implemented in 2003, the KALAHI-CIDSS[25] is a community-driven

[25] KALAHI stands for Kapitbisig Laban sa Kahirapan (Linking Arms against Poverty). CIDSS stands for Comprehensive and Integrated Delivery of Social Services.

development project that aims to empower communities through their enhanced participation in community projects that reduce poverty. Within 6 years, the project aims to cover 25 percent of the poorest municipalities in the poorest 42 (out of 79) provinces of the Philippines, equivalent to more than 4,000 villages in 182 municipalities. It strengthens community participation in local governance and develops local capacity to design, implement, and manage development activities. Community grants are used to support the building of low-cost, productive infrastructure such as roads, water systems, clinics, and schools (see World Bank web site and click on KALAHI-CIDSS Project).

The five types of KALAHI Special projects includes rural and urban projects; social projects that construct farm to market roads and water systems, and water supply, electrification and drainage for resettlement sites. KALAHI programs serve as a liaison between the targeted barangay and the national level agency (ADB, 2005).

Certain features of the national government have been devolved to local government units to fight poverty. Local Poverty Reduction Action Officers have been appointed by all provinces and cities/municipalities to help formulate action plans to reduce poverty. However Reyes comments that the weakest link in the chain to fight poverty remains at the village level. A large part of village budgets often goes to village officials instead of the chronic poor and accountability needs to be strengthened.

Social safety nets. Compared to other Asian countries, Philippines has a wide range of social protection schemes but generally provides low coverage and inadequate level of benefits. The low coverage is partly due to the lack of funding. The persistent budget deficits accumulated over the years have led to the government to substantially reduce spending on social services. During 2001–2005, social spending was only 22 percent of the central government spending as compared with 45 percent in Thailand and 37 percent in Malaysia.

The National Health Insurance Program covers poor residents in the backward regions although the richer areas of Luzon get the lion's share of the benefits. Approximately three-fifth of the beneficiaries are in Luzon, another one fifth in Mindanao, and the remaining 20 percent in the Visayas. There is an attempt to include the indigent population and they comprise nearly 8 percent of the total estimated household population for 2002. Medicare Para sa Masa program aims at providing medical care to the marginalized groups. The beneficiaries are identified using the community-based information system for minimum basic needs. The payment of the health premium is shared between the local government units and the national government, with premium payment discounted according to the income classification of the indigents' residence.

The Health Sector Reform Agenda (HSRA) proposes to

(i) Expand health insurance coverage for the poor. While one third of the population is covered by insurance coverage, about only 1 percent of the poor is covered (Department of Health, 1999). Payment for health care by the poor are almost entirely out of the pocket.
(ii) Improve the quality and accessibility of health care for the poor in public primary facilities.
(iii) Reduce the cost of medicine and expenditures on hospital stays. Realizing the heavy burden of high medicine prices on the poor (approximately 50 percent of household medical expense), the government has initiated a parallel drug importation program such as India where the same patented drug is sold at a fraction of its price in the Philippines.
(iv) Improve the quality of government hospitals.

Social inclusion. The Magna Carta for Disabled People creates a national mandate to eliminate discrimination against disabled people and to integrate them into social and economic mainstream of society. It stipulates that 5 percent of the contractual personnel of the national government engaged in social development should be reserved for qualified people with disabilities (ADB, 2005). Employment is also encouraged for the private sector and local government units.

However more would have to done as violators of the law are rarely prosecuted.

7.8.6 *Future policy agenda and challenges*

Poverty reduction efforts in the Philippines are fragmented and suffer from a lack of consistent policy commitment. Many programs funded from foreign sources have been successful but they often do not fit into a long term agenda for poverty reduction. There is a distinct bias toward programs that offer assistance in Luzon and to a lesser extent in Viscayas. Mindanao is often overlooked. The civil unrest that has plagued Mindanao in the past is partially responsible for the lack of attention by successive governments based in Manila. Aside from this bias many poverty programs are not well focused on the poor. Balisacan (2007) suggests a reorientation that would have six major objectives. Amending his list to include a focus on chronic poverty we highlight the need to

1. Stress basic education, especially teaching and technical and skills development in rural areas. Reduce emphasis on tertiary education while still selectively supplying scholarships for the poor.
2. Stress basic health and family planning with focus on the poorest villages and regions. Cut back spending on tertiary health care and stress importance of cost recovery for the existing programs.
3. Increase spending on rural infrastructure such as rural roads and power. Cut back on public works equipment programs.
4. Target supplementary feeding programs for the poor and coordinate with food stamp program. Keep the non poor from using these programs. Do away with general food price subsidies.
5. Stimulate research and development for small holder agriculture and also development more small scale irrigation projects and systems. Cut back on post harvest facilities supplied by the government. These activities should be left to the private sector.
6. Build administrative capacity for local government units and microfinance with stress on providing finance for the chronically poor. Reduce emphasis on livelihood programs.

7.9 Cambodia

Box 7.18. A Snapshot of Cambodia's Chronic Poor

- About 5.6 million people are poor in Cambodia. 40 percent of the poor survive on less than US$1.25 per day. Empirical data on the incidence of chronic poverty in Cambodia is not available from the CPRC (2008) report.
- Chronic poverty is likely to be highest in the uplands. The poorest live in the districts bordering Thailand and Laos in the north and north-east, and Vietnam in the east.
- The chronic poor tend to be (i) those unable to engage in productive activity; (ii) farmers who sell their labor to larger farms; and (iii) subsistence farmers who have no marketable surplus.
- Cambodia was categorized as a "chronically deprived country" along with countries like Afghanistan, Angola and Zimbabwe.

Table Box 7.18 Selected Indicators

Proportion of poor who are chronically poor over 5 years (low estimate)[1]	..
Proportion of poor who are chronically poor over 5 years (high estimate)[1]	..
Population (2005)	14.1 mil
Percentage of poor living on less than US$1.25 per day (2005PPP)*	40.2
Average depth of poverty (number of % points by which the poor fall below the poverty line[2] in 1997)	28.4
Income share held by lowest 20 percent	6.9
Gini index of inequality	17.6
Healthcare indicators	
Under five mortality rate (per 1,000 live births) in 2004	141
Infant mortality rate (per 1,000 live births) in 2004	97
Proportion of children under five who are stunted (2000)[2]	45
Life expectancy at birth, 2004	56.5
Educational indicators	
Adult illiteracy rate for women aged 15 years and above (2000–2004)	36

(*Continued*)

Box 7.18 (*Continued*)

Adult illiteracy rate for men aged 15 years and above (2000–2004)	15
Child labor	
Percentage of children aged between 7–14 in the labor force (1999–2004)	52.3

Source: CPRC (2008) Annex E and F and *Bauer *et al.* (2008).
Note: [1]
[2]Most recent year.

Economic growth in Cambodia has been rapid with an average growth rate of 7.7 percent per annum between 1994 and 2004 (World Bank, 2007c). Growth was due primarily to a vibrant industrial sector especially garment manufacturing, which contributes about 85 percent of the country's exports. Tourist visits to the Angkor Heritage Park also contributed to growth. Urban centers and in particular Phnom Penh, Siem Reap Town and Sihanoukville have benefited from the rise in economic activities.

Poverty has fallen from 47 percent in 1993/4 to 31 percent in 2001 (World Bank, 2007c and ADB, 2008). However recent estimates using the revised poverty line puts the proportion of the population that is poor in Cambodia at 40 percent (Table Box 7.18). The rate of poverty reduction has been slow. There have been improvements in non-material aspects such as greater access to infrastructure and amenities like clean water and electricity. Although the proportion of the poorest population with access to improved water is still very small, it jumped 20 folds from 0.1 percent to 2.2 percent. Similarly, the proportion of the poorest population who enjoyed reliable lighting experienced a 4-fold increased to 18 percent in 2004 (World Bank, 2007c). Health outcomes with the exception of maternal mortality rates have improved dramatically. Gender gaps in literacy and schooling have also been narrowed.

Nevertheless, the rate of poverty reduction has been slow. After decades of war and internal conflict, Cambodia remains one of the poorest countries in Asia. 90 percent of Cambodians depend on agriculture for their livelihood, yet the countryside has millions of land mines, hidden and yet to be exploded. The landmines pose a potential health hazard to rural dwellers and impede the pace of agricultural development. Inequality in the distribution of income and consumption has been on the rise. Consumption of goods and services per capita per day of the poorest fifth of the population rose by a mere 8 percent as compared to 45 percent for the richest fifth households in 2004 (World Bank, 2007c). The alarming increase of land ownership in the hands of the rich and insecure land tenure risk aggravating income inequality further.

General information on poverty and per capita consumption levels are available from the Socio-Economic Survey of Cambodia (SESC) and Cambodia Socio-Economic Survey (CSES). The Cambodia Development Resource Institute has also conducted Moving out of Poverty Survey and the Participatory Poverty Assessment to better understand the causes and nature of poverty in Cambodia. Key sources of information on health outcomes can be gathered from the Cambodia Demographic and Health Survey. However it is difficult to establish trends in poverty in Cambodia as questionnaire design and sampling methods have changed over time. The geographical sampling frame has expanded over time to include remote peripheral areas and those previously under Khmer Rouge control.

7.9.1 *Incidence of poverty*

About 5.6 million people are poor in Cambodia. 40 percent of the poor survive on less than US$1.25 per day (Table Box 7.19). 90 percent of Cambodians reside in rural areas and at least 12 percent of poor people do not have any access to land at all (IFAD, 2008a). Results from a study conducted in 2005 by the Cambodia

Development Resource Institute (CDRI 2007)[26] showed that approximately 14 percent of the survey respondents in the study remained chronically poor between 2001 and 2004. Within that period, 22 percent of the surveyed households fell into poverty. On the other hand, 26 percent managed to move out of poverty. Furthermore, all sampled villages experienced rising income inequality. Incomes of the chronic poor rose by 33 percent whereas incomes of the non-poor increased by twice as much (61 percent), thus creating a widening income gap.

Chronic poor households generally tend to (i) be located in poor villages and their livelihoods dependent common property resources; (ii) have high dependency ratios; (iii) have a higher probability of having old, disabled or single female household heads; (iv) possess small land holdings or are rural landless; (v) have few economic opportunities and are often locked in discriminating labor arrangements which frequently leads to indebtedness; (vi) suffer from food insecurity and the children need to work to support the family. The CDRI (2007) report highlighted the importance of internal characteristics (family demographics, human capital, and physical capital) and location and geographical endowment of the villages in the determination of chronic poverty rates.

While the CDRI (2007) study did not specifically focus on the study of chronic poverty, it can be inferred from the national surveys that chronic poverty is likely to be more prevalent in the uplands where general poverty rates are highest (see Table 7.23). The chronically poor live in the districts bordering Thailand and Laos in the north and north-east, and Vietnam in the east. Average years of schooling completed for an individual living on the northeast highland is 1.7 years as compared to someone living in Phnom Penh, where school completion rate averages 7.7 years. Kompong Speu, which is located in the uplands, had the worse outcomes in the country in terms of child survival rates, female anemia

[26] The Moving out of Poverty study tracked movements of households out of poverty over a three year period based on data from 9 villages from all four of Cambodia's rural ecological zones — the Tonle Sap plains, Mekong plains, uplands and the coastal region.

Table 7.23 Poverty Rates in Cambodia
(Poverty Headcount percentage below poverty line)

Upland Plateau and Mountains	52
Kompong Speu	57
Other plateau/mountain	46
Tonle Sap	43
Kompong Thom	52
Siem Reap	52
Kompong Chhnang/Pursat	40
Banteay Meanchey	37
Battambang	34
Plains	32
Prey Veng	37
Kompong Cham	37
Svay Rieng	36
Takeo	28
Kandai	22
Coast	27
Kampot	30
Sihanoukville/Kep/Koh Kong	23
Phnom Penh	5

Source: World Bank (2007c).

and babies delivered outside a facility or without trained assistance. The poverty rate is generally less severe in the Southern provinces and bordering the coast. Phnom Penh has the lowest poverty rate in Cambodia.

Cambodia's poorest people are often isolated and live in remote villages (see Table 7.24). Many have to travel more than 5 km to reach a health clinic, and still others live more than 5 km from the nearest road. Remote areas are more likely to have poorer soils and limited access to irrigation. Only 10 percent of upland dwellers and approximately 25 percent of population living in the rural Plains, Tonle Sap and coastal areas have access to electricity (World Bank, 2007c).

The vulnerable groups include subsistence farmers, rural landless people as well as internally displaced persons and mine victims.

Table 7.24

Village Size	Distance to the Nearest all-weather Road	
	Less than 5 km	More than 5 km
More than 1,000 people	33 percent of the population are poor	38 percent of the population are poor
Less than 1,000 people	43 percent of the population are poor	53 percent of the population are poor

Source: *Cambodia Socio-Economic Survey* (2004).

Women, children, the elderly and indigenous ethnic minorities are generally the most disadvantaged. Domestic violence is not viewed as a crime. Up to a quarter of the poorest group who had suffered from domestic violence in the CDRI (2007) study mentioned an average loss of 2 months' income due to inability to work (World Bank, 2007c). The indigenous ethnic minorities are significantly poorer than the Khmer majority. 60 percent of them fall in the lowest two consumption quintiles. Young children are also at risk. A child born into the poorest quintile is twice as likely to suffer from severe malnutrition and three times unlikely to survive beyond the fifth year. Those who survive early childhood are often exploited as child labor. There is no universal social security system, so the elderly must depend on family and community networks for assistance. Without such assistance they could quickly fall into the poverty trap.

7.9.2 *Determinants of poverty*

Macroeconomic growth has not been evenly distributed through the country. There are limited multiplier effects from the expansion in the garment manufacturing industry, with some trickle down effects to the construction and trade sector. Likewise, the strong growth of tourism is limited to Siem Reap town and its surrounding areas, particularly in construction and food retail industries (see Box 7.19 for more details). The vast countryside which is pre-dominantly agricultural based has lagged significantly behind.

Box. 7.19 A Tale of Four Districts in Cambodia

Case studies in 4 different districts, namely Malai, Mesang, Phnom Sruoch and Puok are presented below to illustrate the differences in growth and poverty reduction.

Malai District: Increase in Cash Crop Cultivation

Malai is located in the Banteay Meanchey province which is near the Thai border. It used to be under the full control of the Khmer Rouge till 1996. Households grow cash crops for a living. After the Khmer Rouge integration, each household received a distribution of land of approximately 5 hectares. The subsequent increase in agricultural production led to an increase in incomes. Average income of the cash crop farmer has increased five fold since 1996. Because of competition for farm workers from neighboring Thailand, the daily wage is 40 percent higher than in other parts of Cambodia. However growth is likely to slow down due to less land for expansion and soil degradation. Being a war prone area in the past, land mines pose a difficulty to further increasing agricultural production. High cost of inputs, poor road access and lack of credit further constrains farmers.

Mesang District: Remittances from Garment Factory Workers

Mesang is located in the Prey Veng province, in the plains. Agriculture is its main economic activity. Residents are now much better off due to improvement in road conditions linking the district to the market. Many families have sent their daughters to work in garment factories in Phnom Penh City. They remit home roughly about US$30 per month, which is very high compared to the annual income from those working in rice fields of around US$100 per hectare. However inequality has been on the rise in the Mesang district. Those with assets such as land and livestock are able to expand agricultural activities. Some are also able to afford the commission fee that has to be paid to middle

(*Continued*)

Box 7.19 (*Continued*)

men in order to find work in Phnom Penh City. On the other hand, those without assets like the rural landless tend to be worse off. The gradual depletion of common resources like fish stocks has reduced their income sources.

Puok District: Spillover Effects from Tourism Boom

Puok district is located in the Siem Reap province. Residents used to rely on agricultural production for income growth in the past. It has profited handsomely from its strategic location next to the tourism town of Siem Reap which is adjacent to the popular tourist site of Angor Wat. Residents work at construction sites, restaurants and hotels in Siem Reap and there is increased demand for villagers' agricultural produce from hotels and restaurants in Siem Reap. In addition, growers also provide mulberry and silk to local artisans. Income from tourism-related employment accounted for as much as 40 percent of income of rice farmers. Nevertheless, villagers are employed in lowly skilled occupations due to their lack of education. Furthermore the lack of capital and technological know-how has prevented Puok farmers from expanding agricultural output sufficiently to satisfy the strong demand from Siem Reap.

Phnom Sruoch District: Poor Land Governance & Exhaustion of Forests

Phnom Sruoch is located in the uplands. After the Khmer Rouge integration, 53 new villages have been incorporated into the district. There is a significant difference between the livelihood strategies of those residing in the old villages and new villages. The former depend on farming whereas the latter depend on logging and land sales from the large forest lands in the new villages. However residents of the new villages often find their sources of income diminishing once the forest is cleared or they have sold off their land to speculators. Currently a few

(*Continued*)

Box 7.19 (*Continued*)

elite Phnom Penh families holds most of the lands in Phnom Sruoch district. With limited off-farm opportunities, the landless poor are trapped in poverty.

Source: Economic Institute of Cambodia (2006).

Land ownership in Cambodia is highly skewed (see Table 7.25). The CDRI study highlights the importance of patronage relationships (*khnang*) which have allowed certain rich families to grab land from the poor. The richest 20 percent of the population control up to two-thirds of available land. An alarming proportion of land is held by powerful and rich individuals that do not reside in the community. These include wealthy businessmen (31 percent), *okhna* — individuals who made financial contributions of US$100,000 or more (23 percent), military officers (15 percent) and members of the National Assembly (8 percent).

There are over half a million landless rural poor and nearly half of all rural households are either landless or own less than 0.5 hectare of land while even more land is being bought by the rich for speculative purposes.

The share of land held by the poorest two-fifth of the population has been reduced from 8.4 percent to 5.4 percent between 1999 and 2004 (UNDP, 2007). Some had to sell land in a hurry

Table 7.25. Land Ownership in Selected Asian Countries

Country	Gini Coefficient of Land Ownership
Thailand	0.41
Indonesia	0.49
Malaysia	0.51
India	0.55
Cambodia	0.65

Source: World Bank (2007c).

to pay for urgent medical expense. Others are landless because of displacement including refugees returning from the Khmer Rouge camps on the border with Thailand, or after long military service either in the Khmer Rouge or government armed forces. Indigenous minorities are particularly vulnerable to land loss as they lack secure land tenure. Furthermore illegal logging, land sales and purchase and land grabbing for private ownership are prevalent in Cambodia (UNDP, 2007). Government efforts to re-allocate mine-cleared land to those displaced have faced resistance from powerful interest groups.

Low level of education and limited access to capital keep farmers from off-farm employment or pursuing self-employment options. Markets are not readily accessible for farmers in poorly connected provinces like Kompong or inland province like Tonle Sap provinces. Such provinces tend to lag behind the rest of the country and are likely to stagnate if the government does not intervene. Subsistence farmers are unable to sell off their excess agricultural output because they have limited market access whereas well-connected provinces such as Battambang with links to Thailand and provinces that border Phnom Penh such as Kandal continue to enjoy the fruits of economic growth. There are few spillover effects on the remote parts of the country.

7.9.3 *Micro policies*

Food security. The Special Programme on Food Security, a component of the National Programme for Food Security and Poverty Reduction, is coordinated by three different government ministries to help poor households deal with food insecurity.

Recent increases in the cost of living have resulted in a fall in real income and purchasing power of the poor. The price of rice has doubled and price of meat and fish has risen 30 to 50 percent. Input prices such as fertilizer prices have also increased. To help offset these cost increases the Asian Development Bank (ADB) will provide Cambodia's poorest families with $35 million in emergency food assistance. Poor families living around the Tonle Sap Lake, and in Phnom Penh's urban slums, will receive free rice and other food subsidies. Poor children attending early childhood learning centers and primary schools will be given free meals.

Most of the food security projects are funded with external assistance. More needs to be done on the part of the government to address food insecurity issues and the fundamental need to increase the rural livelihoods of the chronic poor. CPRC (2008) recently simulated a model to see the effect of cash transfers on three types of households with characteristics typical of the chronically poor: (i) those unable to engage in productive activity; (ii) farmers who sell their labor to larger farms; and (iii) subsistence farmers who have no marketable surplus.

The recommended scale of the transfer is relatively modest at 2.5 percent of household income. The CPRC (2008) findings suggest that cash transfers are pro-poor, aid in raising consumption of the poor, stimulate production and economic growth. The chronically poor farm worker and farmers benefit (in groups ii and iii) more since they can work to increase income once their basic food needs have been satisfied. In turn, both groups could make transfers to those who are old and disabled (groups i) and unable to work and thus create a win-win situation. The study strongly advocates cash transfers to aid the chronic poor.

To reduce the vulnerability of the chronic poor to price shocks, CPRC (2008) argues that Cambodia should increase public investment in agriculture and infrastructure. This kind of intervention will also stimulate local agriculture production as well as reduce Cambodia's reliance on imported food. With greater accessibility to markets, the chronic poor can buy directly from food producers at lower prices rather than depend on middlemen.

Education. Education in Cambodia is not gender biased at the primary level. However many girls in Cambodia tend to drop out of school after grade 6. In addition, many parents do not allow girls to travel long distances and live away from home to attend upper secondary schools. To stimulate enrolment of poor boys and girls the government has developed scholarship schemes where cash or in-kind benefits are given to poor families. The condition stipulates that children regularly attend lower secondary school (grades 7–9).

More reforms are critically needed before the education scheme would truly benefit the poor. Primary schools are often understaffed and the general quality of instruction is poor. More needs to be done to provide incentives for teachers in remote areas. Students also have to pay "informal" fees to teachers which, combined with costs of school uniforms, often make education unaffordable for the poor. Teacher salaries need to be raised and school lunch programs can help improve attendance as well as nutrition. (See the current challenges facing free meal program in schools in Box 7.20).

Box: 7.20 Rising Inflation and School Breakfast Program

Destitute schools were selected to take part in the breakfast program in Cambodia. Funds were provided by the World Food Program under the charge of United Nations agency. 450,000 students in 1,344 schools across Cambodia have benefited from the program. The Sun primary school is one such school and located in Pray Viev. Pray Viev is one of the poorest villages in Cambodia's most impoverished province, Kampong Speu.

When the free breakfast was first introduced here eight years ago by the World Food Program, it was an instant hit. "Students brought their brothers and sisters, 2, 3 and 4 years old," said Yim Soeurn, the principal at Sun. "It was very hard to control." Breakfast has been a magnet for students ever since, as well as the teachers' best friend. Well-fed students are more attentive, tardiness is no longer a problem (breakfast is served at 6:30 a.m., before classes begin) and attendance by girls, who for years had been kept home by their parents, has increased sharply.

(*Continued*)

Box 7.20 (*Continued*)

When food prices increased in 2008 the breakfast program was scheduled to be suspended. Poor students will not come to school if the program is eliminated. The United Nations agency has appealed worldwide for an additional $500,000 million to be able to continue with the program.

Source: *New York Times* (April 30, 2008).

Social funds. With the assistance of external donors like ADB, World Bank and IFAD, the Cambodian government has implemented various community projects such as food-for-work program and other rural development projects. For example, ADB Northwest Rural Development Project geographically targeted the war-torn northwestern part of Cambodia (specifically Seam Reap, Oddar Meanchey, Banteay Meanchey, and Battambang) and directed assistance towards female-headed households, war widows, disabled, and displaced soldiers. In the Southern provinces, ADB is working with NGOs to provide farmers with access to agricultural services and resource. It also emphasizes the participation of women in income-generating activities. Current ongoing IFAD projects include the Rural Livelihoods Improvement Project in Kratie, Preah Vihear and Ratanakiri to build the capacity of the rural poor. Local interest groups are involved in the projects and the various target groups are involved in planning and implementation.

Social protection. Social protection is minimal in Cambodia. Insurance covers only the small formal sector and there are no general safety nets or social insurance. Furthermore most social assistance is implemented with external resources. Progress in pro-poor poverty alleviation schemes lags far behind neighbouring countries Vietnam and Thailand.

Health Care. One rather successful pro-poor scheme that Cambodia has adopted is that of the health equity funds (HEF).

A contract is signed between the NGO or community organization responsible for managing the program and identifying poor patients and the external donor who funds the scheme. Under the scheme, the poor can receive free treatment at healthcare facilities. In turn, the healthcare facilities are compensated via the fund. In some districts, poor patients are even compensated for their travel costs, which can be quite substantial especially those chronic poor living more than 4 or 5 km away from a health centers. It effectively tilts demand for health care services away from expensive private practitioner towards public health facilities (see Box 7.21).

As of 2006, the project has covered up to 21 out of 61 operational districts. It is set to cover up to one-third of the population. HEF appears to have successfully aided the poor at rather low cost. Total monthly subsidies to the beneficiaries amounts to $200–300 at the health care centers and around $3,000–6,000 at referral hospitals. There have been large declines in average out-of-pocket health spending among the poorest half of the population in districts with contracted out health services. Incidence of a health-related debt was found to be 3.4 times lower in a poor village with an equity fund than one without (World Bank, 2007c). Leakage to the non-poor is limited. Because of its success other low-income developing countries have expressed interest in adopting health equity funds in their countries.

Box. 7.21 Success of Health Equity Fund (HEF)

With funding from UNICEF, the HEF has been successfully launched in the village of Svay Rieng since 2002. Svay Rieng is one of Cambodia's poorest villages with 500,000 residents. Half of the funds are used to support the operational costs of the hospital, while the other half is given to the health workers to supplement their meager monthly government salary of just $15–$30, which is only one-third of the estimated living wage in Cambodia.

(*Continued*)

Box 7.21 (*Continued*)

Village-based representatives first identify those most in need in their communities. The UNICEF provincial staff and staff from the Provincial Health Department and Operational Health District will then verify the status of the household to see if they are eligible to qualify for assistance. Points are awarded based on various aspects such as the number of dependents and amount of assets such as land, animals owned and the type of housing.

The approved household with most points will receive a health exemption card that grants them exemption of all fees at the provincial hospital, while others can secure entitlement to either 50 or 75 per cent subsidy based on their points. Nearly 125,000 people in Svat Rieng are expected to benefit from the scheme. About 200 to 300 poor patients are given free treatment at the hospital each month. Families are also pro-actively bringing their sick children to seek medical treatment.

Source: UNICEF (2005).

Despite HEF the maternal mortality rate in rural areas remains high at over 450 per 100,000 live births (UNDP, 2007). It remains a lagging indicator among the Cambodian Millennium Development Goals. Maternal mortality rates are likely to be even higher in chronically poor households, where mothers often have low levels of education. Cambodia should increase the geographical coverage of HEF and could specifically target females of reproductive age in poor villages. Health awareness would have to be built among the poor. It will require increasing the proportion of deliveries that occur in health facilities and with trained staff, and strengthening the referral system to ensure that women with difficult deliveries are transferred to accessible hospitals (World Bank, 2007c).

7.9.4 *Sector policies*

Telecommunication. The number of mobile phones per capita in Cambodia is quite low in relation to its neighboring countries.

In order to increase connectivity of by-passed regions UNDP has worked with several Cambodian microfinance institutions, Nokia-KTH, the German Technical Cooperation Agency and Camshin to set up a private sector-led village phone initiative in 40 communes in Kampong Cham, Kampong Chhnang and Siem Reap in 2007.

Under the scheme, each village is supplied with a mobile phone package, which includes the phone itself along with a solar panel recharger, a phone book and phone credit. The village phone operator then provides phone service at a subsidized rate to the community for a three- to six-month trial period to generate income. With access to telecommunication, farmers would be able to check out demand and prices of agricultural products in different markets and satisfy demand according. Depending on the success of the pilot experiment, it would be extended to 80 percent of the Cambodia's communes (UNDP, 2007). More could be done on the part of the government in coordination with external donors especially in the northeast part of the provinces where poverty headcount ratios are above 50 percent.

Rural roads. Connectivity to roads has improved over the years. In rural areas, the poorest quartile group on average traveled 2.8 km to get to the nearest motor road in 1997. By 2004, they traveled less than 1 km. With the expansion of rural roads, the proportion of poorest population with access to market in their villages has increased by 3 times to 9.1 percent, still a small degree of access (World Bank, 2007c).

There are no empirical study on investment in rural roads and poverty reduction in Cambodia, however the beneficial effects of roads on rural well-being have been well-documented (TRIP, 2004; TRIP, 2002, MRD, 2002). As shown earlier in Table 7.27, the more isolated and the smaller the village, the higher is the probability of poverty. Cambodia has recently set up the Integrated Rural Accessibility Planning mechanism to identify underserved rural areas so that priority attention is given to those areas (Government of Cambodia, 2008). By 2010, Cambodia aims to rehabilitate 25,000 km out of 28,000 km rural roads.

Rehabilitation of existing rural roads has also helped to alleviate poverty in food deficit areas by providing employment opportunities to the unemployed. Payment of wages under the labor-intensive projects operated by WFP ("food for work") and ILO has improved the health and productivity of the rural poor, and has tided them over the ups and downs of seasonal unemployment. While it is a short-term solution, Beresford *et al.* (2004) comments that it is far better for the poor than to have no increase in their income at all.

Rural electrification. War has badly damaged Cambodia's power supply facilities and the process of power rehabilitation is still underway with support from external donors. Currently, electricity supply in Cambodia is fragmented into 24 isolated power systems centered in provincial towns and cities. All are fully reliant on diesel power stations. (United Nations, 2008). Cambodia has one of the lowest per capita usage of electricity as electricity prices are relatively expensive as compared to Thailand or Vietnam where prices below ten cents per kilowatt-hour are normal (UNDP, 2006).

According to data from year 2000, the average tariff in Cambodia is about 14.6 US cents/kWh in Phnom Penh, and 25 to 50 US cents/kWh in rural areas. The high price of electricity is partly due to the extensive use of small older generators, heavy dependence on imported diesel fuel, and large losses due to the low quality of the distribution systems.

The Cambodia Rural Electrification and Transmission Project aims to provide electricity coverage to all villages in Cambodia by the year 2020 and to provide grid quality electricity to 70 percent of households in Cambodia by the year 2030. Under the Rural Electrification Fund, there will be a subsidy scheme with grants from the government and the Global Environment Facility for licensed rural electricity enterprises when they connect power supplies to poor households in rural areas. A grant assistance of US$45 is given per new household connection. It aims to make power affordable to the rural population and should help improve the livelihood of the rural poor.

Rural electrification efforts have had a late start as the scheme has only been in operation since April 2007. Disbursements intended for solar power home systems and hydro and bio mass project have also stalled. Some constraints include the high floor limit of 40 watt capacity for the solar home system which far exceeds the needs of the rural poor. In addition, the chronically poor cannot afford the initial cost of home solar power, estimated at betweenUS$400 to US$500 per home. Instead, the rural poor continue to rely on kerosene lamps and lead batteries to provide electricity.

Experiments have been conducted to assess the potential for using biomass as a source of renewable energy in Cambodia. According to the New Energy and Industrial Technology Development Organization, they have identified Kompong Cham province as the region with the highest potential for biomass energy. There is ample annual production of rice, sugar cane and maize within the province and transporting biomass residues to energy production facilities is possible since Kompong Cham is close to the capital with adequate road and waterway access. Given the high incidence of poverty (see Table 7.23), Kompong Cham would benefit from pro-poor renewable biomass energy project for farmers. It would spur production of the needed farm crops; the biomass energy would help power the province and the income of the poor would be raised.

Clean water. In 2004, the proportion of people getting potable drinking water among the lowest income groups was just 4 percent (UNDP, 2007). Potable drinking water is scarce outside of Phnom Penh, Prey Veng and Svay Rieng. Coverage tends to be worse in rural and peri-urban areas. In an effort to connect the poor, the government first piloted the Output Based Approach (OBA) in four towns in the province of Kompong Chom. Under the scheme, private operators received a subsidy payment for connecting targeted poor households. The poorest are identified by a community-administered survey and verified by an independent consultant. Various permutations of this approach are already being piloted in Brazil, Cambodia, Honduras, India, Indonesia, and Uganda. See Box 7.22 for more details.

Box 7.22 Output-based Aid (OBA) and Service Delivery for the Poor

The OBA scheme in Cambodia utilizes local private operators to deliver water to the poor. Private operators will design, build, and run water supply and sanitation systems through different forms of subsidized, concession-style contractual arrangements. The operators are selected under least-cost subsidy bidding. Operators are assured payment for connecting the poor, but are for the most part paid *after* service delivery.

Subsidies would be targeted directly to individual households. Of the 13,000 households in the four towns, close to 3,000 poorest households (approximately 23 percent of all households) would receive a subsidized connection.

The initial success of the project has prompted Cambodia to extend the outreach of water delivery in Kompong Cham. The first set of projects was in towns with relatively large populations and good transport networks, largely in accordance with the design of the OBA scheme to target sufficient number of poor people with economic viability for the private operators. A second batch of four towns is being prepared for a similar OBA mechanism. More than 1,660 poor households have been identified as eligible for a connection subsidy. However these towns are in less accessible areas.

Sources: Mumssen (2004) and Navarro and Tavares (2008).

Some challenges to the OBA approach include the difficulties in attracting private operators to deliver water to the more peripheral and remote areas. For instance, two of the eight towns in the Kompong Cham did not receive any bids by private operators as the relative subsidy was perceived to be lower than for the first batch of towns. Income levels were assessed to be lower, making operations more risky for private operators. In addition, the poor households tend to limit their consumption (currently 15 liters per capita per day on average) for cooking and drinking purposes. This very low consumption level may affect private operator's viability and unless the utility is able to connect non-poor households with higher income and higher potential consumption, the sustainability of the system could be at risk.

Although still at an early stage and limited solely to the province of Kompong Cham, the OBA scheme has been generally quite successful and has further potential. There has been strong community involvement in deciding who receives the connection subsidy and the poor has been targeted effectively. Opportunities for rent seeking and corruption were successfully controlled as payments to the private operator were only made after ensuring service delivery. However with the limited availability of grant financing from external agencies, it is probably not a long-term solution (Navarro and Tavares, 2008). If royalties from the exploitation of recently discovered off-shore oil and gas reserves are well managed, it could help Cambodia to fund the scheme.

Irrigation. Cambodia is neither mountainous nor landlocked and 90 percent of its land lies in the catchment area of the Tonlé Sap River and the Mekong River. The Cambodian plain carries more water than most other countries, hence the potential to expand surface irrigation is great (UNDP, 2007). Nevertheless, only 20 percent of cultivable land is irrigated in Cambodia. During the rainy season, the plains tend to have recurring floods which spoil agricultural output. During the dry season, irrigation facilities are not sufficiently integrated hence limiting paddy output. Many Cambodian farmers harvest just once a year because of a lack of water. Vietnam and Thailand, with their superior irrigation systems, manage two or three crops per year.

Multicropping would raise farm incomes dramatically and Cambodia is working with ADB to rehabilitate 700 plus canals and irrigation dikes which were installed by the Khmer Rouge (*International Herald Tribune*, 2008). The Ministry of Interior is leading experimental projects to use water from the existing canals to irrigate fields of hybrid rice that yields 4 times as much as the traditional varieties that are in place. In addition to increasing paddy output, it also provides employment opportunities for the surplus rural poor. Rural workers receive a stipend of $55 per month from the government, thus alleviating some of impoverished households in the region.

Water pumps can also be utilized to redirect surface water and water pumped from tube wells. Treadle pumps are a cost effective and powerful tool for raising incomes of small farmers in Cambodia (UNDP, 2007). It has a high cost benefit ratio estimated at five to one, with an internal rate of return of 100 percent. Other, smaller devices are in operation in Cambodia as well, such as the *Snaup Tuk Rova* (an ingenious locally designed cheap rope pump). Cambodia will need to work in cooperation with NGOs and external organizations to subsidize the sales of water pumps to impoverished families. Currently the usages of water pump is still low. Only 3 percent of poor farmers own water pumps while richer farmers usage is only 12 percent (World Bank, 2007c). Without external assistance, it is unlikely the poor would be able to afford the one-off cost of buying water pumps, and not to mention recurrent costs such as fuel and maintenance. It is also unclear what proportion of the chronically poor own enough land to make double cropping feasible with water pump assistance.

Agricultural extension. Not many farmers make use of agricultural extension services. Specialized courses in agricultural extension did not start till 1991. The university graduates specializing in the field are posted mainly in ministerial and provincial departments, and are too far away from the district or commune level to provide direct consultations with farmers. Their salaries are also low. As a result farmers have limited access to extension services and continue to rely on traditional farming techniques (Beresford *et al.*, 2004).

To further increase agricultural productivity of poor Cambodian farmers, Farmer Field Schools were been set up (FAO, 2004). Currently there are 180 such schools. The curriculum is based on the needs of the poor farmers, including hands on field work and experimentation. Participation rates are still small. So far 5,000 poor farmers from six provinces have participated in the scheme. Over half of the participants have been females. There have been some successes with the implementation of the scheme. It resulted in the formation of 73 rice banks, 106 fertilizer banks and one well construction unit. To further aid the very poor in the uplands, UNDP (2007) recommends that Cambodia learn from Farmer Field Schools in neighboring Thailand and Vietnam regarding highland farming practices. To reach minority groups who practice shifting cultivation, they recommend giving small plot of lands as well as 'starter packs' of small amounts of seed and fertilizer with instructions. However this would have to work together with better land governance from the authorities and strengthened land tenure rights for the poor (see next section).

Land reforms. Under the Land Law of 2001 Cambodia has implemented social land concessions to redistribute state land to poor landless households for housing and agricultural use. Ownership rights will only be granted after 5 years of continuous occupation and use. However implementation faces some challenges: (i) The government will need to settle any disputed land claims before distribution can take place. Often, there are competing land claims from other government agencies. At times, the government will need to recover illegally-claimed land tracts; (ii) If the rural landless do move to the offered land parcels, they might have to relocate to the surplus lands in the northeast, northwest and coastal areas; (iii) Information on the quality of the distributed land is not readily available to the rural landless beforehand. They would need to relocate first before they can ascertain the suitability of the land for agricultural production; and (iv) even for those households who are willing to relocate, the sustainability of their livelihoods are not guaranteed (See Box 7.19 for a case study of Phnom Sruoch, where new villagers could not sustain a living once the forests have been cleared).

It is not adequate simply to provide the poor with land. Linkages of the new small land holders to the rest of the supply chain have to be in place before their livelihoods can improve. In this connection access to rural electricity, credit and roads are of utmost importance as well as the arability and potential productivity of the land.

Currently 60 percent of the poorest families do not possess proof of ownerships of the land they till. This is particularly true for poor households who occupy land at the borders whose claims are often contested by the state. Since 2004, the government has begun systematic land titling to improve tenure security and welfare of the rural people. The Ministry of Land has issued close to 1 million titles under the Land Administration and Distribution Program (World Bank, 2007d). Complete titling of 2.5 million more plots of land is supposed to reduce the national poverty rate by 8 percentage points (see Table 7.26). It has significantly reduced land conflicts and makes it easier for the owner to sell land to buyers outside the local community to raise capital. Furthermore titles can be used as collateral when applying for micro credit. Evidence also shows that farmers are more willing to invest in long-term investment when they have secure land tenures.

However there are various limitations to systematic titling that does not benefit the chronic poor. First, systematic titling has generally benefited the densely settled and more stable communities like Phnom Penh, urban areas in the southern provinces, the Mekong Plains and Tonle Sap plains. It has yet to be extended to the more conflict prone or marginal areas where the chronic poor are in greater numbers.

Cases of land grabbing from the poor is another problem. The rich are able to obtain titles by buying the land, whereas the poor has to wait for the government to proceed with systematic titling for their

Table 7.26. Simulated Effect of Titling Programs on Poverty

No. of Titles Issued	No. of Households Affected	No. of Households Escaping Poverty	No. of Individuals Escaping Poverty	Change in National Poverty Rate (% points changes)
650,000	361,988	50,135	284,924	–2.19
1,000,000	556,904	77,131	438,345	–3.36
2,000,000	1,113,808	154,262	876,690	–6.73
2,500,000	1,392,260	192,828	1,095,863	–8.41

Source: World Bank (2007d).

lands. Speculators have an unfair advantage over farmers and sellers as they have prior knowledge as to which lands are to be developed and the nature of the development. According to the Ministry of Planning's Commune Council Database, approximately 28,000 land conflicts were reported in 2005 (UNDP, 2007). With the rise in demand for land, conflicts over land claims are likely to increase in the future.

Second, the titling program is regressive. The landless, who constitute the bulk of the poor households, are excluded. A large number of the chronic poor that operates on state land or illegal settlements are also excluded from the program. At the same time, the newly added provisions in the Land Law of 2001 do not adequately protect the ethnic minorities, whose traditional homelands have often been allocated to others.

Third, the area based formula for titling fees makes it prohibitive for the poor with large plots of land to participate. Fees are paid to the titling teams based on the area of the land plot, leading to a preference for the teams to work first in areas with large number of small, easy to measure plots and low incidence of land conflicts. Titling cannot proceed if there are conflicts.

Lastly, the law does not make concessions for the quality of the land which could be poorer in remote areas. Such concessions could include lower costs of purchase and titling.

More time is needed to fully ascertain the impact of the land reforms on the poor as they have only been recently implemented. The World Bank (2007c) lists some recommendations to make the project more pro-poor. (1) To better benefit the landed poor with large plots of inferior land, Cambodia should lower the rate charged for poor quality land especially in remote areas. (2) Reclassification of state lands would have to proceed at a faster pace if land titling is to benefit the poor living in remote areas and illegally farming on state land. Systems for better land management would have to be in place. (3) Incentives should be created for the titling teams to visit remote, less densely populated northeast areas with lower productivity like Otdar Meanchey, Preah Vihear, Stueng Treng and Rattankiri, where the chronic poor are likely to reside. Pay of the teams could be based on the area titled and number of plots. Given that the chronic poor reside in the northeast province where mine causalities are likely to be high, the government would need to speed up on its mine clearing program. This would ensure that the arable land is safe for cultivation and the chronic poor will be able to farm without fear of mines exploding. There has been progress in the mine clearing program but much work still remains (Government of Cambodia, 2008). Better implementation of new technology could also reduce the number of child laborers who are involved in mine clearing. Reported annual casualties from landmines, many of them children, decreased from 1,743 in 1996 to 797 in 2005.

Micro credit. Rural finance is typically underdeveloped and does not currently serve the needs of the chronic poor. Less than 330,000 rural households have accessed institutional credit. Despite the presence of microfinance institutions like the ACLEDA Bank which charge relatively low interest rate at 3.5 percent per month, most chronically poor are ineligible because they lack collateral. They also lack the ability to join any borrowing groups (Economic Institute of Cambodia, 2006). Cambodia could look into subsidized loans for the poor, which would reduce the relative cost to the borrower. Moreover if titling speeds up, farmers could use the land titles as collateral for credit which could stimulate the micro-credit sector.

7.9.5 *Macroeconomic policies*

Cambodia plans to lower the rate of poverty to 25 percent by 2010. To do this it has launched the "National Strategic Development Plan 2006 to 2010" and the "Rectangular Strategy for Growth, Employment, Equity and Efficiency". Under these plans over 60 percent of government development resources will be diverted to the development of rural areas, with increased attention to productive activities like agriculture, rural development and to provision of basic services to enhance human capital. Any improvement in agricultural productively is likely to be pro-poor. The elasticity of reduction in the incidence of poverty with respect to increases in agricultural yields has been estimated at 0.95 (UNDP, 2007) so that an increase in agricultural yield of 10 percent will result in a 9.5 percent reduction in poverty. Priority strategies as outlined in the National Strategic Development 2006–2010 include focusing on increasing rice yields to at least an average of 2.4 ton per hectare; encouraging cultivation of cash crops to diversify food output; initiating "one village-one product" to promote high value agricultural products and giving direct grants to poor farmers for increased production of crops of their choice.

Cambodia has also launched its trade development policy to promote the export of agricultural-related products, rubber, silk and footwear. 15 special economic zones (SEZ) around the borders and urban areas were approved. The SEZs are located near the borders of Thailand and Vietnam, Phnom Penh, Kampot, and at Sihanoukville. The Manhattan SEZ approximately 5 kilometers from the Vietnamese border has been in operation since late 2006, while Phnom Penh SEZ has partially completed the construction of its industrial complexes. Foreign investment is meant to generate employment opportunities and economic growth. However as to whether the Manhattan SEZ will generate backward linkages to benefit the local rural economy is uncertain as no sub-contracting arrangement has been made with the local enterprises yet.

The Cambodia PRSP stated: "Estimates show that for every tourist dollar, 75 cents are returned to Thailand to import fresh vegetables, fruit, flowers, handicrafts and furniture." If local rural farmers are able to supply these required inputs it would significantly aid in poverty reduction (Bolwell and Weinz, 2008) and bring added income to local farmers, rural industry and the local poor. In addition, Cambodia has started the Pro-Poor Sustainable Tourism Programme since 2006 which concentrates on the northeast regions especially Kratie and Stung Treng Provinces along the Mekong River. Other than Angkor, the government has taken actions to develop other ecotourism spots such as the Kulen Mountain, Kos Ker temple, Preah Vihea temple, and Ta Mok house in Anlong Veng. Work could be created for the local poor by getting them to maintain the temples, tourist sites, and tourist infrastructure. The government could also promote private investment in ecotourism in mountainous and coastal regions. However they will need to consider how to efficiently manage and/or balance between heritage protection and economic development.

Fiscal budget and infrastructure. Public spending as a percent of GDP is much lower than it is in other low income countries in Asia. Total expenditure averaged 15 percent of GDP between 1994 and 2004 while other low income countries spend up to 25 percent of GDP (World Bank, 2007d). The challenge for Cambodia is to increase revenue while increasing transparency and accountability with its oil and gas revenue. It ranks 49 out of 51 low income countries in terms of revenue collection as a share of GDP (World Bank, 2007d).

It is commendable that Cambodia has increased spending on provision of social services like health and education, which led to improvements in service delivery and human development outcomes. The Health Coverage Plan was implemented to ensure geographical equity in the provision of health care services. There is one health centers for every 10,000 people and one Operational District with a Referral Hospital for every 100,000 people. Cambodia has also done remarkably well to close the gap in distance to schools. School construction has increased substantially in recent years. As a result, the average distance to the nearest primary school within rural areas in the upland zone for the poorest quintile was comparable to that of the richest quintile between 2.0 km to 2.5 km (World Bank, 2007c).

However its spending on economic sectors (agriculture, transport and rural development) is inadequate to stimulate labor intensive employment and alleviate poverty in impoverished rural areas. Cambodia will need to improve rural infrastructure such as roads, access to electricity and irrigation before rural residents can benefit from more rapid economic growth and income generating activities. The chronic poor in remote areas do not benefit much from the expansion of health care facilities. Given that the poor generally live beyond 4.5 km radius of a health center, utilization rates of the poor are extremely low (World Bank, 2007c).

Maintenance of the public sector infrastructure is of utmost importance. Delayed maintenance on roads is expensive: US$1 not spent on maintenance typically results in a US$3 penalty to the economy (OECD, 2007). Most ministries and developmental partners are forced to utilize piecemeal and project-approaches which adversely affect delivery outcomes, owing to lack of a cohesive overarching road development framework.

Labor laws. The incidence of child labor in Cambodia is alarmingly high. Over 50 percent of children between 7–14 years are in the labor force Table Box 7.18. Although Cambodia's Labor Law sets the minimum age for employment at 15 years, children aged 12–14 years are allowed to do light work that is not hazardous and does not affect regular school attendance or participation in other training programs. According to ILO, UNICEF and the World Bank (2006), there are various loopholes in the child labor legislations. For instance, the labor law does not cover informal sector enterprises where the overwhelming majority of child laborers are concentrated. This means family-based agriculture and domestic service are not covered by the legislation. The Law also does not specifically define what constitutes child labor in terms of type of work, conditions of work, or work hazards. Cambodia has also established community-based child protection networks in many districts. International Labor Organization has declared that the garment and footwear industries in Cambodia are free of forced labor, child labor or discrimination (Government of Cambodia, 2008).

Migration and remittances. Internal migration has risen due to growing landlessness, displaced populations looking for settlement, and a rapidly growing labor force in search of livelihood. According to Sarthi (2003), the top destination was Phnom Penh, which alone received about one third of all inter-provincial migrants, followed by Kandal, Banteay Meanchey and Koh Kong (another 30 percent). Phnom Penh and Kandal are the main urban/non-agricultural destinations, while the two rural provinces of Koh Kong and Banteay Meanchey have high average farm sizes and low population densities.

The garment industry employs 300,000 mostly female workers from rural areas (UNDP, 2007). Garment sector workers typically remit an average of 35 percent of their earnings back to rural families (Dahlberg, 2006). These remittances have enabled rural households to sustain current consumption and to invest in equipment, seeds, fertilizers and livestock. However to obtain a job in the garment industry, one needs to have a certain level of education and some household savings to fund the move to Phnom Penh. A bribe is sometimes needed for middlemen. Hence few of the chronically poor are able to find a job in the garment industry. This is substantiated by the World Bank (2007c) who found that only 12 percent of the poorest quintile has a family member working in the garment industry. Such remittances often accounted for less than a tenth of the recipient's household income (UNDP, 2007). They found that the internal migration to Phnom Penh City promoted gender equality rather than income equality.

Increased numbers of Cambodians are also (informally) migrating to Thailand. They are usually employed in low-end labor intensive jobs such as construction workers, porters, farm workers and garment workers. At times, bribes to cross the border or escape prosecution and payments to middlemen can cost the illegal migrants their entire earnings (Sarthi, 2003). Other international migration destinations for the chronically poor are even less likely.

The Cambodian policy framework for international migration is still in its infancy. It does not have an official policy to promote or control migration. Cambodian migrant workers are generally unaware of their rights and the possible adverse consequences of migration are low. Many migrants have their rights or interests undermined at some stage in the migration process by brokers or government officials (Sarthi, 2003).

7.9.6 *Future policy agenda and challenges*

Cambodia has made some progress in poverty alleviation through political and macroeconomic stability and from greater integration into the international arena through trade and tourism. However rural development (where 90 percent of the poor resides) and poverty reduction schemes in Cambodia are excessively dependent on international aid. This is not likely to be a viable long term strategy. Cambodia should focus on crafting and initiating cohesive anti-poverty policies to target the poor before looking for partners to fund the schemes. If the royalties from the recently discovered oil and gas reserves are well managed, it would enable Cambodia to take greater ownership of poverty reduction strategies. CDRI (2007a) and UNDP (2007) have made some suggestions that are augmented with special consideration for the chronically poor.

1. Introduce food security programs and/or in-kind transfers to the chronically poor.
2. Provide more options for local employment. Promote economically viable public works programs aimed at creating/maintaining rural infrastructure while also providing jobs for the poor in the off season. Help diversify occupational choices for fishermen.
3. Ensure greater access to social services like health and education. Pilot health insurance schemes should be introduced. More educational scholarships for children of poor households including early childhood development are needed. Increase net primary school enrolments and completion rates by reducing costs to families of poor rural students, providing mid-day meals to encourage attendance and completion, and motivate teachers with adequate salaries.
4. Ensure efficient and equitable land use. Cambodia should continue with protecting land tenure through systematic titling and addressing landless-related poverty with social land concessions and non-farm employment. Excessive land fragmentation needs to be checked, land grabbing by the rich stopped and community management of excessively small lands introduced.
5. Expand various types of irrigation, especially irrigation that also increases the potable water supply. Reduce impediments to competitive input and output markets. Increase access to affordable credit through improved microfinance regulations and incentives. Invest in rural electrification and development and rehabilitation

of rural feeder roads. Facilitate development of farmer groups and associations to improve price negotiating power, post harvest systems, and conditions for contract farming.

6. Develop stronger and more accountable local government to protect the poorer households and address their needs. Ensure that fair and effective implementation of laws on land, forestry and fisheries keep the rich from monopolizing these resources.

Implementing these objectives will be challenging given projections that show economic growth slowing over the next few years as a result of the removal of US safe guards on the garment industry in 2008 and increasing competition from Vietnam and China in export markets for apparel.

7.10 Laos

Box 7.23. A Snapshot of Laos's Chronic Poor

- About 2 million people are poor in Laos. 36 percent of the population lives below the poverty line.
- 47 districts were identified as very poor and 25 districts as poor and needy of government intervention.
- Poverty is most severe in the Northern region at 52.5 percent, and its inhabitants generally live in mountainous terrains. However the Central region has the largest number of poor as almost one in two poor live in the lowlands.
- Laos was categorized as a "partially chronically deprived country" along with India, Nepal, Pakistan, Philippines and Sri Lanka.

Table Box 7.23. Selected Indicators

Proportion of poor who are chronically poor over 5 years (low estimate)	..
Proportion of poor who are chronically poor over 5 years (high estimate)	..

(*Continued*)

Box 7.23 (*Continued*)

Population	5.7 m
Percentage of poor living on less than US$1.25 per day* (2005PPP)	35.7
Average depth of poverty (number of % points by which the poor fall below the poverty line[1] in 2002)	22.6
Income share held by lowest 20 percent	81
Gini index of inequality	34.6
Healthcare indicators	
Under-5 mortality rate (per 1,000 live births) in 2004	83
Infant mortality rate (per 1,000 live births) in 2004	65
Proportion of children under 5 who are stunted (2000)	42
Life expectancy at birth, 2004	55.1
Educational indicators	
Adult illiteracy rate for women aged 15 years and above (2000–2004)	39
Adult illiteracy rate for men aged 15 years and above (2000–2004)	23
Child labor	
Percentage of children aged between 7–14 in the labor force (1999–2004)	25.4

Sources: CPRC (2008) Annex E and F, Government of Laos (2003), World Bank (2006c) and *Bauer *et al.* ADB (2008) and Table 1.1.
Note: [1] Most recent year.

Laos is a small landlocked nation in Southeast Asia which borders China in the north, Vietnam to the east, Cambodia in the south and Thailand and Myanmar to the west and northwest. Population size is currently at 5.7 million. Agriculture is the most important sector in Laos and employs nearly 80 percent of the workforce but less than 50 percent value added. Industry and services account for 30 percent and 26 percent of value added respectively. Rapid economic growth in 2008 was driven by strong external demand for the country's hydropower and minerals (ADB, 2008).

Poverty in Laos declined steadily from 46 percent in 1992 to 35 percent by 2002. The poverty gap fell from 11.2 percent to

8.0 percent over the same period (World Bank, 2006c). About 137,500 poor families were said to have escaped from poverty during that period (Government of Laos, 2006). However the rate of poverty reduction (approximately 1 percent per annum) is much slower than the economic growth rate of more than 5 percent per annum suggesting a small elasticity of poverty reduction with respect to economic growth. Revised poverty figures from Bauer *et al.* (2008) indicate over one third of the population in Laos is suffering from poverty (Table Box 7.23).

Inequality has risen. Consumption of the poorest quintile has fallen from 9.3 percent to around 8 percent between 1992 and 2002 (Bechstedt *et al.*, 2007). Laos also has low health and educational outcomes relative to the Asian region (Table Box 7.23). Life expectancy is 55 years compared to a regional average of 70; the primary school net enrolment rate is 84 percent compared to the region's 99 percent; and child mortality, at 98 per 1,000, is more than double the regional average of 37 (Bird, 2009). Approximately two thirds of the rural population suffers from food insecurity and every second child in rural areas is chronically malnourished (United Nations, 2007).

7.10.1 *Incidence of poverty*

Laos is divided into 3 regions, 18 provinces and 141 districts. Over 80 percent of the population lives in rural areas and it is estimated that over 30 percent are living in poverty (see Box 7.23). Although poverty has declined in all regions of the country, this decline has been slow and uneven (see Table 7.27). Vientiane, the capital city of Laos located on the banks of the Mekong River, has the lowest incidence of poverty in the country at 12.2 percent.

Poverty is most severe in the Northern region at 52.5 percent where most families generally live in mountainous terrain. The Northern region also often have to faces chronic rice deficits. Due to its remoteness and the high cost of transportation, inhabitants often have to import rice from neighboring countries and are unable to partake in the rice surplus of southern and central regions. Poverty in the central and southern regions is in the range of 35 percent to 38 percent.

Table 7.27 Incidence of Poverty Over Time (%)

	1992–93	1997–98	Annual Rate in Decrease of Poverty
Vientiane municipality	24.4	12.2	13.9
Northern region	**58.4**	**52.5**	**–2.1**
Phongsaly	68.7	64.2	–1.3
Louang Namtha	60.3	57.5	–1.0
Oudomxay	51.1	73.2	7.2
Bokeo	63.5	37.4	–10.6
Louang Prabang	62.7	49.4	–4.8
Houa Phanh	78.4	74.6	–1.0
Xaygnaboury	30.1	21.2	–7.0
Central region	**39.5**	**34.9**	**–2.5**
Xieng Khoang	57.3	34.9	–9.9
Vientiane province	28.1	24.3	–2.9
Borikhamxay	10.6	25.8	17.8
Khammuane	43.7	41.6	–1.0
Savannakhet	45.7	37.1	–4.2
Xaysomboom-SZ		55.0	
Southern region	**45.9**	**38.4**	**–3.6**
Saravanh	36.7	39.6	1.5
Xékong	65.9	45.7	–7.3
Champasak	43.6	35.6	–4.1
Attapeu	72.2	45.3	–9.3
Lao PDR	**45.0**	**38.6**	**–3.1**

Source: Government of Laos (2003).
Note: The Municipality of Vientiane is normally treated as a separate region and the Xaysomboon province has been dissolved since 2006. Note that the aggregate level of poverty is somewhat higher than the level in Box 7.23 which is a more recent estimate from 2005.

Poverty is being monitored at three levels in Laos using the following criteria:

(1) Rural households are considered poor if their income is less than US$8.20 per person per month at 2001 prices.
(2) Villages are considered poor if at least 51 percent of households are poor and lack access to schools, dispensaries, traditional healers, safe water and roads.

(3) Districts are considered as poor if over 51 percent of the villages are poor and where over 40 percent of villages do not have local or nearby schools, a dispensary or a pharmacy, an access road or safe water.

Although there are no studies on chronic poverty in Laos, some deductions can be made based on data from Laos Consumption and Expenditure Survey, Laos' National Growth and Poverty Eradication Strategy (NGPES) and Bechstedt *et al.* (2007).

According to NGPES, the very poor make up 17 percent of the population. Thus near to 1 million people in Laos are likely to be chronically poor with few assets and coping mechanisms to escape poverty. The very poor live at least 15 km from a main road and 70 percent have no road access during the rainy season.

At the district level, the government has identified 47 districts as very poor and 25 districts as poor and needing government intervention. Close to three-fifth of the very poor priority districts are located in the Northern region. The severity of poverty in the 47 very poor districts is almost 4 times as high as non–poor districts (World Bank, 2006c). Living conditions are difficult and human capital is low–particularly in the more isolated areas (UN, 2007). For instance, Houa Phanh, which is located in the northern region, is one of the poorest provinces in the Laos. Five of its eight districts are included in the list of 47 poorest districts of Laos. Houa Phanh has 758 villages, of which 78 percent are poor with the majority of the population relying on upland agriculture (ADB, 2008d).

Ethnic minority communities are particularly susceptible to chronic poverty. While the ethnic Lao mainly engage in agriculture, fishing, and commercial activities in the fertile lowlands, the ethnic minorities mainly live in the hills, where infrastructure is underdeveloped and access to services is poor, particularly in the rainy season. Such upland minority groups make up about 80 percent of the nation's poor, although they are only about 33.5 percent of the total population (Lee, 2003). The Mon Khmer and Tibeto-Burman groups are considered to be among the poorest (see Box 7.24).

Box 7.24. Ethnic Minorities in Laos

Among the 47 different ethnic minorities in Laos, the Tibeto-Burman groups are generally considered as very poor. Most are subsistence farmers who practice slash and burn cultivation and depend on hunting and collection of forest products to make a living in the uplands. Poverty has increasingly driven them out of isolation and into the marginal commercial activities of towns such as selling firewood.

The Mon-Khmer are generally poor. They usually reside on the slopes of mountains, in forests and valleys midlands. They practice traditional *swidden* or shifting cultivation, hunting, and collecting forest products for their own consumption. The shifting cultivation they practice allows for the forest to regenerate, and usually does not require resettlement. Some also work as casual laborer for the Lao majority in the rice fields.

The Hmong-Yao have mainly settled at high altitude in the northern mountains. They are a relatively better off group. They engage in agricultural and off farm activities. The Hmong usually practice an environmentally harmful shifting cultivation that forces them to periodically move to a new location. Many Hmong families receive overseas remittances from relatives who migrated to the United States. The government is trying to resettle Hmong villages by building social services in new locations.

The Tai-Kadai group is generally better off than the rest of minorities as they live in the lowlands and are able to grow rice and cash crops. The adult literacy rate is 72.9 which is three times that of Mon Khmer and four times that of Tibeto-Burman. They generally reside in large villages and enjoy more modern lifestyles.

Source: ADB (2000).

7.10.2 *Determinants of poverty*

According to the Laos' Expenditure and Consumption Survey 2002/03, poor households are characterized by large household size, high dependency ratios, low levels of human capital, poor access to agricultural inputs and technology, and limited access to essential infrastructure and basic services.

In particular, Bechstedt *et al.* (2007) highlighted the lack of adequate land for growing rice for own consumption as one key reason for poverty. About two-thirds of the country is mountainous. Poor farmers have small plots averaging only 0.25 hectare of arable land per family member during the wet season, and no more than 0.05 hectares during the dry season in 2003 (World Bank, 2006c). This has led to seasonal food shortages and hunger in poor families. Malnutrition is common among poor rural women and children, particularly in upland forested areas. The mountainous terrain has made it difficult and costly to provide all-weather roads. Consequently, many villages are isolated and lack access to markets and services available in most lowland areas. Upland farmers also receive low prices for their farm products as they have little negotiating power with agriculture traders. Other factors contributing to poverty include a high incidence of disease in livestock due to a lack of veterinary services and environmental degradation. Some policy changes such as land allocation and resettlement efforts to "stabilize" shifting cultivation among ethnic minorities have had the reverse effect on rural well-being, causing some households to slide further into poverty.

Within the different geographic regions, some causes of poverty appear to be more significant than others (Government of Laos, 2003). Households in the northern and eastern regions suffer from small plot size and environmental degradation; those in the southern regions are subject to natural disasters while villages in the central regions have large families. Furthermore opium addiction is also a problem in the northern region where minority women are involved in opium production and distribution.

7.10.3 *Micro policies*

Health. Healthcare facilities are unevenly distributed in Laos. Access to primary healthcare is irregular and unsystematic, especially in the northern provinces of Bokeo, Houa Phan, Louang Namtha, and Phongsali. More than 60 percent of residents in these four provinces have no access to public primary healthcare facilities (ADB, 2000). The poor often have to travel for more than half a day to the nearest health facility, and more than a day for emergency services.

Distance to health centers for the poor actually increased from 10.7 km in 1993 to 11.7 km in 2003 while it fell from 7.4 km to 6.5 km for the non-poor (World Bank, 2006c). Poor ethnic groups often rely on spiritual healing instead of seeking medical care in public health centers (see Table 7.28 for access to health services by different ethnic groups). The very poor like the Tibeto-Burman have few resources outside the family to call on and are especially at risk if they are subject to a health shocks. In comparison, other ethnic minorities such as the Tai-Kadai and Mon-Khmer receive more support from family members for health care. Furthermore an informal mutual fund or credit system has been developed in some communities to allow households to access services first with payment later, thus allowing time to arrange for contributions from relatives or sale of livestock or other assets. Formalizing such a system is being studied in Borikhamxai Province with the help of the German Technical Cooperation (ADB, 2000).

In order to help the poor, the government provides subsidies to the poor for hospital services. Hospitals are to identify the poor on the basis of a card or document issued by the Ministry of Labor and Social Welfare or by the village head. About 40 percent of patients receive subsidized services in district hospitals (ADB, 2000). However because access is difficult and hard for the poor to reach, services are frequently under utilized by the very poor. There are also substantial leakages to the non-poor as the richest quintile captures

Table 7.28 Access to Health Services (%)

Indicator	Tai-Kadai	Mon-Khmer	Hmong-Mien	Tibeto Burman
Persons using a government facility first when sick	46	22	23	18
Villages accessible by road	87	53	35	50
Villages within 4 hrs of district headquarter	85	66	45	47
Villages within 1 hr of health centers	62	33	9	16
Villages within 1 hr of private pharmacy	79	48	13	26
Villages having a village health provider	96	80	74	56

Source: ADB (2000).

27 percent of public subsidies for health services, compared with 13 percent for the poorest (World Bank, 2007d). More needs to be done to protect the poor, especially for those who live outside the targeted 47 priority districts designated for poverty alleviation efforts by the government.

Priority has been given to increase the number of health care facilities and health care workers especially in the poorest 47 districts. The government has established primary health care training centers in the Northern Region (Luangnamtha, Xayaboury, Phongsaly, Houa Phanh and Bokeo). Particular efforts are being made to attract trainees from ethnic minority groups to overcome the language barrier as most minority groups do not understand the official Lao language. 50 percent of the trainees are targeted to be female.

The government has set up Village Drug Revolving Funds so as to provide drug kits to poor villagers. Most drugs in Laos are imported and drug prices are generally high and costly for the poor. The poor often buy illegal and fake drugs, which have further adverse effects on their health. As access to health facilities is often limited especially in remote areas, the drug kit gives a range of medicine which can provide some form of emergency relief for the poor. They are dispensed by a village health worker. The scheme is expected to be of particular benefit to villagers in remote areas. About 94 percent of villages have been provided with drug kits (Government of Laos, 2006) and the government has actively trained village health volunteers to dispense medication. However more would have to be done to reform the weak management of the fund (Government of Laos, 2003).

Education. Primary and secondary enrolment has grown over the years. Female enrolment has also increased but mainly for the majority Lao-Tai women. At the secondary level enrolment rates among the poorest are less than half the national average (see Table 7.29). The situation is worse in the Northern region where 9 out of 10 primary schools in the poorest districts are unable to provide the full 5 years of schooling to its pupils (Government of Laos, 2006). Female enrolment in the Northern region also lags behind the rest of the

Table 7.29 Enrolment Rates of Children from Different Quintiles (%)

	Poorest	II	III	IV	Richest	Total
Primary	91	110	120	127	128	112
Lower secondary	23	41	51	71	88	53
Upper secondary	12	17	27	38	53	29

Source: World Bank (2007e).

other regions due to the high cost of transport. Language poses a serious barrier to the enrolment of ethnic minorities.

Drop out rates for the poor at primary school level are substantial due to lack of interest, need to work, and distance to the school (World Bank, 2006c). Furthermore primary school classroom expansion has been unable to keep up with the increase in demand since the early 1990s. For instance, in 1992/3, less than one in ten households lived in villages without a primary school. By 2002/3, one in six households had to send their children to neighboring villages for education. Most ethnic minorities have to walk at least 1.5 km to the next village's primary school. In particular, the Mon Khmer and Chine-Tibet children have to walk 2.5 to 7.5 km to reach the nearest primary school.

More schools need to be built to reverse these trends. Multi language (other than Lao) curricula are also needed in order to the reach the poor. The government has recently approved an Ethnic Group Development Plan as part of its ongoing consideration of how best to respond to the education needs of the multi-ethnic Lao population.

In 2002, Laos began a School Feeding Program to enable poor and vulnerable children, especially girls to attend school in the food insecure northern regions of Phongsaly, Oudomxay and Luangnamtha. Currently more than 1,000 children in the northern region benefit from the program. School children are provided with mid-morning snacks and take-home rations of rice, canned fish and iodized salt to share with their families upon enrolment; and at the end of the school year conditional on 80 percent of attendance during the year. To encourage girls of poor families to come to school, girls are given bigger take-home rations than boys. Students who live further from school are also given bigger take-home rations than those living close to the school. The program will be extended to the poor southern provinces of Attapeu, Saravane and Sekong in 2009, where key educational indicators like enrolment rates and ratio of girls to boys attending school have been lagging behind the national average. The program is supported under the United Nations World Food Programme which is expected to benefit almost 115,000 primary school children and their families in six provinces. (see http://laos.usembassy.gov/econ_dec4_2008.html.

Migration and remittances. Almost one in ten Hmong-Iu Mien families and one in thirty Lao-Tai families receive remittances from abroad. These remittances help reduce poverty in the recipient households. (World Bank, 2006c). Remittances come from the large number of Hmong who have resettled overseas after the US- Vietnam war and Lao migrant workers in neighboring Thailand. Such remittances make up approximately 250 percent to 300 percent of an average household's monthly expenses and significantly reduce poverty. However, only a small fraction of the chronically poor benefit from these remittances. The World Bank estimates that only 3 percent of all poor households are able to supplement their household income with cash remittances from abroad (World Bank, 2006c). Poor ethnic minorities like the Mon-Khmer and the Chine-Tibet generally do not receive any overseas remittances.

Social funds. Many initiatives were begun in the last decade, many of them initiated with the help of foreign assistance. Under the NGPES, the government has set up Village Development Funds (VDF) to reduce poverty in 47 very poor districts. VDF promotes livelihood activities related to cultivation and animal husbandry, the clearing of land for agricultural production, handicraft, processing, and trade. Village participation and ownership of funds are promoted. As of the end of June 2007, the scheme has been extended to 315 villages (World Bank, 2008h). However developmental targeting of poor districts did not appear to be effective in reducing the severity of poverty as 2 out of every five persons are still poor in the participating districts (World Bank, 2006c). The program needs to be further revamped to better address the chronically poor.

Under the Village Investment for the Poor program, block-grants between US$500 to US$1500 are given to poor villages for small-scale sub-projects identified by the community. A village committee together with village volunteers implements the project under the supervision of the District Agricultural and Forestry Office. Currently, more than 200 villages in 15 districts have benefited from the given block-grants (World Bank, 2008h). Some of the funds were also used to form credit and savings groups which provide low interest rates to villagers.

With assistance from International Development Assistance branch of the World Bank, Laos implemented the Poverty Reduction Fund (PRF) to empower those in the poorest districts to assess their own needs and priorities and to plan, manage and implement their own public investments. The poor decide the priority of their needs, such as access to clean water, roads, education, health services, irrigation and agriculture and income generation activities etc. Each project costs around US$8,000 and is shared between the PRF and the community. Four-fifths of the cost is borne by the PRF and the remaining is raised by the community in cash, provision of labor and raw materials. Guides and trainers aid them in project implementation. Since 2002, more than 1,200 subprojects have been selected, implemented and completed by poor communities in five provinces, 20 districts and nearly 2,000 villages with an investment of US$8.6 million. PRFs have improved health and education outcomes, and access to roads (World Bank, 2008h).

Respondents in Hua Phan and Saravane have expressed satisfaction with the implemented projects and an increase in their well-being. However the implementation of sub-projects in the uplands was hindered by language barriers with the ethnic minority communities which made facilitation between the district organizers and the individual communities difficult (World Bank, 2008i).

Pilot experiments supported by the World-Bank-funded Health Services Improvement Project have been in place to establish community health insurance to help the poor afford large medical expenses. The poor will be cross-subsidized to a limit of up to 10 percent of the population and 10 percent of revenues. However the chronic poor are unlikely to afford the monthly payments. Also, the amount of subsidies is likely to be insufficient, considering the large number of rural poor. A mechanism to pay for the poor, such as equity funds from the government, will be necessary.

7.10.4 *Sector initiatives*

Data from the World Bank (2006c) study provides a snapshot picture of infrastructure connectivity of the poor in Laos in 2003. The poor are more likely to live in a village without passenger transport (60 percent), electricity (45 percent), development project (25 percent), permanent market (7 percent) and primary school (7 percent).

Rural roads. Overall, rural road connectivity expanded more quickly for the non-poor than the poor between 1998 and 2003. In 2003, the poor were on average 6.7 km away from a road, compared to only 2.9 km for the non-poor (World Bank, 2006c). Access to villages is impeded especially in the rainy season. More than 10 percent of all district centers and over 40 percent of villages report having no year-round road access (World Bank, 2007d).

Road expenditure is dependent on funding by external donors and generally concentrated on construction and rehabilitation of national roads. Feeder roads at the village level where the poor reside are generally given a lower priority. In order to better maintain road conditions, the government established the Road Maintenance Fund based on a user pay principle and funding from the fuel levy. However the fund does not sufficiently address the problem of connectivity of the rural poor. The government has to do more to overcome transportation problems especially in remote rural areas.

Rural electrification. Access to electricity across the nation has improved over the past decade. The percentage of rural households with access to electricity has risen from 15 percent in 1995 to 44 percent of rural population by 2004. Support was obtained from IDA to connect poor households to solar home systems and small, village-based hydro schemes in isolated areas without grid coverage. Village electricity committees were set up to facilitate the planning and implementation process. It also enabled job creation as SMEs were involved in provision of off-grid electrification. (see World Bank, 2008j). However the probability of a poor family living in a village without electricity is 45 percent higher than the same probability for a non-poor family (World Bank, 2006c). The government is attempting to rectify this situation by making rural electrification an explicit component of the NGPES. It aims to provide at least 70% of all households with electricity by 2010.

Irrigation. Access to irrigation schemes improved somewhat but mainly for non-poor farmers in non-priority districts. Irrigation investments are targeted mainly in the Mekong Corridor and in particular in the Vientiane Municipality, which has received almost as much funds as all the districts in the poor northern highlands (World Bank, 2007e). Again the chronic poor do not benefit. They are particularly at risk during the mid season dry period from October to April since they are unable to farm due to lack of irrigation facilities. Hence the poor are likely to face food shortages and hunger. More needs to be done to provide dams and tube wells for the poor, particularly in the northern region.

Agricultural extensions. Research centers are to be established and production of improved varieties of rice, corn and community forestry will be promoted in the provinces of Vientianne, Luang Namtha and Champasak (Government of Laos, 2006). In drought and flood prone areas efforts should be made to implement varieties that are adapted to these conditions. This could help in increasing crop output and may considerably reduce poverty in Luang Namtha where over 50 percent of the population is poor.

Land allocation. According to IMF (2008), land allocation is expected to be completed in 423 villages in the 47 poorest districts with the number of poor households practicing shifting cultivation being reduced from 21,000 in 2007 to 15,000 by the end of 2008. The government has also actively promoted other forms of livelihood strategies such as rearing livestock, permanent paddy rice production, secondary food crop production and handicrafts. However responses from the poor appear to be mixed as some households have expressed dissatisfaction with resettlement programs to the newly allocated lands and livelihoods do not seem to have improved. Chamberlain and Phomsombath (2002) criticized such land and forest allocation programs for seriously reducing fallow periods from 15 years to as little as two years and leading to serious nutrient depletion and unsustainable rural livelihoods in the long term. Further monitoring of the scheme is needed to evaluate its effectiveness.

Land clearance. Areas of high unexploded military weapons (UXO) contamination are strongly associated with poverty. The minority groups like the Mon Khmer are particularly susceptible to UXO contamination (World Bank, 2006c). The Lao National Unexploded Ordinance Program has been in place since 1999 to clear land of UXO left from the Indochina conflict (1964 to 1973). An estimated rate of at least 200 to 400 of UXO causalities occur each year. Land has been cleared in about 40 percent of the rural cultivated area and approximately 6 percent of land area in targeted poverty districts. Regression studies also show that government efforts in UXO clearance correspond favorably to poverty reduction. It frees up previously tied-up arable land and allows farmers to work the land safely. However it is acknowledged by the authorities that they will need 10 more years to fully clear all UXO.

Microfinance. Micro credit at low interest rates is available to the poor from the credit and savings groups formed under the Village Development Fund and Village Investment for the Poor. However, the chronic poor do not usually qualify since they do not have any collateral to offer for the loan. Furthermore a vicious cycle was generated by the low interest rate loans which caused excessive competition for funds and increased favoritism towards middle-income households who had the ability to repay the loans. Low interest rates also discouraged households from contributing to the fund. This has led to problems with sustaining the profitability and viability of the fund. Even when the poorest families obtained loans, they encountered difficulties sustaining the investment (e.g. livestock). They were forced into default since they couldn't make the required monthly repayments. Alternatively some families simply ran out of cash to continue to rear the livestock. Alternative schemes need to be explored that enable the poor to borrow for worthwhile projects without collateral, where repayment terms are flexible enough to help borrowers deal with income shocks.

7.10.5 *Macroeconomic policies*

According to Kakwani and Pernia (2000), economic growth in Laos has been weakly pro-poor. The government will need to improve its poverty performance in order to accelerate the rate of reduction in poverty. Under the NSEDP, Laos targets to reduce poverty headcount to less than 25 percent by 2010 and has undertaken significant economic reforms to move from a command economy towards a market economy. The government has aggressively promoted foreign investment in sectors like energy, mining, agriculture, textiles, agriforestry, telecommunications, transportation and tourism. Major projects such as Nam Theun 2 and Sesaman 3 hydropower projects have been implemented. The former is due for completion by 2009. New mining projects like the Phu Kham copper and gold mine are expected to start production this year. In addition, Laos has actively fostered trade and investment relationships with other countries in the emerging Greater Mekong Sub-Region Economic Cooperation Program and AFTA. Efforts have been made to improve trade and investment conditions for Laos to join the World Trade Organization in 2010. The reforms seem in line with the long-term development strategy of sustaining economic growth at an average rate of 7 percent by 2020.

As noted above the government has identified the 47 poorest districts and 25 poor districts requiring government intervention based on the household, village and district level indicators of basic minimum needs. Several initiatives such as village development funds and provision of basic services to remote areas appeared to have yielded results. According to the World Bank (2006c), vulnerability to poverty fell at a faster pace than poverty itself. The probability of being poor in the next period declined from 37 percent in 1992/3 to 23 percent in 2002/3. However the vicious cycle of poverty is still hard to break. The poor were still more than twice as likely to be residing in the 47 priority districts as the non-poor.

Poverty reduction projects have been implemented to encourage the poor to give up slash and burn practices and switch to permanent paddy cultivation in the lowlands. Plans are also in place to eradicate opium growing which occurs mainly in the North. Other sources of income will have to be generated or migration to other areas organized. See Bird 2009, Bechstedt *et al.*, 2007 and Box 7.25 for more discussion.

Box 7.25

Approximately 50,000 households in about 1,600 villages in the remote Northern highlands cultivate poppy as a source of livelihood. Poppy cultivation occurs in almost 70 percent of the 47 poorest districts. However it often causes the poor to fall deeper into poverty as family members become addicted to opium.

Under the National Drug Control Programme, the government has destroyed almost 19,000 ha of opium fields. By 2005, ten provinces — Oudomxay, Luang Namtha, Bokeo, Vientiane, Phongsaly, Huaphan, Xiengkhuang, Xayaboury and Bolikhamxay — and one special zone were officially declared to be free from opium production. Laos seeks to increase awareness of the harmful effects of opium and at the same time, help the rural poor develop alternative income sources.

(*Continued*)

Box 7.25 (*Continued*)

With the ban on opium cultivation Bird (2009) argues that it leaves the poor with little choice but to resettle to the lowland areas. However this tends to hurt the poor. First, they lose assets such as land and access to forest resources. Secondly, they often experience difficulties in adjusting to lowland rice production, leading to lower yields and rice production and ultimately food shortages. Thirdly, they often experience social tensions with the original residents of the lowland villages (for example, Khmu, Xiengmoon and Hmong joining the Lao villagers). To make a living, some decide to work as casual laborers for the Lao farmers. The women hire out their labor to domestic employers, migrate to Thailand or get drawn into prostitution. Quite a substantial number of the resettled migrants are highly likely to remain trapped in chronic poverty for an extended period.

It is of utmost importance that the government re-thinks its strategy and ensures that re-settlers are able to maintain a certain living standard. They could be trained to use lowland farming technology and the government could develop a program where entire villages would be relocated to avoid ethnic tensions. Alternatively the government could elect village committees to look into integrating the ethnic minorities into the existing villages.

Sources: Bird (2009), Bechstedt *et al.* (2007) and Government of Laos (2006).

With the help of village groups, the government aims to shift 15–20 percent of agricultural labor to small-scale industry. Other than continuing with assistance for the 47 poorest districts, Laos also intends to invest in infrastructure development along the borders so as to further reduce poverty. More investments are intended to stimulate trade and tourism at the borders with neighboring countries like Myanmar, China, Vietnam and Thailand. This should help to promote economic growth and raise income levels and benefit residents of provinces like Xiengkhuang near Myanmar, Boten near China and Nam Kan near Vietnam. There should also be positive spillover effects on nearby areas.

The government has plans to spur economic development and income levels in the lagging North region, where there are a substantial number of poor districts. For instance, there are plans to develop the Luang Prabang City into a provincial capital which will also serve to attract tourists to the region. The government also aims to increase the share of non-agricultural sector for the Northern region, to provide alternative employment opportunities for the rural poor. Greater emphasis is to be placed on industries like mining, community forestry and agricultural processing. The Luang Namtha Industrial Zone will serve to further promote the industrial sector. There are also opportunities for tourism in the north, particularly from China which has relaxed its tourist travel policy to Laos.

Public spending and budget. According to World Bank (2007d), the government spends approximately US$12 per person on road construction and maintenance, US$9 for agriculture, US$7 for education, and US$5.50 for health. Public expenditure on health and education will have to be increased in the future since health and education outcomes are low even when compared to other low-income countries.

Despite the targeted health and education interventions in priority districts, the gap in health and education outcomes between priority and non-priority districts has not been substantially reduced (Bechstedt *et al.*, 2007). This could be partially due to the decentralization of spending to the provinces and excessive autonomy on the part of the provincial authorities.

National priorities, provincial spending and the needs of the poor communities are somewhat disconnected. For instance, recurrent expenditures in education in fiscal years 2003–04 were US$5.40 per capita for Luangnamtha Province, three times as much as Bolikhamxay Province (World Bank, 2007). Also more needs to be done to improve the accountability of provincial spending to the central authorities to be in line with national poverty reduction objectives. The provincial authorities also need to take greater account of the needs of the poor under their jurisdiction and formulate appropriate policy interventions. There is also an urgent need to increase allowance of health and educational workers in remote areas where language barriers of ethnic minorities would have to be overcome.

Laos is heavily dependent on external funding. Official development assistance makes up 85 percent of public investments and almost 40 percent of total public expenditures (IMF, 2008). Heavy reliance on such off-budget funds compromises the effectiveness of the budget process and is likely to affect the sustainability of implemented pro-poor policies once funds start running low (World Bank, 2007d). To overcome this dependence, revenues from the hydropower and mining projects can be use to aid in provision of pro-poor services and allow Laos to ensure greater ownership of its poverty programs and implementation schemes.

Social protection. Only a small proportion of workers are covered under the formal social security systems. Less than 5 percent of the labor force has social security coverage. The figure goes up to 28 percent for formal sector workers in Vientiane City (Government of Laos, 2006). Workers in the informal sector who comprise the bulk of the rural poor are not covered. To provide minimum living and health standards it is important to consider widening the social security system or at a minimum, the provision of food and income subsidies.

7.10.6 *Future policy agenda and challenges*

Under the NGPES, the government clearly spelled out a focal area approach in reducing poverty. There has been active government intervention in the four priority sectors (agriculture and forestry, education, health and infrastructure), particularly for the identified targeted 72 poor districts. It has made a good head start in identifying the very poor. However the outcomes on Lao's poverty reduction scorecard have been rather mixed. Food security, educational and health indicators are especially lacking. Many of the policies are still in the process of implementation and difficult to evaluate their effectiveness. There is a great need for pro-poor policies to attain the long term objectives of eradicating poverty.

Below are some recommendations for future policy agenda. We incorporate some suggestions from the 6th National Socio-Economic Development Plan and add in our recommendations:

1. Conduct quantitative and qualitative data survey on the chronically poor in Laos to further investigate the sources and nature of vulnerability.
2. Continue with poverty reduction schemes in the 47 poorest districts. Supply necessary infrastructure for isolated villages. Implement other development alternatives for non-priority districts since about six in ten poor people live outside the 47 poorest priority districts. Offer non-farm opportunities to people in the lowlands.
3. Setting up food-for-work activities, accessing rice banks where they can borrow rice especially during the dry spell season to improve food security. Develop assets such as livestock by participating in livestock groups.
4. Invest in education and health services for the poor. Speed up construction of healthcare facilities and schools in remote villages so as to reduce distance and traveling time of the poor. Delivery of preventive services such as immunization. Equity funds could be set up for the chronically poor so that they could access medical services. Conditional cash transfers to be given to school children especially rural ethnic minority girls. Training of health and educational workers should be accelerated.
5. Provide assistance to socially excluded groups like ethnic minorities, disabled, orphaned and disadvantaged people. There is a need to prepare and implement community driven projects with the informed participation of the ethnic minorities.
6. Further strengthen micro-credit facilities with subsidized loans for the very poor.
7. To align provincial spending with national priorities, establish monitoring and evaluation of poverty reduction schemes at the local levels.

8. Set up social safety nets such as disaster alleviation funds and short term fund relief for the formerly poppy cultivating households who have re-settled in the lowlands.
9. Begin farm extension programs to improve yields in drought and flood prone areas using technology recently developed by IRRI.

7.11 Vietnam

Box 7.26 A Snapshot of Vietnam's Chronic Poor

- About 19 million people are poor in Vietnam, Bauer *et al.* (2008) reports that 22.8 percent of the population in Vietnam survives on less than US1.25 per day.
- The chronic poor account for approximately 35 percent to 45 percent of the poor.
- Chronic poverty tends to be concentrated in the North West and Central Highlands, which has a high concentration of ethnic minorities.
- The chronic poor include the 53 ethnic minorities who face discrimination by the Kihn majority.
- Vietnam was categorized as a "consistent improver" together with China and Indonesia. Vietnam has a high overall level of literacy.

Table Box 7.26 Selected Indicators

Proportion of poor who are chronically poor over 5 years (low estimate)[1]	0.35
Proportion of poor who are chronically poor over 5 years (high estimate)[1]	0.45
Population	83 mil
Percentage of poor living on less than US$1.25 per day (2005PPP)*	22.8
Average depth of poverty (number of % points by which the poor fall below the poverty line[2] in 1998)	18.6
Income share held by lowest 20 percent	7.5
Gini index of inequality	37.0

(*Continued*)

Box 7.26 (*Continued*)

Healthcare indicators	
Under-5 mortality rate (per 1,000 live births) in 2004	23
Infant mortality rate (per 1,000 live births) in 2004	17
Proportion of children under 5 who are stunted (2003)[2]	32
Life expectancy at birth, 2004	70.8
Educational indicators	
Adult illiteracy rate for women aged 15 years and above (2000–2004)	13
Adult illiteracy rate for men aged 15 years and above (2000–2004)	6
Child labor	
Percentage of children aged between 7–14 in the labor force (1999–2004)	17.5

Sources: CPRC (2008) Annex E and F and *Bauer *et al.* (2008) and Bauer *et al.* (2008).

Notes: [1]Based on Vietnam Living Standards Survey (VLSS) 1992/93, 1997/1998 and 2002–2004. [2]Most recent year

Vietnam's Five-Year Plan 2006–2010 has set an ambitious target to further halve poverty over the next five years to approximately 10 to 11 percent by 2010. Based on Vietnam's post success in poverty reduction, the target appears plausible. Poverty, as measured by the per capita consumption, has more than halved in the last 12 years, falling from 58 percent in 1993 to around 20 percent in 2004 (Pham, 2008 and Table Box 7.30). Progress has been made in both rural and urban areas. No region has been left out in its inclusive development drive, not even Northern Mountains and Central Highlands where poverty rates have been historically high. Improvements in living standards and poverty reduction were most pronounced in the Mekong and Red River Delta area. In Asia, Vietnam joins China and Indonesia in the highest poverty reduction category "consistent improver".

7.11.1 *Incidence of poverty*

According to the Chronic Poverty Research Center (2008), the chronically poor account for approximately 35 percent to 45 percent of the

Table 7.30. Poverty Rates Across Region, 1993 and 2004

	1993	2004	Difference in Poverty Gap, 1993–2004
General Poverty	58.1	19.48	–13.8
Northern Mountains	81.5	35.39	–19.5
North East	86.1	29.38	–22.6
North West	81	58.57	–5.0
Red River Delta	62.7	12.14	–16.2
North Central Coast	74.5	31.90	–16.6
South Central Coast	47.2	19.01	–12.1
Central Highlands	70	33.15	–15.7
South East	37	5.37	–8.9
Mekong Delta	47.1	15.82	–10.8

Source: Pham (2008).

poor in Vietnam. Using data from the Vietnam Living Standard Survey which was conducted in 1992/93 and 1997/98, Gunther and Klasen (2007) arrive at a similar conclusion regarding the extent of chronic poverty. They are also able to further decompose the level of chronic poverty for adults and children. Chronic poverty for children (38.2 percent) is substantially higher than that of adults. Labor force participation of children between the ages of 7 and 14 is also high (see Table Box 7.26). Nutrition and educational indicators of children are also quite low.

The eight regions in Vietnam may be classified into 3 main groups according to living standards and general economic well being: poor, middle and well-off (see Table 7.30). The poor regions include the North mountainous areas, the North Central Coast and the Central Highlands. Together these regions house over half of the Vietnamese population and all have poverty rates of 30 percent or higher. These three regions are also the home of most ethnic minorities. The highlands are also characterized by poor economic infrastructure and are often prone to malaria attacks.

The middle group of regions includes the North East, the South Central Coast and the Mekong River Delta. The Red River Delta and the South East are the most prosperous. Fertile soils near the Red River Delta and Mekong River are conducive to productive agriculture and higher crop yields. The natural ports along the east coast and relatively well-developed infrastructure also foster trade and development. The ethnic Vietnamese, the Kinh, are clustered especially in the delta areas while the Chinese minority can be found in the urban areas of the South. Between 1993 and 2004, rapid reduction in the incidence of poverty took place in the North East (57 percent), Red River Delta (51 percent), North Central Coast and Central Highlands (more than 35 percent). The pace of poverty reduction was slowest in the North East, where poverty fell by a modest 22 percent.

Ethnic minorities who reside in the mountainous and forested areas of Vietnam have been and continue to be particularly vulnerable to chronic poverty. The share of poor ethnic minorities in the population has risen in the North West from 12 percent to 20 percent between 1998 and 2002 (Swinkels and Turk, 2004). These ethnic minorities are highly dependent on agriculture and the North West has poorly developed infrastructure and living conditions are harsh. Only 4 percent of the ethnic minorities have access to safe water and only 19 percent have access to sanitation. They generally grow maize on extensive areas of sloping land where yields are lower than the rice wetlands. As a result crop yields and farmer's incomes are substantially lower. Furthermore, only 14 percent of ethnic minority farmers have access to irrigated land as compared to 54 percent of the majority Kinh farmers (Swinkels and Turk, 2006). Many ethnic minorities are unable to take advantage of government subsidies on newly improved seed varieties due to the poor quality of soil, lack of irrigation and agricultural extension services. Despite the efforts of the Vietnamese government to reduce poverty, 61 percent of ethnic minorities remained poor as compared to 14 percent of Kinh and Chinese people. Furthermore the Kinh and Chinese that are poor have a smaller poverty gap to bridge than the ethnic minorities as they often are just below the poverty line. The poor ethnic minorities face a significantly larger poverty gap of 19.2 percent, which is more difficult to bridge (Swinkels and Turk, 2006).

7.11.2 *Determinants of chronic poverty*

Many of the factors responsible for chronic poverty in Vietnam relate to geography, market access and social exclusion such as discrimination against ethnic minorities. Minot *et al.* (2006) used poverty mapping analysis of Vietnam's 614 districts. They found spatial poverty traps in the North mountainous areas, North Central Coast and the Central Highlands as they investigated the geographical determinants of district-level poverty such as distance to city, soil type and topography. All of these were significant factors affecting local poverty rates. Market access explained about three quarters of the variation in rural poverty at the district level and the proximity to small towns plays a larger role in affecting rural poverty rather than access to larger cities. Sandy and acidic soils that are ill suited to high agricultural yields were a contributing factor to the higher incidence of rural poverty in these regions. Similarly, poverty was reported higher in districts with sloped land and bare and rocky land cover. Surprisingly Minot *et al.*, 2006 found a surprising low correlation between chronic poverty income and non-chronic income poverty. They suggest this is because there is a low correlation between income and non-income poverty in individual years even though both variables tend to move together over time.

7.11.3 *Microeconomic policies*

In 2005 Vietnam adopted a Comprehensive Poverty Reduction and Growth Strategy (CPRGS) which was integrated with its five-year Socio-Economic Development Plan (SEDP). This strategy has placed special emphasis on social equity and reducing chronic poverty. In conjunction with the CPRGS its National Targeted Program aims to increase the level of available resources to poor communities and individuals located in geographically isolated areas and ethnic and demographic groups. Political stability has allowed the smooth functioning of macroeconomic policies and aided economic growth with beneficial trickle-down effects to the poor. See Table 7.31 for a breakdown of government spending on various pro-poor programs as targeted in Vietnam's Five-Year Plan, 2001–2005.

Table 7.31 Vietnam's Five Year Plan (2001–2005)

	Breakdown of Total Investment	*VDN (Thousand bil.)*
1.	Poverty reduction and employment	27–28
2.	Clean water and hygienic rural environment	8.0–8.5
3.	Population and family planning	3.5–4.0
4.	Program to prevent communicable and dangerous diseases and HIV/AIDS	5.0–5.5
5.	Cultural development program	1.5–2.0
6.	Training and education program	6.5–7.0
7.	Program for the social and economic development of communes experiencing special difficulties	8.5–9.0
8.	Five million hectare forestry project	10.0–11.0
	Total	70–75 (USD 5–5.5 billion).

Source: Socialist Republic of Vietnam (2002, p. 98, Table 5.7).

Vietnam has made efforts to ensure that the chronic poor are reached. A complex structure of identifying the poor was implemented by the Ministry of Labor and Social Assistance (MOLISA). MOLISA acts as the lead government agency to provide guidelines and assistance to provincial, district and commune level authorities to identify poor households under their jurisdiction. Households whose expenditure falls below the threshold are considered as poor. The village head makes the first selection in agreement with village residents and sends in the list of poor households which is submitted to the commune authority and posted in a public place for feedback. Then it goes on to the district level. Finally the consolidated list is sent to the province which approves it and sends it to MOLISA. The selected poor households become eligible for support from the government. The effectiveness of their poverty reduction scheme can be attributed to local officers being able to identify and target the poor effectively. However its outreach can be improved further according to CPRC (2008). The central government should consider abolishing its current quota for each locality to allow all chronic poor to be included. Efforts should also be made to target excluded groups like drug addicts or HIV-positive individuals (among the most needy) who are often left out of the scheme due to discrimination at the village level. Also more needs to be done for migrants and their families. Migrants often face restrictions in registering for residence; hence they are not recognized in the official poor list and are not eligible for government assistance. Rural households who have a family member remitting money and working in urban centers are also unfairly excluded from the poor list in the home village (Pham, 2008).

Government assistance to the poor includes spending under the poverty targeting programs such as National Targeted Program for Hunger Eradication and Poverty Reduction (HEPR) and Program 135[27] to improve the access of the poor to basic services like education, healthcare and infrastructure. The HEPR generally targets all the poor in Vietnam based on MOLISA poverty guidelines whereas Program 135 explicitly targets socio-economic development of ethnic minorities and those living in mountainous regions. Program 135 funds construction of infrastructure at the village and commune level (roads, health centers, schools, irrigation systems, water supply systems, markets, etc.), inter-commune center infrastructure development, relocation planning, agricultural and forestry extension and training of commune level cadres for management and monitoring of works in remote and mountainous regions. On the other hand, the HEPR is not a program but rather coordinates a range of support policies and projects for the poor under different ministries. The HEPR incorporates (i) provision of health care, education, housing, special assistance for ethnic minorities, temporary migrants, disaster-affected people and aid with production tools and land; and (ii) policies like access to credit for poor, small loans for small-scale employment generation projects and infrastructure construction in the rest of the country not covered under Program 135.

[27] Program 135 is simply named after the Prime Minister's executive Decision 135 on poverty reduction in disadvantaged communes. There is no particular significance behind the numerical figures. Funding for projects in the poorest communes is allocated from the State budget and provincial funds. For more details on Program 135 and HEPR, please refer to Pham (2008) for more details.

There appears to be overlaps between the assistance given by HEPR and Program 135 and the structural set up of oversight is very similar. The two seems to be working quite closely together following a similar relationship to the poverty reduction scheme in Dien Bien (see Box 7.27).

Box 7.27. Poverty Reduction in Dien Bien Province, 1998–2005

Dien Bien, a province located in the North West mountainous region, has about 21,435 households. Close to 45 percent of households were classified as poor. Ethnic minorities like Thai accounted for 40.4 percent, H'mong: 28.8 percent, Kinh (Viet): 19.7 percent, Kho Mu 3.2 percent of the inhabitants in Dien Bien.

Between 1998 and 2005, the poor in Dien Bien has benefited from the following national level programs (NTP) and projects:

1. Credit for the poor	(part of NTP on HEPR)
2. Production support	(part of NTP on HEPR)
3. School fee exemption for the poor	(part of NTP on HEPR)
4. Healthcare for the poor	(part of NTP on HEPR)
5. Agricultural and forestry extension	(part of Programme 135)
6. Infrastructure at commune and village levels	(part of Programme 135)
7. Infrastructure at cluster-cluster level	(part of Programme 135)
8. Settlement and sedentarisation of ethnic minorities	(part of Programme 135)
9. Training of commune-level cadres	(part of Programme 135)
10. Cultivate land for the poor	
11. NTP on rural water supplies and sanitation	
12. Production model for hunger eradication	

The provincial steering committee for Program 135 was made up of almost the same committee as the HEPR. The provincial

(*Continued*)

Box 7.27 (*Continued*)

Committee on Ethnic Minorities was the coordinating agency for the former whereas the Department of Labor, Invalid and Social Affairs was the lead agency for HEPR.

By the end of the period, HEPR committees have been set up in all communes and poverty reduction was achieved at 5 percent per annum in Dien Bien. The poor were given free health services and could access subsidized credit. There was a similar degree of success for projects under Program 135. Over 400 infrastructural projects were constructed at the commune and village level. About 750 ethnic minority households had been successfully re-settled. From 2006 onwards, Dien Bien provincial government has taken ownership and leadership in its long-term plan for socioeconomic development and hunger eradication and poverty reduction.

Source: Pham (2008).

Spending on HEPR and Program 135 makes up of 2 percent of GDP in Vietnam. Such transfers are generally progressive where poorer regions and households receive more aid. For instance in 2004 the North West received the most aid in 2004 followed by the Central Highlands and North East. Redistribution at the household level is also pro-poor. The poorest quintile benefits more from social spending than other quintiles. In addition, special programs are set up for ethnic minorities and administered by the Commission for Ethnic Minorities and Mountain Areas.

Program 135 has been credited with the sharp rate of annual poverty reduction in the Central Highlands and North West regions of 5.8 percent and 4.8 percent respectively, from 2002 to 2006 (Tran and Ha, 2008). The first phase of Program 135 provided support to about 2400 communes, of which 80 percent were chosen owing to their geographical remoteness or high poverty levels. It has also included: (i) settling shifting cultivators into communities and resettling small mountainous communities in large villages to facilitate access to basic services. Reactions to resettlement have been mixed with only about one-third expressing approval of their new environment.

Education and health spending has been on the rise. The share of public spending on education rose to 5.6 percent of GDP higher than the average level in the Asian region of 3.8 percent of GDP (see VASS, 2007). The government emphasizes its "Education for All" policy and has special programs in place to give access to education for children in disadvantaged regions. Swinkels and Turk (2006) reports that school fee exemptions are much higher for ethnic minorities than Kinh households. For instance, 95 percent of ethnic minorities enjoyed exemption from primary school tuition fees and 60 percent enjoyed an exemption from lower secondary tuition fees. This has led to a significant increase in school enrolment rates of ethnic minorities. Between 1993 and 2004, enrolment rates of ethnic minorities has increased from 64 percent to 83 percent at the primary level, 7 percent to 56 percent at the lower secondary level (an 8-fold increase) and 2 percent to 25 percent at the upper secondary level (more than 12-fold increase), according to Pham (2008).

One important early healthcare intervention was a family planning campaign that helped to reduce population growth from an annual 2.2 percent in the early 1980s to 1.5 percent in the late 1990s. A "two-child policy" was implemented in 1988 and aided in controlling population growth especially in the more prosperous regions. Special healthcare centers were set up at the commune or district level. "Poor household certificates" and "free health cards" were issued to the poor. The two schemes entitle recipients to free medical treatment in public hospitals. This health coverage helps to alleviates the risk of falling into poverty due to health shocks. However the indirect costs like transportation, board and other related costs for warded patients are likely to be substantial for the chronic poor (Pham, 2008) and could deter them from utilizing the services. Health insurance in Vietnam is mandatory for the wage-employed, voluntary for the better-off self employed and subsidized for the poor. The percentage of the poorest having health insurance has increased dramatically from 6.22 percent in 1998 to 22.69 percent in 2004. Up to 42 percent of the poorest are covered by both health insurance and the free health-care card program (VASS, 2007).

Other pro-poor organizations include the Motherland Front, Women's Union, Farmers' Association and Veterans' Association. Unemployment insurance and benefit and voluntary insurance have been legalized in June 2006 and will be enforced from 2008 and 2009 respectively. These programs are likely to increase the spread of unemployment insurance to more people including the poor.

Access to credit has increased over the years especially due to an expansion in the outreach of the Vietnam Bank for Social Policy. The Bank tends to favor ethnic minorities, although coverage is still minimal. Only 4 percent of Kinh individuals have accessed the bank for credit compared with more than 10 percent of ethnic minorities (Swinkels and Turk, 2006). To enhance the outreach to all ethnic minorities in remote areas, the Bank has started to collaborate with NGOs. However the range of savings products has to be increased and there is a need to lower minimum deposits. Mobile banking facilities would also enhance the effectiveness of the schemes in reaching the poor.

7.11.4 *Sectoral policies*

Improving connectivity. Regional development policies around Hanoi, Da Nang and Ho Chi Minh City have promoted the growth of nearby provinces and encouraged greater linkages with poorer regions. The construction of the National Highway No. 5 has led to further development within the provinces of Hung Yen and Hai Duong. Likewise, the rehabilitation of the Hai Phong Harbor has contributed to the development of Northern Vietnam and its surrounding areas. Pham, Rama and Larsen (2004) investigated Vietnam's public spending from 1996 to 2000. While the elasticity is not high they report that an increase of 1.0 percent of GDP spending on infrastructure leads to a 1.5 percent reduction of the poverty rate. Results from Fan, Huong, and Long (2004) indicate that for every Dong invested in roads, the value of agricultural production would increase by three Dong. Plans are still underway regarding upgrading the existing railway network, opening new railways to important economic centers and developing trans-national traffic corridor comprising of trans-Asia railway and road networks connecting ASEAN capital cities, industrial centers and important ports.

Under the National Targeted Programme, there are also plans to improve infrastructure development, including power systems, schools, clinics, roads and markets, for disadvantaged ethnic minority communes. Program 135 provides basic infrastructure in poor communes. These include provision of electricity and clean water supplies, development of roads that link to more developed provinces, building schools and health clinics and small-scale irrigation projects. The VASS (2007) reported on the success of the investment works. 90 percent of poor communes now have access to electricity, nursery and primary schools as well as small-scale irrigation. 97 percent have passable roads to the commune centers. 100 percent of communes enjoy access to health clinics and upper secondary schools. There are also proposals in the Draft National Targeting Programme on Poverty Reduction 2006–2010 to improve infrastructure development for communes with special difficulties in coastal and island areas.

Land, forestry and agricultural extension services. Extension centers for agriculture in Vietnam have created new job opportunities for some ethnic minorities in lagging regions. Program 135 and HEPR program provided assistance by subsidizing or giving free seeds of improved varieties of rice, maize or cassava to the poor in these regions. The programs have benefited some ethnic minorities. Some are still unable to participate since they lack resources such as irrigation and fertilizers and pesticides to take advantage of these new technologies and high yielding varieties. As pointed out earlier in the chapter, only 14 percent of ethnic minority farmers have access to irrigated land. Only the few who have access to reliable irrigation will be able to make use of the improved varieties. The other farmers have little choice but to continue growing their traditional varieties that do not require pesticides, irrigation or fertilizers. As a result there has been negligible progress in raising agricultural output and incomes for these farmers. Another difficulty is that improved varieties are not always popular with the consumers. For example, in Cai Bang and Ha Giang, the crossbred maize is considered to be of poor quality and not favored by local population (VASS, 2007).

Despite the provision of special funds for the ethnic minorities through the Committe for Ethnic Minorities and Mountaineous Affairs, poverty rate in the mountainous regions remain high. There is a vast difference in how incomes can be raised for ethnic minorities compared with the Kinh majority. As a result the typical pro-growth strategies that benefit the Kinh do not benefit the poorest. Other than improved targeting, Vietnam would also need to customize growth strategies to meet the needs of the ethnic poor (Besley and Cord, 2007). Furthermore, the mountainous and forested areas where the ethnic minorities reside are generally under the strict protection of the government. Hence the poor who reside here do not have opportunities to access forest resources. There is a need to redraft the forestry program and to integrate poverty reduction objectives for the locals that reside in these protected areas. Currently the emphasis of Program 327 on "re-greening barren hills" and its successor Program 661 (also called 5 million hectare program) has centered mostly on improving conditions of the forest and ignoring the plight of the poor who live there. This could be quite a challenge as field studies have generally found conflicts between the objectives of forest studies, conservation and poverty reduction. Swinkels and Turk (2006) suggest hiring of ethnic minorities in areas like bio-diversity conservation, management of protected areas and tourism. See Swinkels and Turk (2006) for more details on the difficulties of agricultural extension services for ethnic minorities.

7.11.5 *Macroeconomic policies*

In summarizing Vietnam's rapid growth and general success in poverty reduction, Klump (2007) notes three key factors:

(i) Policies adopted deliberately fostered job creation;
(ii) Institutional and macroeconomic policies that led to and reinforced economic growth and development and

(iii) Targeted transfer of public goods and public expenditures to the poor.

This is all the more surprising when it is recognized that before 1990, Vietnam's political, social and economic conditions appeared anything but conducive to economic growth and poverty reduction. Under the communist regime that ruled the country following the end of the Vietnam War land was collectivized of land, markets abolished and prices controlled. The private sector was eliminated and emphasis placed on heavy industry and SOEs. The ethnic Chinese who had been the backbone of South Vietnam's market economy before the war fled the country. Vietnam was generally politically and economically isolated, except for some support from Soviet Union which had also declined over the years.

After poor harvests and economic mismanagement left millions facing famine and malnutrition in 1990, Vietnam began to actively pursue a transition towards a market-oriented society and fostered economic liberalization policies (also known as *doi mo,* the Vietnamese phrase for renovation). Reforms in agriculture and rural areas helped to increase agricultural output. It raised income of about 70 percent of the population. Land was generally evenly distributed to farming households. The Land Law of 1993 enabled land to be legally transferred, mortgaged and inherited and played an important part in reducing poverty. By 2000, Vietnam had issued almost 11 million land titles (Klump, 2007). Constraints on fertilizer imports were relaxed and agricultural productivity improved tremendously. Vietnam became self-sufficient in food with satisfactory food reserves, and now exports over three million tons of food each year (Socialist Republic of Vietnam, 2003).

The land reform and trade liberalization for coffee and rice and the boom in the world coffee market in the 1990s generally benefited the agricultural sector and its workers. In the Central Highlands, the introduction of coffee crops in 1995 paid off handsomely and resulted in pro-poor growth of 5 percent. (Klump, 2007). Vietnam had a comparative advantage as a coffee grower and coffee exports grew at an annual rate of nearly 60 percent between 1993 and 1998.

Farm job opportunities expanded rapidly in the Central Highlands and employment and agricultural incomes rose. In fact, the coffee boom sparked inward migration into the rural Central Highland regions. In the South, farmers in the rice exporting regions mainly in the South Central Coast, Southeast and Mekong River Delta also benefited from export sales of surplus rice. Hence rice-producing and coffee-growing rural households enjoyed a relative higher probability of moving out of poverty than other rural households. However the increase in price of rice appeared to be a double-edged sword as it increased the income of rice producers but increased the cost of food consumed by the poor. Negative rates of pro-poor growth persisted in the Northwest region where the increase in agricultural productivity led to a fall in demand for workers. It also resulted in surplus labor and generated fewer change of non-farm opportunities in the labor market.

The opening up of the Vietnam economy since the late 1990s has resulted in the creation of export-oriented manufacturing industries and employment opportunities which have increased migration opportunities from poor rural locations to urban areas. This has facilitated the ability of many more families to escape from the poverty trap. After joining the WTO, the impetus to further economic growth was also enhanced. Workers for businesses that export goods to the US have grown rapidly from 16.5 percent in 2002 to 23.5 percent in 2004 (VASS, 2007). Female workers in Vietnam's internationally competitive SOEs such as footwear, leather, textile and garments receive fairly high compensation for their services. FDI has also accelerated and economic growth has stepped up. The economic growth elasticity of poverty reduction is estimated at 0.95 percent for 1988–1993 and has further increased to 1.32 percent for 1998–2004, showing the beneficial effects of economic growth on poverty reduction. In addition, with the opening up of the economy, Vietnam has also received generous increases in official development assistance (ODA) from foreign governments and international institutions to develop its infrastructure and improve its industrial capacity.

With *doi moi* reforms, there has an increase in geographic and occupational labor mobility and this has facilitated access of rural workers to non-rural jobs. Internal migration is an option for most rural households and remittances from family members working away from home have increased to between 4 percent and 11 percent of total income in 2004. The more prosperous regions like North Central, South East and Mekong Delta have remittances of approximately 10 percent of total income of households. Remittances to poorer regions like North West and Central Highlands are about half that of the most prosperous regions, and could have contributed to the persistence of poverty. VASS (2007) highlights the importance of remittances to poverty alleviation in Vietnam and points out that the prosperous region of South East could have had much higher poverty rates if not for remittances (see Table 7.32).

7.11.6 *Future policy agenda and challenges*

After a steep reduction in the poverty rate from 58 percent of the population in 1993 to around 22 percent in 2007, many households are slipping back again below the poverty line (International Herald Tribune, 2008a). Inflation has increased as well as the number of households going hungry. Some farmers and other rural residents who migrated to seek jobs in the cities and industrial zones have

Table 7.32 Significance of Remittances in Regions

	Average Household Remittance (VND thousand)	Average Household Income (VND thousand)	Ratio (1)/(2)(%)
North East	1,556	22,330	6.3
North West	850	16,891	4.2
Red River Delta	2,898	26,885	9.9
North Central Coast	2,224	18,779	9.8
South Central Coast	2,080	24,387	7.8
Central Highlands	1,342	24,181	5.2
South East	5,830	46,850	11.0
Mekong River Delta	3,178	28,071	9.7
Vietnam	2,965	28,087	9.1

Source: VASS (2007, p. 59, Box 1).

Table 7.33 Socio-Economic Development Plan (SEDP), 2006–2010

SEDP Initiatives	Objective
• To continue to promote agricultural growth of 3–3.2 percent so as to reduce rural poverty. Higher priority is to be given to agricultural R&D and extension services.	Enhancing the participation of the poor
• To implement market-oriented reforms with emphasis on the private sector and increase efficiency of state-owned enterprises so as to continue to foster job creation for workers.	Enhancing the participation of the poor
• To further speed up labor distribution among regions and further shift migrants towards higher share of wage employment and better paid jobs. It aims to reduce the employment of agriculture workers in the labor force to 50 percent and increase industry and construction labor to 24 percent and service related industries to 27 percent by 2010.	Enhancing the participation of the poor
• To develop insurance policies for agricultural production and farmers such as social insurance, natural disaster insurance and insurance against market risks such as fluctuations in price. Unemployment benefits and universal old age pensions are to be considered. The pension scheme could benefit from the success of the health insurance scheme (mandatory for the self-employed, voluntary for the better off self-employed and subsidized for the poor) and have a comparable delivery system for all in Vietnam.	Improving social protection scheme
• To continue with Program 135 with high priority given to improving welfare of ethnic minorities in Vietnam and to ensure all communes have essential public works.	Accelerate poverty reduction among ethnic minorities and "Lagging Regions"
• To introduce more unified control over forest land under the district and commune authority and to increase the ability of the ethnic minorities in the highlands to use forestry land in a profitable manner.	Accelerate poverty reduction among ethnic minorities and "Lagging Regions"

Source: VASS (2007, pp. 65–76).

moved back home to the countryside. This has put more pressure on the Government to increase the pace of economic growth in rural areas.

In view of the challenges ahead for sustaining fast poverty reduction, the Socio-Economic Development Plan (SEDP) 2006–2010 outlined in Table 7.33 proposes the following initiatives.

Although rather general in nature these objectives seem reasonable. They will have to be fleshed out further and prioritized, implementation schedules developed and budgets put in place before they can be integrated into the national government planning process.

Chapter 8

Final Thoughts on Policy

In conclusion to its study of poverty written by Duncan Green (2008), Oxfam says

> The fight against the scourges of poverty, inequality and the threat of environmental collapse will define the twenty — first century as the fight against slavery or for universal suffrage defined earlier eras. Fail, and future generations will not forgive us. Succeed and they will wonder how the world could have tolerated such needless injustices and suffering for so long. (Green, 2008, p. 429)

How will the countries of Asia participate in addressing these challenges? In previous chapters we have learned that there are many ways that families can fall into poverty traps. We also learned that those who become immersed in chronic poverty often have great difficulty in escaping this trap. In this final chapter we examine the array of policy measures that have been adopted to reduce the incidence of chronic poverty in the most vulnerable Asian economies and how these policies can be adjusted to achieve even greater success in the future.

Those families who are chronically poor may have gotten there for many different reasons. If they were already poor they could have been driven further into poverty by a poor crop, illness or accident that prevents the breadwinner from working, a natural disaster or other crisis. Without resources families would have to sell off farm implements or livestock or borrow from loan sharks or the landowner to maintain enough consumption to keep from starving. Without much education, having lost their physical assets and in debt, the chronically poor have little hope of escaping the poverty trap without outside help.

What should be the nature and structure of that assistance? How and when should it be delivered and by whom? And what role does the institutional setting play in effectively delivering the assistance? As we have seen in previous chapters there are many modalities of assistance and government agencies and NGOs to provide it. We summarize what we believe are the most effective and powerful policy tools to address chronic poverty that have been adopted by the Asian economies.

8.1 Where Chronic Poverty Fit into Overall Poverty Reduction Agenda in Asia

The most recent Chronic Poverty Research Center (2008) estimates that there are about 800 million poor people in Asia and that the number of chronically poor is between 175 million and 250 million (Chronic Poverty Research Center (2008) Annex E). Using the low estimate of chronically poor and assuming that it would take a dollar a day to lift everyone of these chronically poor out of poverty, then it would take 175 million times 365 days in a year or around $US64 billion to help eliminate chronic poverty in Asia for one year. This assumes that every dollar would get to the chronically poor. However this is being overly optimistic. Administrative costs can eat up some of the resources of poverty programs. However, research in Latin America suggests that these costs are not that high, averaging only around 10 percent of total program costs (see Caldes *et al.*, 2004 and Coady *et al.*, 2005).

On the other hand the chronically poor are not all completely indigent, so that it would take less than a dollar per day per person to lift all of the chronically poor out of poverty. Allowing for these distortions it still seems useful to work with the dollar a day benchmark as a way to assess both the cost of dealing effectively with eliminating chronic poverty and the capacity of governments to deliver the needed assistance.

The subsequent on-going cost of keeping the chronically poor above the poverty threshold would be lower still, since some of the chronically poor would find jobs as a result of the dollar a day subsidy.

So let's take $64 billion as a first round guess as to the cost of eliminating chronic poverty in Asia, setting aside the logistical problems of identifying where they are, the costs of delivering the assistance, keeping greedy government officials from subverting the money to their own pockets and the possible negative impact on work efforts of the poor.

We can compare this US$64 billion to wipe out chronic poverty in Asia with a variety of budgetary items for industrial and developing countries. For example the United States spent almost three times this much (about US$170 billion) on the wars in Afghanistan and Iraq in 2007. US official development assistance to poorer countries was US$23.5 billion in 2006 of which US$18 billion went to Iraq. The next largest donor was the United Kingdom ($12.46b) followed by Japan ($11.19b), France ($10.60b) and Germany ($10.43b). Other European countries along with Australia and New Zealand gave smaller amounts.

Current estimates of the budgetary costs of all forms of social protection in a few countries are reported in Table 8.3. These estimates range from 2 percent or less in Cambodia, Laos, Indonesia and Pakistan to 5.7 percent in Sri Lanka. For our set of chronic poverty countries and using 3 percent as a notional average for the region as a whole, this amounts to about US$150 billion at current exchange rates.[28] From these notional calculations and assuming that the full allocation of social spending is spent on the chronically poor, there are sufficient resources available in the Asian region to wipe out chronic poverty.

If we look at the budget for chronic poverty reduction from a more disaggregated point of view a somewhat different picture emerges. Comparing the 3 percent of GDP figures with the dollar a day costs on a country by country basis there are three countries that would not have sufficient resources, India and Bangladesh and Nepal. A few countries would have somewhat more than needed and a few would have a large surplus. The calculations are displayed in Table 8.1. China and Indonesia have the biggest surplus resource gap. 3 percent

[28] Using PPP to value GDP, the figure would be more than double.

Table 8.1 Cost Comparisons of a Dollar a Day Subsidy for the Poor with a Social Spending Allocation of 3 Percent of GDP for a Panel of Asian Economies (in billion US dollars)

Country	Cost of a US One Dollar a Day Program for the Chronically Poor Given to All Chronically Poor in the Country (billion US)	Cost of a US One Dollar a Day Program for the Chronically Poor Given to All Chronically Poor in the Country (as percent of GDP)
China	11.92	.003
Indonesia	.92	.002
Philippines	1.42	.010
Vietnam	1.49	.020
Bangladesh	**4.01**	**.055**
India	**35.92**	**.033**
Nepal	**1.18**	**.110**
Pakistan	2.50	.017

Source: CIA factbook and Chronic Poverty Report (2008 and 2009).
Note: Highlighted countries have a ratio in column 3 of over 0.03. The assumption is that $1US equivalent is given to all the chronically poor. The number of chronically poor was calculated at the lower bound estimate of the proportion of poor who are chronically poor by CPRC 2008/2009. GDP was estimated at current exchange rate from CIA factbook.

of GDP is about 10 times as big as the cost of a dollar a day subsidy for all the chronically poor in China and around 15 times the dollar a day resource cost in Indonesia. In the Philippines, Pakistan and Vietnam the surpluses are somewhat smaller.

For the other three countries (shown in bold face) — India, Bangladesh and Nepal — there is a deficit. The cost of a dollar a day poverty reduction program for the chronically poor is 11 percent of GDP in Nepal, 5.5 percent in India and 3.3 percent in Bangladesh. Assuming that a dollar per day per person would eliminate chronic poverty for a family, even in the best case scenario where the chronically poor were well targeted and overhead expenses were low, these three countries would still not be able to eliminate chronic poverty without outside assistance. This assumes that they could not muster more than 3 percent of GDP to address chronic poverty.

The point of this exercise is not to give accurate estimates of the cost of poverty reduction but rather to point out that the financial capacity of countries to finance a comprehensive poverty reduction effort varies dramatically. India, Nepal and Bangladesh would need additional resources to eradicate chronic poverty while China and Indonesia are quite capable of handling the financial burden should they wish to embark on such a program to tackle chronic poverty. Also note that this ignores the resources required to deal with other families in poverty that don't fit into the chronically poor category. Whatever the nature of government efforts to address chronic poverty these financial realities have to be kept in mind.

The World Bank and the United Nations have a somewhat broader perspective on poverty. The United Nations Millennium Development Goals (MDG) looks at the poverty challenge through a wider lens than chronic poverty. In particular MDG sets out goals for physical and social infrastructure that need to be implemented by 2015. These goals deal with poverty reduction as but one of several others including health, education, nutrition, physical infrastructure as well as gender equality. The MDG was adopted by 189 countries and signed by 147 heads of state and governments during the UN Millennium Summit in September 2000. The eight goals can be broken down into 21 quantifiable targets that are measured by 60 indicators.

Briefly the goals are

- eradicate extreme poverty and hunger,
- achieve universal primary education,
- promote gender equality and empower women,
- reduce child mortality,
- improve maternal health,
- combat HIV/AIDS, malaria and other diseases,
- ensure environmental sustainability and
- develop a global partnership for Development.

Refer to the UN millennium project website http://www.unmillennium project.org/reports/fullreport.htm for more on UN Millennium Development Goals.

To assess the actual cost of achieving these objectives five countries were selected for in depth analysis by the United Nations, including two in Asia, Bangladesh and Cambodia. Interestingly the estimates of needs in the eight specific goal defined areas are nearly identical in these two Asian countries, going for around \$70 per capita in 2006 to \$100 per capita in 2010. Recognizing that these are estimates for the entire populations of these two countries we note that these amounts are much less than the amount required to eliminate chronic poverty using the dollar a day benchmark ($\$365 \times 0.3) = \$109$.

The breakdown of projected per capita costs of these programs in 2010 for Bangladesh and Cambia are displayed in Table 8.2. Of these, infrastructure expenditures and spending to reduce hunger, improving health and education and extending the rural road network would have the biggest impact on chronic poverty. The small allocation for hunger is a bit puzzling unless malnutrition reduction is not considered part of the investment package.

Table 8.2 Per Capita MDG Investment Needs for Bangladesh and Cambodia in 2010 (US dollars)

MGD Investment Needs	Bangladesh	Cambodia
Hunger	4	7
Education	17	19
Gender equality	3	3
Health	19	21
Water supply and sanitation	5	5
Slum improvement	3	3
Energy	19	13
Roads	21	21
Others such as higher education, research and environmental sustainability	9	9

Source: United Nations Development Program Millennium Development Goals available at http://www.undp.org/mdg/goal1.shtml, Chapter 17, Table 17.1.

In any event there is minimal overlap between such a MDG program and a subsidy program to eradicate chronic poverty such the $64 billion program described earlier in this section. These MDG programs would certainly complement a direct subsidy program by increasing the social and physical infrastructure required to sustain chronic poverty reduction and eventual elimination. They would address the problems that arise for those in the chronic poverty trap including.

For children:

- Brain damage from malnutrition
- Stunting
- Low school attendance
- Illness, disease, morbidity
- High infant mortality
- Perpetuation of poverty
- Child labor and child bonding.

For adults:

- Poor health
- Low life expectancy
- Gender discrimination
- Indebtedness and bonded labor
- Limited assets
- Vulnerability to shocks
- Hunger
- Illiteracy.

The World Bank Poverty Reduction Strategy Papers (PRSP) are prepared by governments through a participatory process involving local interest groups and international development partners including the World Bank, the IMF and regional development institutions such as the Asian Development Bank and the Inter-American Development Bank.

They describe a country's macroeconomic, structural and social policies and programs to promote growth and reduce poverty, as well as associated external financing needs. Each country in conjunction with the World Bank prepares a PRSP every few years. The PRSP guides the poverty reduction strategy of the country and is monitored and reviewed by the World Bank. Each PRSP contains detailed assessments of critical sectors in the poverty reduction effort. For example the Bangladesh PRSP includes analysis of sectors that promotes pro poor growth and social safety nets and human development as well as supporting analysis of good government, social inclusion and empowerment. PRSPs have a somewhat narrower focus than the MGD. The two together provide countries with a comprehensive assessment of development needs to reduce poverty. Bangladesh Cambodia, Lao PDR, Indonesia and Vietnam currently have PRSPs. China, India, Pakistan and Philippines do not. For example estimates of required spending per capita (in US$) for Bangladesh and Cambodia are presented in Table 8.2.

Taken together PRSPs and the Millennium Development Goals give governments a good idea of the thinking among external donors and interested foreign groups. However it is up to each country in consultation with these interested foreign parties to implement its own poverty reduction strategy. From the perspective of chronic poverty a more detailed and focused analysis such as the work of the Chronic Poverty Research Center and this monograph can provide useful additional insights into poverty reduction priorities and strategies.

8.2 Social Protection and Social Assistance

Setting aside the strategy of providing a cash subsidy to each person who is chronically poor, social protection is another avenue for dealing with chronic poverty. Social protection can be achieved in two ways — by subsidizing the purchases of the poor either by lower prices for the goods that the poor purchase or by offering the poor particular staples (rice, wheat, other grains) at highly subsidized prices. Alderman (2002) makes a case for using pricing policies and subsidies rather than income transfers to aid the poor. His argument is based on the assumption that pricing policies are easier to administer than subsidies which could require a means test. He also argues that lower prices for staple foods that are key components in the expenditures of the poor will raise their real incomes and supplementary budget allocations to the poor are not required. The effectiveness of food subsidies for staple foods such as rice and other grains as support for the chronically poor is questionable because of the substantial leakage to other groups, some of them poor and some not so poor.

Targeted assistance to chronically poor families could do a better job that food subsidies and pricing policies and is far less expensive. This assistance may come in several different forms. In India the states provide some benefits to the poor like pension benefits for the elderly, families where the bread winner has died and poor mothers. However they are not comprehensive and not nearly sufficient to enable these families to escape from poverty. There is also a targeted food subsidy program, AAY. AAY offers special ration cards to very poor families which gives households an entitlement of 35 kg of wheat and rise at highly subsidized prices. Still this is not nearly enough to sustain a poor household below the poverty line and, as noted in Chapter 4, although the AAY program operates nationwide it only reaches a fraction of the poor in the poorest states of India.

A review of programs in Bangladesh, China and Philippines summarized in Chapter 4 suggests that ration cards, food entitlements and social security programs are not very effective in these countries either. From this evidence it seems that none of the targeted assistance programs for the chronically poor have been particularly effective. But this does not mean that social assistance is, by nature, ineffective. In richer developing countries and industrial countries social security and unemployment compensation are the main sources of support for the poor. Properly funded and targeted social security programs can also be effective in Asia. So far, there has not been the political will and budgetary commitment to go the next step.

Conditional cast transfers (CCT) programs which are very popular in Latin America have a number of advantages in assisting families to build up their human capital endowment and reduce the incidence of child labor. In Asia, CCT programs in Bangladesh and Indonesia have been successful. The program targets families and villages which have been identified as locations where chronic poverty is most prevalent. CCT programs have a number of other advantages which were discussed in Chapter 4. Using the accumulated experience from existing CCT programs, new programs could be introduced in the rest of South Asia, the Mekong countries and the Philippines. CCT programs are not particularly costly and have proven to be cost effective when targeted to poor families with school age children. Evaluation of CCT programs have demonstrated the positive impacts made in reducing the level of poverty and chronic poverty. However poor households are often not able to take advantage of increased school access simply because it is too expensive for them to send their children to school. Subsidies for these families should also be considered for CCT programs. This will enable the program to reach all of the chronically poor more effectively and ensure their participation.

As noted in Chapter 4 work fare programs can be very effective if the poor are well targeted and good infrastructure projects selected that can employ surplus labor. One key to achieving greater success involves community involvement in both the planning and implementation of infrastructure and social programs. Attention should be focused on poor regions where there is surplus labor during the slack season and workfare projects can be very beneficial. Aside from India there is little work fare program experience in Asia. There is scope for exploring the use of work fare programs in other countries where poor communities can use surplus labor to upgrade infrastructure and build community involvement as well as supplement income of poor agricultural laborers. Social funds run by international agencies have many of the same objectives as work far projects and have been implemented in several Asian countries. Cross fertilization and shared experience of work fare and social fund projects would be a good way for both programs to improve efficiency of operation and targeting of recipients as well as to avoid duplication of effort.

The Asian Development Bank has recently completed a comprehensive analysis of social protection in the Asian region by a team of

Table 8.3 Social Spending and Human Development Index in Selected Asian Economies

Country	SPEXP	SPDIST	SPIMP	HDI Ranking
China	4.6	69	44	82
Indonesia	1.9	71	8	107
Philippines	2.2	30	6	90
Vietnam	4.1	71	17	105
Laos	1.3	40	7	130
Cambodia	1.4	43	4	131
Bangladesh	5.3	53	24	140
India	4.0	100	26	128
Nepal	2.3	35	7	142
Pakistan	1.6	8	3	136
Sri Lanka	5.7	85	26	99

Source: Asian Development Bank (2008a, Chapter 4) and UNDP (2008).
Note: HDI is the UN Human Development Index, SPEXP is social protection expenditure as a percent of GDP, SPDIST is the percent of the poor receiving some social protection and SPIMP is the per capita social protection expenditures as a percent of the national poverty line. See Table 6.7 for alternative estimates of SPEXP.

researchers who systematically studies social programs across the Asian region (Asian Development Bank, 2008). Three components of social protection for the Asian countries analyzed in this book are summarized in Table 8.3 — social protection expenditure as a percent of GDP, the percent of the poor receiving some social protection and per capita social protection expenditures as a percent of the national poverty line. Social protection expenditures as a percent of the national poverty line SPIMP are the most revealing. Aid reaching the poor is a fraction of the poverty line requirements of around a dollar a day. If each individual received a dollar a day, SPIMP would be 100.

6 of the 11 countries (Indonesia, Philippines, Laos, Cambodia, Nepal and Pakistan) had SPIMP values less than 10 percent, an abysmal performance of assisting the poor through social programs. Social programs in Bangladesh, India and Sri Lanka were somewhat more effective. Social capital expenditures were about one fourth of

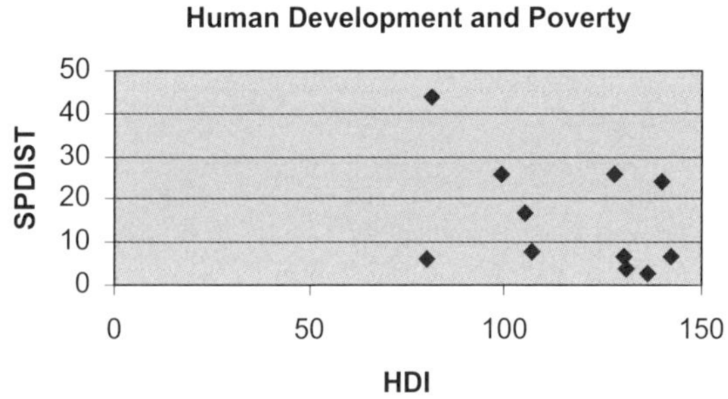

Chart 8.1 Human Development Index Rank and Percent of Poor Receiving Social Protection

Source: UNDP (2008) and Asian Development Bank (2008a).

the per capita poverty line, perhaps spillovers from other programs discussed in this chapter and in Chapter 4 such as conditional cash transfers (CCT) and food subsidy programs.

Comparisons of SPDIST and country rankings from the Human Development Index of the United Nations are displayed in Chart 8.1. The correlation between the two variables is not high. The Philippines ranks relatively high in the HDI ranking and yet very low in terms of social protection while Bangladesh and India are ranked only behind China in the effectiveness of delivery of social protection to the poor and yet are at the lower end of the HDI rankings. This spread between the two indices could be because HDI measures longer term attainment in raising life expectancy and literacy as well as the level of GDP per capita while social protection is a more specialized index relating more directly to poverty reduction.

Another useful aspect of the ADB study is the country reports which explore individual country poverty reduction and social protection programs in more depth. Some of their analyses have been compiled in the country reports reviewed in Chapter 7.

Despite the recent success of social protection programs in a few countries the direct impact on chronic poverty is still questionable. Going back to the analysis underlying Table 8.1, government expenditures to reduce chronic poverty are still insufficient if countries relied only on domestic resources especially in countries with the largest numbers of chronically poor — Bangladesh, India and Nepal. This is not to say that more effective social protection for Asian countries should be neglected. However it does bring the focus back to chronic poverty and underscores the conclusion that direct interventions to reduce chronic poverty are probably the most effective while other programs only help at the margin.

8.3 Assisting Isolated Poor Communities

Geography plays an important role in the perpetuation of chronic poverty. The importance of connectivity for poverty reduction in isolated rural communities was stressed in Chapter 4. Bauer *et al.* (2008) also note that those living in drought or flood prone areas as well as the upland poor are particularly vulnerable and need special assistance. It is, however, difficult to analyze the long term cost benefit ratio of investment in physical infrastructure projects such as telecommunications and roads. There are many dynamic externalities involved. Clearly feeder and other secondary roads yield high rates of return even using narrow criteria of wear and tear on vehicles and reduction in transportation cost of goods. However certain benefits are difficult to quantify including better access to rural markets, lowering costs of retail products, better selection and wider access to local labor markets and better access to educational and health facilities. When these benefits are included as part of the desired outcome, road investments become even more effective in addressing chronic poverty in rural communities. After ascertaining which isolated poor communities can best benefit from the development of secondary and feeder roads, each country has to make these road projects a priority. Furthermore road projects should be coordinated with other poverty reduction strategies that develop the physical and social infrastructure network including schools and health facilities. By establishing a cohesive network of communications and social infrastructure the chronically poor in remote areas can be more easily integrated into the economic mainstream.

Recent developments in telecommunications, particularly laptop computers, cell phones and the internet have also improved connectivity and increased efficiency. Telecommunications investment at the individual and village level is best left to the private market. However extension of the relay infrastructure is a priority for governments and it is a good long term investment with significant external benefits to poor communities as outlined in Chapter 4.

Additional infrastructure should also be provided to isolated communities where the chronically poor reside. For the communities that derive their livelihood from the land, irrigation is key. Without irrigation dry land farming on poor quality land is a sure recipe for poverty. Tube well or canal irrigation should be developed where possible. Evidence from field studies reviewed in Chapter 4 show that some form of irrigation for rain fed areas would lift incomes dramatically by making a second crop possible while increasing yields and possible adaptation of higher yielding varieties for the first crop. The Bethma system of irrigation used in Sri Lanka and described in Box 5.1 is a form of irrigation that may also be appropriate in other locations. If irrigation is not possible agricultural extension can provide advice for planting crops that do well with less water. IRRI is developing such varieties. Wetlands require assistance in planting varieties that are flood resistant as well as additional maintenance of dikes and paddy buns to contain and redirect irrigation water.

8.4 Migration as a Strategy for the Chronically Poor

Out migration is a viable strategy for the chronically poor but only if they can afford the cost of moving to a new location and are able to find work. We outlined the impediments and benefits of an internal migration strategy in Chapter 4 and also pointed out that income constraints and limit international migration of the chronically poor. Internal migration presents a different story. It was noted that for the chronically poor with little education migration of a family member can be the most significant force to lift the family above the poverty line. Steady remittance not only allow poor families to save and build a capital base but also serves as a cushion against income shocks that force borrowing from landlords and loan sharks. Large families with a few men in the work force have often received a sustained increase in income from internal migration and the extent of this migration is extensive, particularly in the poorest regions of China and India. Successful migration by one family member can also serve as motivation for further migration by other family members.

For these reasons public policy should encourage rural to urban migration and also international migration from rural areas. Urban areas that are swelling with new migrants and urban slums are growing rapidly although policy makers who live in these cities have been averse to providing incentives to migrate. They have even suggested policies to slow the trend toward further urbanization. The Chinese policies requiring proof of residence to receive state subsidies is a good example of such a policy.

We believe that such policies should be reviewed and greater labor market flexibility encouraged. Greater migration to urban areas from the poorer rural regions provides an opportunity to reverse the trend toward unequal regional income imbalances and growing social tensions between the urban elites and the countryside. Resources should be provided by the central government to key destination cities to deal with the increases in social services that new immigrants require. Higher taxes and user fees for public utilities in cities could be used to finance the required capital spending.

Instead of discouraging immigration additional resources should be devoted to recruiting qualified workers from rural areas, particularly poor by-passed and tribal areas. New communications modalities created by the increased availability of information technology can be harnessed to achieve this objective by looking at new ways to spread information about available job opportunities in the cities to rural villages. This could include internet job fairs and recruiting visits from large industrial firms located in nearby urban locations.

8.5 Creation of Assets for the Chronically Poor

It has been noted that the poor have few personal assets to absorb shocks in their lives. In this context it is important to understand the dynamics of chronic poverty and to recognize that a crippling illness, a poor crop or some other disaster can be overcome only by having a cushion of assets to rely on. Without such a shield to protect them the chronically poor are often forced to seek short term solutions such as sending children to work or borrowing from landlords and money lenders. This undermines their long term chances for breaking out of the poverty trap. In addition to providing social safety nets, work fare and conditional cash transfers to help with education and health of their children, it is important to recognize the importance of building up individual and collective assets such as better roads, irrigation network, fertilizers, livestock, farm equipment, clean water and sanitation and better schools and health facilities. These assets will provide the capital and wherewithal for poor residents to earn more money and will also serve to smooth out variations in income that arise from poor harvests, droughts, floods and other disasters. Such support not only provides the opportunity to break the poverty trap but also gives these poor families the hope of a better life for themselves and their children. Writing about the plight of the poor in Europe in the 18th century, one of the world's leading authorities on income distribution and poverty has written as a comment on the current global crisis in Europe:

> When reading accounts of life in OECD countries a 100 or more years ago, one cannot but be struck by the difference between the insecurity of the poor compared with the security of the rich. (Atkinson, 2008).

And speaking of the current predicament in industrial countries:

> On what resources can they draw in the event of job loss? How exposed are their retirement savings? Politicians talk about confidence. This is not just a matter of the Dow Jones or the FTSE, but of the very real concerns of households for their future and that of their children and grandchildren. (Atkinson, 2008).

The concerns of all citizens in all countries are the same. This is why it is important to protect the rights and the livelihoods of the poorest in every global location whether it is a well to do country or one which is not so well to do. Security is important for us all.

8.6 Discrimination and Gender Empowerment

Discrimination has a devastating effect on living standards and opportunities for the chronically poor. Minorities have lower levels of education and health, receive lower pay for similar work and discrimination forces them into low paying jobs. Women are subject to discrimination at work and at home, where girls' nutrition is lower than boys' and their infant mortality rates are higher. These forces of discrimination can be fought thru legal means, by greater political representation and by reforms that give the poor more access to financial markets, education, health and better jobs. In some countries bonded labor has been outlawed but still persists. In others, outright discrimination against minorities is still being practiced in the provision of health care, in the educational systems and by employers. Where women have been empowered at the local level there are been significant improvements in welfare of families and children. For example when women in India hold positions of authority in local villages more investment in clean drinking water as well as higher rates of immunization and closing of the gender gap in schooling have been observed (see Beaman *et al.*, 2007).

More needs to be done; money is not enough. Unless those who discriminate realize that in continuing these discriminatory practices they are imposing a high cost to society and, in the long run, to their own welfare, discrimination can not effectively be eliminated. Continued discrimination runs the risk of creating a society of haves and have nots which is not sustainable in the long run. Discrimination creates a toxic social fabric that can contribute to intensified tension, disruption and riots. It eventually undermines the economic, political and social viability of the country and contributes to the overthrow of entrenched regimes. The volatile political situation in Thailand, the turmoil surrounding the end of the Marcos era in the Philippines and of Suharto's rule in Indonesia are examples of how an entrenched elite aggrandized their own positions, discriminated widely against their opponents and neglected the poor.

Required changes include vigorous enforcement of antidiscrimination laws already on the books. These include labor market discrimination, illegal contracts that force workers and their children to continue working for the same employer to whom they are in debt and denial of legal rights. New financial instruments and institutions have to be forged to address the financial needs of minorities and other chronically poor groups. Without recourse to borrowed funds at affordable rates, these groups will continue to be at risk of further indebtedness. In order to meet these financial challenges, efforts by lenders like the Grameen Bank have to be extended to families with fewer resources. These financial initiatives can be reinforced with broader social security programs such as the dollar a day supplement to the chronically poor suggested above and possibly combined with programs to increase the stock of physical assets. Active involvement by the poor and their advocates can also serve to mobilize public awareness, increase opportunities and give the poor more control over their destinies (see Green, 2008 for additional ideas for mobilizing resources to empower the poor).

8.7 Chronic Poverty and the Global Financial Crisis

As this draft is being written the global financial crisis continues to deepen. In the United States stock market averages continue to decline. The Dow Jones has fallen more than 40 percent in the past year to the end of October 2008 and 23 percent in the month of October alone. Asian markets have fallen even further. Output, employment and international trade have been affected across the board in industrial and developing countries alike. Some economists predict that unemployment in the US could reach 10 percent by the fall of 2009, the highest level in over 25 years.

While Asian banks have limited exposure to the toxic mortgage assets that have undermined confidence in industrial countries, slower growth in the USA and Europe are expected to take a toll on growth in developing economies of Asia. For example at the end of October 2008 the central banks of Korea lowered its key lending rates as their stock market indices have retreated further.

In addition to sagging exports, financial flow in the form of development assistance, foreign direct investment and portfolio placements are also expected to decline. Despite these difficulties, analysis by the Asian Development Bank and the International Monetary Fund in September 2008 (Asian Development Bank, 2008b and International Monetary Fund, 2008) suggests that the impact of the global financial crisis would be broadly limited to a decline in import demand by industrial countries for Asian manufactured goods along with a diminution in the flow official lending and private capital inflows. In Asia this would be reflected by sagging exports and industrial production and an increase in unemployment. There is also likely to be further softening of aggregate economic activity.

The Asian Development Outlook Update (2008) notes that the slowdown in the import demand of the US, Europe and Japan is particularly acute for clothing, footwear and computers. A continuation of this trend is predicted and is likely to result in a decline in the volume of world trade as well as in intraregional trade in intermediate parts and components. The IMF does not believe that this slowdown in Asia will be as severe as the 2001/2002 recession and certainly not as severe as the financial crisis of 1997/98 which took a much larger toll on economic growth (see Table 2.26 for comparisons in the five countries that were most adversely affected by the Asian financial crisis). If the fallout from the ongoing global financial crisis is of similar magnitude to the Asian crisis, then poverty and chronic poverty in Asia will escalate sharply. As was pointed out in Chapter 2, the poorly educated are likely to be most vulnerable.

It is anticipated by some observers that the recession will have a more modest impact on Asia. Even the most pessimistic projections of global growth by the IMF still show expected global growth of 3 percent and a 70 percent confidence interval of growth between 2 percent and 4 percent. Furthermore the Asian Development Bank has GDP growth forecasts for 2008 and 2009 which are not much below growth the previous two years (see Table 8.4). While this is not business as usual it does not reflect a serious downgrading of

Table 8.4 Projected Macroeconomic GDP Growth in Selected Asian Economies

Country	2006	2007	2008	2009 ADB
China	11.7	11.9	10.0	7.0
Indonesia	5.5	6.3	6.2	3.6
Philippines	5.4	7.2	4.5	2.5
India	9.6	9.0	7.4	5.0
Bangladesh	6.6	6.4	6.2	5.6
Nepal	4.1	2.6	5.6	5.6
Pakistan	5.8	6.8	5.8	2.8
Sri Lanka	7.7	6.8	6.0	4.5
Cambodia	10.8	10.2	6.5	2.5
Laos	8.3	7.9	7.5	5.5
Vietnam	8.2	8.5	6.5	4.5

Source: Asian Development (2008b, Table A1).

growth prospects in 2008 and 2009. And if growth is not going to be that much slower then other macroeconomic variables including unemployment, tax revenues and spending on poverty reduction are also not likely to be seriously threatened.

Nevertheless there is a chance that the global downturn will be more serious than the ADB and IMF anticipated in their September 2008 reports as the recession has begun to deepen more sharply in the United States at the end of 2008. At the beginning of November 2008 the IMF further lowered its forecast for global economic growth from 3 percent to 2.2 percent and it noted that

> Prospects for global growth have deteriorated over the past month as financial sector deleveraging has continued and producer and consumer confidence have fallen. (AFP press release on 2 November 2008).

The IMF went on to predict that nearly all advanced economies would contract including the US by 0.7 percent, Japan by 0.2 percent, the Eurozone by 0.5 percent and the UK by 1.3 percent. As a result the advanced economies will shrink by 0.3 percent in 2009 compared with a forecast of growth of 0.5 percent in October 2008. This would be the first time since World War II that GDP in the advanced economies would decline. It went on to say that

> Markets have entered a vicious cycle of asset deleveraging price declines and investor redemptions and that as the financial crisis has become more entrenched, households and firms are increasingly anticipating a prolonged period of poor prospects for jobs and profits. (AFP press release on November 2 2008).

The IMF did note that Asia would remain relatively robust although less so than forecast a month ago. It now forecasts China's growth at 8.5 percent and ASEAN at 4.2 percent in 2009. It said that developing countries that are heavily dependent on exports and in need of foreign credit would be affected the most. Among the Asian economies Malaysia, Taiwan and China are likely to be hit the hardest.

Euroframe, a forecast group in Europe (see www.euroframe.org) predict even slower growth for China than the IMF. In 2009 and 2010 growth is projected to slow to 7.6 and 7.1 percent respectively and Taiwan is already in recession. The countries with large pockets of the chronically poor are less likely to be hard hit. Because their exposure to international trade is not as large as countries in Southeast Asia and East Asia, India, Bangladesh and Pakistan are not likely to be experience an export slump that could radiate through the rest of the economy. Furthermore, Indonesia is also less dependent on exports than Malaysia and Thailand.

If the revised forecasts of the IMF and other international organizations turn out to be true then the likely negative impact on international trade both intraregionally and on industrial countries will be much stronger than anticipated. The chronically poor in rural areas will be adversely affected and there will be fewer resources available for essential poverty reduction programs and social programs. Return migration to rural towns from city residents who have lost their jobs will also increase the burden on the resources of the chronically rural poor as well as other rural residents. Remittances from international migrants will also be adversely affected by the global slowdown. The Philippines is likely to be heavily impacted.

Governments need to prepare further for this contingency by setting aside some funds to protect the poor should this negative scenario materialize. They also need to adopt appropriate countercyclical macroeconomic policies to compensate for the slowdown in exports. Governments also need to be ready to provide resources to protect the chronically poor from further deterioration in their living standards. In our view a deeper recession scenario becomes more probable every day the global crisis persists and the possibility of further contagion spreading to stock markets and banking systems in Asia increases.

On the positive side, even if the recession in industrial countries does deepen, developing Asia is now generally much better positioned to withstand this external shock than it was during the Asian financial crisis of a decade ago. International reserves have been built up, economic growth has accelerated in many countries, and financial systems have been restructured. Furthermore lower oil prices should have a beneficial impact on the external balance of the regions oil importers — basically the entire region with the exception of Indonesia and Malaysia. China has also taken steps to shore up its economy by announcing a US$586 billion infrastructure investment program to be implemented over 2009 and 2010 (about 6 percent of GDP where GDP is measured by purchasing power parity and much more using the exchange rate method). The projects will include low income housing, electricity, water, rural infrastructure, environmental protection and technological innovation. This package is intended to shore up consumer confidence as well as to provide jobs and additional spending to offset the anticipated slowdown in exports. China can well afford such a large stimulus package since government debt is less than 20 percent of GDP. A similar though smaller package was implemented following the 1997 Asian financial crisis. By comparison this package is slightly larger than the $700 billion financial sector bailout in the United States when measured as a percent of income. The US bailout package is about 5 percent of GDP.

Malaysia, South Korea and Thailand have already announced stimulus packages and Singapore will probably announce a package soon. However there are still large budgets deficits in several countries

Table 8.5 Economic Growth, International Reserves and Government Deficits for Asian Economies

Country	International Reserves $million 2007	Central Government Budget Balance as Percent of GDP 2007 (2003)	Average GDP Growth 2003/2004 in Percent	Average GDP Growth 2006/2007 in Percent	Current Account Surplus/ Deficit as a Percent of GDP 2007
China	1,540,000	0.7 (–2.2)	10.0	11.3	11.3
Indonesia	56,920	–1.2 (–1.7)	4.9	5.9	2.4
Philippines	33,754	–0.2 (–4.6)	5.6	6.4	4.4
India	306,488	–5.5 (–8.5)	8.0	9.2	–1.5
Bangladesh	5,077	–3.2 (–3.4)	5.8	6.6	1.4
Nepal	2,401	–2.0 (–1.4)	4.1	2.7	–0.1
Pakistan	13,345	–5.8 (–3.6)	6.1	6.8	–4.8
Sri Lanka	3,100	–7.7 (–7.8)	5.6	7.2	–4.2
Cambodia	1,621	–3.2 (–6.7)	9.2	10.2	–7.8
Laos	530	–3.1 (–7.9)	6.3	8.1	–18.6
Vietnam	19,931	–4.9 (–4.8)	7.5	8.3	–8.0

Source: Asian Development Bank (2008c).

although they have come down in several countries including China, India, Philippines, Cambodia and Laos. Current account deficits are still large, particularly in parts of South Asia (Pakistan and Sri Lanka) and in the Mekong countries (see Table 8.5) and financial inflows from private sources are likely to dry up. The Institute of International Finance expects a 30 percent decline in global private capital flows to developing countries compared with 2007 (see Economist, 2008a). Despite potential weak spots, recent strong economic growth in South Asia and the Mekong countries is noteworthy; particularly considering that twenty five years ago they were still emerging from the shadow of the Vietnamese war. They are now among the fastest growing countries in the developing world and this should hold them in good stead as they deal with the global slowdown in the coming months. In India export dependence is much lower than in China and Southeast Asia. However it has other difficulties in financing its investments because of weak local equity markets and lacking willingness of overseas lenders to invest. It already has high debt to GDP ratio which constrains its options to provide further fiscal stimulus.

As the global crisis has intensified assistance is being offered by donors. The IMF has recently approved a loan of $7.6 billion to Pakistan to rebuild its economy and expand its safety net for the poor and it is not unlikely that similar requests will be made from Cambodia and Laos. In late October 2008 the IMF also said it will create a Short-term Liquidity Facility (SLF) that comes with no conditions attached and offers large upfront financing to help countries restore confidence and combat financial contagion.

8.8 Medium Term Prospects for Reducing Chronic Poverty

Bauer *et al.* (2008) have made some projection for reducing chronic poverty based on three alternative scenarios — a baseline business as usual, pro-poor and pro-rich alternative policy frameworks. Pro-poor policies stress more equitable distribution of income and policies that address the problems of the poor. Under this scenario South Asia[29] can reduce poverty from 42.5 percent in 2005 to around 16 percent by 2015. Southeast Asia which includes the Mekong countries goes from 18.8 percent to 7.3 percent and China (and Mongolia) from 15.9 percent to 2.6 percent.

Even if the scenario presented above in Section 8.1 using a US$1 a day assumption is not fully realized it seems plausible that these benchmarks proposed by Bauer *et al.* (2008) can be attained if there is a continued commitment to reduce poverty. If governments neglect the poor and pursue pro-rich policies, work in reducing poverty will make much less progress relative to the 2005 baseline. For the Asia and Pacific region as a whole, Bauer *et al.* (2008) project that poverty will fall from around 900 million in 2005 to 500 million by 2015 rather than to 342 million if pro-poor policies are adopted.

[29] This excludes Pakistan which is included in West and Central Asia in this exercise.

160 million fewer people will be raised out of poverty if pro-rich policies were adopted.

While Bauer *et al.* did not directly address the status of the chronically poor; we can infer that a similar undesirable outcome will result if pro-poor policies are not generally adopted. The Bauer *et al.* scenarios are constructed to measure the impact of policies on poverty after the impact of growth on poverty has already been accounted for. While more rapid economic growth works to reduce poverty through raising incomes for everyone, pro-poor policies have additional beneficial effects on the poor and chronically poor.

Bibliography

Abbott, DA, S Sharma and S Verman (2004). The emotional environment of families experiencing chronic poverty in India. *Journal of Family and Economic Issues*, 25(3), 387–409.

ACC/SNN (2000). United Nations Administrative Committee on Coordination's Sub Committee of Nutrition and IFPRI (International Food Policy Research Institute) 4th Report on the world nutrition situation: Nutrition throughout the life cycle. Geneva: ADD/SCN, IFPRI.

Adams, RH and J He (1995). *Sources of Income Inequality and Poverty in Rural Pakistan*. Washington, DC: International Food Policy Research Institute.

Adams Jr, RH and J Page (2005). Do international migration and remittances reduce poverty in developing countries? *World Development*, 33(10), 1645–1669.

Adato, M and L Haddad (2002). Targeting poverty through community-based public works programs: Experiences from South Africa. *Journal of Development Studies*, 38(3), 1–36.

Adhikari, P. Rural Electrification in Nepal: Cooperative Concepts in Rural Electrification. http://www.smecc.org/rural_electrification_in_nepal.htm (accessed 19 May 2008).

AFD, BMZ, DFID and World Bank (2005). *Pro-Poor Growth in the 1990s: Lessons and Insights from 14 Countries*. Washington, DC: International Bank for Reconstruction and Development & World Bank.

Aghion, C and J Stachurski (2005). Poverty traps. In *Handbook of Economic Growth*, eds. Aghion P and S Durlauf. Amsterdam: Elsevier.

Ahmed, AU and C Ninno (2002). Food for education program in Bangladesh: An evaluation of its impact on educational attainment and food security. *Food Consumption and Nutrition Division*, Discussion paper no. 138. Washington DC: IFPRI.

Ahmed, AU, AR Quisumbing, JF Hoddinott, M Nasreen, E Bryan and the Data Analysis and Technical Assistance Limited (2007). *Relative Efficiency of Food and Cash Transfers in Improving Food Security and Livelihoods of the Ultra-Poor in Bangladesh*. Washington DC: IFPRI.

Ahmed, R and JW Mellor (1988). Agricultural price policy: The context and the approach. In *Agricultural Price Policy for Developing Countries*, eds. Mellor, JW and R Ahmed. Baltimore: Johns Hopkins Press.

Ahmed, R and M Hossain (1990). *Development Impact of Rural Infrastructure in Bangladesh*. Washington, DC: International Food Policy Research Center (IFPRI).

Ahmed, N (2006). Bangladesh Institute of Development Studies (BIDS), Ad hoc Expert Meeting in preparation for the Mid-Term Review of the Programme of Action for the Least Developed Countries for the Decade 2001–2010, Geneva, 29–30 May 2006.

Ahuja, V and D Filmer (1996). Educational attainment in developing countries: New estimates and projections disaggregated by gender. *Journal of Educational Planning and Administration*, 3(4), 229–254.

Akter, S (2005). Occupational segregation, wage discrimination and impact on poverty in rural Bangladesh. *Journal of Developing Areas*, 39(1), 16–38.

Alatas, V and L Cameron (2003). The impact of minimum wages on employment in a low income country: An evaluation using the difference-in-differences approach. *World Bank Policy Research Working Paper* 2985. Washington DC: World Bank.

Albert, JRG (2007). Household Vulnerability to Income Poverty. *PIDS No.* 2007–05. Philippine Institute for Development Studies (PIDS).

Alderman, H (1996). Saving and economic shocks in Pakistan. *Journal of Development Economics*, 51(2), 343–365.

Alderman, H (2002). Subsidies as a social safety net: Effectiveness and challenges. *Social Protection Discussion Paper*, Series No. 0224. Washington DC: World Bank, Social Protection Unit.

Alderman, H and JV Braun (1984). The effects of the Egyptian food ration and subsidy system on income distribution and consumption. *IFPRI Report* 45. Washington, DC: International Food Policy Research Institute.

Alderman, H, JR Behrman, DR Ross and R Sabot (1996). Decomposing the gender gap in cognitive skills in a poor rural economy. *The Journal of Human Resources*, 31(1), 229–254.

Alisjahbana, A and AA Yusuf (2003). Poverty dynamics in Indonesia: Panel data evidence. Working Paper in *Economics and Development* studies no. 200303. Center for Economics and Development Studies, Department of Economics, Padjadjaran University.

Alston, JM, C Chan-Kang, MC Marra, PG Pardey and TJ Wyatt (2000). *A Meta-Analysis of Rates of Return to Agricultural R&D: Ex Pede Herculem?* Washington, DC: International Food Policy Research Institute (IFPRI).

Anderson, JR and G Feder (2004). Agricultural extension: Good intentions and hard realities. *World Bank Research Observer*, 19(1), 41–60.

Arif, GM and M Ahmad (2001). Poverty Across the Agro-climatic Zones in Rural Pakistan. Paper presented at the National Workshop on Pro-poor Intervention Strategies in Irrigated Agriculture in Asia. Pakistan: International Water Management Institute, Lahore, March 12.

Ariyabandu, MM (2000). Impacts of hazards on women and children situation in South Asia. In *Reaching Women and Children In Disasters*. Laboratory of Social and Behavioral Research, Florida International University.

Arsenic Poisoning in Bangladesh/India. www.sos-arsenic.net [18 March 2007].

Arya, S (1989). Infant nutrition and mother-child dyad. *Indian Journal of Clinical Psychology*, 16, 34–40.

Asian Development Bank (ADB) (2000). Report and Recommendation of the President to the Board of Directors on a Proposed Loan to the Lao People's Democratic Republic for the Primary Health Care Expansion Project. Manila: ADB.

Asian Development Bank (ADB) (2001). *Social Protection in Asia and the Pacific.* Manila: ADB.

Asian Development Bank (ADB) (2002). *Poverty in Pakistan: Issues, Causes, and Institutional Responses.* Islamabad, Pakistan: ADB.

Asian Development Bank (ADB) (2005). *Poverty in the Philippines: Income, Assets and Access.* Manila: ADB.

Asian Development Bank (ADB) (2006). *From Poverty to Prosperity A Country Poverty Analysis for Indonesia.* Manila: ADB.

Asian Development Bank (ADB) (2006a). *Social Protection in Asia and the Pacific.* Manila: ADB.

Asian Development Bank (ADB) (2006b). *Asian Development Outlook* 2006. Manila: ADB.

Asian Development Bank (ADB). *Asian Development Outlook* (2009). Manila: ADB.

Asian Development Bank (ADB) (2006c). *Background Paper 1. Poverty, Economic Growth and Inequality: A Review of Pakistan's Poverty Literature.* Pakistan Poverty Assessment Update. Islamabad, Pakistan: ADB.

Asian Development Bank (ADB) (2006d). *Lao People's Democratic Republic 2007–2010.* Country Strategy and Program. Manila: ADB.

Asian Development Bank (ADB) (2007). Bridging the Digital Divide to Fight Rural Poverty. ADB Operational Report. http://www.adb.org/Documents/Periodicals/NPRS-PRF/newsletter/documents/Feature-Bridging-Digital.pdf [5 April 2008].

Asian Development Bank (ADB) (2007a). *Philippines: Critical Development Constraints.* Manila: ADB.

Asian Development Bank (ADB) (2008). *Asian Development Outlook.* Manila: ADB.

Asian Development Bank (ADB) (2008a). *Impact Stories: Philippines.* Manila: ADB.

Asian Development Bank (ADB) (2008b). Nepal 2005–2009. *Country Partnership Strategy Mid-term Review.* Manila: ADB.

Asian Development Bank (ADB) (2008c). Poverty Estimates and Projections for 1990, 2005, and 2020 for Selected DMCs (including PRC and India). Mimeo paper. Manila: ADB.

Asian Development Bank (ADB) (2008d). Lao People's Democratic Republic: Alternative Livelihood for Upland Ethnic Groups in Houaphanh Province. ADB Project Number: 41096. Manila: ADB.

Asian Development Bank (ADB) (2008d). Social Protection Index for Committed Poverty Reduction Volume 2: Asia. Manila: ADB.

Asian Development Bank (ADB) (2008e). *Asian Development Outlook Update.* Manila: ADB.

Asian Development Bank (ADB) (2008f). Country Partnership Strategy: Sri Lanka 2009–2011. Washington DC: World Bank.

Asian Development Bank and World Bank (2005). *Sri Lanka-Improving the Rural and Urban Investment Climate.* Colombo: World Bank Colombo Office.

Asra, A (2000). Poverty and Inequality in Indonesia. *Journal of Asia Pacific Economy,* 5(1/2) 2000, 91–111.

Athukorala, P (2005). The Indian Ocean Tsunami: Economic Impact and Disaster Management and Lessons. *Asian Economic Papers,* Winter, 1–18.

Atkinson, AB (2008). Unequal growth, Unequal recession. *OECD Observer,* 270/271.

Azariadis, C and J Stachurski (2006). Poverty traps. In *Handbook of Economic Growth Volume 1A,* eds. Aghion P and SN Durlauf. Amsterdam: North Holland Publishing.

Baulch, B and E Masset (2003). Do Monetary and Non Monetary Indicators tell the same story about Chronic Poverty? A Study of Vietnam in the 1990s. *World Development,* 31(3), 441–454.

Badal, R (2005). Social Security System in Nepal. Paper presented in *Social security Seminar* in Beijing, November.

Balisacan, AM (2003). Poverty comparisons in the Philippines: Is what we know about the poor robust? In *Reducing Poverty in Asia: Emerging Issues in Growth, Targeting and Measurement,* ed. Edmonds C. Cheltenham, UK: Edward Elgar.

Balisacan, AM (2007). Why Does Poverty Persist in the Philippines? Facts, Fancies and Policies. *Southeast Asian Regional Cener for Graduate Study and Research in Agriculture,* Discussion Paper 2007–1.

Balisacan, AM (2007b). *An Analysis of Chronic Poverty in the Philippines.* University of the Philippines, Diliman, Quezon City.

Balisacan, AM and N Fuwa (2004). Going beyond cross-country averages: Growth, inequality and poverty reduction in the Philippines. *World Development,* 32(11), 1891–907.

Balisacan, A and J Tubianosa (2004). *The Population-Poverty Nexus: The Philippines in Comparative East Asian Context.* Quezon City: Asia Pacific Policy Center/Philippine Center for Population and Development.

Banerjee, AV, R Benabou and D Mookherjee eds. (2006). *Understanding Poverty.* UK: Oxford University Press.

Banerjee, AV and M Ghatak (1996). Empowerment and efficiency: The economics of tenancy reform. Mimeo. MIT and University of Chicago.

Banerjee, AV, PJ Gertler and M Ghatak (2002). Empowerment and efficiency: Tenancy reform in West Bengal. The Journal of Political Economy, 110(2), 239–280.

Banerjee, L (2007). Flood disasters and agricultural wages in Bangladesh. *Development and Change,* 38(4), 641–64.

Bangladesh Department of Agricultural Extension (1999). Agricultural Extension Manual Department of Agricultural Extension Dacca. Bangladesh.

Basu, K (1999). Child Labor: Causes, Consequences and Cure: With remarks on International Labor Standards. *Journal of Economic Literature,* 37(3), 1083–1119.

Basu, K and KH Van (1998). The Economics of Child Labor. *American Economic Review,* 88(3), 412–427.

Bardan, PK (1974). On Life and Death Questions. *Economic and Political Weekly* 9, 32–34 (August), 1293–1304.

Bardan, PK (1982). Little Girls and Death in India. *Economic and Political Weekly* 17, 36(September), 1448–1450.

Bardan, PK (1984). *Land, Labor and Rural Poverty.* Delhi: Oxford University Press.

Barrientos, A (2007). Does Vulnerability Create Poverty Traps? *Chronic Poverty Research Center,* Working paper 76. Manchester, UK: CPRC.

Barrientos, A and D Hulme, eds. (2008). *Social Protection for the Poor and the Poorest: Concepts, Policies and Politics.* Hampshire, UK: Palgrave Macmillan.

Barro, R and X Sala-i-Martin (1995). *Economic Growth.* New York: Mc Graw Hill.

Barro, RJ (1991). Economic Growth in a Cross Section of Countries. NBER Working Papers 3120. National Bureau of Economic Research, Inc.

Bauer, A, R Hasan, R Magsombol and G Wan (2008). *The World Bank's New Poverty Data: Implications for the Asian Development Bank. ADB Sustainable Development,* Working Paper Series No. 2. Manila: ADB.

Baulch, B and J Hoddinott (2001). Simulating the Impact of Policy Upon Chronic and Transitory Poverty in Rural Pakistan. In *Economic Mobility and Poverty Dynamics in Developing Countries,* eds. Baulch B and J Hoddinott. London: Frank Cass.

Baulch, B, J Wood and A Weber (2006). Developing a Social Protection Index for Asia. *Development Policy Review* 24(1), 5–29.

Beah, I (2007). *A Long Way Gone Memoirs of a Boy Soldier.* New York: Sarah Crichton Books, Farrar, Straus and Giroux.

Beaman, L, E Duflo, R Pande and P Topalova (2006). Women politicians, gender bias, and policy-making in rural India. Background Paper for The State of the World's Children 2007. United Nations, New York: UNESCO.

Bechstedt, HD, V Gilbos and O Souksavat (2007). Impact of Public Expenditures on Ethnic groups and Women — Lao PDR, Phase 2. Poverty and Social Impact Assessment (PSIA) Final Report Part 1.

Behrman, JR and J Knowles (1999). Household Income and Child Schooling in Vietnam. *World Bank Economic Review* 13(2), 211–256.

Benjamin, D, L Brandt and J Giles (2005). The Evolution of Income Inequality in Rural China. *Economic Development and Cultural Change,* 53(4), 769–824.

Beresford, M, N Sokha, R Roy, S Sisovanna and C Namazie (2004). *The Macroeconomics of Poverty Reduction in Cambodia.* Kathmandu: UNDP, Asia-Pacific Regional Programme on the Macroeconomics of Poverty Reduction.

Berg, A and A Krueger (2002). Lifting All Boats: Why Openness Helps Curb Poverty. *Finance and Development,* 39(3).

Besley, T and R Burgess (1998). Land Reform, Poverty Reduction and Growth: Evidence from India. *Development Economics,* Discussion Paper Series No. 13.

Sutory and Toyota International Centers for Economics and Related Disciplines, London School of Economics.

Besley, T and R Burgess (2003). Halving Global Poverty. *Journal of Economic Perspectives,* 17(3), 3–22.

Besley, T and LJ Cord, eds. (2008). *Delivering on the Promise of Pro-Poor Growth: Insights and Lessons from Country Experiences.* Palgrave Macmillan and the World Bank.

Bhatta, SD and SK Sharma (2006). The determinants and consequences of chronic and transient poverty in Nepal. *CPRC Working Paper* 66. Manchester. UK: CPRC.

Bhide, S and AK Mehta (2004). Chronic Poverty in Rural India: Issues and Findings from Panel Data. *Journal of Human Development,* 5(2), July.

Bhuiya, A and K Streatsfield (1991). Mothers' Education and Survival of Female Children in a Rural Area of Bangladesh. Population Studies, 45(2), 253–264.

Bihar Times (2007). September 7.

Binswanger, H, K Dillinger, G Feder (1988). Power Distortions, Revolt and Reform in Agricultural Land Reforms. In *Handbook of Development Economics,* eds. Behrman J and T Srinivasan. North Holland: Amsterdam.

Binswanger, H and S Khandker (1993). How infrastructure and financial institutions affect agricultural output and investment in India. *Journal of Development Economics,* 41(2), 337–366.

Binswanger, H, S Kandker and M Rosenzweig (1989). How Infrastructure and Financial Institutions Affect Agricultural Output and Investment in India. *World Bank Working Paper* No. 163. Washington, DC: World Bank.

Bird, K, A McKay and I Shinyekwa (2007). Isolation and Poverty: The Relationship Between Spatially Differentiated Access to Goods and Services and Poverty. Paper prepared for the *CPRC International Workshop Understanding and Addressing Spatial Poverty Traps,* 29 March 2007. Stellenbosch, South Africa.

Bird, K (2009). 'Voluntary' Migration in Lao People's Democratic Republic. Policy Brief No 3. Prepared for the *World Development Report 2009.* Overseas Development Institute.

Birner, R and J Anderson (2007). How to make agricultural extension demand driven: The case of India's agricultural extension policy. *IFPRI Discussion Paper* 00729.

Bloom, DE, D Canning and PN Malaney (1999). Demographic change and economic growth in Asia. *Center for International Development Working Paper* 15. Harvard University.

Bolwell, D and W Weinz (2008). *Reducing Poverty through Tourism.* Working Paper No. 266. Geneva: International Labour Office.

Borooah, VK, B Gustafsson and L Shi (2006). China and India: Income inequality and poverty north and south of the Himalayas. *Journal of Asian Economics* 17, 797–817.

Borooh, VK (2005). Caste, Inequality and Poverty in India. *Review of Development Economics*, 9(3), 399–414.

Boserup, E (1989). *Women's Role in Economic Development*. London: Earthscan.

Bowles, S and H Gintis (2002). Social Capital and Community Governance. *Economic Journal*, 112(483), F419–F436.

Brown, W and C Churchill (2000). Providing Insurance to Low-Income Households. Part 1: A Primer on Insurance Principles and Products. Microenterprise Best Practices Project. Bethesda, MD: DAI/USAID. www.mip.org. [20 May 2008].

BPS-Statistics Indonesia, Bappenas and UNDP Indonesia. 2004. *Indonesia Human Development Report 2004: The Economics of Democracy: Financing Human Development in Indonesia*. Indonesia: BPS-Statistics Indonesia.

Bradsher, K and A Martin (2008). World's Poor Pay Price as Crop Research is Cut. *New York Times*, 18 May.

Bramall, C (2001). The Quality of China's Household Income Surveys. *China Quarterly*, 167 (September), 689–705.

Caldes, N, D Coady and JA Maluccio (2004). The Cost of Poverty Alleviation Transfer Programs: A Comparative Analysis of Three Programs in Latin America. Food Consumption and Nutrition, FCND Discussion Paper 172. Washington, DC: IFPRI.

Caldwell, JC (1976). Toward a Restatement of Demographic Transition Theory. *Population and Development Review*, 2(3/4), 321–366.

Caldwell, JC (1977). The economic rationality of high fertility: An investigation illustrated with Nigerian survey data. *Population Studies*, 31(I), 5–28.

Caldwell, JC (1978). A theory of fertility: From high plateau to destabilisation. *Population and Development Review*, 4(4), 553–578.

Calvo, C and S Dercon (2005). Measuring Individual Vulnerability. Department of Economics Discussion Paper Series, No. 229. Oxford University.

Cambodia Development Resource Institute (CDRI) (2007a). *We are Living with Worry all the Time. A Participatory Poverty Assessment of the Tonle Sap*. Ed. Ballard, B., Phnom Penh. April 2007.

Cambodia Development Resource Institute (CDRI) (2007b). *Moving out of Poverty Study*. Moving Out of Poverty: Trends in Community Well-being and Household Mobility in Nine Cambodian Villages. Cambodia Development Resource Institute. Phnom Penh.

Campen, BV, D Guidi and G Best (2000). *Solar Photovoltaics for Sustainable Agriculture and Rural Development*. Rome: FAO.

Capistrano, LO and MLC Maria (2007). The Impact of International Labor Migration and OFW Remittances on Poverty in the Philippines. Mimeo paper. Quezon City: School of Economics, University of the Philippines.

Card, D and A Krueger (1995). *Myth and Measurement: The Economics of the Minimum Wage*. Princeton, NJ: Princeton University Press.

Cardoso, E (1992). Inflation and Poverty. *NBER Working Paper* 4006. National Bureau of Economic Research, Cambridge Mass.

Centre for Science and Environment (2008). NREGA: Opportunities and Challenges. http://www.cseindia.org/programme/nrml/pdf/NREGA_Policy_Paper_2008.pdf [15 May 2008]

Chamberlain, J and P Phomsombath (2002). *Poverty Alleviation for All: Potentials and Options for People in the Uplands.* Sida mimeo. Vientiane.

Chambers, R, NC Saxena and T Shah (1989). To the Hands of the Poor: Water and Trees. London, UK: Intermediate Technology Publications.

Chan, KW and W Buckingham (2008). Is China Abolishing the Hukou System? *China Quarterly*, 195, 582–606.

Chaudhuri, S, J Jalan and A Suryahadi (2002). Assessing Household Vulnerability to Poverty from Cross-sectional Data: A Methodology and Estimates from Indonesia. Columbia University Department of Economics Discussion Paper Series, Discussion Paper 0102–52.

Chaudhury, N and JS Hamer (2004). Ghost Doctors: Absenteeism in Rural Bangladeshi Health Facilities. *World Bank Economic Review*, 18(3), 423–442.

Chen, S and Y Wang (2001). China's Growth and Poverty Reduction: Recent Trends between 1990 and 1999. *World Bank Policy Research Working Paper* 2651. Washington, DC: World Bank.

Chen, S and M Ravallion (2008). China is poorer than we thought, but no less successful in the fight against poverty. *Policy Research Working Paper 4621.* Washington DC: World Bank.

Chronic Poverty Research Center (CPRC) (2000). *Understanding Chronic Poverty in South Asia.* Chronic Poverty Research Center, University of Manchester.

Chronic Poverty Research Center (CPRC) (2003). *Chronic Poverty Report for 2003 — Understanding Chronic Poverty in South Asia.* Chronic Poverty Research Center, University of Manchester.

Chronic Poverty Research Center (CPRC) (2004). *The Chronic Poverty Report 2004–05.* Chronic Poverty Research Centre, University of Manchester.

Chronic Poverty Research Center (CPRC) (2007). Chronic Poverty in India: Policy Responses. Policy Brief March 2007 No. 4. Chronic Poverty Research Centre, University of Manchester.

Chronic Poverty Research Center (CPRC) (2008). *The Chronic Poverty Report 2008–09.* Chronic Poverty Research Centre, University of Manchester.

Chung, W and MD Gupta (2007). Why is Son's Preference Declining in Korea. *World Bank Policy Research Working Paper* 4373. Washington DC: World Bank.

CIA Factbook (2008). https://www.cia.gov/library/publications/the-world-factbook/geos/pk.html [19 August 2008].

Coady, D, M Grosh and J Hodditott (2002). Targeting Outcomes Redux. *Food Cconsumption and Nutrition Division Discussion Paper* No. 144. Washington, DC: IFPRI.

Coady, D (2003). Alleviating Structural poverty in developing countries: The approach of PROGESSA in Mexico. Background paper. World Development Report. Washington, DC: World Bank.

Coady, D (2004). Designing and Evaluating Social Safety Nets: Theory, Evidence and Policy Conclusions. *Food Consumption and Nutrition Division Discussion Paper* No. 172. Washington, DC: IFPRI.

Coady, D, R Perez and H Vera-Ilamas (2005). Evaluating the cost of poverty alleviation transfer programs: An Illustration base on PROGRESA in Mexico. Food Consumption and Nutrition Division, *FCND Discussion Paper* No. 199. Washington, DC: IFPRI.

Collard, D (2000). Generational transfers and the Generational Bargain. *Journal of International Development*, 12, 453–462.

Collier, P and D Dollar (2001). Can the World Cut Poverty in Half? How Policy Reform and Effective Aid Can Meet International Development Goals. *World Development*, 29, 1787–1802.

Connell, J, B Dasgupta, R Laisley and M Lipton (1976). *Migration from Rural Areas: The Evidence from Village Surveys.* Delhi: Oxford University Press.

Corbett, S (2008). Can the Cellphone Help End Global Poverty? *New York Time,* April 13.

Corrie, BD (1995). A Human Development Index for the Dalit Child in India. *Social Indicators Research,* 34, 395–409.

Coudouel, A, AA Dani and S Paternostro, eds. (2006). *Poverty and Social Impact Analysis of Reforms: Lessons and Examples from Implementation.* Washington DC: World Bank.

Croll, EJ and P Huang (1997) Migration for and Against Agriculture in Eight Chinese Villages. *The China Quarterly*, 149, 128–146.

Dahlberg, E (2005). *Insights into migration and spending patterns based on a small-scale study of garment workers in Phnom Penh.* Working Paper 221, Stockholm School of Economics, December 2005.

Dalton, R and N Ong (2005). Civil Society and Social Capital in Vietnam *Urban Studies*, 42(10), 1693–1710.

Dalton, R, PM Hac, PT Nghi and N Ong (2002). Social Relations and Social Capital in Vietnam: The 2001 World Value Survey. *Comparative Sociology*, 1(3–4), 369–386.

Das Gupta, Monica (1987). Selective discrimination against female children in rural Punjab, India. *Population and Development Review*, 13(1), 77–100.

Das Gupta, Monica (2005). Explaining Asia's missing women: A new look at the data *Population and Development Review*, 31(3), 529–535.

Das, A (1999). Socio-economic development in India: A regional analysis. *Development and Society*, 28(2), 313–345.

Dasgupta, A (2007). Floods and Poverty Traps: Evidence from Bangladesh. *Economic and Political Weekly*, 28 July 2007.

Dasgupta, P and D Ray (1986). Inequality as a determinant of malnutrition and unemployment: Theory. *Economic Journal* 96, 1011–34.

Dasgupta, S, U Deichmann, C Meisner and D Wheeler (2003). The Poverty/Environment Nexus in Cambodia and Lao People's Democratic Republic. *World Bank Policy Research Working Paper 2960.*

Dasuki, AS, M Djamin and AY Lubis (2001). The Strategy of Photovoltaic Technology Development in Indonesia. *Renewable Energy*, 22(1), 321–326.

Datta, KL and S Sharma (2000). Level of Living in India: An Analysis of Consumption and Poverty. Perspective Planning Division, Planning Commission of India, New Delhi.

Davidson, AP, M Ahmad and T Ali (2001). Dilemmas of Agricultural extension in Pakistan: Food for Thought. Network Paper 116. Agricultural Research and Extension Network, UK Department for International Development.

Davidson, J and R Smith (1990). Traumatic Experience in Psychiatric Outpatients. *Journal of Traumatic Stress Studies*, 2, 459–475.

Davis, P (2006). Poverty in time: Exploring poverty dynamics from life history interviews in Bangladesh. *CPRC Working Paper 69.* Chronic Poverty Research Centre.

de Haan, A and A Dubey (2003). Extreme deprivation in remote areas of India: social exclusion as explanatory concept. Paper presented at Staying Poor: Chronic Poverty and Development Policy, Manchester, April. http://idpm.man.ac.uk/cprc/Conference/conferencepapers/ [20 March 2008].

de Janvry, AF Finan, El Sadoulet and R Vakis (2006). Can conditional cash transfer programs serve as safety nets in keeping children at school and from working when exposed to shocks? *Journal of Development Economics,* 79, 349–373.

de Tray, D (1983). Children's Work Activities in Malaysia. *Population and Development Review*, 9(3), 437–455.

Deininger, K and W Zakout (2004). Land Policy, Management, and Administration. Processed. Washington, DC: World Bank.

Deolalikar, A (1993). Gender differences in returns to schooling and in school enrollment rates in Indonesia. *Journal of Human Resources*, 28(4), 899–932.

Department of Health (1999). *Health Sector Reform Agenda.* Philippines. Mimeo. Manila.

Dercon, S, T Bold and C Calvo (2008). Insurance for the Poor? In *Social Protection for the Poor and the Poorest Concepts, Policies and Politics*, eds. Barrientos A and D Hulme. New York: Palgrave Macmillan.

Desai, S (1993). The impact of family size on children's nutritional status: insights from a comparative perspective. In *Fertility, Family Size and Structure Consequences for Families and Children*, ed. Lloyd CB, 155–191. New York: Population Council.

Deshingkar, P, S Kumar HK Chobey and D Kumar (2006). *The Role of Migration and Remittances in Promoting Livelihoods in Bihar.* Department for International Development, Overseas Development Institute, London, UK.

Deshingkar, P and D Start. 2003. Season Migration for Livelihoods in India: Coping, Accumulation and Exclusion. Mimeo. *Overseas Development Institute Working Paper* 220, London, UK.

Dessing, M (2004). Implications for minimum-wage policies of a S-shaped labor supply curve. *Journal of Economic Behavior and Organization,* 53(4), 543–568.

Dev, MS (2006). Safety Nets for the Chronic Poor in India: An overview. In *Chronic Poverty and Development Policy in India*, eds. Mehta AK and Shepherd A. New Delhi: Sage Publication.

Devereux, S (2005). Can Minimum Wages Contribute to Poverty Reduction in Poor Countries. *Journal of International Development*, 17, 899–912.

Doanne, D (2007). Living in the Background: Home-based Women Workers and Poverty Persistence. Chronic Poverty Research Center Working Paper 97. Manchester UK.

Dollar, D and A Kray (2001). Growth is Good for the Poor. *World Bank Policy Research Working Paper 2587.* Washington DC: World Bank.

Dollar, D and A Kraay (2001a). Trade Growth and Poverty. Mimeo. Washington DC: World Bank.

Donnges, C, G Edmonds and B Johannessen (2007). *Rural Road Maintenance: Sustaining the Benefits of Improved Access.* Geneva: ILO.

Dorosh, P, MK Niazi and H Nazli (2003). Distributional Impacts of Agricultural Growth in Pakistan: A Multiplier Analysis. *Pakistan Development Review*, 42(3), 249–75.

Dowling, JM (2007). *Future Perspectives on the Economic Development of Asia.* London, New York and Singapore: World Scientific Publishing Co.

Dowling, JM and C Yap (2007). *Modern Developments in Behavioral Economics Social Science Perspectives on Choice and Decision Making*, London, New York and Singapore: World Scientific Publishing Co.

Dreze, J and A Sen (1989). *Hunger and Public Action.* Oxford, UK: Oxford University Press.

Dreze, J and A Sen (1991). Public action for social security: Foundations and strategy. In *Social security in developing countries*, eds. Ahman E, J Dreze, J Hills and A Sen. Oxford: Clarendon Press.

Dreze, J and A Sen (1995). *India: Economic Development and Social Opportunity.* Oxford and New Delhi: Oxford University Press.

Dreze, J and PV Srinavasan (1997). Widowhood and Poverty in Rural India: Some Inferences from Household Survey Data. *Journal of Development Economics*, 54(2), 217–234.

Dreze, J (2002). Ending Destitution. *The Hindu*, July 29.

Du, Y, A Park and S Wang (2005). Migration and Rural Poverty in China. *Journal of Comparative Economics*, 33, 688–709.

Duclos, J, A Araar and J Giles (2006). Chronic and Transient Poverty: Measurement and Estimation, with Evidence from China. IZA DP No. 2078. Bonn, Germany: IZA.

Duflo, E (2000). Grandmother and Granddaughters: The Effects of Old Age Pensions on Child Health in South Africa. Working paper, Department of Economics MIT.

Dyson, T and M Moore (1983). On kinship structure, female autonomy, and demographic behavior in India. *Population and Development Review*, 9(1), 35–60.

Easterley, W and S Fisher (2001). Inflation and the Poor. *Journal of Money, Credit and Banking*, 33, 160–178.

Economic Institute of Cambodia (EIC) (2006). *Paths to Poverty Reduction in Cambodia: A Tale of Four Districts.*

Economist (2008). *On the Poverty Line, May 22.*

Edmonds, E (2005). Does Child Labor Decline with Improvements in Economic Status? *Journal of Human Resources*, 40(1), 77–99.

Elbers, C, T Fujii, P Lanjouw, B Ozler and W Yin (2004). Poverty Alleviation through Geographic Targeting: Does Disaggregaton Help? Policy research working paper. Washington DC: World Bank.

Engle, PL, S Castle and P Menon (1996). Child Development: Vulnerability and Resilience. *Social Science and Medicine*, 43(5), 621–635.

Erfe, J (2007). Determining the Motivations for Internal Remittances in Uttar Pradesh and Bihar. Ph.D. dissertation, Stanford University.

Evenson, RE and M Rosegrant (2003). The Economic Consequences of Crop Genetic Improvement Programmes. In *Crop Variety Improvements and Its Effect on Productivity: The Impact of International Agricultural Research*, eds. Evenson RE and D Gollin. Wallingford, Oxford: CABI Publishing.

Evenson, RE and D Gollin (2003). Assessing the Impact of the Green Revolution, 1960 to 2000. *Science*, 300(5620), 758–762.

Family Planning Foundation in India (1988). *Focus on Population* Jan–Mar; 2(1), 2–3, 12.

Fan, S and C Chan-Kang (2005). Road Development, Economic Growth and Poverty Reduction in China. Research Report No 138. Washington, DC: IFPRI.

Fan, S, J Brzeska and G Shields (2008). Reducing Poverty and Hunger in Asia Investment Priorities for Economic Growth and Poverty Reduction in Asia. *Focus 15* (March). Washington, DC: IFPRI.

Fan, S, L Zhang and X Zhang (2002). Growth, Inequality and Poverty in Rural China: The Role of Public Investments. Research Report 125. Washington DC: IFPRI. originally appeared as Fan, S, L Zhang and X Zhang (2000). Growth and Poverty in Rural China: the Role of Public Investments, E PTD Discussion Paper 66. Washington DC: IFPRI.

Fan, S, Jitsuchon and N Methakunnavut (2002a). Rural Infrastructure Development and Poverty Reduction in Rural Thailand. IFPRI project report submitted to ADB and TDRI. Bangkok, Thailand.

Fan, S, P Hazell and S Thorat (1999). Linkages between Government Spending, Growth and Poverty in rural India, Research Report 110 IFPRI, Washington, DC.

Fan, S, PL Huong and TQ Long (2004). Government Spending and Poverty Reduction in Vietnam. Project Report. International Food Policy Research Institute, Washington DC, and Central Institute for Economic Management, Hanoi.

Farrington, J, NC Saxena, T Barton and R Nayak (2003). Post Offices, Pensions and computers: New Opportunities for Combining Growth and Social Protection in Weakly Integrated Areas. *Natural Resource Perspectives,* 2003 (87), May. London: Overseas Development Institute.

Feder, G, R Murgai and JB Quizon (2004). Sending Farmers Back to School: The Impact of Farm Field Schools in Indonesia. *Review of Agricultural Economics,* 26(1), 45–62.

Feder, G, A Willett and W Zijp (1999). Agricultural Extension Generic Challenges and Some Ingredients for Solutions. *Policy Research Working Paper 2129.* Washington, DC: World Bank.

Filmer, D (2000). The Structure of Social Disarities in Education Gender and Wealth. World Bank Policy Research Working Paper No. 2268. Washington, DC: World Bank.

Filmer, D and L Pritchett (1997). Child Mortality and Public Spending on Health: How Much does Money Matter? Mimeo. Development Research Group. Washington, DC: World Bank.

Filmer, D, EM King and L Pritchett (1998). Gender Disparity in South Asia: Comparisons between and within Countries. Mimeo. World Bank, Washington, DC.

Fitchett, D (1999). Bank for Agriculture and Agricultural Cooperatives (BAAC), Thailand Case Study, Consultative Group to Assist the Poorest (CGAP) Working Group on Saving Mobilization, GTZ and BMZ. Mimeo.

Gamage, DT and P Sooksomchitra (2004). Decentralization and school-based management in Thailand. *International Review of Education*, 50, 289–305.

Gangopadhyay, S and W Wadhwa (2003). Are Indian female-headed households more vulnerable to poverty? *India Development Foundation.*

Gannon, C and Z Liu (1997). Poverty and transport. TWU discussion papers TWU-30. Washington, DC: World Bank.

Garcia, M (1988). Food Subsidies in the Philippines: Preliminary Results. In *Nutrition and Development,* eds. Biswas, M. and Per Pinstrup-Andersen. Oxford, UK: Oxford Medical Publications.

Ge, W (2009). China's Urban Employment Challenge, Department of Economics, Bucknell University mimeograph.

Genicot, G (2002). Bonded Labor and Serfdom: A paradox of voluntary choice. *Journal of Development Economics,* 67(1), 101–127.

George, PS (1988). Costs and Benefits of Food Subsidies in India. In *Food Subsidies in Developing Countries Costs, Benefits and Policy Options,* ed. Pinstrup-Anderson. Johns Hopkins Press, Baltimore for IFPRI.

Ghate, P (1992). *Informal Finance: Some Findings from Asia.* Manila: Asian Development Bank.

Ghazala, M (2006). Migration, sex bias, and child growth in rural Pakistan. Policy Research Working Paper 3946. Washington, DC: World Bank.

Ghura, D, CA Leite and C Tsangarides (2002). Is Growth Enough? Macroeconomic Policy and Poverty Reduction. *IMF Working Paper 118*. Washington DC: IMF.

Gibson, J (2006). The Constraints Associated with Infrastructure faced by Non-Farm Enterprises at the Kabupaten Level. Background paper for the Rural Investment Climate Assessment. University of Canterbury, New Zealand.

Gill, I and H Karas (2006). *An East Asian Renaissance: Ideas for Economic Growth.* Washington, DC: World Bank.

Government of Bangladesh (2005). Poverty Reduction Strategy Paper. http://go.worldbank.org/Y9T2YBF2A1 [23 May 2008]

Government of Cambodia (2002). *National Poverty Reduction Strategy 2003–2005.* Council for Social Development.

Government of Cambodia (2004). Rectangular Strategy: Address of Samdech Hun Sen, Prime Minister, RGC to the First Cabinet Meeting, Phnom Penh.

Government of Cambodia (2008). *National Strategic Development Plan 2006–2010.*

Government of Cambodia (2008a). *Rural Electrification Fund. Strategic Plan For Strategic Plan For Rural Electrification Fund Project and Beyond.*

Government of India (2001). *Indian Population Census.*

Government of India. Population Census and Registrar General of India.

Government of Lao PDR (2003). *National Growth and Poverty Eradication Strategy (NGPES).* Vientiane.

Government of Lao PDR (2006). *Sixth National Socio Economic Development Plan (2006–2010).* Vientiane.

Government of Malaysia (1956). Report of the Education Committee, Kuala Lumpur, Malaysia, Government Printing Office.

Green, D (2008). *From Poverty to Power: How Active Citizens and Effective States Can Change the World.* UK: Oxfam International.

Günther, I and S Klasen (2007). Measuring chronic non-income poverty. *CPRC Working Paper 79.* Chronic Poverty Research Centre.

Gustafsson, B and S Li (2002). Income Inequality within and across Counties in Rural China, 1988 and 1995. *Journal of Development Economics*, 69(1), 179–204.

Hamid, MA and B Frank (1993). Effectiveness of pubic extension service in the transfer of agricultural technology in Bangladesh. Proceedings of Australia Pacific Extension Conference, Brisbane, Autralia.

Hammond, A, RS Katz, J Trand and C Walker (2007). *The Next four Billion Market Size and Business Strategy at the Base of the Pyramid.* Washington DC: World Resources Institute, International Finance Corporation.

Hannum, E (2005). Market Transition: Educational Disparities, and Family Strategies in Rural China: New Evidence on Gender Stratification and Development. *Demography* 42(2), 275–299.

Hao, CT and S Fan (2001). How Can Vietnam Better Target Its Public Spending for Poverty Reduction. Paper presented at Internatinal Conference on Rural Investment, Growth and Poverty Reduction November, Beijing, China.

Hare, D (1999). Women's Economic Status in Rural China: Household Contributions to Male–Female Disparities in the Wage–Labor Market. *World Development*, 27(6), 1011–1029.

Harrison, A and J Scorse (2006). Improving the Conditions of Workers? Minimum Wage Legislation and Anti-Sweatshop Activism. California Management Review, 2 (48), 144–160.

Hausman, R, L Pritchett and D Rodrik (2005). Growth accelerations. *Journal of Economic Growth*, 10, 303–329.

Heller, P (2005). World Bank and IMF analysis of government spending and growth. Paper presented at high level forum on health MGDs in Asia, IMF and World Bank, Washington, DC.

Hill, H (1996). *The Indonesian Economy since 1966*. Cambridge: Cambridge University Press.

Hill, RV and C Christiaensen (2006). Linking Laotian farmers to markets. Mimeo. Washington, DC: World Bank.

Hoff, K and P Pandey (2004). Belief systems and durable inequalities: An experimental investigation of Indian caste. World Bank Policy Research Working Paper 3351. Washington, DC: World Bank.

Holmval, P (2007). Remittances and Poverty — A Case Study of the Philippines. Masters Thesis. Department of Economics, School of Economics, University of Lund, Sweden.

Holzman, R (1990). The Welfare Effects of Public Expenditure Programs Reconsidered. *IMF Staff Papers*, 37, 338–359.

Hossain, M, ML Bose, A Chowdhury and R Meinzen-Dick (2002). Changes in agrarian relations and livelihoods in rural Bangladesh: Insights from repeat village studies. In *Agrarian Studies: Essays on Agrarian Relations in Less Developed Countries*, eds. Ramachandran VK and M Swaminathan. New Delhi: Tulica Books.

Howes, S and R Murgai (2004). Subsidies And Salaries: Issues In The Restructuring Of Government Expenditure In India. Mimeo. www.imf.org/external/np/seminars/eng/2004/fiscal/pdf/howes.pdf [14 February 2008].

Hu, A, L Hu and Z Chang (2003). China's Economic Growth and Poverty Reduction (1978–2002). http://www.imf.org/external/np/apd/seminars/2003/newdelhi/angang.pdf [5 April 2008].

Human Rights Watch Asia (1996). *The Small Hands of Slavery: bonded Child Labor in India*. New York: Human Rights Watch.

Human Rights Watch India (2003). *Small Change: Bonded child Labor in India's Silk Industry*. http://www.hrw.org/reports/2003/india/India0103-05.htm#P1330_294375 [6 May 2008].

Human Rights Watch (1995). *Contemporary forms of slavery in Pakistan*. http://www.hrw.org/reports/1995/Pakistan.htm [6 May 2008].

Human Rights Watch (1995a). *Human Rights Watch World Report* 1995. New York: Human Rights Watch.

Human Rights Watch (1996). *Human Rights Watch Asia* 1996. New York: Human Rights Watch.

Human Rights Watch (1997). *Human Rights Watch World Report* 1997. New York: Human Rights Watch.

Human Rights Watch (2003). *Human Rights Watch World Report* 2003. New York: Human Rights Watch.

Human Rights Watch (2007). *Hidden Apartheid Caste Discrimination against India's Untouchables*. http://www.hrw.org/reports/2007/india0207/ [23 July 2008].

Hussain, A (2003). *Urban Poverty in China: Measurement, Patterns and Policies*. Geneva: International Labour Office.

Hussain, A (2003a). *Pakistan National Human Development Report 2003: Poverty, Growth and Governance*. Karachi: UNDP/Oxford University Press.

Hussain, I and MA Hanjra (2003). Does irrigation water matter for rural poverty alleviation? *Water Policy*, 5(5/6), 429–442.

Hussain, I and MA Hanjra (2004). Irrigation and poverty alleviation: review of the empirical evidence. *Irrigation and Drainage*, 53(1), 1–15.

Hussain, I, Giordano and MA Hanjra (2004). Agricultural Water and Poverty Linkages: Case Studies on Large and Small Systems. In *Water and Poverty: The Realities*, ed. Ahmed R. Manila: ADB.

IFAD (2007). *Rural Poverty Portal: Rural Poverty in Nepal*. http://www.ruralpovertyportal.org/english/regions/asia/npl/index.htm [25 July 2008].

IFAD (2008). *Republic of Indonesia: Country Strategic Opportunities Programme*.

IFAD (2008a). Rural Poverty in Cambodia. http://www.ruralpovertyportal.org/web/guest/country/home/tags/cambodia [18 April 2008]

IFPRI (2002). Evaluation Design for the pilot phase of the Nicaraguan Red de Protection Social: Impact Evaluation. Washington, DC: World Bank.

IFPRI (2007). *The World's Most Deprived: Characteristics and Causes of Extreme Poverty and Hunger*. Washington, DC: IFPRI.

Ilahi, N and S Jafarey (1999). Guest worker migration, remittances and the extended family: Evidence from Pakistan. *Journal of Development Economics*, 58(2), 485–512.

ILO (1997). *Bitter Harvest*. Geneva: International Labour Organization.

ILO (2003). Decent Work in Agriculture. Labor Education Study No 131–132. Geneva: International Labour Organization.

ILO (2004). Report on the Second National Commission on Labor Macroeconomic Reforms and a Labor market Policy for India, International Labour Organization, Geneva.

ILO (2007). Data bank available on ILO web site. www.ilo.org [25 March 2008].
ILO (2008). Promotion of Rural Employment for Poverty Reduction. Geneva: International Labour Organization.
ILO, UNICEF and World Bank (2006). *Children's Work in Cambodia: A Challenge for Growth and Poverty Reduction.*
Independent Evaluation Group (2008). *The Welfare Impact of Rural Electrification: A Reassessment of Costs and Benefits.* Washington, DC: World Bank.
PROBE Team (India), Delhi School of Economics (1999). Centre for Development Economics. India Education Report. *Public Report on Basic Education.* New Delhi: Oxford University Press.
India, Government of (2001). Population Census, Delhi, Government of India.
India, Government of (2007). Special Task Force on Bihar *Road Sector Development — New Dimensions.* New Delhi.
International Fund for Agricultural Development (IFAD) (1999). Rural Poverty Assessment: Asia and the Pacific Region. Draft for Discussion. Rome: IFAD.
International Herald Tribune (2008). A Liquid Legacy from a Murderous Regime, 5 December 2007.
International Herald Tribune (2008a). Highest inflation in Asia stifles tiger economy of Vietnam, 20 August 2008.
International Institute for Population Sciences (1999). *National Family Health Survey* II1998/99, National Report, Mumbai.
International Monetary Fund (IMF) (2004). *Poverty Reduction Strategy Paper.* www.imf.org/external/pubs/ft/scr/2004/cr0424.pdf [21 March 2008].
International Monetary Fund (IMF) (2008). Lao Peopls's Democratic Republic: Poverty Reduction Strategy Paper — Annual Progress Report. *IMF Country Report No. 08/342.* Washington DC: IMF.
International Monetary Fund (IMF) (2008a). *World Economic Outlook* September. Washington, DC: IMF.
International Rice Research Institute (IRRI) (2008). The rice crisis: What needs to be done? A background paper by the International rice Research Institute, Mimeo.
Jacoby, HG (2000). Access to markets and the Benefits of rural roads. *The Economic Journal*, 110, 713–737.
Jalan, J and M Ravallion (1998). Transient Poverty in Post reform Rural China. *Journal of Comparative Economics*, 26, 338–357.
Jalan, J and M Ravalliion (1998a). Are There Dynamic Gains from a poor-area Development Program? *Journal of Public Economics* 67(1), 65–86.
Jalan, J and M Ravallion (1999). Are the poor less well insured? Evidence on vulnerability to income risk in rural China. *American Economic Review*, 92(5), 1420–1447.
Jalan, J and M Ravallion (2000). Determinants of Transient and Chronic Poverty: Evidence from Rural China. *The Journal of Development Studies,* 36(6), 82–99.

Jalan, J and M Ravallion (2002). Geographic Poverty Traps? A Micro Model of Consumption Growth in Rural China. *Journal of Applied Econometrics*, 17, 329–346.

Jenkins, R and E Barr (2006). Social Exclusion of Scheduled Caste Children from Primary Education in India. Mimeo. India: UNICEF.

Jensen, R (2007). The Digital Provide: Information (technology) market performance and welfare in the South Indian fisheries sector, *Quarterly Journal of Economics*, 122(3), 879–924.

Jordans, EH and M Zwarteveen (1997). A Well of One's Own: Gender Analysis of an Irrigation Program in Bangladesh. *IIMI Country Paper, Bangladesh* No. 1. Irrigation Internal Management Institute, Sri Lanka and Grameen Krishi Foundation.

Kabeer, N and M Simeen (2004). Globalization, Gender and Poverty: Bangladeshi Women Workers in Export and Local Markets. *Journal of International Development*, 16(1), 93–109.

Kabeer, N (2000). Inter-Generational Contracts, Democratic Transitions and The Quality-Quantity Tradeoff: Parents, Children and Investing in the Future. *Journal of International Development*, 12, 463–482.

Kabeer, N (2006). Social Exclusion and the MDGs? The Challenge of "Durable Inequalities" in the Asian Context. Institute of Development Studies, U.K.

Kakwani, N and EM Pernia (2000). What is Pro-poor Growth? *Asian Development Review*, 18(1), 1–16.

Kalim, R and M Shahbaz (2008). Remittances and Poverty Nexus: Evidence from Pakistan. Paper presented at Oxford Business and Economics Conference, Oxford, UK.

Kam, S, M Hossain, ML Bose and LS Villano (2005). Spatial patterns of rural poverty and their relationship with welfare-influencing factors in Bangladesh. *Food Policy*, 30(5–6), 551–67.

Kanan, KP and KS Hari (2002). Kerala's Gulf Connection: Remittances and their Macroeconomic Impact. In *Kerala's Gulf Connection: CDS Studies on International Labour Migration from Kerala State in India*, eds. Zachariah KC, KP Kannan, S Irudaya Rajan, Centre for Development Studies (Trivandrum, India). Thiruvananthapuram: Centre for Development Studies.

Karan, A and Pushpendra (2006). Bihar: Including the Excluded and Addressing the Failures of Public Provision in Elementary Education. In *The Economics of Elementary Education in India: The Challenges of Public Finance, Private Provision and Household Costs*, ed. Mehrotra S. New Delhi: Sage Publications.

Kennedy, ET (1988). Alternatives to Consumer-Oriented Food Subsidies for Achieving Nutritional Objectives. In *Food Subsidies in Developing Countries Costs, Benefits and Policy Options*, ed. Pinstrup-Anderson. Baltimore: Johns Hopkins Press.

Kerkvliet, B (2001). An Approach for Analyzing State-Society Relations in Vietnam. *Sojourn*, 16(2), 238–278.

Khan, SH, A Barkat, M Rahman, S Zaman and A Poddar (2002). Economic and Social Impact Evaluation Study of the Rural Electrification Program in Bangladesh. Human Development Research Centre, NRECA and USAID.

Khandker, S, Z Bakht and G Koolwal (2006). *The Poverty Impact of Rural Roads: Evidence from Bangladesh.* World Bank Policy Research Working Paper 3875. Washington, DC: World Bank.

Khandker, SR and GB Koolwal (2006a). Are Pro-Growth Policies Pro-Poor? Mimeo.

Kijima, Y (2006). Case and Tribal Inequality: Evidence from India, 1983–1999. *Economic Development and Cultural Change,* 54(2), 370–404.

King, E and LA Lillard (1987). Education policy and schooling attainment in Malaysia and the Philippines. *Economics of Education Review*, 6, 67–181.

King, EM and MA Hill (1993). *Women's Education in Developing Countries: Barriers, Benefits and Policies.* Baltimore MD: Johns Hopkins Press.

Klasen, S and C Wink (2003). Missing women: Revisiting the Debate. *Feminist Economics,* 9(2–3), 263–299.

Klump, R (2007). Pro-poor Growth in Vietnam: Miracle or Model? In *Delivering on the Promise of Pro-Poor Growth: Insights and Lessons from Country Experiences*, eds. Timothy Besley and Louise J. Cord. Palgrave Macmillan and the World Bank.

Knight, J, L Song and H Jua (1999). Chinese Rural Migrants in Urban Enterprises: Three Perspectives. *Journal of Development Studies,* 35(12), 2163–74.

Knowles, JC, EM Pernia and M Racelis (2000). Social Consequences of the Financial Crisis in Asia, the Deeper Crisis. Asian Development Bank Discussion Paper. Manila: ADB.

Koenig, M, D Bishai and MA Khan (2001). Health interventions and health equity: The example of measles vaccination in Bangladesh. *Population and Development Review,* 27(2), 283–302.

Koenig, M, D Bishai and MA Khan (2003). Measles vaccination improves the equity of health outcomes: Evidence from Bangladesh. *Health Economics,* 12(5), 415–419.

Kola, K (2004). Fighting Poverty in Cambodia. *Contemporary Review*, 284(1658), 164–166.

Krishna, R and A Chibber (1983). Policy Modelling of a Dual Grain Market: The Case of Wheat in India. Research Report 38. Washington DC: IFPRI.

Krishnan, TN (1997). The role to Social Development in Kerala: Social Intermediation and Public Action. In *Development with a Human Face*, eds. Mehrotra S and R Jolly. Oxford, UK: Oxford University Press.

Kristof, N (2008). http://www.facebook.com/Kristof [15 May 2008].

Kristof, N (2009). Opinion: the Face of Slavery Sexual trafficking in Cambodia. New York Times, January 5. Video. http://www.nytimes.com [6 January 2009].

Kumar, SC Bjattacharya and M Anisuzzaman (2003). Role of a regional programme for promotion of photovoltaic based rural electrification in Asia. *International Journal of Global Energy Resource*, 20(2), 139–154.

Kurosaki, T (2003). Measurement of Chronic and Transient Poverty: Theory and Application to Pakistan. *Discussion Paper Series A,* No. 436. Tokyo: Institute of Economic Research, Hitotsubashi University.

Lal, R, PR Hobbs, N Uphoff and DO Hansen, eds. (2002). *Sustainable Agriculture and the International Rice-Wheat System.* New York: Marcel Dekker, Inc.

Lanjouw, P and M Ravallion (1995). Poverty and Household Size. *The Economic Journal*, 105(433), 1415–1434.

Lanjouw, P, M Pradhan, F Saadah, H Sayed and R Sparrow (2001). Poverty, Education and Health in Indonesia: Who Benefits from Public Spending? *World Bank Policy Research Working Paper Series* No. 2739. Washington, D.C.: World Bank.

Leamer, EE (1995). The Heckscher-Olin Model in Theory and Practice. *Princeton Studies in International Finance* 77, 1–50.

Lee, K (2003). *Social challenges for Lao PDR*. In *Social Challenges for the Mekong Region*, eds. Mingsarn Kaosa-ard and John Dore. Bangkok, Thailand: White Lotus.

Leong, CH and TS Hoey (2006). Malaysia: Social Development, Poverty Reduction and Economic Transformation. In *The Economics of Elementary Education in India: The Challenges of Public Finance, Private Provision and Household Costs*, ed. Santosh Mehrotra. New Delhi: Sage Publications.

Lipton, M (1988). Rural Development and the Retention of the Rural Population in the countryside of Developing Countries. In *Staying On: Retention and Migration in Peasant Societies*, ed. Havet J. Ottawa, ON, Ottawa University Press.

Lipton, M (2005). Crop Science, Poverty and the Family farm in a Globalizing world. IFPRI 2020 discussion paper.

Lipton, M and R Martin (1994). Poverty and policy. In *Handbook of Development Economics*, Vol. 3, eds. Behrman J and TN Srinivasan. North-Holland: Amsterdam.

Lipton, M, J Litchfield, R Blackman, D De Zoysa, L Qureshy, H Waddington (2003). Preliminary Review of the impact of irrigation on poverty with special emphasis on Asia. Technical Paper. Rome: FAO.

Liu, AYC (2004). Flying Ducks? Girls' Schooling in Rural Vietnam: A Revisit *Asian Economic Journal*, 18(3), 293–318.

Lloyd, CB (1994). Investing in the next generation: the implications of high fertility at the level of the family. Research Division Papers No. 63. New York: Populating Council.

Lokshin, M, M Bontch-Osmolovski and E Glinskaya (2007). Work-related migration and poverty reduction in Nepal. *Policy Research working Paper* No 4231. Washington, DC: World Bank.

Lucas, RJ (1990). Why doesn't Capital Flow from Rich to Poor countries? *American Economic Review*, 80(2), 92–96.

Lustig, NC and D McLeod (1997). Minimum Wages and Poverty in Developing Countries: Some Empirical Evidence. In *Labor Markets in Latin America*, eds. Sebastian Edwards and Nora Lustig. Washington, DC: Brookings Institution Press.

Luthar, S (1991). Vulnerability and resilience: a study of high-risk adolescents. *Child Development*, 62, 600–616.

MS Swaminathan Research Foundation (MSSRF) (2005). *The Third MSSRF South — South Exchange Travelling Workshop.* M.S. Swaminathan Research Foundation Chennai, India. http://dlist.sir.arizona.edu/854/01/Arun_06.pdf [15 August 2008].

Mahmud, S and JP Mc Intosh (1980). Returns to Scale to Family Size-Who Gains from High Fertility? *Population Studies*, 34(3), 500–506.

Malik, RK, A Yadav, GS Gill, P Sardana, RK Gupta and C Piggin (2004). Evolution and Acceleration of No-till farming in Rice-Wheat Cropping System of the Indo-Gangetic Plains. Proceedings of the 4th International Crop Science Congress, Brisbane Australia.

Malik, SJ (2005). *Agricultural Growth and Rural Poverty: A Review of the Evidence.* Pakistan Resident Mission Working Paper No. 2. Islamabad: ADB.

Mallee, H (1995/96). In Defense of Migration: Recent Chinese Studies on Rural Population Mobility. *China Information*, 10(3–4), 108–140.

Mallick, SK (2008). A Macroeconomic Policy approach to Poverty Reduction. Brooks World Poverty Institute Working Paper 31. Brooks World Poverty Institute, University of Manchester, UK.

Maloney, W and J Nunez (2001). Measuring the Impact of minimum wages: Eevidence from Latin America. *World Bank Policy Research Working Paper* 2597. Washington, DC: World Bank.

Mankiw, N, D Romer and DN Weil (1992). A Contribution to the Empirics of Economic Growth. *Quarterly Journal of Economics*, 107, 407–437.

Marcoux, A (1998). The Feminization of Poverty: Claims, Facts, and Data Needs. *Population and Development Review*, 24(1), 131–139.

Martin, W and M Ivanic (2008). Implications of Higher Global Food Prices for Poverty in Low-Income Countries. *World Bank Policy Research Working Paper* 4594. Washington, DC: World Bank.

Maurer, K (2004). Bank Rakyat Indonesia: Twenty Years of Large-Scale Microfinance. World Bank paper presented at Scaling Up Poverty Reduction: A Global Learning Process and Conference, Shanghai.

Mazumdar, T (2005). Employment and Earnings in the formal sector of India. Mimeo. Washington, DC: World Bank.

Mazumdar, T (2006). Cost and Financing of Elementary Education in West Bengal. In *The Economics of Elementary Education in India: The Challenges of Public Finance, Private Provision and Household Costs*, ed. Mehrotra S. New Delhi: Sage Publication.

McCord, A (2008). The Social Protection Function of short-Term Public Works Programmes in the Context of Chronic Poverty. In *Social Protection for the Poor*

and the Poorest: Concepts, Policies and Politics, eds. Barrientos, A and David Hulme Hampshire, UK: Palgrave Macmillan.
McCulloch, N and B Baulch (1999). Assessing the poverty bias of growth Methodology and an application to Andhra Pradesh Uttar Pradesh. Working Paper 98. Sussex, UK: Institute for Development Studies.
McCulloch, N and M Calandrino (2003). Vulnerability and Chronic Poverty in Rural Sichuan. *World Development*, 31(3), 611–628.
McKay, A and D Lawson (2002). Chronic Poverty in Developing and Transition Countries: Concepts and Evidence. CREDIT Research Paper No. 02/27. Centre for Research in Economic Development and International Trade, University of Nottingham, UK.
McKay, A and B Baulch (2003). How Many Chronically Poor People are there in the World? Some Preliminary Estimates, Chronic Poverty Research Centre Working Paper No. 45, Manchester UK.
McLaughlin, K, A Satu and M Hoppe (2007). Kecamatan Development Program Qualitative Impact Evaluation: Experiences of India and Indonesia. LOGOTRI Research Study.
Mehrhotra, S and M Biggeri (2007). *Asian Informal Workers: Global Risks, Local Protection*. New York, NY, USA and Abingdon, UK: Routledge.
Mehrotra, S, ed. (2006). *The Economics of Elementary Education in India: The Challenges of Public Finance, Private Provision and Household Costs*. New Delhi: Sage Publications.
Mehta, AK and A Shah (2001). Chronic Poverty in India: Overview Study. Working Paper 7. Chronic Poverty Research Center.
Mehta, AK and A Shah (2003). Chronic Poverty in India: Incidence, Causes and Policy, *World Development*, 31, 491–511.
Mehta, AK and A Shah (2006). Chronic Poverty in India: Overview Study. Chronic Poverty Research Center Working Paper 7. Manchester, UK.
Meng, X and J Zhang (2001). The Two-Tier Labor Market in Urban China. *Journal of Comparative Economics*, 29(3), 485–504.
Metraux, D and JW Yoxall (2007). China Today: A Brief Introduction. *Virginia Review of Asian Studies*.
Milanovic, B (2006). Inequality and Determinants of Earnings in Malaysia, 1984–97. *Asian Economic Journal*, 20(2), 191–214.
Miller, BD (1997). Social Class, Gender and Intra household Food Allocations to Children in south Asia. *Social Science and Medicine*, 44(11), 1685–1697.
Miller, BD (1981). The Endangered Sex: Neglect of Female Children in rural North India: Cornell University Press, Ithica, New York.
Ministry of Rural Development (MRD) (2002). Benefit Monitoring and Evaluation (BME): RIIP Final Report and Recommendations for Continuing Activities Within MRD (a report by Kirit Vaidya, Benefit Monitoring and Evaluation Consultant), MRD, Phnom Penh.

Minot, N, B Baulch and M Epprecht (2006). Poverty and Inequality in Vietnam. *Spatial Patterns and Geographic Determinants.* Research Report 148. Washington DC: IFPRI.

Modi, V (2005). Improving Electricity Services in Rural India, CGSD Working Paper No 30. Center on Globalization and Sustainable Development, The Earth Institute at Columbia University.

Mohanan, M (2003). Rural road network in selected states. *Economic Affairs*, 48(3), 162–166.

Monsod, S, TC Monsod and GM Ducanes (2004). Philippines' Progress towards the Millennium Development Goals: Geographical and political correlates of sub-national outcomes. *Journal of Human Development*, 5(1).

Moore, K (2005). Thinking about youth poverty through the lenses of chronic poverty, life-course poverty and intergenerational poverty. CPRC Working Paper 57. Chronic Poverty Research Center, Manchester, UK.

Morduch, J (1999). The Microfinance promise. *Journal of Economic Literature*, 37, 1564–1614.

Morgan, S (2006). http://www.morganstanley.com/GDFdata/digests/20060814-mon.html#anchor3 [10 February 2007].

Morley, S and D Coady (2003). *From Social Assistance to Social Development.* Center for Global Development and IFPRI, Washington DC.

Mumssen, Y (2004). Output-based aid in Cambodia: Private operators and local communities help deliver water to the poor. OBA Approaches. November 2004 Note Number 01. The Global Partnership on Output-Based Aid (GPOBA).

Munasinghe, M (1990). Rural electrification in the Third World. *Power Engineering Journal*, 4(4), 189–202.

Murthi, M, A-C Guio and J Dreze (1995). Mortality, Fertility, and Gender Bias in India: A District-Level Analysis. *Population and Development Review*, 21(4), 745–782.

Nair, A and R Kloeppinger-Todd. (2007). Reaching Rural Areas with Financial Services: Lessons from Financial Cooperatives in Brazil, Burkina Faso, Kenya, and Sri Lanka. Agriculture and Rural Development Discussion Paper 35. Washington, DC: World Bank.

Nanayakkara, H (2008). Creating Sustainable Livelihoods for the Rural Poor: What we do in Sri Lanka. Statement by Minister of Agriculture, Sri Lanka. Special Meeting of CIRDAP Governing Council and Ministerial Retreat, New Delhi, India, 24–26 June 2008.

Narayan, D (1999). *Bonds and Bridges: Social Capital and Poverty.* Poverty Group, World Bank Washington DC.

Narayan, D and E Glinskaya, eds. (2007). Ending Poverty in South Asia: Ideas that Work. Washington, DC: World Bank.

Naseem, SM (2005). Economic Growth Marathon. *Dawn*, March: 7–13.

National Economic Development Authority (NEDA) (2004). *Medium-Term Philippines Development Plan 2004–2010.* Pasig City: National Economic and Development Authority.

Navarro, M and L Tavares (2008). Output-based Aid in Cambodia: Getting Private Operators and Local Communities to Help Deliver Water to the Poor — The Experience to Date. OBA Working Paper Series Paper No. 9, April 2008. The Global Partnership on Output-Based Aid (GPOBA).

NEDA-UNDP (2007). *Philippines Midterm Progress Report on the Millennium Development Goals 2007.* Makati City: National Economic and Development Authority and United Nations Development Programme.

Neef, A, O Tongroj and S Rainer (2003). Access to Natural Resources in Mainland Southeast Asia and Implications for Sustaining Rural Livelihoods — The Case of Thailand *Quarterly Journal of International Agriculture*, 42(3), 329–350.

Nepal Central Bureau of Statistics (2005). *Poverty trends in Nepal, 1995–96 and 2003–04.* Kathmandu: His Majesty's Govt. of Nepal, National Planning Commission Secretariat, Central Bureau of Statistics.

Nepal National Planning Commission (NPPC) (2003). *The Tenth Plan (Poverty Reduction Strategy Paper 2002–2007.* Kathmandu, Nepal: His Majesty's Govt., National Planning Commission.

New York Times (13 Jan. 2008). Lives of Poverty, Untouched by China's Boom http://www.nytimes.com/2008/01/13/world/asia/13china.html?pagewanted=1&_r=1 [1 February 2008].

New York Times (30 April 2008). Soaring Food Prices Imperil Meals for Poor in Cambodia. http://www.nytimes.com/2008/04/30/world/asia/30cambodia.html?ex=1367294400&en=dfb0ceba2266cb10&ei=5124&partner=permalink&exprod=permalink [1 May 2008].

New York Times (7 Sept. 2008). Right at the Edge. http://www.nytimes.com/2008/09/07/magazine/07pakistan-t.html?ex=1378440000&en=7d69ec761586efc3&ei=5124&partner=permalink&exprod=permalink [9 September 2008].

New York Times (27 Sept. 2008). Huge bombing raises stakes for Pakistan. http://www.iht.com/articles/2008/09/21/asia/pakistan.php [28 September 2008].

New York Times (11 October 2008). China may let Peasants Sell Rights to Farmland.

Nienke, MB and G-J Steds (2002). Agricultural R&D capacity and Investment in the Asian Pacific Region. *IFPRI Research Brief* 11.

Oberai, AS, PH Prasad and MG Sardana (1989). *Determinants and Consequences of Internal Migration in India Studies in Bihar, Kerala and Uttar Pradesh.* Delhi: Oxford University Press.

Oberai, AS (1979). Determinants of rural-urban migration and its implications for rural areas with special reference to ILO research, in International Union for the Scientific Study of Population, Economic and demographic change: issues for the 1980s Proceedings of the Conference Helsinki volume 2 Liege, Belgium IUSSP 229–44.

OECD (2007). Infrastructure for Pro-poor Growth: Addressing the Challenges in Cambodia. Workshop Proceedings. Phnom Penh, October 2007.

Ortiz, ID, ed. (2001). *Social Protection in Asia and the Pacific*. Manila: ADB.

Panter-Brick, C (2002). Street children, human rights, public health: A critique and future directions. *Annual Review of Anthropology*, 31, 147–171.

Park, A, W Li and S Wang (2003). School Equality in Rural China. *Journal for International Conference on Chinese Education*, 1–4.

Parker, B and V Kozel (2007). Understanding Poverty and Vulnerability in India's Uttar Pradesh and Bihar: A Q-squared Approach. *World Development*, 35(2), 296–311.

Pathic, DS and RK Shrestha (2002). No Till in the Rice-Wheat System: An Experience from Nepal. In *Sustainable Agriculture and the International Rice-Wheat System*, eds. Lal, R, PR Hobbs, N Uphoff and DO Hansen. New York: Marcel Dekker, Inc.

Paxson, C and N Schady (2002). The allocation and impact of social funds: Spending on school infrastructure in Peru. *World Bank Economic Review*, 16(2), 297–319.

Pellissery, S (2008). Process Deficits in the Provision of Social Protection in Rural Maharasthra. In *Social Protection for the Poor and Poorest: Concepts, Policies and Politics*, eds. Armando Barrientos and David Hulme. University of Manchester. Brooks World Poverty Institute, Chronic Poverty Research Centre.

People's Daily Online (29 May 2007). China lifts 228 million people out of poverty in twenty-eight years. http://english.people.com.cn/200705/29/eng20070529_378772.html [28 June 2007].

Pernia, EM (2007). Migration, Remittances, Poverty and Inequality: The Philippines. Mimeo.

Pham, AT (2008). *Viet Nam Country Case Study Background Paper for the Chronic Poverty Report 2008–09*. University of Manchester, CPRC.

Pham, LH, M Rama and T Larsen (2004). *Vietnam's Public Investment Program and its Impacts on Poverty Reduction*. Hanoi: World Bank.

Pham, T-H and B Reilly (2007). The gender pay gap in Vietnam, 1993–2002: A quantile regression approach. *Journal of Asian Economics*, 18, 775–808.

Pinstrup-Anderson, P (1988) *Food Subsidies in Developing Countries*. Baltimore: Johns Hopkins University Press.

Poerwanto, S, M Stevenson and N de Klerk (2003). *Journal of Epidemiology and Community Health*, (57), 493–498.

Pokharel, B and J Carter (2007). Addressing chronic poverty and spatial poverty traps in Nepal's middle hills: the Nepal Swiss Community Forestry Project. A paper prepared for the international workshop *Understanding and addressing spatial poverty traps: an international workshop*, 29 March 2007, Spier Estate, Stellenbosch, South Africa.

Powell, Alvin (2006). In China, India, Health Care Burden Shifts to the Poor. http://www.news.harvard.edu/gazette/2006/10.12/09-chinaindia.html [11 April 2008]

Pradhan, M and L Rawlings (2002). The Impact and targeting of social infrastructure investments: Lessons from the Nicaraguan social fund. *World Bank Economic Review*, 16(20), 275–295.

Praveen, J (1994). The short-run trade-off between food subsidies and agricultural production subsidies in developing countries. *Journal of Development Studies*, 31(2), December.

Pritchett, L and LH Summers (1996). Wealthier is Healthier. *Journal of Human Resources*, 31(4), 841–868.

Putnam, R (1995). *Bowling Alone: America's Declining Social Capital*. Princeton: Princeton University Press.

Putzel, J (2000). Land Reforms in Asia: Lessons from the Past for the 21st Century. Working Paper Series No. 00–04. LSE Development Studies Institute, London School of Economics and Political Science.

Quibria, MG (2002). Growth and Poverty: Lessons from the Asian Mracle Revisited *ADB Institute Research Paper* 33. Tokyo: Asian Development Bank Institute.

Quisumbing, AR (2007). Poverty transitions, shocks, and consumption in rural Bangladesh: Preliminary results from a longitudinal household survey. CPRC Working Paper 105.

Quisumbing, AR, L Haddad and C Peña (2007). Gender and Poverty: New Evidence From 10 Developing Countries. Food Consumption And Nutrition Division Discussion Paper No. 9. Washington, DC: IFPRI.

Qureshi, SK and GM Arif (2001). *Profile of Poverty in Pakistan, 1998–99*. MIMAP Technical Paper No. 5. Islamabad: PIDE.

Rahman, L and V Rao (2004). The Determinants of Gender Equity in India: Examining Dyson and Moore's Thesis with New Data. *Population and Development Review*, 30(2), 239–268.

Rahman, RI (2005). The dynamics of the labour market and employment in Bangladesh: A focus on gender discriminations. Employment Strategy Paper 13. Employment Policy Unit, Employment Strategy Department, International Labour Organization.

Raiser, M (1998). Subsidizing Inequality: Economic Reforms, Fiscal Transfer and Convergence across Chinese Provinces. *Journal of Development Studies*, 34(3), 1–26.

Ramachandran, V (2007). A School for Every Village The Education Scheme in Madhya Pradesh, India. In *Ending Poverty in South Asia: Ideas that Work*, eds. Narayan D and E Glinskaya. Washington, DC: World Bank.

Ramaswami, B and P Balakrishnan (2002). Food prices and the efficiency of public intervention the case of the public distribution system in India. *Food Policy*, 27, 419–436.

Ramousset, JA (1976). *Rice and Risk Decision: Making among low-income Farmers.* North Holland: Amsterdam.

Ravallion, M (2007). Inequality is bad for the poor. In *Inequality and Poverty Re-examined*, eds. Jenkins S and J Micklewright. Oxford: Oxford University Press.

Ravallion, M, S Chen and P Sangraula (2008). China is poorer than we thought, but no less successful in the fight against poverty. Working paper 4621. Washington, DC: World Bank.

Ravallion, M, S Chen and P Sangraula (2008a). Dollar a day revisited, World Bank Working paper 4620. Washington, DC: World Bank.

Ravallion, M and J Jalan (2002). Geographic Poverty Traps? A Micro Model of Consumption Growth in Rural China. *Journal Of Applied Econometrics*, 17, 329–346.

Ravallion, M (2006). Transfer and Safety Nets in Poor Countries: Revisiting the Trade-Offs and Policy Options. In *Understanding Poverty*, eds. Banerjee AV, Benabou R and D Mookherkee. Oxford: Oxford University Press.

Ravallion, MS and G Datt (2002). Why has economic growth been more pro-poor in some states of India than others? *Journal of Development Economics*, 68, 381–400.

Ravallion, M and M Chen (1997). What can new survey data tell us about recent changes in distribution and poverty? *The World Bank Economic Review*, 11, 357–82.

Ravallion, MS and Q Wodon (2001). Does Child Labour Displace Schooling? Evidence on Behavioural Responses to an Enrollment Subsidy, *Economic Journal* 110(462), 158–175.

Rawlings, L, L Sherburne-Benz and J van Domelen (2002). *Evaluating Social Fund Performance: A Cross-Country Analysis of Community Investments.* Social Protection Network, World Bank, Washington DC.

Ray, R (2000). Child Labor, Child Schooling and Their Interaction with Adult Labor: Empirical Evidence from Peru and Pakistan. *World Bank Economic Review*, 14(2), 347–367.

Ray, S (2006). The cost and financing of Universalizing Elementary Education: A Silver Lining in Rajasthan? In *The Economics of Elementary Education in India: The Challenges of Public Finance, Private Provision and Household Costs*, ed. Mehrotra S. New Delhi: Sage Publication.

Reimers, F, C DeShano da silva and E Trevino (2006). Where is the "Education" in Conditional Cash Transfers in Education? UNESCO Institute for Statistics in Montreal, Montreal.

Reyes, CM (2002). The Poverty Fight: Have We Made an Impact? PIDS Discussion Paper Series No. 2002 20. Makati City. Philippine Institute for Development Studies (PIDS).

Reye, C (2004). An Initial Verdict on Our Fight Against Poverty. Discussion Paper Series No. 2004–48. Philippines Institute for Development Studies (PIDS).

Ridao-Cano, C and D Filmer (2004). Indonesia: Evaluating the Performance of SGP and SIGP: A Review of the Existing Literature and Beyond. Human Development Sector Unit, East Asia and Pacific Region. Working Paper 2004–3. Washington, DC: World Bank.

Riskin, C (1994). Chinese Rural Poverty: Marginalized or Dispersed? *American Economic Review,* 84, 281–84.

Riskin, C and N Bouche (2004). *The Macroeconomics of Poverty Reduction: The Case of China.* Beijing: UNDP-China.

Roemer, M and M Gugerty (1997). Does Economic Growth Reduce Poverty? *Consulting Assistance of Economic Reform (CAER) Discussion Paper 4.* Cambridge Mass, Harvard Institute for International Development.

Rola, AC, SB Jamas and JB Quizon (2002). *Journal of International Agricultural and Extension Education,* 9(1), 65–76.

Romer, PM (1986). Increasing Returns and Long-run Growth. *Journal of Political Economy,* 94(5), 1002–37.

Roos, N, HE Bouis, N Hassan and KA Kabir (2004). Alleviating Malnutrition through Agriculture in Bangladesh, Biofortification and Diversification as Sustainable Solutions. Proceedings of the Workshop on Alleviating Micronutriet Malnutrition through Agriculture in Bangladesh: Biofortification and Diversification as Long-Term Sustainable Solutions, Gazipur and Dhaka, Bangladesh.

Rosenberg, T (2008). A Payoff Out of Poverty, *New York Times,* 21 December.

Rosenzweig, MR and KI Wolpin (1993). Credit market constraints, consumption smoothing and the accumulation of durable production assets in low-income countries: investments in bullock in India. *Journal of Political Economy,* 101, 223–244.

Roy, KC and JCH Chai (1999). Economic reforms, public transfers and social safety nets for the poor: A study of India and China, *International Journal of Social Economics* 26(1/2/3), 222–238.

Rubenson, B, NT Van Anh, B Hojer and E Johansson (2004). Child domestic servants in Hanoi: Who are they and how do they fare? *The International Journal of Child's Rights,* 11, 391–407.

Saget, C (2001). Is the minimum wage and effective tool to promote decent work and reduce poverty? The experience of selected developing countries. ILO Employment Paper 2001/13. Geneva: ILO.

Sah, DC (2007). Chronic Poverty in Tribal Areas: Evidence from Southwestern Madhya Pradesh. *Indian Journal of Agricultural Economics,* 62(2), 193–215.

Sainath, P (1996). *Everybody Loves a Good Drought.* New York: Penguin.

Salih, R (2000). The Samurdhi Poverty Alleviation Scheme. Social Security Division. Geneva: ILO.

Samasinghe, S (1988). Sri Lanka: A Case Study from the Third World. In *Health, Nutrition and Economic Crisis: Approaches to Policy in the Third World,* eds. Bell DE and Reich MR. New York: Auburn House.

Sarewitz, D, R Pielke and M Keykhah (2003). Vulnerability and Risk: Some Thoughts from a Political and Policy Perspective. *Risk Analysis,* 23(4), 805–810.

Sarthi, A (2003). Labour Migration in the Transitional Economies of South-east Asia. Working Paper on Migration and Urbanization. Economic and Social Commission for Asia and the Pacific, United Nations.

Sasikumar, SK and Z Hussain (2007). *Migration, Remittances and Development: Lessons from India*. VV Giri National Labour Institute Research Study Series No. 083.

Save the Children (2006). http://www.savethechildren.org/ [5 April 2007].

Schafgans, MA (1998). Ethnic Wage Differences in Malaysia: Parametric and Semi-parametric Estimation of the Chinese-Malay Wage Gap. Special Issue: Application of Semiparametric Methods for Micro-Data. *Journal of Applied Econometrics*, 13(5), 481–504.

Schultz, TP (1995). Investments in the Schooling of Women and Men: Quantities and Returns. In *Investments in Women's Human Capital*, ed. Schultz TP. Chicago: University of Chicago Press.

Sebastian, G (2007). GIS/Spatial Analysis Contribution to 2008 World Development Report: Technical Note on Data and Methodologies. Background paper for the World Development Report 2008.

Sen, A (1981). *Poverty and Famines. An Essay on Entitlements and Deprivation*. Oxford: Oxford University Press.

Sen, A (1990). More than 100 Million women are Missing. *New York Review of Books*, 39(20), 61–66.

Sen, A (1990a). Public Action to Remedy Hunger. The Hunger Project. http://www.globalpolicy.org/socecon/hunger/general/1990/0802public.htm [28 May 2008].

Sen, A (2003). Drivers of Escape and Descent: Changing Household Fortunes in Rural Bangladesh. *World Development*, 31(3), 513–534.

Sen, B and D Hulme, eds. (2004). The State of the Poorest 2004/2005: Chronic Poverty in Bangladesh — Tales of Ascent, Descent, Marginality and Persistence. Working Paper. CPRC.

Sengupta, S and H Gazdar (1996). Agrarian Politics and Rural Development in West Bengal In *Indian Development: Selected Regional Perspectives*, eds. Drèze J and Sen A. Delhi: Oxford University Press.

Shaffer, P (2001). Poverty Dynamics: An Institutional Approach. Mimeo, Center for International Studies, University of Toronto, Toronto, Canada.

Shah, T, M Alam, D Kumar, RKN Nagar and M Singh (2000). Pedaling out of Poverty: Social Impact of a Manual Irrigation Technology in South Asia. International Water Management Institute Research Paper 45. IWMI, Colombo.

Shah, T, C Scott, A Kishore and A Sharma (2003). Energy-Irrigation Nexus in South Asia: Improving Groundwater Conservation and Power Sector Viability Research Report 70. International Water Management Institute, Battaramulla, Sri Lanka.

Sharma, ML and P Thapa (2007). Women in Rural Micro Finance Programme in the Western Hills of Nepal: Reflection from *Sahakarya* Project Area. Mimeo.

Sharma, RA (1987). Testing between Competing Models of Sharecropping. *Journal of Political Economy*, 95, 893–920.

Singh, S and R Samara (1996). Early Marriage Among Women in Developing Countries. *International Family Planning Perspectives*, 22(4), 148–157.

Skoufias, E and B McClafferty (2001). Is PROGRESA Working? Summary of the Results of an Evaluation by IFPRI. Food Consumption and Nutrition Division Discussion Paper 118. Washington, DC: IFPRI.

Social Weather Stations Website (2008). www.sws.org.ph [15 July 2008].

Socialist Republic of Vietnam (2002). *The Comprehensive Poverty Reduction and Growth Strategy (CPRGS)*. Hanoi: Government of Vietnam.

Society for Development Studies (SDS), India & Urban and Regional Development Institute (URDI). *Innovative Approaches to Poverty Reduction: Experiences in India and Indonesia*. Indonesia.

Sofranko, A and M Khan (1992). Farmers' access to information and its impact on technology adoption in North-West Frontier Province, Pakistan. *Journal of Rural Development* and *Administration,* 24(4), 9–24.

Soil Research (2007). Editorial volume 94, 1–3.

Springate-Baginshi, O and P Blaike (2007). Is Community Forestry in Contemporary Nepal Pro-Poor and Sustainable? Improving Policy-Livelihood Relationships in South Asia, Policy Process Analysis Paper 1. UK Department for International Development (DFID).

Srivastava, R (2005). Bonded Labor in India: Its Incidence and Pattern. *International Labor Office Working Paper 43*. Geneva: ILO.

Srivastava, R and SK Sasikumar (2003). An Overview of migration in India, its impacts and key issues. Regional Conference on Migration, Development and Pro-poor Policy Choices in Asia, June 2002, Dhaka, Bangladesh. http://www.livelihoods.org [23 March 2008].

Stark, O (1991). *The Migration of Labor*. Cambridge: Harvard University Press.

Subbarao K, J Ezemerani, J Randa and G Rubio (1999). Impact evaluation in FY98 Bank Projects: A review. Poverty Reduction and Economic Management Network. Washington, DC: World Bank.

Subbarao, K, A Bonnerjee, J Braithwaite, S Carvalho, K Ezemenari, C Graham and A Thopmson (1997). *Safety Net Programs and Poverty Reduction*. Washington, DC: World Bank.

Suryahadi, A and S Sumarto (2003). Measuring Vulnerability to Poverty in Indonesia Before and After the Economic Crisis. *Asian Economic Journal,* 17(1), 45–64.

Swinkels, R and C Turk (2004). Poverty and remote areas: Evidence from new data and questions for the future, Background paper for PAC conference, 24–26 November.

Swinkels, R and C Turk (2006). Explaining Ethnic Minority Poverty in Vietnam: a summary of recent trends and current challenges. Draft Background paper for CEM/ MPI meeting on Ethnic Minority Poverty. Hanoi, 28 September.

Tan, E CC Kusharto and S Budiyati (2005). Rewarding Educational Performance in Tanah Datar, Sumatra. Prepared for the Making Services Work for the Poor in Indonesia Case Studies. World Bank Office Jakarta, the Ash Institute for Democratic Governance and Innovation, in collaboration with the Ford Foundation International Innovation Liaison Group. www.innovations.harvard.edu [10 February 2008].

TANGO International (2003). Technical Assistance to Non-Governmental Organization Governmental Organizations. *Southeast Rural Livelihoods Baseline.* Report prepared for CARE Bangladesh.

Tertiary Rural Roads Improvement Programme (TRIP) (2002). *Socio-economic Impact Study of Roads Construction 1996–2001.*

Tertiary Rural Roads Improvement Programme (TRIP) (2004). *Socio-economic Impact Study of Roads Constructed During TRIP-Phase III (October 2002–April 2004).*

Thabrany, H (2003). Social Health Insurance in Indonesia: Current Status and the Proposed National Health Insurance. New Delhi.

The Economist (2007). Shoveling for their supper, 26 April 2007.

The Economist (2008). Economic Focus On the poverty line, 24 May 2008.

The Economist (2008a). Into the Storm and A taxonomy of trouble, 25 October 2008.

The Economist (2008b). How to promote the spread of mobile phones among the world's poorest, 29 May 2008.

Thorat, S and S Fan (2007). Public Investment and Poverty Reduction Lessos from China and India. *Economics and Political Weekly*, 24 February 2007.

Timmer, CP (2007). How Indonesia Connected the Poor to Rapid Economic Growth. In *Delivering on the Promise of Pro-Poor Growth: Insights and Lessons from Country Experiences,* eds. Besley T and LJ Cord. Palgrave Macmillan and the World Bank.

Tomkins, R (1997). Extending rural electrification: A survey of innovative schemes. www.gpoba.org/docs/10ch5.pdf [5 May 2008].

Topalova, P (2007). Trade Liberalization, Poverty and Inequality: Evidence from Indian Districts. In *Globalization and Poverty*, ed. A Harrison. Chicago: University of Chicago Press.

Torrens, A (2005). KDP Economic Impact Analysis Study. World Bank Office Jakarta. Mimeo.

Tran, VT and H Quan (2008). A case study of the Program for Socio-economic Development of Communes Facing Extreme Difficulties in Ethnic Minority and Mountainous Areas in Vietnam (P135) Workshop on Strengthening the Development Results and Impacts of the Paris Declaration through Work on Gender Equality, Social Exclusion and Human Rights London, 12, 13 March 2008.

Udry, C (2006). Child Labor in Banerjee. In *Understanding Poverty*, eds. Roland Benabou AV and Dilip Mookherjee. Oxford UK: Oxford University Press.

UNDP (1995). *Human Development Report.* New York: United Nations.

UNDP (2004). *The Macroeconomics of Poverty Reduction in Cambodia.* Kathmandu: UNDP, Asia-Pacific Regional Programme on the Macroeconomics of Poverty Reduction.

UNDP (2006). Insights for Action: A SWOT Analysis of the Cambodian Economy. Discussion Paper No. 1.

UNDP (2007). Cambodia Human Development Report 2007. *Expanding Choices For Rural People*. Ministry of Planning and United Nations Development Programme Cambodia.

UNDP (2008). *Human Development Report*. New York: United Nations.

UNICEF (2005). Free healthcare for Cambodia's poorest families. http://www.unicef.org/infobycountry/cambodia_27370.html [25 July 2008].

United Nations (2001). United Nations Sub-Commission on the Promotion and Protection of Human Rights The enslavement of dalit and indigenous communities India, Nepal and Pakistan through debt bondage. New York: United Nations.

United Nations Economic and Social Commission for Asian and the Pacific (ESCAP) (2004). *Economic and Social Survey of Asia and the Pacific*, ESCAP, Bangkok.

United Nations Economic and Social Commission for Asian and the Pacific (ESCAP). (2008). Bangkok: ESCAP.

United Nations Food and Agricultural Organization (FAO). http://www.fao.org/DOCREP/0040AC385E [3 January 2008].

United Nations Food and Agricultural Organization (2003). Nepal Agricultural Policy and Strategies for Poverty Alleviation and Food Security. FAO SPDD Report, Rome.

United Nations (1996a). *Food security for all, food security for rural women*. Geneva: International Steering Committee on the Economic Advancement of Rural Women.

United Nations (2006). Report on the Aids Epidemic Update. http://data.unaids.org/pub/EpiReport/2006/05-Asia_2006_EpiUpdate_eng.pdf.

United Nations (2008). Cambodia: Energy Sector Strategy http://www.un.org/esa/agenda21/natlinfo/countr/cambodia/energy.pdf [27 July 2008].

United Nations (Various years). Human Development Report. New York: United Nations.

Van de Walle, D (2002). Choosing Rural Road Investments to Help Reduce Poverty *World Development*, 30(4), 575–589.

van de Walle, D and D Gunewardena (2001). Sources of Ethnic Inequality in Vietnam. *Journal of Development Economics*, 65, 177–207, originally published as Policy Research Working Paper 2297, World Bank.

Vietnam Academy of Social Sciences (VASS) (2007). *Vietnam Poverty Update Report: Poverty and Poverty Reduction in Vietnam 1993–2004*. Hanoi: Vietnam Academy of Social Sciences.

Wagstaff, A and N Nguyen (2007). *Poverty and Survival Prospects of Vietnamese Children under Doi Moi*. Washington DC: World Bank.

Warr, P (2005). Road Development and Poverty Reduction: The Case of Lao PDR, *ADB Institute Discussion Paper 25*, Tokyo.

Warr, P (2006). How do Infrastructure Projects Benefit the Poor? *Indian Development Review*, 4(3), 225–39.

Warr, P (2006a). How Road Improvement Reduces Poverty: The Case of Laos Mimeo.

Warr, P (2007). Reducing Rural Poverty: The role of Agricultural Trade and Investment Policy. Session F on Strategies for Rural Growth: Macroeconomic Context, Trade Policies and Foreign Direct Investment, Policy Forum Agricultural and Rural Development for Reducing Poverty and Hunger in Asia: In Pursuit of Inclusive and Sustainable Growth, IFPRI, Washington DC and ADB, Manila.

Waverman, L, M Meschi and M Fuss (2005). The Impact of Telecomms on Economic Growth in Developing Countries, Mimeo. London Business School, London, UK.

West, LA and CPW Wong (1995). Fiscal decentralization and growing regional disparities in rural China: some evidence in the provision of social services. *Oxford Review of Economic Policy*, 11, 70–84.

Widyanti, W, S Sumarto and A Suryahadi (2001). Short-term Poverty Dynamics: Evidence from Rural Indonesia. Working Paper, September, Jakarta: SMERU Research Institute.

Wilson, EO (1975). *Sociobiology: The New Synthesis*. New York: Belnap Press.

Winrock International and International Development Enterprise (IDE) (2001). Study of the Dissemination Potential of Affordable Drip and Other Irrigation Systems and the Concrete Strategies for their Protection. Mimeo.

Wodon, Q (1999). Cost-benefit analysis of Food for Education in Bangladesh. *Policy Research Working Paper*. Background paper for the poverty assessment of Bangladesh. Washington DC: World Bank.

World Bank and IMF (2001). *Interim Poverty Reduction Strategy Paper for Lao PDR*. Washington, DC: World Bank.

World Bank (1990). *World Development Report*. World Bank, Washington DC, Oxford University Press.

World Bank (1993). *The East Asian Miracle: Economic Growth and Public Policy*. Washington DC: World Bank.

World Bank (1994). *World Development Report 1994: Infrastructure for Development*. New York: Oxford University Press.

World Bank (1995). *World Development Report 1995*, Washington DC.

World Bank (2000). *World Development Report*. New York: Oxford University Press.

World Bank (2001). *China: Overcoming Rural Poverty*. http://www.worldbank.org.cn/English/content/poverty.pdf [6 April 2008].

World Bank (2001a). *China's Farmers Need Long-Term Land Tenure Security, Not Land Readjustment*. http://www.worldbank.org/html/prddr/trans/augsepoct00/pages21-23.htm [6 April 2008].

World Bank (2001b). *Philippines Poverty Assessment.* Washington, DC: World Bank.
World Bank (2002). Pakistan poverty assessment — Poverty in Pakistan: Vulnerabilities, social gaps, and rural dynamics. Washington, DC: World Bank.
World Bank (2003). *India: Sustaining Reforms, Reducing Poverty.* Report No 25797-IN. Washington, DC: World Bank.
World Bank (2003a). *World Development Report.* Washington, DC: World Bank.
World Bank (2003b). *World Development Indicators.* Washington, DC: World Bank.
World Bank (2004). *Indian Investment Climate 2004: Improving Manufacturing Competitiveness.* Washington, DC: World Bank.
World Bank (2004a). *Vietnam Development Report 2004: Poverty.* Washington, DC: World Bank.
World Bank (2005). *Bihar Toward a Development Strategy.* Washington, DC: World Bank.
World Bank (2005a). AIDS in South Asia: Understanding and responding to a heterogeneous epidemic. Washington, DC: World Bank.
World Bank (2006). *Cambodia Halving Poverty by 2015?* Poverty Assessment 2006 East Asia and the Pacific Region. Washington, DC: World Bank.
World Bank (2006). *South Asia: The End of Poverty.* Washington DC. http://go.worldbank.org/DZVHB0C0P0 [6 March 2008].
World Bank (2006a). *World Development Indicators.* Washington, DC: World Bank.
World Bank (2006b). *World Development Report 2006.* Washington, DC: World Bank.
World Bank (2006c). *Global Economic Prospects: Economic Implications of Remittances and Migration.* Washington, DC: World Bank.
World Bank (2006d). Inclusive Growth and Services Delivery: Building on India's Success. *Development Policy Review Report No 34580-IN.* Washington, DC: World Bank.
World Bank (2006e). *Making the New Indonesia Work for the Poor.* Washington DC: World Bank.
World Bank (2006f). *Survey of Gender Norms.* Dhaka.
World Bank (2006g). *Sri Lanka: Strengthening Social Protection.* Washington DC: World Bank.
World Bank (2006h). *Nepal Resilience amidst Conflict: An Assessment of Poverty in Nepal, 1995–96 and 2003–04.* Washington DC: World Bank.
World Bank (2006i). *Lao PDR Poverty Assessment Report: From Valleys to Hilltops — 15 Years of Poverty Reduction.* Washington DC: World Bank.
World Bank (2007). *World Development Indicators.* Washington, DC: World Bank.
World Bank (2007a). Reaching Rural Areas with Financial Services: A Fresh Look at Financial Cooperation, processed. Washington, DC: World Bank.
World Bank (2007b). *Sri Lanka Poverty Assessment — Engendering Growth with Equity: Opportunities and Challenges.* Washington DC: World Bank.

World Bank (2007c). *Pakistan: Promoting Rural Growth and Poverty Reduction.* Washington, DC: World Bank.

World Bank (2007d). *Pakistan: Promoting Rural Growth and Poverty Reduction.* Washington DC: World Bank.

World Bank (2007e). *Sharing Growth: Equity and Development in Cambodia: Equity Report 2007.* Washington DC: World Bank.

World Bank (2007f). *Lao PDR Public Expenditure Review Integrated Fiduciary Assessment.* Washington DC: World Bank.

World Bank (2008). *World Development Report.* World Bank Washington DC.

World Bank. 2008a. *World Development Indicators*, World Bank, Washington DC.

World Bank (2008b). Bangladesh: Priorities for Agriculture and Rural Development, http://web.worldbank.org/WEBSITE/EXTERNAL/COUNTRIES/SOUTHASIAEXT/EXTSAREG [8 August 2008].

World Bank (2008c). *Whispers to Voices: Gender and Social Transformation in Bangladesh.* Washington DC: World Bank World.

World Bank (2008d). *Indonesia: Economic and Social update April 2008.* Washington DC: World Bank.

World Bank (2008e). Sri Lanka — Roads Sector Assistance Projects. http://go.worldbank.org/EBDIVN5W90 [9 Feb 2008].

World Bank (2008f). Sri Lanka — Empowering Rural Communities http://go.worldbank.org/HD4TZWG3W0 [9 Feb 2008].

World Bank (2008g). Pakistan — Pakistan Poverty Alleviation Fund. http://go.worldbank.org/B7LAWE8FG0 [16 March 2008].

World Bank (2008h). *Lao PDR Public Expenditure Tracking: Survey in Primary Education and Primary Health.* Washington DC: World Bank.

World Bank (2008i). IDA — Lao's Poverty Reduction Fund. http://go.worldbank.org/GG6E9GQIO0 [8 March 2008].

World Bank (2008j). IDA — Providing Electricity in Rural Lao PDR. http://go.worldbank.org/VJ5AFQBJB0 [8 March 2008].

World Food Programme (2007). *Executive Brief: Lao PDR Comprehensive Food Security and Vulnerability Analy*sis. Rome: WFP.

World Health Organization (2000). Bulletin 78(1), 12.

World Resources Institute and International Finance Corporation (2007). *The Next Four Billion.* Washington, DC: World Resources Institute and International Finance Corporation.

Yao, Y (2001). Social Exclusion and Economic Discrimination: The Status of Migrations in China's Coastal Rural Area. Working Paper no E 2001005 Beijing: China Center for Economic Research, Peking University mimeo.

Yunus, M and W Karl (2007). *Creating a World without Poverty: Social Business and the Future of Capitalism.* New York: Public Affairs Books.

Zhang, A (2003). Poverty alleviation in China: Commitment, Policies and Expenditures. Occasional Paper 27. http://www.hdr.undp.org/docs/publications/ocational_papers/oc27.htm [18 March 2008].

Zhang, F, L Zhang and X Zhang (2002). Investment, Reforms and Poverty in Rural China. *Economic Development and Cultural Change*, 52(2), 395–422.

Zhao, Z (1999). Labor migration and earnings differences: The case of rural China, *Economic Development and Cultural Change*, 47(4), 762–782.

Zhao, Z (2005). Migration, labor market flexibility and wage determination in China: A Review. *The Developing Economies*, 43(2), 285–312.

Subject Index